The
PSYCHOLOGY
OF WOMEN

MARGARET W. MATLIN

SUNY GENESEO

The

PSYCHOLOGY
OF WOMEN

FOURTH EDITION

WADSWORTH

THOMSON LEARNING

Australia • Canada • Mexico • Singapore • Spain
United Kingdom • United States

WADSWORTH

THOMSON LEARNING

Publisher   Earl McPeek
Executive Editor   Carol Wada
Acquisitions Editor   Lisa Hensley
Developmental Editor   Tracy Napper
Project Editor   Claudia Gravier

Art Director   Carol Kincaid
Production Manager   Andrea Archer
Cover Photo   © David Young-Wolff/PhotoEdit
Compositor   Publications Development Company
Printer   R.R. Donnelley, Crawfordsville

Printed in the United States of America
2 3 4 5 6 7 05

For more information about our products,
contact us at:
**Thomson Learning
Academic Resource Center
1-800-423-0563**
For permission to use material from this text,
contact us by:
Phone: 1-800-730-2214   **Fax:** 1-800-730-2215
Web: http://www.thomsonrights.com

**Library of Congress Catalog Card
Number:** 99-61163

ISBN: 0-15-507896-8

Asia
Thomson Learning
60 Albert Street, #15-01
Albert Complex
Singapore 189969

Australia
Nelson Thomson Learning
102 Dodds Street
South Melbourne, Victoria 3205
Australia

Canada
Nelson Thomson Learning
1120 Birchmount Road
Toronto, Ontario M1K 5G4
Canada

Europe/Middle East/Africa
Thomson Learning
Berkshire House
168-173 High Holborn
London WC1 V7AA
United Kingdom

Latin America
Thomson Learning
Seneca, 53
Colonia Polanco
11560 Mexico D.F.
Mexico

Spain
Paraninfo Thomson Learning
Calle/Magallanes, 25
28015 Madrid, Spain

This book is dedicated to

THE STUDENTS
IN MY PSYCHOLOGY OF WOMEN CLASSES

Preface

I prepared the Fourth Edition of *The Psychology of Women* in 1999, the last year of the 20th century. The current study of the psychology of women was born in the late 1960s, developed in its youth and adolescence during the 1970s and 1980s, and is thriving in its adulthood as we cross into the 21st century. Hundreds of professors throughout North America are currently teaching college courses about the psychology of women or the psychology of gender. Increasing numbers of students are selecting these courses because of their personal or academic interest in this endlessly fascinating subject. Research in the psychology of women continues to be energetic and diverse. Topics range from prenatal influences to adolescent friendship patterns, and to the life satisfaction of women of all ages.

When this textbook was first published in 1987, the research on many aspects of women's lives was scanty at best. Publications that were available did not always feature women's own perspectives. Little information about women of color could be found, and cross-cultural studies were virtually nonexistent. In contrast, it's now a unique challenge to keep up with the hundreds of books and thousands of articles published on this subject each year.

The Psychology of Women (Fourth Edition) provides a synthesis of information that can guide readers through important facets of women's lives. I have made a special effort to include significant topics that are omitted or abbreviated in most other textbooks: the development of gender-typing, women and work, love relationships, pregnancy and motherhood, women with disabilities, and later adulthood. The resources cited represent only a fraction of the literature I examined in preparing the sequence and coverage of the subjects. In the first edition of this textbook, I commented that the meager information on the psychology of women made writers reluctant to tackle a textbook in this area. The explosion of research in the past decade has made the task rewarding, but challenging from a different perspective. As this project progressed, I often asked myself, "How can I possibly cover all these dimensions of women's lives without creating a textbook of encyclopedic proportions?"

Text Features and Organization

The Fourth Edition of *The Psychology of Women* combines both developmental and topical approaches. An introductory chapter presents some general concepts and several important cautions about research methods and biases. The stereotypes that help shape gender-related expectations and behavior are then addressed. The next two chapters explore female development, from prenatal experiences and infancy, through childhood and adolescence.

The next nine topical chapters examine components of women's lives, such as gender comparisons, work experiences, love relationships, sexuality, childbirth, physical and psychological health, and violence against women. Young adults are usually the focus of psychological research in these areas, although the implied scope is much broader. (For example, females of all ages may be affected by violence.) Chapter 14 focuses more specifically on women who are middle-aged and elderly. The concluding chapter assesses the current status of women, women's studies, and gender relations as we enter the 21st century.

Organization is an important component of both my teaching and my textbooks. For example, the combination of life-span and topical approaches seems to provide a cohesive framework that my own students appreciate. However, all chapters are self-contained; instructors who prefer a different approach can easily rearrange the sequence of topics. The subdivisions within each chapter have their own summaries, to allow further flexibility.

A second organizational feature is that the book develops four general themes about the psychology of women that can be traced through many components of women's lives. These themes provide a sense of continuity to an area that may otherwise seem overwhelming to students.

The special features that were praised in the first three editions of *The Psychology of Women* have been retained:

- Topical outlines give students an overall structure prior to reading each chapter.
- True–False questions at the beginning of each chapter encourage student interest and foreshadow the key issues to be examined.
- The writing style is clear and interesting; it continually engages the reader, and includes many examples and quotations reflecting women's experiences.
- Boldface type identifies new terms, which are defined within the same sentence. To accommodate professors who may assign chapters in a nonlinear order, a new term that is used in several chapters (e.g., social constructionism) is redefined each time it appears. In addition, the correct pronunciation is provided parenthetically for terms that have potentially ambiguous pronunciations.
- Small-scale demonstrations are included to encourage involvement and to clarify the procedures for key research studies.
- Section summaries (two to five in each chapter) allow frequent review prior to beginning new material.
- A "New Terms" section at the end of each chapter invites students to review the vocabulary.
- The end-of-chapter review questions encourage students to clarify and synthesize concepts; they also offer instructors a wide range of discussion topics or written assignments for students.
- The lists of recommended readings suggest extra resources for students who want to explore in greater detail the topics covered within each chapter. I have annotated each reference.

This book is intended for students from a variety of backgrounds. I have included extensive learning aids, to make it readable for students who have taken only an introductory course in psychology. However, because the coverage of topics is complete and the references are extensive, *The Psychology of Women* should also be useful for advanced-level students. This textbook is primarily designed for courses in psychology of women, psychology of gender, psychology of gender comparisons, and psychology of gender roles. Some instructors focusing on the psychology of gender may wish to supplement the book with one of several textbooks currently available on the psychology of men.

Features of the Fourth Edition

This Fourth Edition continues the special features and writing style that students and professors admired in the earlier editions. Professors who reviewed the Third Edition were pleased with its overall structure; therefore, I retained the same topic sequence for the Fourth Edition. However, readers should note the following changes:

- Whenever possible, I have expanded coverage on women of color living in the United States and Canada.
- Cross-cultural perspectives have been enlarged whenever possible. Research on women living in other cultures has been more forthcoming, and this information provides a broader view of women's lives.
- "Women's voices" are more widely included. Direct quotations from girls and women balance the qualitative and quantitative approaches to research.
- Each chapter is introduced with a vignette or anecdote that represents a perspective on the chapter's content.
- This Fourth Edition is a thoroughly revised and updated textbook featuring more than 1,300 new references; 1,068 of the 2,133 references in the book were published in 1995 or later. It reflects changes in women's lives, changes in their views of themselves, and changes in society's attitudes toward women's issues.

New Coverage in Specific Chapters

For professors familiar with the previous edition, here is a concise guide to some representative changes in this new textbook:

- Chapter 1: Rearranged; expanded coverage of theoretical approaches.
- Chapter 2: Shortened; new section on heterosexism in relationship to sexism.
- Chapter 3: Reorganized; updated research on children's gender knowledge and stereotypes.
- Chapter 4: New research on the premenstrual syndrome, adolescent women and education, and early romantic relationships.
- Chapter 5: Reorganized; incorporates new research on gender comparisons in cognitive abilities.
- Chapter 6: Greater emphasis on cross-cultural issues in social and personality characteristics.

- Chapter 7: Reflects current multidisciplinary research on women and work; new sections on women and welfare and on combating discriminatory treatment.
- Chapter 8: Increased coverage of love relationships from cross-cultural and ethnically diverse perspectives; critiques of the biological perspective on sexual orientation.
- Chapter 9: A more woman-centered approach to sexuality; updated information and cross-cultural perspectives on birth control.
- Chapter 10: New quotations about pregnancy and motherhood; updated coverage of postpartum problems and infertility.
- Chapter 11: Reorganized; approximately 140 new references; up-to-date coverage of social class and susceptibility to disease, AIDS, and substance abuse.
- Chapter 12: New case studies of women and psychological disorders; updated discussion of eating disorders.
- Chapter 13: Explores entitlement in relation to violence against women; updated statistics on the incidence of sexual harassment, rape, and abuse.
- Chapter 14: Updates on the double standard of aging, retirement, and economic issues; alternative views of menopause.
- Chapter 15: Reorganized; expanded coverage of women of color, men's studies, and international issues.

Acknowledgments

This is an especially pleasant section of the book because it gives me the opportunity to thank the people who have provided ideas, references, perspectives, and encouragement. I especially appreciated the useful suggestions and insights about organization, content, current research, and presentation that were received from the manuscript reviewers: Krisanne Bursik, Suffolk University; Joan Chrisler, Connecticut College; Nancy DeCourville, Brock University; Lucinda DeWitt, University of Minnesota; Grace Galliano, Kennesaw State College; Beverly Goodwin, Indiana University of Pennsylvania; Chris Jazwinski, St. Cloud State University; Linda Kinner, Middle Tennessee State University; Letitia Anne Peplau, University of California, Los Angeles; and Jean Poppei, The Sages College.

My continuing thanks go to the reviewers of the first three editions: Harriet Amster, Linda Anderson, Julianne Arbuckle, Ileane Arias, Nancy Betts, Beverly Birns, Krisanne Bursik, Joan Chrisler, Gloria Cowan, Mary Crawford, Kay Deaux, Sheri Chapman De Bro, Joan Fimbel DiGiovanni, Elaine Donelson, Susan K. Fuhr, Grace Galliano, Margaret Gittis, Sharon Golub, Beverly Goodwin, Linda Lavine, Liz Leonard, Wendy Martyna, Maureen O'Neill, Michele A. Paludi, Letitia Anne Peplau, Rebecca Reviere, Barbara Sholley, Myra Okazaki Smith, Susan Snelling, Beverly Tatum, Barbara S. Wallston, Dolores Weiss, Yvonne V. Wells, Barbara J. Yanico, and Cecilia K. Yoder.

I also acknowledge the numerous contributions of Mary Roth Walsh, who died in February 1998. Over a period of nearly 20 years, Mary generously shared with me her perspectives, resources, and insights on the psychology of women, and I miss her deeply.

Lucinda DeWitt agreed to coauthor the Instructor's Manual/Test Bank for this Fourth Edition. Lucinda wrote the Test Item File for my introductory psychology textbook, and I was consistently impressed with her skill in writing clear and interesting multiple-choice items. Her expertise in the psychology of women, combined with her verbal skills and good judgment, greatly enhance the quality of the instructor's supplement.

I would also like to thank friends, relatives, and colleagues for suggesting many important references: Susan Arellano, Christine Beard, Lawrence Casler, Jacques Chevalier, Johanna Connelly, Amy Jo Eldred, Lisa Elliot, Hugh Foley, Joanne Goodrich (from the About Canada Project), Jennifer Gullo, Diane Halpern, Marion Hoctor, Jamie Kerr, Arnold Matlin, Kathy McGowan, Stuart J. McKelvie, Patricia Murphy, Josephine Naidoo, Thaddeus Naprawa, George Rebok, Philip Smith, Helen S. White, and Diony Young.

Several other friends and colleagues also earn my gratitude as superb readers and reviewers during the presentation of this and earlier editions: Mary Clark, Pam Cloonan, Karen Duffy, Evon Eddy, Meda Rebecca, Mary Roth Walsh, and Diony Young.

Many students gave valuable suggestions and feedback: Kate Bailey, Laurie Ciccarelli, Kelly Crane, Patty Curry, Michael Derrick, Jennifer Donlon, Amy Jo Eldred, Susan Flood, Lori Gardinier, Charlie Gilreath, Myung Han, Lisa Kaplan, Karen Kreuter, Heidi Lang, Christine Lauer, Laura Leon, Yau Ping Leung, Amy Liner, Zorayda Lopez, Tracy Marchese, Kathleen Matkoski, Erin Mulcock, Torye Mullins, Cory Mulvaney, Cathleen Quinn, Ralph Risolo, Marriane Rizzo, Kristen Setter, Jennifer Swan, Marcie Trout, and Cindy Zanni. The students enrolled in my Psychology of Women courses have also given me numerous ideas and suggestions.

Constance Ellis, Carolyn Emmert, and Shirley Thompson provided numerous services that permitted me to devote more energy to writing. Three students—Melissa Katter, Barbara Cole, and Colleen O'Loughlin—were especially helpful in locating references and performing clerical tasks. The members of the Milne Library staff at SUNY Geneseo demonstrated their professional expertise in tracking down elusive references, documents, and information. My thanks go especially to Judith Bushnell, Paula Henry, Mina Orman, and Harriet Sleggs.

Claudia Liepold, Ron Pretzer, and Louis Wadsworth deserve special recognition for their creativity and persistence as photographers. Thanks also to Sandra Lord for her excellent work in obtaining additional photos.

The editorial staff at Harcourt College Publishers were exceptionally skilled in guiding this edition of *The Psychology of Women* through development and its production. Tracy Napper is a superb developmental editor. I greatly admire her organizational skills, her useful perspectives on important issues, and her helpfulness in pursuing elusive information. It was a pleasure to work with her. Lisa Hensley, associate editor, shared her expertise in editorial matters, as well as her perspectives on clinical psychology issues. Carol Wada, executive editor, helped us examine our goals for this new edition and provided useful insights at many points in the book's development.

Other people at Harcourt who deserve my thanks include Claudia Gravier, project editor, and Andrea Archer, production manager. I'd also like to acknowledge Carol Kincaid's good work on the textbook's design. I would also like to thank Kathleen Sharp, Harcourt's marketing strategist, for her energetic and thoughtful guidance during the later stages of production.

Thanks are due to Nancy Land and her staff at Publications Development Company of Texas for their expertise and attention to quality during the production process; Darliene Bennett and Jennifer Gage deserve an especially enthusiastic thank-you! I am also very grateful to Maryan Malone of PDC for her outstanding contributions as copyeditor. Her intelligence, wide-ranging expertise, and editorial skills clearly strengthened this Fourth Edition.

Linda Webster prepared the indexes for this book. Linda and I have now worked together on eight textbooks, and I continue to admire her ability to produce such detailed and thoughtful resources.

Finally, I thank the three most important people in my life for their help, suggestions, love, and enthusiasm—my husband, Arnie, and our daughters, Beth and Sally. Their appreciation and pride in my work continue to make writing textbooks a joyous occupation.

MARGARET W. MATLIN
Geneseo, New York

Contents

Preface   vii

CHAPTER
1
Introduction   2

CENTRAL CONCEPTS IN THE PSYCHOLOGY OF WOMEN   5
Sex and Gender   5
Social Biases   6
Feminist Approaches   6
Psychological Approaches to Gender Similarity and Difference   7

A BRIEF HISTORY OF THE PSYCHOLOGY OF WOMEN   10
Early Studies of Gender Comparisons   10
The Emergence of the Psychology of Women as a Discipline   11
The Current Status of the Psychology of Women   12

PROBLEMS AND BIASES IN RESEARCH   14
Formulating the Hypothesis   14
Designing the Study   16
Performing the Study   17
Interpreting the Data   18
Communicating the Findings   19
Critical Thinking and the Psychology of Women   21

WOMEN OF COLOR   22

ABOUT THIS TEXTBOOK   26
Themes of the Book   27
How to Use This Book   29

CHAPTER
2
Gender Stereotypes   34

THE REPRESENTATION OF WOMEN AND MEN   37
A Heritage of Gender Bias   38
Representing Women in Language   40
Representing Women in the Media   45

xiii

PEOPLE'S BELIEFS ABOUT WOMEN AND MEN   51
The Content of Stereotypes   51
The Complexity of Contemporary Sexism   55
Heterosexism   62
The Social Cognitive Approach to Gender Stereotypes   64
Gender Stereotypes, Self-Fulfilling Prophecies, and Behavior 68

GENDER TYPING AND THE ALTERNATIVES   70
Androgyny   71
Moving Beyond Androgyny   75

C H A P T E R
3
Infancy and Childhood   80

THE BEGINNINGS OF GENDER DEVELOPMENT   82
Prenatal Development   83
Gender Comparisons During Infancy   86
How People Respond to Infant Girls and Boys   87

THEORETICAL EXPLANATIONS OF GENDER TYPING   94
Psychoanalytic Theory   94
Gender Schema Theory   95

CHILDREN'S KNOWLEDGE ABOUT GENDER   98
Children's Ideas About Gender Constancy   98
Children's Stereotypes About Personality   99
Children's Stereotypes About Activities and Occupations 101
Factors Related to Children's Stereotypes   101

FACTORS THAT SHAPE GENDER TYPING   104
The Family   104
Peers   108
School   111
The Media   115

C H A P T E R
4
Adolescence   122

PUBERTY AND MENSTRUATION   124
Puberty   124
Biological Aspects of the Menstrual Cycle   125

Menstrual Pain 128
The Controversial Premenstrual Syndrome 129
The Menstrual Cycle and Performance 133
Attitudes Toward Menstruation 133

SELF-CONCEPT AND IDENTITY DURING ADOLESCENCE 136
Body Image 137
Ethnic Identity 139
Self-Esteem 140

EDUCATION AND CAREER PLANNING 141
Young Women's School Experiences 141
Early Experiences in Math and Science 142
Higher Education 144
Career Aspirations 146
Aspirations Versus Reality 148

INTERPERSONAL RELATIONSHIPS DURING ADOLESCENCE 150
Family Relationships During Adolescence 150
Friendships During Adolescence 152
Romantic Relationships During Adolescence 153

C H A P T E R
5

Cognitive Abilities and Achievement Motivation

160

BACKGROUND ON GENDER COMPARISONS 163
Cautions About Research on Gender Comparisons 163
Two Approaches for Summarizing Multiple Studies 165

COGNITIVE ABILITIES 166
Cognitive Abilities That Show No Consistent Gender Differences 167
Verbal Ability 168
Mathematics Ability 171
Spatial Ability 174
Explaining the Gender Comparisons 177

ACHIEVEMENT MOTIVATION AND RELATED TOPICS 181
Biases in the Research on Achievement Motivation 182
Achievement Motivation 183
Fear of Success 184
Confidence in Your Own Achievement and Ability 185
Attributions for Your Own Success 188

CHAPTER
6

Gender Comparisons in Social and Personality Characteristics   194

COMMUNICATION PATTERNS   198
  Verbal Communication   198
  Nonverbal Communication   201
  Potential Explanations for Gender Differences in Communication   209

CHARACTERISTICS RELATED TO HELPING AND CARING   212
  Altruism   212
  Nurturance   214
  Empathy   214
  Moral Judgments Concerning Other People   215
  Friendship   218

CHARACTERISTICS RELATED TO AGGRESSION AND POWER   221
  Gender and Aggression: The Social Constructionists' Concerns   221
  Aggression   222
  Assertiveness   225
  Leadership   226
  Persuasion   227
  Influenceability   229

CHAPTER
7

Women and Work   234

**BACKGROUND FACTORS RELATED TO
WOMEN'S EMPLOYMENT**   237
  Personal Characteristics Related to Women's Employment   237
  Women and Welfare   240
  Discrimination in Hiring Patterns   241

DISCRIMINATION IN THE WORKPLACE   244
  Salary Discrimination   244
  Discrimination in Promotions   248
  Other Kinds of Treatment Discrimination   250
  Discrimination Against Lesbians in the Workplace   251
  What to Do About Treatment Discrimination   252

WOMEN'S EXPERIENCES IN SELECTED OCCUPATIONS   254
  Employment in Traditionally Female Occupations   254
  Employment in Traditionally Male Professions   256
  Employment in Blue-Collar Jobs   259

Why Are Women Scarce in Certain Occupations? 260
Homemakers 263

COORDINATING EMPLOYMENT WITH PERSONAL LIFE 264
Marriage 265
Children 268
Personal Adjustment 270

CHAPTER
8

Love Relationships 276

DATING AND LIVING TOGETHER 278
The Ideal Dating Partner 280
Explanations for Gender Differences in Preference Patterns 283
Characteristics of the Love Relationship 284
Living Together 287
Breaking Up 288

MARRIAGE AND DIVORCE 290
Getting Married 291
Marital Satisfaction 293
Responsibility and Power in Marriage 295
Marriage Patterns Among People of Color 296
Divorce 298

LESBIANS AND BISEXUAL WOMEN 301
The Psychological Adjustment of Lesbians 303
Characteristics of Lesbian Relationships 304
Lesbian Women of Color 307
Bisexual Women 308
Theoretical Explanations About Sexual Orientation and Preference 310

SINGLE WOMEN 314
Characteristics of Single Women 314
Attitudes Toward Single Women 316
Advantages and Disadvantages of Being Single 316
Single Women of Color 317

CHAPTER
9

Sexuality 322

FEMALE SEXUAL ANATOMY AND SEXUAL RESPONSES 324
External Sexual Organs 324
Sexual Responses 326

Theories About Orgasms   327
Gender Comparisons in Sexual Responses   327

SEXUAL BEHAVIOR AND ATTITUDES   330
Sex Education   330
Adolescent Sexual Behavior   332
The Double Standard   333
Sexual Scripts   335
Sexual Activities   335
Communication About Sexuality   336
Sexuality Among Lesbians   338
Sexuality and Older Women   339

SEXUAL PROBLEMS   341
Disorders of Sexual Desire   341
Female Orgasmic Disorder   342
Painful Intercourse   342
How Gender Roles Contribute to Sexual Problems   343
Therapy for Sexual Problems   344

BIRTH CONTROL AND ABORTION   345
Birth Control Methods   347
Who Uses Birth Control?   347
Obstacles to Using Birth Control   349
Family Planning in Developing Countries   351
Abortion   352

CHAPTER

10

Pregnancy, Childbirth, and Motherhood   360

PREGNANCY   362
The Biology of Pregnancy   363
Physical Reactions to Pregnancy   363
Emotional Reactions to Pregnancy   364
Attitudes Toward Pregnant Women   366
Pregnant Women and Employment   368

CHILDBIRTH   369
The Biology of Childbirth   370
Expectations About Childbirth   371
Emotional Reactions to Childbirth   371
Alternative Models of Childbirth   372

MOTHERHOOD   375
Stereotypes About Motherhood   375
The Reality of Motherhood   376

Motherhood and Women of Color   378
Lesbian Mothers   380
Postpartum Disturbances   382
Breastfeeding   384
Deciding Whether to Have Children   385
Infertility   388

CHAPTER
11
Women and Physical Health   **394**

THE HEALTH CARE AND HEALTH STATUS OF WOMEN   397
Biases Against Women   397
Health Issues for Women in Developing Countries   400
Gender Differences in Life Expectancy   402
Gender Differences in Overall Health   403
Heart Disease, Breast Cancer, and Other Specific Health Problems   404

WOMEN WITH DISABILITIES   411
Work Patterns of Women with Disabilities   412
Personal Relationships of Women with Disabilities   414

AIDS AND OTHER SEXUALLY TRANSMITTED DISEASES   416
Background Information on AIDS   416
Medical Aspects of AIDS   418
How AIDS Is Transmitted   418
Living with AIDS   419
Preventing AIDS   419
Other Sexually Transmitted Diseases   421

WOMEN AND SUBSTANCE ABUSE   423
Smoking   423
Alcohol Abuse   425
Other Substance-Abuse Problems   428

CHAPTER
12
Women and Psychological Disorders   **432**

DEPRESSION   435
Characteristics of Depression   435
Explanations for the Gender Difference in Depression   436

ANXIETY DISORDERS   442
Specific Phobias   442
Agoraphobia   442

EATING DISORDERS AND RELATED PROBLEMS   444
    Anorexia Nervosa   444
    Bulimia Nervosa   445
    The Emphasis on Being Slim   446
    Being Overweight and Dieting   449

TREATING PSYCHOLOGICAL DISORDERS IN WOMEN   451
    Psychotherapy and Sexism   451
    Psychotherapy with Women of Color   453
    Traditional Therapies and Women   456
    Gender-Sensitive Therapy   460

CHAPTER
13

Violence Against Women   466

SEXUAL HARASSMENT   470
    Why Is Sexual Harassment an Important Issue?   471
    How Often Does Sexual Harassment Occur?   472
    Effects of Harassment on the Victim   473
    Attitudes Toward Sexual Harassment   473
    What to Do About Sexual Harassment   474

RAPE   477
    Acquaintance Rape   478
    How Often Does Rape Occur?   482
    Fear of Rape   483
    Women's Reactions to Rape   484
    Attitudes Toward Rape   486
    Myths About Rape   486
    Child Sexual Abuse   488
    Marital Rape   490
    Rape Prevention   491

THE ABUSE OF WOMEN   496
    How Often Does the Abuse of Women Occur?   498
    The Dynamics of Abuse   498
    Women's Reactions to Abuse   499
    Characteristics of the Abusive Relationship   499
    Attitudes Toward the Abuse of Women   501
    Myths About the Abuse of Women   502
    How Abused Women Take Action   503
    Society's Response to the Problem of Abuse   505

CHAPTER
14
Women and Older Adulthood

510

ATTITUDES TOWARD OLDER WOMEN 513
  The Media 513
  The Double Standard of Aging 515
  Cross-Cultural Views of Older Women 518

OLDER WOMEN, RETIREMENT, AND
ECONOMIC ISSUES 519
  Planning for Retirement 520
  Adjusting to Retirement 520
  Economic Issues 521

MENOPAUSE 522
  Physical Symptoms 523
  Hormone Replacement Therapy 524
  Psychological Reactions 525
  Attitudes Toward Menopause 526

SOCIAL ASPECTS OF OLDER WOMEN'S LIVES 529
  Family Relationships 529
  Widowhood and the Death of Life Partners 532
  Older Women of Color 533
  Satisfaction with Life 534
  Rewriting Our Life Stories 536
  Final Words 536

CHAPTER
15
Moving Onward . . .

542

THE FUTURE OF THE DISCIPLINE OF PSYCHOLOGY
OF WOMEN 545
  The Increasing Number of Women Within Psychology 545
  Developing a More Inclusive Psychology of Women 546
  Specific Predictions About the Future of Psychology of Women 547

FEMINISM AND WOMEN OF COLOR 548

THE MEN'S MOVEMENT 550

SOME DISCOURAGING TRENDS   553
   The Rigid Interpretation of Feminism   554
   The Backlash Against Feminism   556
SOME HELPFUL TRENDS   556
   Women's Studies Courses   557
   The Women's Movement in North America   558
   The Women's Movement Worldwide   558
   Helping to Change the Future: Becoming an Activist   560

References   564

Name Index   641

Subject Index   655

Credits   681

The
PSYCHOLOGY
OF WOMEN

$\mathcal{I}$NTRODUCTION

TRUE OR FALSE?

_____ 1. An example of sexism is a corporation that refuses to consider hiring a male for a receptionist position.

_____ 2. Feminism is based on the principal that women should be highly regarded as human beings.

_____ 3. Feminists disagree among themselves about whether men and women are quite different from each other or whether the two genders are fairly similar.

_____ 4. In the early 1900s, psychologists had already demonstrated that the menstrual cycle did not have a major effect on intellectual abilities.

_____ 5. Research on the psychology of women grew rapidly in the 1950s in both the United States and Canada.

_____ 6. The number of psychology articles and books about gender written each year has more than tripled since the 1980s.

_____ 7. Many large-scale medical studies have been conducted using only male participants.

_____ 8. A problem in research on gender is that researchers' expectations can influence the results of the study.

_____ 9. Native Americans in the United States have about 200 different tribal languages.

_____ 10. Gender differences are larger when researchers observe people in real-life situations, rather than in a laboratory setting.

CHAPTER 1

Central Concepts in the Psychology of Women
Sex and Gender
Social Biases
Feminist Approaches
Psychological Approaches to Gender Similarity and Difference

A Brief History of the Psychology of Women
Early Studies of Gender Comparisons
The Emergence of the Psychology of Women as a Discipline
The Current Status of the Psychology of Women

Problems and Biases in Research
Formulating the Hypothesis
Designing the Study
Performing the Study
Interpreting the Data
Communicating the Findings
Critical Thinking and the Psychology of Women

Women of Color

About This Textbook
Themes of the Book
How to Use This Book

Consider the following items, reported in recent months:

- Women at the Mitsubishi Corporation in Illinois reported that as many as 500 female employees had experienced sexual harassment. For example, one woman reported that the male employees would surround her, fondling her breasts and grasping at her crotch. Many of the men said that they had thought there was nothing wrong with this behavior (Benokraitis, 1997a).
- One of my students brought in a copy of a flyer that had been posted at her father's workplace, a company that manufactures chemicals. The sheet of paper described the "chemical analysis of the element Woman." The physical properties included "Boils at nothing—freezes without reason" and "Found in various states from virgin metal to common ore." A chemical property was "Most powerful money-reducing agent known." A chemical test was "Turns green when placed beside a better specimen."
- According to newspaper reports, a woman in Afghanistan was beaten in a public shopping area because she was "improperly dressed." She had failed to follow the religious dress code of covering her ankles.

These examples illustrate a pattern that we will encounter throughout this book. Even as the twenty-first century begins, women are frequently treated differently from men. This differential treatment is often relatively subtle, but it can also be life-threatening.

Furthermore, women and issues important to them are frequently neglected by the popular media and the academic community. For example, I searched for topics related to women in the index of a popular introductory psychology textbook. Pregnancy isn't mentioned, but the index has an entry for a relatively rare insect: "praying mantis, disinhibitory mechanism in." The topic of rape is similarly missing from the index, but the letter-r listings includes multiple references to reflexes, regional cerebral blood flow, and rats.

The reason we study the psychology of women is to explore a variety of psychological issues that specifically concern women. Some life experiences are directly experienced only by women; these include menstruation, pregnancy, childbirth, and menopause. Other events are inflicted almost exclusively on women, such as rape, domestic violence, and sexual harassment. When we study the psychology of women, we can also focus on women's experiences in areas that are usually approached from the male point of view, such as achievement, work, sexuality, and retirement. Still other issues compare females and males. For example, what factors in childhood encourage little girls and boys to behave differently? Do women and men differ substantially in their intellectual abilities or their social interactions? Are women and men *treated* differently? These important topics, which are neglected in most psychology courses, will be our central focus throughout this book.

Our exploration of the psychology of women begins with some important concepts in the discipline. Then we'll briefly consider the history of the psychology of women, as well as some important research issues. The fourth section of the chapter provides a background on women of color, to give you a context for the discussion of ethnicity in later chapters. The final section describes the themes of this book, as well as the features of its design and presentation that can help you learn more effectively.

CENTRAL CONCEPTS IN THE PSYCHOLOGY OF WOMEN

Let's first consider two interrelated terms—*sex* and *gender*—which are crucial to the psychology of women. Other central concepts we'll explore are: several forms of bias, various approaches to feminism, and two psychological viewpoints on gender similarities and differences.

Sex and Gender

The terms *sex* and *gender* have provoked considerable controversy (e.g., Howard & Hollander, 1997; Nicholson, 1994). **Sex** is a relatively narrow term that refers only to those inborn physiological characteristics relating to reproduction such as *sex chromosomes* or *sex organs* (Howard & Hollander, 1997; Lott & Maluso, 1993).

In contrast, *gender* is a broader term. **Gender** refers to psychological characteristics and social categories that are created by human culture. For example, a friend of mine recently showed me a photo of her 7-month-old son, whom the photographer had posed with a football. This photographer is providing gender messages for the infant, his mother, and everyone who sees the photo. As you might guess, the North American understanding of gender is likely to differ strongly from the gender concept in Kenya, China, or Brazil (Howard & Hollander, 1997). Because this textbook focuses on psychology—rather than biology—you'll see the word *gender* more often than the word *sex*. For example, you'll read about gender comparisons, gender roles, and gender stereotypes.

Unfortunately, the distinction between sex and gender is not maintained consistently in psychology articles and books (Howard & Hollander, 1997; Unger &

Crawford, 1993). For instance, a highly regarded scholarly journal is called *Sex Roles,* though a more appropriate title would be *Gender Roles.*

Social Biases

An important term throughout this book is *sexism* (which probably should be renamed *genderism*). **Sexism** is bias against people on the basis of their gender. A person who believes that women cannot be competent lawyers is sexist. A person who believes that men cannot be competent nursery school teachers is also sexist. Sexism can reveal itself in social behavior, in media representations of women and men, and in job discrimination. Sexism can be blatant. For example, Yale Law School students distributed a flyer rating the physical appearance of five women students and describing them in sexual terms (Benokraitis, 1997a). Sexism can also be more subtle, as in using the word *girl* to refer to an adult woman.

Numerous other biases permeate our social relationships. For example, **racism** is bias against differing racial or ethnic groups. For instance, many White college students report that their parents had not allowed Black friends to visit their homes when they were younger (Tatum, 1992). Like sexism, racism provides special privileges to some humans, based on their category membership (Burnham, 1994). As we'll see throughout this book, sexism and racism combine in complex ways. As a result, the experiences of women of color may be quite different from the experiences of European American men.

We'll also examine several other forms of bias. For example, **classism** is bias on the basis of social class, defined in terms of factors such as income, occupation, and education (Howard & Hollander, 1997). Another important problem is **heterosexism,** or bias against lesbians, gay males, and bisexuals—groups that are not exclusively heterosexual. Heterosexism is revealed in the behaviors of individuals, but is also found in the policies of institutions such as the legal system (Herek, 1994). Two other common biases are **ableism,** or bias based on an individual's disability, and **ageism,** or bias (usually against the elderly) based on an individual's age.

Feminist Approaches

A central term throughout this book is feminism—the principle that women should be highly regarded as human beings. **Feminism** values women's experiences and ideas; it argues that women and men should be socially, economically, and legally equal (Hunter College Women's Studies Collective, 1995; L. Jackson et al., 1996).

We must emphasize several additional points about feminists. First, reread the definition of feminism and notice that it does not exclude men. Indeed, men as well as women can be feminists. Many current books and articles discuss feminist males (e.g., Kilmartin, 1994; Levant & Pollack, 1995; O'Neil & Nadeau, 1998). Think about some men you know, or have read about, who advocate feminism more than some of the women you know. (We'll discuss male feminists and the growing discipline of men's studies in the final chapter of this book.)

Second, many of your friends would probably qualify as feminists, even though they may be reluctant to call themselves feminists (L. Jackson et al., 1996). You have probably heard someone say, "I'm not a feminist, but I think men and women should be treated the same." This person may mistakenly assume that a feminist must be a person who hates men, or a person who believes that all males in positions of power should be replaced by females. However, remember that the defining feature of feminism is a high regard for women, not antagonism toward men.

Third, feminism encompasses a variety of ideas and perspectives, rather than a single feminist viewpoint. Let's consider three perspectives:

1. **Liberal feminism** focuses on the goal of gender equality, giving women and men the same rights and opportunities. Liberal feminists argue that this goal can be achieved by reducing our culture's rigid gender roles and by passing laws that guarantee equal rights for women and men (Enns, 1997; Humm, 1995).

2. **Cultural feminism** emphasizes the positive qualities that are presumed to be stronger in women than in men—qualities such as nurturing and caretaking. Cultural feminism therefore emphasizes gender differences that value women, rather than the gender similarities of liberal feminism (Bohan, 1997; Humm, 1995). Cultural feminists often argue that society should be restructured to emphasize cooperation rather than aggression (Kimball, 1995).

3. **Radical feminism** argues that the basic cause of women's oppression lies deep in the entire sex and gender system, rather than in some superficial laws and policies (Bell & Klein, 1996; Tong, 1998). Radical feminists argue that sexism permeates our society, from the personal level in male–female relationships to the national and international level (Hunter College Women's Studies Collective, 1995). Radical feminists often argue that our society especially needs to overhaul its policies on sexuality and on violence against women. They maintain that the oppression of women is so pervasive that massive social changes will be required in order to correct the problem (Tong, 1998).

In Chapter 15, we'll further explore perspectives on feminism and women studies. A central point, however, is that feminism isn't simply one unified point of view. Instead, feminists have created a variety of perspectives on gender relationships and on the ideal pathways for achieving better lives for women. To clarify the three feminist approaches we discussed in this section, try Demonstration 1.1 on page 8.

Psychological Approaches to Gender Similarity and Difference

Psychologists interested in women's studies and gender usually adopt either a similarities perspective or a differences perspective. Let's explore these two approaches.

Differentiating Among Three Approaches to Feminism

Imagine that, in a discussion group, each of these six individuals makes a statement about feminism. Read each statement and write down whether the approach represents liberal feminism, cultural feminism, or radical feminism. The answers are on page 33 (Based on Enns, 1997).

1. Cora: "The way marriage is currently designed, women are basically servants who spend most of their energy improving the lives of other people." _____

2. Nereyda: "Laws must be made to guarantee women the right to be educated the same as men—women need to reach their full potential, just like men do."_____

3. Sylvia: "My goal as a feminist is to value the kind of strengths that have traditionally been assigned to women, so that women can help society learn to be more cooperative."_____

4. María: "Society needs to change in a major way so that we can get rid of the oppression of women."_____

5. Alex: "I think women should be given exactly the same opportunities as men, with respect to promotion in the workplace."_____

6. Terry: "Because women are naturally more peaceful than men, I think women need to organize and work together to build a peaceful society."_____

The Similarities Perspective.   Those who emphasize the **similarities perspective** believe that men and women are generally similar in their intellectual and social skills. These psychologists argue that social forces may create some temporary differences. For example, women may be more submissive than men in the workplace because women typically hold less power in that setting (Kimball, 1995; Lott, 1996). Supporters of the similarities perspective also tend to favor liberal feminism; by reducing gender roles and increasing equal-rights laws, they say, the gender similarities will increase still further.

If the similarities perspective is correct, then why do women and men often *seem* so different? Let's consider an explanation called the social constructionist view. First, however, read the following passage:

Chris was really angry today! Enough was enough. Chris put on the gray suit, marched into work, and went into the main boss's office and yelled: "I've brought in more money for this company than anybody else and everybody gets promoted but me!" . . . The boss saw Chris's fist slam down on the desk. There was an angry look on Chris's face. They tried to talk but it was useless. Chris just stormed out of the office in anger. (Beall, 1993, p. 127)

Most people envision that Chris is a man, though Chris's gender is not stated. Instead, readers *construct* a gender, based on their cultural information about gender.

According to **social constructionism,** individuals and cultures construct or invent their own versions of reality based on prior experiences, social interactions, and beliefs (Beall, 1993; Howard & Hollander, 1997; Hyde, 1996b). Social constructionists argue that we can never objectively discover reality because our observations will always be influenced by our beliefs. (Chapter 2 shows how our thought processes are colored by our culture's myths and practices.) As a result, we tend to perceive, remember, and think about gender in a way that exaggerates the differences between women and men. This textbook (and most other current psychology of women textbooks) supports both the similarities perspective and the social constructionist view.

The Differences Perspective. In contrast, other psychologists interested in women's studies emphasize the **differences perspective,** which argues that men and women are generally different in their intellectual and social skills. Feminist psychologists who support the differences perspective usually emphasize the positive characteristics that have been undervalued because they are associated with women. These psychologists might emphasize that women are more likely than men to be concerned about human relationships and caregiving (Kimball, 1995; Tavris, 1992). As you might imagine, those who favor the differences perspective also tend to be cultural feminists.

People who endorse the differences perspective believe that gender differences can be explained by essentialism. **Essentialism** argues that gender is a basic, stable characteristic that resides *within* an individual. According to the essentialist perspective, all women share the same psychological characteristics—which are very different from the psychological characteristics that all men share. Thus, say the essentialists, women are more concerned than men about caregiving because of their internal nature—not because society currently assigns women the task of taking care of children (Bohan, 1993; Hare-Mustin & Marecek, 1994; Kimball, 1995). We'll explore essentialist views on caregiving in more detail in Chapter 6.

 SECTION SUMMARY *Central Concepts in the Psychology of Women*

1. *Sex* **refers only to physiological characteristics related to reproduction (e.g., sex chromosomes);** *gender* **refers to psychological characteristics (e.g., gender roles).**

2. **Some of the social biases to be discussed in this book include sexism, racism, classism, heterosexism, ableism, and ageism.**

3. **Feminism focuses on high regard for women as human beings; men can be feminists, and many people endorse feminist principles, even if they don't identify themselves as feminists.**

4. **Three feminist perspectives are: liberal feminism, cultural feminism, and radical feminism.**

5. **Psychologists typically support either a gender similarities perspective (combined with social constructionism) or a gender differences perspective (combined with essentialism).**

A BRIEF HISTORY OF THE PSYCHOLOGY OF WOMEN

Psychology's early views about women were generally negative (Bohan, 1992). Consider the perspective of G. Stanley Hall, who founded the American Psychological Association and pioneered the field of adolescent psychology. He opposed college education for young women because he believed academic work would "be developed at the expense of reproductive power" (Hall, 1906, p. 592). As you might imagine, views like Hall's helped promote biased research about gender. Let's briefly examine some of this early work, then trace the emergence of the psychology of women, and finally outline the discipline's current status.

Early Studies of Gender Comparisons

Most of the early researchers in psychology were men, although a few women made valiant attempts to contribute to the discipline of psychology (Pyke, 1998; Scarborough & Furumoto, 1987). The early research on gender specifically focused on gender comparisons, and it was often influenced by sexist biases. Helen Thompson Woolley (1910)—an early woman psychologist—claimed that this early research was permeated with "flagrant personal bias . . . unfounded assertions, and even sentimental rot and drivel . . ." (p. 340).

For example, one early "hot topic" involved the relative size of structures within male and female brains. Early scientists believed that the highest mental capacities were located in the frontal lobes of the brain. Not surprisingly, early researchers reported that men had larger frontal lobes than women. Several years later, researchers decided that the most important mental processes occurred in the parietal lobes, not the frontal lobes. Interestingly, researchers hastily revised their earlier statements. Suddenly, women were found to have *larger* frontal lobes (Shields, 1975). Researchers also "discovered" that women had stunted parietal lobes (Patrick, 1895). In other words, findings were revised to match whatever brain theory was currently fashionable.

During this early period in psychology's history, dozens of researchers assessed gender differences in areas as diverse as fear responses, reading speed, and color preferences (Morawski, 1994). In that same era, two female psychologists conducted important gender-fair research. Helen Thompson Woolley discovered that men and women had similar intellectual abilities and that women actually received superior scores on some memory and thinking tasks (E. James, 1994; H. Thompson, 1903). Leta Stetter Hollingworth demonstrated that the menstrual cycle had little effect on intellectual abilities (Benjamin & Shields, 1990)—a finding we'll discuss in Chapter 4.

The Emergence of the Psychology of Women as a Discipline

Most psychologists paid little attention to research on gender in the early years of psychology. During the 1930s, women constituted roughly one-third of the members of the American Psychological Association (M. Walsh, 1987). However, most of these women were employed in applied areas and social services. Women were seldom hired for faculty positions at research universities—the primary location for conducting psychological research and constructing theories (Furumoto, 1996; Scarborough, 1992). As a result, the psychology of women did not move forward substantially during the first half of the twentieth century (Morawski & Agronick, 1991).

By the 1970s, a greater percentage of psychologists were female. Feminism and the women's movement had gained recognition on college campuses, and courses in women's studies were increasingly introduced. This rapidly growing interest in women had an impact on the field of psychology. For example, the Association for Women in Psychology was founded in 1969. In 1973, the American Psychological Association established a new Psychology of Women division, which is currently one of the largest divisions in the organization (M. Walsh, 1996). In 1974, the Canadian Psychological Association Task Force on the Status of Women in Canadian Psychology was founded (Pyke, 1994). In both countries, the psychology of women became a popular course of study.

Many psychologists found themselves asking questions about gender that had never occurred to them before. Looking back over his life of social activism, one prominent psychologist remarked, "We were actively opposed to anti-Semitism and also to anti-Black policies. I must confess, however, that in those days we remained 'blind' to the evidence of widespread sex discrimination that has recently become salient in American social science" (Stagner, 1997, p. 14). Similarly, I recall suddenly realizing in 1970 that I had completed my undergraduate degree in psychology at Stanford University and my PhD in psychology at the University of Michigan with only one female professor during my entire academic training! [Fortunately, this one female professor was Eleanor Maccoby, whose classic book with Carol Jacklin (1974) helped shape the discipline of the psychology of women.] I wondered why these universities hadn't hired more women professors, and why so little of my training had focused on either women or gender.

During the mid-1970s, the field of the psychology of women expanded dramatically. Researchers eagerly explored topics such as women's achievement motivation and domestic violence, two topics that had previously been ignored (A. Stewart, 1994).

During the late 1970s, historians began to identify important women in psychology's annals. Some of the classic studies in psychology had actually been conducted by courageous women who had not received credit for their achievements (O'Connell & Russo, 1983). We also discovered the obstacles—such as "family responsibilities"—that blocked the majority of women who aspired to professional goals (Scarborough & Furumoto, 1987).

Looking back on the 1970s from the perspective of the current decade, many people have remarked on that decade's sense of excitement and discovery. However, the work done in the 1970s typically had two problems. First, we did not realize that the issue of gender was extremely complicated. Most of us thought, optimistically, that just a handful of factors could explain, for example, why so few women held top management positions. Now we realize that the explanation encompasses numerous factors, including many that have not yet been identified.

A second problem with the 1970s framework is that women were sometimes blamed for their own fate. In trying to determine why women were scarce in management positions, researchers typically constructed two answers. Women were (a) not assertive enough and (b) afraid of success. The alternate idea—that the *situation* might be faulty—received little attention (Henley, 1985; Unger, 1983). Some of the research (and most of the treatment of that research in the popular media) was emphatic: The fault rested in women's personalities, rather than in social structure, stereotypes, and institutions.

The Current Status of the Psychology of Women

During the current era, we have learned that questions about the psychology of women are likely to generate complex answers. Research in this area continues to increase rapidly. For example, Worell (1996) located 589 psychology articles and books on gender published in 1983, compared to 2,782 in 1993. Three journals that are especially likely to publish relevant articles are *Psychology of Women Quarterly, Sex Roles,* and *Feminism & Psychology.*

A related development is that psychologists are increasingly aware how factors such as ethnicity, social class, and sexual orientation interact in complex ways with gender. As you'll see throughout this book, we typically cannot make statements that apply to *all women.* Contrary to the essentialist approach, women are far from a homogeneous group. As we'll note in Chapter 12, for example, the incidence of eating disorders seems to depend on factors such as ethnic group and sexual orientation.

The current psychology of women is also interdisciplinary. In preparing all four editions of this book, I consulted resources in areas as varied as biology, medicine, sociology, anthropology, history, philosophy, media studies, economics, political science, business, education, religion, and linguistics. In preparing this current edition, I accumulated a stack of reprints that was literally more than 6 feet tall, in addition to more than 500 relevant books, all published in the past 4 years!

Still, research on the psychology of women is relatively young, and several important issues are not yet clear. At many points throughout this textbook, you will read a statement such as, "We don't have enough information to draw conclusions." My students tell me that these disclaimers irritate them: "Why can't you just tell us what the answer is?" In reality, however, stating a firm conclusion would be dishonest.

Another issue is that our knowledge base continues to change rapidly. Because new research often requires revision of a previous generalization, this current edition is substantially different from the three earlier editions. For example, the coverage of gender comparisons in cognitive abilities bears little resemblance to the material on that topic in the first edition. Other areas that have changed dramatically include adolescence, women and work, substance abuse, and sexually transmitted diseases.

The field of psychology of women is especially challenging because both women and men continue to change in some ways as we begin the new century. We'll see, for example, that the number of women working outside the home has changed dramatically. Other human characteristics—such as the nature of long-term memory or shape perception—remain constant from year to year. However, women in 1999 are somewhat different from women in 1959. It is fascinating to contemplate the future of the psychology of women in the twenty-first century!

 A Brief History of the Psychology of Women

1. **Early research on gender examined gender differences and often seemed focused on establishing female inferiority; however, Helen Thompson Woolley and Leta Stetter Hollingworth conducted gender-fair research.**

2. **Gender research was largely ignored until the 1970s, when psychology of women became an emerging field in both the United States and Canada; however, researchers in that era did not anticipate the complexity of the issues, and blame for the fate of women was often placed on the women themselves.**

3. **In the current era, research on gender is continually increasing, and it is interdisciplinary; the knowledge base continues to change as a result of this research.**

PROBLEMS AND BIASES IN RESEARCH

The previous section mentioned the biased research that characterized the early history of the psychology of women. Let's now shift our focus to the important topic of research in this discipline. Specifically, let's explore the kinds of problems that are likely to arise today, when people conduct research on gender or the psychology of women.

Anyone conducting research in psychology faces the problem of potential biases. However, biases are a particular problem in research on the psychology of women because researchers are likely to have strong preexisting emotions, values, and opinions about the topics being investigated. In contrast, most researchers in the area of shape perception probably did not acquire strong emotional reactions to topics such as the retina and the visual cortex as they were growing up! These preexisting reactions may be especially strong in connection with research on women who do not conform to the traditional feminine stereotypes (e.g., unmarried women or lesbian mothers).

Table 1.1 shows how biases can influence each step within the research process. As you can see, inappropriate procedures can create problems when researchers formulate the hypothesis, design the study, perform the study, interpret the data, and communicate the findings. Let's look at each phase in more detail.

Formulating the Hypothesis

Researchers are often strongly committed to a certain psychological theory. If this theory is biased against women, the researchers may be predisposed toward biased findings before they even begin to conduct their study (Caplan & Caplan, 1999). For example, one of Sigmund Freud's theories argued that women are **masochistic** (pronounced "mass-owe-*kiss*-tick"); they actually enjoy suffering. Psychologists who endorse this concept will be biased when they conduct research about women who have experienced domestic violence.

A second problem is that psychologists may formulate a hypothesis based on previous research that is unrelated to the topic they want to study. Several decades ago, for example, researchers wanted to determine whether children were psychologically harmed when their mothers worked outside the home. Psychologists' own biases against employed mothers led them to studies showing that children raised in low-quality orphanages often developed psychological problems. The situation of a child whose mother works outside the home is very different from the situation of a child raised in an institution without a mother or father. Still, these early researchers argued that the children of employed mothers would develop similar psychological disorders.

The final way biases can influence hypothesis formulation concerns the kinds of questions that researchers ask. For example, researchers who are

TABLE 1.1	Stages at Which Biases Can Influence the Research Process

I. Formulating the hypothesis
   A. Using a biased theory
   B. Formulating a hypothesis on the basis of unrelated research
   C. Asking questions only from certain content areas
II. Designing the study
   A. Selecting the operational definitions
   B. Choosing the participants
   C. Choosing the experimenter
   D. Including confounding variables
III. Performing the study
   A. Influencing the outcome through experimenter expectancy
   B. Influencing the outcome through participants' expectancies
IV. Interpreting the data
   A. Emphasizing statistical significance rather than practical significance
   B. Ignoring alternate explanations
   C. Making inappropriate generalizations
   D. Supplying explanations that were not investigated in the study
V. Communicating the findings
   A. Leaving out analyses that show gender similarities
   B. Choosing a title that focuses on gender differences
   C. Journal editors rejecting studies that show gender similarities
   D. Secondary sources emphasizing gender differences instead of gender similarities

studying Native American women typically examine issues such as alcoholism or suicide. The biased attitude that these women are somehow "deficient" keeps researchers from asking questions that might reveal the strengths of these women. For example, do women with extensive tribal experience have different attitudes about growing old?

So far, we have seen that biases can be influential, in several ways, in the early stages of hypothesis formulation. Specifically, biases can influence the theoretical orientation, the previous research that psychologists consider relevant, and the content areas that are investigated.

Designing the Study

An important early step in designing a research study is selecting the operational definitions. An **operational definition** tells exactly how a **variable** (or characteristic) in a study will be measured. Consider a study investigating gender differences in **empathy,** which involves feeling the same emotion that someone else is feeling. For our operational definition, suppose we decide to ask people questions such as, "When your best friend is feeling sad, do you also feel sad?" In other words, we will measure empathy in terms of self-report.

This operational definition for empathy may look perfectly innocent until we realize that it contains a potential bias. Women and men may really be equal in their empathy, but men may be more hesitant to *report* that they feel empathic. Gender stereotypes emphasize that men should not be overly sensitive. Perhaps if we had used another measure (maybe watching people's faces as they look at a sad movie), we might have reached a different conclusion about gender differences in empathy. In fact, a hypothesis should ideally be tested with several different operational definitions to provide a richer perspective of the research question.

The second source of bias in research design is the choice of participants. Some researchers have studied men more than women. For example, Chapter 11 points out that medical researchers used only male participants in conducting many large-scale studies on important health questions. At present, psychologists study roughly equal numbers of men and women (Ader & Johnson, 1994). However, they typically conduct research with participants who are European American, middle-class individuals—most often, college students. As a result, we know relatively little about people of color and people who are economically poor (Reid & Kelly, 1994; Yoder & Kahn, 1993). The choice of research topics also influences the choice of participants. Studies on welfare mothers or on female criminal behavior have typically focused on African American women and Latinas, but studies on body image or employment equity have usually been limited to European Americans.

A third source of bias in designing a study is the choice of the experimenter who will conduct the study. The gender of the experimenter may make a difference (e.g., Levine & Le De Simone, 1991). Let's imagine that a researcher wants to compare women's and men's interest in babies. If the experimenter is a man, males may be embarrassed to demonstrate a strong interest in babies; gender differences may be large. The same study conducted by a female experimenter could produce minimal gender differences.

A final source of bias is the inclusion of confounding variables. A **confounding variable** is any characteristic—other than the central variable being studied—that is not equivalent in all conditions. In studies that compare women and men, a confounding variable is some variable other than gender that is different for the two groups of participants. For example, if we want to compare the mathematics performance of college men and women, a potential confounding variable is the number of courses in mathematics and science they have taken

(M. Crawford, 1989). Because college men are likely to have taken more of these courses, any gender difference in math performance might be traceable to the discrepancy in the number of previous math courses, rather than to a true difference in the actual mathematics ability of college women and men.

The reason we want to be wary of confounding variables is that we need to compare two groups that are as similar as possible in all characteristics except the central variable we are studying. Careless researchers may fail to take appropriate precautions. For example, suppose that researchers want to study whether sexual orientation influences psychological adjustment, and they decide to compare married, heterosexual women with women who are lesbians. The two groups are not appropriate for comparison (Herek et al., 1991). For example, some of the lesbians may not currently be in a committed relationship. Depending on the goals of the researchers, a more appropriate study might compare single heterosexual women in a committed relationship and single lesbians in a committed relationship.

Each of these problems in designing a study may lead us to draw inadequate or inappropriate conclusions. The underrepresentation of females in some research means that we do not know much about their behavior in certain areas. Furthermore, decisions about operational definitions, the gender of the experimenter, and the inclusion of confounding variables may influence the nature of the conclusions.

Performing the Study

Further complications arise when the study is actually performed. One source of bias at this point is called experimenter expectancy (Rosenthal, 1976, 1993). According to the concept of **experimenter expectancy** or **researcher expectancy,** the bias that researchers bring to the study can influence the outcome. If researchers expect males to perform better than females on a test of mathematics ability, they may somehow treat the two groups differently; males and females may therefore respond differently. Any researcher—either male or female—who has different expectations for males and females can produce these expectancy effects.

Others areas of psychology also encounter the problem of experimenter expectancy. However, researchers in those areas can reduce the effect by designing the study so that the experimenter is not aware of which participant is in which condition. If the experimenters in a study on memory don't know which people received a special memory-improvement session and which did not, they won't have different expectations for the two groups. However, in gender research, the investigators can't help noticing which participants are female and which are male! Suppose that researchers are rating female and male adolescents on their degree of independence in working on a difficult task. These ratings may reflect the researchers' expectations and stereotypes about female and male behavior, rather than reality. Parents, teachers, and other observers may supply different ratings for females and males, when an objective frequency tally of their actual behavior would reveal no gender differences.

Participants, as well as researchers, are likely to have absorbed expectations and stereotypes about their own behavior. For example, many women have learned that they are supposed to be moody and irritable just before their menstrual periods. If a woman is told that she is participating in a study on how the menstrual cycle affects mood, she may supply more negative ratings during the premenstrual phase of the cycle. If she had been unaware of the purpose of the study, her responses might have been different. When you read about a study that uses self-report, keep this potential problem in mind. In summary, the expectations of both the researchers and the participants may bias the results so that they do not accurately reflect reality.

Interpreting the Data

The data from studies on gender and the psychology of women can be misinterpreted in many ways. For example, some researchers confuse statistical significance and practical significance. As Chapter 5 discusses, a difference between male and female performance on a math test may be *statistically* significant. **Statistical significance** means that the results are not likely to occur by chance alone. The mathematical formulas used in calculating statistical significance are influenced by sample size. For example, almost any gender difference is likely to be statistically significant if a study has tested 10,000 males and 10,000 females.

Suppose, however, that closer inspection shows that the males received an average score of 40.5, in contrast to females' average score of 40.0. The difference would be statistically significant, as would virtually *any* difference with such an enormous sample size. However, this difference has minimal *practical* significance. **Practical significance,** as the name implies, means that the results have some important implications for the real world. A half-point difference in these hypothetical math scores would have no imaginable implications for how males and females should be treated with respect to mathematics. Unfortunately, researchers often discuss only statistical significance when they should also discuss whether a gender difference has practical significance.

When researchers interpret the data they have gathered, they may be ignoring alternate explanations. For example, suppose researchers claim that males' superior performance on a math test is due to their superior math ability. The researcher may be ignoring an alternate explanation that we mentioned earlier: Males often take more math courses than females. Furthermore, if females score higher on a test measuring anxiety, the difference might really be caused by males' reluctance to *report* anxiety that they feel, rather than by any gender differences in true anxiety. Unbiased research considers alternative interpretations.

An additional problem occurs when researchers make inappropriate generalizations—for example, when they sample unusual populations and draw conclusions from them about the psychological characteristics of normal populations. For instance, after investigating infants who had been exposed to abnormally high levels of male hormones before they were born, researchers might draw conclusions about the way that male hormones influence normal infants (Halpern, 1992). Or, researchers might examine a sample of European American female and male college students and then assume that their findings apply to all people, including people of color and people who have not attended college (Reid & Kelly, 1994). Researchers might also generalize beyond the setting they have tested. For example, they might study social interactions in a laboratory and generalize these findings to a real-life situation, in which the context and social cues would be much richer and more complex (Worell & Robinson, 1994).

Finally, some researchers supply explanations for their results, even when these explanations were never investigated in their study. For example, some researchers investigating females' and males' mathematics ability have detected gender differences and concluded that these differences can be traced to biological sex differences. However, biological components of mathematics ability were never examined as part of their investigation (Caplan & Caplan, 1999; Jacklin, 1983).

In summary, the interpretation phase of research contains several additional possibilities for distorting reality. Researchers have been known to ignore practical significance, bypass alternate explanations, overgeneralize their findings, and supply explanations that were never properly tested.

Communicating the Findings

After researchers conduct the planned studies and perform the related analyses, they usually want to report their findings in writing. Other sources of bias may now enter. One important point to keep in mind is that gender similarities are seldom considered to be startling psychological news (Caplan & Caplan, 1999; M. Crawford, 1989; McHugh et al., 1986). Therefore, when researchers summarize the results of a study, they may leave out a particular analysis showing that females and males had similar scores. However, any gender *difference* that was discovered is likely to be reported. As you can imagine, this kind of selective reporting underrepresents the gender similarities that are found in research, and it overrepresents the gender differences.

Biases are even likely to influence the choice of a title for a research report. Until recently, titles of studies focusing on the psychological characteristics of men and women were likely to include the phrase *gender differences*. Thus, a study examining aggression might be titled "Gender Differences in Aggression," even if it reported one statistically significant gender difference and five comparisons that showed gender similarities. The term *gender differences* focuses on dissimilarities, and it suggests that we should search for differences. Accordingly, I prefer to use the more neutral term *gender comparisons*.

After researchers have written a report of their findings, they send their report to journal editors, who must decide whether it deserves publication. Journal editors, like the researchers themselves, may be more excited about gender differences than gender similarities. Selective publication therefore overrepresents gender differences still further, so that gender similarities receive relatively little attention.

Even further distortion occurs when the published journal articles are discussed by "secondary sources" such as textbooks, newspapers, and magazines. For example, an introductory psychology textbook might discuss one study in which men are found to be more aggressive than women and ignore several other studies that report gender similarities in aggression.

The distortion of results is typically even more blatant when research on gender is reported in the popular press. For example, an article on women and men who own businesses showed a small number of gender differences in decision-making style, and many gender similarities (National Foundation for Women Business Owners, 1994). However, the article summarizing this report in *The Washington Post* carried the headline, "Different Strokes for Different Genders" (Mathews, 1994). Similarly, a newsletter intended for college educators featured the headline "Gender Affects Educational Learning Styles, Researchers Confirm" (1995), even though the original research did *not* find a statistically significant gender difference (Philbin et al., 1995).

In an attempt to entice their audience, the media may even misrepresent the species population. A study on response to pain in male and female mice was later summarized for the *Los Angeles Daily News* with the following leap to the human species: "Women have a gender-specific, natural pain-relief system that depends on estrogen, say researchers at UCLA" ("Gender-Specific Pain Relief," 1993, p. C1; Mogil et al., 1993). Try Demonstration 1.2 to see whether you find similar media biases.

Researchers may have been unbiased in formulating their hypothesis, designing and performing a study, and interpreting the data. However, the publication process often introduces its own variety of bias, and readers may receive a distorted version of the truth. The published version may represent gender differences as being larger than they really are, it may misinterpret the findings, or it may misrepresent women's experiences. Ironically, this distorted version of the truth may then serve as the basis for future theories, because re-

---

DEMONSTRATION 1.2

Analyzing Media Reports About Gender Comparisons

During the next few days, inspect the magazines and newspapers you normally read. Look for any reports on gender comparisons or the psychology of women. Check Table 1.1 as you read each article. Can you discover any potential biases? Can you find any areas in which the summary does not include enough information to make a judgment (e.g., the operational definition for the relevant variables)?

searchers examine the published literature to discover ideas for new studies. As a result, the cycle will begin all over again. Researchers know that publishers and secondary sources favor studies demonstrating gender differences. Therefore, they may tend to examine areas where gender differences are likely, ignoring areas where they expect to find gender similarities.

Critical Thinking and the Psychology of Women

As we have discussed, people must be cautious when they encounter information about gender; published material must be inspected for a variety of potential biases. This vigilance is part of a more general approach called critical thinking. **Critical thinking** requires you to:

1. Ask good questions about what you see or hear;
2. Determine whether conclusions are supported by the evidence that has been presented;
3. Suggest alternative interpretations of the evidence.

One of the most important skills you can acquire in a course on the psychology of women and gender is the ability to think critically about the issues. Unfortunately, the popular culture does not encourage this skill. We are often asked to believe what we see or hear, without asking good questions, determining whether the evidence supports the conclusions, or suggesting other interpretations.

Consider, for example, a scenario described by psychologist Sandra Scarr (1997). She was invited to discuss the topic of mothers' employment on National Public Radio, and she described eight recent research studies, all showing that maternal employment had no impact on infants' emotional security. The other female guest on the show was a psychotherapist, the author of a new book arguing that mothers should stay home. The source of her evidence was presumably her own clients, who reported that they had been emotionally harmed by having a caretaker other than their mother. The psychotherapist argued that she must speak for young infants, because she knows their pain and they are too young to express their distress.

Scarr reports that both the talk-show host and those who called the show seemed to consider her research evidence and the other guest's intuitive evidence to be equally persuasive. Critical thinkers, however, would ask good questions, examine the evidence, and think of other interpretations. For example, they might ask whether we should generalize from the retrospective reports of a small number of therapy clients in order to draw conclusions about infants in the 1990s. They might also ask whether the psychotherapist ever directly measured distress in the young infants she claimed to represent. Naturally, critical thinkers would also examine Scarr's more research-based findings for evidence of potential bias.

Because accuracy is an important aim of research, we must identify and eliminate the sources of bias that can distort accuracy and misrepresent women. We must also use critical thinking skills to examine the research evidence. Only then can we have a clear understanding about women and gender.

 Problems and Biases in Research

1. **During the hypothesis-formulation stage of research, biases can influence researchers' theoretical orientation, the research they consider relevant, and the content areas they choose to investigate.**

2. **During the study-design stage of research, biases can influence the choice of an operational definition, the choice of participants, the choice of the experimenter, and the inclusion of confounding variables.**

3. **When the study is performed, biases include experimenter expectancy, as well as the participants' expectations.**

4. **When the results are interpreted, biases include ignoring practical significance, ignoring alternate explanations, overgeneralizing the findings, and supplying expectations that had not been tested.**

5. **When the findings are communicated, gender differences may be overreported, or the title may emphasize gender differences; articles on gender difference may receive preference, and the popular media may distort the research.**

6. **Being alert for potential biases is part of critical thinking, which requires asking good questions, determining whether the evidence supports the conclusions, and proposing alternative interpretations for the evidence.**

WOMEN OF COLOR

At the start of this chapter, we introduced the term *racism,* or bias against certain ethnic groups. In the section just completed, we discussed how bias in designing a research study may lead psychologists to examine only European American* individuals and to ignore people of color. In this section, we'll specifically focus on ethnicity, in order to provide a framework for future discussions.

Peggy McIntosh (1998) discusses how North American culture is based on the hidden assumption that being White is normative in our culture. As the normative group, White people have certain privileges that they often take for granted. For example, as a White woman, McIntosh can be certain that her children will be taught material that focuses on their ethnic group. In contrast, a

---

*At present, our terminology for ethnicity is in flux. I will use the terms *European American* and *White* interchangeably.

child from any other ethnic background has no such guarantee. If a White woman acts in an impolite manner, people will not assume that her impolite behavior is characteristic of all White people. She can use a credit card or a check and not arouse suspicions about its legitimacy. Can you think of other hidden assumptions that are customary in our White-normative culture?

Many people of color report that their personal identity changed during childhood, as they grew to understand racism. For example, in her book *Black Feminist Thought,* Patricia Hill Collins recalls her childhood experiences as a Black female:

> When I was five years old, I was chosen to play Spring in my preschool pageant. Sitting on my throne, I proudly presided over a court of children portraying birds, flowers, and other, "lesser" seasons. Being surrounded by children like myself—the daughters and sons of laborers, domestic workers, secretaries, and factory workers—affirmed who I was. When my turn came to speak, I delivered my few lines masterfully, with great enthusiasm and energy. I loved my part because I was Spring, the season of new life and hope. All of the grown-ups told me how vital my part was and congratulated me on how well I had done. Their words and hugs made me feel that I was important and that what I thought, and felt, and accomplished mattered.
>
> As my world expanded, I learned that not everyone agreed with them. Beginning in adolescence, I was increasingly the "first," or "one of the few," or the "only" African American and/or woman and/or working-class person in my schools, communities, and work settings. I saw nothing wrong with being who I was, but apparently many others did. My world grew larger, but I felt I was growing smaller. I tried to disappear into myself in order to deflect the painful, daily assaults designed to teach me that being an African-American, working-class woman made me lesser than those who were not. And as I felt smaller, I became quieter and eventually was virtually silenced. (P. Collins, 1990, p. xi)

Incidentally, Collins uses two terms—*Black* and *African American*—to refer to her own ethnicity. In general, I'll use the term *Black* because it is more inclusive. *African American* seems to exclude many North Americans who feel a strong connection to their Caribbean roots (e.g., in Jamaica, Trinidad, or Haiti), as well as Blacks who live in Canada. As the Black Poet Laureate Gwendolyn Brooks said in an interview, she likes to think of Blacks as family, who happen to live in countries throughout the world. *Black* is a welcoming term, like an open umbrella (B. Hawkins, 1994).

Table 1.2 shows the estimated number of U.S. residents in the major ethnic groups, and Table 1.3 indicates the geographic origins of people who immigrated to Canada. As the U.S. data indicate, Blacks constitute the second largest ethnic group in the United States. Blacks may include people who live in cities, suburbs, and rural areas. Some may have arrived recently from Africa or the Caribbean, whereas the families of others may have lived in North America since the 1700s.

Latinas/Latinos are currently the third largest ethnic group in the United States. At present, most individuals in this ethnic group prefer this term rather than *Hispanic,* the term used by the U.S. Bureau of the Census (Espín, 1997; E. Martínez, 1997). The problem is that *Hispanic* focuses on Spanish origins, rather than Latin

TABLE 1.2	Projected Estimate for the U.S. Population, by Ethnic Group, for the Year 2000 (Day, 1996)

Ethnic Group	Estimated Population
White	226,000,000
Black	35,000,000
Latina/o	31,000,000
Asian American	11,000,000
Native American	2,000,000

Note: Some individuals may list themselves in more than one category.

American identity. Unfortunately, though, the term *Latinos* has an *-os* ending that renders women invisible when speaking about both males and females. I will follow the current policy of using *Latinas* to refer to women of Latin American origin and *Latinas/Latinos* or *Latinas/os* to refer to both genders. Incidentally, Mexican Americans are often called *Chicanas* or *Chicanos*, so you'll sometimes see this term used to refer to individuals with Mexican origins (E. Martínez, 1997).

Latinas/os share a language and many similar values and customs. However, a Chicana growing up in a farming community in central California has different experiences from a Puerto Rican girl living in Manhattan. Furthermore, a Latina whose family has lived in Iowa for three generations has different experiences from a Latina who recently left her Central American birthplace because her family had been receiving death threats. Even under ideal circumstances, an immigrant experiences a series of losses that are unfamiliar to someone with deep

TABLE 1.3	Origins of Canadian Immigrants (Based on Colombo, 1998)

Origin by Geographic Region	Number of Residents
Europe	1,392,000
Asia	973,000
Caribbean	240,000
Latin America	210,000
Africa	98,000

Note: Total population of Canada is about 27,000,000.

roots in a community. Oliva Espín describes her own experiences with these losses:

> Indeed, the loss experienced by an uprooted person encompasses not only the big and obvious losses of country, a way of life, and family. The pain of uprootedness is also activated in subtle forms by the everyday absence of familiar smells, familiar foods, familiar routines for doing the small tasks of daily life. (Espín, 1997, p. 23)

Like Hispanics, Asian Americans come from many different countries. Asian Americans include—in order of population in the United States—Chinese, Filipinos, Japanese, Vietnamese, Koreans, Asian Indians, and more than 23 other ethnic-cultural groups (True, 1990). Consider a Laotian woman who is one of the 10,000 refugees belonging to the Hmong tribe and now living in Minnesota. She may have little in common with an Asian Indian woman who is a physician in New Jersey or a Taiwanese woman living in Toronto's Chinatown.

Asian Americans are often stereotyped as the "ideal minority group," and they are often academically successful. For example, Asian American women are twice as likely as European American women to earn a college degree (Root, 1995). However, we'll see throughout this book that women from an Asian background face many roadblocks. Kang, a Korean doctor, addressed this issue:

> At the professional level, it is hard for a woman or a foreigner to take an important position as a chairman or a director of a department or an association. First of all, people don't feel comfortable with anyone who is different. They tend to think of difference as inferiority before I even have a chance to say anything. (as quoted in Chow, 1994, pp. 210–211)

Native Americans and Canadian aboriginals (as this ethnic group is often called in Canada) may share a common geographic origin and a common history of being invaded and dispossessed by White North Americans. However, their languages, values, and current lifestyles may have little in common (LaFromboise et al., 1990). In fact, they may represent the most diverse ethnic group. In the United States, for example, they have about 200 different tribal languages and 517 separate native backgrounds (Garbarino & Kostelny, 1992; LaFromboise et al., 1993).

Many Native American women struggle as they try to integrate their own aspirations with the values of their culture. For example, a Native American teenager explained this conflict:

> As a young woman, I should have been starting a family. When Grandma told them I was going to college, they'd look away. But in my eyes, going to college wasn't going to make me less Indian or forget where I came from. (Garrod et al., 1992, p. 86)

We have seen that each ethnic group consists of many different subgroups. Even if we focus on one specific subgroup—perhaps Chinese Americans—the variability within that one subgroup is always greater than the variability between groups (Bronstein & Quina, 1988). In focusing on how the various ethnic groups differ from one another, keep in mind the difficulty of drawing any generalizations that also reflect this within-group diversity. As we noted at the beginning of this section, we must reexamine the perspective that routinely considers European Americans to be normative. Elsa Brown (1990) writes:

> One of the central problems that confronts those of us who attempt to teach or write about nonwhite, non-middle class, non-Western persons is how to center our work, our teaching, in the lives of the people about whom we are teaching and writing. . . . No matter how much prior preparation they have had, in large measure our students come to us having learned a particular perspective on the world, having been taught to see and analyze the world in particular ways, and having been taught that there are normative experiences and that they are those of white, middle-class Western men and women. (pp. 9–10)

The majority of the research on women still describes the experience of White, middle-class people, but the focus of the discipline is broadening. Whenever possible, the chapters in this book examine the diversity of experiences for all women.

 SECTION SUMMARY   *Women of Color*

1. **In North American culture, being White is normative; people of color often report painful early lessons about racism.**

2. **Blacks constitute the second largest ethnic group in the United States; Blacks differ from one another with respect to their residential community and their family background.**

3. **Latinas/os share a language, as well as many values and customs, but other characteristics vary tremendously.**

4. **Asian Americans also come from diverse backgrounds; although they are considered the "ideal minority," they often experience discrimination.**

5. **Even though Native Americans and Canadian aboriginals share a common geographic origin and history, they are perhaps the most diverse of all ethnic groups.**

6. **The variability within any ethnic group—or subgroup—is always greater than the between-group variability.**

ABOUT THIS TEXTBOOK

This book has been designed to help you understand and remember concepts and information about the psychology of women. Let's first consider the four themes of the book, and then we'll examine some features that will help you learn more effectively.

Themes of the Book

The subject of the psychology of women is impressively complex, and the discipline is so young that we cannot point out a large number of general principles that summarize this diverse field. Nevertheless, you'll find that several important themes are woven throughout this textbook. Let's discuss them now, to provide a framework for a variety of topics you will encounter.

Theme 1: Psychological Gender Differences Are Typically Small and Inconsistent.   The earlier section on research biases noted that the published results may represent the gender differences as being larger than they really are. However, even the published literature on men's and women's abilities and personalities shows that the gender similarities are usually more impressive than the gender differences. In terms of permanent, internal psychological characteristics, women and men simply are not very different (Aries, 1996; S. Bem, 1993). In gender research, one study may demonstrate a gender difference, but a second study—apparently similar to the first—may demonstrate a gender similarity. As Unger (1981) remarked, gender differences often have a "now you see them, now you don't" quality.

You'll recognize that Theme 1 is consistent with the similarities perspective discussed on page 8. Theme 1 also specifically rejects the notion of essentialism. As we noted earlier, essentialism argues that gender is a basic, stable characteristic that resides within an individual.

Let's clarify two points, however. First, I am arguing that men and women are *psychologically* similar; obviously, their sex organs make them anatomically different. Second, men and women acquire some different skills and characteristics in our current culture because they occupy different social roles (Aries, 1996). Men are more likely than women to be chief executives, and women are more likely than men to be secretaries. However, if men and women could have similar social roles in a culture, those gender differences would be almost nonexistent.

Throughout this book, we will see that gender differences may appear in some situations, but not in others. Gender differences are most likely to occur in these three contexts:

1. When people evaluate themselves, rather than when a researcher records behavior objectively;

2. When people are observed in real-life situations, rather than in a laboratory setting;

3. When people are aware that they are being evaluated by others.

In these three kinds of situations, people drift toward stereotypical behavior. Women tend to respond the way they think women are supposed to respond; men tend to respond the way they think men are supposed to respond.

Theme 1 focuses on **gender as a subject variable,** or a characteristic within a person that influences the way she or he acts. We will see that the gender of the subject—that is, the person who is being studied—typically has little impact on behavior.

Theme 2: People React Differently to Men and Women.   We just pointed out that gender as a subject variable is usually not important. In contrast, gender as a *stimulus variable* is important. When we refer to **gender as a stimulus variable,** we mean a characteristic of a person to which other people react. Psychologists studying memory might examine word length as a stimulus variable: Do people remember short words better than long ones? Psychologists studying gender often examine gender as a stimulus variable: Do people react differently to people who are female than to people who are male?

Gender is an extremely important social category—perhaps the most important—social category in North American culture (S. Bem, 1993; Unger, 1988). To illustrate this point, try ignoring the gender of the next person you see!

Throughout the book, we will see that gender is an important stimulus variable. In general, we will see that males are more valued than females. For example, many parents prefer a boy—rather than a girl—for their firstborn child. Men are also more valued in the workplace. Chapter 2 will discuss how males are represented more positively in religion and mythology, as well as in current language and the media.

If people react differently to men and women, they are illustrating that they believe in gender differences. We could call this phenomenon "the illusion of gender differences." As Rhoda Unger (1979) emphasizes, "Men and women are especially alike in their beliefs about their own differences" (p. 1086).

Theme 3: Women Are Less Visible Than Men in Many Important Areas.
Men are typically featured more prominently in areas that our culture considers important. A quick skim through a current newspaper will convince you that males and "masculine" topics receive more emphasis. Chapter 2 discusses the research on all forms of media, confirming that men are seen and heard more than women. Another example is the relative invisibility of girls and women in the classroom, because teachers tend to ignore females (Sadker & Sadker, 1994). Females may also be relatively invisible in the English language. In many respects, our language has traditionally been **androcentric:** the male experience is treated as the norm (S. Bem, 1993, 1996). Instead of *humans* and *humankind,* many people still use words such as *man* and *mankind* to refer to both women and men.

Psychologists have helped keep some important topics invisible. For example, several major biological events in women's lives have received too little attention from psychology researchers. These events include menstruation, pregnancy, childbirth, and breastfeeding. Women *are* visible in areas such as the women's magazines, advertisements for laundry soap, the costume committee for the school play, and low-paying jobs. However, these are all areas that our culture does not consider important or prestigious.

As we noted in the previous section, women of color are even less visible than White women (Caraway, 1991). Chapter 2 emphasizes how women of color are absent in the media. Psychologists have only recently paid attention to this invisible group (Guthrie, 1998). During the early 1990s, urban school systems throughout the United States began discussing special programs aimed at raising the achievement levels of Black boys. This is certainly an admirable goal, but who is paying attention to Black girls? And when was the last time you saw a newspaper article or television show about Asian American women, Latinas, or Native American women?

Theme 4: Women Vary Widely from One Another. This textbook will explore how women differ from one another in their psychological characteristics, their life choices, and their responses to biological events. In fact, individual women show so much variability that we often cannot draw any conclusions about women in general. Notice that Theme 4 contradicts the essentialism perspective, which argues that all women share the same psychological characteristics that differentiate them from men.

Think about the variability among women you know. They probably differ dramatically in their aggressiveness or in their sensitivity to the emotions of others. Women also vary widely in their life choices, in terms of careers, marital status, sexual orientation, desire to have children, and so forth. Furthermore, women differ in their responses to biological events. Some women have problems with menstruation, pregnancy, childbirth, and menopause; others find these experiences neutral or even positive.

In the previous section, we discussed ethnicity and we noted that the diversity within each ethnic group is remarkable. Later, when we examine the lives of women in countries outside North America, we will gather even further evidence that women vary widely from one another.

We have emphasized that women show wide variation. As you might imagine, men show a similarly wide variation among themselves. These within-gender variabilities bring us full circle to Theme 1 of this book. Whenever variability *within* two groups is large, the difference *between* those two groups is not likely to be statistically significant. Chapter 5 discusses this statistical issue in more detail. The important point to remember now is that women (and men) show wide variability.

How to Use This Book

This textbook has been carefully planned to provide many features that will help you learn the material more effectively. Read this section carefully to make the best use of these features.

Each chapter begins with an outline. When you start a new chapter, read through the outline to acquaint yourself with the scope of the chapter. Some of the outline topics relate directly to the four major themes of the book. For example, two of the topics in the Chapter 3 outline are "Gender Comparisons During Infancy" and "How People Respond to Infant Girls and Boys." You might expect to learn in these sections that the actual gender differences are small, but people respond differently to infant girls and boys.

A second feature is a set of ten true–false questions. You can find the answers at the end of each chapter, together with the page number on which each item is discussed. These questions will encourage you to think about some of the controversial and surprising findings you'll encounter in the chapter.

The chapters themselves contain a number of demonstrations, such as Demonstrations 1.1 (page 8) and 1.2 (page 20). Try them yourself, or invite your friends to try them. Each demonstration is simple and requires little or no equipment. The purpose of the demonstrations is to make the material more concrete and personal. Research on memory has demonstrated that material is easier to remember if it is concrete and is related to personal experience (Matlin, 1998; Rogers et al., 1977).

In the text, new terms appear in boldface type (e.g., **gender**), and are defined in the same sentence. I have also included some phonetic pronunciations, with the accented syllable appearing in italics. (My students tell me that they feel more confident about using a word in discussion if they know their pronunciation is correct.) Concentrate on these definitions. An important part of any discipline is its terminology.

Many textbooks include summaries at the end of each chapter, but I prefer section summaries at the end of each major section. For example, this chapter has five section summaries. This feature helps you review the material more frequently, so that you can feel confident about small, manageable portions of the textbook before you move on to new material. At the end of each section, you may wish to test yourself to see whether you can recall the important points. Then check the section summary to see whether you were accurate. Incidentally, some students have mentioned that they learn the material more effectively if they read one section at a time, then take a break, and review that section summary before reading the next portion.

A set of chapter review questions appears at the end of each chapter. Some questions test your specific recall, some ask you to interrelate information from several parts of the chapter, and some ask you to apply your knowledge to everyday situations.

At the end of each chapter is a list of the new (boldface) terms, in the order they appear within the chapter. You can test yourself to see whether you can define each term. Each of these terms also appears in the subject index at the end of the book, so you can check on the terms you find difficult.

A final feature, also at the end of each chapter, is a list of several recommended readings. These are important articles, books, or special issues of journals that are particularly relevant to that chapter. These readings should be useful if you are writing a paper on one of the relevant topics or if an area is personally interesting to you. These resources should encourage you to go beyond the information in the textbook and learn on your own about the psychology of women.

 About This Textbook

1. **Theme 1 states that psychological gender differences are typically small and inconsistent.**
2. **Theme 2 states that people react differently to men and women.**
3. **Theme 3 states that women are less visible than men in many important areas.**
4. **Theme 4 states that women vary widely from one another.**
5. **Features of this book that will help you learn more effectively include the chapter outline, the true–false questions, demonstrations, new terms, section summaries, chapter review questions, the new-terms lists, and recommended readings.**

CHAPTER REVIEW QUESTIONS

1. The terms *sex* and *gender* have somewhat different meanings, although they are sometimes used interchangeably. Define each term, and then decide which of the two terms should be used in connection with each of the following topics: (a) how boys learn "masculine" body postures and girls learn "feminine" body postures; (b) how hormones influence female and male fetuses; (c) a comparison of self-confidence in adolescent males and females; (d) how body characteristics develop during puberty, such as breasts in females and pubic hair; (e) people's beliefs about the personality characteristics of women and men.

2. Apply the two terms *feminism* and *sexist* to your own experience. Do you consider yourself a feminist? Can you identify examples of sexism you have observed during the past week? How do the terms *feminism* and *sexism*—as used in this chapter—differ from the popular use in the media? Also, define and give an example for each of the following terms: classism, heterosexism, ableism, and ageism.

3. Describe the three kinds of feminism discussed in this chapter. How are the two psychological approaches to gender comparisons related to those three kinds of feminism? How are social constructionism and essentialism related to the two psychological approaches?

4. Describe the early research related to gender and the psychology of women. The chapter's section on problems in research discusses biases that arise in

formulating hypotheses. How might these problems be relevant in explaining some of this early research?

5. Briefly trace the development of the psychology of women, from its early beginnings to the current state of the discipline.

6. Imagine that you would like to examine gender comparisons in leadership ability. Trace how a number of biases might influence your research.

7. Suppose that you read an article in a news magazine that concludes, "Women are more emotional than men." From a critical thinking perspective, what questions would you ask in order to uncover potential biases and problems with the study? (Check Table 1.1 to see whether your answers to Questions 6 and 7 are complete.)

8. Turn back to Tables 1.2 and 1.3. Does the information about the diversity of racial and ethnic groups match the diversity at your own college or university? If not, what are the differences? How does the information on ethnicity relate to two of the themes of this book?

9. Describe each of the four themes of this book, providing an example for each theme. Do any of the themes contradict your previous ideas about women and gender? If so, how?

10. What is the difference between gender as a subject variable and gender as a stimulus variable? Suppose that you read a study comparing the aggressiveness of men and women. Is gender a subject variable or a stimulus variable? Suppose that another study examines how people judge aggressive men versus aggressive women. Is gender a subject variable or a stimulus variable?

NEW TERMS

sex (5)
gender (5)
sexism (6)
racism (6)
classism (6)
heterosexism (6)
ableism (6)
ageism (6)
feminism (6)
liberal feminism (7)
cultural feminism (7)
radical feminism (7)
similarities perspective (8)
social constructionism (9)
differences perspective (9)

essentialism (9)
masochistic (14)
operational definition (16)
variable (16)
empathy (16)
confounding variable (16)
experimenter expectancy (17)
researcher expectancy (17)
statistical significance (18)
practical significance (18)
critical thinking (21)
gender as a subject variable (27)
gender as a stimulus variable (28)
androcentric (28)

RECOMMENDED READINGS

Caplan, P. J., & Caplan, J. B. (1999). *Thinking critically about research on sex and gender* (2nd ed.). New York: Longman. Paula Caplan is a well-known psychologist whose work on the psychology of women is discussed throughout this textbook. She and her son Jeremy wrote this excellent book on applying critical thinking principles to the research on gender.

Kimball, M. M. (1995). *Feminist visions of gender similarities and differences.* Binghamton, NY: Haworth. Meredith Kimball has written a wonderfully thoughtful book that explores the similarities and differences perspectives within the psychology of women. She argues that both viewpoints are necessary for a full appreciation of the complexity of gender.

Landrine, H. (Ed.). (1995a). *Bringing cultural diversity to feminist psychology: Theory, research, and practice.* Washington, DC: American Psychological Association. Many excellent books are now available on women of color. This is one of my favorites. In addition to general chapters on cultural diversity, it includes useful chapters on Native Americans, Latinas, Asian American women, and Black women.

Scarborough, E., & Furumoto, L. (1987). *Untold lives: The first generation of American women psychologists.* New York: Columbia University Press. If you are searching for interesting women in the early history of psychology, this book is ideal. It focuses not only on these important women, but also on the forces that shaped their lives.

Walsh, M. R. (Ed.). (1996). *Women, men, and gender: Ongoing debates.* New Haven: Yale University Press. I strongly recommend this book to anyone who would like to examine crucial controversies in the psychology of women. Mary Roth Walsh includes two articles by experts for each of 18 important debates. A short history of the discipline of the psychology of women is an added bonus.

ANSWERS TO DEMONSTRATION 1.1

1. radical feminism; 2. liberal feminism; 3. cultural feminism; 4. radical feminism; 5. liberal feminism; 6. cultural feminism.

ANSWERS TO THE TRUE–FALSE QUESTIONS

1. True (p. 6); 2. True (p. 6); 3. True (pp. 8–9); 4. True (p. 11); 5. False (p. 11); 6. True (p. 12); 7. True (p. 16); 8. True (p. 17); 9. True (p. 25); 10. True (p. 27).

GENDER STEREOTYPES

TRUE OR FALSE?

_____ 1. Women provided the majority of the food consumed by prehistoric humans.

_____ 2. Prior to about 1900, all prominent philosophers maintained that women were clearly inferior to men.

_____ 3. When people hear a sentence like "Each student took his pencil," they tend to think about males more than females.

_____ 4. At present, about one-third of radio talk-show hosts are women.

_____ 5. Latinas and Latinos account for about 2% of all characters on prime-time television.

_____ 6. In cross-cultural research on gender stereotypes, the greatest degree of stereotyping is found in the most developed countries where the major religion is Protestant.

_____ 7. Current surveys indicate that between 10% and 25% of lesbians and gay males have been assaulted.

_____ 8. Most contemporary psychologists explain gender stereotypes as an unconscious desire to discriminate against women.

_____ 9. According to the current theory, masculinity and femininity are exact opposites of each other; if you are high in masculinity, you must be low in femininity.

_____ 10. Research shows that women who are very feminine have higher self-esteem than those who are very masculine.

The Representation of Women and Men
A Heritage of Gender Bias
Representing Women in Language
Representing Women in the Media

People's Beliefs about Women and Men
The Content of Stereotypes
The Complexity of Contemporary Sexism
Heterosexism
The Social Cognitive Approach to Gender Stereotypes
Gender Stereotypes, Self-Fulfilling Prophecies, and Behavior

Gender Typing and the Alternatives
Androgyny
Moving Beyond Androgyny

Dr. Taraneh Shafii, the chief resident at a children's hospital in Louisville, Kentucky, frequently notices the impact of stereotypes. One day, in the emergency department, she introduced herself to the father of a sick child: "Hi, I'm Dr. Shafii." Then she proceeded to ask detailed questions about the child's illness. When it came time for the physical exam, the father said, "Come on, get up for the nice nurse." On that same day, another parent watched Dr. Shafii examine her children and then asked, "Can you tell me when the doctor will be in?" A third time that day, Dr. Shafii again introduced herself and examined a patient, a teenage boy. As she was preparing to put a splint on his broken hand, the boy asked, "So, how long did you have to go to school to be a nurse?" As Dr. Shafii explains, she admires nurses, and she also has many friends and relatives who are nurses. However, her patients often fail to understand that a woman can be a doctor, rather than a nurse. Apparently, their gender stereotypes are so powerful that they counteract the "Dr." in her name, the M.D. on her nametag, and all her medical expertise (Shafii, 1997).

Gender stereotypes are organized, widely shared sets of beliefs about the characteristics of females and males (Golombok & Fivush, 1994). Notice that a stereotype is a *belief*. Stereotypes refer to thoughts, which may not correspond to reality. Even when a gender stereotype may be partly accurate, it still won't apply equally to all individuals (Eagly et al., in press). As Theme 4 points out, individual differences in psychological characteristics are large.

A study by Carol Martin (1987) highlighted the inaccuracy of gender stereotypes. She asked male and female students to rate themselves on personality characteristics such as independence. The self-ratings supplied by males were quite similar to the self-ratings supplied by females. She also asked the same students to rate the "typical male" and the "typical female" on those personality characteristics. The students rated the typical male as being much more independent than the typical female. The same discrepancy occurred for additional "typically masculine" characteristics such as hostility, as well as "typically feminine" characteristics such as helpfulness and gentleness. The study was later replicated by Allen (1995). Consistent with the themes of the book, men's and

36

TABLE 2.1	Comparing Stereotype, Prejudice, and Discrimination— with Respect to Women	
Term	**Brief Definition**	**Example**
Stereotype	Belief about women	Chris believes that women aren't very smart.
Prejudice	Attitude about women	Chris has a negative attitude toward female lawyers.
Discrimination	Behavior about women	Chris won't hire a woman for a particular job.

women's self-ratings suggest gender similarities, though both genders believe that men and women are quite different. Apparently, gender differences are typically smaller than our stereotypes reveal them to be (Deaux & Major, 1987).

Two additional terms are related to stereotypes. **Prejudice** is a negative attitude toward a group of people, such as women (Lott & Maluso, 1995a). **Discrimination** refers to action against a person or a group of people. A person can discriminate against an individual woman by making sexist remarks. Social institutions can also discriminate against groups of women, for example, when a religion has a policy that women cannot take part in a particular ceremony (Lott & Maluso, 1995a). Table 2.1 contrasts these three terms.

Let's begin our examination of gender stereotypes by noting how women have been represented in history, philosophy, and religion, and how they are currently represented in language and the media. The second section of this chapter focuses on the content of contemporary stereotypes: What are the current stereotypes? How are these stereotypes related to thought processes? How can stereotypes influence behavior? In the final section, we'll examine how people sometimes apply these gender stereotypes to themselves, so that they adopt a gender-stereotyped identity. However, they may also create a self-identity that is not constrained by these rigid categories.

THE REPRESENTATION OF WOMEN AND MEN

A systematic pattern emerges when we look at the way women are portrayed. As we'll see in this section, women are the "second sex" (de Beauvoir, 1961). Consistent with Theme 2, women are often represented as being inferior to men. In addition, consistent with Theme 3, women are frequently invisible.

A Heritage of Gender Bias

A few pages of background discussion cannot do justice to a topic as broad as our legacy of gender bias. However, we need to summarize several topics in order to appreciate the origin of current views about women.

The Invisibility of Women in Historical Accounts.   In recent decades, scholars have begun to realize that we know very little about how half of humanity has fared throughout history. What *have* women been doing for all these centuries? Archaeologists interested in prehistoric humans typically focused their research attention on tools associated with hunting, which was most often men's activity. They ignored the fact that women provided the majority of the diet by gathering vegetables and grains (Hunter College Women's Studies Collective, 1995).

Similarly, what were the women doing while the men of Europe were enjoying the Renaissance period? Did they also have a Renaissance? One important goal of women's studies is to look for missing information about women. Women have been invisible in our history books. We need to know about women food-providers, artists, and philosophers.

Women have been left out of many history books because their work was confined to home and family. Women artists often expressed themselves in music, dance, embroidered tapestries, and quilting. These relatively fragile and anonymous art forms were less likely to be preserved than men's artistic efforts in painting, sculpture, and architecture.

In addition, many of women's accomplishments have been forgotten. Did you know that women often presided over monasteries before the 9th century A.D. (Hafter, 1979)? Did your history book tell you that the Continental Congress chose Mary Katherine Goddard to print the official copy of the Declaration of Independence in 1776? Traditional historians—whether consciously or unconsciously—have ensured women's invisibility in most history books. Scholars interested in women's history, however, are uncovering information about women's numerous accomplishments. Many college history courses now focus on women's experiences, making women central rather than peripheral.

Philosophers' Representation of Women.   Philosophers throughout the centuries have commented on women but have typically depicted them as inferior to men. For example, the Greek philosopher Aristotle (384–322 B.C.) believed that women's inferiority was biologically based. He believed that women could not develop fully as rational beings. Aristotle also believed that women are more likely than men to be envious and to tell lies (Book IX, Chapter 1, cited in Miles, 1935, p. 700).

Philosophers since the classical Greek period have adopted the same framework. For instance, Jean Jacques Rousseau (1712–1778) argued that the function of women was to please men and to be useful to them (Hunter College Women's Studies Collective, 1995). In other words, this prominent Enlightenment philosopher was not enlightened about the roles of women! Rousseau's views were echoed by political figures. The French emperor Napoleon Bonaparte (1769–1821) wrote: "Nature intended women to be our slaves. . . . They are our property. . . . Women are nothing but machines for producing children" (cited in Mackie, 1991, p. 26).

Prior to the 20th century, perhaps the only well-known philosopher whose views would be acceptable to current feminists was John Stuart Mill (1806–1873), a British philosopher whose viewpoint was strongly influenced by his wife, Harriet Taylor Mill (1807–1858). John Stuart Mill argued that women should have equal rights and equal opportunities. They should be able to own property, to vote, to be educated, and to choose a profession. John Stuart Mill is prominently featured in philosophy textbooks, but his views on women were omitted until recently (Hunter College Women's Studies Collective, 1995).

Images of Women in Religion and Mythology. We've seen that history and philosophy have not been kind to women. In general, women are also treated differently from men in religion and mythology.

For example, Jews and Christians share the story of Adam and Eve. In this account, God created man "in his own image." Later, God made Eve, constructing her from Adam's rib. In other words, women are made from men, and women are therefore secondary in the great scheme of things. In addition, Eve gives in to temptation and leads Adam into sin. Women's moral weakness therefore contaminates men. When Adam and Eve are expelled from paradise, the curses they receive show an interesting asymmetry. Adam's curse is that he must work for food and survival. Eve's curse is that she must endure the pain of bearing children, and she must also obey her husband.

In the Jewish religion, further evidence of the position of women can be found in the traditional prayer for men, "Blessed art Thou, O Lord our God, King of the Universe, that I was not born a woman." Furthermore, the Torah specifies 613 religious rules, but only three of them apply to women. In these important Jewish traditions, women are relatively invisible (Carmody, 1994; R. Siegel et al., 1995). In addition, women must sit apart from men during Orthodox religious services.

For Christians, many parts of the New Testament treat men and women differently. For example, a letter of St. Paul notes: ". . . the women should keep silence in the churches. For they are not permitted to speak, but should be subordinate, as even the law says" (I Corinthians 14:34).

Key interpreters of the Bible for the Christian religion continued in the same tradition. For instance, Augustine in the 5th century and Thomas Aquinas in the 13th century argued that women's major function was to have children.

As the 21st century begins, Jewish women have become rabbis and scholars (R. Siegel et al., 1995). Women have also assumed leadership responsibilities in

Protestant religions. However, women typically constitute less than 10% of the clergy in both the United States and Canada (Ruether, 1994).

Other religions promote negative views of women. Consider the yin and yang in traditional Chinese beliefs. The yang, the masculine side, represents light and goodness; the feminine yin represents darkness and evil (Levering, 1994).

In the Hindu religion, a woman is defined in terms of her husband. As a consequence, an unmarried woman or a widow has no personal identity (R. Siegel et al., 1995). The Hindu goddess Kali is a dark monster with fangs, crossed eyes, and bloodstained tongue, face, and breasts. Hindus believe her wild dancing brings death on the world.

When we combine views of women from various religions and from traditional Greco–Roman mythology, we can derive several views of women:

1. *Women are evil.* Women may be bloodthirsty, like Kali. They can also bring harm to men, as Eve did to Adam.

2. *Women are terrifying sorceresses.* Women can cast spells, like the wicked witches and evil stepmothers in fairy tales. Scylla, in Greek mythology, was a six-headed sea monster who squeezed men's bones together and ate them.

3. *Women are virtuous.* Women can also be virtuous and saintly, especially when they nurture men and small children. For example, the Virgin Mary represents the essence of caring and of never demanding anything for oneself. Mythology may also represent women as "earth mothers" who are fertile and close to nature (Mackie, 1991).

Notice that these images are sometimes negative and sometimes positive. However, each image emphasizes how women are *different* from men. In these androcentric traditions, men are normal; women are "the second sex."

Representing Women in Language

Language, like religion, encourages a second-class status for women. Specifically, people often use subordinate or negative terms to refer to women. In addition, women are often invisible in language—for example, when the term *he* is used in reference to both men and women. Incidentally, we'll consider a related topic in Chapter 6 when we compare how men and women use language.

Terms Used for Women.   In many situations, people use different terms to refer to men and women, and the two terms are not parallel. For example, John Jones, M.D., will be called a *doctor,* whereas Jane Jones, M.D., may be called a *lady doctor.* This usage implies that being a male doctor is normal, and a female doctor represents an exception.

Sometimes, the female member of a pair of words has a much more negative or sexual connotation than the male member. Think about the positive connotations of the word *bachelor*—a happy-go-lucky person, perhaps with many romantic partners. How about *spinster?* Here the connotation is much more negative; no man wanted to marry her. Similarly, compare *master* with *mistress, major* with *majorette, wizard* with *witch,* and *dog* with *bitch* (Penelope, 1990).

Language may also infantilize women. For example, women are often referred to as "girl" or "gal" or "little lady" in situations where men would not be called "boy" or "little man." In my husband's pediatric practice, drug-company sales representatives—referring to an office staff member who is age 50—often ask, "May I leave this with your *girl?*" They are usually surprised by the answer, "Not unless you want me to tell her the *boy* left it."

Furthermore, men and women are addressed in different ways. Andrea Schmidt may be called "Mrs. George Schmidt" or simply "Andrea," rather than "Andrea Schmidt." In contrast, her husband will be called "George Schmidt." In addition, women are often addressed by strangers as "honey," "dear," and "sweetheart"—terms that would not be used in speaking to men (Benokraitis & Feagin, 1994).

Do terms such as "lady doctor," or infantilizing words such as "girl," have any significance? A study by Dayhoff (1983) showed that words really do matter. She prepared two versions of a fictitious newspaper article about a woman named Joan Delaney, who was a candidate for a local political office. One version described her in sexist terms such as "lady candidate," "gal," "woman reporter," and "girl." The other version used nonsexist language (e.g., "candidate" and "woman"). People tended to rate the candidate as being more competent, more serious, and more intelligent when they had read the nonsexist version rather than the sexist version. Notice the implications of this study: When the media refer to a female political candidate in a sexist fashion, they may be reducing her chances of being elected.

The Masculine Generic. Several years ago, I read a newspaper article about a male counselor at a local elementary school. The counselor was quoted as saying, "When a child sees that he has something in common with me, it's like a miracle the way he opens up." I visualized a troubled boy, feeling comfortable with the counselor and sharing his troubles. But then I wondered: What happens with the troubled girls? Had the counselor's choice of the pronoun *he* reflected a greater concern about the problems of male students? Are their problems more conspicuous? Do the troubled girls feel they have little in common with the counselor, so they rarely "open up"? Most important to our subject here, does the counselor's use of the word *he* tend to limit his thinking so that he provides more service to boys than to girls?

More recently, I opened a cognitive psychology textbook with a 1998 copyright. The first paragraph read: "Who and what are we? What is the mind and how does it function? . . . Such questions certainly have been with us as long as man has existed . . . ." I found myself wondering: Were women really included in the author's term *man?* Women surely pondered the questions too.

The language problem we are considering focuses on the masculine generic. The **masculine generic** is the use of masculine nouns and pronouns to refer to all human beings—both males and females—instead of males alone. Table 2.2 shows some of these masculine generic terms. You've probably heard that masculine pronouns are supposed to refer to both males and females. For example, a teacher may have said that *his* really includes *her* in the sentence, "Each student took his pencil." Essentially, you were supposed to consider *his* in this sentence as being gender neutral.

Researchers have now provided clear evidence that these masculine generic terms are not really gender neutral. The issue is no longer simply a grammatical one; it has become both political and practical.

About 40 studies have demonstrated that terms such as *man* and *he* produce thoughts about males rather than thoughts about both genders (e.g., M. Hamilton, 1988; Ivy et al., 1995; Matlin, 1985; Switzer, 1990). For instance Wilson and Ng (1988) used a machine called a tachistoscope to present—very briefly—either a male or a female face. These photographs were shown so quickly that viewers could not really determine the gender of the person in the photo. Nevertheless, the experimenter asked the participants to guess "male" or "female" for each face. Each face was accompanied by a sentence, which remained on the screen for a long time and was clearly visible. When the sentence contained a masculine generic term (e.g., "All men are created equal"), participants were likely to report that they had seen a male face. In contrast, when the sentence was gender neutral (e.g., "All people are created equal"), participants were much more likely to report having seen a female face. Thus, the word *men* is not really gender neutral, and it biases perception so that people frequently believe they have seen a male face when the stimulus was ambiguous.

TABLE 2.2	Examples of Masculine Generic Terms (American Psychological Association, 1994; Maggio, 1991; C. Miller & Swift, 1988)

businessman	man on the street
chairman	manfully
fellow man	mankind
forefathers	manpower
fraternize	Neanderthal man
he/his/him (to refer to both genders)	patronize
	working man

DEMONSTRATION 2.1

Imagery for Masculine Generic and Gender-Neutral Pronouns

Ask a friend to listen as you read sentence 1 aloud. Then ask the friend to describe out loud any image that comes to mind. Repeat the process with the remaining sentences. For each of the target (T) sentences, note whether your friend's image represents a male, a female, or some other answer.

　　　　1. Fire hydrants should be opened on hot days.

(T)　2. The average American believes he watches too much TV.

　　　　3. The tropical rain forests of Brazil are a natural wonder.

(T)　4. Pedestrians must be careful when they cross the street.

　　　　5. The apartment building was always a mess.

(T)　6. After a patient eats, he needs to rest.

　　　　7. In the corner sat a box of worn-out shoes.

(T)　8. Teenagers often daydream while they do chores.

　Did your friend supply more male images for sentences 2 and 6 than for sentences 4 and 8? To obtain a broader sample of replies, try this demonstration with several friends, or combine data with a number of other classmates.

(Based on Gastil, 1990.)

　Demonstration 2.1 illustrates part of a second study, conducted by John Gastil (1990). Gastil presented a number of target sentences. These were interspersed with irrelevant sentences, so that participants would not suspect the purpose of his study. Some of the target sentences used a masculine generic pronoun (e.g., "The average American believes he watches too much TV"), and some used a gender-neutral pronoun (e.g., "Pedestrians must be careful when they cross the street"). Gastil asked the participants to describe the mental image evoked by each sentence. He then calculated the number of male images and female images reported.

　As Figure 2.1 shows, female participants reported four times as many male images as female images when they responded to sentences containing "he" pronouns. In contrast, females reported an equal number of male and female images (i.e., a 1:1 ratio) when they responded to sentences containing "they" pronouns. Figure 2.1 also shows that males, in responding to the "he" sentences, reported an astonishing 13 times as many male images as female images, but

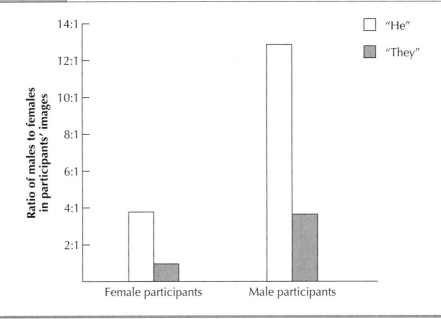

FIGURE 2.1   **The ratio of male images to female images, as a function of the pronoun condition and the gender of the participant. (Based on Gastil, 1990)**

only a 4:1 ratio in response to the "they" sentences. In short, masculine generic terms do indeed produce more thoughts about males than do gender-neutral terms.

Some research has shown that the masculine generic issue has important implications for people's lives. For example, Briere and Lanktree (1983) showed students different versions of a paragraph describing careers in psychology. One group saw a masculine generic version that began: "The psychologist believes in the dignity and worth of the individual human being. He is committed to increasing man's understanding of himself and others. . . . " Other groups saw a gender-neutral version of the paragraph. Then the students were asked to rate whether psychology would be an appealing future career for men and for women. Students who had seen the gender-neutral version rated psychology as more appealing for women than did those who had seen the masculine generic version.

In many sections of this textbook, we will see that attitudes toward gender issues have not changed substantially in several decades. In contrast, the use of gender-biased language has decreased. For example, the masculine generic term "man" is typically replaced by "people." In fact, some observers have stated that the shift to avoid the masculine generic may be one of the most important

TABLE 2.3	Suggestions for Nonsexist Language (Based on American Psychological Association, 1994)

1. Use the plural form. "Students can monitor their progress" can replace "A student can monitor his progress."

2. Use "you." The sentence, "Suppose that you have difficulty recalling your social security number" is less sexist—and also more engaging—than "Suppose that a person has difficulty recalling his social security number."

3. Use "his or her" or "her or his," as in the sentence, "A student can monitor her or his progress." The order of these pronouns may sound awkward, but females do not always need to appear second.

4. Eliminate the pronoun. "The student is typically the best judge of the program" can replace "The student is usually the best judge of his program."

changes in English in the past four centuries (C. Miller et al., 1997). Johnson and Dowling-Guyer (1996) reported a related finding: College students rate psychology counselors more positively if they use gender-neutral language rather than masculine generic language.

Some defenders of the masculine generic argue that language change is too difficult. They complain that "he or she" is so much more work than a simple "he." However, people have learned to use the terms *Black* or *African Americans* rather than the older term *Negroes.* In fact, researchers have found that high school students can easily increase their use of nonsexist language after they have seen appropriate examples (Cronin & Jreisat, 1995).

Many books and articles have been written about converting gender-biased language to gender-neutral phrases (e.g., American Psychological Association, 1994; Foertsch & Gernsbacher, 1997; Maggio, 1991). Table 2.3 provides some suggestions.

Language change does require some effort, and we may find ourselves slipping back into the masculine generic. For example, a truck driver once passed my car when the visibility was poor, and I shouted, "What in the world does he think he is doing?" My daughter, then 9 years old, gently reminded me, "Or *she,* Mom."

Representing Women in the Media

An advertisement for perfume in an upscale magazine shows a woman reclining with her eyes closed, adorned by flowers, as if it is her funeral. An ad for anti-wrinkle cream suggests that women should fight the signs of age because it is a "smart career move" (Faludi, 1991). Can you imagine switching the genders—

using a corpselike male model to advertise men's cologne, or an ad suggesting that an antiwrinkle cream will enhance a man's career? If you want to test whether an advertisement is sexist, switch the genders and note whether the revision seems bizarre.

In Chapter 3, we'll consider media directed at children. In the present chapter, let's first examine gender stereotypes found in media directed at adults, and then we'll discuss the effects of these stereotyped representations.

Stereotyped Representations.   Hundreds of studies have examine how women are represented in the media. From this research, we can draw the following conclusions:

1. *Women are relatively invisible.* Recent studies show that women are underrepresented in the media. For example, women are relatively invisible in the news. Studies of the front pages of newspapers in the United States and Canada show that the articles refer to women only 15–25% of the time (Bridge, 1994; United Nations, 1995; Wheeler, 1994).

Men also dominate entertainment. For example, music videos feature roughly twice as many males as females (Sommers-Flanagan et al., 1993). An analysis of characters on TV shows found 2.4 times as many males as females (Gerbner, 1997).

One place where women *are* seen is in television advertisements, where the numbers of females and males are roughly equal (Furnham & Skae, 1997; Hotaling, 1994). As we'll see, however, the ads portray women in sexist contexts.

2. *Women are relatively inaudible.* Women are not seen much, and they are *heard* even less. For example, only 5% of radio talk-show hosts are women (Flanders, 1997). Women are also inaudible in advertisements. Try to recall a typical television ad. Whose voice of authority is praising the product's virtues? As it turns out, it is almost always a man's voice. The percentage of males in these voice-overs has remained reasonably constant in recent years. Studies in the United States report that 75–90% of voice-overs are male; similar data are reported in Great Britain and Australia (Furnham & Skae, 1997; Hotaling, 1994; Hurtz & Durkin, 1997). Even a March 1999 sample reported that 67% of ads with voice-overs featured males (Rickard, 1999).

3. *Although most women are said to be employed, they are seldom shown working outside the home.* For example, television advertisements are much more likely to show men—rather than women—in an employment setting (Hurtz & Durkin, 1997). In television programs, ironically, women and men are both likely to be described as having professional careers—lawyers, doctors, and architects—an employment pattern that doesn't reflect the real-life distribution of jobs (Kolbe & Albanese, 1997). In addition, women on television shows are seldom shown actually *working* on the job.

In Chapter 4, we'll see that adolescent girls may have ambitious career plans. However, they frequently abandon these plans as they work on cultivating romantic relationships. An analysis of *Seventeen* magazine showed a similar emphasis. Only 7% of the content concerned career planning, independence, and other self-development topics, in contrast to 46% focusing on physical appearance (Peirce, 1990). In other words, the coverage implied, teenage girls should worry about their appearance and they should focus on finding a boyfriend. In magazines intended for adult women, the articles on careers and other serious topics are far outnumbered by advertisements for food, cosmetics, and home products (French, 1992).

4. *Women are shown doing housework.* Here, unfortunately, the percentages probably capture reality quite accurately. For example, the women in the Sunday comics are much more likely than the men to be cleaning the house (Brabant & Mooney, 1997). Television commercials overwhelmingly show women performing household chores—whether the sample is gathered in the United States, Canada, Europe, or Africa (Mwangi, 1996). A recent cartoon portrayed a male advertising executive explaining why he won't use a female copywriter's proposed layout for an ad: "Destereotyping the housewife can't be done overnight, Angela. Be a good kid and let her sing to her mop in this one, and I promise next time she can do something else with it" (Rhode, 1997, p. 71).

5. *Women and men are represented differently.* The media are likely to treat men more seriously than women. Consider the 1992 Senate election in Pennsylvania, where Lynn Yeakel ran against Arlen Specter. *The Washington Post* described in detail Ms. Yeakel's silk suit, her haircut, and her husband's profession. The article did not begin to discuss her political credentials until halfway through the profile. A similar article on Mr. Specter discussed his former employment in detail, never mentioning one word about his wardrobe or his haircut (Bridge, 1993).

The media also portray women and men as having different personalities. The women are relatively powerless and passive, and the men are often aggressive and "macho," both on television and in the movies (Haskell, 1997; Scharrer, 1998). In addition, careful analyses show that the characters in television scripts respond differently to men and women. Lott assessed distancing behavior, which was operationally defined as any head or body movement that increased the physical distance between the characters (Lott, 1989; Lott & Maluso, 1995a). Male characters on TV showed this distancing behavior toward women twice as often as they showed it to men. In other words, men keep their attention focused on other men, but they soon turn away from women.

6. *Women's bodies are used differently from men's bodies.* In magazines, images of overweight women are rarely seen. In action comic books, the women have perfect bodies, and they wear short skirts and clinging body suits (Fraser, 1997a; Massoth, 1997). If you glance through magazine advertisements, you'll also notice that the women are more likely than the men to serve a decorative function. Women recline in seductive clothes, caressing a liquor bottle, or they drape themselves coyly on the nearest male. In contrast, the men are strong and muscular, and they adopt rigid body posture (Kolbe & Albanese, 1996). The research confirms that women are frequently shown lying down or bent at an

angle, whereas men are posed to look more dignified (Belknap & Leonard, 1991; Jones, 1991). Also, women's whole bodies are typically shown, whereas a photo of a man is likely to show only his face (Belknap & Leonard, 1991; C. Hall & Crum, 1994).

7. *Women of color are underrepresented and they are often shown in a particularly biased way.* On television, people of color appear primarily in the situation comedies (C. Wilson & Gutiérrez, 1995). African Americans are now represented in a reasonable number of TV programs and advertisements. However, other ethnic groups are virtually invisible. For example, Latinas/os now represent more than 10% of the U.S. population, but they account for only about 2% of all characters on prime-time television (Espinosa, 1997). Most often, these Latinas/os are featured only in minor supporting roles (Cortés, 1997).

In the earlier discussion of women and religion, we noted that religions represent women as either saints or sinners. The same polarized representation is often true for women of color in the media. Most women of color are either "good girls" or "bad girls"—either asexual or sexpots. The characters are seldom well enough developed to reveal the interesting combination of traits depicted in the media for European American individuals (Espinosa, 1997; Goodwin, 1996; Rodríguez, 1997b). Sadly, researchers have noted that even the movies directed by men of color tend to perpetuate sexist stereotypes (G. Cowan, 1995). In summary, women of color are both underrepresented and misrepresented by the media.

Now that you are familiar with some of the ways in which women are represented in the media, try Demonstration 2.2. Also, start analyzing magazine

---

DEMONSTRATION 2.2

The Representation of Women and Men on Television

Keep a pad of paper next to you during the next five television programs you watch, so that you can monitor how women and men are represented. Use one column for women and one for men, and record the activity of each individual who appears on screen for more than a few seconds. Use simple codes to indicate what each person is doing, such as working outside the home (W), doing housework (H), or performing some activity for other family members (F). In addition, record the number of female and male voice-overs in the advertisements. Can you detect any other patterns in the representations of women and men, aside from those mentioned in the text?

advertisements to assess stereotyped representations. Pay particular attention to any nontraditional advertisements. Is the female lawyer who is arguing the case looking both confident and competent? How about the father who is changing the baby's diaper?

You may want to share your views with the advertisers. (You can obtain companies' addresses from a library; many companies are also on the World Wide Web.) Sponsors are often very attuned to public opinion. For example, I once wrote to the chief executive of a hotel after seeing its extremely sexist ad in *Toronto Life.* He replied that the advertisement had already been discontinued, due to complaints from the public. You should also be ready to compliment companies about nonstereotyped ads.

The Effects of Stereotyped Representations.   Does the biased representation of women in the media simply *reflect* reality, or does it actually *influence* reality? Both of these outcomes are possible. The media reflect the reality that women are often unseen and unheard and that they are more likely than men to do housework. The media also reflect the reality that women are too frequently believed to be decorative and subservient. However, the ads certainly do *not* reflect reality in other respects. For example, do you have a single friend who obsesses about ring-around-the-collar or who invites neighbors in to smell her toilet bowl?

Research evidence suggests that the media may be important in shaping reality. Stereotypes in magazines and on television actually do change some people's behaviors and beliefs. In one classic study, researchers prepared two kinds of commercials similar to those seen on television. In the traditional version of one ad, a woman proudly served her husband a packaged "TV dinner." In the nontraditional version, the husband proudly served his wife the same dinner. Compared to the college women who had seen the traditional version, those who had viewed the nontraditional version were more self-confident when delivering a speech several minutes later. The women in the nontraditional group also showed less conformity when making judgments in a group setting (Jennings et al., 1980).

Other research investigated women's self-images. When women looked at advertisements showing beautiful female models, they tended to be less satisfied with their own attractiveness (Richins, 1991; Wolf, 1991).

Advertisements can also influence gender-role attitudes. For example, men who are initially nontraditional are likely to become even more nontraditional after looking at nonstereotyped ads. In contrast, men who look at stereotyped ads become more traditional (Garst & Bodenhausen, 1997). Other research shows that both men and women hold less feminist attitudes after viewing stereotyped ads (MacKay & Covell, 1997). In general, too, people who have been exposed to sexually aggressive media are more likely to believe that violence against women is acceptable (J. D. Johnson et al., 1995; Lanis & Covell, 1995; MacKay & Covell, 1997; Wester et al., 1997). In other words, people who have watched violent music videos or videos that show women in subordinate roles may be more likely to believe that women are largely responsible for being raped.

Even subtle differences in the representation of women and men may be important. When you were reading that men's faces are emphasized in advertisements—whereas women's entire bodies are shown—you may have responded, "So what?" However, Archer and his coauthors (1983) found that photographs in which the face was prominent, with little of the remaining body visible, were rated as being more intelligent, attractive, and ambitious. In summary, the media can perpetuate stereotypes. More optimistically, the media also have the power to create new possibilities for nontraditional gender roles.

SECTION SUMMARY   *The Representation of Women and Men*

1. **A gender stereotype is an organized, widely shared set of beliefs about the characteristics of females and males. Prejudice applies to negative attitudes, and discrimination applies to biased action.**

2. **We have little information about women's activities throughout history. In general, philosophers emphasized women's inferiority.**

3. **Judaism and Christianity both perpetuate women's inferiority; Chinese and Hindu religions also portray negative images of women. Various religions and ancient myths have represented women as evil people, sorceresses, and virtuous mothers.**

4. **The terms used for women often emphasize their secondary status, or these terms may be negative or infantilizing; women are often addressed by their first name or in relation to their spouse's name.**

5. **Numerous studies have demonstrated that the masculine generic encourages people to think about males more often than females; gender-neutral terms can be easily substituted.**

6. **The media represent women in a stereotyped fashion. Women are seen and heard less than men. They are seldom shown working outside the home, though they are shown doing housework. The media treat men more professionally, and male TV characters distance themselves from women; women's bodies are also represented differently. Women of color are particularly likely to be underrepresented or to be represented in a stereotypical fashion.**

7. **The media's stereotyped representations of women promote stereotyped behaviors, self-images, and attitudes; sexually aggressive media tend to promote the view that violence against women is acceptable.**

PEOPLE'S BELIEFS ABOUT WOMEN AND MEN

In the first section of this chapter, we looked at the ways in which women and men are represented in history, philosophy, religion, mythology, language, and the media. Now let's turn to the man and woman on the street—or, more likely, on the college campus. What is the nature of their gender stereotypes? Why is sexism such a complex topic? What kinds of thought processes produce these stereotypes and keep them powerful? Finally, how can gender stereotypes influence people's behavior?

The Content of Stereotypes

Try Demonstration 2.3 before you read this section. Notice that this demonstration does not ask you to assess your own stereotypes or beliefs about men and women. Instead, you must try to guess what *most people* think. You will probably find that your answers are very accurate.

DEMONSTRATION 2.3

Stereotypes About Women and Men

For this demonstration, you are asked to guess what *most people think* about women and men. Put a W in front of those characteristics that you believe most people associate with women more than men. Put an M in front of those associated more with men than women.

_____ self-confident	_____ fickle
_____ gentle	_____ greedy
_____ kind	_____ warm
_____ competitive	_____ nervous
_____ active	_____ capable
_____ emotional	_____ talkative
_____ loud	_____ show-off
_____ compassionate	_____ patient
_____ modest	_____ courageous
_____ inventive	_____ powerful

The answers appear at the end of the chapter, based on responses that researchers have obtained (Cota et al., 1991; Street, Kimmel, et al., 1995; J. Williams & Best, 1990).

If you check the list of characteristics associated with women and with men, you'll see that those two lists are fairly different. Theorists use the term **agency** to describe a concern with one's own self-interests. Terms associated with agency (such as *self-confident* and *competitive*) are often stereotypically masculine. In contrast, the term **communion** emphasizes a concern for one's relationship with other people. Terms associated with communion (such as *gentle* and *warm*) are often stereotypically feminine (Di Dio et al., 1996; Kite, 1996).

Interestingly, these stereotypes have remained fairly consistent across time. For example, Bergen and Williams (1991) found that gender stereotypes remained highly stable when they tested college students in 1972 and 1988. Furthermore, in studies that examined general stereotypes about men and women, college students and college faculty members shared almost identical stereotypes about men and women (Street, Kimmel, et al., 1995; Street, Kromrey, et al., 1995). Let's now look at the stereotypes about men and women from various ethnic groups. Then we'll consider how certain variables influence our stereotypes.

Stereotypes About Women and Men from Different Ethnic Groups. We humans move beyond simple gender stereotypes to create stereotypes about women and men from different ethnic groups (Deaux, 1995). For example, Yolanda Niemann and her coauthors (1994) asked college students from four ethnic groups to list the first 10 adjectives that came to mind when they thought of particular categories of people. These categories included males and females from four different ethnic groups, so eight ethnic categories in all were represented. Table 2.4 combines the data from all participants and shows the three most commonly listed terms for each group. As you can see, people do not have one unified gender stereotype that holds true for all four ethnic groups. Instead, gender and ethnicity combine to produce a variety of gender stereotypes.

In reality, however, we probably create subtypes within each of these gender-ethnicity categories. For example, the stereotypes often distinguish between the "good women" and the "bad women" in each ethnic group. Ethnic Studies scholars note that African American women are stereotyped as either warm but sexless "mammies" or sexually promiscuous females (Comas-Díaz & Greene, 1994a). Latinas are portrayed, with similar polarization, as either chaste virgins or promiscuous women (Comas-Díaz & Greene, 1994a; Peña, 1998). Asian American women are seen as either shy and unassertive homebodies or as threatening "dragon ladies."

Interestingly, we don't know much about people's stereotypes about Native American women. Niemann and her colleagues (1994) did not study Native Americans, so they are not listed in Table 2.4. When most people hear the term "Native American" or "Indian," they think of a male, or they may possibly think of Pocahontas. In any event, most Native Americans do not have clear stereotypes about this least visible group of women of color (Comas-Díaz & Greene, 1994a).

TABLE 2.4	**The Three Most Frequently Supplied Adjectives for Females and Males from Four Different Ethnic Groups (Based on Niemann et al., 1994)**

European American Females	*European American Males*
Attractive	Intelligent
Intelligent	Egotistical
Egotistical	Upper-class
African American Females	*African American Males*
Speak loudly	Athletic
Dark skin	Antagonistic
Antagonistic	Dark skin
Asian American Females	*Asian American Males*
Intelligent	Intelligent
Speak softly	Short
Pleasant/friendly	Achievement-oriented
Mexican American Females	*Mexican American Males*
Black/brown/dark hair	Lower-class
Attractive	Hard workers
Pleasant/friendly	Antagonistic

The research on ethnic subtypes within gender stereotypes illustrates the complexity of these stereotypes. There is no simple, unified stereotype that could represent all women. Instead, we've created subtypes to reflect social class, ethnicity, and other characteristics of the group we are judging.

Factors Influencing Stereotypes.   We've just seen that various characteristics of the target—the person we are judging—can influence our stereotypes. For example, ethnicity as a stimulus variable can affect these stereotypes. Now let's switch gears and examine characteristics of the subject—the person who holds these stereotypes. Subjects' variables are often important. (You may want to review the distinction between stimulus variables and subject variables, on pages 27–28.)

Are stereotypes influenced by subject variables such as gender, ethnicity, and the culture in which we are raised? Alternately, do we all share the same gender stereotypes, no matter what our own background may be? The answer seems to be somewhere between these two possibilities.

Consider the influence of the respondents' gender. Typically, men and women hold similar gender stereotypes, but men's beliefs are somewhat more traditional (e.g., Larsen & Long, 1988; Spence & Hahn, 1997; Twenge, 1997a).

That is, male participants are more likely than female participants to believe in strong gender stereotypes. However, there are wide individual differences in stereotypes. Some women hold strong gender stereotypes; other women believe that men and women are quite similar.

Several studies have explored how ethnic background influences gender stereotypes. For example, Blacks are often less gender-stereotyped than Whites (Dugger, 1996; P. A. Smith & Midlarsky, 1985). Dugger (1996) analyzed data that had been gathered as part of a national poll of Black and White women. Compared to the White women, the Black women in this sample had less stereotyped views about adult women. Dugger pointed out that this finding makes sense. Black women have had a long history of employment in North America, so they know that women can be strong and competent.

Any attempt to explore ethnicity must acknowledge the diversity of people within each ethnic group. Puerto Ricans in the South Bronx and Chicanas/os in Texas would both be categorized as Latinas/os. However, their experiences may be vastly different, and their gender stereotypes may also differ widely. Similarly, recent immigrants from Cambodia may have little in common with third-generation Chinese Americans. Still, these diverse groups are combined in the single category called Asian Americans.

LaFromboise and her coauthors (1990) emphasized the diversity among North American Indian tribes. Some tribes specified very different gender roles for men and women. However, many tribes, such as the Klamath, gave equal treatment to men and women. Each gender may have performed separate but complementary tasks; however, "male tasks" and "female tasks" were considered equally important. LaFromboise and her coauthors argued that anthropologists (the majority of whom have been non-Indian males) have underestimated the high frequency of egalitarian relationships found in Indian tribes.

Do people in other countries differ in their stereotypes? Cross-cultural research presents a unique set of challenges. As Gibbons and her colleagues (1997) have pointed out, some tests that are commonly used to measure gender stereotypes cannot be easily used in some cultures. Consider the item, "It is all right for a girl to want to play rough sports like football." In some parts of the world, football means soccer; in other parts of the world, the game called football is unknown. A test containing this item would not be valid in many cultures outside North America.

The most extensive cross-cultural research on gender stereotypes has been conducted by Deborah Best and John Williams (Best & Williams, 1993; Williams & Best, 1990). They assessed gender stereotypes for 100 university students (50 females and 50 males) in each of 25 countries. In general, people in these diverse cultures shared similar gender stereotypes. In fact, the correlations were significant between each pair of the 25 countries.*

---

*Psychologists often calculate correlations to determine whether two groups of scores are related to each other. In this case, the researchers discovered a statistically significant positive correlation for each pair of countries. This means that if we consider two countries—say,

Best and Williams (1993) also found that some countries held stronger stereotypes than others. The Netherlands, Finland, Norway, and Germany had especially polarized views of women and men. In contrast, Scotland, Bolivia, and Venezuela saw women and men as more similar. Incidentally, of the 25 countries, the United States showed the seventh-highest amount of stereotyping, and Canada ranked tenth. The stereotyping seemed strongest in the most developed countries that were Protestant. This finding probably doesn't match your own stereotypes about cross-cultural comparisons, and the authors could not locate a persuasive explanation for their results.

In summary, factors such as gender, ethnicity, and culture have complex influences on people's gender stereotypes. Overall, however, the consistency of the gender stereotypes is more prominent than any differences among the groups.

The Complexity of Contemporary Sexism

In 1989, a Texas state senator remarked, "Do you know why God created women? Because sheep can't type." (Armbrister, cited in Starr, 1991, p. 41). This quotation is clearly sexist—no doubt about it! However, much of the sexism in the current decade is less obvious, and more subtle, elusive, and complex (Benokraitis, 1997a). Let's begin by considering several studies that focus on discrimination against women in interpersonal interactions. Then we'll examine attitudes toward women's competence, as well as toward their "pleasantness." A related topic is a recent scale designed to test the complicated, ambivalent sexism that is now operative. Finally, we'll briefly note some cross-cultural issues.

Discrimination in Interpersonal Interactions.   Bernice Lott examined discrimination in the most basic kind of interpersonal situation (Lott, 1987; Lott & Maluso, 1995a). Pairs of unacquainted students were instructed to work together in building a structure out of dominoes. Meanwhile, observers watched from behind a one-way mirror and recorded comments and behaviors of the participants.

Figure 2.2 shows the average incidence of negative behavior. Negative behavior included both verbal behavior (negative comments) and nonverbal behavior (moving the head or body away from the partner). As you can see, women seldom responded negatively to their partners (either male or female). Also, men seldom responded negatively when their partners were other men. However, men were much more likely to respond negatively to women partners. In another similar study, men reported that they would prefer to work with other men, rather than with women, on a variety of tasks (Lott et al., 1990).

We've considered laboratory studies on gender discrimination. What happens in real life? One study asked attorneys to report on gender-biased behavior (Stepnick & Orcutt, 1996). According to the results, 85% of the female attorneys

---

Norway and Bolivia—the people in the two countries tend to give the same ratings to the same characteristics. For example, when judging the characteristic *strong,* Norwegians and Bolivians might both give high ratings for males, but low ratings for females.

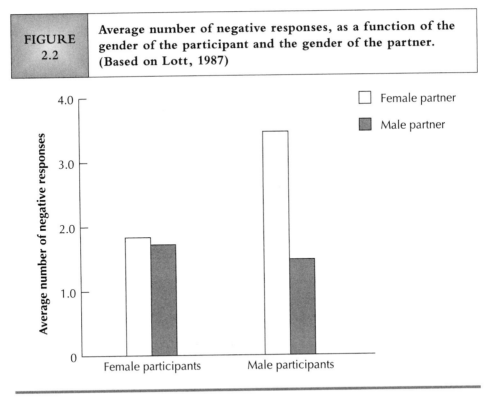

FIGURE 2.2 Average number of negative responses, as a function of the gender of the participant and the gender of the partner. (Based on Lott, 1987)

agreed that "In professional settings, men are assumed to be attorneys, whereas women are not." (Only 51% of the male attorneys agreed with that statement.) Similarly, 70% of the female attorneys agreed that, in professional settings, "Jokes or demeaning remarks are made about women." (Only 45% of male attorneys agreed.) In another study, male and female students were asked to assess the advantages and disadvantages of being the other gender. The males generally concluded that becoming a female would create more disadvantages, whereas the females generally concluded that becoming a male would create more advantages (Cann & Vann, 1995).

The most extensive study of interpersonal discrimination was conducted by Hope Landrine and Elizabeth Klonoff (1997). These researchers surveyed 1,279 women from a wide variety of ethnic and social-class backgrounds. The purpose of their survey was to determine how often women reported sexist events. Their results suggested that most women had experienced sexism. For example, about 80% noted that they had experienced sexism from a boyfriend, had been called a sexist name, or had been treated in a sexist fashion by a clerk or someone else in a service profession. For example, a 20-year-old Latina reported:

I couldn't go out with friends because I was a girl, but my brother was allowed to . . . [In addition] I was told by my uncles and men neighbors that all I was good for was cleaning, housewife, and gossip because I was a female!" (p. 15)

In Chapter 7, we will explore other forms of interpersonal discrimination when we look at sexism in the workplace. In Chapter 12, we'll see that interpersonal discrimination may contribute to the relatively high rate of depression in women, a point that Landrine and Klonoff (1997) also emphasize. In other words, the interpersonal discrimination that women experience does not evaporate quickly. Instead, these gender-biased experiences often reduce the overall quality of women's lives. In short, this section provides abundant evidence for Theme 2: Women are often treated differently than men.

Attitudes Toward Women's Competence.   Dozens of studies conducted in the past 30 years have focused on people's reactions to women's achievements. You are certain to be frustrated if you like reading about orderly, clear-cut results; these studies highlight the complexity of contemporary sexism.

The prototype study on women's competence was conducted by psychologist Philip Goldberg (1968), in a study entitled, "Are Women Prejudiced against Women?" Goldberg asked college women to evaluate articles that had presumably been published in professional journals. One-third of the articles represented stereotypically masculine professions (e.g., law), one-third represented stereotypically feminine professions (e.g., dietetics), and one-third represented neutral professions (e.g., art history).

The most important variable was the gender of the author's name, which appeared in a conspicuous location on the paper. Half of the students were given a male author's name (John T. MacKay), and half were given a female author's name (Joan T. MacKay). Except for the author's name, the two versions were identical. In each case, students were instructed to evaluate the quality of the paper. For the two stereotypically masculine professions and one of the neutral professions, students rated the article significantly higher in quality if they had been led to believe that it was written by a man. (Men received somewhat higher ratings in most other conditions, but the differences were not statistically significant.) The results led many people to conclude that women were indeed prejudiced against women.

Following Goldberg's original study, other researchers repeated the study, varying numerous characteristics of the participants, the target person, the stimulus material, and so forth. A meta-analysis by Janet Swim and her colleagues (1989) of 123 studies surprised many of us. Overall, there was no convincing evidence for prejudice against women. Even when the stimulus material was concerned with a stereotypically masculine area, the gender of the presumed author produced only a modest bias. The analysis did suggest, however, that women will be rated less favorably than men when little additional information is provided about the person's qualifications.

Researchers have tried to identify the circumstances in which women's competence is likely to be devalued. For example, Haslett and her coauthors (1992) pointed out that evaluators who have expertise are more likely to devalue women. According to this perspective, students would not be especially biased—and research using students is especially common for studies based on Goldberg's design. In contrast, in real-life occupational settings, women are more likely to be evaluated by "experts," who may well be biased. In addition, women's competence is likely to be devalued when the evaluators are men rather than women (Eagly et al., 1992; Eagly & Mladinic, 1994).

So far, we have seen that bias against women is most likely in the following conditions: (1) when competence is being judged in a traditionally masculine area; (2) when little information is available about a person's qualifications; (3) when experts are doing the evaluating; and (4) when males are doing the evaluating. A final factor—perhaps one of the most important—is that bias may be strongest when a woman is acting in a stereotypically masculine fashion (Eagly et al., 1992; Eagly & Mladinic, 1994; Fiske et al., 1993).

Consider the case of gender discrimination that accountant Ann Hopkins brought to court (Fiske et al., 1991; Fiske & Stevens, 1993). Hopkins was working at a prestigious accounting firm. She was being considered for promotion to partner, the only woman among 88 candidates that year. She had brought in business worth $25 million, the top amount of the 88 candidates. However, the company did not promote her. The firm claimed that Hopkins lacked interpersonal skills, and they branded her "macho" because of her hard-driving managerial style. A sympathetic coworker suggested that she would improve her chances if she would "walk more femininely, talk more femininely, dress more femininely, wear makeup, have her hair styled, and wear jewelry" (Fiske et al., 1991, p. 1050).

Notice that this bias against strong women presents a double bind. If they act feminine and sweet, they are unlikely to be persuasive; would Ann Hopkins have brought in $25 million in business if she had batted her eyelashes and worn frilly blouses? But if they act masculine and assertive, their superiors give them negative evaluations.

Attitudes Toward Women's Pleasantness. People don't think that women are especially competent, but they frequently *do* think that women are generally pleasant and nice. A series of studies was conducted by Alice Eagly, whose work on gender comparisons forms the core of Chapter 6. In this research, college students were asked to rate the category "men" and the category "women" on scales with labels such as "pleasant–unpleasant," "good–bad," and "nice–awful" (Carter et al., 1991; Eagly & Mladinic, 1994; Eagly et al., 1991). Compared to men, women typically receive higher positive ratings on these scales. For example, the subtype "macho men" receives the lowest rating; these men are rated as much less pleasant than the comparable female subtype "sexy women."

Fiske and Stevens (1993) provided the following summary of the research on attitudes:

. . . people seem to view women simultaneously as likeable but also as unworthy of much respect. . . . Respect, which translates into rewards in the public marketplace, is differentially awarded to male stereotypic traits precisely because of their association with the group having more power and prestige.

The power and prestige asymmetry can also explain the prescription that women, the stereotypically less competent group, should limit themselves to their stereotypic (less valued) domains of expertise. And clearly, it explains why men traditionally would not aspire to "feminine" traits, the devalued alternative. (p. 183)

We also know that people are not equally positive about all kinds of women. Haddock and Zanna (1994) asked Canadian college students to rate their attitude toward two groups of women, "housewives" and "feminists." Figure 2.3 shows their responses, on a scale where 100 was labeled "extremely favorable" and 50 was labeled "neither favorable nor unfavorable." As you can see, females gave higher ratings to both groups of women than did males. Also, both females and males gave higher ratings to housewives than to feminists, a finding that has been replicated with U.S. college students (Kite & Branscombe, 1998).

| FIGURE 2.3 | Attitudes toward housewives and feminists, as a function of respondents' gender (100 = extremely favorable; 50 = neither favorable nor unfavorable). (Based on Haddock & Zanna, 1994) |

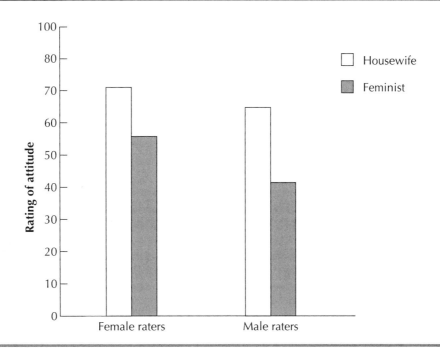

DEMONSTRATION 2.4

The Ambivalent Sexism Inventory

The following items are selected from Glick and Fiske's (1996) Ambivalent Sexism Inventory. For each item, indicate the degree to which you agree or disagree with each statement, using the following scale:

0	1	2	3	4	5
disagree strongly	disagree somewhat	disagree slightly	agree slightly	agree somewhat	agree strongly

_____ 1. Many women are actually seeking special favors, such as hiring policies that favor them over men, under the guise of asking for "equality."

_____ 2. Women should be cherished and protected by men.

_____ 3. Most women fail to appreciate fully all that men do for them.

_____ 4. Many women have a quality of purity that few men possess.

_____ 5. A good woman should be set on a pedestal by her man.

_____ 6. Most women interpret innocent remarks or acts as being sexist.

_____ 7. Once a woman gets a man to commit to her, she usually tries to put him on a tight leash.

_____ 8. In a disaster, women should be rescued before men.

_____ 9. Women seek to gain power by getting control over men.

_____ 10. No matter how accomplished he is, a man is not truly complete as a person unless he has the love of a woman.

When you have finished this test, check the scoring instructions at the end of the chapter. You may also want to ask friends to take the test, to see whether you obtain the same gender differences that Glick and Fiske did. Incidentally, the complete test includes 22 items, some of which are worded so that a highly sexist person would disagree with them.

Note: Readers should be aware that this shortened version of the Ambivalent Sexism Inventory has not been validated. Anyone who is interested in using the scale for research or assessment purposes should refer to Glick and Fiske (1996).

In summary, a strong, feminist woman—one who is not stereotypically feminine—will often receive low ratings for competence. She may also be downgraded in the "pleasantness" category.

Try Demonstration 2.4 before you read further.

Ambivalent Sexism.   We have seen that contemporary sexism is complicated. Women may not be judged to be very competent, but they *are* judged to be fairly nice. But, wait, not all women are nice. . . .

Peter Glick and Susan Fiske (1996, 1997) have tried to capture the complexity of sexism with a scale they call the "Ambivalent Sexism Inventory." They argue that sexism is a prejudice based on a deep ambivalence toward women, rather than uniform dislike. This scale contains items that tap two kinds of sexism. **Hostile sexism,** the more blatant kind of sexism, is based on the idea that women should be subservient to men and should "know their place." **Benevolent sexism** is the kind of sexism that argues for women's special niceness and purity; however, it still emphasizes that women are *different* from men.

You tried a short version of the Ambivalent Sexism Inventory in Demonstration 2.4. As Glick and Fiske (1996) anticipated, men tended to score higher than women on the benevolent sexism subscale, but the gender differences were even stronger on the hostile sexism subscale. Later research with male students showed that men who score high on the benevolent sexism subscale tend to have positive attitudes toward women who are homemakers (Glick et al., 1997). In addition, men who score high on the hostile sexism subscale tend to have negative attitudes toward career women (Glick et al., 1997). In short, the development of the Ambivalent Sexism Inventory is especially valuable because it highlights both the subtlety and the complexity of contemporary sexism.

Cross-Cultural Sexism.   Most of the research discussed in this textbook was conducted in the United States, Canada, or other English-speaking cultures. In many countries, however, the kind of discrimination we've discussed—such as moving away from a female—would be considered relatively minor.

Consider, for example, the story told by a woman named Rajbala (1986), which I found in *Manushi,* a feminist journal from India. Rajbala had given birth to a daughter. She found that people in her village referred to daughters as "stones," indicating their low value in contrast to sons. At the age of 18 months, her daughter died. Rajbala writes:

> But when our fellow villagers came to condole with us, their words, which still resound in my ears, were: "Stop crying now, she was a worm from hell and has gone back to hell." Another woman said, "Don't sorrow so much, she was a tempest. After the tempest comes the rain (a son)." Yet another said, "You must have committed some sin in your former birth. First you gave birth to a girl and then god called her away." (p. 3, translated from Hindi)

Sexism is certainly evident in North America. However, as we'll see throughout this book, the differential treatment of males and females in other cultures is even more exaggerated (Chia et al., 1997).

Heterosexism

In the previous discussion of contemporary sexism, we saw that people make a distinction between men and women. People may be hostile toward women, or they may be benevolent toward women, but a major conclusion is that they think about women as being very different from men. As we also emphasized in our discussion of Theme 2, people react differently to men and women. As we'll see throughout this chapter, people divide the world into two categories, male and female.

This gender categorization has an important implication for love relationships. Specifically, gender categorization encourages people to believe that a person from the category "male" must fall in love with a person from the category "female." Most people are troubled by same-gender love relationships (S. Bem, 1995a).

A **lesbian** is a woman who is psychologically, emotionally, and sexually attracted to other women. A **gay male** is a man who is psychologically, emotionally, and sexually attracted to other men. A **bisexual** is someone who is psychologically, emotionally, and sexually attracted to both women and men. In Chapter 8, we will discuss potential explanations for sexual orientation, as well as the love relationships of women who are lesbians and bisexuals.

In this current section, however, let's focus on heterosexism. As we noted in Chapter 1, **heterosexism** is bias against lesbians, gay males, and bisexuals—or any group that is not exclusively heterosexual. You've probably heard a related term, homophobia. **Homophobia** refers to irrational fear, hatred, and intolerance of people who are lesbian, gay, or bisexual (Obear, 1991). However, theorists point out that people don't really have a *phobia*—or fear—regarding gay people (Fernald, 1995). As a result, we'll typically use the word *heterosexism* throughout this book. Let's consider some examples of heterosexism and then see what factors are correlated with it.

Examples of Heterosexism. Some types of heterosexism are relatively subtle, but they still reveal that our culture values people who love someone from the other gender category rather than someone from the same gender category. Consider Jane and her longtime partner Marilyn, who were guests at the wedding of Jane's cousin. After the ceremony, Jane's aunt was gathering family members together for a photo. The aunt called out to Jane to join them, but she didn't call Marilyn (Berzon, 1996). From the aunt's perspective, a longtime lesbian relationship didn't have the same status as a heterosexual relationship.

In many instances, heterosexism is more intentionally hurtful. For example, surveys suggest that between 50% and 90% of lesbians and gay males have been verbally harassed about their sexual orientation (Pilkington & D'Augelli, 1995). Carla was the president of her senior class when she told her classmates she was gay. The next day, someone had spray-painted "Carla will die" in big red letters across one of the walls of the school building (Owens, 1998).

Surveys also indicate that between 10% and 40% of lesbians and gay males have been chased or followed, and between 10% and 25% have been assaulted. Jaime, a lesbian college student, recalls a situation where she was assaulted:

> There were some frat boys . . . out looking for trouble . . . and I was walking with my girlfriend. And they had a baseball bat. They whacked me a good one and broke two ribs. And they broke her nose . . . with the butt of the bat. (Owens, 1998)

We've seen that gays and lesbians frequently experience interpersonal discrimination—heterosexist biases, verbal harassment, and physical assault—because of their sexual orientation. They also face institutional discrimination;

DEMONSTRATION 2.5

Attitudes Toward Lesbians and Gay Men

Answer each of the following items either "yes" or "no." (Please note that the original questionnaire was designed for heterosexuals, so some items may seem inappropriate for lesbian, bisexual, and gay male respondents.)

———— 1. I would not mind having gay friends.

———— 2. I would look for a new place to live if I found out that my roommate was gay.

———— 3. I would vote for a gay person in an election for a public office.

———— 4. Two people of the same gender holding hands in public is disgusting.

———— 5. Homosexuality, as far as I'm concerned, is not sinful.

———— 6. I would mind being employed by a gay person.

———— 7. I would decline membership in an organization if it had gay members.

———— 8. I would not be afraid for my child to have a gay teacher.

———— 9. Gay people are more likely than heterosexuals to commit deviant sexual acts, such as child molestation.

———— 10. I see the gay movement as a positive thing.

To obtain a rough idea about your attitudes, add together the number of "yes" answers you provided for items 1, 3, 5, 8, and 10. Then add together the number of "no" answers you provided for items 2, 4, 6, 7, and 9. Scores close to 10 indicate positive attitudes toward gay people.
(Based on Kite & Deaux, 1986.)

that is, the government, corporations, and other institutions discriminate against gays, lesbians, and bisexuals. For example, the U.S. military does not permit its members to discuss their sexual orientation. Most insurance companies deny benefits to same-gender partners. I recall a friend discussing with irony that her insurance benefits could not cover her lesbian partner, with whom she had lived for 20 years. In contrast, a male colleague's wife could receive benefits though the couple had been married less than three years and were now separated.

Factors Correlated with Heterosexism.   Attitudes toward lesbians, gays, and bisexuals are very complicated. In the current era, U.S. and Canadian residents generally believe that homosexuals should be allowed equal rights in terms of job opportunities. However, most argue that homosexuality is morally wrong (Fernald, 1995).

Gender comparisons in heterosexism show similarly complex patterns. Men and women have similar attitudes about civil rights for homosexuals—again, in terms of job opportunities (Kite & Whitley, 1996). However, men are much more negative than women in their attitudes toward homosexual individuals—especially gay males (Kite & Whitley, 1996). This gender difference may be partly explained by attitudes toward gender roles (Kite & Whitley, 1996, 1998). Men are more likely than women to endorse traditional gender roles: A man should be a man, and he shouldn't have any feminine traits, and he certainly shouldn't be in love with another man (LaMar & Kite, 1996).

In general, people with heterosexist attitudes tend to be politically and religiously conservative. They also tend to be racist (Fernald, 1995; Kite & Whitley, 1998). However, students become more tolerant and less heterosexist as they go through college (Lottes & Kuriloff, 1994). To assess your own attitudes toward lesbians and gay men, try Demonstration 2.5.

The Social Cognitive Approach
to Gender Stereotypes

The social cognitive approach is currently the major theoretical explanation for gender stereotypes, heterosexist stereotypes, and stereotypes based on categories such as ethnicity, social class, and age. According to the **social cognitive approach,** stereotypes are belief systems that guide the way we process information—including information about gender (D. Hamilton & Sherman, 1994).

One cognitive process that seems nearly inevitable is our tendency to divide the people we meet into social groups (Cross & Markus, 1993; D. Hamilton & Sherman, 1994). We categorize people as females versus males, White people versus people of color, people with high occupational status versus people with low occupational status, and so forth.

The social cognitive approach argues that stereotypes help us simplify and organize the world by creating categories (Macrae et al., 1994; Snyder & Miene, 1994). The major way we categorize people is on the basis of their gender (S. Bem, 1993; Geis, 1993). This process of categorizing others on the basis of gender is habitual and automatic. If you doubt that fact, after you finish reading today, try *not* to pay attention to the gender of the first person you meet!

The problem, however, is that this process of categorizing and stereotyping encourages us to make errors. These errors, in turn, produce further errors. That is, because we have a stereotype, we tend to perceive women and men differently, and that perception adds further "evidence" to our stereotype. A strengthened stereotype leads to an even greater tendency to perceive the two genders differently (Barone et al., 1997). As a result, stereotypes are especially resistant to change.

Let's look at several topics in the area of the social cognitive approach and gender stereotyping. As we'll see, people tend to exaggerate the contrast between women and men. People also tend to see the male as normative and the female as nonstandard. In addition, people make biased judgments on the basis of stereotypes, and they often selectively remember characteristics that are consistent with gender stereotypes.

Exaggerating the Contrast Between Women and Men.   We tend to exaggerate the similarities *within* a group and exaggerate the contrast *between* groups. When we divide the world into two groups—male and female—we tend to see all males as being similar, all females as being similar, and the two gender categories as being different, a tendency called **gender polarization** (S. Bem, 1993). Gender polarization forces us to condemn individuals who deviate from this rigid role definition. As we saw in the discussion of gender discrimination, accountant Ann Hopkins experienced job discrimination because she did not have typically feminine mannerisms.

As we will emphasize throughout this textbook, the characteristics of women and men tend to overlap. Unfortunately, however, gender polarization often creates an artificial gap between women and men. People tend to believe that gender differences in personality are larger than they really are (B. Allen, 1995; C. Martin, 1987). Human cognitive processes seem to favor clear-cut distinctions, rather than the blurry differences that are more common in everyday life. Our contemporary culture especially encourages distinctions based on gender.

The Normative Male.   The concept of the "normative male" is pervasive in our culture. According to the **normative male** concept, the male experience is considered to be the norm—the neutral standard for the species as a whole. In contrast, the female experience is a deviation from that supposedly universal standard. Another term for this male-centered view of the world is **androcentrism** (S. Bem, 1993, 1996).

One example of the normative male principle is that when we hear the word "person," we tend to believe that this individual is a male rather than a female (M. Hamilton, 1991a; Merritt & Kok, 1995).

The normative male principle also reveals itself when people discuss gender differences (Tavris, 1992). As you'll learn in Chapter 5, men and women sometimes differ in their self-confidence. However, the research typically assumes that males have the "normal" amount of self-confidence, and females are some-how defective. In other words, men are serving as the standard of comparison (McGill, 1993). However, the truth may be that females actually have the appro-priate amount of self-confidence; they may judge the quality of their perfor-mance fairly accurately. From that perspective, males would be *over*confident and overly self-serving.

When Miller and his colleagues (1991) asked people to visualize a "typical American voter," 72% of their participants described a male rather than a fe-male. Participants also tended to explain gender differences in male normative terms. For example, when asked to explain gender differences in the number of visits to a doctor, people tended to say, "Women are more likely to be worried about illness." They seldom provided a statement in which females were stan-dard, such as: "Men are less likely to be worried about illness."

Making Biased Judgments About Females and Males.   Our stereotypes often lead us to interpret certain behaviors in a biased manner. After all, social behavior is often ambiguous and can be interpreted in several different ways (D. Hamilton et al., 1990). In a classic example of this phenomenon, Condry and Condry (1976) prepared videotapes of an infant responding to a variety of stim-uli. For example, the infant stared and then cried in response to the opening of a jack-in-the-box. College students who participated in this study were predom-inantly middle-class European Americans between the ages of 18 and 25. The students received a rating sheet that listed either a male or a female name for the infant. Then everyone watched the same, identical video.

The results showed that when people thought the infant was a boy, they tended to judge that "he" was showing anger. Those who thought the infant was a girl judged that "she" was showing fear. Everyone saw the same crying infant, but this ambiguous negative reaction was given a more masculine label (anger, rather than fear) when the infant was perceived to be a boy. We are evidently reluctant to believe that baby girls can express such a forceful negative emotion as anger or that baby boys can be afraid.

People display the same stereotyped interpretations when they make judg-ments about adults' emotional reactions. Robinson and Johnson (1997) asked college students to read a variety of short scenarios. A representative scenario described an average woman (or man) who was becoming concerned about the future of an important relationship that the person did not want to end. When the participants were making judgments about a woman, they tended to say that she would feel "emotional." In contrast, when making judgments about a man, they tended to say that he would feel "stressed." These gender stereotypes were much more influential when participants evaluated other people than when they evaluated themselves (M. Robinson et al., 1998). Once again, the stereo-types about gender differences are larger than the actual gender differences.

Naturally, our tendency to make stereotyped judgments is influenced by several variables. Specific information about individuals can sometimes be so persuasive that it overrides a stereotype (Kunda & Sherman-Williams, 1993). A woman may be so well qualified for a job that her strengths outweigh the "problem" that she is female. However, we are more likely to apply a stereotype if we are busy working on another task at the same time (D. Gilbert & Hixon, 1991; Valian, 1998).

Many studies have been conducted on a particular kind of judgment called attributions. **Attributions** are explanations about the causes of a person's behavior. Chapter 5 discusses people's attributions about their own behavior. Now let's see how stereotypes are revealed in people's attributions about the behavior of other people.

The research on this topic is both extensive and complex. It shows that people often think that a woman's success on a particular task can be explained by the fact that she tried hard (Swim & Sanna, 1996). For example, research has been done on parents' attributions for their children's success in mathematics. When daughters do well in math, parents attribute their success to hard work. In contrast, they attribute their sons' success to their high ability (Eccles, 1987; Eccles (Parsons) et al., 1982). Notice the implications of this research: People think that females need to try harder to achieve the same level of success as males.

The same "effort and hard work" explanation may be used when people are trying to explain the success of a group that is commonly believed to be inferior. Yarkin and her colleagues (1982) extended the attribution research to include judgments about both gender and ethnicity. Students read about a highly successful banker who was either male or female, Black or White. They were then asked to judge the importance of four factors in determining the banker's success. Was ability, effort, task difficulty, or luck most responsible for this individual's success? The participants explained the White male's success as being due to his high ability. However, they showed a different attributional pattern when judging the White female, Black male, and Black female. For those three individuals, hard work and luck were judged to be the most important reasons. I'm reminded of a highly successful African American couple I know. She's a professor and he's a surgeon. They were visiting their son's math teacher to discuss the young man's less-than-ideal performance. The teacher said to them, "Well, I wouldn't worry too much . . . you're both overachievers." In the teacher's eyes, the only way these two African Americans could have achieved their professional prominence was by hard work, not natural intelligence and ability.

Let's review what we know so far about the social cognitive approach to gender stereotypes. We know that stereotypes simplify and bias the way we think about people who belong to the social categories of *female* and *male*. Because of gender stereotypes, we exaggerate the contrast between women and men. We also consider the male experience to be "normal," whereas the female experience is the exception that requires an explanation. We also make biased judgments about females and males—for instance, when we judge whether they are feeling emotional or stressed. Research in the area of social cognition also emphasizes one final component of stereotypes: people's memory for stereotyped characteristics.

Memory for Personal Characteristics. People sometimes—but not always—recall gender-consistent information more accurately than gender-inconsistent information. In one relevant study, Cann (1993) found that students recalled sentences like "Jane is a good nurse" better than "Jane is a bad nurse." When people work in a gender-*consistent* occupation, we expect successful performance, and so we recall their *competence*. In contrast, Cann's participants recalled sentences like "John is a bad nurse" better than "John is a good nurse." When people work in a gender-*inconsistent* occupation, we expect unsuccessful performance, and so we recall their *incompetence*. Notice how this memory bias could encourage a supervisor to remember a greater number of negative characteristics than positive characteristics for individuals who work in nontraditional occupations.

As you might imagine, not everyone shows the same selective memory. For instance, Furnham and Singh (1986) tape-recorded 30 supposed findings about gender differences. Fifteen of these findings were pro-female (e.g., that females are not as susceptible as males to disease), and 15 of them were pro-male (e.g., that males greatly outnumber females in physics courses). Adolescents listened to these sentences and tried to recall them. The results showed that men and women who had a negative attitude toward females recalled a relatively small number of pro-female items and a relatively large number of pro-male items.

We also use stereotypes to fill in gaps in our memory. Halpern (1985) had high school students read a short story about a person named either Linda or David. When they were trying to remember the story but forgot a detail, they often filled in the blank with gender-stereotypical information. Think about it: Suppose you are female, and a male tells you he went shopping. If you can't recall the nature of the shopping, aren't you likely to "recall" a sporting goods store or some similarly masculine destination?

The research in social cognition shows that we are especially likely to recall stereotype-consistent material when we have other tasks to do at the same time—such as remembering other information—and when we have a strong, well-developed stereotype (Burn, 1996; D. Hamilton & Sherman, 1994; Hilton & von Hippel, 1996; Macrae et al., 1993). When we have nothing else to do and when stereotypes are weak, we may sometimes remember material inconsistent with our stereotypes.

Gender Stereotypes, Self–Fulfilling Prophecies, and Behavior

We began this section by discussing the content of gender stereotypes and the complex nature of contemporary sexism. The social cognitive approach helps us understand how errors in our thinking can arise, and how these errors, in turn, generate further errors. However, if we focus entirely on our thought processes, we may forget an extremely important point: Stereotypes can influence our behavior (D. Hamilton et al., 1990). That is, stereotypes can influence actions and choices, in ourselves and in other people.

Stereotypes can influence behavior through a **self-fulfilling prophecy;** your expectations about someone may lead him or her to act in ways that confirm your original expectation (Rosenthal, 1993). For example, if people expect a young girl to be quiet, passive, and gentle, she may begin to act that way.

Self-fulfilling prophecies are difficult to study, but let's consider two representative examples. Skrypnek and Snyder (1982) arranged to have pairs of students participate in an experiment without ever seeing or talking to each other. One member of each pair was male, and the other was female, but this fact was not revealed to the participants. These researchers found that females chose more masculine tasks to perform when their male partners had been led to believe they were working with other males. When the male partners believed they were working with females, the females tended to select feminine tasks. Presumably, the men's stereotypes influenced the way they treated their partners; they used different strategies toward people whom they believed to be male rather than female. The women then behaved in a fashion that was consistent with the men's expectations.

Self-fulfilling prophecies can also influence how people acquire important skills. Eccles and her coauthors (1990) argued that parents expect their sons to be better than their daughters in mathematics. Parents communicate these expectations to their children, so that boys become more optimistic about their math ability. As a result, boys end up with greater interest in acquiring skills in mathematics.

Think of occasions when self-fulfilling prophecies may operate in your own life. As Burn (1996) points out, a man might believe that women are not good drivers. If he states this belief to a woman while she is driving, she may become so nervous that she indeed does not drive well. His stereotype will be confirmed even though his opinion indirectly influenced her behavior.

However, people are not always at the mercy of other people's stereotypes (Fiske, 1993). We are not marionettes, with other people pulling our strings. Our own self-concepts and abilities are usually stronger determinants of behavior than are the expectancies of other people. Still, we should be concerned about the potentially powerful effects of self-fulfilling prophecies. They have the power to keep women and men from living up to their potential.

 SECTION SUMMARY *People's Beliefs About Women and Men*

1. **People believe that men and women differ substantially on a number of characteristics. Men are considered to be higher in agency, and women are considered to be higher in communion. These stereotypes have remained consistent throughout recent decades.**

2. People have different stereotypes about women from different ethnic groups.

3. The strength of a person's gender stereotypes is influenced by factors such as his or her gender, ethnicity, and culture. However, the consistency of stereotypes is impressive.

4. Research shows evidence of gender discrimination in interpersonal interactions (e.g., negative statements against women, or reports of sexist comments).

5. Women's competence is likely to be downgraded in a traditionally masculine area, when little other information is available, when the evaluators are experts, when the evaluators are males, and when women act in a stereotypically masculine fashion.

6. People typically rate women higher than men on scales assessing pleasantness, but men tend not to rate feminists favorably.

7. Men score higher than women on both the benevolent sexism and the hostile sexism subscales of the Ambivalent Sexism Inventory. Sexism in other cultures may have more serious consequences than in North America.

8. Heterosexism is encouraged by strict gender categorization, and it includes both interpersonal and institutional discrimination. Gender differences are found in some aspects of heterosexism; also, heterosexism is greater among politically and religiously conservative individuals.

9. According to the social cognitive approach to stereotypes, we exaggerate the contrast between women and men, we consider the male experience to be normative, we make biased judgments about females and males, and we remember gender-consistent information more accurately than gender-inconsistent information.

10. Stereotypes influence behavior through self-fulfilling prophecies, according to research on topics such as choice of work tasks and parents' expectations for their children's mathematical skills.

GENDER TYPING AND THE ALTERNATIVES

This chapter has explored the representation of gender stereotypes in areas such as religion, language, and the media, as well as the nature of people's current stereotypes. Now we'll change our focus somewhat in order to investigate **gender typing,** which occurs when people acquire the preferences, skills, personality attributes, behaviors, and self-concepts considered by our culture to be "gender appropriate" (S. Bem, 1983). In other words, many people believe that the stereotypes we've explored represent ideal standards that they should strive to reach. According to the traditional view, women *should* try to be "feminine," and men *should* try to be "masculine."

In contrast to these stereotyped approaches, the concept of androgyny encourages individuals to develop both feminine and masculine characteristics. However, we'll see in this section that androgyny may not be the perfect alternative. Instead, the answer could lie in a transcendence of gender roles.

Androgyny

The word *androgyny* comes from the Greek words for men *(andro-)* and women *(-gyny)*. Currently, **androgyny** (pronounced "an-*drah*-jih-nee") is a term applied to people who are high in both feminine and masculine qualities. Think about a friend you know who is competent in areas that are stereotypically masculine, as well as in areas that are stereotypically feminine. Your friend may be an excellent athlete, a superb cook, and a "born leader." This friend may build an impressive oak bookcase on Thursday and spend several hours comforting a depressed friend on Friday. This friend may work well independently when the occasion demands, but may also work cooperatively with a group on other occasions.

Androgyny sounds like an appealing alternative to the adoption of oppressive gender stereotypes. Let's explore the concept of androgyny more thoroughly, first focusing on how the concept was developed. Then we will briefly look at some of the research on androgyny. Finally, we'll discuss why androgyny may not be an ideal alternative.

The Development of the Androgyny Concept. As we saw in the previous section, people often believe that men and women are quite different from one another. In the early research on gender typing, psychologists viewed masculinity and femininity as being quite different from one another—in fact, they were considered exact opposites. That is, the traditional scales designed to measure femininity–masculinity were **bipolar.** Femininity was at one pole and masculinity at the other, as shown in Figure 2.4. Notice, though, that you'd have difficulty placing your androgynous friend on this bipolar scale, because

| FIGURE 2.4 | **The bipolar view of femininity and masculinity.** |

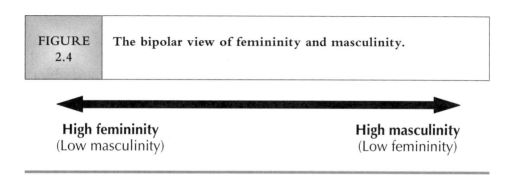

High femininity
(Low masculinity)

High masculinity
(Low femininity)

your friend is high in *both* femininity and masculinity. On a bipolar scale, a person who is high in femininity *must* be low in masculinity, and vice versa. (Throughout the rest of this book, the terms *femininity* and *masculinity* will be used to describe characteristics that have been *traditionally considered more appropriate* for females and males, respectively.

The traditional femininity–masculinity scale also specified certain ideal standards. Females "should" have scores toward the feminine pole, and males "should" have scores toward the masculine pole. Females with more masculine scores and males with more feminine scores were considered to have gender-role confusion, certainly not an enviable diagnosis.

In the 1970s, several new methods of assessing gender typing captured psychologists' attention. These methods proposed that femininity and masculinity should be measured on separate, independent scales. The best known androgyny measure is the Bem Sex-Role Inventory (BSRI), which was developed by Sandra Bem (1974, 1977). Before reading further, try Demonstration 2.6, which contains items similar to those on the BSRI.

DEMONSTRATION 2.6

Items Similar to Those on the BSRI

Rate yourself on the following items, which are similar to the 60 items on the Bem Sex-Role Inventory (BSRI). Use a scale in which 1 = never or almost never true and 7 = always or almost always true.

1. pleasant	7. enjoys eating
2. honest	8. affectionate
3. independent	9. self-confident
4. studious	10. enjoys feminine activities
5. active	11. traditional
6. easily convinced by others	12. enjoys masculine activities

Check the end of the chapter for instructions on how to score your answers to this demonstration.

Note: The BSRI is now owned by a company called Mind Garden, and so it could not be reproduced here. For more information on the BSRI, you may wish to read descriptive articles by Bem (1974, 1977) or to purchase a copy of the test from Mind Garden, 1690 Woodside Road, Suite 202, Redwood City, CA 94061.

The BSRI provides scores on a Femininity Scale and on a Masculinity Scale for each person who takes the test. Typically, each of these scores is then compared to a group median (or midpoint) for each of the two scales. Table 2.5 shows how the scores on each of the two scales can produce four categories of people:

1. **Undifferentiated people,** who rated themselves low on both the femininity and masculinity scales.
2. **Feminine people,** who rated themselves high on the femininity scale and low on the masculinity scale.
3. **Masculine people,** who rated themselves high on the masculinity scale and low on the femininity scale.
4. **Androgynous people,** who rated themselves high on both the femininity and masculinity scales.

Bem and other theorists argued against encouraging people to conform to outdated standards in which women should be traditionally feminine and men should be traditionally masculine. Instead, these theorists encouraged both women and men to be flexible in their gender roles, or androgynous: "That is, they should be encouraged to be both instrumental *and* expressive, both assertive *and* yielding, both masculine *and* feminine—depending upon the situational appropriateness of these various behaviors" (S. Bem, 1975, p. 634).

Soon, androgyny captured popular attention. It was no longer confined to psychology journals; schools, corporations, and therapists began advocating the concept of androgyny.

TABLE 2.5	Categories from the Bem Sex-Role Inventory

	Masculinity	
	Low	**High**
Femininity High	**Feminine** High femininity and Low masculinity	**Androgynous** High femininity and High masculinity
Femininity Low	**Undifferentiated** Low femininity and Low masculinity	**Masculine** Low femininity and High masculinity

The Bem Sex-Role Inventory and other methods of measuring androgyny have now been used in hundreds of studies on gender roles. Let's first consider the research on the most popular topic: Do people who rate themselves as androgynous have higher self-esteem and better adjustment than other people? Then we'll consider several other factors that are potentially related to androgyny.

Research on Self-Esteem and Adjustment.   Dozens of studies show that people who rate themselves high in masculinity also rate themselves higher in self-esteem and adjustment, compared to those who rate themselves low in masculinity (e.g., Aube et al., 1994; Whitley, 1985, 1988; D. Williams & D'Alessandro, 1994). However, femininity scores are generally *not* related to the opinions people have about their own worth. In fact, women who rate themselves very high in their concern for other people—while neglecting their own personal needs—may be at risk for depression (Fritz & Helgeson, 1998; V. S. Helgeson & Fritz, 1998).

Notice, then, that this research does not provide clear-cut evidence of the advantages of androgyny. In general, androgynous people—those who score high on the feminine scale as well as on the masculine scale—are no more positive about themselves than people who score high on the masculine scale but low on the feminine scale.

You may have detected another problem with the research: the measures of self-esteem and adjustment are typically gathered from self-reports. However, Aube and her colleagues (1994) obtained a more objective measure of each person's social adjustment—other students' ratings of that person's popularity. Masculinity was not correlated with this more objective measure of social adjustment.

In short, we've seen no strong evidence that androgynous people are relatively well adjusted. Masculinity—rather than androgyny—is correlated with self-rated adjustment. And when we obtain an objective measure of adjustment, we see that masculinity may not be related to a person's actual adjustment.

Additional Research on Androgyny.   Let's consider a representative sample of other research on androgyny. In most cases, only a single study has been reported for each attribute.

1. Androgynous people helped a "victim" who was chocking on food more than did masculine men and feminine women (Senneker & Hendrick, 1983).

2. Androgynous people are more tolerant of men and women holding nontraditional jobs than are people in the other three categories (Motowidlo, 1982).

3. Androgynous people are not more likely than people in the other three categories to have a mature, complex view of themselves and their relationships with others (Bursik, 1995).

4. Scores on the Bem Sex-Role Inventory have changed somewhat over time. Specifically, both women and men tended to have higher scores on the masculinity scale during the 1990s, in comparison with 20 years earlier. Men also

tended to have somewhat higher scores on the femininity scale in recent years, but women's femininity scores remained stable (Twenge, 1997b).

5. Two studies on ethnic comparisons indicate that European American women are less likely than women from other ethnic groups to be androgynous (Binion, 1990; De León, 1995). However, another study showed no significant ethnic differences among White, Black, Latina, and Asian American women (Landrine et al., 1992). An important barrier in studying ethnic comparisons is that ethnic groups may differ in their interpretation of terms on the BSRI. For example, Landrine and her colleagues found that European American women defined the word *passive* as "laid-back and easygoing." In contrast, women of color defined *passive* as "not saying what you really think." Both of these definitions fail to capture the inactivity and submissiveness that psychologists mean when they use the term *passivity*. In summary, we do not have clear-cut ethnic differences in androgyny.

This brief summary hints at the complexity of the issue. Androgynous people sometimes perform more admirably than other people. However, androgyny does not deliver the special advantages psychologists had once envisioned.

Problems with Androgyny. Psychologists in the current era have increasingly acknowledged the flaws of the androgyny concept. Let's look at some of the problems that are related to both the experimental results and the theory.

1. As we've just seen, the research suggests that people who are androgynous are not especially different from other individuals.

2. An androgynous person is presumably high in both feminine and masculine characteristics. However, the concept of androgyny was created in an effort to move *beyond* femininity and masculinity. Androgyny is not really an alternative to those stereotypes if femininity and masculinity are actually part of the definition of androgyny!

3. The concept of androgyny suggests that all adults must meet two standards: they must be both masculine *and* feminine. In other words, a competent adult should be able to split half a cord of wood and then proceed to the kitchen to prepare a seven-course Thai dinner. These are probably unrealistic standards for most people.

4. Androgyny tempts us to believe that the solution to gender bias lies in changing the individual. However, androgyny won't solve our present social problems of discrimination against women and institutional sexism. We need to improve the situation, not simply individual women and men.

Moving Beyond Androgyny

Psychologists now agree that the androgyny theory has problems. However, they have not suggested many alternative models. In fact, many critics of androgyny turn back to a classic article by Meda Rebecca and her colleagues (1976), which argued for gender-role transcendence.

Gender-role transcendence means that people do not merely combine gender roles, as androgyny recommends; instead, they go beyond these gender roles, because these roles are no longer relevant. People who have transcended gender roles are free to express their human qualities without worrying about violating stereotypes. They choose strategies that are personally meaningful, rather than forcing themselves into "gender-appropriate" behaviors.

Androgyny stress that people could be flexible, either feminine or masculine as a situation demanded. Rebecca and her coauthors' concept of transcendence goes further. For instance, they suggest that many professions now seem to require a competitive, aggressive style in order to get ahead. An androgynous person would behave in a "masculine" fashion, becoming competitive and aggressive. A person who has transcended gender roles, however, might choose to change her or his interpretation of that profession, no longer acting in a competitive or aggressive fashion. In other words, if a person who transcends gender roles were asked the question, "Are you masculine or feminine?" he or she would answer "None of the above" (Sedney, 1989).

Other authors have developed alternate conceptions of androgyny. For example, Heilbrun and Mulqueen (1987) argued that ideal androgyny is not simply a "more is better" approach, in which high levels of both masculine and feminine traits provide advantages. Instead, these theorists suggested that ideal androgyny blends masculine and feminine qualities to create new strengths, an approach called **blended androgyny.** For example, Stake (1997) asked people to describe real-life situations in which they had to demonstrate this kind of blending. One woman described her job as a bookkeeper, where she was expected to work on her own accounting tasks in a competent and efficient manner, while also answering—in a sensitive and helpful manner—questions from the professional staff about their own projects.

Other authors have devised programs to help people consider how they can transcend gender roles in their own lives. For example, James O'Neil describes a workshop in which men and women trace their own initial acceptance of gender roles, followed perhaps by ambivalence and then anger (O'Neil, 1996b; O'Neil & Egan, 1992). A next step may be activism, in which people use their energy to address sexism in constructive ways. The goal is an integration of gender roles, and in fact a freedom from gender roles in both personal and professional interactions.

Even Sandra Bem (1993), who wrote the classic analysis of psychological androgyny, now argues against the concept. She points out that we should not perceive the world in terms of a split between feminine and masculine characteristics. Instead, we should de-emphasize the distinction between females and males, so that the two groups are not segregated in many aspects of their lives. In short, we should move beyond gender as a way of responding to the world.

Institutions must change, as well as individuals. At present, institutions such as schools, corporations, and the government encourage gender stereotypes. The challenge will be to modify institutions so that they can encourage self-fulfillment in all individuals.

Section Summary *Gender Typing and the Alternatives*

1. Gender typing occurs when people acquire characteristics such as skills and personality attributes that are considered to be appropriate for their gender.

2. Androgynous people are high in both femininity and masculinity; however, androgynous people are typically no better adjusted than people who are high in masculinity (but not femininity); androgynous people may be more helpful and more nontraditional in their beliefs.

3. The problems with androgyny include the following: (a) androgyny is not strongly correlated with other behaviors; (b) androgyny is based on the femininity–masculinity concept; (c) androgyny forces people to meet two standards; and (d) changing institutions is more appropriate than changing individuals.

4. Some psychologists have devised ways of moving beyond androgyny with concepts such as gender-role transcendence, blended androgyny, and programs designed to integrate gender roles.

CHAPTER REVIEW QUESTIONS

1. How would you define the term *gender stereotype?* Based on the information in this chapter, would you suppose that the stereotype of a female can accurately represent a specific woman? Why or why not?

2. This chapter examines how women have been left out of history. Discuss the kinds of topics related to women that scholars have previously ignored. Mention several reasons why women have not received much attention in history books.

3. Review the positions that philosophers have proposed with respect to women. In your answer, pay attention to gender differences. How do these views compare with Theme 1 of this textbook?

4. The chapter discusses how women often seem invisible—for example, men are normative whereas women are secondary. Summarize the information about women's invisibility, mentioning history, religion, mythology, language, the media, and relevant parts of the social cognitive approach to stereotypes.

5. The chapter points out that people are often more negative about women than about men. Discuss this statement, citing support from philosophers, religion, mythology, language, and the media. Then point out why the issue is more complicated when we consider current assessments of women.

6. We discussed factors that influence the strength of people's stereotypes. Review these factors. From this information, predict what kind of person is most likely to believe that men and women are fairly *similar*.

7. The social cognitive approach proposes that stereotypes arise from normal cognitive processes, beginning with the two categories *men* and *women*. Describe some of the cognitive biases that would encourage people to believe that women are more talkative than men (a stereotype that isn't correct).

8. What is heterosexism, and how are gender stereotypes related to heterosexism? The social cognitive approach proposes that our normal cognitive processes would encourage people to develop stereotypes about lesbians and gay males. Describe how some of the cognitive biases would encourage these exaggerated stereotypes.

9. What is a self-fulfilling prophecy? Why is it relevant when we examine how stereotypes can influence behavior? Identify one of your own behaviors that is more gender stereotyped than you might wish, and point out how a self-fulfilling prophecy might be relevant.

10. Define *androgyny* and describe why this approach offers some advantages over the traditional idea that masculinity and femininity are exact opposites. Point out some problems that the concept of androgyny has encountered in recent years, and discuss some of the other alternatives.

NEW TERMS

gender stereotypes (36)
prejudice (37)
discrimination (37)
masculine generic (42)
agency (52)
communion (52)
hostile sexism (61)
benevolent sexism (61)
lesbian (62)
gay male (62)
bisexual (62)
heterosexism (62)
homophobia (62)
social cognitive approach (64)

gender polarization (65)
normative male (65)
androcentrism (65)
attributions (67)
self-fulfilling prophecy (69)
gender typing (70)
androgyny (71)
bipolar (scales) (71)
undifferentiated people (73)
feminine people (73)
masculine people (73)
androgynous people (73)
gender-role transcendence (76)
blended androgyny (76)

RECOMMENDED READINGS

Bem, S. L. (1993). *The lenses of gender: Transforming the debate on sexual inequality*. New Haven, CT: Yale University Press. Sandra Bem, who developed the concept of androgyny, turns her attention in this book to three of our culture's assumptions: androcentrism, gender polarization, and biological essentialism.

Burn, S. M. (1996). *The social psychology of gender*. New York: McGraw-Hill. This engaging book examines the limitations of the traditional male and female roles, as well as the social cognitive approach to stereotypes, cross-cultural views of gender, and how to change gender roles.

Frieze, I. H., & McHugh, M. C. (Eds.). (1997). Measuring beliefs about appropriate roles for women and men. [Special issue]. *Psychology of Women Quarterly, 21*(1). This special issue is devoted entirely to measuring stereotypes and attitudes toward women; it's an excellent resource for current research.

Lott, B., & Maluso, D. (Eds.). (1995b). *The social psychology of interpersonal discrimination*. New York: Guilford. I'd recommend this volume for anyone who would like an overview of various "-isms"; it examines sexism, racism, heterosexism, classism, and ageism.

Rodríguez, C. E. (Ed.). (1997b). *Latin looks: Images of Latinas and Latinos in the U.S. media*. Boulder, CO: Westview Press. This book was the most interesting one I found on media representations and ethnicity. Topics covered include the news media's ignoring of Latinas/os, the representation of Chicanas in films, and documentaries by Latinas.

ANSWERS TO THE DEMONSTRATIONS

Demonstration 2.3: Most people believe that the following items are characteristics of women (W): gentle, kind, emotional, compassionate, modest, fickle, warm, nervous, talkative, patient. They also believe that the following items are characteristic of men (M): self-confident, competitive, active, loud, inventive, greedy, capable, show-off, courageous, powerful.

Demonstration 2.5: Add together the total number of points from the following items: 1, 3, 6, 7, 9. These represent the hostile sexism subscale. Then add together the total number of points from the following items: 2, 4, 5, 8, 10. These represent the benevolent sexism subscale. Adding these two subscale scores together provides an index of overall sexism.

Demonstration 2.6: Add up the ratings for feminine-typed items (1, 6, 8, 10) to obtain a score on the Femininity Scale. Add up the ratings for masculine-typed items (3, 5, 9, 12) to obtain a score on the Masculinity Scale. The remaining items are "filler items" and are not scored.

ANSWERS TO THE TRUE–FALSE QUESTIONS

1. True (p. 38); 2. False (p. 39); 3. True (p. 42); 4. False (p. 46); 5. True (p. 48); 6. True (p. 55); 7. True (p. 63); 8. False (p. 64); 9. False (pp. 72–73); 10. False (p. 74).

Infancy and Childhood

TRUE OR FALSE?

_____ 1. During the first few weeks of prenatal development, females and males have similar sex glands and external genitals.

_____ 2. Infant girls are substantially more advanced than infant boys in their social development; this early advantage lays the foundation for adult females' social skills.

_____ 3. If a baby is introduced as "Johnny," people typically hand the baby a football; if the same baby is introduced as "Jenny," people typically hand the baby a doll.

_____ 4. Researchers have found fairly strong evidence for the Freudian concept of penis envy; girls do feel that their own genitals are inferior.

_____ 5. By the age of 6 months, infants can perceive that a female face belongs in a different category from a series of male faces.

_____ 6. Young children often believe that a man can easily become a woman—for example, by holding a purse.

_____ 7. In general, girls are more likely than boys to prefer an occupation that is considered nontraditional for their gender.

_____ 8. Parents are consistently more critical of aggressive girls, compared to aggressive boys.

_____ 9. Teachers typically give more educational feedback to boy than to girls.

_____ 10. Research conducted during the past 10 years shows that boys and girls are now almost equally represented in children's television programs, and children rarely act in gender-stereotyped ways in these programs.

The Beginnings of Gender Development
Prenatal Development
Gender Comparisons During Infancy
How People Respond to Infant Girls and Boys

Theoretical Explanations of Gender Typing
Psychoanalytic Theory
Gender Schema Theory

Children's Knowledge About Gender
Children's Ideas About Gender Constancy
Children's Stereotypes About Personality
Children's Stereotypes About Activities and Occupations
Factors Related to Children's Stereotypes

Factors That Shape Gender Typing
The Family
Peers
School
The Media

A friend who teaches Women's Studies keeps me informed about her son Brian's experiences with gender in his fourth-grade classroom. The teacher routinely holds reading contests, with the boys competing against the girls. The losers in each contest must act as individual "slaves" for the children who won the event—carrying books, running errands, and so on. When my friend complained to Brian's teacher, she replied, "He's the only one who has a problem with the game. . . . All the other children love it!" Recently, the teacher assigned the children to each read a biography of a famous person. They were then to give the book reports orally, dressed in a costume appropriate for that person. Brian asked if he could read a biography about a famous woman, and the teacher replied that he could not; after all, it would be inappropriate for him to dress in a woman's outfit.

In Chapter 2, we introduced the term **gender typing,** which refers to the acquisition of preferences, skills, personality attributes, behaviors, and self-concepts that our culture considers to be "gender appropriate" (S. Bem, 1983). In this chapter, we'll consider how infants and children learn about gender. We'll start by considering the very beginnings of gender, during prenatal development and infancy, and then we'll examine several important theories of gender typing. A major part of this chapter then focuses on children's knowledge and stereotypes about gender. Finally, we'll consider the factors responsible for gender typing—such as the school experiences with which 9-year-old Brian is currently struggling.

THE BEGINNINGS OF
GENDER DEVELOPMENT

Some important components of gender—specifically, the sex organs—develop during the **prenatal period,** the time prior to birth. Other gender messages are conveyed during **infancy,** the period between birth and 18 months of life.

Prenatal Development

At conception, an egg with 23 chromosomes unites with a sperm, which has 23 chromosomes. Together, they form a single cell that contains 23 chromosome pairs. One of those pairs is called the **sex chromosomes**—the chromosomes that determine whether the embryo will be genetically female or male.

The egg from the mother always supplies an X sex chromosome. The father's sperm, which fertilizes the egg, contains either an X chromosome or a Y chromosome. If the egg is fertilized by an X chromosome, then the chromosome pair is symbolized XX, and the child will be a genetic female. If the egg is fertilized by a Y chromosome, then the chromosome pair is symbolized XY, and the child will be a genetic male. Isn't it ironic that a characteristic our culture considers to be so important—whether someone is an XX person or an XY person—should be determined simply by whether an X-bearing sperm or a Y-bearing sperm is the first to reach the egg cell?

Normal Prenatal Development.   Until about 6 weeks after conception, female and male embryos look identical. They differ only in their chromosomes. For instance, each human fetus has two sets of primitive, internal reproductive systems. The female system, called **Müllerian ducts,** will eventually develop into a uterus, egg ducts, and part of the vagina in females. The male system, called **Wolffian ducts,** will eventually develop into the appropriate internal reproductive system in males.

The sex glands, or **gonads,** of males and females, also look identical during the first weeks after conception. If the embryo has an XY chromosome pair, a tiny segment of the Y chromosome guides the gonads to develop into male testes, beginning about 6 weeks after conception (Marx, 1995). In contrast, if the embryo has an XX chromosome pair, the gonads begin to develop into female ovaries, beginning about 10 weeks after conception (D. Ruble & Martin, 1998).

In about the third month after conception, the fetus's hormones encourage further sex differentiation. In males, the testes secrete two substances. One of these, the Müllerian regression hormone, shrinks the (female) Müllerian ducts. The testes also secrete **androgen,** often called the male sex hormone. Androgen encourages the growth and development of the Wolffian ducts (Breedlove, 1994; Collaer & Hines, 1995). Androgen also encourages the growth of the external genitals (Figure 3.1). The genital tubercle becomes the penis in males.

At about the same time, the ovaries in females begin to synthesize large quantities of **estrogen,** one of the female sex hormones. Consistent with the "invisible female" theme, we know much less about prenatal development in females than in males. However, some researchers argue that estrogen encourages the growth and development of the Müllerian ducts, while shrinking the Wolffian ducts. Estrogen also seems to encourage the development of the external genitals in females. Note, in Figure 3.1, that the genital tubercle becomes the penis in males but it develops into the clitoris in females.

FIGURE 3.1	**Prenatal development of the external genitals. (Money & Ehrhardt, 1972)**

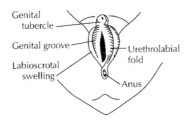

Sexual appearance of fetus at second to third month of pregnancy

Male and Female Identical

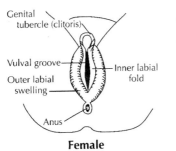

Female

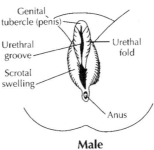

Male

Sexual appearance of fetus at third to fourth month of pregnancy

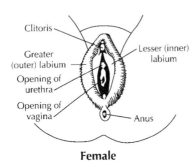

Female

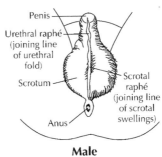

Male

Sexual appearance of baby at time of birth

Normal sexual development, then, involves a complex sequence prior to birth. The first event is conception, when genetic sex is determined. Female and male embryos are anatomically identical for the first weeks after conception. Four further processes then begin the differentiation of females and males: (1) the development of the internal reproductive system, (2) the development of the gonads, (3) the production of hormones, and (4) the development of the external genitals.

Atypical Prenatal Development. The scenario we've just examined is the typical one. However, this elaborate developmental sequence sometimes takes a different pathway. As a result, an infant is born whose biological sex is ambiguous. Let's consider two atypical patterns of development in which the hormone production does *not* match the genetic pattern.

One atypical pattern is called **androgen-insensitivity syndrome,** a condition in which genetic males (XY) produce normal amounts of androgen, but a genetic defect makes their bodies not respond to androgen (Breedlove, 1994). Because the developing fetus is not sensitive to androgen, the genital tubercle does not grow into a penis. These persons are usually labeled girls because they lack a penis. However, they have a shallow cavity instead of a complete vagina, and they have no uterus. They also do not menstruate. Individuals with androgen-insensitivity syndrome who are raised as girls generally play with stereotypically feminine toys and appear satisfied with the female gender role (Money & Ehrhardt, 1972; D. Ruble & Martin, 1998).

A second atypical pattern is called **congenital adrenal hyperplasia,** a condition in which genetic females (XX) receive too much androgen during prenatal development. The excess androgen causes their genitals to look somewhat masculine. When these children are raised as girls, they are usually treated with surgical adjustment of the genitals and supplemental hormone therapy to reduce the androgen level. In general, girls with this disorder may be more likely than other girls to enjoy playing with boys. However, like other girls, they avoid rough play (M. Hines & Kaufman, 1994; Ruble & Martin, 1998).

An ongoing controversy in psychology focuses on whether children's ideas about their gender are firmly shaped by their biological makeup—either their genetic pattern or their exposure to hormones. For many years, psychologists argued that psychological factors were more important than biological factors (Golombok & Fivush, 1994; Money & Ehrhardt, 1972). In other words, a child who was labeled a girl and treated like a girl would come to identify herself as a girl, even if she was genetically a male or even if she had received an excess of prenatal androgen. However, some psychologists are now arguing that we have underestimated the importance of biological factors (e.g., Diamond, 1996).

The problem is that we cannot draw clear-cut conclusions about the relative importance of psychological and biological factors because the studies on atypical prenatal development cannot be carefully controlled. For example, parents certainly know when their child has atypical genital development, so they may treat this child differently from most girls. These children are likely to develop more masculine-looking faces and bodies, so they may not be treated like feminine-looking girls (Ruble & Martin, 1998). In reality, we cannot objectively determine the relative contribution of psychological and biological factors.

To me, the most interesting aspect of atypical prenatal development focuses on a different issue: Why does our culture force all infants into either the female category or the male category (S. Kessler, 1998)? Why can't we accept that some people are **intersexuals**—neither female nor male? Many adult intersexuals now argue that such children should *not* be forced to adopt one gender just because it is socially acceptable (Diamond, 1996). As one intersexual writes:

> I was born whole and beautiful, but different. The error was not in my body, nor in my sex organs, but in the determination of the culture. . . . Our path to healing lies in embracing our intersexual selves, not in labeling our bodies as having committed some "error." (Diamond, 1996, p. 144)

We pointed out in the previous two chapters that gender polarization forces us to see the two genders as being very different from one another. Can we overcome this polarization and accept the fact that we humans are not limited to just two options?

Gender Comparisons During Infancy

We will discuss gender comparisons in most chapters of this book. However, the reason we focus on gender comparisons during infancy is that research on infants could potentially clarify an important question: Can gender differences be traced to biological explanations ("nature"), rather than explanations in which females are treated differently than males ("nurture")? Suppose, for example, that researchers were to find that 1-day-old female infants are much more responsive to human faces than 1-day-old male infants are. Given that finding, we would be inclined to believe that an inborn, biological difference exists in this area. After all, we could not explain this gender difference by arguing that baby girls are treated much differently than baby boys during their first 24 hours of life.

We'll see, however, that gender differences during infancy are actually small and inconsistent, supporting Theme 1 of this book. In general, girls and boys are fairly similar during infancy.

Physical and Temperamental Comparisons.   Besides the obvious differences in their genitals, infant boys and girls show several minor physical differences. At birth, boys weigh about 5% more than girls—a fairly subtle difference. Infant girls are somewhat more advanced in their motor development; they may sit, crawl, and walk slightly earlier than boys do (Beal, 1994). However, boys and girls are similar in their perceptual development (Beal, 1994).

Baby boys may be slightly more active than baby girls (Beal, 1994; Eaton & Enns, 1986; Valian, 1998). However, the gender differences are not large, and many studies have reported gender similarities (Beal, 1994; Cossette et al., 1991;

Rothbart, 1983). Thus, a staff member at a child care center is likely to notice that the typical male infant is more active than the typical female infant. However, many girls will be more active than the norm for a typical boy. No clear-cut gender differences have been found in the amount of time spent sleeping or crying (Beal, 1994; Rothbart, 1983).

Social Comparisons.   In social behavior, no clear gender differences emerge. For example, one study showed that infant girls are more likely than infant boys to vocalize to their mothers, but other research showed just the opposite (Brooks-Gunn & Matthews, 1979; G. Wasserman & Lewis, 1985).

In general, girls and boys are similar in their smiles and other social interactions with their mothers (Cossette et al., 1996; Gunnar & Donahue, 1980; G. Wasserman & Lewis, 1985). In some studies, girls have been found to be slightly more social than boys at some ages or in some kinds of social situations. In Chapter 6, you'll see that gender differences are prominent in some social situations but disappear in others. The results on infant social interactions suggest that, even during infancy, we cannot draw conclusions about gender differences unless we know something about the social setting.

Do infant girls and boys differ in their dependency on adults? The answer here seems to be a tentative "No." An early study reported that 11-month-old baby girls cried more than boys did when a barrier separated them from their mothers (S. Goldberg & Lewis, 1969). Other research, however, maintained that males and females do not differ in dependency during infancy (Brooks-Gunn & Matthews, 1979; Maccoby & Jacklin, 1974). However, you may still find the popular media making unjustified claims like, "Researchers have proven that girls are more dependent than boys, even during infancy."

In general, the research on infancy suggests gender similarities. Some differences have occasionally been discovered, but none is large enough to suggest that infant girls behave much differently from infant boys. Gender differences are typically reported in studies of older infants. By late infancy, the differences may well have been produced by people's differential treatment of girls and boys during earlier infancy. Let's now consider that topic.

How People Respond to Infant Girls and Boys

We consider a person's gender—the label "female" or "male"—to be very important, as we saw in Chapter 2. Furthermore, when people hear that a baby has been born, their most likely question is: "Is it a boy or a girl?" One pair of researchers stood by as the parents of newborns telephoned friends and relatives to announce their baby's birth (Intons-Peterson & Reddel, 1984). In 80% of the calls, the first question to the parents concerned the baby's sex. To some parents, sex and gender are so important that their own child may be a tragic disappointment. A friend of mine once shared a room on a maternity ward with a woman who was planning to give up her infant girl for adoption. She and her husband had wanted a boy.

In general, research in the United States and Canada demonstrates that men and women tend to prefer a boy for their firstborn child (M. Hamilton, 1991b; Krishnan, 1987), although one study showed that women slightly prefer a girl (Pooler, 1991). The birth of a daughter will therefore be a disappointment—at least initially—for many people you know. At some point in the near future, try Demonstration 3.1, which focuses on gender preferences.

Parents in some other cultures have even stronger preferences for boys. Favoritism toward boys is so strong in India that doctors often conduct a prenatal sex determination, and the mother requests an abortion if the fetus is female. This selective-abortion policy has had long-term effects on the country's population. For example, Kishwar (1995) has estimated that, in India, almost 30 million fewer baby girls have been born than baby boys, primarily because of selective abortion. Selective abortion and female infanticide also operate in China, where the discrepancy in the female population has important social consequences. For example, a 1990 news release announced that the country had almost seven times as many single men as single women (Berscheid, 1993). This preference for male babies is an important example of Theme 2 of this book.

A preference for male babies may also have important health consequences. For example, I know a female student who had been born in Korea, in a premature delivery. Her father recently told her that that family had decided not to put her in an incubator, because she was a girl, but they would have chosen the incubator option if she had been a boy.

How do people respond to infant girls and boys? Do they think baby girls and baby boys have different characteristics, and do they treat them differently?

DEMONSTRATION 3.1

Preferences for Males Versus Females as the Firstborn Child

You've just read that most North Americans who have been surveyed prefer a boy as their firstborn, but this preference is not universal. To perform this demonstration, locate 10 women and 10 men who do not have children, and ask them whether they would like a boy or a girl as their firstborn child. Be sure to select people with whom you are comfortable asking this question, and interview them one at a time. After noting each person's response, ask for a brief rationale for the answer. Do your male and female respondents differ in their preferences? Do you think their responses would have been different if they had filled out an anonymous survey?

Let's first consider parents' responses, and then we'll examine the responses of strangers.

Parents' Behavior. Katherine Karraker and her colleagues (1995) studied 40 mother–father pairs, two days after their infant son or daughter had been born. All the parents were asked to rate their newborn infant on a number of scales. Each scale was anchored with a masculine adjective (e.g., *strong*) on the left and a feminine adjective (e.g., *weak*) on the right.

Even though the boys and girls were objectively similar in terms of size and health, the parents rated them differently (Figure 3.2). Parents of girls rated their daughters as being relatively weak, whereas parents of boys rated their sons as being relatively strong. Greater distinctions were made between daughters and sons of three other dimensions: (1) large featured–fine featured; (2) hardy–delicate; and (3) masculine–feminine. Mothers and fathers responded similarly in this study; in other research, we'll find that fathers often have stronger gender stereotypes.

FIGURE 3.2	Average ratings for newborn girls and boys on four dimensions. (Based on Karraker et al., 1995)

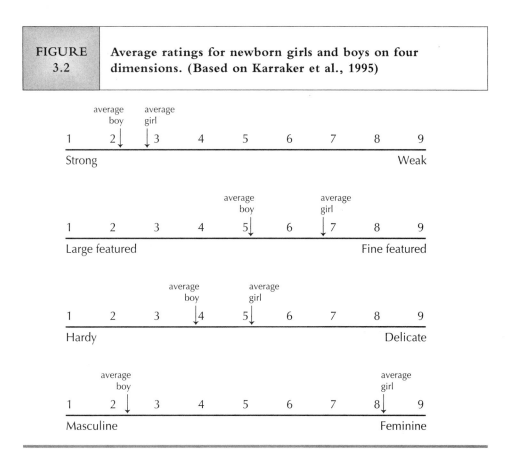

Some researchers have watched parents interacting with their young infants. For example, Moss (1974) asked parents to encourage their 7-week-old infants to perform certain tasks. Both mothers and fathers spent more time encouraging their female infants to smile and to make sounds. Must girls be social creatures, even if they are only 7 weeks old? (Chapter 6 shows that adult women smile much more than adult men. Perhaps we ensure this later gender difference because we were trained early.) Moss also found that parents were more likely to call baby girls—rather than baby boys—affectionate terms such as "angel," "honey," and "precious."

Some studies suggest that parents talk more to their infant daughters than to their infant sons; other studies show no differences (Golombok & Fivush, 1994; Huttenlocher et al., 1991). Parents may treat their children differently with respect to clothing. Paul and Paula might both wear neutral T-shirts and pants for most of their infancy. Still, for special occasions, Paul is likely to be sporting a tailored blue outfit, whereas Paula wears a dress with flowers, bows, and frills.

Parents typically decorate boys' rooms with animal themes and bold colors. In contrast, girls' rooms are likely to have pastels, lace, and ruffles (Pomerleau et al., 1990). Youngsters' toys also differ. In one study, boys had an average of 12 toy vehicles, in contrast to 5 for girls. Girls owned an average of 4 dolls, in contrast to 1 for boys (Pomerleau et al., 1990).

Strangers' Behavior.   Have you ever assumed an infant was a boy, and then learned it was a girl? Most of us find this experience puzzling. We try to maintain a nonsexist perspective, yet we find ourselves immediately justifying this gender transformation: "Oh, of course, she has long eyelashes" or "Yes, her hands are so delicate." In other words, strangers—as well as parents—make distinctions based on gender.

In general, the research evidence confirms that people judge infants differently when they are perceived to be female rather than male. For instance, in a classic study, adults were introduced to a neutrally dressed 3-month-old infant whose gender was not specified (Seavey et al., 1975). Later, these people were asked to guess the baby's gender and provide reasons for their answers. Those who had concluded that the baby was a boy remarked about the strength of the baby's grasp or the lack of hair. Those who thought that the baby was a girl commented on how round, soft, and fragile "she" was.

Let's consider a study by John Delk and his colleagues (1986) in more detail. These researchers prepared a videotape of a diaper-clad White toddler walking, sitting, and playing with assorted gender-neutral toys. Half of the observers were told the baby was female, and half were told the baby was male. Every 15 seconds, the observers rated the baby's most recent activity as either masculine or feminine.

As Figure 3.3 illustrates, people who thought that the toddler was female tended to label the various activities as feminine. In contrast, those who thought that the toddler was male tended to label the activities as masculine.

Incidentally, one limitation of this study—and of most other research on gender—was that the toddler was White and the participants were primarily White

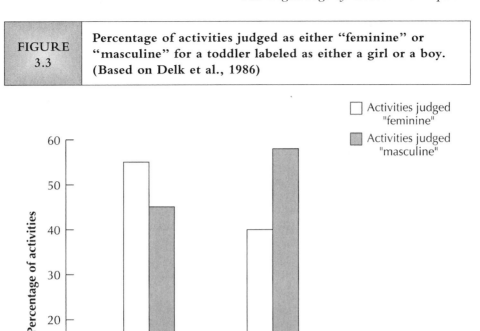

| FIGURE 3.3 | Percentage of activities judged as either "feminine" or "masculine" for a toddler labeled as either a girl or a boy. (Based on Delk et al., 1986) |

middle-class students. Would the labeling have had similar results if both the toddler and the judges represented other ethnic and socioeconomic groups?

A variety of other studies have shown that people make somewhat different judgments, depending on whether they believe an infant to be a boy or a girl (e.g., Demarest & Glinos, 1992; C. Lewis et al., 1992; Paludi & Gullo, 1987). Recall, in Chapter 2, the study by Condry and Condry (1976) in which adults watched videotapes of an infant crying in response to the opening of a jack-in-the-box. Those who thought the infant was a boy tended to judge that "he" was showing anger. Those who thought the infant was a girl tended to judge that "she" was showing fear.

Other research has demonstrated that people hand different toys to infants they perceive to be female rather than male. In one study, college students who thought they were playing with a baby girl handed "her" a doll 80% of the time and a football 14% of the time. Students who thought they were playing with a baby boy handed "him" a doll 20% of the time and a football 64% of the time

(Sidorowicz & Lunney, 1980). Repeated play with stereotyped toys may keep children from developing broader competencies.

Marilyn Stern and Katherine Karraker (1989) reviewed the research in which infants are given male or female labels. More than two-thirds of the studies showed at least one gender-label effect. In general, gender labels make a bigger difference when people judge infants' activities and physical characteristics or when people actually interact with the infants. In contrast, gender labels are less likely to influence judgments of developmental achievements and personality characteristics. In summary, we may be encouraging gender-stereotyped behavior in infant boys and girls, even though we are not consciously aware that we are treating them differently (Golombok & Fivush, 1994).

Relatives and friends may convey gender stereotypes through their choice of greeting cards. Figure 3.4 illustrates a typical contrast between cards intended for parents of newborn girls versus newborn boys. Bridges (1993) gathered a sample of 61 newborn-girl cards and 61 newborn-boy cards from 18 stores in a

FIGURE 3.4	**Representative cards to be sent to the parents of a baby boy or a baby girl. (*Note:* The original card for the boy is blue, and the card for the girl is pink.)**

variety of neighborhoods. She found that the boy cards showed physical activity and action toys, whereas the girl cards emphasized the baby's sweetness. In addition, boy cards were more likely to mention how happy the parents must be. Bridges suggests that this emphasis may reflect the greater value our culture places on males. Parents therefore receive a strong gender message as soon as they open the envelopes!

Notice that all these studies on adults' treatment of infants tend to support a social constructionist approach. As we discussed in Chapter 1, **social constructionism** argues that we tend to construct or invent our own versions of reality based on our prior experiences and beliefs. For example, when we are told that an infant is female, we tend to "see" delicate, feminine behavior. When we are told that the same infant is male, we tend to "see" sturdy, masculine behavior. That is, we create our own versions of reality, based on our prior beliefs about gender.

The available information on prenatal and infant development gives us some partial insights into the puzzle of gender typing. For example, the research on atypical prenatal development suggests that genetic makeup and prenatal hormones do not completely determine whether an individual acts stereotypically feminine or masculine. Thus, we must look beyond biology for explanations. We have also seen that baby boys and baby girls are more similar than different in their personal characteristics. A partial explanation of gender typing lies in the way people respond to infant girls and boys: Both parents and strangers make some gender distinctions. However, differential treatment by adults is still not a complete answer. Instead, as we'll see in the remainder of this chapter, part of the explanation comes from girls' and boys' own ideas about the importance of gender. They acquire these ideas from adults, other children, and the media, and they exaggerate these ideas still further.

 SECTION SUMMARY *The Beginnings of Gender Development*

1. **During normal prenatal development, male and female embryos initially look identical; male testes begin to develop at 6 weeks, and female ovaries begin to develop at 10 weeks.**

2. **An embryo's neutral external genitals grow into either female or male genitals during prenatal development.**

3. **In atypical prenatal development, genetic males with androgen-insensitivity syndrome—raised as girls—appear generally satisfied with the female gender role; genetic females with congenital adrenal hyperplasia (too much androgen)—raised as girls after surgery—seem generally satisfied with stereotypically feminine play patterns.**

4. **From the studies on atypical prenatal development, we cannot draw clear-cut conclusions about the relative contribution of psychological**

and biological factors; interestingly our culture insists upon creating two distinctly different categories, male and female.

5. Gender differences in physical build, temperament, and social behavior are typically small and inconsistent.

5. Parents tend to prefer male offspring in the United States and Canada; gender preferences are so strong in some other countries that female fetuses may be aborted, and parents make extra effort to keep male babies healthy.

7. Parents tend to have different initial reactions to sons and daughters, to interact with their sons more vigorously, and to buy different clothing, room furnishings, and toys for their sons and daughters.

8. Strangers tend to respond to babies differently, depending on whether they believe a baby is a boy or a girl.

THEORETICAL EXPLANATIONS OF GENDER TYPING

How can we account for gender typing? What theoretical explanations can we offer for children's acquisition of preferences, skills, personality attributes, behaviors, and self-concepts? Let's first summarize the psychoanalytic theory, which is not supported by the research. Then we'll consider Sandra Bem's gender schema approach, which integrates several theoretical explanations that have generally been supported by the research.

Psychoanalytic Theory

Psychoanalytic theory, which originated with Sigmund Freud, emphasizes childhood experiences and unconscious motivations and conflicts. Sigmund Freud was a Viennese physician who lived from 1856 to 1939. Freudian theory has had a tremendous influence on psychological theory, psychotherapy, and our culture in general. As we'll see in Chapter 12, Freud's theory contributed to negative views about women. We summarize his approach here because it influenced attitudes toward women, not because it explains gender-role development accurately.

Freud proposed that children's sexual emotions are vitally important. Specifically, sexual identity begins to form at about the age of 4 years, during the **phallic stage** of development, when children focus on their genitals. Boys in the phallic stage intensify their love for their mothers. They also suffer from a **castration complex,** or fear that their genitals will be mutilated. Freud proposed that girls who are in the phallic stage experience different emotions. Girls presumably develop **penis envy;** they notice that they do not have a penis, and they therefore feel inferior (Freud, 1993/1965).

Before continuing this description, I want to emphasize that this concept is not supported by research (Jacklin & Reynolds, 1993; Roopnarine & Mounts,

1987). Most young girls either don't notice genital differences or express relief that they are not similarly burdened. Consider a little girl who, during a bath with her young male cousin, silently observed the genital differences. When her mother tucked her into bed that night, she said softly to her mother, "Isn't it a blessing he doesn't have it on his face?" (Tavris & Offir, 1977, p. 155).

Freud argued that penis envy was central to girls' development and that girls blame their mothers for not supplying them with the proper equipment. A disappointed daughter turns from her mother to her father, hoping that he will give her a penis as a gift. Freud theorized that penis envy is eventually partly resolved when girls begin to identify with their mothers.

This brief description of Freud's theory of female development provides only an introduction to his complex ideas. Freud himself acknowledged that his ideas about women were the weakest part of his theories (Slipp, 1993). More current revisions of psychoanalytic theory downplay the importance of penis envy and are less emphatic about females' presumed psychological inferiority (Notman, 1991; Slipp, 1993).

Gender Schema Theory

Most psychologists currently support some variation of gender schema theory. We'll examine the version developed by Sandra Bem, whose work on gender typing and on androgyny we explored in Chapter 2. **Gender schema theory** is complex; it blends together two prominent earlier approaches: (1) the cognitive developmental approach and (2) the social learning approach (S. Bem, 1981, 1985, 1993). Let's consider these two components.

The Cognitive Developmental Component. Gender schema theory proposes that children use gender as a cognitive organizing principle or **schema** (pronounced "*skee*-mah"). Cognitive psychologists point out that we acquire schemas from our past experience. For example, you have a schema for a professor's office; your general knowledge suggests that the office should have a desk, a chair, and books—but not a pet rabbit or a waffle iron.

Sandra Bem argues that the gender schema has particular salience, as we noted in Chapter 2. She proposes that children organize information about themselves and about the rest of the world according to the definitions of maleness and femaleness found in their culture. These gender schemas include everything children know about gender, and they encourage children to act in gender-stereotyped ways that are consistent with the gender schemas (G. Levy & Fivush, 1993).

This portion of Bem's theory, which emphasizes children's thoughts about gender, is partly based on Lawrence Kohlberg's theories about gender typing (Kohlberg, 1996; Kohlberg & Ullian, 1974). Kohlberg's **cognitive developmental theory** proposes that children are responsible for shaping their own gender typing; they actively work to understand gender-related concepts. Kohlberg pointed out that the first major step in gender typing is **gender identity**—a girl's realization that she is a girl, and a boy's realization that he is a boy. Most children are quite accurate in labeling themselves by the time they are 2 or 3 years old.

Soon after children label themselves accurately, they learn how to classify males and females. At this point, Kohlberg notes, they begin to prefer things that are consistent with their own gender identity. A child who realizes that she is a girl, for example, likes feminine objects and activities. A woman in one of my classes provided a vivid example of these preference patterns. Her 4-year-old daughter asked about the sex of every dog she met. If it was a "girl dog," she would run up and pat it lovingly. If it was a "boy dog," she would cast a scornful glance and walk in the opposite direction. Girls prefer stereotypically feminine activities because these activities are consistent with their female gender identity, according to Kohlberg.

Sandra Bem elaborates on Kohlberg's description of children's gender ideas. Specifically, Bem (1981, 1985, 1993) argues that children evaluate their own adequacy in terms of the gender schema. Mary realizes that she should be gentle and attentive to her baby brother in order to rate high on the nurturance dimension, which adults will use to evaluate her. Bem observes that a culture determines what kind of schema is most important. In the United States and Canada, gender is emphasized more than other social categories. For example, this chapter began with a description of Brian's fourth-grade classroom. The teacher instructs the children to form "boys' lines" and "girls' lines" when they leave the classroom. The teacher does not line up the children according to race. We try to de-emphasize racial distinctions, but we continue to emphasize gender distinctions.

So far, our examination of gender schema theory has emphasized the importance of *children's thoughts* in encouraging gender typing. The other major force in gender schema theory is *children's behavior*.

The Social Learning Component.   Gender schema theory proposes that traditional learning principles explain an important part of gender typing. This portion of Bem's gender schema theory is based on Walter Mischel's (1966, 1970) version of social learning theory. **Social learning theory** proposes two major mechanisms for explaining how girls learn to act "feminine" and boys learn to act "masculine":

1. Children are rewarded for "gender-appropriate" behavior, and they are punished for "gender-inappropriate" behavior.
2. Children watch and imitate the behavior of other people of their own gender.

Let's first see how rewards and punishments might operate. Jimmy, age 2, grabs a toy truck and, racing it back and forth, produces an impressive rumbling-motor sound. The doting parents smile, thereby rewarding Jimmy's behavior. His parents would not respond so positively if he donned his sister's pink tutu and waltzed around the dining room. His parents would probably produce either a punishing silence or active efforts to discourage him. Now imagine how

Sarah, also age 2, might win smiles for the pink-tutu act, but possible frowns for the roaring-truck performance. According to this first social learning component, children learn many gender-related behaviors by trial and error; they notice and modify their behavior in response to other people.

According to the second social learning component, children also learn by watching others and imitating them, a process called **modeling.** They are especially likely to imitate a person of their own gender or a person who has been praised for a behavior. For example, a little girl would be most likely to imitate her mother, especially if her mother has been praised for her actions. Children frequently imitate characters from books, films, and television, as well as "real" people. As we'll discuss later, gender-stereotyped models help explain why children reared in strongly feminist homes may still develop stereotyped views. For example, a woman who is a physician overheard her young son telling the child next door, "No, ladies can't be doctors; they gotta be nurses."

General Comments About Gender Schema Theory.   In summary, gender schema theory provides two major components of gender typing, with the second component featuring two mechanisms:

1. Children's thoughts are important, as suggested by cognitive developmental theory.
2. Children's behavior is important, as suggested by social learning theory.
   a. Children are rewarded and punished for gender-related behavior.
   b. Children model their behavior after same-gender individuals.

Current theorists generally favor gender schema theory because it integrates both cognitive and learning approaches (e.g., Reid et al., 1995; Ruble & Martin, 1998). However, it's unclear exactly how these two approaches blend together. Do children's beliefs about gender come first? Or, do children first observe how they are rewarded and punished for gender-related behavior, and then use that information to construct their beliefs about gender? Gender typing is such a complex topic that many interesting theoretical questions remain to be solved.

Let's now turn our attention to the research. We'll first see how children's thoughts about gender develop. Then we'll consider the external forces that encourage gender typing, including the parents and teachers who reward and punish children's gender-related behavior, and the media that provide models of gender-stereotyped behavior.

 SECTION SUMMARY *Theories of Gender Typing*

1. **According to psychoanalytic theory, girls presumably develop penis envy during the phallic stage (a concept not supported by research). Girls next turn to their fathers but ultimately identify with their mothers.**

2. Sandra Bem's gender schema theory combines the cognitive developmental approach (in which children's thought processes shape gender typing) with the social learning approach (in which children are rewarded for "gender-appropriate" behavior and punished for "gender-inappropriate" behavior; in addition, they imitate the behavior of same-gender individuals).

CHILDREN'S KNOWLEDGE ABOUT GENDER

In Chapter 2, we explored adults' stereotypes about males and females. Now let's examine children's knowledge, beliefs, and stereotypes about gender.

Interestingly, even infants as young as 6 months of age know something about gender; they can place males and females in different categories (Fagot & Leinbach, 1993, 1994; P. Katz & Kofkin, 1997; Leinbach & Fagot, 1993). In a typical study, researchers showed each infant a series of slides of the heads and shoulders of different women. (The slides showed a variety of clothing, hairstyles, facial expressions, and so forth.) After a number of slides, the infant lost interest in these female stimuli. Then the researchers presented a test slide, showing either a male or a female. Katz and Kofkin (1997) found, for example, that 6-month-olds looked significantly longer at a slide of a male than at a slide of a female. This looking pattern tells us that young infants recognize that a new slide belongs to a different category than the slides previously shown. (Infants also looked longer at a slide of a female after seeing a series of slides showing males.)

This series of studies shows us that, long before they are able to say their first word or take their first step, infants divide people into two categories on the basis of gender. Some exploratory research suggests that hair length is one critical factor that infants use to determine category membership (Fagot & Leinbach, 1994).

As you can imagine, gender knowledge is much easier to test in children who are old enough to talk. Let's begin by examining children's knowledge about gender constancy. Then we'll look at children's stereotypes about personality characteristics, as well as their stereotypes about activities and occupations. We'll also examine some factors that influence the strength of children's stereotypes.

Children's Ideas About Gender Constancy

Gender constancy means that a person's gender stays the same, even when outward physical appearance changes. Young children fail to appreciate gender constancy, so they believe that a person can easily change genders. A woman can "become" a man by cutting her hair very short, and a man can "become" a woman by holding a purse.

Young children also believe that children can easily change genders as they mature into adults. For example, Kohlberg (1966) recorded a conversation between Jimmy, almost 4 years old, and Johnny, who is 4½:

Johnny: I'm going to be an airplane builder when I grow up.
Jimmy: When I grow up, I'll be a Mommy.
Johnny: No, you can't be a Mommy. You have to be a Daddy.
Jimmy: No, I'm going to be a Mommy.
Johnny: No, you're not a girl, you can't be a Mommy.
Jimmy: Yes, I can. (p. 95)

By about the age of 5, children achieve gender constancy (Golombok & Fivush, 1994). They understand that a person's gender remains stable both across situations (for example, when a boy plays with a doll) and across time (for example, when a girl grows into an adult). In general, children who have gender constancy are more likely to show gender-stereotyped preferences and behaviors (Ruble & Martin, 1998).

Children's Stereotypes About Personality

Demonstration 3.2 shows how one team of researchers assessed children's stereotypes about personality characteristics (J. Williams et al., 1975; J. Williams & Best, 1990). Using questions like those shown, the researchers found that even 5-year-olds were well aware of gender stereotypes. For example, 78% of the 5-year-olds in the study responded to the question about aggression (Item 1 from Demonstration 3.2) by pointing to the male. Males were seen as being strong, aggressive, dominant, and cruel. In contrast, these 5-year-olds saw females as being emotional, gentle, weak, and affectionate.

Gloria Cowan and Charles Hoffman (1986) tested even younger children (from 2½ to 4 years of age). These children were shown two pictures of infants who actually looked gender neutral. The researchers said that the baby on the left was a boy named Tommy and the baby on the right was a girl named Susie. The children were than asked a series of eight questions such as: "One of these babies is strong, and one is weak; point to the baby which is strong." The results showed that the children chose the gender-stereotyped response 64% of the time. That is, they tended to say that the baby boy was big, mad, strong, and hard. In contrast, they thought that the baby girl was small, scared, weak, and soft. The results were statistically significant, suggesting that even preschoolers have stereotypes about gender.

Children also associate men and women with different metaphorical properties. For example, 4- and 5-year-olds assign the terms *bears, fire,* and *something rough* to males. In contrast, they assign *butterflies, birds,* and *flowers* to females (Fagot et al., 1997; Leinbach et al., 1997). They may have noticed that men tend to light barbecue fires, and that women tend to wear flowered fabrics. But how many regularly see men together with bears, or women next to butterflies? These answers are more likely to reveal children's gender schemas: Men are

DEMONSTRATION 3.2

Children's Beliefs About Men and Women

Enlist, with a parent's permission, the help of a child who is between the ages of 4 and 8 years. Explain that you would like to ask a few questions about women and men as part of your coursework. Show the child the two pictures below. Say that you are going to read a little story, and you want the child to point to the person that it is about. Then read the child the list below.

1. One of these people likes to boss others around. This person yells a lot and tells people what they should do. Which person likes to be the boss? [Continue in the same fashion with the remaining questions.]

2. One of these people is emotional. This person cries when something good happens as well as when everything goes wrong. Which is the emotional person?

3. One of these people is appreciative. This person is always very thankful when you do something nice. Which person always says "Thank you"?

4. One of these people is very loud. This person always makes a lot of noise and talks in a great, big voice. Which person talks loudly?

5. One of these people is meek and mild. This person doesn't make a big fuss and is shy around new people. Which person is the shy person?

6. One of these people is very confident. This person always seems to know what to do. Which person is self-confident?

(Adapted from J. Williams et al., 1975, pp. 636–637; J. Williams & Best, 1990, p. 154.)

strong and dangerous; women are gentle and delicate. In short, young children seem to have elaborate and well-developed gender schemas, even before they are old enough to attend school.

Children's Stereotypes About Activities and Occupations

Children have clear ideas about the activities that are performed by females and males (e.g., Bauer, 1993; G. Levy & Fivush, 1993). For instance, children associate women with objects such as brooms and baby bottles (Serbin & Sprafkin, 1986). In addition, children remember activities better when they are consistent with their own gender. Girls remember stereotypically feminine activities better than boys do, and boys remember stereotypically masculine activities better than girls do (Signorella et al., 1997). As S. Bem (1985, 1993) proposed, children categorize objects and activities according to their gender schemas. And as Kohlberg (1966) proposed, children show favoritism for items that match their own gender.

These gender schemas extend to occupations. In one study of 2- and 3-year-olds, 78% selected a male for the job of a construction worker, and only 23% selected a male for the job of a teacher (Gettys & Cann, 1981). Stroeher (1994) found similar results for kindergartners. Some of the girls had said that only boys could be firefighters and astronauts. When asked to justify their responses, the girls said, "Boys are braver and stronger."

We'll see throughout this chapter that gender roles are somewhat more lenient for females than for males. For example, in a study conducted by Labour Canada (1986), children could imagine women entering traditionally masculine professions such as dentistry and medicine. In contrast, they had trouble imagining men becoming secretaries or nurses. Some of their specific answers revealed their rigid thinking. When asked why forest rangers had to be men, one child responded that a ranger might have to run away from a nearby fire—and women can't run very fast in their high-heeled shoes!

Sadly, children also show strong stereotypes when thinking about their own future occupations. Etaugh and Liss (1992) asked children in kindergarten through eighth grade to describe their occupational aspirations. Figure 3.5 shows the results when their occupational choices were categorized as traditionally feminine or traditionally masculine. Notice two interesting results in this figure. First, not one of the boys in the study even mentioned a feminine career! Second, the younger girls tended to prefer feminine careers, but the older girls listed feminine and masculine careers equally often. (About 10% of the children listed gender-neutral careers.)

Factors Related to Children's Stereotypes

A variety of factors influence the strength of children's stereotypes. We have just seen that boys and girls differ in their tendency to choose gender-stereotyped

FIGURE 3.5	Percentage of girls and boys selecting feminine and masculine occupations, as a function of children's grade in school. (Based on Etaugh & Liss, 1992)

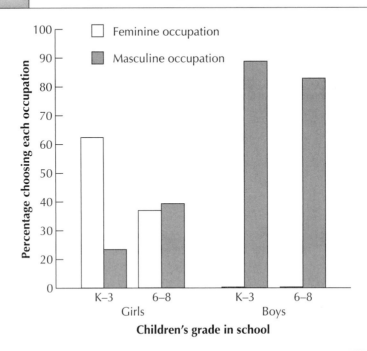

careers. Adults probably send stronger messages to boys than to girls. They may think that 5-year-old Susie is charming when she says she wants to be a surgeon, but they may frown if 5-year-old Bobby announces that he wants to be a nurse. Boys also have much more accurate knowledge of the details related to a masculine activity (e.g., building a birdhouse) than about those related to a feminine activity (e.g., doing laundry). In contrast, girls tend to know an equal amount about each kind of gender-typed activity (Boston & Levy, 1991). Their knowledge is less restricted to "gender-appropriate" topics.

Researchers have examined social class and ethnic differences in children's stereotypes. In general, middle-class children are somewhat more flexible than lower-class children in their ideas about gender (P. A. Katz, 1987; Romer & Cherry, 1980). Ethnic differences in children's stereotyping are often inconsistent (e.g., P. A. Katz, 1987). In some studies, White children tend to give more stereotyped responses than Black children. For example, White children are likely to say that women are more emotionally expressive than men, whereas Black children believe that men and women are equally expressive (Romer &

Cherry, 1980). However, Hispanic children and European American children do not seem to differ substantially in their degree of stereotyping (Bardwell et al., 1986).

Cross-cultural research shows that children in different cultures tend to have similar views of the personality characteristics associated with males and females (Best & Williams, 1993; J. Williams & Best, 1990). However, some cultures showed stronger stereotypes than others. In general, children's stereotypes tended to be fairly strong in Canada, New Zealand, and Pakistan, and intermediate in the United States, Peru, and Japan. Stereotypes were relatively weak in France, Spain, and Thailand. (I cannot discover any pattern in these results; can you?) Another cross-cultural finding is that children have consistently stronger stereotypes about males than about females. Once again, masculine stereotypes are relatively rigid.

Are children's gender ideas influenced by their family's views? You probably won't be surprised to learn that, of the children surveyed, those raised in traditional families had stronger gender stereotypes than those raised in nontraditional, egalitarian families (Fagot & Leinbach, 1995). However, girls enrolled in all-female schools were just as stereotyped as girls enrolled in coeducational schools (Signorella et al., 1996).

Age has an important effect on the nature of children's stereotypes, as shown in an analysis of the research (Signorella et al., 1993). Some studies assess children's *knowledge* about culturally accepted gender stereotypes. The older children clearly know more than the younger children. After all, the older children have had more opportunities to learn their culture's traditional notions about gender. However, other studies have assessed the *flexibility* of children's stereotypes. A typical question might be: "Who can bake a cake? Can a woman do it, can a man do it, or can they both do it?" Older children were generally more flexible than younger children; that is, they were more likely to reply, "Both can do it." Thus, older children know more about gender stereotypes, but they are also aware that people do not need to be bound by them (Fagot & Rodgers, 1998).

 SECTION SUMMARY *Children's Knowledge About Gender*

1. **Even 6-month-olds show some ability to distinguish males and females.**

2. **By about the age of 5 years, children achieve gender constancy.**

3. **Even preschoolers have strong stereotypes about personality characteristics, women's and men's activities, and occupations.**

4. **The strength of children's stereotypes is influenced by factors such as their gender, social class, ethnicity, culture, and age.**

FACTORS THAT SHAPE GENDER TYPING

We have seen that, beginning at an early age, children acquire clear-cut ideas about males and females. We have also mentioned that the family, the school, and the media provide models of gender-typed behavior and may also reward gender-typed behavior. We need to look at these influential factors in more detail. Let's begin with the family, and then move on to peers, the school, and the media.

The Family

We know most about parents' role in gender typing, so parents will be our primary focus in this section. However, remember how important siblings were when you and your friends were growing up. An older brother might tease little Carlos about choosing an Anastasia lunchbox to bring to kindergarten. An older sister may complain about having to walk to school with her younger sister, who wears "dirty" clothes or styles more suitable for boys. In most families, siblings have numerous opportunities to convey information about gender roles. Unfortunately, researchers seldom examine how siblings may influence gender typing (Ruble & Martin, 1998).

We saw, in an earlier discussion, that parents react somewhat differently to male and female infants. Those reactions tend to be stereotyped because they do not yet know their infants' unique characteristics (Jacklin & Maccoby, 1983). By the time children become toddlers, however, the parents know much more about each child's unique personality (Lott & Maluso, 1993). Therefore, parents often react to toddlers on the basis of personality characteristics, rather than on the basis of gender.

In this section, we'll see that parents sometimes encourage gender-typed activities, conversational patterns, and household chores. They also treat sons and daughters somewhat differently with respect to two characteristics: (1) aggression and (2) independence. However, parents don't make as strong a distinction between boys and girls as you might expect (Fagot, 1995; Lytton & Romney, 1991; Ruble & Martin, 1998). In this section, we'll also consider the factors related to parents' gender-typing tendencies.

Gender-Typed Activities.   Parents often encourage their children to develop gender-typed interests by providing different kinds of toys for daughters than for sons (Fisher-Thompson, 1990, 1993; Grusec & Lytton, 1988). However, one study showed that when parents rated toys without the child present, they had gender-typed opinions about the toys. In contrast, when a child was present and actively engaged in playing with the toys, parents showed less stereotypical behavior (Idle et al., 1993). In other words, if parents notice that 3-year-old Tanya likes playing with the Fisher-Price gas station, they won't interfere by handing her a doll. Parents and adults may have gender stereotypes, but they are also sensitive to each child's individual preferences (Fisher-Thompson et al., 1995).

In addition, parents encourage gender-typed activities by the way they interact with their children. For instance, parents are more likely to play ball and wrestle with their sons than with their daughters (Leaper, Leve, et al., 1995; MacDonald & Parke, 1986).

Another kind of gender-typed activity focuses on conversations. Parents are more likely to talk with their daughters than with their sons about three topics: (1) earlier events, (2) other people, and (3) emotions (S. Adams et al., 1995; Fivush, 1998; Flannagan et al., 1995).

Perhaps the most interesting aspect of parent–child conversations is that parents typically discuss different emotions with daughters than with sons. The section on infancy mentioned that adults tended to judge a crying baby boy as "angry," whereas a crying baby girl was "afraid." Related research examined mothers' conversations with children between the ages of 2½ and 3 years. During a session that lasted about half an hour, 21% of mothers discussed anger with their sons, whereas 0% of mothers discussed anger with their daughters. Instead, they talked with their daughters about fear and sadness (Fivush, 1989).

Additional studies confirm that parents are much more likely to discuss sadness with their daughters than with their sons (S. Adams et al., 1995; Kuebli & Fivush, 1992). In Chapter 12, we'll see that when women are sad, they may dwell on their sad emotions. In contrast, when men are sad, they often try to *do* something, to avoid thinking about sadness (Nolen-Hoeksema, 1990). These gender differences may be encouraged by early family interactions.

We've seen that parents often encourage gender typing through the toys they provide and the topics they discuss. As you might expect, girls are more likely to be assigned domestic chores such as washing the dishes or dusting the furniture, whereas boys are typically assigned outdoor work such as mowing the lawn or taking out the garbage (Antill et al., 1996).

Perhaps an even stronger force than encouragement of gender-typed activity is parents' *discouragement* of activities they think are inappropriate. Sons—rather than daughters—are particularly likely to be the targets of active protest about the wrong kind of activities (C. Martin, 1990). That is, parents are much more negative about boys' being "sissies" than about girls' being "tomboys."

Why are parents more worried about a boy who puts on lipstick and wears high heels than about a girl who outlines a mustache above her lip and wears cowboy boots? To some extent, "gender-inappropriate" behavior in boys may be more anxiety-arousing because we tolerate a wider range of dress in adult women than in adult men. Adult women can wear cowboy boots, and jeans are often the norm rather than the exception. A well-known designer has produced a line of underwear for women that mimics men's T-shirts and jockey shorts. However, no prestigious designer has yet offered pink lace bikinis for men! A possible explanation is that adults tend to interpret feminine behavior in a boy as a sign of gay tendencies, but they are less likely to view masculine behavior in a girl as a sign of lesbian tendencies (C. Martin, 1990).

Theme 2 of this book, that males are more valued than females, is another reason why people are more concerned about "gender-inappropriate" behavior in boys. A boy who doesn't act masculine is failing to show the traits and behaviors that our culture values most highly (M. Crawford, 1984).

Just as male children are the most likely recipients of messages about "gender-appropriate" behavior, male adults are more likely than females to offer these messages (Leve & Fagot, 1997; Lytton & Romney, 1991). For example, fathers are more likely than mothers to encourage their daughters to play with stereotypically feminine items such as tea sets and baby dolls, and to encourage their sons to play with stereotypically masculine items such as footballs and boxing gloves (Jacklin et al., 1984).

In summary, parents do seem to promote some gender-typed activities in their children. They often encourage gender-typed play activities and conversational patterns, and they may assign gender-typed household chores. However, many parents conscientiously try to treat their sons and daughters similarly. Among any group of friends, a wide variety of parenting styles is often represented.

Aggression.   In popularized accounts about gender-role development, you may read that parents discourage aggression in their daughters but tolerate or even encourage aggression in their sons. This description may be intuitively appealing. However, the research findings are inconsistent; some studies show that parents are more likely to discourage aggression in their daughters than in their sons, but other studies show no differences (Lytton & Romney, 1991; Ruble & Martin, 1998). For example, among children who had been attacked by other children, boys and girls were equally discouraged from hitting back.

Try Demonstration 3.3. Do your own observations show that parents respond differently to aggressive daughters than to aggressive sons?

Chapter 6 discusses how adult males are sometimes more aggressive than adult females. Most of this difference cannot be explained by parents' rewarding and punishing boys differently from girls. However, parents can provide information

---

DEMONSTRATION 3.3

Tolerance for Aggression in Sons and Daughters

For this demonstration, you will need to find a location where parents are likely to bring their children. Some possibilities include public playgrounds, toy stores, and fast-food restaurants. Place yourself so that you can simultaneously observe several families with more than one child. Be alert for examples of verbal or physical aggression from the children, directed toward either a parent or a sibling. What is the parent's response to this aggression? Does the parent respond differently to aggression as a function of a child's gender?

about aggression and power in other ways. As the second component of social learning theory emphasizes, boys can learn to be aggressive by imitating their aggressive fathers. Furthermore, the structure of the family provides information for children's thoughts about proper "masculine" and "feminine" behavior, as emphasized by cognitive developmental theory. Children notice in their own families that fathers make decisions and announce which television show will be watched. Fathers may also use physical intimidation to assert power. By watching their parents, children learn that aggression and power are "boy things" rather than "girl things."

Independence.   According to popularized accounts of gender-role development, parents encourage their sons to explore and do things on their own, but they overprotect and overhelp their daughters. Once again, the evidence is not clear-cut.

To some extent, independence is encouraged more in boys than in girls. In research on toddlers, boys were more often left alone in a room (Fagot, 1978). In contrast, girls were more likely to be supervised and "chaperoned" (Grusec & Lytton, 1988). However, parents give the same kinds of verbal directions to their sons and their daughters (Bellinger & Gleason, 1982). Considering a wide variety of measures of independence, parents treat their sons and daughters fairly similarly (Lytton & Romney, 1991).

Factors That Influence Parents' Gender Typing.   We have seen that parents may encourage gender-typed activities. However, they do not consistently encourage aggression and independence in their sons more than in their daughters (Jacklin & Baker, 1993; Lytton & Romney, 1991; Ruble & Martin, 1998). Some parents treat their sons and daughters very differently, and others actively try to avoid gender bias. Tenenbaum and Leaper (1997) studied Mexican American fathers interacting with their preschool children in a feminine setting: playing with toy foods. Fathers who had traditional attitudes toward gender did not talk much with their children in this setting. In contrast, nontraditional fathers asked their children questions such as "What is on this sandwich?" and "Should we cook this egg?" By asking these questions, the fathers sent a message to their children that men can feel comfortable with traditionally feminine tasks.

Several studies have focused specifically on ethnic differences in parents' treatment of sons and daughters. As might be expected when the variability is so great within each ethnic group, the results are often contradictory. For example, L. Hoffman and Kloska (1995) found that Black parents had more stereotyped views of child rearing than did European American parents. In contrast, P. A. Katz (1987) and Price-Bonham and Skeen (1982) found that Black parents were *less* stereotyped. The difference in results may depend on the region of the country or the social class and education level of those sampled.

Most theorists argue that Puerto Rican girls are more likely than European American girls to receive gender-typed messages from their families. Describing the typical Puerto Rican girl, Vázquez-Nuttall and Romero-García (1989) wrote:

The sexes are strictly separated, with the female's role more narrowly defined than the male's. Since early childhood she is restricted in dress, conduct, freedom, language usage, and social association. (p. 65)

Even nontraditional families may have trouble overcoming the customary ideas about gender. For example, Weisner studied European American families in unconventional living arrangements such as communes (Weisner, 1992; Weisner et al., 1994). Even in this environment, parents tended to divide household tasks in a traditional manner. Parents were also fairly conventional with respect to gender-typed activities. For example, they were much more likely to encourage doll play in their daughters, rather than in their sons.

In summary, we know that ethnicity seems to have a complex influence on parents' treatment of daughters and sons. We also know that even unconventional families may send traditional gender messages. However, we need to reemphasize the general conclusions about parents. Parents encourage gender typing by their reactions to "masculine" and "feminine" activities. However, they often treat their daughters and sons similarly with respect to aggression and most kinds of independence. Taking everything into account, parents are not as consistent about encouraging gender typing as articles in the popular media would suggest. We need to consider additional forces that are responsible for gender typing.

Peers

Once children begin school, a major source of information about gender is their peer group—other children approximately their own age. A child may have been raised by relatively nonsexist parents. However, on the first day of class, if Jennifer wears her hiking boots and Johnny brings in a new baby doll, their peers may respond negatively.

Peers encourage gender typing in four major ways: (1) they downgrade children who act in a nonstereotypical fashion; (2) they encourage gender segregation; (3) they are prejudiced against children of the other gender; and (4) they treat boys and girls differently. Let's examine these four areas.

Rejection of Nontraditional Behavior.   In general, children tend to reject peers who act in a fashion that is more characteristic of the other gender. For example, children tend to think that girls should not play the aggressive, "fighting" electronic games (Funk & Buchman, 1996). Also, girls who dominate discussions about fund-raising ideas are downgraded as being too bossy (Zucker et al., 1995). Women who had been "tomboys" as children often report that their peers were influential in convincing them to act more feminine (Morgan, 1998).

Nontraditional boys also receive rejecting messages. Elementary school children are much more positive toward a boy who watches Superman cartoons and plays with racing cars than toward a boy who watches Wonder Woman cartoons and plays with Barbie dolls (Zucker et al., 1995).

Gender Segregation.   The tendency to associate with other children of the same gender is called **gender segregation.** Children begin to prefer playing with same-gender children by age 3 or 4 years, and this tendency increases. One study showed that, by age 5 years, 86% of children chose a same-gender playmate (P. Katz & Kofkin, 1997). On the school playground or in the cafeteria, the peer pressure can be so strong that a girl who plays with a particular boy in her neighborhood may refuse to say hello to him once they reach school (Thorne, 1993). The preference for friends of the same gender continues to increase until about the age of 11 (Maccoby, 1998). As romantic relationships develop in early adolescence, boys and girls then increase their time together.

Gender Prejudice.   A third way in which peers encourage gender typing is with prejudice against members of the other gender. As we discussed in connection with gender schema theory, children strongly prefer their own gender (Etaugh et al., 1984; Olsen & Willemsen, 1978). For example, Powlishta (1995) showed children a series of brief videotaped interactions between children and adults. Three of the segments featured girls, and three featured boys. The children who viewed the films were 9 and 10 years old; their ethnic diversity was fairly close to the percentages in the U.S. population. After viewing each video, the children rated the child in the video, using a 10-point scale of liking that ranged from "not at all" to "very, very much."

As you can see in Figure 3.6, girls liked the girl targets in the videos better than the boy targets, and boys preferred the boy targets to the girl targets. This kind of prejudice arises from children's clear-cut gender schemas, and it reinforces children's beliefs that females and males are very different kinds of people.

Differential Treatment.   A fourth way in which peers promote gender typing is with different responses to boys and girls. One of the most interesting observations is that children respond to girls on the basis of their physical attractiveness, but attractiveness is largely irrelevant for boys. Smith (1985) observed middle-class European American preschoolers for 5-minute sessions in a classroom setting, on 5 separate days. He recorded how other children treated each child. Were the other children prosocial—helping, patting, and praising the child? Or were the other children physically aggressive—hitting, pushing, or kicking the target child? How was each measure related to the child's attractiveness?

The results showed that attractiveness (as previously rated by college students) was correlated with the way the girls were treated, but not the boys. Specifically, attractive girls were much more likely to receive prosocial treatment. Figure 3.7 shows a strong positive correlation. In other words, the "cutest" girls were most likely to be helped, patted, and praised; the most attractive girl (with a rating of 6.8), received four prosocial actions. In contrast, the less attractive girls received few of these positive responses, and the girl with a rating of 2.5 received no prosocial actions. However, Smith found no relationship

| FIGURE 3.6 | Ratings supplied by female and male children for the girls and boys in videos. The data show prejudice against the other gender. (Based on Powlishta, 1995) |

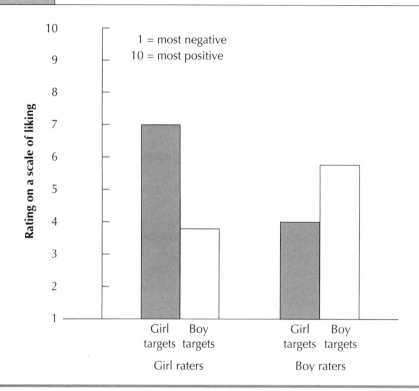

between attractiveness and prosocial treatment of boys; attractive and less attractive boys received a similar number of prosocial actions.

Smith (1985) also found a comparable pattern for physical aggression scores. That is, the less attractive girls were more likely to be hit, pushed, and kicked, whereas the cutest girls rarely received this treatment. However, attractiveness was not related to the aggression directed toward boys. Very young girls learn a lesson from their peers that will be repeated throughout their lives. Physical attractiveness is important for females, and pretty girls and women will receive better treatment.

The influence of peers on gender typing has not been examined as thoroughly as the influence of parents (Jacklin & Baker, 1993). However, we have seen that, in several ways, children can influence others who are their own age. Specifically, they can reject nontraditional behavior in their peers. They can encourage gender segregation, so that boys and girls have minimal contact with

FIGURE 3.7 | Relationship between attractiveness and prosocial treatment of girls (*r* = + .73). (Smith, 1985)

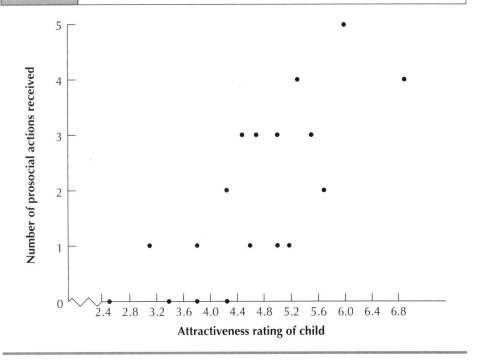

one another. They can also express prejudice against children of the other gender. Finally, they can respond differently to girls and boys, for example, by emphasizing attractiveness for girls but not for boys.

School

The typical elementary school child spends more waking hours in school with teachers than at home with family members. As a result, teachers and schools have rich opportunities to influence gender typing. Let's investigate how the structure of a school can inform children that males have more prestige and power than females, and how teachers' behavior can influence that message. Then we'll look briefly at the international literacy rates for girls and boys. Finally, we will explore how schools can encourage change.

School Structure. The structure of the typical school provides children with a sadly representative view of the status of employed women. Think about the number of women and men who taught in your own school system. Were any of your elementary school teachers males? Were your high school teachers equally likely to be males or females? Did the men teach math and science and the women teach English and foreign languages? What gender were the principals and superintendents? If your school was typical, most of your elementary school teachers were female; in contrast, only about half of your high school teachers would have been female. The percentage of females drops even lower when we consider the highest-ranking individuals in school systems, the principals and the superintendents. Children see that women dominate in the least prestigious positions, in the classrooms of the youngest students. The "big kids" are important enough to be associated with a reasonable number of male teachers. The real power in a school lies with the administrators, almost all of whom are male. Schoolchildren therefore have abundant opportunity to learn that male activities are more valued than female activities, an important component of Theme 2.

Teachers' Behavior.   Beginning in the early 1990s, the media finally discovered what many of us had been reporting for years: Girls do not receive equal treatment in the classroom (AAUW Educational Foundation, 1992; Sadker & Sadker, 1994). The publicized reports highlighted the invisibility of girls in the educational system, a point that is clearly consistent with Theme 3 of this textbook. According to the reports, classroom activities are often selected to appeal to boys, teachers typically pay more attention to boys in the classroom, and females are absent or misrepresented in the textbooks and other teaching materials.

Boys generally receive more positive attention in the classroom. They are more likely to receive positive feedback. They are also more likely to be recognized for their creativity, called on in class, and included in class discussions (AAUW Educational Foundation, 1992; S. M. Bailey et al., 1993; Sadker & Sadker, 1994). Sadker and Sadker cite a typical example: The teacher asks, "What is an adjective? Maria?" Maria answers appropriately, "A word that describes something." Simultaneously, Tim calls out, "Adjectives describe nouns." The teacher responds, "Good, Tim" (p. 74). Notice how the teacher reinforces Tim, ignoring Maria's correct answer. A moment later, the teacher asks the children to identify the adjective in a sentence. When Donna appropriately answers "Beautiful," the teacher doesn't even comment that she is correct.

Boys also receive more negative attention than girls. Researchers have reported that boys are scolded much more frequently than girls—for the same misbehavior. Also, the scolding directed toward boys is stronger and louder (Eccles, 1989; Sadker & Sadker, 1994).

In addition, teachers are more likely to offer "remediation statements" to boys. For example, a boy writing a poem might be asked, "Is that image as strong as what you're trying to convey?" In contrast, the only feedback a girl might receive would be a bland and imprecise "OK" (Sadker & Sadker, 1994). The girl would not be told whether her poem is excellent or just barely adequate, or how she can make it more powerful.

We have seen that teachers tend to ignore girls and pay attention to boys, whether the boys are behaving properly or improperly. The end result is that, compared to boys, girls are relatively invisible in the classroom. In another study, teachers were asked to name the students whom they often thought about after school hours. The teachers listed 61% more boys than girls (BenTsvi-Mayer et al., 1989). This pattern of invisible girls illustrates an important theme of this textbook, and the invisibility continues throughout adulthood and old age.

Besides ignoring them, teachers may actively discourage the girls in their classrooms. For example, Sadker and Sadker (1994) observed second-graders in an expensive private school in Washington, DC. Two young girls were excitedly investigating the contents of a large box, pulling out wooden blocks, colored balls, and counting sticks. A teacher suddenly loomed in front of them and shouted impatiently, "Ann! Julia! Get your cotton-pickin' hands out of the math box. Move over so the boys can get in there and do their work" (p. 2).

Teachers may also encourage girls to become dependent. Teachers tend to like dependent, compliant girls, and they rate these girls as being more competent than girls who are eager to express their own opinions (Gold et al., 1987). This emphasis on girls' "niceness" was illustrated in the class awards one teacher distributed at kindergarten graduation. The "Boys' Awards" were listed as "Very Best Thinker, Most Eager Learner, Most Imaginative, Mr. Personality, and Hardest Worker." The "Girls' Awards" were "All-Around Sweetheart, Sweetest Personality, Cutest Personality, Best Manners, and Best Helper" (Rhode, 1997, p. 55).

Sadker and Sadker (1994) also observed that female students of color are especially likely to be ignored in the classroom. L. Grant (1994) reported that Black girls often assume adultlike social roles in elementary classrooms, distributing material to other students and keeping them in line when the teacher must leave the classroom. However, teachers don't seem to encourage Black girls to take on *academic* responsibilities, such as tutoring or showing a new student how to prepare an assignment.

In short, several factors in the school system operate so that girls are often shortchanged. They may be ignored, they may not be given appropriate feedback, and they may be encouraged to be dependent or socially skilled rather than academically competent.

Gender and Education on the International Level.   At the international level, we often encounter a more extreme problem about education for young girls. In many countries, girls are much less likely than boys to be enrolled in school. For example, in many parts of India, boys are encouraged to go to school, but girls are kept at home to care for younger siblings. As a result, the literacy rate in India is 64% for males and 39% for females (Kulkarni, 1997).

A United Nations report on countries in the developing world showed that about 20% fewer females than males were enrolled in the primary grades (Aidoo, 1991). In the secondary grades, about 30% fewer females than males were enrolled (Aidoo, 1991). Where food and other essentials are limited, the education of females is considered a luxury.

Unfortunately, women who have not been educated will experience a lifelong handicap. They will not be able to read newspapers, write checks, sign contracts, or perform numerous other activities that can help make them independent and economically self-sufficient. The gap between the developing countries and the wealthy countries continues to widen. In addition, the governments of wealthy countries rarely subsidize literacy programs or other socially responsible projects that could make a real difference in the lives of women in the developing countries.

Encouraging Change.   So far, our exploration of gender and education has emphasized that school structure and teachers' behavior are likely to favor boys over girls. We also noted that educational systems in developing countries discourage girls from pursuing education—a policy that is not likely to change in the near future.

Fortunately, however, the North American educational scene has begun to change in recent years. Many colleges and universities that train teachers now require courses that focus on gender and ethnic diversity. Media coverage of the "silenced female" problem has also alerted teachers about the need for more equal attention to girls and boys (Streitmatter, 1994).

Some programs have been designed to change children's stereotypes (B. Bailey & Nihlen, 1990; Gash & Morgan, 1993). Tozzo and Golub (1990) addressed children's stereotypes about males' and females' occupations. In their program, a third-grade classroom was visited by four individuals in nontraditional occupations—a female police officer, a female letter carrier, a male nursery school teacher, and a male registered nurse. Children in this program were much less stereotyped after the class visits. In contrast, children in a control-group classroom of third graders showed no change in their beliefs.

Teachers can also help children become less stereotyped by de-emphasizing gender schemas. For example, Bigler (1995) assigned 6- to 9-year-old children either to control classroom or to gender-emphasis classrooms during a four-week summer school program. Teachers in the control classrooms were instructed not to emphasize gender in their remarks or in their treatment of the children. Meanwhile, teachers in the gender-emphasis classrooms used gender-segregated seating, with girls' and boys' desks on opposite sides of the classroom. The teachers also displayed girls' and boys' artwork on different bulletin boards, and they frequently instructed boys and girls to perform different activities.

The most interesting results concerned those children who initially had no strong gender schemas. The children from the classrooms that did not emphasize gender were 50% less likely than the children in the gender-emphasis classrooms to make stereotyped judgments about which jobs males and females could hold.

We cannot expect that a life history of learning gender stereotypes can be erased with brief interventions. The approach must be more comprehensive, so that teachers from kindergarten onward are encouraged to pay equal attention to girls and to reduce inappropriate stereotypes about gender. One 4-year-old girl revealed her awareness about gender equity when she explained why her class had changed the words to a song about "Mr. Sun." As she pointed out, "You've just gotta sing about Mrs. Sun to make it fair" (Bailey, 1993, p. 100).

The Media

In recent years, the media have improved somewhat with respect to gender stereotypes, although children's books and television programs are a long way from gender equity. Keep in mind, too, that children are still exposed to earlier, stereotyped material. Libraries and schools keep circulating the older books, and children still watch television reruns from the 1950s and 1960s. As a result, children have ample opportunity to learn gender typing from the media.

Books.   Early studies on children's books showed that more than 70% of the main characters were male. In addition, both genders were presented in a stereotyped fashion, and women were invisible in math, science, and history textbooks (e.g., Bordelon, 1985; Marten & Matlin, 1976; Women on Words & Images, 1972).

Analyses of children's books from the 1990s are slightly more optimistic. One study of picture books showed that "only" 64% of the main characters were male (Kortenhaus & Demarest, 1993). Another analysis focused on books that received the Coretta Scott King awards, which honor Black illustrators of picture books. Again, "only" 64% of the illustrations showed males (R. Clark et al., 1993).

What are the males and females *doing* in these children's books? According to one analysis, boys help others, solve problems, and play actively (Kortenhaus & Demarest, 1993). In contrast, girls need help and play quietly indoors. In all, males were almost three times as likely as females to be accomplishing goals, and females were almost five times as likely as males to be shown in passive or dependent activities. Males are also portrayed in a wider variety of occupations, compared to females (Crabb & Bielawski, 1994; McDonald, 1989).

As you've been learning about the general lack of female role models in children's literature, perhaps you felt uneasy. Should we really worry about what children read? As it turns out, these biases do have consequences for children (Ashton, 1983; McArthur & Eisen, 1976). Ochman (1996) designed a study in which children watched videotapes of an actor reading a series of stories. Each story required the main character to solve a problem, which enhanced this character's self-esteem. The same stories were presented to classrooms of 7- to 10-year-olds, except that the main character was a boy for half of the classes and a girl for the remaining classes.

A standard measure of self-esteem was administered at the beginning of the study. Then the stories were read to the children over a period of about six weeks, and the self-esteem measure was administered a second time. The researchers then calculated the change in the children's self-esteem. As Figure 3.8

| FIGURE 3.8 | Improvement in girls' and boys' self-esteem (compared to baseline) after hearing stories about a female character or a male character. (Based on Ochman, 1996) |

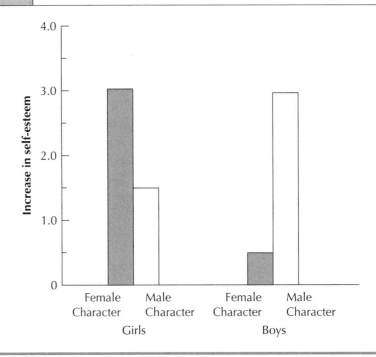

shows, girls had a greater increase in self-esteem if they had heard the stories about an achieving girl rather than an achieving boy. The boys showed a comparable pattern; their self-esteem increased after they heard stories about an achieving boy rather than an achieving girl.

You can appreciate the implications of this research. If children hear stories about strong, competent boys—but not girls—the boys are likely to experience a boost in self-esteem. Meanwhile, the girls' self-esteem will remain stable.

Conscientious parents and teachers can review the books that children will see and can make sure that competent females are well represented (S. Bem, 1995b). They can also be alert for new resources. For example, a new feminist magazine called *New Moon* is edited by girls and young women. (See Figure 3.9; the address is P.O. Box 3620, Duluth, MN 55803-3620.)

Television.   Preschoolers average more than 27 hours of television per week (Centerwall, 1992). By the time teenagers graduate from high school, they have spent an average of 15,000 to 18,000 hours in front of the TV set, in contrast to

FIGURE 3.9	*New Moon,* a magazine for girls and young women, discusses issues such as gender, racism, and ecology.

Reprinted, with permission, from New Moon®: The Magazine for Girls and Their Dreams; Copyright New Moon Publishing, Duluth, MN 55803-3587. Subscriptions $29.00/6 issues. 1-800-381-4743.

12,000 hours in classroom instruction (B. Gunter & McAleer, 1997; Strasburger, 1991). Chapter 2 examined stereotyping in programs intended for adult audiences. Now let's consider the television programs and advertisements aimed at children. As we'll see, 15,000 hours of television can provide a good "education" in gender stereotypes.

Males are shown much more frequently than females in children's television programs (Furnham et al., 1997). A sample of network and cable cartoon programs contained 106 major and 127 minor female characters, and 326 major and 587 minor male characters (T. Thompson & Zerbinos, 1995). Many cartoon programs have no female characters (Golombok & Fivush, 1994). I recall seeing an adventure cartoon in which the only female was the young male hero's mother. She fainted within the first five minutes and never appeared again. *Sesame Street* has more than twice as many male characters as females (Hallingby, 1993).

Males and females also perform different activities on television. For example, males are more likely to be shown in the workplace, whereas females are shown as caregivers (T. Thompson & Zerbinos, 1995). Males are more likely to show leadership, ingenuity, and aggression. Females are more likely to be affectionate and helpless (T. Thompson & Zerbinos, 1995).

Another problem is that boys and girls are shown playing with different toys in the advertisements. In a sample of 135 toy ads from Saturday morning children's programs, the 15 depicting action figures showed only boys. Of the ads for dolls, 52 showed only girls, 10 showed both boys and girls, and 1 showed only a boy (Rajecki et al., 1993). Perhaps we should be happy that a total of 11 ads showed a boy together with a doll. However, even children reared by nonsexist parents will quickly understand from TV commercials that girls and boys are supposed to enjoy playing with different kinds of toys.

We have seen that females are underrepresented. We've also seen that females and males are shown in quite different roles. Again, skeptics might ask whether children even notice the gender patterns on television. Thompson and Zerbinos (1997) asked 4- to 9-year-olds about the number of boy and girl characters who appeared on the television shows they watched. The researchers found that 78% of the children reported more boy characters, 12% reported more girls, and 10% reported the same number of boys and girls. In general, then, children do notice that males are more common in the cartoons.

But can children learn gender-role stereotypes by watching television? Let's consider a careful study conducted by Signorielli and Lears (1992). They tested 530 fourth- and fifth-graders, using a sample of ethnic groups that resembled the distribution in the United States. They found a significant correlation between the amount of time the children watched television and their scores on a test of gender stereotyping. (This particular test focused on whether certain chores—such as washing the dishes or mowing the lawn—should be done by boys only, girls only, or either girls or boys.)

If you are considering some of the research issues we raised in Chapter 1, you might wonder whether those results might be explained by confounding variables. For example, maybe well-educated parents limit their children's television viewing, and they also discourage gender stereotypes. However, Signorielli and Lears (1992) conducted a second analysis, statistically controlling for potential confounding variables such as gender, ethnic group, reading level, and parents' education. The correlation between TV viewing and gender stereotyping still remained significant, although not very strong. In general, the research tends to show a modest relationship between television viewing and gender stereotypes (e.g., Golombok & Fivush, 1994; B. Gunter & McAleer, 1997).

A cautious parent who wants to raise nonstereotyped children should probably limit television viewing. In addition, children should be encouraged to watch programs in which women are shown as competent people and men are shown in nurturant roles—especially because children who watch nontraditional programs tend to have less stereotyped gender roles (Rosenwasser et al., 1989). Parents can also select educational and entertaining videos that avoid stereotypes and feature competent females. Furthermore, parents can occasionally stop these videos at appropriate intervals to discuss gender-related issues (B. Gunter & McAleer, 1997). Television and videos have the potential to present admirable models of female and male behavior, and they *could* even make children less stereotyped. So far, unfortunately, the media have not lived up to that potential.

Factors That Shape Gender Typing

1. **Parents tend to encourage gender-typed activities (e.g., toy choice, discussion of emotions, and chore assignment); they also treat sons and daughters somewhat differently with respect to children's aggression and independence, but the differential treatment is not consistent.**

2. **Peers react negatively to nonstereotypical behavior; they encourage gender segregation; they are prejudiced against children of the other gender; and they treat boys and girls differently.**

3. **Schools encourage gender typing via the distribution of men's and women's occupations. Boys receive more attention and useful feedback in the class, compared to girls. In developing countries, literacy rates are lower for girls than for boys. Educators are now better informed about gender issues, and some programs can help children reduce stereotypes, but a comprehensive approach is necessary.**

4. **Children's books and television continue to underrepresent females and to show males and females in stereotyped activities. According to research, the media have a moderate impact on children's ideas about gender.**

CHAPTER REVIEW QUESTIONS

1. Early in prenatal development, infant boys and girls are similar. By the time they are born, they differ in their gonads, internal reproductive systems, and external genitals. Discuss how these three kinds of differences emerge during normal prenatal development.

2. According to a well-known proverb, beauty is "in the eye of the beholder." Apparently, the masculinity or femininity of an infant is also in the eye of the beholder. Discuss this concept.

3. Five-year-old Darlene is playing with a doll. Discuss how gender schema theory would explain her behavior. Be sure to mention both the cognitive developmental component of this theory as well as the two mechanisms proposed by social learning theory.

4. Suppose that you are working at a day care center, and you interact with children between the ages of 6 months and 5 years. How do you know that the 6-month-olds already have some information about gender? Describe

what the older children of different ages will know about gender and gender stereotypes.

5. As children grow older, they know more about gender stereotypes, but these stereotypes are also more flexible. Describe the research that supports this statement. What implications does this statement have for the influence of peers on gender typing?

6. Imagine that a family has twins, a boy named Jim and a girl named Sandra. Based on the information on families and gender typing, how would you predict that their parents would treat Sandra and Jim? Discuss four topics: (a) gender-typed activity, (b) discussion of emotion, (c) aggression, and (d) independence.

7. Discuss four ways in which peers encourage gender typing. How might a skillful teacher minimize gender typing? What other precautions should this teacher take, to make certain that females and males are treated fairly in the classroom?

8. Describe as completely as possible how books and television convey gender stereotypes. Also describe how these media can influence children's toy preferences and other activities.

9. A friend who has a 2-year-old child asks you: "What can I do to encourage my child *not* to be restricted by gender stereotypes?" How would you reply?

10. At several points throughout the chapter, we mentioned that gender stereotypes are more restrictive for boys than for girls, and that fathers are more likely than mothers to encourage these stereotypes. Discuss this issue, being sure to mention parents' encouragement of gender-related activities, children's ideas about occupations, and any other topics you consider to be relevant.

NEW TERMS

gender typing (82)
prenatal period (82)
infancy (82)
sex chromosomes (83)
Müllerian ducts (83)
Wolffian ducts (83)
gonads (83)
androgen (83)
estrogen (83)
androgen-insensitivity syndrome (85)
congenital adrenal hyperplasia (85)
intersexuals (86)

social constructionism (93)
psychoanalytic theory (94)
phallic stage (94)
castration complex (94)
penis envy (94)
gender schema theory (95)
schema (95)
cognitive developmental theory (95)
gender identity (95)
social learning theory (96)
modeling (97)
gender constancy (98)

RECOMMENDED READINGS

Beal, C. R. (1994). *Boys and girls: The development of gender roles.* New York: McGraw-Hill. Beal's book is an interesting examination of gender development. The topics include theories about gender-role development, and how peers, teachers, and the media influence children's ideas about gender.

Golombok, S., & Fivush, R. (1994). *Gender development.* New York: Cambridge University Press. This book offers a comprehensive survey of theories of gender typing, factors that encourage gender typing, and gender stereotypes.

Gunter, B., & McAleer, J. (1997). *Children and television* (2nd ed.). London: Routledge. Here's a good, general overview of television's effects on children. In addition to TV's impact on children's gender typing, the book also explores its effects on aggression, prosocial behavior, and schoolwork.

Maccoby, E. E. (1998). *The two sexes: Growing up apart, coming together.* Cambridge, MA: Harvard University Press. Eleanor Maccoby's book is especially strong in exploring gender segregation, children's play patterns, and the implications of these behaviors.

Ruble, D. R., & Martin, C. L. (1998). Gender development. In W. Damon (Series Ed.) & N. Eisenberg (Vol. Ed.), *Handbook of child psychology: Vol. 4: Social, emotional, and personality development* (pp. 933–1016). New York: Wiley. Diane Ruble and Carol Martin are two prominent researchers in the field of gender; this chapter traces the development of gender-related concepts and behaviors and includes a detailed exploration of gender-development theories.

Sadker, M., & Sadker, D. (1994). *Failing at fairness: How America's schools cheat girls.* New York: Charles Scribner's Sons. Intended for a general audience, this book provides many interesting anecdotes about teachers' treatment of boys and girls. Anyone concerned about gender equity in a local school should figure out a diplomatic way to present a copy of this book to the school administration!

ANSWERS TO THE
TRUE–FALSE QUESTIONS

1. True (p. 83); 2. False (p. 87); 3. True (p. 91); 4. False (p. 95); 5. True (p. 98); 6. True (p. 98); 7. True (p. 101); 8. False (p. 106); 9. True (p. 112); 10. False (p. 117).

$\mathcal{A}$DOLESCENCE

TRUE OR FALSE?

_____ 1. Researchers believe that there is no physical explanation for menstrual pain.

_____ 2. A clear-cut cluster of symptoms, often called premenstrual syndrome (PMS), consistently affects between 35% and 50% of North American adolescent females.

_____ 3. Women's performance on intellectual tasks does not vary greatly with the menstrual cycle.

_____ 4. Recent research confirms that young women's self-esteem consistently drops during adolescence, especially in relation to young men's self-esteem.

_____ 5. Adolescent females with extremely feminine characteristics tend to be higher in self-esteem than those with less feminine characteristics.

_____ 6. During the current era, schools, teachers, and peers offer strong support for young women who want to pursue careers in math and science.

_____ 7. For all major ethnic groups in the United States, women are more likely than men to attend college.

_____ 8. Adolescent males and females are interested in pursuing careers that are similar in level of prestige.

_____ 9. According to research, the majority of adolescents get along fairly well with their parents.

_____ 10. The friendships of adolescent men have been consistently shown to be just as intimate as the friendships of adolescent women.

Puberty and Menstruation
  Puberty
  Biological Aspects of the
    Menstrual Cycle
  Menstrual Pain
  The Controversial Premenstrual
    Syndrome
  The Menstrual Cycle and
    Performance
  Attitudes Toward Menstruation

**Self-Concept and Identity
During Adolescence**
  Body Image
  Ethnic Identity
  Self-Esteem

Education and Career Planning
  Young Women's School
    Experiences
  Early Experiences in Math
    and Science
  Higher Education
  Career Aspirations
  Aspirations Versus Reality

**Interpersonal Relationships
During Adolescence**
  Family Relationships During
    Adolescence
  Friendships During Adolescence
  Romantic Relationships During
    Adolescence

In human development, **adolescence** is a transition phase between childhood and adulthood. Adolescence begins at **puberty,** the age at which the young person is physically capable of sexual reproduction (McClintock & Herdt, 1996). For females, a major biological milestone of puberty is **menarche,** or the beginning of menstruation. No specific event marks the end of adolescence and the beginning of adulthood. We usually associate the beginning of adulthood with living separately from our parents, holding a job, and finding a romantic partner. However, none of these characteristics is essential for adulthood.

Adolescents find themselves caught between childhood and adulthood. They may sometimes be treated as children—a mixed blessing that eases their responsibility but limits their independence. As they face issues of sexuality and development into adults, adolescents receive mixed messages. Parents tell them not to grow up too quickly. On the other hand, their models tend to be adolescents who *have* grown up too quickly—sexy teenage television and movie stars, teenagers in advertisements, and maybe even the girl next door.

In this chapter, we will examine four important topics for adolescent females: (1) puberty and menstruation, (2) self-concepts, (3) education and career planning, and (4) interpersonal relationships. We'll mention other relevant topics—such as sexuality and eating disorders—but those will be discussed more completely in later chapters.

PUBERTY AND MENSTRUATION
Puberty

Most girls enter puberty between the ages of 8 and 16 (Golombok & Fivush, 1994; Golub, 1992). Many factors influence the age at which a young woman begins to menstruate. For instance, early menarche is more common among young women who are above-average in body weight and who have not trained intensively as athletes or dancers (Golub, 1992). Ethnicity is another important factor.

Black girls in the United States begin menarche at an average age of 12.2 years, whereas European American girls begin about three-fourths of a year later, at an average of 12.9 years (Herman-Giddens et al., 1997). Part of the explanation may be that Black girls, on average, weigh slightly more, but extensive research has not yet uncovered a satisfactory explanation for this ethnic difference.

Young women who reach menarche at the typical age—between 11 and 13 years—are significantly more positive about it than young women who reach it either earlier or later than average (Dubas et al., 1991). Emotional reactions to menarche vary widely; in part, they depend on girls' understanding of menstruation, and the reaction of family and friends. One young woman recalled the positive status that menarche conveyed:

> It was common knowledge who had started and who hadn't, and it became quite an object of envy. I remember being highly envious of girls who had begun. And the word spread like wild-fire: "She started! She did!" And then we would all look at her differently. That girl certainly gained status in our eyes, if she had started. (Lee & Sasser-Coen, 1996)

In contrast, some young women respond neutrally, as if the experience were disconnected from their own bodies: "I can remember it was in August and I woke up and I had pains, so I went to the bathroom, and *there it was*" (K. Martin, 1996, p. 24). Young women who are not informed about menstruation may react with panic. When a young Egyptian woman awoke to find blood on her thighs, she assumed that a man had crept into her bedroom and had somehow harmed her (Saadawi, 1998). In short, the varied emotional reactions to menarche provide evidence for the individual differences theme of this textbook.

In addition to menarche, young women experience changes with respect to **secondary sex characteristics,** or the parts of the body related to reproduction but not directly involved in it. For instance, breast development precedes menarche by about two years. Looking back on adolescence, many women report feeling self-conscious about breasts that they considered either too large or too small (K. Martin, 1996; P. Robinson, 1997). During puberty, young women also accumulate body fat through the hips and thighs—often a source of resentment in a culture that emphasizes slender bodies (Fredrickson & Roberts, 1997).

Biological Aspects of the Menstrual Cycle

Let's briefly examine the biological components of menstruation, as well as the sequence of events in the menstrual cycle. The average woman menstruates about 450 times during her life. Naturally, then, this information on the menstrual cycle is relevant for most women for about 40 years after menarche. However, we'll discuss it here for the sake of continuity.

Structures and Substances Responsible for Menstruation.   The hypothalamus, a structure in the brain, is crucial in menstruation because it monitors the body's level of estrogen during the monthly cycle. When estrogen levels are low, the hypothalamus signals a second brain structure, the pituitary gland. The pituitary gland produces two important hormones: follicle-stimulating hormone and luteinizing hormone.

In all, four hormones contribute to the menstrual cycle:

1. Follicle-stimulating hormone acts on the follicles (or egg holders) within the ovaries, making them produce estrogen and progesterone;

2. Luteinizing hormone is needed for the development of the follicles;

3. Estrogen, primarily produced by the ovaries, stimulates the development of the uterine lining;

4. Progesterone, also primarily produced by the ovaries, regulates the system by inhibiting overproduction of the luteinizing hormone.

Figure 4.1 shows how the estrogen and progesterone levels change during the menstrual cycle.

Several major structures in menstruation are illustrated in Figure 4.2, together with other important internal organs in the female reproductive system. The two **ovaries,** which are about the size of walnuts, contain the follicles that hold the **ova,** or eggs, and produce estrogen and progesterone. Midway through the menstrual cycle, one of the eggs breaks out of its follicle. It moves from an ovary into a fallopian tube and then into the uterus. The **uterus** is the organ in which a fetus develops. The lining of the uterus, called the endometrium, can serve as a nourishing location for a fertilized egg to mature during pregnancy. If a fertilized egg is not implanted, the endometrium is shed as menstrual flow, and the egg disintegrates on its way out of the uterus.

FIGURE 4.1	**Levels of estrogen and progesterone throughout the menstrual cycle.**

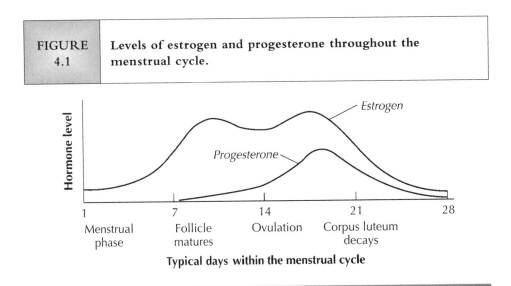

| FIGURE 4.2 | **Female internal reproductive organs.** |

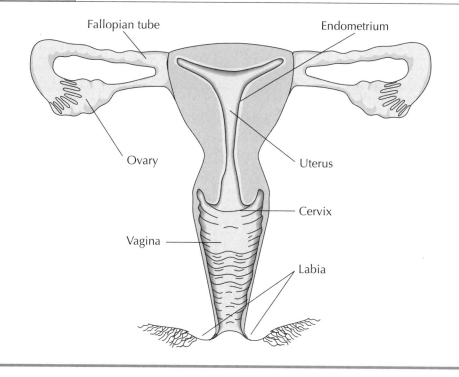

Fallopian tube

Endometrium

Ovary

Uterus

Vagina

Cervix

Labia

The Events in the Menstrual Cycle.   Now that you know some of the important components of the menstrual cycle, let's see how they interact. The important thing to remember is that brain structures, hormones, and internal reproductive organs are carefully coordinated to regulate the menstrual cycle. When the level of a particular hormone is too low, a structure in the brain is signaled, and the chain of events that follows produces more of that hormone. When the level of a hormone is too high, a signal to a structure in the brain begins a chain of events that decreases that hormone. Here are the major events in this monthly cycle:

1. In response to a low estrogen level, the hypothalamus signals the pituitary gland.
2. The pituitary gland responds by releasing follicle-stimulating hormone, which stimulates the follicles to become more mature; this hormone also signals the ovaries to increase their production of estrogen.

3. The increased level of estrogen stimulates the development of the endometrium (essentially preparing for possible pregnancy every month). It also signals the pituitary to stop producing follicle-stimulating hormone.

4. The pituitary stops producing follicle-stimulating hormone and starts producing luteinizing hormone.

5. Luteinizing hormone suppresses growth in all follicles except one; therefore, only one egg typically reaches maturity.

6. The follicle then releases the ovum, or egg, on approximately the 14th day of the menstrual cycle, a process called **ovulation** (pronounced "ov-you-*lay*-shun").

7. The empty follicle matures into a round structure called the corpus luteum, which secretes progesterone and estrogen. As Figure 4.1 illustrates, the levels of these hormones rise after ovulation.

8. The high level of progesterone inhibits the production of additional luteinizing hormone, resulting in the decomposition of the corpus luteum.

9. When the corpus luteum decomposes, the production of progesterone and estrogen falls rapidly, as Figure 4.1 shows. With such low levels of hormones, the endometrium can no longer be maintained in the style to which it has grown accustomed. The endometrium is sloughed off, and it passes out of the vagina as menstrual flow.

10. The low level of estrogen signals the hypothalamus, causing a new cycle to begin.

Notice the checks and balances that are required to orchestrate the menstrual cycle. This complex set of interactions encourages the production of an egg, leads to menstrual flow if no fertilized egg is implanted, and then begins another cycle.

Most people are amazed to learn that a woman typically loses only 40 to 80 cubic centimeters—or about 3 to 6 tablespoons—of blood during each menstrual period (Emans, 1997). However, this relatively trivial blood loss is often accompanied by menstrual pain and is sometimes associated with a variety of premenstrual reactions. Let's examine these two phenomena.

Menstrual Pain

Menstrual pain, or **dysmenorrhea** (pronounced "diss-men-or-*ree*-ah"), typically refers to painful cramps in the abdominal region. It may also include headache, nausea, dizziness, and pain in the lower back (Golub, 1992; A. Walker, 1998). (Dysmenorrhea is *not* the same as premenstrual syndrome, or PMS, which will be discussed in the next section.)

How common is menstrual pain? Estimates range from 50% to 75% for high school and college women (Golub, 1992; A. Walker, 1998). Dysmenorrhea is also the leading cause of young women's absence from school or work (Golub, 1992). Consistent with Theme 4 of this book, women's reactions to life events—such as menstruation—vary widely. Pain during menstruation is certainly common, but it is *not* inevitable.

Junior high school females who have not yet begun to menstruate report that they expect to experience substantial pain—even more pain than is reported by their classmates who have already menstruated. These expectations can produce a self-fulfilling prophecy. Those who expect pain actually experience more severe symptoms (Brooks-Gunn et al., 1986; Ruble & Brooks-Gunn, 1982).

Expectations about pain may play a role, but menstrual pain is clearly *not* "all in the head." The contractions of the uterus that cause menstrual pain are encouraged by prostaglandins (pronounced "pross-tuh-*glan*-dins"). **Prostaglandins** are substances produced by the body in high concentrations just prior to menstruation, and they cause severe cramps. However, the relationship between prostaglandins and menstrual pain is complex. The two factors are strongly correlated, but some women with severe dysmenorrhea do not have elevated prostaglandin levels (Golub, 1992; A. Walker, 1998). Menstrual pain seems to be caused by a combination of physiological and psychological factors.

Many different treatments have been used to reduce menstrual pain. Some drugs are helpful, including those that inhibit the synthesis of prostaglandins. Oral contraceptives can be useful in severe cases, but they may bring unwanted side effects. Heat, exercise, muscle relaxation, and dietary changes often produce additional relief (Golub, 1992; Hyde & DeLamater, 1997).

The Controversial Premenstrual Syndrome

Menstrual pain is well accepted as being part of the menstrual cycle. In contrast, the premenstrual syndrome is controversial among both professionals and laypeople (Chrisler, 1996; Figert, 1996). **Premenstrual syndrome (PMS)** is the name given to a variety of symptoms that may occur a few days before menstruating. These symptoms often include headaches, breast soreness, swelling in some body regions, acne, and various psychological reactions. These psychological reactions typically include depression, irritability, anxiety, and lethargy (Chrisler, 1996; S. Johnson, 1995).

One reason the premenstrual syndrome is controversial is that researchers do not agree on its definition (Chrisler, 1996; Figert, 1996). Read the previous list of symptoms once more, and add on others that you've heard about in popular accounts of PMS. Some critics have discovered as many as 200 different symptoms presumably connected with PMS (Chrisler, 1996; E. Mitchell et al., 1992). Think of the problem created by this confusion. One researcher may be studying women whose primary symptom is anxiety; another may be studying women with depression. How can researchers study PMS systematically when we don't even have a clear-cut operational definition for the problem?

Another reason PMS is so controversial is that some experts claim that virtually all menstruating women experience it. This claim is unfair because it suggests that all women are at the mercy of their hormones. An alternate view argues that the premenstrual syndrome is a myth created by our culture. This view, if taken too far, would be equally unfair because some women do experience genuine symptoms more often premenstrually than at other times in their cycle.

Our discussion of the premenstrual syndrome takes an intermediate position between the two extremes of the biologically driven explanation and the psychological/cultural explanation. Apparently, a small percentage of women (maybe 5%) have significant symptoms that are related to their menstrual cycle (Hardie, 1997; S. Johnson, 1995). Other women do not. This is an example of the general principle that large individual differences exist among women. No single rule holds true for all females.

Let's examine the aspect of PMS that has received the most attention: the presumably dramatic mood swings during the menstrual cycle. We'll also consider a new concept, called "menstrual joy," as well as methods of coping with the premenstrual syndrome.

Mood Swings.   Much of the research that supposedly supports the concept of PMS is plagued by biases. For example, many researchers ask women to recall what their moods had been during various times throughout previous weeks of the menstrual cycle. Problems with this kind of retrospective study are easy to anticipate. For example, women may recall their moods as being more negative premenstrually than they actually were.

Some well-controlled studies report modest cyclical variation in moods during the menstrual cycle. For example, Alagna and Hamilton (1986) asked women to rate their emotions on a day-by-day basis. Later, each woman's responses were categorized according to whether she was premenstrual, menstruating, or midcycle. Relative to the other groups, the premenstrual women rated themselves as more indifferent, more negative, more dominant, and more energetic. However, ratings of tension showed no significant differences between the groups. Other research by the same authors demonstrated that women's moods were influenced as much by the day of the week as by the phase of the menstrual cycle (Alagna & Hamilton, 1986). In other words, their mood was just as likely to be influenced by whether a day was a Monday or a Friday, as by whether they were premenstrual or midcycle.

During the 1990s, most of the research produced results that should make us skeptical about the mood-swings component of the premenstrual syndrome (e.g., Figert, 1996; Gallant et al., 1992; McFarlane & Williams, 1994; Nash & Chrisler, 1997). Klebanov and Jemmott (1992) examined the effects of expectations on PMS symptoms. They gave women a fictitious "medical test" that misinformed the women that they were either midcycle or premenstrual. Then the women took a standard scale called the Menstrual Distress Questionnaire. Those who believed that they were premenstrual—even if they were not—reported more symptoms than did those who thought they were midcycle.

Let's consider another study that was critical of the PMS concept. Hardie (1997) asked 83 menstruating women who were employed by a university to keep records in a booklet titled *Daily Stress & Health Diary*. Each day, for 10 weeks, they recorded their emotional state, stress level, general health, exercise, laughter, crying, menstrual bleeding, and so forth. At the end of the 10 weeks, the women completed a questionnaire about women's health issues. Included in this questionnaire was a crucial item: "I think I have PMS."

To assess PMS, Hardie used a criterion that several others had used; it took into account the emotional states during both the premenstrual phase and the postmenstrual phase, and the woman's range of emotions during the entire menstrual cycle. Not one of the 83 women met this criterion for two menstrual cycles during the 70-day study. In addition, the women who believed they had PMS did *not* have more negative emotions premenstrually than did the women who reported no PMS. In other words, both groups actually reported similar cyclic changes.

Researchers who endorse the psychological/cultural explanation for PMS argue that our current culture clearly accepts PMS as an established "fact" (Figert, 1996; A. Walker, 1998). You've probably heard dozens of jokes and references to PMS, such as, "What is the difference between a pit bull and a woman with PMS?" The answer? "A pit bull doesn't wear lipstick" (Figert, 1996, pp. 12–13). With this kind of cultural endorsement, women believe that PMS is "normal." If a woman is feeling tense, and she is premenstrual, she blames her emotions on PMS (Hardie, 1997). Hormonal factors may indeed cause premenstrual problems in a small percentage of women (Hardie, 1997; Schmidt et al., 1998). However, cultural and psychological factors are probably more important (Chrisler, 1996).

Menstrual Joy.   Go ahead; read the title of this section again. Yes, menstrual *joy*. Joan Chrisler and her colleagues noticed that American magazines had published hundreds of articles on the negative—and often exaggerated—aspects of changes associated with the menstrual cycle (Chrisler et al., 1994; Chrisler & Levy, 1990). Surely some women must have *some* positive reactions to menstruation! Therefore, they administered the Menstrual Joy Questionnaire (Delaney et al., 1988), which is similar to Demonstration 4.1. Interestingly, women who first completed the Menstrual Joy Questionnaire were likely to rate their level of arousal more positively when they later completed a questionnaire about menstrual symptoms. Compared to women who hadn't been encouraged to think about the positive side to menstruation, these women were more likely to report feelings of well-being and excitement, and bursts of energy (Chrisler et al., 1994).

In a second study, Chrisler and her colleagues (1994) demonstrated that the Menstrual Joy Questionnaire encouraged women to think about their menstrual symptoms in a different way. The women also reported that they would be likely to think about some of these positive qualities during their next menstrual cycle. Chrisler and her coauthors do not anticipate that they can convince the world that menstruation is truly joyous, rather than unpleasant. However, isn't it interesting that so little research has been conducted on the potentially positive side of menstruation?

DEMONSTRATION 4.1

Positive Symptoms of Menstruation

If you are a female who has menstrual cycles, complete the following questionnaire, which is based on the Menstrual Joy Questionnaire (Chrisler et al., 1994; Delaney et al., 1988). If you do not have menstrual cycles, ask a friend if she would be willing to fill out the questionnaire.

Instructions: Rate each of the following items on a 6-point scale. Rate an item 1 if you do not experience the feeling at all when you are menstruating; rate it 6 if you experience the feeling intensely.

_____ high spirits   _____ affection

_____ sexual desire   _____ self-confidence

_____ vibrant activity   _____ euphoria (extreme well-being)

_____ revolutionary zeal   _____ creativity

_____ intense concentration   _____ power

Did you or your friend provide a positive rating for one or more of these characteristics?

Coping with the Premenstrual Syndrome.   It's difficult to talk about coping with or treating PMS when we have no clear-cut definition of the problem and no comprehensive theory about its origins (Golub, 1992; A. Walker, 1998). The research certainly suggests that women should monitor their emotional reactions throughout the menstrual cycle to determine whether anxiety and tension are equally likely to occur during phases that are not premenstrual. The best strategy may be to figure out how to reduce the problems that create those emotions at *all* phases of the menstrual cycle.

Physicians—and other health professionals who believe that PMS is a genuine, biologically driven problem—often recommend exercise as therapy. They also suggest avoiding fat, salt, alcohol, and caffeine ("PMS," 1994; A. Walker, 1998). Some may also recommend specific vitamin supplements. None of these remedies can hurt, though their value has not been established. Some physicians are currently recommending low doses of antidepressants such as Prozac (Steiner et al., 1995; A. Walker, 1998). These drugs can cause side effects and, for many women, may not be necessary (A. Walker, 1998). Most psychologists who currently conduct research on PMS would not recommend antidepressants unless a woman and her health care provider are convinced that she has serious premenstrual problems.

The Menstrual Cycle and Performance

We have discussed the most publicized aspects of the menstrual cycle: menstrual pain and the premenstrual syndrome. Now let's turn to another question: Do certain kinds of abilities vary with the phase of the menstrual cycle? Let's specifically consider physical and cognitive abilities.

Physical Abilities. Performance of physical tasks may show some variations throughout the menstrual cycle (e.g., Kimura & Hampson, 1993). However, this variation is neither large nor universal. Performance in sports does not seem to suffer substantially during the premenstrual or menstrual phases. Young women have set world records and won Olympic competitions during these "critical times" (Brooks-Gunn et al., 1986; Brooks-Gunn & Matthews, 1979). The rate at which women perform physical tasks such as typing is also unrelated to menstrual phase (A. Walker, 1998).

Cognitive Abilities. The earliest research on cognitive abilities and the menstrual cycle was conducted by Leta Hollingworth in 1914. She found no effects. Since then, researchers have tested a wide variety of skills, including memory, spelling, mathematical tasks, spatial tasks, and scores on psychology exams. The results demonstrate that women's cognitive performance is no worse during premenstrual and menstrual phases than during other parts of the cycle (Asso, 1987; Chrisler, 1991; Golub, 1992; A. Walker, 1998). The rare publication that *does* find cyclical variation in cognitive performance becomes a media sensation, featured on the front pages of newspapers and discussed seriously on television (e.g., Kimura & Hampson, 1994). Meanwhile, the dozens of studies that show no cognitive impairment don't even make it into the fine print of the newspapers' Women's Section. As Golub (1992) concludes:

> Thus, researchers find, over and over and over again, with increasingly sophisticated research methodology, no meaningful menstrual-cycle-phase effects on women's cognitive or work performance. Yet there is something to worry about here: We seem to be doomed by the negative stereotypes to continue to search for adverse effects. (p. 106)

Please, do not misinterpret this conclusion. Some women, some of the time, on some tasks, surely perform worse before or during their periods than they might at midcycle. As we emphasize throughout this book, individual differences among women are vast. In general, though, the menstrual cycle has no substantial effect on women's cognitive achievements.

Attitudes Toward Menstruation

Throughout this book, you will see a contrast between people's beliefs about women and women's actual experiences. For example, people's stereotypes about women (Chapter 2) often differ from women's actual cognitive skills (Chapter 5) and women's social characteristics (Chapter 6). Similarly, we will see in this section that people's attitudes about menstruation often differ from women's experiences.

Menstrual Myths and Taboos.   Some cultures have a taboo against contact with menstruating women. For example, a New Guinea tribesman reportedly murdered his wife because she had slept on his blanket while menstruating (Delaney et al., 1988). Contemporary Creek Indians in Oklahoma do not allow menstruating women to use the same plates or utensils as other tribe members (A. Bell, 1990). Many similar menstrual practices reflect a belief in female pollution and the devaluation of women (A. Walker, 1998).

Some menstrual myths and taboos persist in less dramatic forms in mainstream North American culture. Many women believe, for example, that swimming during menstruation is harmful. Some also think that hair permanents will not "take" when a woman is menstruating, and that flowers will wilt if handled by a menstruating woman (A. Walker, 1998; L. Williams, 1983). Some women are known to avoid shaving, gardening, and baking when they are menstruating (Jurgens & Powers, 1991).

This section has been a testimonial to one of the themes of the book: Something associated with women—in this instance, their menstrual periods—will often be negatively evaluated (Chrisler, 1996). But are menstrual attitudes *always* negative? Assess these attitudes among your friends by trying Demonstration 4.2.

Menstrual Expressions.   The topic of menstruation is relatively invisible in our popular culture, consistent with Theme 3 of this book. We usually do not speak openly about menstruation, because it is often a taboo topic. Instead, we enlist euphemisms, or more pleasant ways of saying the same thing. For example, you'll rarely hear the word *menstruation* on television. An ad referring to "that time of the month" probably does not mean the date the car payment is due! Some common euphemisms include "on the rag," "Aunt Flo is visiting," and "I've got my friend" (Gordon, 1993; A. Walker, 1998). Even the customary term "period" is actually a euphemism that manages to avoid the word *menstrual*. (The term *PMS* does not seem to be taboo, even during TV shows that are popular with children—but notice that the use of initials avoids saying the word *menstrual*.)

Young girls' attitudes may be shaped by advertisements in the teen media. Havens and Swenson (1988) examined the advertisements in the popular magazine *Seventeen*. Most readers of *Seventeen* are probably in early puberty, so the advertisements may have a strong influence on young women at the time of menarche. The dominant message conveyed by the advertisers is that menstruation represents a hygienic crisis that can be overcome with an effective "security system." A secondary theme is that menstruation is embarrassing and odorous, and a woman's clothing may become stained. I examined a recent issue of the teen magazine *Jump*. In addition to the usual ads for menstrual products, *Jump* featured an article titled "Seeing Red, Feeling Blue? Cramps!

DEMONSTRATION 4.2

Attitudes Toward Menstruation

Present the questions below to several close friends. You may wish to ask both females and males, to see whether they differ in their answers.

1. Have you heard of any activities that menstruating women should not do?

2. Have you ever been told that a menstruating woman is bad luck?

3. Which people can you discuss menstruation with? Which friends? Which relatives?

4. Would you feel embarrassed if your biology professor discussed menstruation? Would if matter if the professor was a male or female?

5. Do you feel that there is something dirty or unclean about a menstruating woman?

6. Do you think couples should change their sexual activities when a woman is menstruating?

7. What kinds of menstrual slang words have you heard? How about menstrual jokes?

8. Have you ever heard anything positive about menstruation? Can you yourself think of anything positive concerning menstruation?

9. How do you feel when TV ads describe the qualities of sanitary napkins or tampons? Do you react differently when watching these ads with people of the other gender?

10. Describe some of the things that you've recently heard about the premenstrual syndrome (PMS). What percent of women would you guess experience PMS each month?

Bloating! Breakouts!" (Marston, 1998). I read two paragraphs before seeing the word *menstruation,* though "the Curse" was prominent and the article firmly endorsed PMS and hormone-dependent emotions. As you might imagine, no hint of "menstrual joy" appears in those teen magazines!

Positive Images of Menstruation.   We've been discussing the negative images of menstruation, but women's personal accounts sometimes provide more positive images. Anne Frank wrote a passage in her diary that captures the bittersweet emotions she felt about her menstrual periods:

> Each time I have a period . . . I have the feeling that in spite of all the pain, unpleasantness, nastiness, I have a sweet secret and that is why, although it is

nothing but a nuisance to me in a way, I always long for the time that I shall feel that secret within me again. (1972, p. 117)

A friend mentioned another positive image: Menstruation represents sisterhood to her. When she is menstruating, she is reminded that women all over the world, of different races, shapes, and ages, are menstruating as well. Less poetically—but very significantly—many women greet a menstrual period with joy because it means they are not pregnant. Menstrual cramps and other problems will not disappear if you simply adopt a more positive attitude. However, the issues are easier to deal with if you know their cause and remind yourself that other women share similar experiences.

 *Puberty and Menstruation*

1. **Adolescence begins at puberty; for females, menarche is the crucial milestone, and young women vary greatly in their reactions to menarche.**

2. **The menstrual cycle requires a complex coordination of brain structures, hormones, and internal reproductive organs.**

3. **Dysmenorrhea, or menstrual pain, is common in young women and is at least partially caused by prostaglandins.**

4. **The premenstrual syndrome is a controversial set of symptoms that presumably includes headaches, breast soreness, depression, and irritability. Although some research supports mood variation for some women, we do not have solid evidence for a biological basis of PMS. The psychological/cultural explanation suggests that cultural expectations encourage women to explain mood swings in terms of PMS. Still, some women report positive reactions to menstruation.**

5. **Physical and cognitive abilities show little variation as a function of the phase of the menstrual cycle.**

6. **Menstrual myths are found in many cultures, including mainstream North American culture. These myths demonstrate the negative evaluation of women's bodily processes. Numerous euphemisms have been created to refer to menstruation, but some positive images can be found.**

SELF-CONCEPT AND IDENTITY DURING ADOLESCENCE

We have seen that adolescent females are very aware of the changes in their bodies during puberty, and that they experience a major transition when they reach menarche. Because adolescents have the cognitive capacity to think abstractly, they can begin to ask complex questions such as "Who am I?" **Identity** refers to an individual's self-rating of personal characteristics, along biological, psychological, or social dimensions (Whitbourne, 1998). We'll consider three components of identity in this section: body image, ethnic identity, and self-esteem.

Body Image

In Chapter 3, we saw that attractiveness is more important for preschool girls than for preschool boys. Compared to less attractive little girls, cute little girls are more likely to be patted and praised—and less likely to be hit and pushed. However, attractiveness is generally irrelevant for little boys.

This same emphasis on female attractiveness is exaggerated during adolescence. Young women constantly receive the message that good looks and physical beauty are the most important dimension for females (Brumberg, 1997; Nielsen, 1996). Their skin must be clear, their teeth straight and gleaming, and their hair lustrous.

The most important component of female attractiveness in North America is body weight. Theorists argue that the typical European American female is obsessed about her weight (Brumberg, 1997). Among some adolescents, concern about their body's appearance reveals itself in life-threatening eating disorders. (We will discuss these disorders and our culture's emphasis on thinness in more detail in Chapter 12.) Consider how a young woman named Samantha focused so much attention on her weight that she developed anorexia. Samantha enjoyed a fairly normal life until her high school boyfriend started dating someone else. As Samantha interpreted his actions and his choice of a new girlfriend, he wanted someone thinner. Samantha became obsessed with food and weight, until her anorexia became so severe that she was seriously underweight and fainted from hunger. Nothing else but her weight mattered; her academic and social successes were largely irrelevant (Pipher, 1995b).

The media encourage this emphasis on beauty and slenderness (Higginbotham, 1996). Try Demonstration 4.3 to appreciate the narrow view provided to female adolescents by teen magazines.

Your investigation of magazines in Demonstration 4.3 probably will not reveal many young women of color—even though teen magazines sell well when their covers feature Black women (Higginbotham, 1996). The European American models remind women of color that their features do not conform to the "standard" (Freedman, 1986). Ironically, these idealized images of White women may actually allow women of color to escape from the constraints of imitating the women in the advertisements. For example, an Asian American adolescent recalled watching the models in TV ads and realizing that their appearance was impossibly different from her own (Melpomene Institute, 1992). The media images seemed irrelevant; she could never become blond and blue-eyed.

The small number of women of color who do appear in the ads usually look "White." For example, a recent catalog designed exclusively for Black women

DEMONSTRATION 4.3
Representation of Females in Teen Magazines

Locate several magazines intended for adolescent women. (In the late 1990s, *Seventeen, YM, Jump,* and *'Teen* are most popular.) Glance through the magazine for photos of women, in either advertisements or feature articles. What percentage of these women would be considered overweight? How many look nearly anorexic? Then inspect the magazines for ethnic representation. If you find any women of color, are they pale-skinned, with features typical of White women, or do they seem typical of their own ethnic group?

Notice the body posture of the women pictured. Would a young man look ridiculous in these positions? What percentage of the photos seems aimed at encouraging sexual relationships? How many of the women look competent? What other messages do these images provide for high school females?

showed skin the shade of a well-tanned European. And all the Black models pictured had straightened hair. Of course, some women of color develop a concept of beauty consistent with their own racial features. One woman wrote:

> Through solidarity with other women and my reading, I learned to develop a positive self-image. I went through a period of being born again black, of experiencing a transformation. My relaxed hair was changed to an Afro look. . . . This was the beginning of a period in my life of feeling the rage, coming to terms with the guilt, healing the shame, and breaking the silence. (Valcarcel, 1994)

However, most adolescent women—both women of color and European Americans—tend to accept media messages, and their self-concepts are shaped by whether they are attractive. Consider an important study by Kwa (1994). She found that physical appearance was the strongest predictor of self-worth in females. For males, athletic competence was the strongest predictor of self-worth. Notice, then, that females feel valued for how their bodies look. In contrast, males feel valued for how their bodies *perform* in athletics and other activities that enhance their self-image.

In recent years, researchers have begun to discover that girls who participate in athletics can often escape from the dominant images presented to adolescent females. They may even enjoy long-term health benefits (Rongé, 1996). For example, Erkut and her coauthors (1996) collected information on 362 females from the five major ethnic groups. In response to the question, "What activities make you feel good about yourself?" almost half mentioned an athletic activity. The media occasionally feature female athletes, and these images of strong women might make a difference. Adolescent women watching the various U.S. women's teams in the Olympics and other sports events may realize that women's bodies can be competent and athletic rather than anorexic.

Ethnic Identity

Some research suggests that young girls are more likely than young boys to have a strong sense of ethnic identity (Fine & Bowers, 1984). Unfortunately, no clear conclusions can be drawn about gender comparisons during adolescence. The statistics will vary, depending on the ethnic group that is being examined and the operational definition of "ethnic identity." Research on Asian Americans and Hispanic students has reported that females are more concerned about ethnicity than males are (Ethier & Deaux, 1990; Phinney & Alipuria, 1990). Other research suggests that Black and Latina females are more strongly identified with their ethnic group than are Black and Latino males (Rotheram-Borus et al., 1996).

We can reach different conclusions from a different perspective, however. Black males receive more criticism than Black females do for "acting White" (Fordham, 1988; Waters, 1996). A Black male may be teased by his friends if he speaks standard English and tries to do well in school; his friends may even question his masculinity. In contrast, Black females seem to have more latitude for adopting an identity that includes both Black and mainstream White cultures (Waters, 1996). A possible conclusion is that females are often more strongly linked to their ethnic group than males are. However, a threat to a male's masculinity may drive him to adopt a very strong ethnic identity.

Other researchers focus on the process of adolescents' ethnic identity, rather than the issue of gender comparisons in that domain. In general, European American adolescent females are not concerned about their ethnic identity (Peplau, Veniegas et al., 1998; Waters, 1996). When being White is considered standard or "normative," White individuals don't notice their privileged status.

Some young women of color may initially try to reject their ethnicity. Consider, for example, an African American woman's description of herself:

> For a long time it seemed as if I didn't remember my background, and I guess in some ways I didn't. I was never taught to be proud of my African heritage. Like we talked about in class, I went through a very long stage of identifying with my oppressors. Wanting to be like, live like, and be accepted by them. Even to the point of hating my own race and myself for being a part of it. Now I am ashamed that I ever was ashamed. I lost so much of myself in my denial of and refusal to accept my people. (Tatum, 1992, p. 10)

However, some adolescents find that their ethnic identity may clash with their nontraditional ideas about gender. A young Asian American woman commented:

> My parents are sort of old-fashioned, so they tell me that I have to do things. . . .
> Like I am a girl so I am always sent to the kitchen to cook. . . . I am more

Americanized and I don't believe in that girl thing. We end up in an argument and it does not get solved. (Phinney & Rosenthal, 1992, p. 153)

Researchers are just beginning to explore these complex issues that arise at the intersection of ethnicity and gender (Peplau, Veniegas et al., 1998).

Self-Esteem

Do adolescent males and females differ in their self-esteem? As with ethnic identity, we cannot reach a clear-cut conclusion because the answer seems to depend on how self-esteem is measured.

A well-publicized study by the American Association of University Women (AAUW) concluded that boys and girls are similar in self-esteem during elementary school. However, females drop in self-esteem—relative to males—during high school (cited in Sadker & Sadker, 1994). For example, 67% of elementary school boys and 60% of elementary school girls replied "Yes" to the statement: "I'm happy the way I am." When high school students were asked the same question, 46% of the males and only 29% of the females answered "Yes." Further analysis showed that the drop was especially dramatic for Latinas, but Black females actually reversed the trend and showed an *increase* in self-esteem during high school.

Various studies have reported a gender difference in self-esteem (e.g., K. Kelly & Jordan, 1990; Widaman et al., 1992). However, others have not shown a substantial gender difference (e.g., Cate & Sugawara, 1986; Côté, 1996; Dusek & Flaherty, 1981). In an effort to clarify the puzzling findings, researchers have examined several components of self-esteem. For example, A. Rose and Montemayor (1994) found that adolescent males had higher self-esteem in athletic and social skills, whereas adolescent females had higher self-esteem with respect to "romantic appeal." Most important, no gender differences were found in areas such as scholastic competence or general self-worth. In short, we *cannot* conclude that young women inevitably experience a drastic plunge in self-esteem, relative to young men.

One finding is fairly consistent. Adolescents who receive high scores on measures of masculinity tend to be high in self-esteem, whether they are male or female. Apparently, young people who are high in *instrumentality*—who believe they can accomplish goals—have higher self-esteem. In contrast, femininity scores are generally unrelated to self-esteem in adolescence (Cate & Sugawara, 1986; A. Rose & Montemayor, 1994; J. Stein et al., 1992; Worell, 1989). These findings are consistent with a large number of studies conducted with adults, which we discussed in connection with androgyny in Chapter 2.

We need to be especially concerned about another issue. Young women who have frequent contact with a boyfriend—or with friends in general—are likely to be lower in academic competence (Feiring & Lewis, 1991). We'll explore these social connections at the end of this chapter.

Self-Concept During Adolescence

1. **Physical attractiveness is emphasized for adolescent women, and the current emphasis on thinness can lead to eating disorders. The focus on European American models in the media can create conflict for some young women of color; others may be able to ignore those media images.**

2. **Some research suggests that adolescent young women may have a stronger sense of ethnic identity than young men; however, young men of color may develop strong ethnic identity if their masculinity is threatened.**

3. **Gender differences in self-esteem are inconsistent; some studies report that males have higher self-esteem, but others do not. One consistent finding is that males and females who have high masculinity scores are generally higher in self-esteem than other individuals. Social pressures may undermine academic competence.**

EDUCATION AND CAREER PLANNING

In Chapter 3, we saw that young girls are often relatively invisible in the elementary school classroom. In contrast, boys receive more praise, more scolding, and more helpful feedback. Now we'll examine gender and education in the lives of adolescents, and their effect on young people's preparation for careers. Then, after investigating cognitive skills and achievement motivation in Chapter 5, and social and personality characteristics in Chapter 6, we will be in a good position to discuss women and employment in Chapter 7. In the current section, we'll be tracing young women's experiences in junior high and high school, early encounters with math and science, opportunities for higher education, career choices, and the discrepancy between aspirations and reality.

Young Women's School Experiences

A female seventh-grader described the complex challenge of blending school and social roles:

> For school we got an open mind, good grades, participation, we've got the attitude, a certain perspective. You have to suck up sometimes, you have to be quiet, you have to know certain people, you have to be yourself, you have to be attentive, on task, you have to study a lot. And for the crowd you have to wear the right clothes, you have to have the attitude, you have to be willing to bully people, you also have to suck up to like your friends or whatever, you have to be

outgoing, daring, you have to know certain people . . . and sometimes you have to be mean. (Cohen et al., 1996, p. 60)

According to a study by the American Association of University Women (AAUW), some young women respond to the challenge of blending school and social roles by **doing school,** or conforming to traditional expectations. These young women do what the teachers ask. They speak in turn in the classroom, or they may not speak at all. Depending on the school's culture, they may be admired or rejected by their peers for this behavior. Other young women who speak out freely in class may be perceived as troublemakers or acknowledged as leaders. Still others are **border crossers,** skillful communicators with both adults and peers (Cohen et al., 1996).

Some of the adolescent characteristics we've been discussing make it especially challenging for young women to achieve academic success. Their bodies are changing, they may be tempted to starve themselves, and they may be preoccupied about their physical appearance. They may also have low self-esteem, especially if they are low in instrumentality. Under these circumstances, many young women will not select a challenging career, choose rigorous courses, or study diligently (Arnold et al., 1996a; Kerr, 1994).

According to the AAUW report, young women are most likely to maintain their academic aspirations if schools make gender issues a priority, institute a mentoring system, and encourage young women to become leaders (Cohen et al., 1996). Schools can also arrange programs in nontraditional careers, through organizations such as the Society for Women Engineers or the Association for Women in Science (Betz, 1994b).

Early Experiences in Math and Science

Zelda Ziegler remembers sitting in a high school classroom, preparing to take an engineering exam. She was the only female among those taking the test. The proctor stood in front of the room and announced that the exam would be reasonable. "Nobody would have trouble with it except for one person—and she knows who she is" (J. Kaplan & Aronson, 1994, p. 27). Fortunately, Ziegler was not discouraged by these words. She went on to earn a PhD in chemistry and now acts as a mentor for young women interested in science.

Most young women do not face such overt sexism, but they typically experience subtler biases that discourage all but the most persistent students. For example, the teachers may treat females as if they were largely invisible, and they may give them less helpful feedback than they provide to males (J. Kaplan & Aronson, 1994). They may also fail to encourage talented females to pursue careers in math and science. Junior high school (middle school) is often the crucial time in which young women start to form negative attitudes toward these traditionally male courses (Eccles, 1997). In high school, they may then take only the required math and science courses. College-bound female high school graduates have typically had one year less of physical science and a half-year less of mathematics, compared to their male peers. The females are *not* weaker students; indeed, they often earn better grades in these classes than the males do (Catsambis, 1994; Eccles, 1989).

Several additional factors contribute to the gender differences in pursuing math and science: (1) male peers may tease and harass females interested in these areas (J. Kaplan & Aronson, 1994); (2) females are less likely to join extracurricular groups focusing on math and science (Catsambis, 1994); (3) females often feel less competent and effective in these courses—even though they may actually perform very well (Catsambis, 1994; Betz, 1997); and (4) students see few female role models in the sciences; for example, the typical college chemistry department has only *one* female member (Betz, 1994a).

Some school systems are beginning innovative programs to bring females into the sciences—and keep them there. For example, some school districts encourage high school females to enroll in special science schools. Others develop summer programs in which talented young women can conduct science research

---

DEMONSTRATION 4.4

Reasons for Seeking a College Degree

Take a moment to consider the reasons you are pursuing your college degree. Look at each of the factors listed below. Place a 1 in front of any reason you consider *very unimportant,* and place a 5 there if you consider it to be *very important.* Assign ratings between 1 and 5 for factors of intermediate importance. Then check page 158 at the end of this chapter to evaluate your score for this demonstration.

_____ 1. Your own skills and abilities.

_____ 2. The financial worth of a college degree.

_____ 3. Couldn't arrange anything better to do.

_____ 4. The lifestyle that results from getting a college degree.

_____ 5. Your desire for self-fulfillment.

_____ 6. Luck, accidental, unplanned.

_____ 7. The prestige of a college degree.

_____ 8. Drifting along, easier to finish than not.

_____ 9. Your enjoyment of the process of earning your college degree.

(Based on Bank, 1995.)

with a mentor (Betz, 1997; Callahan et al., 1996). Other schools encourage young women to participate in science clubs. In these settings, they can learn to take risks, make mistakes, and enjoy being successful in a nontraditional area (Travis, 1993).

Parents can encourage a daughter's interest in nontraditional fields by seeking nonsexist career guidance. They can also encourage her college plans and value her academic interests more than her physical appearance (Kerr, 1994).

Higher Education

Currently, women are more likely than men to pursue higher education. Women now constitute 56% of students in U.S. colleges and universities (Gose, 1997); the comparable figure for Canada is 52% (Normand, 1995a). However, relatively few college professors are women. At present, only 35% of all full-time faculty members at U.S. colleges and universities are female (*The Nation,* 1998). Consequently, female students may receive a message that they have entered a male-dominated environment. But what factors predict whether they will complete their college degrees? Is the college environment somewhat hostile to women? And what is college like for women of color? Before you read further, try Demonstration 4.4.

Predicting Educational Achievement.   As you might expect, parental characteristics are correlated with the number of years of education a woman achieves. For example, Reeder and Conger (1984) found, in a sample of Black and White women, that the father's education and the mother's occupation were significantly related to the number of years of college (including graduate school) that their daughters had attained. These authors also found that parents' encouragement was more important than parents' education for the Black women in the sample. Economic barriers may well have kept highly motivated Black parents from achieving their own educational goals when they were younger. Now, they can encourage their daughters toward pursuing the educational opportunities they never had.

Ultimately, though, most high school students will not enroll in college unless they have their own motivational reasons. Bank (1995) asked students to complete a questionnaire about their reasons for pursuing a bachelor's degree; Demonstration 4.4 lists nine items from the questionnaire. The top two kinds of answers, for both males and females, focused on *internal reasons* (e.g., self-fulfillment) and *instrumental reasons* (e.g., financial advantages and other assets that a bachelor's degree could bring). In these two categories, females gave slightly higher ratings than males. Both groups gave low ratings to *academic-drift* reasons, such as luck or drifting along. However, more males than females admitted to being in this category. In summary, males and females have fairly similar reasons for attending college. Check your own answers and note their relative importance.

The Academic Environment.   Once women are enrolled in college, how are they treated? In the early 1980s, some observers suggested that female students in higher education were experiencing a "chilly classroom climate" (e.g., R. Hall & Sandler, 1982). Where the concept of the **chilly classroom climate** persists, faculty members treat men and women differently in the classroom, and women may feel ignored and devalued. As a result, some women may participate less in discussions and may be less likely to feel academically competent.

Most professors who teach women's studies courses have heard reports from their students about faculty members who call on male students in class but ignore the females. We also hear about professors who tell sexist jokes or who otherwise devalue women. Unfortunately, it's difficult to document how often professors create these chilly classroom climates for the women in their classes.

In one survey, Crawford and MacLeod (1990) questioned students in two institutions. The students did not report favoritism toward men. However, students may not be sensitive to subtle differences in treatment, or they may choose to ignore differential treatment. Perhaps professors give slightly more eye contact to males, call on them more, and praise them more. Research that uses videotapes of classes and is based on objective measures would be useful in future studies.

Another factor that inhibits women's success is the **null academic environment,** in which faculty members do little to support or encourage students (Betz, 1989; Freeman, 1989). For example, an adolescent female who announces that she plans to go to medical school is likely to receive a lukewarm response. Consider the reaction that psychologist Nancy Betz (1989) received from her high school guidance counselor when she told him she wanted to be a physician. He told her that:

> Being a physician would rule out the chance for a husband and family because most men weren't interested in "brainy" women and, anyway, by the time I finished medical school I'd be too old to find a husband. (p. 139)

Teachers at all levels need to correct this kind of inequity by responding positively to female students. Instead of perpetuating the null academic environment, college professors need to ask talented undergraduate women about their career plans and invite them to work on independent research projects.

Women of Color and Higher Education.   We mentioned earlier that women are more likely than men to attend college. This observation is true for all major U.S. ethnic groups—White, Latina/o, Asian, Native American, and Black. In fact, Black women are almost twice as likely as Black men to earn a bachelor's degree (Gose, 1997; Malveaux, 1997). The complex reasons for this discrepancy are not clear, although Black theorists suggest that part of the problem is a cultural climate that values athletic ability more than academic achievement in young males (B. Hawkins, 1996).

We have seen that women students—especially in the sciences—are likely to receive a message: "You don't fit." Students of color are also likely to receive, from their educational institutions, a message that they do not match the university's expectations. Consider the experience of a group of Latinas who were enrolled at two Ivy League colleges that are especially steeped in European American traditions. Some of these women felt uncomfortable, tense, and aware of being different. Other Latinas, in contrast, perceived little discomfort or prejudicial treatment. These powerful individual differences clearly illustrate Theme 4 of this book.

A small number of universities offer special programs for people of color. For example, Pennsylvania State University's American Indian Leadership Program was designed to train leaders in the field of education. Napier (1996) describes the experience of nine Native American women who received PhDs through this program. The women encountered resistance from family members. One elderly father said, "You've got enough education. Why do you want to go there? It's so far away" (p. 139). However, support from helpful faculty members—and from each other—provided a warm academic climate rather than a chilly one.

Our discussion so far has focused on the difficulty of blending school with peer relationships, early experiences in math and science, and the challenges of higher education. Now let's turn to women's career plans.

Career Aspirations

A variety of studies have asked adolescents about their career aspirations. In general, adolescent females and males have similar career goals. Here are some of the findings:

1. Adolescent males and females aspire to similarly prestigious careers, according to an overview of the research (e.g., Belansky et al., 1993; Reis et al., 1996; Signorielli, 1993).

2. Adolescent females are more likely than adolescent males to choose careers that are nontraditional for their gender (Belansky et al., 1993). For example, Reis and her coauthors (1996) surveyed gifted adolescents. Of the females, 37% aspired to be doctors, whereas fewer than 1% of the males aspired to be nurses.

3. Adolescent females are more likely than adolescent males to emphasize the importance of marriage and children (Belansky et al., 1993; Eccles, 1994; Reis et al., 1996).

Before you read further, try Demonstration 4.5 to help you appreciate some of the factors related to young women's career choices.

Women who plan on a nontraditional career are likely to have parents who are well educated and from middle- or upper-class backgrounds (Betz & Fitzgerald, 1987; Kastberg & Miller, 1996). Their mothers are also likely to be employed outside the home and to have feminist beliefs (Belansky et al., 1992; Betz & Fitzgerald, 1987; J. Steele & Barling, 1996). Other influential background characteristics include a supportive and encouraging family, female role models, and

DEMONSTRATION 4.5

Women's Career Choices

Think about the female student from your high school who seemed most likely to pursue a high-prestige career considered to be traditionally male (e.g., lawyer, doctor, physicist). Review the list of factors in the left-hand column below, and place a + in the "Nontraditional" column to indicate each item that describes this nontraditional woman. Then think of a female student from your high school who has planned a career considered to be traditionally female (e.g., nurse, elementary school teacher, secretary). Review the list of factors once more, and place a + in the "Traditional" column for each item that describes this second student. When you have finished, count whether the first student has more + marks than the second one.

Factors Associated with Choosing a Nontraditional Career	Female Students	
	Nontraditional	Traditional
Good grades in school	_____	_____
Feminist orientation	_____	_____
Highly educated parents	_____	_____
Mother employed outside the home	_____	_____
Female role models	_____	_____
Independent	_____	_____
Emotionally stable	_____	_____
Work experience as adolescent	_____	_____
Supportive family	_____	_____

(Based on Betz, 1994a; Betz & Fitzgerald, 1987.)

work experience as an adolescent (Betz, 1994a; Betz & Fitzgerald, 1987; Holms & Esses, 1988).

What personal characteristics are typical for women who aspire to nontraditional careers? Not surprisingly, they receive high grades in school (Betz & Fitzgerald, 1987; Holms & Esses, 1988). They also tend to be independent, self-confident, assertive, emotionally stable, and satisfied with their lives (Betz, 1994a; Eccles, 1994; T. Ruble et al., 1984). Notice that these nontraditional women typically have characteristics that should serve them well in a traditionally masculine occupation. Also, their emotional stability and life satisfaction indicate that they are well adjusted. You may already have assumed, correctly, that they tend to express feminist attitudes and to transcend traditional gender roles (Belansky et al., 1992; Betz, 1994a; Vincent et al., 1998).

Social scientists typically study women's interest in high-prestige, high-paying professions such as medicine, law, and the sciences. They seldom focus on women's decisions about vocational occupations. What factors determine whether a woman will choose to be an auto mechanic or a welder, rather than a hairdresser or a florist? Research on students from several ethnic groups suggests that the most important factor is support and encouragement from family members, friends, teachers, and guidance counselors (Houser & Garvey, 1985). Encouragement from other women who pursued nontraditional training programs is also important, as are personality characteristics considered stereotypically masculine.

Social scientists know little about women's occupational choices in developing countries. However, Gibbons and her colleagues (1993) remind us that cross-cultural research must emphasize each culture's construction of career options. In the United States, for instance, doctors are well paid. In India—where a greater percentage of doctors are female—a doctor's salary is relatively low. The ideal doctor in India must therefore be kind, honest, and dedicated to serving the poor. An Indian woman considering a career in medicine would therefore be motivated by altruism, rather than money.

In this section, we have explored women's aspirations about future careers, as well as the factors associated with nontraditional career choices. But how do women's aspirations match their actual career pathways?

Aspirations Versus Reality

Women may graduate from high school with admirable life goals. However, women may be more likely than men to downscale their dreams as they move through college. For example, K. D. Arnold traced students who had graduated either first or second in their high school classes. The males and females performed similarly well in college. However, the women were much more likely to pursue nonprofessional employment or homemaker roles after college graduation (cited in Betz, 1994a).

A book called *Educated in Romance: Women, Achievement, and College Culture* follows the lives of a group of Black women and a group of White women while they progress through two universities in the South and enter the workforce (D. Holland & Eisenhart, 1990). The research showed that ethnicity influenced two variables: (1) the Black women were usually less focused than the White women on finding a husband, and (2) the Black women were less likely than the White women to expect a man to support them economically.

These differences, however, were overshadowed by similarities. In two-thirds of both groups, the women's aspirations about careers diminished as they progressed through college. Instead, both Black and White women spent a great deal of time and energy on romantic relationships. In a cyclical fashion, increased attention to romance produced more boredom with schoolwork and further erosion of their career identities. Ultimately, their education in romance became far more important than their career-related education.

Consider a Black woman named Paula, who entered college with a straight-A average in high school and planned to become a doctor. She found her pre-med courses boring, though not especially difficult. By the end of her first year, she decided to switch to nursing, yet she missed the deadline for the application. Instead, she decided to pursue an education degree, and then she switched to a social science area. After graduating from college, she worked in a department store and got married, choosing to support her husband in his career goals, rather than pursuing her own.

Educated in Romance raises some intriguing questions. What will happen to these women if they discover that problems can arise from depending on men for their identity? Will they later regret their decisions to forgo more ambitious careers? Do these same patterns of career erosion apply throughout other regions of the United States?

Educated in Romance examined the lives of relatively affluent women who could afford to go to college. Columnist Molly Ivins (1997) reminds us that the aspirations of these individuals are not relevant for many young women. Ivins describes the situation of Shanika, who is 24, unmarried, and has three children. She has no high school degree, no job, and little prospect of obtaining either. When asked what she had dreamed before her children were born, she replied, "You know, I really didn't have a dream."

 SECTION SUMMARY   *Education and Career Planning*

1. **Adolescent females must negotiate the conflicting demands of social interactions and schoolwork.**

2. **Young women face subtle biases, from teachers and school systems, that discourage them from careers in science and math; however, some schools offer innovative programs to promote these nontraditional careers.**

3. **Educational achievement is predicted by factors such as parents' education level; both males and females emphasize internal and instrumental reasons for their decision to attend college.**

4. **Some research has suggested that women in higher education sometimes encounter a chilly classroom climate, but the experience is not universal.**

5. **Women of color sometimes report that they do not feel comfortable in academic environments, but some universities offer programs designed to be supportive.**

6. **Gender differences are minimal in adolescents' career aspirations.**

7. **Factors associated with women's choice of a prestigious nontraditional career include parental education, mothers' employment and feminist beliefs, high grades, self-confidence, emotional stability, and feminist beliefs. Women who choose nontraditional vocational occupations emphasize the importance of support from other people.**

8. **As women advance through college, they are likely to adopt less ambitious plans; meanwhile, they increasingly emphasize romantic relationships.**

INTERPERSONAL RELATIONSHIPS DURING ADOLESCENCE

So far in this chapter, we have explored three clusters of issues that are important to young women: (1) puberty and menstruation; (2) self-concept and identity; and (3) education and career planning. However, as the third section suggested, adolescent females are perhaps most concerned about their social interactions.

Consider Ruby, a 14-year-old African American, who has six younger siblings. Her narrative, as recorded by Taylor and her colleagues (1995) illustrates the centrality of interpersonal relationships for adolescent females. For example, she describes the circle of support that the women in her family offer when she wants to discuss her future plans:

> [My mother] says if I want something, I can always accomplish it. I believe that, too. And my aunt and my grandmother. There's lots of people.

Ruby also emphasizes the support offered by her classmates—for example, when they elected her to a special team in her history class:

> The kids are all—I guess they accepted me for that, so maybe they like me. . . .
> You know you're wanted. That's all I can say. (p. 42)

In this final section of the chapter on adolescence, we will begin by exploring relationships with family members. Then we'll examine connections with peers, specifically in friendships and in love relationships.

Family Relationships During Adolescence

If you believe the popular media, you might conclude that adolescents and their parents inhabit different cultures, interacting only long enough to snarl at each other. The data suggest otherwise. The majority of adolescents—both females and males—actually get along quite well with their parents. Although they may disagree on relatively minor issues such as music or messy rooms, they typically agree on more substantive matters such as religion, politics, education, and social values (Nielsen, 1996; Smetana, 1996). Still, adolescents believe they have the right to question their parents. A study of data from 46 different countries discovered that only 16% of young women and 19% of young men agreed that "You should never question the word of your mother" (Gibbons et al., 1991).

In general, both female and male adolescents feel closer to their mothers than to their fathers (Blyth & Traeger, 1988; Vitulli & Holland, 1993). In a cross-cultural study, 49% of girls and 44% of boys said that "For me, the mother is the dearest person in the world" (Gibbons et al., 1991). Also, the majority of female students in a Wellesley College study identified their mother as the most important person in their life (A. Kaplan et al., 1991).

In most areas, female and male adolescents report similar family experiences. However, you may remember from Chapter 3 that parents tend to discuss fear and sadness with their daughters, but they talk about anger with their sons. Interestingly, adolescent females are much more likely than adolescent males to endorse statements such as, "In our family, it's okay to be sad, happy, angry, loving, excited, scared, or whatever we feel" (Bronstein et al., 1996). In addition, adolescent females are more likely than adolescent males to report intense sadness, shame, and fear (Stapley & Haviland, 1989). Family discussions about emotions may encourage young women to think about them and to experience them. We'll explore some of the consequences of these emotions in Chapter 12, when we discuss depression.

As young women mature, they begin to notice gender issues in their families. For example, Taylor and her colleagues (1995) reported that the young Latina and Portuguese American women in their study complained that their parents gave their brothers many more privileges and much more freedom. Their parents also emphasized that young women must be modest about their bodies and not sexually interested.

Older adolescents begin to notice gender issues focusing on their parents' experiences. One young White adolescent named Victoria commented on the unfairness that her mother should be called "Mrs. Jim Hanson," rather than "Ms. Elaine Hanson." As she pointed out to the interviewer:

> Victoria: . . . that's unfair because it makes it look like she's not even there.
> Interviewer: Why does that bother you?
> Victoria: Well, because, like, my mother, she's good and she's smart and she's understanding, but, like, everything about these names and stuff is kind of draining her, draining off her potential and stuff.
> Interviewer: Why because of the name?
> Victoria: Just because, because like everything always points to the man, like the man is most important and the woman is not even alive . . . to put it that way, the men are the most important people. (L. Brown & Gilligan, 1992, pp. 145–146)

An interesting possibility for further research would be young women's increasing awareness of gender inequities during adolescence.

Friendships During Adolescence

Chapter 6 examines whether gender differences can be found in friendship patterns during adulthood. We have somewhat less information about friendships during adolescence, and the research on gender differences is not clear-cut. In many studies using self-report, females' friendships seem to be closer and more intimate than males' friendships (e.g., Berndt, 1994; Blyth & Traeger, 1988), but some studies find no gender differences. You might wonder whether gender differences are found when researchers use a more objective measure of intimacy, such as analyses of recorded conversations. The problem here is that adolescents must be told when their conversations are being recorded, so their remarks are rarely very intimate. The research is split. Some studies reveal that female friendships are more intimate, and some suggest no gender differences (Berndt, 1994).

Berndt (1994), who reviewed the literature on adolescent friendships, pointed out that he had not yet heard of any study in which female friendships were *less* intimate than male friendships. He concluded that female friendships may be somewhat more intimate, but the differences are not enormous.

A more interesting question might focus on the importance of close friendships in the lives of adolescent females and males. Although I'm not aware of gender comparisons on this topic, Carol Gilligan and her colleagues (1990) recorded in-depth interviews with young women. Their research examined friendships at Emma Willard School, a private all-female high school in Troy, New York. The Gilligan book is especially important because, consistent with Theme 3 of this textbook, adolescent females have been generally ignored by researchers. The young women at this school had apparently incorporated the message that young women's lives are not especially noteworthy. When the researchers described the proposed project to the students, one young woman raised her hand and asked, "What could you possibly learn by studying us?" (Gilligan, 1990a, p. 2). Adolescent females doubt the value of their own voices.

The researchers found that the young women focused on their friendships with other students. Many of these conscientious students even ignored the "lights out" deadline at night when they knew a friend needed comforting (Lyons, 1990).

These young women emphasized the importance of communication with their friends. When asked to identify the worst thing that could happen in a relationship, most mentioned some aspect of failing to talk openly. One student responded that the worst thing would be:

> That you grow up, or sideways, and not be able to talk to each other, especially if you depend on being able to talk to someone and not being able to. That hurts a lot, because you have been dependent on that. It is like walking fifty miles for a glass of water in a hot desert and you have been depending on it for days and getting there and finding it is not there anymore; you made the wrong turn ten miles back. (Gilligan, 1990b, p. 24)

Adolescent females face a major challenge as they try to develop a clear sense of themselves in relationships with others. Some emphasize interdependence with others; these young women may spend so much attention on others that they fail to take care of their own needs. Other young women are more autonomous in relation to others—concerned about other people, but not compromising their own integrity for the sake of friends (Lyons, 1990).

Carol Gilligan and the other researchers in the Emma Willard project have identified, in their exploration of relationships, a central choice that weaves through women's lives. At many turning points, from youth through old age, women will be faced with conflicts between doing something that is best for themselves or doing something for another person—a parent, a female friend, a male friend, or a spouse.

In two later chapters of this book, we attend to topics related to women's focusing on themselves: cognitive ability and achievement (Chapter 5) and work (Chapter 7). Several other chapters emphasize women in relationships: social characteristics (Chapter 6), love relationships (Chapter 8), sexuality (Chapter 9), and pregnancy, childbirth, and motherhood (Chapter 10). We'll see that women frequently have to balance their own needs and priorities against the wishes of other people who are important in their lives.

Romantic Relationships During Adolescence

For most individuals, adolescence marks the beginning of romantic relationships. Chapter 8 explores these experiences in more detail, but let's consider some of the issues that young women face in heterosexual and lesbian relationships during adolescence.

Heterosexual Relationships.   Before you read further, try Demonstration 4.6, on page 154. This demonstration focuses on early heterosexual romances.

As you recall from Chapter 3, young girls and boys practice gender segregation; they inhabit different worlds for many years. As a result, they reach early adolescence with only limited experience regarding the other gender (Feiring, 1998). How do they figure out how they should interact with this unfamiliar person in a romantic relationship? An important source of information is the media—movies, television, music, books, and computer games (Feiring, 1998). Not surprisingly, the media typically portray stereotyped romances. Women are likely to be less powerful and more passive (Hedley, 1994).

Many teenagers may incorporate these media messages into their romantic interactions. However, Feiring (1998) reminds us about the tremendous individual differences in the gender typing of adolescents' romantic relationships, consistent with Theme 4 of this book. For example, if you check the answers to Demonstration 4.6, you're likely to find that some adolescents behave in a gender-stereotypical fashion, but some clearly transcend these stereotypes.

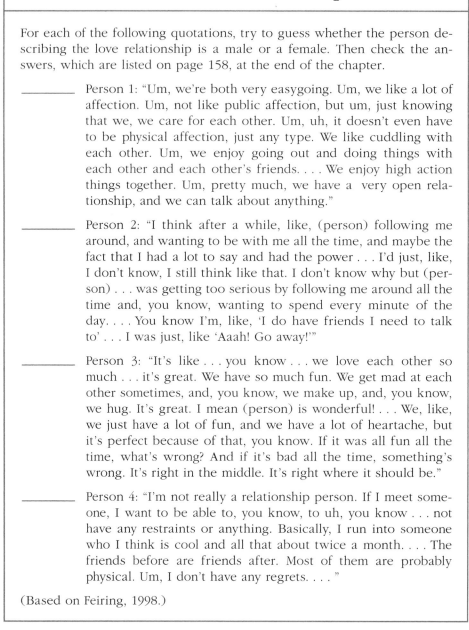

DEMONSTRATION 4.6

Gender and Love Relationships

For each of the following quotations, try to guess whether the person describing the love relationship is a male or a female. Then check the answers, which are listed on page 158, at the end of the chapter.

_____　Person 1: "Um, we're both very easygoing. Um, we like a lot of affection. Um, not like public affection, but um, just knowing that we, we care for each other. Um, uh, it doesn't even have to be physical affection, just any type. We like cuddling with each other. Um, we enjoy going out and doing things with each other and each other's friends. . . . We enjoy high action things together. Um, pretty much, we have a very open relationship, and we can talk about anything."

_____　Person 2: "I think after a while, like, (person) following me around, and wanting to be with me all the time, and maybe the fact that I had a lot to say and had the power . . . I'd just, like, I don't know, I still think like that. I don't know why but (person) . . . was getting too serious by following me around all the time and, you know, wanting to spend every minute of the day. . . . You know I'm, like, 'I do have friends I need to talk to' . . . I was just, like 'Aaah! Go away!'"

_____　Person 3: "It's like . . . you know . . . we love each other so much . . . it's great. We have so much fun. We get mad at each other sometimes, and, you know, we make up, and, you know, we hug. It's great. I mean (person) is wonderful! . . . We, like, we just have a lot of fun, and we have a lot of heartache, but it's perfect because of that, you know. If it was all fun all the time, what's wrong? And if it's bad all the time, something's wrong. It's right in the middle. It's right where it should be."

_____　Person 4: "I'm not really a relationship person. If I meet someone, I want to be able to, you know, to uh, you know . . . not have any restraints or anything. Basically, I run into someone who I think is cool and all that about twice a month. . . . The friends before are friends after. Most of them are probably physical. Um, I don't have any regrets. . . . "

(Based on Feiring, 1998.)

Research on early heterosexual romances suggests that these relationships typically last an average of only 4 months (Feiring, 1996). Both females and males are likely to describe their romantic partners in terms of positive personality traits, such as "nice" or "funny." However, males are more likely to mention physical attractiveness, whereas females are more likely to emphasize personal characteristics such as support and intimacy. (In Chapter 8, we'll see that males' emphasis on attractiveness in a dating partner continues through adulthood.)

Chapter 9 examines in some detail an important component of heterosexual romantic relationships during adolescence—decision making about sexuality. As we'll see, these decisions can have a major impact on a young woman's life, especially because they can lead to pregnancy and life-threatening sexually transmitted diseases.

Romantic relationships can also have a major impact on a young woman's career. In our discussion of career preparation, we mentioned Holland and Eisenhart's (1990) observation that female college students paid less attention to career plans as they became "educated in romance." These researchers also found that the women spent large amounts of time trying to make themselves attractive by dieting and exercising; the White women also worked on their tans. Once a woman found a boyfriend, she arranged her life to be available to her boyfriend, to help her boyfriend, and to participate in social activities chosen by her boyfriend. Holland and Eisenhart (1990) reported:

> Women also find time to wash their boyfriends' clothes, buy their food, clean their apartments, and work out refunds or repairs for defective purchases. In exchange for their efforts, women hope that their boyfriends will provide them with attention, gifts, and emotional closeness. (p. 98)

We do not know how widespread this pattern of "education in romance" may be. Does this description sound like the norm for women at your college? Do you know several women who do more work for their boyfriends than for their own careers? Or do these descriptions seem to apply to women on another planet—or at least women from another decade?

Lesbian Relationships.   In Chapter 8, we will examine many aspects of lesbian relationships. Young women who are just beginning to discover their lesbian identity rarely have the opportunity to see positive lesbian images in the movies or on television. They are also likely to hear negative messages about lesbians and gay males from their peers. By fourth or fifth grade, the words "queer," "dyke," and "fag" are serious insults. Adolescent lesbians are likely to be threatened or attacked (Owens, 1998). They also receive negative messages from their parents, who may believe that being gay or lesbian is a sin. Parents may also feel guilty for not recognizing the signs early enough to "change" their child's sexual orientation (Savin-Williams & Dube, 1996).

As we'll see in Chapter 8, lesbians typically overcome these negative messages from their family and community, and they construct positive self-images.

Consider the words of 'Lizabeth, who came out as a lesbian when she was 18 years old:

> I have a sense of peace about me that I've never had. I don't have to play any games. I don't have to pretend that I'm straight when I'm not. It's like a weight had been lifted off my shoulders. . . . My mother keeps telling me that the heterosexual norm would be so much easier. . . . But I had to live that way for eighteen years and it wasn't easier. It was screwing me up in my head. (Owens, 1998, p. 224)

In Chapters 3 and 4, we have considered how children and adolescents develop gender typing. Chapter 3 pointed out that infant boys and girls are quite similar, though the world may treat them differently. Factors such as the family, the media, and schools "educate" them further, so that they develop elaborate ideas about gender throughout their childhood. In this chapter, we examined how puberty and menstruation help define young women's views of themselves. We also noted that gender may influence an adolescent's body image, ethnic identity, and self-esteem. Gender also has important implications for an adolescent's career planning and interpersonal relationships.

In the following chapters, we'll examine adult women. We'll explore gender comparisons in cognitive and achievement areas (Chapter 5) and in personality and social areas (Chapter 6). Then we'll consider women in work settings (Chapter 7) as well as in social relationships (Chapters 8, 9, and 10). Chapters 11, 12, and 13 will focus on issues women face with respect to health, psychological disorders, and violence. Chapter 14 returns to a developmental framework as we consider women's journeys during middle age and old age, and our final chapter examines some trends in gender issues that we will face in the 21st century.

 SECTION SUMMARY   *Interpersonal Relationships During Adolescence*

1. **Adolescent women generally get along well with their families; they generally feel closer to their mother than their father.**

2. **Compared to adolescent men, adolescent women may have somewhat more intimate friendships; research at Emma Willard School emphasized the importance of close friendships in young women's lives.**

3. **Adolescents' heterosexual relationships show wide individual differences in the extent to which they are gender stereotyped, but the research by Holland and Eisenhart (1990) emphasizes that young women spend a great deal of time assisting their boyfriends.**

4. **Adolescent lesbians often hear negative messages from classmates, community members, and parents. These messages must be overcome in order to develop a positive self-image.**

CHAPTER REVIEW
QUESTIONS

1. The section on menstruation covered three topics that are occasionally mentioned in the popular media: (a) menstrual pain, (b) the premenstrual syndrome (PMS), and (c) the influence of the menstrual cycle on performance. What did you learn in this section that was different from the impressions the media convey?

2. At several points in this chapter, we discussed the emphasis on young women's attractiveness. Summarize this topic and relate your material to adolescent women you know.

3. Throughout this book, we have discussed the social constructionist perspective, in which people construct or invent their own versions of reality, based on prior experiences and beliefs. How does this perspective help explain the following issues: (a) premenstrual syndrome; (b) young women's emphasis on slenderness; and (c) how romantic relationships "should" be?

4. Throughout this book, we emphasize that research findings about gender comparisons often vary, depending on operational definitions. How is this statement relevant when we consider the research on ethnic identity and on self-esteem?

5. This chapter argues that some people—but not everyone—may treat young women in a biased fashion during the process of guiding and educating them. Summarize the information on these issues. If you were conducting a large-scale study on gender biases during high school and college, what other issues, not mentioned here, would you consider examining?

6. Define the concepts of "chilly classroom climate" and "null academic environment." How would you evaluate your own college or university with respect to these two potential problems?

7. Portions of this chapter examined ethnic comparisons. Describe information about relevant comparisons, including age of menarche, reactions to media images, self-esteem, and experiences with higher education.

8. Contrast adolescent males' and females' career aspirations. What factors modify these aspirations for young women? Although we do not have similar research on young men, speculate about whether these same factors influence the aspirations of adolescent males.

9. Relate the material in the section on self-concept to the material on career aspirations, as well as the material on social interactions. Focus on the struggle between commitment to one's own pursuits and commitment to social relationships.

10. The research on friendships at the Emma Willard School emphasized young women's struggles to develop a clear sense of themselves in relationships with others. Relate this topic to the information on women's relationships with family and friends, as well as their romantic relationships.

NEW TERMS

adolescence (124)

puberty (124)

menarche (124)

secondary sex characteristics (125)

ovaries (126)

ova (126)

uterus (126)

ovulation (128)

dysmenorrhea (128)

prostaglandins (129)

premenstrual syndrome (PMS) (129)

identity (137)

doing school (142)

border crossers (142)

chilly classroom climate (145)

null academic environment (145)

RECOMMENDED READINGS

Arnold, K., Noble, K. D., & Subotnik, R. F. (Eds.). (1996b). *Remarkable women: Perspectives on female talent development.* Cresskill, NJ: Hampton Press. This book's 25 chapters examine different components of methods for encouraging (or discouraging) intellectually talented women; some chapters focus on contemporary European American women, some on women of color, and some on women in earlier eras.

Leadbeater, B. J. R., & Way, N. (Eds.). (1996). *Urban girls: Resisting stereotypes, creating identities.* New York: New York University Press. In addition to topics from the present chapter, this book examines issues such as adolescent females' thoughts about their fathers, their relationships with nonparent adults, and sexual risk taking.

Walker, A. E. (1998). *The menstrual cycle.* New York: Routledge. Here's an excellent, current account of the biological components of menstruation, as well as the research on menstruation and on cognitive performance and the premenstrual syndrome.

Walsh, W. B., & Osipow, S. H. (Eds.). (1994). *Career counseling for women.* Hillsdale, NJ: Erlbaum. This book contains two excellent chapters by Nancy Betz; the other chapters examine topics such as career assessment, counseling women of color, gifted women, and special careers.

ANSWERS TO THE DEMONSTRATIONS

Demonstration 4.4: Add together the total number of points from items 1, 5, and 9; these represent internal reasons. Then add together the points from items 2, 4, and 7; these represent instrumental reasons. Finally, add together the points from items 3, 6, and 8; these represent "academic drift."

Demonstration 4.6: Person 1 is a male; Person 2 is a female; Person 3 is a female; Person 4 is a male.

ANSWERS TO THE
TRUE–FALSE QUESTIONS

1. False (p. 129); 2. False (p. 130); 3. True (p. 133); 4. False (p. 140); 5. False (p. 140); 6. False (p. 142); 7. True (p. 145); 8. True (p. 146); 9. True (p. 150); 10. False (p. 152).

Cognitive Abilities and Achievement Motivation

TRUE OR FALSE?

_____ 1. Males typically score higher than females on a wide variety of memory tests.

_____ 2. In the United States, females score consistently higher than males on tests of language and verbal ability; the differences are small but statistically significant.

_____ 3. On most tests of mathematical ability, the gender differences are negligible.

_____ 4. In general, females receive better grades than males in mathematics courses.

_____ 5. The largest gender difference in any measure of cognitive ability is that males are typically faster in rotating a geometric shape.

_____ 6. Basically, men and women are similar in their motivation to achieve success.

_____ 7. Women are more worried than men that being very successful can bring bad social consequences.

_____ 8. When estimating their grade point averages in the presence of other people, men provide higher estimates than do women.

_____ 9. Women are more likely than men to find that their self-confidence is influenced by evaluations from other people.

_____ 10. When a woman succeeds on some tasks, she typically says that her success is due to ability, whereas a man tends to attribute his success to hard work.

Background on Gender Comparisons
Cautions About Research on Gender Comparisons
Two Approaches for Summarizing Multiple Studies

Cognitive Abilities
Cognitive Abilities That Show No Consistent Gender Differences
Verbal Ability
Mathematics Ability
Spatial Ability
Explaining the Gender Comparisons

Achievement Motivation and Related Topics
Biases in the Research on Achievement Motivation
Achievement Motivation
Fear of Success
Confidence in Your Own Achievement and Ability
Attributions for Your Own Success

Y ou've probably heard the media motto, "Sex sells!" We can add a second motto, related to the topic of this chapter: "Sex differences sell!" (Halpern, 1995). The March 27, 1995, cover of *Newsweek* featured a prominent headline: "The new science of the brain: Why men and women think differently." The accompanying article, which featured brain scans and a prominent chart, emphasized the gender differences in brain structure (Begley, 1995). Casual readers might have assumed that those brain differences had been well established. They might have failed to notice that the long article reported on only four brain-scan studies, each of which tested just 20 to 61 individuals. Readers certainly *did not* learn that men and women actually perform similarly on most cognitive tasks.

To understand the psychology of women, some knowledge of gender comparisons is necessary. The present chapter explores two general questions regarding comparisons of women and men:

1. Do women and men differ in their cognitive abilities?
2. Do women and men differ in their patterns of achievement motivation?

By addressing these questions, we gain the background information needed to answer a more important question. In Chapter 7, we'll see that men and women tend to pursue different careers; for example, men are much more likely than women to become engineers. Can we trace this gender difference in career choice to major cognitive differences (such as ability in math) or to major motivational differences (such as an interest in achieving)?

The present chapter focuses on the school-related comparisons that assess intellectual abilities and achievement motivation. In contrast, Chapter 6 will focus on more interpersonal gender comparisons—specifically, social and personality characteristics. Perhaps males and females pursue different careers because they differ in some important personality qualities, such as communication patterns, helpfulness, and aggressiveness.

BACKGROUND ON
GENDER COMPARISONS

Before we address any of these specific gender comparisons, we need to consider some research issues that are relevant here and in Chapter 6. We'll first examine some cautions about the way research in psychology is conducted and interpreted. Then we'll briefly describe two approaches for summarizing a large number of studies on the same topic.

Cautions About Research
on Gender Comparisons

As pointed out in Chapter 1, a variety of biases can have a powerful effect when psychologists conduct research on women or on gender comparisons. In addition, we need to be cautious about interpreting the results. Let's consider five specific cautions:

1. *Expectations can influence results.* As we noted in Chapter 1, biases can interfere during every stage of the research process. For example, researchers who expect to find gender differences will often tend to find them.

2. *Biased samples can influence results.* Almost all the research on cognitive abilities focuses on college students (Halpern, 1995). We know almost nothing about the majority of adults who don't attend college. In addition, most of the research on gender comparisons examines U.S. samples (J. Archer, 1996). Our conclusions about gender comparisons might be different if the research participants were more diverse.

3. *The scores of males and females typically produce overlapping distributions.* In order to discuss the concept of overlap, we need to consider frequency distributions. A **frequency distribution** tells us how many people in a sample receive each score. Imagine that we give a vocabulary test to a group of women and men, and the frequency distribution for each gender is as shown in Figure 5.1. The two distributions show only a small overlap, which tells us that these two distributions are very different. The average woman received a score of 80, whereas the average man received a score of 40.

In real life, however, distributions of female and male characteristics rarely show the separation illustrated in Figure 5.1. They are much more likely to show a very large overlap, as illustrated in Figure 5.2. As we have often emphasized in our discussion of Theme 1, men and women are reasonably similar, which means that their scores will overlap considerably. Notice in Figure 5.2 that the average woman received a score of 80, and the average man received a score of 75. This 5-point difference between the average scores looks meager when we compare it to the difference *within* each distribution—a range of about 50 points. As Theme 4 emphasizes, women differ widely from one another; men also show wide variation.

| FIGURE 5.1 | Scores achieved by males and females on a hypothetical test. The small overlap indicates a large gender difference. |

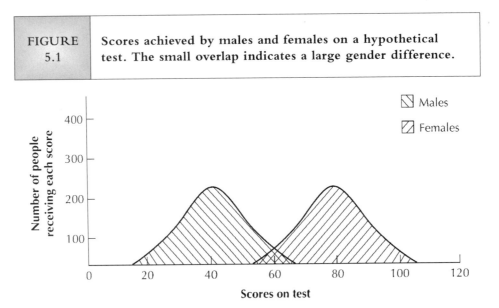

| FIGURE 5.2 | Scores achieved by males and females on a hypothetical test. The large overlap indicates a small gender difference. |

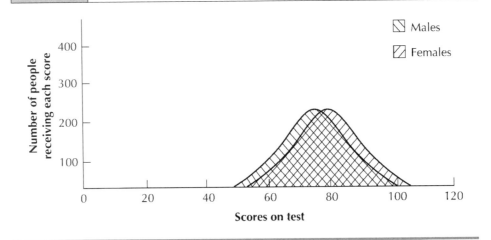

4. *Most females and males receive similar scores.* Whenever the male and female distributions show a large overlap—as in Figure 5.2—the scores for the two groups are likely to be similar. In that distribution, most men and women receive scores between about 65 and 90. (Notice, too, that we could easily find a pair of individuals in Figure 5.2 in which the man receives a *higher* score than the woman.)

5. *Gender differences are not likely to be found in all situations.* You are certainly familiar with this issue from our earlier discussion of Theme 1. Throughout this chapter as well, you will notice that we cannot make general statements about gender differences. Instead, the gender differences often disappear when we test certain kinds of people or when we look at particular situations (Lott, 1996). This observation suggests that gender differences are modifiable, rather than inevitable.

We can draw an important practical conclusion from these last two cautions. Many men and women, in many situations, have remarkably similar psychological characteristics.

Two Approaches for Summarizing Multiple Studies

When psychologists want to obtain an overview of a specific topic, they typically review the research by examining all the studies on that topic. For many years, psychologists who wanted to draw general conclusions about gender comparisons used the box-score approach to reviewing research. When using the **box-score approach,** researchers read through all the appropriate studies on a given topic and draw conclusions based on a tally of their outcomes. Specifically, how many studies show no gender differences, how many show higher scores for men, and how many show higher scores for women? Unfortunately, however, the box-score approach often produces ambiguous tallies. Suppose that 10 studies find no gender differences, 5 show higher scores for men, and 1 shows higher scores for women. One researcher might conclude that no gender differences exist, whereas another might conclude that men score somewhat higher. The box-score approach does not have a systematic method for combining individual studies.

A newer alternative, called the **meta-analysis** technique, provides a statistical method for integrating numerous studies on a single topic. Researchers first locate all appropriate studies on the topic. Then they perform a statistical analysis that combines the results from all these studies. The meta-analysis yields a single number that tells us whether a particular variable has an overall effect. For example, in the case of verbal ability, a meta-analysis can combine numerous previous studies into one enormous super-study that can provide a general picture of whether gender has an overall effect on verbal ability (Kimball, 1995).

A meta-analysis yields a number known as effect size or *d*. Psychologists tend to use the following guidelines: A *d* value of less than 0.35 indicates that the variable being studied has only a small influence. A *d* in the region of 0.50 is generally considered to be a moderate difference. A *d* greater than 0.65 is considered a large difference (J. Cohen, 1969; Hyde & Plant, 1995).

To provide a "yardstick" for effect size, consider that the *d* for the gender difference in height is 2.0—a huge difference in which the overlap between the male and the female distributions is only 11% (Kimball, 1995). Compared to a *d* of 2.0, the *d* values for psychological gender differences are relatively small. In fact, an examination of 171 different meta-analyses from psychology showed that 60% had small effect sizes (*d* less than 0.35); 27% had medium effect sizes (0.36 to 0.65), and only 22% had large effect sizes (greater than 0.66). Only 3% had *d* values greater than 1.0 (Hyde & Plant, 1995).

 Background on Gender Comparisons

1. **In considering research on gender comparisons, we need to emphasize that: (a) expectations and biased samples can influence results; (b) frequency distributions for the scores of males and females typically overlap, so that most females and males receive similar scores; and (c) gender differences are present in some situations and absent in others.**

2. **In contrast to the earlier box-score approach, the meta-analysis technique provides a systematic statistical method for integrating studies on a single topic.**

COGNITIVE ABILITIES

We'll begin our examination of the research by focusing on cognitive abilities. Topics related to achievement motivation will be discussed later in the chapter. Within this current section, we'll focus on three kinds of cognitive abilities for which we have some evidence of gender differences: (1) verbal, (2) mathematical, and (3) spatial abilities.

Throughout this chapter, however, we must emphasize a practical point: The gender differences are so small that they should *not* be considered when people are making career choices. For example, women's scores may be slightly lower than men's scores on tasks that require spatial skills. Specifically, about 7% of males and 3% of females place in the top 5% of the population (Hyde, 1981). This means that, about 2.3 times as many males as females have superior spatial abilities.

Some people argue that women seldom pursue careers in engineering because they lack spatial skills. At present, only 8% of U.S. engineers are women—about 1 female to 12 males (U.S. Department of Labor, 1994). The 2.3:1 ratio for high spatial ability explains only a small portion of the 12:1 gender imbalance among engineers. We need additional explanations to account for the small number of women in fields such as engineering.

We also should keep in mind that the women who are especially competent in areas such as spatial skills perform better than most men in the general population. Therefore, we would be shortsighted to discourage women from professions such as engineering. It would be equally ridiculous to discourage men from professions that require color sensitivity—on the grounds that men are about 20 times as likely as women to have color-vision deficiencies.

Cognitive Abilities That Show No Consistent Gender Differences

Before we examine some areas that show gender *differences,* let's first consider some general categories where gender *similarities* are typically observed.

General Intelligence.   One major area in which females and males are similar is general intelligence, as measured by total scores on an IQ test (e.g., Bishop et al., 1990; Stumpf, 1995). Many intelligence tests have been standardized by eliminating items on which gender differences are found. As a result, gender similarities are encouraged because of the way tests are constructed (Stumpf, 1995). Other research also shows gender similarities in general knowledge about history, geography, and other basic information (Meinz & Salthouse, 1998).

Memory.   In general, men and women are similar in memory ability, though occasional studies report that women are somewhat more accurate (Feingold, 1993; Herlitz et al., 1997; Maccoby & Jacklin, 1974; Meinz & Salthouse, 1998; Skowronski & Thompson, 1990). We'll have to wait for a current meta-analysis to figure out whether gender differences are likely to emerge in certain tasks. The nature of the instructions—and the kinds of items to be remembered—may make a difference. For example, Herrmann and his coauthors (1992) gave men and women a list of items to remember. The list was labeled either "Grocery store list" or "Hardware store list." The items on the list were equally likely for both settings (e.g., brush, nuts, salt, chips). Women remembered more items than men when the list was labeled "Grocery store," but men remembered more items than women when it was labeled "Hardware store."

Complex Cognitive Tasks.   A variety of other challenging intellectual tasks show no gender differences. For example, males and females are equally competent when they form concepts, solve problems, or perform reasoning tasks (Kimura, 1992; Meinz & Salthouse, 1998). Males and females are also similar in their performance on creativity tasks like the one shown in Demonstration 5.1 (Hargreaves, 1977; Maccoby & Jacklin, 1974; Singleton, 1987).

DEMONSTRATION 5.1

A Measure of Creativity

Take a round object such as a glass or a can, and trace 10 circles on a piece of paper. As soon as you are done, go back to the first circle and draw in additional details to create your own design of a real or imaginary object. When you have completed that circle, move on to the next one, and continue with additional circles for a total of 2 minutes. Your goal is to work quickly to produce creative designs.

We have seen that women and men are fairly similar in their general intelligence, memory, and performance on complex cognitive tasks. Keep these important similarities in mind as we explore the three areas in which modest gender differences have sometimes been identified.

Verbal Ability

Females score somewhat higher than males on a small number of verbal tasks, though the overall gender similarities are much more striking. Let's look at three areas of research: the general studies, the Verbal SAT scores, and the research on language disabilities.

General Research.   Some research suggests that girls have larger vocabularies than boys prior to the age of 2, but these gender differences disappear by 3 years of age (Eisenberg et al., 1996; Huttenlocher et al., 1991; Jacklin & Maccoby, 1983). The similarities are more striking than the differences when we consider young school-age children (Cahan & Ganor, 1995; Maccoby & Jacklin, 1974). Therefore, if you plan to teach elementary school, the girls and boys in your class should be comparable in their language skills.

When we consider adolescents and adults, occasional studies find that females excel on verbal tasks. However, other research shows gender similarities in such areas as spelling, vocabulary, and reading comprehension (Collaer & Hines, 1995; Feingold, 1993; Halpern, 1997; Hedges & Nowell, 1995). Small gender differences may be found in some specific areas. For example, females seem to be somewhat better at **verbal fluency,** or naming objects that meet certain criteria, such as beginning with the letter *S* (Halpern, 1997; Kimura, 1992). Ironically, the one general area in which females occasionally have the advantage—verbal abilities—has been studied less extensively than spatial or mathematical skills (Halpern, 1992).

We emphasized earlier that meta-analysis is the ideal statistical tool for combining the results of a number of studies on a specific topic. Janet Hyde and Marcia Linn (1988) conducted a meta-analysis on overall gender comparisons in verbal ability. The average effect size *(d)* was only 0.11, just slightly favoring females. This value is so close to zero that Hyde and Linn concluded that overall gender differences do not exist. Furthermore, the most recent studies were especially likely to show gender similarities. Other researchers have reached the same conclusions, based on standardized test scores for U.S. students (Feingold, 1988; Hedges & Nowell, 1995; Willingham & Cole, 1997).

The Verbal Portion of the SAT.   You may have taken the Scholastic Achievement Test (SAT) when you decided to apply for college admission. The verbal portion of this test covers skills such as reading comprehension, verbal analogies, and sentence completion. In the early years of the SAT, women received somewhat higher scores than men on the verbal portion. In the 1970s, the test was revised; science items were substituted for some humanities items and questions that measured verbal fluency were dropped. After these two adjustments, men began receiving somewhat higher scores than women (Halpern, 1992; Kimball, 1995). For example, in 1997, the average SAT verbal score was 507 for men and 503 for women ("The Nation," 1998).

We've looked at general verbal ability, as well as performance on standardized tests of verbal skills. Let's explore the related topic of language disabilities.

Reading Disabilities and Other Language Problems.   Some research suggests that males are more likely than females to be diagnosed as having language problems. For instance, school systems report reading disabilities about five times as often for boys as for girls (Halpern, 1992).

An important study by Shaywitz and her colleagues (1990) used more objective methods of categorizing students. These researchers pointed out that the term **reading disability** refers to poor reading skills that are not accounted for by the level of general intelligence. Accordingly, they defined reading disability in statistical terms. Specifically, a child's IQ was used to predict a score on a standardized test of reading achievement. Any child whose actual score on the reading test was more than 1.5 standard deviations below the predicted score was categorized as having a reading disability.* The target population for this study included children in 12 cities throughout the state of Connecticut.

As Figure 5.3 shows, when the school systems evaluated the two gender groups, they classified roughly four times as many boys as having reading disabilities. This ratio was consistent with earlier reports (Halpern, 1992). In contrast, when the *objective* test scores were measured, roughly the same number of boys and girls met the criterion of having reading disabilities.

Why do the schools identify so many more boys as having reading problems? Shaywitz and her coauthors (1990) proposed that teachers target more

---

*A score that is 1.5 standard deviations below the prediction means that a child has a reading score in the bottom 7% of those children at his or her IQ level.

FIGURE
5.3

Number of boys and girls with reading disabilities, according to the schools' criterion and the objective research criterion. (Based on Shaywitz et al., 1990)

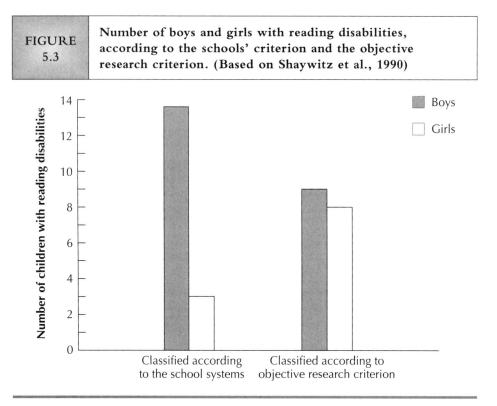

active, less attentive boys as having reading disabilities. They may be referred to a reading clinic on the basis of their behavior, not their reading skills. Equally disturbing is the likelihood that some girls have objective reading disabilities, but they sit quietly in their seats and hide their disabilities (J. Richardson, 1997a). These well-behaved, neglected girls will miss out on the additional tutoring in reading that could help them thrive in school. As Chapter 3 emphasized, girls are often invisible in our schools, and they lose out on educational opportunities.

Incidentally, other research suggests that males are three to four times as likely as females to be classified as stutterers (Halpern, 1994; Skinner & Shelton, 1985). Once again, we might wonder: Is the classification system objective? Are quiet, female stutterers being ignored?

Throughout this section on verbal skills, we have seen a consistent pattern of minimal gender differences, based on a variety of measures. In addition, gender differences in reading disabilities can be traced, at least partially, to a bias in teachers' referrals to reading clinics.

Mathematics Ability

Of all the topics associated with cognitive gender differences, mathematics receives the most attention from researchers and from the popular press. Media reports might create an expectation of large gender differences favoring males. Instead, as you'll see, most of the research shows gender similarities in math ability, and females actually receive higher grades in math courses. Males perform substantially better than females only on the mathematics section of the SAT.

General Research.   Many comparisons of males' and females' ability on mathematics achievement tests show gender similarities (Feingold, 1988; Hedges & Nowell, 1995). Consider, for example, a meta-analysis of 100 studies, based on standardized-test scores of more than 3 million people. (This analysis did not include math SAT scores, which we'll consider shortly.) Averaging across all samples and all tests, Hyde and her coauthors (1990) found a *d* of only 0.15, which is illustrated in Figure 5.4. As you can see, the two distributions are almost identical.

Hyde and her coauthors (1990) found some interesting patterns in the data. For example, females performed somewhat better than males in elementary

| FIGURE 5.4 | **Performance of females and males on all mathematics tests except the SAT, showing an effect side (d) of 0.15.** |

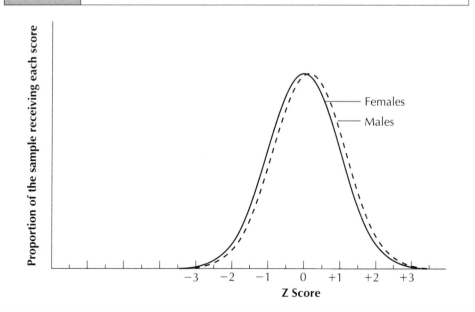

school and junior high. Males performed somewhat better than females during late adolescence and adulthood, especially on tests that measured mathematical problem solving.

Grades in Mathematics Courses.   I often ask students in my classes to raise their hands if they have heard that males receive higher average scores on the math section of the SAT. The hands fly up. Then I ask how many have heard that females receive higher average grades in mathematics *courses*. The hands all drop. Representative studies show, for example, that females earn higher grades in college statistics and in tenth-grade mathematics (C. Brooks, 1987; S. Smith & Walker, 1988).

Meredith Kimball (1989, 1995) reviewed the research on grades in mathematics courses. She found fairly consistent evidence for females' receiving higher grades in their classes, and a recent, comprehensive review reached the same conclusion (Willingham & Cole, 1997). Kimball proposed that females perform better when dealing with familiar situations, such as exams on material covered in a mathematics course. In contrast, boys seem to perform better when dealing with unfamiliar situations, especially the kinds of problems included on the SAT. In any event, Kimball points out that females' high grades in math courses deserve wider publicity. This publicity would encourage females, their parents, and their teachers to have greater confidence in girls' and women's competence in mathematics.

The SAT.   Of all the research in cognitive gender differences, the topic that has received the most media attention is performance on the math portion of the SAT when it was given to an unusual sample—seventh- and eighth-grade students. We'll first address these studies of junior high students and then consider the gender comparisons when the test is given to high school students. Finally, we will examine general issues concerning the math portion of the SAT.

Beginning in 1980, Camilla Benbow and Julian Stanley began analyzing data in what they called a Study of Mathematically Precocious Youth, or SMPY (e.g., Benbow, 1988; Benbow & Stanley, 1980). In this project, students who received high scores on a standardized math achievement test were invited to take the SAT. As we discuss the SMPY, keep in mind that we are discussing a small, select sample of 12- to 14-year-olds taking a test designed for high school students. These points are often omitted from discussions of the study in the popular press (Hyde, 1997).

The SMPY research with junior high school students demonstrated consistent gender differences favoring males on the mathematics part of the SAT. In a typical report, for example, the ratio of boys to girls was 13 to 1 for those scoring above 700. We should emphasize that a score above 700 is astonishing for such young students, especially because they couldn't have taken courses such as trigonometry to prepare them for the SAT problems.

Everyone agrees that a 13-to-1 ratio is impressive. However, the nature of any frequency distribution guarantees that ratios will be extreme when we consider only the very highest portion of a distribution for which we have a gender difference. Also, we really don't know whether the school personnel encouraged the very brightest girls to take the SAT, or whether the girls were less likely than the boys to practice their math skills before taking the SAT (Kimball, 1995).

What happens when the math portion of the SAT is given to the high school populations for which it is intended? According to the data for 1998, women received an average score of 493, in contrast to 530 for men ("The Nation," 1998). Part of this gender difference can be explained by the fact that females are more likely than males to take the SAT; as we saw in Chapter 4, in every ethnic group, females are more likely than males to attend college. The sample of females therefore includes a greater percentage of average-ability students, whereas the sample of males has a greater percentage of high-ability students.

Let's shift now to the more general question of the validity of the SAT. A test has high **validity** if it measures what it is supposed to measure. For example, the SAT is supposed to predict students' grades in college courses. In general, the SAT is valid, because it does predict college grades (D. Leonard & Jiang, 1999; Willingham & Cole, 1997). However, the math SAT has a specific validity problem because it *underpredicts* the grades that women will receive in college math courses.

Let's consider this underprediction problem in more detail. Wainer and Steinberg (1992) conducted a large-scale study of roughly 47,000 students at 51 different colleges and universities. Each of these students had taken the SAT and had also completed a mathematics course in the first semester of college. Wainer and Steinberg then matched male and female students in terms of the type of college math course taken and the grade received. The researchers found that the women had received SAT-math scores that were an average of 33 points lower than those of the men with whom they were matched. For example, suppose that Susan Jones and Robert Smith both received a B in calculus at College X. Looking back at their SAT-math scores, Susan might have had a score of 600, compared to 633 for Robert. Susan's SAT-math score *underpredicted* her grade in calculus, relative to Robert's score (Linn & Kessel, 1995).

Using similar methods, Leonard and Jiang (1999) analyzed the scores of about 10,000 students at the University of California at Berkeley. They discovered that the SAT scores underpredicted women's undergraduate grade-point averages by 0.1. This may sound trivial until you realize the implications: Each year, between 200 and 300 women are denied admission to this university because the SAT underpredicts their college grades. In addition, women are shortchanged when college scholarships are awarded on the basis of scores on tests similar to the SAT (Winerip, 1994).

Based on validity studies like these, universities such as Rutgers, MIT, and Penn State have modified their policies by reducing the score required on the SAT-math. Other institutions—such as Bates College, Middlebury College, and

Union College—have stopped using the SAT (Linn & Kessel, 1995). Colleges and universities need some adjustments in their admissions policies when the SAT underpredicts college performance for female students.

Spatial Ability

Most people are very familiar with the first two cognitive abilities discussed in this chapter—verbal and mathematics abilities. Spatial abilities are less well known. **Spatial abilities** assess skill in understanding, perceiving, and manipulating shapes and figures. Spatial ability is important in many everyday activities, such as playing electronic games, reading road maps, and arranging furniture in a dormitory room.

Most researchers have concluded that gender differences in spatial ability, with males performing better than females, are larger than in any other cognitive area (M. Crawford et al., 1995; Geary, 1995; Halpern, 1997). They also agree that spatial ability is not unitary. Instead, it has three separate components (Linn & Petersen, 1986; Voyer et al., 1995). Let's consider each of these components separately.

Spatial Visualization.   Tasks that use **spatial visualization** require complex processing of spatially presented information. For example, an embedded-figure test requires locating a particular pattern or object that is hidden in a larger design. Demonstration 5.2a illustrates three examples of an embedded-figure test. As a child, you may have tried similar games, perhaps searching for faces in a woodland scene.

Several meta-analyses and large-scale studies have concluded that males and females perform fairly similarly on tasks requiring spatial visualization (e.g., Feingold, 1988; Hedges & Nowell, 1995; Linn & Petersen, 1986). For example, a recent meta-analysis of 116 studies produced a d of 0.19, a small gender difference suggesting that males are slightly better on this task (Voyer et al., 1995). Glance again, however, at Figure 5.4 for a graph of a similar effect size ($d = 0.15$). As you can see, the overlap for the two distributions is very substantial.

Let's consider one component of visualization, the ability to learn map information. One study found that males performed better, but a similar study reported no gender differences (Beatty & Bruellman, 1987; Galea & Kimura, 1993). Related research showed that males were better than females in finding their way back to the starting point, from a distant location. However, other measures revealed no gender differences (Lawton, 1996; Lawton et al., 1996). Other studies suggest that males score higher on tests of geography map skills (Henrie et al., 1997). As you can see, the picture is mixed; gender differences are not consistent.

Spatial Perception.   In **spatial perception** tests, the participants are asked to identify a horizontal or vertical location without being distracted by irrelevant information. One example of this skill, a water-level test, is shown in

DEMONSTRATION 5.2

Examples of Tests of Spatial Ability

Try these three kinds of tests of spatial ability.

a. EMBEDDED-FIGURE TEST. In each of the three units, study the figure on the left. Then cover it up and try to find where it is hidden in the figure on the right. The left-hand figure may need to be shifted in order to locate it in the right-hand figure.

b. WATER-LEVEL TEST. Imagine that this woman is drinking from a glass that is half-filled with water. Draw a line across the glass to indicate where the water line belongs (Based on Kalichman, 1989.)

c. MENTAL-ROTATION TEST. If you mentally rotate the figure on the left, which of the five figures on the right would you obtain?

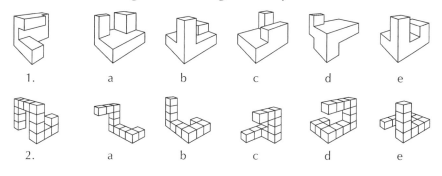

The answers to these three tests appear at the end of the chapter.

Demonstration 5.2b. Spatial perception is also assessed by the rod-and-frame test, in which participants sit in a darkened room and look at a single rod, which is surrounded by a rectangular frame. The participants are instructed to adjust the rod so that it is in a true vertical position, without being distracted by the cues from the obviously tilted frame. Meta-analyses of gender comparisons for spatial perception show that males receive somewhat higher scores, with effect sizes in the range of 0.40 (Linn & Petersen, 1986; Voyer et al., 1995).

Vasta and his colleagues (1996) discovered that females performed as accurately as males, following a brief training session. Schools offer remedial training for children who have reading problems. Why not offer remedial training in spatial skills—the one area where females experience the greatest disadvantage (Hyde & McKinley, 1997)?

Mental Rotation.   A test of **mental rotation** measures the ability to rotate a two- or three-dimensional figure rapidly and accurately. This skill is illustrated in the two problems of Demonstration 5.2c. The mental rotation task produces the largest gender differences of all spatial skills, when measured in terms of performance speed. The effect sizes are generally in the range of 0.50 to 0.75 (Linn & Petersen, 1985; Voyer et al., 1995). Even though the gender differences on mental-rotation tasks are relatively large, we still need to keep the data in perspective. An effect size as large as 0.75 is certainly larger than the other cognitive effect sizes. However, it is trivial compared to the effect size of 2.00 for height, which we discussed earlier (Kimball, 1995).

Furthermore, Favreau (1993) pointed out that significant gender differences often arise from studies in which most males and females actually receive similar scores. Look at Figure 5.5, which Favreau derived from earlier research by Kail and his colleagues (1979). As you can see, most males and females received scores between 2 and 8. The statistically significant gender difference can be almost entirely traced to 20% of the females, who had very slow mental-rotation speeds (Favreau & Everett, 1996).

Other research (e.g., Sharps et al., 1993) shows that gender differences on mental rotation tasks depend on how the task is described to participants. For example, Sharps and his colleagues (1994) found that men performed much better than women when the instructions emphasized the usefulness of these spatial abilities in stereotypically masculine professions, such as piloting military aircraft. When the instructions emphasized how these abilities could help in stereotypically feminine occupations—such as interior decoration—the gender differences disappeared.

What can we conclude about spatial abilities? Even the most well-established gender difference—mental rotation—turns out to be elusive. In fact, any potential deficit is limited to only a small proportion of females, and the differences seem to evaporate when the instructions emphasize that a spatial skill is related to a traditionally feminine area of interest. In short, this erratic gender difference should not have major implications for women's lives. And this erratic difference certainly cannot explain why only 8% of U.S. engineers are female!

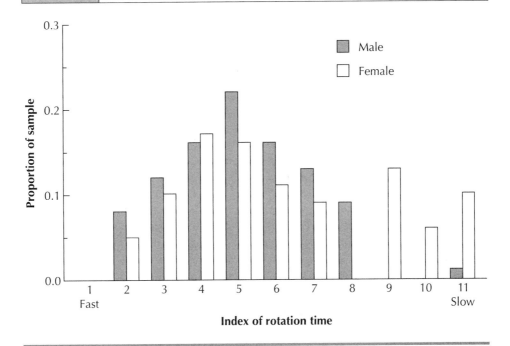

| FIGURE 5.5 | Amount of time required to mentally rotate a geometric figure. Note that faster scores represent better performance. (Based on Favreau, 1993; Kail et al., 1979) |

Explaining the Gender Comparisons

We began this chapter by considering a large number of cognitive skills on-which males and females are similar. Then we saw that the gender differences in most verbal skills and most mathematical skills are minimal. However, the gender differences in mathematical problem solving, spatial perception, and mental rotation are large enough to deserve a closer look. We'll first consider the biological explanations, and then the social explanations.

Biological Explanations.   A major article in *Newsweek* proclaimed that "Men and women use their brains differently" (Begley, 1995, p. 48) and clearly implied that gender differences in cognitive performance can be explained by biological factors. As Carol Tavris (1992) pointed out earlier, it's ironic that the media and some researchers are so eager to embrace a biological explanation for gender differences that are not even well established.

In a clear presentation of biological perspectives, Diane Halpern (1992) divided the biological explanations into three major categories: (1) genetics, (2) hormones, and (3) brain organization. Let's consider each of these:

1. A genetic explanation suggests that spatial ability is a recessive trait carried on the X chromosome. However, research has not supported this theoretical possibility (Halpern, 1992; J. Richardson, 1997b).

2. Hormones are critically important before birth and during puberty. Could the level of circulating hormones in males and females also account for gender differences in cognitive skills? Here, the results are often complex or contradictory (J. Richardson, 1997b). For example, men seem to perform better on spatial tasks if they have low levels of the "male hormone" testosterone, whereas women seem to perform better if they have high levels of this hormone (Kimura, 1987).

3. The last category of biological explanations focuses on brain organization. Chapter 1 noted that researchers at the beginning of the 20th century searched for differences in male and female brain structures; that search continues today.

Current researchers in the area of gender differences typically favor some version of an explanation that emphasizes brain lateralization. **Lateralization** means that the two halves (or hemispheres) of the brain function somewhat differently. In general, the left hemisphere specializes in language or verbal tasks, whereas the right hemisphere typically specializes in spatial tasks. (For easy recall, remember that *left* and *language* both begin with the letter *l*.) For most people, either hemisphere *can* process both language and spatial material. However, the left hemisphere tends to be faster and more accurate on language tasks, and the right hemisphere tends to be faster and more accurate on spatial tasks.

Numerous theories have tried to account for how lateralization might explain gender differences. Most of these theories argue that males have more complete lateralization or processing specialization. For example, males may process spatial tasks exclusively in the right hemisphere, whereas females may display less complete lateralization (Breedlove, 1994; Halpern, 1996). When females work on a spatial task, verbal information may "spill over" into the right hemisphere and interfere with that hemisphere's ability to process spatial information.

More recent theories about lateralization are more complex. For instance, some theorists suggest a complicated relationship among handedness, gender, and performance on spatial tasks (e.g., Casey, 1996; Halpern, 1996).

These brain organization theories have one problem: They do not provide convincing evidence that males have more complete lateralization. For example, one study was widely cited as "proof" that men's brains show more lateralization (B. Shaywitz et al., 1995). The popular media failed to emphasize that 8 of the 19 female participants showed strong lateralization, rather than the balanced-hemisphere pattern proposed by those favoring gender differences in brain organization (Favreau, 1997b).

In addition, the media typically fail to mention that much of the research uses small samples—only nine individuals participated in one study (Witelson et al., 1995). Still other research acknowledges gender similarities that you'll never read about in your local newspaper. For instance, a study by Gur and his colleagues (1995) concluded that the results "remind us that the two cerebral hemispheres and the brains of men and women are fundamentally more similar than different" (p. 530).

Another major problem with lateralization theories is that people whose brains are more lateralized do not *consistently* perform differently on cognitive tasks (Bleier, 1991; Fausto-Sterling, 1992). In addition, even if we could demonstrate major gender differences in brain lateralization, no one has yet shown that these brain differences actually *cause* the gender differences on cognitive tests (Hyde, 1996b). An alternative possibility is that males and females have different kinds of experiences (for example, with toys emphasizing spatial tasks). We know that brain development is influenced by experience, and the spatial experience may produce greater lateralization in male brains.

Conceivably, at some time in the future, researchers may identify a biological component that helps explain gender differences. However, we need to remember that the differences requiring explanation are neither widespread nor extraordinarily large. Indeed, biological explanations may be more powerful than they need to be, in order to explain such small and inconsistent gender differences. Relying on biological explanations is like trying to kill a fly with a baseball bat when a "subtler" instrument—such as a fly swatter—would be more appropriate.

Social Explanations.   Many theorists have provided social explanations for cognitive gender differences. These explanations can be divided into two categories: (1) different experiences for males and females; and (2) different attitudes among males and females.

Experience with a subject clearly influences a person's competence. If you've had frequent experience with maps and other spatial tasks, you'll perform a mental rotation task quickly (M. Crawford & Chaffin, 1997). Let's examine gender differences in experience.

1. College-bound males are about 10% more likely than their female classmates to take four or more years of high school mathematics. They are also much more likely than females to take science courses such as physics, which provide extra practice in solving math problems (Chipman, 1996).

2. Males and females differ in the amount of experience they have with mathematics outside of school. Young boys are more likely to own math and spatial electronic games (J. Richardson, 1997a). Boys are also more likely to belong to a chess club, be members of a math team, learn about numbers in sports, and attend computer summer camp (Hyde, 1996a; L. Jackson et al., 1995; Subrahmanyam & Greenfield, 1994).

3. When they show how people use mathematics, elementary textbooks may include more pictures of boys than girls. The girls may also be shown in helping roles (Kimball, 1995). Illustrations in computer magazines show twice as many men, compared to women (Ware & Stuck, 1985). As Chapters 2 and 3 emphasized, images of competent females can boost the performance of girls and women. If they have more positive visions, young girls may not develop the expectation that "women and mathematics don't mix" (Henrion, 1997).

4. Teachers may provide different experiences for males than for females. For example, teachers tend to explain boys' poor performance in math by saying that they didn't try hard enough. To explain girls' poor performance, the teachers cite a lack of ability (Fennema, 1990). This experience can certainly influence girls' attitudes and feelings of competence, a topic we'll now consider.

We have reviewed four ways in which males and females may differ in mathematics *experience*. Let's now turn to gender differences in *attitudes* about mathematics.

1. By early adolescence, boys perceive themselves as more competent in math than girls do, even though boys may actually receive lower grades (Eccles, 1994; L. Jackson et al., 1994; C. Steele, 1997).

2. By high school, many students believe that math is a male domain, even though females are almost as likely as males to be enrolled in math courses (Chipman, 1996; Henrion, 1997). As gender schema theory points out (Chapter 3), people prefer activities that are consistent with their gender role. Accordingly, many females may avoid math because it seems "too masculine."

3. Males generally have more positive attitudes toward math, and they are less anxious about it (Eccles, 1994; Hyde et al., 1990; Tobias, 1993). Students with negative attitudes about math are likely to avoid careers in this area, even if their math skills are strong (Chipman et al., 1992).

4. Parents' attitudes may influence their children's self-confidence in an indirect fashion. Specifically, if parents hold strong stereotypes about females' poor performance in math, they may convey these stereotypes to their children (Eccles, 1994; Eccles et al., 1993).

5. Females may be more cautious and careful in their test-taking strategies (Cahan & Ganor, 1995; Willingham & Cole, 1997). This approach may lead them to pause and double-check an answer on a mental rotation task. A strategy of risky guessing is often useful in mathematics problem solving and on the SAT.

We have examined a large number of factors that can contribute to gender differences in spatial and mathematics tasks. Some factors may turn out to be less important as we move into the 21st century. For example, one relatively recent study showed that girls and boys in this sample had similarly positive attitudes toward math, and their teachers treated the children in a gender-fair manner (M. Gilbert, 1996). If parents and schools could encourage this kind of equity, we might see a further reduction in cognitive gender differences.

 Cognitive Abilities

1. **No consistent gender differences are found in general intelligence, memory, concept formation, problem solving, reasoning, or creativity.**

2. **At present, gender differences in verbal skills and language disabilities are minimal.**

3. **Gender differences in mathematics ability are negligible on most tests, though males excel in problem-solving ability after junior high. Females generally receive higher grades than males in their math courses. Males receive higher scores on the SAT mathematics test, a test that underpredicts women's college grades.**

4. **Gender differences are minimal on spatial visualization tasks, moderate on spatial perception tasks, and more substantial on mental rotation tasks. Still, most males and females receive similar scores. Also, gender differences on spatial tasks disappear after a training session and when task instructions are altered.**

5. **Biological explanations for gender differences in cognitive skills include genetics, hormones, and brain organization (typically, lateralization); none of these explanations is strongly supported by the research.**

6. **Social explanations for gender differences in cognitive skills include several that emphasize gender differences in experience (coursework, extracurricular activities, textbook illustrations, and classroom treatment). Several other social explanations focus on math attitudes (perceptions of math competence, stereotypes about math being masculine, attitudes toward math, parents' attitudes, and test-taking strategies).**

ACHIEVEMENT MOTIVATION AND RELATED TOPICS

In the preceding section on gender comparisons in cognitive abilities, we concluded that men and women are generally similar in their thinking skills. The differences are never large enough to explain the tremendous imbalances in the gender ratios found in many professions. Some observers argue that these imbalances can be traced, instead, to women's lackof motivation; perhaps women simply don't want to achieve. As A. Kahn and Yoder (1989) noted, many theorists have tried to explain women's absence in certain prestigious fields in terms of personal "deficiencies" that inhibit their achievement. However, you've seen that females actually earn higher grades in school than males do, and females are more likely than males to enroll in college. As we'll see in this section, the research reveals similarities in almost every area related to achievement. (We'll explore other explanations for women's career patterns in Chapter 7.)

Biases in the Research on Achievement Motivation

Before we examine the research on achievement motivation, we should note some interesting biases in this field. First, the tasks on which success is measured are usually stereotypically masculine (Todoroff, 1994). Success may be represented by achievement at a prestigious occupation, academic excellence, and other accomplishments associated with traditionally masculine values. Achievements that are associated with traditionally feminine values receive little or no attention. An adolescent woman may manage to entertain a group of six toddlers, so that they are all playing cooperatively. However, psychologists don't typically include this kind of accomplishment among the topics of achievement motivation. Psychologists also don't broaden their views of achievement to include comforting a distressed friend or making a stranger feel welcome. As Theme 3 emphasizes, topics that are traditionally associated with women are underrepresented in the psychological literature.

A second bias applies to most of psychology. Nearly all research on achievement motivation is conducted with college students. Academic achievement is especially important for people in this selected sample. Researchers rarely examine achievement motivation in older populations (Todoroff, 1994). Also, researchers rarely investigate achievement in people of color or in populations outside North America (Dabul & Russo, 1996; Mednick & Thomas, 1993).

It's interesting to speculate about alternative definitions that might need to be developed for these other groups, who might not focus on academic achievement. For example, think how achievement motivation might be defined for middle-age employed individuals, or for people who have recently retired. Also, think how achievement motivation might be defined in a culture that places less emphasis on individual achievement—and more emphasis on the well-being of the community—in comparison to North Americans. Perhaps achievement motivation might be measured in terms of a person's ability to work well with others, or a person's knowledge about the community's history. As you read through this section, keep in mind that almost all the research on gender comparisons focuses on academic achievement, rather than a broader perspective.

Let's begin our exploration of motivation by discussing how women and men are fairly similar in their desire for achievement, as well as their concerns about the negative consequences of success. We'll see that gender differences are sometimes found in self-confidence, though gender similarities are often reported. We'll also see that women and men provide similar reasons for their achievements.

DEMONSTRATION 5.3

The Thematic Apperception Test

Look at the picture below and write a paragraph about it. Who are the people involved? What are they doing, and what are they thinking?

Achievement Motivation

Try Demonstration 5.3, which illustrates achievement motivation. **Achievement motivation** is the desire to do well on tasks and to persist on these tasks (Graham, 1994; Reeve, 1997). A person who is high in achievement motivation might try for the highest A in organic chemistry, the leading part in the college musical, or a top award in athletics.

Achievement motivation is often measured with the Thematic Apperception Test (TAT), which asks people to create stories for pictures similar to the one in Demonstration 5.3. A person receives a high achievement-motivation score if these stories emphasize working hard and excelling. The research—conducted with both Black and White participants—shows that males and females are similar in achievement motivation (Mednick & Thomas, 1993; Spence & Helmreich, 1983; A. Stewart & Chester, 1982).

DEMONSTRATION 5.4

Completing a Story

Write a paragraph in response to one of the following beginning sentences.

If you are a female, complete this sentence with a paragraph: "After first-term finals, Anne finds herself at the top of her medical school class. . . . "

If you are a male, complete this sentence with a paragraph: "After first-term finals, John finds himself at the top of his medical school class. . . . "

Travis and her colleagues (1991) assessed achievement motivation by using another approach. They asked students to recall and describe an event that had occurred in their lives within the past year. Later, they rated the event on a number of scales, such as the extent to which the event described mastering skills (e.g., receiving grades or getting a job). Gender differences were not significant; both men and women emphasized mastery in their descriptions.

Try Demonstration 5.4 before reading further.

Fear of Success

At the end of the 1960s, Matina Horner proposed that women are more likely than men to be afraid of success (e.g., Horner, 1968, 1978). Despite dozens of studies showing gender similarities, the idea captured media attention and the concept became very popular (Mednick & Thomas, 1993).

More specifically, Horner proposed that a woman who is high in **fear of success** is afraid that success in competitive achievement situations will produce unpleasant consequences, including unpopularity and a loss of femininity. Men are not afraid of success, Horner said, because achievement is part of the masculine gender role.

When Horner used a technique like the one illustrated in Demonstration 5.4, she found that 62% of the women and 9% of the men showed fear of success, a highly significant gender difference. Women tended to write stories in which Anne was socially rejected. Men tended to write stories in which John's hard work brought rich rewards. The popular press was delighted—at last, here was a reason to justify why women were less successful than men!

In the years following Horner's original study, the research showed consistent gender similarities in the fear of success in European American populations (e.g., Mednick & Thomas, 1993; Paludi, 1984; Zuckerman & Wheeler, 1975). Some studies hinted that Mexican American, Black, and Hopi Indian women may be reluctant to do their best when their achievement might diminish the self-esteem of men (Gonzalez, 1988; Weisfeld et al., 1982, 1983). It's not yet clear whether the pattern of gender similarities can be extended to all ethnic groups (Frieze et al., 1991).

Confidence in Your Own Achievement and Ability

Self-confidence is another concept that is intertwined with achievement motivation. As we'll see, gender differences do sometimes emerge in two areas: (1) men often report more self-confidence than women; and (2) men's self-confidence may be less influenced by the evaluations of other people.

Level of Self-Confidence.   Several studies suggest that men are more self-confident about their ability than women are (Eccles et al., 1998). For example, a study by Furnham and Rawles (1995) found that males estimated their own IQs at an average of 118, in contrast to an estimated average of 112 for females. However, the research on self-confidence generally shows that the specific conditions of a task influence the results. Let's consider several relevant factors:

1. Men are more self-confident than women when making public estimates; gender similarities are found for private estimates (J. Clark & Zehr, 1993; Daubman et al., 1992). An interesting study demonstrated that women were especially likely to give low estimates for their grade point average when another student had already announced she had received a C average (Heatherington et al., 1993). One possible explanation is that women are more likely than men to prefer presenting themselves in a modest fashion to other people (Daubman et al., 1992; Wosinska et al., 1996).

2. Men are more self-confident than women on a task that is considered traditionally masculine; gender similarities are found for neutral or traditionally feminine tasks (Carr et al., 1985; Lenney, 1977; Nicholls, 1975). On one traditionally feminine task—anticipated self-confidence in comforting a friend—women were actually *more* confident than men (Clark, 1993).

3. Men are more self-confident than women when no feedback is provided; gender similarities are found when people are given clear feedback about how they had performed. For example, in one study, people were told that they would be asked to unscramble some anagrams. They were then instructed to rate how well they expected to do on this task (Sleeper & Nigro, 1987). At this point, before they had any feedback about their performance, males were significantly more self-confident than females. Then everyone actually worked on the anagram task and could see how well they performed on the task. In other words, they received clear performance-based feedback about their skills. Once again, everybody rated their self-confidence. Women and men now provided similar estimates. (Try Demonstration 5.5 before reading further.)

DEMONSTRATION 5.5

Reactions to Comments from Other People

Imagine that you have given a presentation on a project to an important group of people. Afterward, someone approaches you and says that you did a very good job: you were clear and articulate, and your ideas were interesting. Someone else rejects everything you had to say, and disagrees with all of your proposals. Then a third person comments, not on the content of your presentation, but on your excellent speaking style.

How much would the feedback from these other people influence your self-confidence? Would your confidence rise or fall, depending on the nature of the comments, or would your self-evaluations tend to remain fairly constant?

(Based on Roberts, 1991, p. 297.)

An interesting question to consider is one we originally raised in Chapter 2. Many studies show gender differences in self-confidence. Does this mean that women are *underconfident,* underestimating how well they perform? Alternately, are men *overconfident,* inflating their estimates of their abilities? Theorists have often discussed the research as if the male level of confidence is standard or normative, whereas the female level is defective. In reality, most of the research doesn't tell us which gender's self-evaluations are more accurate, though this would be useful information when designing future research. Until we have this information, be suspicious of any media reports that women need to boost their self-confidence!

Self-Confidence and Evaluation of Others.   We've seen that gender differences in self-confidence sometimes emerge, especially for public estimates of ability, for traditionally masculine tasks, and when no feedback is provided. Now let's consider a second issue, focusing on the *stability* of a person's self-confidence. Specifically, research by Tomi-Ann Roberts and Susan Nolen-Hoeksema (1989, 1994) suggests that women's self-confidence is influenced by comments from other people. In contrast, men's self-confidence is more stable. Compared to these findings, how did you respond to Demonstration 5.5?

In an important study on responses to others' comments, Roberts and Nolen-Hoeksema (1989) asked students to work on a series of challenging cognitive tasks. After several minutes, the participants rated their self-confidence in terms of the likelihood that they could do well on the task. A few minutes later, half of the participants—chosen at random—received positive comments from the researcher. ("You are doing very well. You are above average at this point in the task.") The other half of the participants received negative comments. ("You are not doing very well. You are below average at this point in the task.") Several minutes later, they all rated their self-confidence a second time.

Figure 5.6 shows the change in self-confidence between the first rating period and the second. Notice that the men's self-confidence ratings were not significantly changed by the nature of the comments other people provided. When the men received positive comments, their self-confidence barely rose; their self-confidence dipped only slightly following negative comments. In contrast, the women's self-confidence rose dramatically after receiving positive comments, and it fell even more dramatically after receiving negative comments.

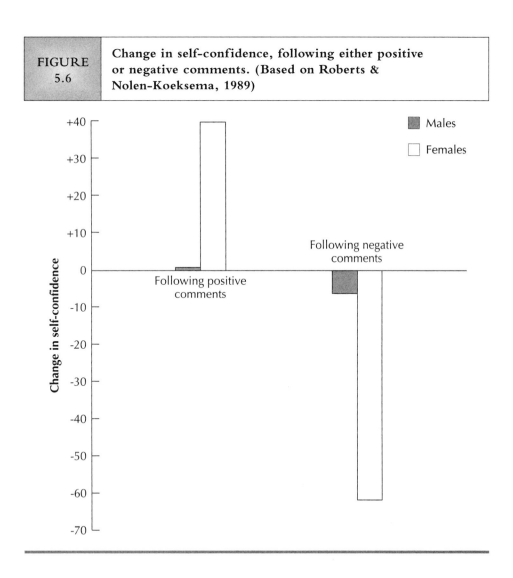

| FIGURE 5.6 | Change in self-confidence, following either positive or negative comments. (Based on Roberts & Nolen-Koeksema, 1989) |

DEMONSTRATION 5.6

Explaining Successful Performance

Think about the last time you received a good grade on a test. A number of different factors could have been responsible for your success. Four possible factors are listed below. You have 100 points to divide among these four factors. Assign points to reflect the extent to which each factor contributed to your success; the points must add up to 100.

_____ I have high ability for the subject that was covered on that test.

_____ I put a lot of effort into studying for that test.

_____ The test was easy.

_____ It was just luck.

But *why* should men and women react so differently to people's comments? In further research, Roberts and Nolen-Hoeksema (1994) replicated these general findings. They also discovered that women were more likely than men to believe that other people's evaluations were accurate assessments of their performance. Women are therefore more likely to use the information from these evaluations in assessing their own performance—even when the evaluations are not accurate.

When I first read about these gender differences in response to others' comments, I'll confess that I was dismayed. Men apparently trust their own judgments, whereas women seem to adjust their self-confidence in response to whatever comments they happen to hear. But then I recalled the male-as-normative issue, discussed in Chapter 2. Maybe we shouldn't conclude that men are stable and women are fickle. Instead, men may be overly rigid, trusting their initial judgment, even when it may be inappropriate. In contrast, women may be appropriately flexible—willing to listen and respond to new information!

Ideally, people *should* respond to evaluations from well-informed experts (presumably including the researcher conducting a psychology experiment). We don't yet know whether women are influenced by people whose judgments are untrustworthy.

Attributions for Your Own Success

Be sure to try Demonstration 5.6 before reading further. This demonstration asks you to make attributions about your own performance on an achievement task. **Attributions** are explanations about the causes of your behavior. When you have been successful on an achievement task, you generally attribute that success to some combination of four factors: (1) ability, (2) effort, (3) task easiness, and (4) luck. Keep your own answers to Demonstration 5.6 in mind as we examine the research on gender comparisons in attribution patterns.

Incidentally, this topic of attributions may seem somewhat familiar; we examined a similar topic in Chapter 2. In that chapter, we saw that the gender of the *stimulus* influences attributions; specifically, when people make judgments about men, they tend to attribute the success of men to their high ability. In contrast, when people make judgments about women, they tend to attribute the success of women to other factors, such as an easy task or luck. In this chapter, however, we are examining the gender of the *subject.* In particular, we will see whether women and men use different attributions when making judgments about *their own* success.

The research on attribution illustrates once more the value of meta-analysis. During the 1970s, several studies suggested that, when males are successful, they give credit to their ability. In contrast, when females are successful, they choose explanations other than ability (e.g., Deaux, 1979). For example, a woman who has received a high exam score might say, "Well, this test was relatively easy, and I really studied hard for it, so that's why I received an A."

However, two meta-analyses have now been conducted on the attribution data (Sohn, 1982; Whitley et al., 1986). Combined with additional reviews by Frieze and her coauthors (1982) and Mednick and Thomas (1993), the research suggests that the overall gender differences are minimal. In the analysis of Whitley and his colleagues (1986), for instance, no effect size was larger than 0.20.

Consider some representative research. Russo and her colleague (1991) asked public administrators to evaluate the importance of a variety of factors in explaining their own professional success. Both men and women explained their success in terms of ability and hard work, and the two genders supplied similar ratings for these two factors. Male and female students also provided similar attributions for a recent personal achievement, according to Travis and her coauthors (1991). Finally, Gaeddert (1987) found gender similarities when people made attributions for outcomes in a wide variety of areas, such as scholastics, friendship, and sports.

In short, attributions for success tend to show the same pattern of gender similarities that we observed in this chapter's discussion of cognitive abilities, achievement motivation, and fear of success. (Remember, however, that gender differences are somewhat common in areas related to self-confidence.)

Although gender similarities in attributions are most common, gender differences are found in some social settings and on some kinds of tasks:

1. Women are likely to avoid saying "I did well because I have high ability" when making public statements, whereas men are somewhat more comfortable about mentioning "high ability" in public. When men and women provide attributions in private, their responses may be similar (Berg et al., 1981).

2. Men are more likely than women to cite ability as an explanation for their success on stereotypically masculine tasks, such as mathematics tests or

performance as a manager (Eccles et al., 1984; Stipek, 1984). However, women are more likely than men to use ability explanations on stereotypically feminine tasks, such as comforting a friend (R. A. Clark, 1993).

3. Women who are low in ability and general achievement motivation—and who support traditional gender roles—are more likely than men to attribute their success to luck. In contrast, women who are high in ability and general achievement motivation—and who are nontraditional—are fairly similar to men; they typically attribute their success to ability (Crombie, 1983; Eccles et al., 1984).

At the beginning of this section on achievement motivation, we saw that theorists have often favored a "blame-the-person" rationale to explain why women are less likely than men to hold prestigious positions in society. However, the discussion of attributions reveals the same pattern we have found throughout most parts of this chapter. Consistent with Theme 1, women and men are typically similar. When gender differences do emerge, they can usually be traced to characteristics of the social setting or the task. In the case of attribution patterns, the gender differences are so small and readily modifiable that a blame-the-person explanation does not seem useful.

This chapter has illustrated that women resemble men in both cognitive ability and motivational factors. In Chapter 6, we will consider gender comparisons in social and personality characteristics. Then, in Chapter 7, we will turn our attention to women's work experiences to try to identify external factors that account for gender differences in employment patterns.

 SECTION SUMMARY *Achievement Motivation and Related Topics*

1. **The research on topics related to achievement motivation typically focuses on stereotypically masculine tasks and typically studies European American college students.**

2. **Women and men are similar in their achievement motivation.**

3. **Horner proposed that women are more likely than men to have a fear of success. Current researchers conclude that there are gender similarities in this area.**

4. **Men are often more self-confident than women on achievement tasks, especially those involving public estimates of self-confidence, traditionally masculine tasks, or no feedback on performance.**

5. **Women's self-confidence is more likely than men's to be influenced by comments from other people.**

6. **Women and men tend to use similar attributions when explaining their successes. However, gender differences may emerge when making statements in public, and when performing gender-stereotyped**

tasks; traditionally feminine women who have low ability and motivation are likely to avoid attributing their success to ability.

CHAPTER REVIEW
QUESTIONS

1. Suppose that your local newspaper carries the headline: "Test Shows Males More Creative." The article reports the average male scored 78 on a creativity test, compared to 75 for females. Based on the cautions discussed at the beginning of this chapter, why would you be hesitant to conclude that the gender differences in creativity are substantial?

2. At the beginning of the discussion of cognitive abilities, we emphasized that we should not discourage people from pursuing careers on the basis of their gender. Considering the information about cognitive abilities and topics related to achievement motivation, what evidence do we have for this point?

3. Recall the cognitive abilities for which no consistent gender differences have been reported. Think of several men and several women whom you know well. Do the conclusions about those abilities match your observations about these individuals?

4. Imagine that a third-grade teacher comments to you that the girls in her class have much better verbal abilities than the boys. What would you answer, based on the information in this chapter?

5. The sections on mathematics and spatial abilities showed inconsistent gender differences. Which areas showed the largest gender differences, and which showed the smallest? Which potential biological and social explanations might account for these differences?

6. A woman you know has read an article about fear of success in a popular magazine marketed to young businesswomen. She asks you whether the article is correct: Do women have a significantly higher fear of success than men do? Answer her with the information from this chapter.

7. The research on topics related to achievement motivation illustrates how gender differences rarely apply to all people in all situations. Describe some variables that determine whether gender differences will be found in self-confidence and in attributions for one's own success. Although the research on fear of success shows gender similarities, which of these variables may also apply to fear of success?

8. We discussed three factors that influence whether gender differences will be found with respect to self-confidence in achievement settings. Keeping these factors in mind, think of a concrete situation in which gender differences are likely to be very large. Then think of an example of a situation in which gender differences should be minimal.

9. In Chapter 6, we'll see that, in comparison to men, women are somewhat more attuned to the emotions of other people. How does the information in this chapter support another observation, that women are somewhat more attuned to the emotions of other people in making self-confidence judgments and attributions for success, and are also more influenced by the judgments of others.

10. To solidify your knowledge in preparation for the chapter on women and work (Chapter 7), think of a profession in which relatively few women are employed. Review each of the cognitive abilities and motivational factors discussed in this chapter. Note whether any of these factors provides a sufficient explanation for the relative absence of women in that profession.

NEW TERMS

frequency distribution (163)
box-score approach (165)
meta-analysis (165)
verbal fluency (168)
reading disability (169)
validity (173)
spatial abilities (174)

spatial visualization (174)
spatial perception (174)
mental rotation (176)
lateralization (178)
achievement motivation (183)
fear of success (184)
attributions (188)

RECOMMENDED READINGS

Caplan, P. J., Crawford, M., Hyde, J. S., & Richardson, J. T. E. (Eds.). (1997). *Gender differences in human cognition.* New York: Oxford University Press. I strongly recommend this book, which contains five chapters on topics such as meta-analyses, social influences on cognitive abilities, and the interesting issue of our culture's enchantment with gender differences.

Eccles, J. S., Wigfield, A., & Schiefele, U. (1998). Motivation to succeed. In W. Damon (Series Ed.) & N. Eisenberg (Vol. Ed.), *Handbook of child psychology: Vol. 4: Social, emotional, and personality development* (pp. 1017–1095). New York: Wiley. I could not locate a current review of research on adult motivational factors; this chapter provides a comprehensive review of the research on childhood and adolescence.

Halpern, D. F. (Ed.). (1995–1996). Psychological and psychobiological perspectives on sex differences in cognition [Two special issues]. *Learning and Individual Differences, 7*(4) and *8*(1). These two issues contain 17 articles on the issue of cognitive gender differences; although the majority emphasize biological explanations, many focus on social influences.

Kimball, M. M. (1995). *Feminist visions of gender similarities and differences.* New York: Haworth Press. Chapter 1 of Kimball's book explores ways of interpreting difference and similarity, a theoretical issue relevant to the current chapter. In addition, Chapter 4 focuses on gender comparisons in mathematics ability.

ANSWERS TO DEMONSTRATION 5.2

a.1: Rotate the pattern so that it looks like two mountain peaks, and place the left-most segment along the top-left portion of the little white triangle. a.2: This pattern fits along the right side of the two black triangles on the left. a.3: Rotate this figure about 100° to the right, so that it forms a slightly slanted Z, with the top line coinciding with the top line of the top white triangle. b. The line should be horizontal, not tilted. c. 1 = c. 2 = d.

ANSWERS TO THE TRUE–FALSE QUESTIONS

1. False (p. 167); 2. False (pp. 168–169); 3. True (p. 171); 4. True (p. 172); 5. True (p. 176); 6. True (p. 183); 7. False (p. 184); 8. True (p. 185); 9. True (p. 187); 10. False (p. 189).

Gender Comparisons in Social and Personality Characteristics

TRUE OR FALSE?

_____ 1. Gender differences in social behavior tend to be especially large when other people are present.

_____ 2. In most situations, adult women talk more than adult men.

_____ 3. With fairly strong consistency, men touch women much more often than women touch men.

_____ 4. Women look at their conversational partners more than men do, especially when listening rather than speaking.

_____ 5. Women are more helpful to other people than men are.

_____ 6. Women are typically more interested in infants than men are.

_____ 7. The research clearly demonstrates that women make moral decisions on the basis of caring relationships with others, whereas men make moral decisions on the basis of laws and regulations.

_____ 8. One consistent gender difference is that men are more aggressive than women.

_____ 9. According to current research, men evaluate female leaders as positively as they evaluate male leaders.

_____ 10. Men are more likely to be persuaded by a woman who uses tentative language rather than assertive language.

CHAPTER 6

Communication Patterns
Verbal Communication
Nonverbal Communication
Potential Explanations for
    Gender Differences in
    Communication

**Characteristics Related to
Helping and Caring**
Altruism
Nurturance
Empathy
Moral Judgments Concerning
    Other People
Friendship

**Characteristics Related to
Aggression and Power**
Gender and Aggression:
    The Social Constructionists'
    Concerns
Aggression
Assertiveness
Leadership
Persuasion
Influenceability

As I was preparing to revise this chapter on social and personality charac- teristics, I thought about the male and female students who had visited me dur- ing a recent office hour. Jim came by to pick up some material for his friend Todd, who couldn't attend class because he had broken his leg and needed treatment in the hospital emergency room. While I was handing the material to Jim, the phone rang; Carol was calling. I explained to Carol that I was talking to another student, and I'd call her right back. However, Carol kept on with her conversation, oblivious to my response. Some minutes later, Angela came in to thank me for my help in preparing her for some medical school interviews and to tell me that she had been accepted at three schools so far. Angela was warm and generous in expressing her gratitude, and I realized that the medical school she chose would benefit from a student whose social skills equaled her cogni- tive skills. A fourth student, Leon, had made a 12:15 appointment with me to discuss his poor performance on the introductory psychology examination. He was visibly angry with me when he arrived at 12:35 and I told him we would need to reschedule the appointment because I had a department meeting at 12:45.

In Chapter 5, we saw that gender similarities are common when we consider cognitive abilities and achievement. In this chapter, once again, we observe oc- casional gender differences, but many gender similarities. For example, we'll see that men may be more aggressive than women in some situations. Most female students would not have been as aggressive as Leon, especially when he had created the problem. We'll also see that females often have closer friendships than males do. Jim's obvious concern about his friend Todd was a reversal of the typical pattern.

As you read this chapter, keep in mind some of the gender-comparison issues we raised in Chapter 5. For example, we saw that people's self-confidence and their attribution patterns are influenced by the social setting. Social factors have a modest impact on cognitive and achievement tasks, but these tasks are typi- cally performed in relative isolation. The social situation is even more important when we consider social and personality characteristics. Humans talk, smile, help, and act aggressively in the presence of other people. The social situation provides a rich source of information that people examine in order to make sense out of the world.

At several points throughout this textbook, we have emphasized that the social constructionist perspective is especially useful in examining social behavior. According to the **social constructionist explanation,** we construct or invent our own versions of reality, based on prior experiences in our culture.

A colleague provided an excellent example of the way we construct personality characteristics. Quickly answer the following question: Who is more emotional, men or women? Most people immediately respond, "Women, of course." But what kinds of emotions did you consider—only sadness and crying? Why don't we include anger, one of the primary human emotions? When a man pounds his fist into a wall in anger, we don't comment, "Oh, he's so emotional." The fact is that our culture constructs "emotional" to refer primarily to the emotions associated with women (Bursik, personal communication, 1997). As we'll see in the final section of this chapter, social constructionism also shapes the way we view aggression; we define aggression primarily in terms of the kinds of aggression associated with men.

Every day, we construct what it means to be male and female in our society (Beall, 1993). Social constructionists focus on a central question: "How is gender produced and sustained by human agents in interaction with one another?" (Hare-Mustin & Marecek, 1994).

Each of us does not construct gender independently. Instead, our culture provides us with schemas and other knowledge; together, they operate like a set of lenses through which we can interpret the events in our lives (Beall, 1993; S. Bem, 1993). In Chapters 2 and 3, we examined how the media provide cultural lenses for both adults and children. Females are represented as gentle, nurturant, and submissive, whereas men are represented as independent, self-confident, and aggressive. Our culture holds these models as ideals or standards, so we should find that people—at least in some situations—want to live up to these ideals (Eagly, 1987).

Several factors influence the size of the gender differences in social and personality characteristics (Aries, 1996; Eagly & Karau, 1991; Eisenberg & Lennon, 1983; J. James, 1997). Here are some examples:

1. *Gender differences are largest when behavior is measured in terms of self-report.* For instance, women are more likely than men to *report* that they are extremely nurturant. In contrast, differences are smaller when behavior is measured by some method less influenced by people's ideas about how they should behave. For example, we'll see that women and men are fairly similar when we measure their *behavior* objectively.

2. *Gender differences are largest when other people are present.* For instance, women are especially likely to react positively to infants when other people are nearby.

3. *Gender differences are largest when gender is prominent and other shared roles are minimized.* For example, at a singles bar, gender is emphasized strongly, and gender differences are likely to be large. In contrast, at a conference of accountants—where men and women share the same work role—the work role will be emphasized, and gender differences will be small.

4. *Gender differences are largest when the behavior requires specific gender-related skills.* For example, men might be especially likely to volunteer to change a tire, or perform a similar skill traditionally associated with men in our culture.

Notice, then, that gender differences are especially prominent when a social situation encourages us to think about gender and to wear an especially strong set of "gender lenses." In other social situations, however, women and men behave with remarkable similarity. Our exploration of social characteristics in this chapter will focus on three clusters: (1) communication patterns, (2) characteristics related to helping and caring, and (3) characteristics related to aggression and power.

COMMUNICATION PATTERNS

The word *communication* typically suggests verbal communication, or communication with words. Many people have strong gender stereotypes about this topic; for example, they often think that women are more "chatty." The research results may surprise you.

Communication can also be nonverbal. **Nonverbal communication** refers to all human communication that does not use words—touching, hand or eye movements, tone of voice, and facial expression. Nonverbal communication can effectively convey messages of power and emotion, but we typically pay less attention to nonverbal communication than to verbal communication. Still, research has uncovered some substantial gender differences in nonverbal communication that are worth exploring.

Both verbal and nonverbal communication are essential in our daily interactions. Unless you are reading this sentence before breakfast, you have already seen and spoken to many people, smiled at others, and perhaps avoided eye contact with still others. Now let's examine these two communication areas for gender comparisons.

Verbal Communication

John Gray's best-selling book, *Men Are From Mars, Women Are From Venus,* claims that men and women "almost seem to be from different planets, speaking different languages" (Gray, 1992, p. 5). Gray's book is based on speculation and informal observations rather than actual research. In reality, within each gender, we find great variation in verbal communication patterns, and social factors influence whether we observe gender differences (Aries, 1998). Let's consider the research.

Talkativeness.   According to some stereotypes, women chatter for hours. In reality, however, males are typically more talkative, based on data gathered in elementary classrooms, college classrooms, and college students' conversations (M. Crawford, 1995; J. Hall, 1984). In an interesting demonstration, Spender (1989) recorded pairs of faculty members in conversation; each pair consisted of one man and one woman. In each pair, the man spoke for more minutes than the woman. Afterward, Spender asked each person whether he or she had contributed a fair share of the conversation. Most of the men believed they had *not* had a fair share, even when they had spoken for 58% to 75% of the time.

Do men also interrupt more than women? Early research suggested they did (J. Hall, 1984; Zimmerman & West, 1975). However, because the research sometimes compared high-status men in conversation with low-status women, power—rather than gender—could explain the interruptions. More recent studies suggest that men interrupt more than women do in conversations with relative strangers and in competitive task settings. However, gender differences may be minimal in other situations (Aries, 1996; C. Johnson, 1994).

Language Style.   Some theorists suggest that women's language style is very different from men's (e.g., Lakoff, 1990). Men *are* more likely to use slang and obscene words (Jay, 1992; Selnow, 1985). However, other research shows minimal gender differences in politeness during conversations or in writing style (Cameron et al., 1993; D. Rubin & Greene, 1992, 1994). Carli (1990) studied disclaimers such as "I'm not sure" and "I suppose." When women were talking to other women, they used these disclaimers rarely, as did men in their conversations with other men. However, in conversations with men, women used these disclaimers often. Once again, we need to know the social setting before we can draw conclusions about language and other social behavior.

The Content of Language.   We have discussed *how* women and men talk, but what do they talk about? Bischoping (1993) asked student assistants to record the conversations of other students in classrooms and public places at the University of Michigan. As you can see from Figure 6.1, the most popular topic for both women and men was work and money, a category that included subjects such as jobs, studying, and career plans. Men were significantly more likely than women to talk about leisure activities, such as sports and entertainment events. The most striking gender difference was that women talked about men almost *four* times as much as men talked about women! These results were generally similar to those from two earlier studies (Aries & Johnson, 1983; Levin & Arluke, 1985). However, men and women are equally likely to gossip (Levin & Arluke, 1985).

Women's interest in talking about men may remind you of our observation, in Chapter 4, on how adolescent women are educated in romance as well as in

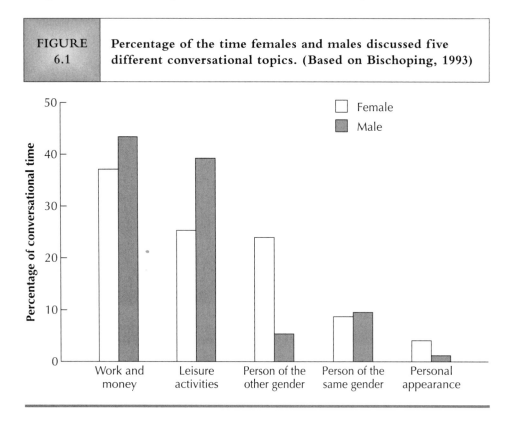

| FIGURE 6.1 | **Percentage of the time females and males discussed five different conversational topics. (Based on Bischoping, 1993)** |

academic topics (D. Holland & Eisenhart, 1990). Other research shows that women are more likely than men to report that they value the discussion of emotions (Shields, 1994, 1995). It's likely that these emotional conversations often focus on romantic relationships. Recall that Chapter 3 pointed out that parents emphasize emotions more in conversations with their daughters than with their sons (Kuebli & Fivush, 1992). Shields's observations suggest that women have learned their parents' lessons well.

Let's consider one other important point about conversations. In our list of four generalizations about gender comparisons, we noted that gender differences are small when other roles are emphasized. A study by Wheelan and Verdi (1992) illustrates this point clearly. These researchers observed professionals in business, government, and service-oriented occupations, who were attending a four-day group relations conference—in other words, this was a setting in which work-related roles would be prominent. Men and women were found to be similar in the nature of their verbal contributions to the discussion groups. For example, men and women were similar in the number of statements that challenged the leadership, and also in the number of statements that supported other people's remarks.

The groups in Wheelan and Verdi's study met for extended periods of between 4½ and 6 hours; most other studies have recorded relatively brief conversations. In Chapter 2, we saw that stereotypes are especially likely to operate when people have little additional information about a person's qualifications. These stereotypes may initially contribute to the suppression of a competent woman's comments. As time passes, however, other group members begin to appreciate the woman's remarks, and their expectations become less gender-based. As a consequence, gender differences may grow smaller as conversations become longer. Looking at a wide range of conversations, Aries (1996) confirmed that gender is a relatively unimportant factor when groups have met for a long time.

Nonverbal Communication

Try turning off the sound on a television game show, and observing the nonverbal behavior. As you watch the TV program, notice that a written transcript of the conversation between Mr. Game Show Host and Ms. Contestant would fail to capture much of the subtle communication between these two people. The nonverbal aspects of conversation are extremely important in conveying social messages. As we'll note below, gender differences are often substantial in certain kinds of nonverbal behavior, such as personal space, body position, and smiling.

Let's examine several components of nonverbal communication, beginning with the nonverbal messages that people send via their personal space, body posture, touch, gaze, and facial expression. A final topic, decoding ability, examines gender comparisons in interpreting those nonverbal messages. As we'll see in this section, gender differences in nonverbal communication are typically larger than other kinds of gender differences (J. Hall, 1984). We'll also consider individual differences in nonverbal communication, as well as explanations and implications of these gender comparisons.

Personal Space. The term **personal space** refers to the invisible border around each person that other people must not invade during ordinary social interactions. You are probably most aware of personal space when a stranger comes too close and makes you feel uncomfortable. In general, women have smaller personal-space zones than men (Briton & Hall, 1995; J. Hall, 1984; M. LaFrance & Henley, 1997). For example, when two women are talking to each other, they sit closer together than two men do (Sussman & Rosenfeld, 1982). Even preschool children approach more closely to female adults than to male adults (Eberts & Lepper, 1975).

Try Demonstration 6.1 before you read further.

Judith Hall (1984) summarized some important points in her superb book on nonverbal gender comparisons. On the topic of personal space, she concluded

---

DEMONSTRATION 6.1

Gender Differences in Body Posture

Which of these figures is a girl, and which is a boy? What cues did you use in reaching your decision?

---

that females tend to set smaller distances when they approach other people. In other words, contrary to the general pattern in Theme 1 of this book, men and women differ in this behavior. That is, *gender as a subject variable* has an influence on personal space because females approach closer to others than males do. However, as Theme 2 proposes, people treat women and men differently. Hall concludes that *gender as a stimulus variable* has an even greater influence than gender as a subject variable. Specifically, people are especially likely to approach closely to females rather than to males. Combining these two factors, we see that two females will stand or sit close to each other, but two males will remain farther apart. The next time you have the opportunity to "people watch," look for these gender differences in personal space.

Body Posture.   Gender differences in body posture develop early in life. The drawings in Demonstration 6.1 were traced from yearbook pictures of two fifth-graders, and then other cues about gender were equated. The figure on the left can be easily identified as a girl, whereas the one on the right is clearly a boy. A glance through magazines will convince you of further gender differences in body posture. Notice that females keep their legs together, with their arms and hands close to their bodies. In contrast, males sit and stand with their legs apart, and their hands and arms move away from their bodies. Men look relaxed; even at rest, women keep their postures more tensely contained (J. Hall, 1984).

Notice how this observation meshes with the gender differences we have discussed. Men often use more "conversational space" in their verbal interactions. Similarly, they use more personal space (distance from other people), and their own body postures require greater physical space. As Demonstration 6.1 illustrates, even young children have mastered "gender-appropriate" body language.

Women and men also walk differently. Frable (1987) attached reflective tape to the body joints of students dressed in dark clothes. She then videotaped them as they walked through a darkened room. A different group of students then viewed these videotapes of moving spots of light, without the benefit of cues such as clothing. Even with this minimal information, viewers rated the videos of males as being significantly more masculine than the videos of females.

Tight skirts and spike heels can restrict women's motion, causing even greater gender differences in body movement (Freedman, 1986; J. Hall, 1984). Several years ago, I followed a guide on a tour of Washington, DC. Her 4-inch spike heels provided compelling evidence for the way fashion restricts women's movement. I can still recall her mincing, wobbly gait as we climbed the steps to the Capitol, her near-disastrous teetering as we negotiated busy streets, and her decision to go barefoot for the last hour of our tour.

Touch. You won't be surprised to learn that, in ordinary interactions, two women touch each other more than two men do. For instance, J. Hall and Veccia (1990) observed 4,500 **dyads** (pairs of interacting people) in public places in the Boston area. The female–female dyads touched each other significantly more than the male–male dyads. Most of the pairs were European American. Gender differences might be reduced among some other ethnic groups.

The picture is more complex for mixed-gender dyads. In the Boston study, J. Hall and Veccia (1990) discovered no overall differences between the number of men who touched women and the number of women who touched men. However, as Figure 6.2 shows, an interesting pattern emerged when the couples were classified according to their estimated age. In younger couples, the males touched the females. In older couples, the females touched the males. The authors pointed out that these age effects may be traceable to differences in the nature of the pairs' relationships. Younger males touch their dates; older females touch their husbands.

Judith Hall (1996) observed how professional men and women touch each other. She instructed undergraduate students to observe professors interacting in dyads at professional conventions for psychologists and for philosophers. Overall, the students detected no gender differences with respect to touching.

FIGURE 6.2	**Percentage of women touching men versus men touching women in mixed-gender dyads, as a function of estimated age. (Based on J. Hall & Veccia, 1990)**

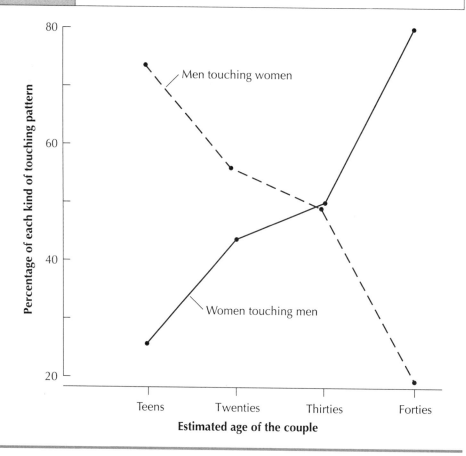

However, when the male and the female in the dyad had equal status (as assessed by their publication record and the "prestige" of their university), males touched females more than females touched males.

In summary, clear gender differences are found only for same-gender dyads: Women touch each other more than men do. In mixed-gender dyads, the patterns of touching depend on age, status, and probably many other factors we haven't yet identified.

Gaze. A classic film on gender includes a fairly lengthy interview with a married couple named Richard and Carol, who are doing their best to avoid a gender-stereotyped relationship. However, their gaze patterns reveal that they are still somewhat traditional. When Richard speaks, Carol gazes at him admiringly. When Carol speaks, Richard looks around the room.

Research has shown that females gaze more at their conversational partners than males do (Briton & Hall, 1995; J. Hall & Halberstadt, 1986; M. LaFrance & Henley, 1997). This gender difference emerges during childhood; even young girls spend more time looking at their conversational partners.

In mixed-gender dyads, women who are listening—rather than speaking—are especially likely to look at their partners. This pattern of gaze is characteristic of people who are relatively low in power and expertise (Dovidio et al., 1988; Valian, 1998). Try to imagine a male employee who is meeting with a male boss. When the employee listens, he gazes at his boss's face to show respect. However, when the employee speaks, he shows respect by *not* consistently gazing at the boss. In contrast, people who are high in power will gaze about the same amount, whether they are listening or speaking. This generalization about power applies to a male speaking to a female, as well as a boss speaking to a subordinate. Gaze is an important way to convey messages of power and submission.

Judith Hall (1984, 1987) concluded that people gaze *at* females more than they gaze *at* males. As we noted in connection with personal space, gender as a stimulus variable seems to be even more powerful than gender as a subject variable. The result with gazing is that two women speaking to each other are likely to have frequent eye contact. In contrast, two men in conversation are likely to avoid looking at each other for long periods of time. Prolonged eye contact—like touching—is relatively uncommon between two men.

Facial Expression.   Gender differences in facial expression are substantial. The most noticeable difference is that women smile more than men (Halberstadt & Saitta, 1987; J. Hall, 1998; Stoppard & Gruchy, 1993). The magazines you examine in Demonstration 6.2 are likely to reveal smiling women and somber men. An inspection of yearbooks will probably confirm this gender difference (J. Mills, 1984; Ragan, 1982). Ragan examined nearly 1,300 portrait photographs and found that women were nearly twice as likely as men to smile broadly. In contrast, men were about eight times as likely as women to show *no* smile. Once again, however, we must consider various social roles; for example, men in the arts smile as much as women in the arts (Willson & Lloyd, 1990).

The gender differences in smiling have important social implications. For example, we know that positive responses—such as smiling—can have an effect on the person who receives these pleasant messages. Specifically, the recipients begin to act more competently (P. Katz et al., 1993; Word et al., 1974). When a typical man and woman interact, the woman's smiles may produce feelings of competence and self-confidence in the man. However, the typical man does not produce many smiles to encourage a woman.

The gender difference in smiling has an additional dark interpretation, in answer to the question: "When do women smile?" You may have noticed that some women smile bravely when someone makes fun of them, tells an embarrassing

---

DEMONSTRATION 6.2

Gender Differences in Smiling

For this demonstration, you will first need to assemble some magazines that contain photos of people. Inspect the photos to identify smiling faces. (We'll define a smile as an expression in which the corners of the mouth are at least slightly upturned.) Record the number of women who smile, and divide it by the total number of women to calculate "percentage of women who smile." Repeat the process to calculate "percentage of men who smile." How do those two percentages compare? Does the gender comparison seem to depend on the kind of magazine you are examining (e.g., fashion magazine versus news magazine)?

Next, locate a high school or college yearbook. Examine the portraits and calculate the percentages of women and of men who are smiling. How do these two percentages compare?

---

joke in their presence, or sexually harasses them. Frances (1979) discovered that the women who laughed and smiled the most in the sample tended to describe themselves as shy, uncomfortable in social settings, and yielding to others' wishes. In other words, the women smiled because they were uncomfortable and were trying to please others—not because they enjoyed the social interaction. As J. Hall and Halberstadt (1986) reported, social tension is the strongest predictor of smiling in women.

So far, our exploration of facial expressions has mentioned only smiling. Another gender difference focuses on the ability to "send" various nonverbal messages through facial expression. In these studies, the research participants are asked to portray a range of emotions, from great happiness to great sadness. Other people try to guess what emotion is being portrayed. Women are typically better at conveying these emotions (Briton & Hall, 1995; Shields, 1995). Combining this information with the information in the previous paragraphs, we can conclude that if a woman is genuinely happy, she will probably produce a broad smile. However, women also smile when they are feeling much more negative emotions.

Decoding Ability. So far, we have seen evidence of gender differences in several kinds of nonverbal behavior: personal space, body posture, touch, gaze, and facial expression. Decoding ability is somewhat different because it requires receiving messages rather than sending them. **Decoding ability** refers to competence in figuring out, from another person's nonverbal behavior, what that person is feeling. A person who is a skilled decoder can notice a friend's facial expression, body posture, and voice, and deduce whether that person is in a good mood or a bad mood.

According to reviews of the research, females are more likely than males to decode nonverbal expressions accurately (Brody & Hall, 1993; J. Hall, 1984, 1998; M. LaFrance & Henley, 1997). For example, one meta-analysis of the research yielded a moderate effect size ($d = .41$); women were better decoders in 106 of 133 gender comparisons. When decoding facial expression, most research shows that females are more accurate than males for every facial expression except anger. In decoding anger, females are *less* accurate than males (Rotter & Rotter, 1988; Shields, 1995). These findings are consistent with Fivush's (1989) observation, which we discussed in Chapter 3: Parents are much more likely to discuss anger with their sons than with their daughters. Boys are trained to recognize, understand, and pay attention to anger.

Females seem to be better decoders than males as early as elementary school. The gender difference also holds up cross-culturally, in studies conducted in countries as varied as Greece, New Guinea, and Singapore (J. Hall, 1984). Incidentally, North American research typically examines European Americans. It would be interesting to see whether the gender differences operate for all ethnic groups.

So far, we have focused on gender differences in decoding emotion from facial expressions. Bonebright and her coauthors (1996) examined people's ability to decode emotion from *vocal* cues. They instructed trained actors to record paragraph-long stories, each time portraying a specified emotion—fear, anger, happiness, sadness, and neutral emotion. Then undergraduate students were asked to listen to each paragraph and determine which emotion the speaker was trying to portray. As you can see from Figure 6.3, women were more accurate than men in decoding voices that expressed fear, happiness, and sadness. No gender differences were found for anger—the one where we might have expected men to be more accurate—or for neutral emotions.

Individual Differences in Communication Styles. The gender differences in nonverbal behavior are often larger than other gender differences. However, we must emphasize that many people do not display the nonverbal behavior that is characteristic of their gender. As always, the behaviors of men and women show some overlap. For example, LaFrance and Carmen (1980) studied students whose scores on a personality measure indicated they were androgynous. (As you'll recall from Chapter 2, androgynous people are high in both feminine and masculine qualities.) These authors found that androgynous individuals tend to blend both feminine and masculine nonverbal behaviors. Androgynous males tend to adopt some characteristically female nonverbal behavior, and androgynous females tend to adopt some characteristically male nonverbal behavior.

Similar evidence of individual differences comes from research by Gallaher (1992), who examined a dimension of nonverbal style called expansiveness. She

FIGURE 6.3	**Male and female accuracy in decoding emotions from vocal cues (maximum score = 6). (Based on Bonebright et al., 1996)**

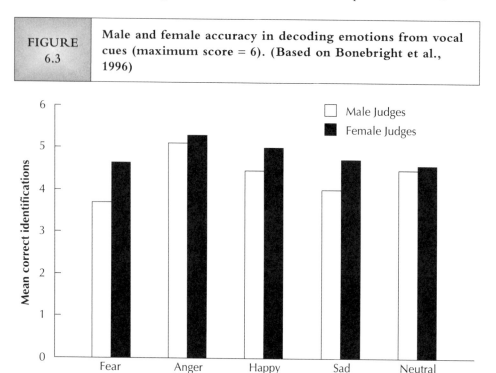

concluded that people who were more masculine, "regardless of their sex, were also rated as more expansive: They tend to sit with legs wide apart, walk with a heavy step, and speak in a loud voice" (p. 138). In other words, masculine people—whether they are male or female—typically take up more space, both physically and psychologically. In contrast, Gallaher found that feminine people are relatively self-contained and quiet, whether they are female or male.

We need to keep in mind the large individual differences within each gender, consistent with Theme 4 of this book. For example, women differ from one another in the size of their personal-space zones, their body posture, touching behavior, gazing, facial expression, and decoding ability. These within-gender variations are so great that you can probably think of several women whose nonverbal behavior is more "masculine" than the average male. For example, you probably know some women who rarely smile, and other women who have no idea what emotions you are feeling unless you make a public pronouncement.

Potential Explanations for Gender Differences in Communication

Even though individual differences are substantial, we need to explain the gender differences in some kinds of verbal and nonverbal communication. Specifically, men often talk more, have larger personal-space zones, use more relaxed body postures, gaze less, and smile less; they are also less skilled at decoding other people's facial expressions. Given these reasonably large gender differences, we might expect that theorists would have developed a coherent theory for these differences. Unfortunately, they haven't. Let's consider two general approaches, which primarily address the gender differences in decoding ability.

Power and Social Status.   Marianne LaFrance and Nancy Henley (1997) argue that the single most effective explanation for gender differences in communication is that men have more power and social status in our culture. Powerful people are allowed to talk at length; less powerful people must listen. Powerless people should use phrases such as "I'm not sure" and "I suppose" when talking with powerful people. Powerful people also have large personal-space zones that less powerful people should not penetrate. Powerful people can sprawl in a chair in a relaxed body position. Also, as we noted, powerful people don't need to convey respect by looking at a less powerful person who is speaking. Powerful people don't need to smile.

LaFrance and Henley (1997) are especially interested in explaining the gender differences in decoding ability. They argue that low-power individuals must be especially attentive to powerful individuals so that they can respond appropriately (M. Conway et al., 1996). Imagine a male boss and his low-ranking male assistant. The assistant must be vigilant for signs of unhappiness on his boss's face, because those signs suggest the boss shouldn't be interrupted or brought any bad news. In contrast, the boss doesn't need to be equally sensitive. According to the power-based explanation, the boss has little to gain from decoding his assistant's facial expression.

LaFrance and Henley (1997) argue that our current culture awards dominant status to men and subordinate status to women. As a consequence, even when a man and a woman are equivalent in other characteristics—such as age and occupation—the man will generally have more power. In that status, he will use the verbal and nonverbal communication patterns that are characteristic of bosses, leaving the woman in the position of a relatively submissive assistant.

Social Learning Explanations.   Judith Hall and Amy Halberstadt (1997) believe that social status and power cannot account for the gender differences in nonverbal decoding ability. As evidence, they cite some of their own research. For example, they found that women in low-ranking jobs at a university were *not* more skilled than high-ranking women in decoding men's facial expressions (J. Hall & Halberstadt, 1994). In another study, they gathered measures of "subordination" among undergraduates; these measures included social-class background, a personality test of subordination, and self-rated social status in high school (J. Hall et al., 1997). In general, the more powerful students were *more* skilled at decoding facial expression than were the more subordinate students—the opposite of the predicted relationship predicted by the power-based explanation.

Instead, Hall and Halberstadt (1997) argue that our culture provides roles, expectations, and socialization experiences that teach males and females how to communicate. As children grow up, for instance, they are reinforced for using nonverbal behavior consistent with their gender. They are also punished for using nonverbal behavior that is more typical of the other gender. Thus, a young girl may be scolded and told, "Let's see a *smile* on that face" when she has been frowning. The girl also notices that females often smile and gaze intently at their conversational partners. In contrast, a boy will be criticized if he uses "feminine" hand gestures, and he can certainly notice stereotypically masculine body movements by watching the men in his family, his community, and the media. (This explanation represents a social learning approach, as discussed in Chapter 3.) Young girls also learn that they are supposed to pay attention to people's emotions (Brody & Hall, 1993).

Conclusions.   Like so many debates in psychology, both perspectives are probably at least partially correct. My own sense is that both the power hypothesis and the social learning approach combine fairly well to explain the gender differences in verbal and nonverbal behavior—the kind of communication that people *send* to others. However, the social learning approach seems relevant for more situations than the power hypothesis in explaining people's ability to *receive* and decode emotions in other people. Consistent with J. Hall and Halberstadt's (1997) argument, I've known some executives and other high-power individuals who are skilled at reading other people's emotions from relatively subtle cues. (In a 1997 article, social commentator Henry Louis Gates, Jr., predicted that U.S. voters will elect the next President based on these social skills.) Social sensitivity makes some people popular, and so they rise to positions of power.

Even if we aren't certain about the explanations, the gender differences remain. What are the important implications? Henley (1977) suggested that an awareness of the gender differences carries a prescription for change. Women do not have to smile when they are unhappy, and they can stop restraining their body posture. With respect to verbal communication, they should feel comfortable about claiming their fair share of the conversation. Men can stop invading women's personal space, they can smile more, and they can sit so that they occupy less space.

In discussing how nonverbal behavior can be changed, we must remember that women should not necessarily strive to be more masculine in their behavior; that would assume that male behavior must be normative. A recent article in a magazine intended for women executives illustrated how a woman can master "powerful, masculine nonverbal behavior." However, as J. Hall (1984) pointed out, we should not assume that women's behavior is deviant and in need of change. Instead, we should note that men may be the victims of years of learning. They have much to gain from adopting some of the nonverbal behaviors and decoding skills of women.

 SECTION SUMMARY   *Communication Patterns*

1. The social constructionist perspective helps us understand why our culture has different standards for the ideal social behavior of women and men.

2. Gender differences are largest when self-report is used, when other people are present, when gender roles are emphasized, and when gender-related skills are required.

3. Men talk more than women; in some circumstances, they also interrupt more.

4. With respect to language, women may be less likely to use profanity, and they use disclaimers (e.g., "I suppose") more in speech with men. Gender similarities are found in other areas.

5. Women are more likely to discuss individuals of the other gender in conversation; otherwise, gender differences in conversational topics are minimal.

6. Women generally have smaller personal-space zones than men do, and they are less relaxed in body posture.

7. Female–female dyads touch each other more than male–male dyads do; patterns of touching are inconsistent in mixed-gender dyads.

8. In comparison to males, females gaze more at their conversational partners, especially when they are listening.

9. Women smile more than men, but their smiles may indicate social tension rather than pleasure.

10. Women are generally better than men at decoding most nonverbal messages sent by other people.

11. Individual differences in nonverbal behavior are large; androgynous people blend the nonverbal behavior of males and females.

12. Some gender differences in communication can be traced to gender differences in power; social learning explanations (e.g., roles, expectations, socialization) are also very important.

13. Suggestions for changing nonverbal behavior emphasize not only the ways in which women should become more "masculine," but also the ways in which men should become more "feminine."

CHARACTERISTICS RELATED TO HELPING AND CARING

Take a moment to form a mental image of a person helping someone else. Try to picture the scene as vividly as possible. Now inspect your mental image—is the helpful person a male or a female?

In North America, we have two different stereotypes about gender differences in helpfulness. Females are considered more helpful and generous in offering assistance and emotional support to family members and close friends (Barbee et al., 1993). In contrast, males are considered more helpful in activities requiring heroism; they are supposed to take risks, even to help strangers.

If you look through journals for articles on helpfulness, you are likely to find mostly research on helping strangers. For many years, psychologists ignored helpfulness in long-term, close relationships, where so many of our everyday interactions occur (Eagly & Wood, 1991). This helpfulness to friends and family members is likely to be called social support rather than helpfulness. We'll explore how women provide social support in the discussion of parenting (Chapter 7), love relationships (Chapter 8), and care of elderly relatives (Chapter 14). Social support is a less noticed kind of helpfulness; it contributes to the relatively low visibility of women (B. Houston, 1989).

Women's paid employment frequently amounts to a low-visibility kind of helpfulness. Women are more likely than men to enter occupations in the "helping professions," such as nursing and social work (Schroeder et al., 1995). In summary, helpfulness includes activities that are both stereotypically masculine and stereotypically feminine.

Alice Eagly has written extensively about gender and helpfulness (Eagly, 1987; Eagly & Crowley, 1986). One meta-analysis of 182 gender comparisons yielded an overall effect size of only 0.13; men were only slightly more helpful (Eagly & Crowley, 1986). A more refined analysis showed that, compared to women, men were substantially more likely to help if the task was perceived to be dangerous to women. For example, men were much more likely to give a ride to a hitchhiker, but men and women were equally likely to place a stamped letter (presumably lost) in a mailbox. Men were also substantially more likely than women to help on tasks for which they had greater experience, such as changing a tire.

In short, men and women probably do not differ in terms of their general helpfulness. However, gender differences emerge on tasks that are dangerous or require expertise. Let's now consider several more specific topics related to helping and caring: altruism, nurturance, empathy, moral judgments, and friendship.

Altruism

Altruism means providing unselfish help to others who are in need, without anticipating any reward for that assistance (Schroeder et al., 1995). Research has

---

DEMONSTRATION 6.3

A Personal Dilemma

Suppose you have been looking forward to watching a special television program that you have wanted to see for quite some time—an old movie you have always wanted to see, a sports championship game, or a special program such as "Masterpiece Theater." Just as you are all settled in and the show is about to begin, your best friend calls and asks you to help with something you had promised several days ago you would do—for example, painting a room or hanging wallpaper. You had assumed that your friend would need you sometime during the week, but had not expected it to be right now. You want nothing else but to stay in your comfortable chair and watch this show, but you know your friend will be disappointed if you do not come over to help (R. Mills et al., 1989, p. 608).

For purposes of this demonstration, assume that you cannot record the program for future viewing. What would you choose to do in this dilemma?

---

not uncovered consistent, overall gender differences in altruism, either with children or adults (Eisenberg et al., 1996). In a representative study with adults, R. Mills and her coauthors (1989) distributed questionnaires to visitors at a Canadian science museum. Each person read three stories, such as the one in Demonstration 6.3, and was instructed to choose between two specified options.

The results of this study showed that both women and men selected the altruistic choice 75% of the time. In other words, the researchers found no gender differences.

Males may be somewhat more likely than females to offer unsolicited help, such as helping a stranger pick up dropped pencils (Deaux, 1976; Latané & Dabbs, 1975). In contrast, when someone directly requests help, the studies typically show either no gender differences or more helpfulness from females. For example, Belansky and Boggiano (1994) found that female students were more likely than male students to report that they would respond to a friend's request for help with a personal problem. These authors also reported gender differences in the *kind* of help people would offer. For example, one scenario described a friend from high school who was considering dropping out of school. Women were likely to say that they would encourage the friend to talk about the situation. Men were likely to use two strategies, the "let's talk about it" strategy and a problem-solving strategy such as encouraging the friend to make a list of pros and cons about dropping out.

Notice the complex relationship between gender and altruism. Gender differences depend on the nature of the task and the nature of the request, as well as factors such as danger and expertise.

Nurturance

Nurturance is a kind of helping in which someone gives care to another person, usually someone who is younger or less competent. The stereotype suggests that women are more nurturant than men, and women indeed rate themselves higher than men do (Feingold, 1994; P. Watson et al., 1994). However, gender similarities are often found.

According to Deaux and Major (1987), gender similarities are found when people's response to a situation is clear. For example, both men and women will quickly respond to the screams of a child who is clearly in pain. However, gender differences may emerge when the situation is more ambiguous—for example, when a child begins to whimper softly. Interestingly, advice books tell mothers to be less emotional in response to their children, but they tell fathers to be more emotionally expressive (Shields et al., 1995). This advice may actually encourage gender similarities.

Here's a related question: Do women find babies more interesting and engaging then men do? Berman (1980) examined this question in terms of three different **operational definitions,** or precise descriptions of how a variable is measured in a research study. Berman concluded that women and men are equally responsive to babies when the operational definition requires a physiological measure (e.g., heart rate) or a behavioral measure (e.g., playing with the baby). However, when the operational definition is based on self-report, women rate themselves as being more attracted to babies. The choice of an operational definition has a major impact on the research conclusions.

As you might expect, the social situation also influences the conclusions. For example, Berman (1976) asked women and men to judge the attractiveness of infants when they were either alone (private) or together with other people (public). Women reported greater attraction in the public condition than in the private condition. The men showed exactly the opposite pattern; they reported greater attraction in the private condition than in the public condition. Notice that, in the public condition, people act according to the socially constructed ideal: Women are supposed to show great excitement; men are supposed to yawn. When people are by themselves, however, men and women are similar in their reaction to babies.

Empathy

You show **empathy** when you feel the same emotion that another person is feeling. An empathic person who watches someone lose a contest can experience the same feelings of anger, frustration, embarrassment, and disappointment that the loser feels.

According to the stereotype, women are more empathic than men. However, Nancy Eisenberg and her colleagues have found substantial gender differences only when the results are based on self-reports (Eisenberg et al., 1989, 1996; Eisenberg & Lennon, 1983). Their findings will remind you of Berman's (1980) analysis of responsiveness to children. Here are the conclusions of Eisenberg and her coauthors about empathy:

1. *Women and men are equally empathic when the operational definition requires physiological measures.* Specifically, measures such as heart rate, pulse, and blood pressure show no gender differences in empathy.

2. *Women and men are equally empathic when the operational definition requires nonverbal measures.* For example, some studies have measured empathy in terms of the observer's facial, vocal, and gestural measures. A typical study examined whether children's facial expressions changed in response to hearing an infant cry. Using this nonverbal measure, boys and girls did not differ in their empathy.

3. *Women are more empathic than men when the operational definition is based on self-report.* For instance, one questionnaire assessing empathy contained statements such as: "I tend to get emotionally involved with a friend's problems." In every self-report study that Eisenberg and Lennon (1983) located, females scored higher than males.

As we have seen, we cannot answer the question, "Are males or females more empathic?" unless we know how empathy is measured. Once again, we see an illustration of Theme 1. Gender differences certainly are not found in every condition.

Moral Judgments Concerning Other People

Do males and females tend to make different kinds of decisions when they make moral judgments that have implications for other people's lives? This is a controversial topic. We'll explore it in some detail because it lies at the heart of the research on helping and caring. First, let's consider some theoretical background, emphasizing the important contributions of Carol Gilligan. Then we'll review other research, which generally supports the similarities perspective. Finally, we'll summarize the issues.

Theoretical Background.　Several prominent feminist theorists have argued that characteristics traditionally associated with women have been undervalued. For example, Judith Jordan (1997) summarized the perspective of a group of theorists working at the Stone Center at Wellesley College. According to their **relational model** (sometimes called the **self-in-relation theory**), we humans grow through our relationships with other people, via mutual empathy and responsiveness to others; in addition, women are more likely to feel that connections with others are central to their psychological well-being.

The relational model is consistent with the differences perspective emphasized in Chapter 1. Those who support the **differences perspective** tend to exaggerate gender differences; they view males and females as being different and as having mutually exclusive characteristics. The relational model is also consistent with cultural feminism. As Chapter 1 outlined, **cultural feminism** emphasizes the positive qualities that are presumably stronger in women than in men—qualities such as nurturing and caring for others.

The **similarities perspective,** in contrast, tends to minimize gender differences, arguing that males and females are generally similar. As you know from Theme 1, this book typically favors a similarities perspective. The similarities perspective is most consistent with the framework of **liberal feminism;** by reducing gender roles and increasing equal-rights laws, the gender similarities will increase still further. Those who favor the similarities perspective admire some aspects of the relational model and Gilligan's model—which we'll discuss next. However, the supporters of the similarities perspective argue that women and men are fairly similar in their concerns about helping and caring; the two genders do not live on separate planets.

Working in parallel with those who support the relational model, Carol Gilligan eloquently expressed the differences perspective in her 1982 book, *In a Different Voice.* (We already discussed Carol Gilligan's interesting research on the friendships of adolescent women in Chapter 4.) Gilligan's book was partly a feminist response to the research on moral development conducted by Lawrence Kohlberg. Kohlberg (1981, 1984) had asked people to make judgments about a series of moral dilemmas. In the most well-known dilemma, for example, a man must decide whether to steal a medication that might prolong the life of his dying wife. Kohlberg argued that most men eventually reach Stage 4 of his theory of moral development. (Stage 6 is the highest level.) In contrast, Kohlberg argued, most women reach only Stage 3.

Carol Gilligan (1982) pointed out that many of Kohlberg's moral dilemmas have a masculine bias. She also noted that Kohlberg's original theory was based on observations of males rather than of both genders. For our purposes, however, the most interesting aspect of her book was that she provided a feminist approach to moral development. According to Gilligan, women are not morally inferior to men, but they do "speak in a different voice," a voice that had been ignored by mainstream psychology.

Gilligan (1982) contrasted two approaches to moral decision making. The **justice perspective** emphasizes that an individual is part of a hierarchy in which some people have more power and influence than others. Gilligan proposed that men tend to emphasize justice and the legal system when making moral decisions. In contrast, the **care perspective** emphasizes that individuals are interrelated with one another in a web of interconnections. Gilligan proposed that women tend to favor the care perspective; women view "life as dependent on connection, as sustained by activities of care, as based on a bond of attachment rather than a contract of agreement" (p. 57). Gilligan favored in-depth interviews to explore women's ideas about care and connection in the context of moral decisions. Her book described several of these interview-based studies. For example, in one study, she interviewed women who were making decisions about unwanted pregnancies (Gilligan, 1982).

Numerous feminists, including many from disciplines outside psychology, embraced Gilligan's emphasis on gender differences (described by Kimball, 1995). Others argued that men and women are more likely to show similar styles of moral reasoning. The dissenters also pointed out that if we were to glorify women's special nurturance and caring, men would be less likely to recognize and develop their own competence in that area (Lerner, 1989; Tavris, 1992).

Subsequent Research.   A variety of studies have been conducted to examine gender comparisons in moral reasoning. Most of the results support the similarities perspective: Men and women typically respond similarly (e.g., Colby & Damon, 1983; Söchting et al., 1994; L. J. Walker, 1984, 1989). In general, these studies have examined participants' responses to standardized hypothetical dilemmas, whereas Gilligan's technique asked individuals to describe moral dilemmas from their own life experiences.

Clopton and Sorell (1993) examined moral reasoning using both standardized dilemmas and participants' own examples. These authors limited the dilemmas to child-rearing situations, so that all dilemmas focused on comparable circumstances. They tested two standardized moral dilemmas about parent–child relationships. Parents were also asked to describe a dilemma they had faced in parenting their own child. Trained raters assessed the mothers' and fathers' responses for evidence of both the justice perspective and the care perspective.

The results showed no gender differences for either the standardized dilemmas or the participants' real-life dilemmas. Clopton and Sorell (1993) concluded:

> In their daily lives, women and men may reason differently about moral problems primarily because of differences in the type of moral problem they encounter. When they encounter similar problems, women and men may employ similar modes of moral reasoning. (p. 99)

These conclusions are consistent with a point we made at the beginning of the chapter: Gender differences are small when the situation emphasizes roles other than gender. Specifically, when men and women focus on the parenting role, they provide similar moral judgments about child-rearing dilemmas.

Some critics of Gilligan's theory argue that her approach is based on European American values. For example, Stack (1994) was teaching a course on women and justice. One Black male student from the South pointed out to the class, "If Carol Gilligan is right, my brothers and I were raised to be girls as much as boys. . . . We were raised in a large family with a morality of care as well as justice. We were all raised to be responsible to kin, and to be able to face injustices at an early age" (p. 291). This young man's comments inspired Stack to present moral dilemmas to Black male and female adolescents living in the

South. She found no gender differences in their relative emphasis on justice versus care.

Similarly, Brabeck (1996) interviewed teenage boys in Guatemala. When asked about the characteristics they most valued, they emphasized helping other people and improving the community.

Summary on Moral Judgments.   Carol Gilligan contributed an important framework. She emphasized that the standard theory had downplayed the ethic of care, a value traditionally associated with women. However, I'm persuaded by the research that demonstrates how men and women respond similarly to a wide variety of moral dilemmas. Especially when people provide judgments about similar moral dilemmas—and when we consider the values of people who are not European American—men and women seem to live in the same moral world, sharing the same basic values.

Friendship

For many decades, psychologists ignored the topic of friendship; aggression was a much more popular topic! However, in recent years, many books and articles have been published that are relevant to friendship and the psychology of women (e.g., Fehr, 1996; J. T. Wood, 1996). Let's first focus on gender comparisons in friendship, and then we'll briefly explore the nature of women's friendships with other women.

Gender Comparisons in Friendship.   Try to create a mental image of two women who are good friends with each other, and think about the nature of their friendship. Now do the same for two men who are good friends. Are female–female friendships basically different from male–male friendships? You can

---

DEMONSTRATION 6.4

Characteristics of Friendships

Think about some of the friendships you have with other people of the same gender. What do you mean by the term "intimacy" when it is used in reference to your same-gender friends? In your reply, please indicate how you and your same-gender friends express intimacy in your relationships. This issue will be discussed shortly in the text.

(Based on Monsour, 1992, p. 282.)

probably anticipate the conclusion we will reach in this section: Although gender differences are sometimes observed, gender similarities are more striking.

We find gender similarities when we assess what friends do when they get together. Specifically both female friends and male friends are most likely to "just talk." They are somewhat less likely to work on a specific task or project together. And they rarely meet for the purpose of working on some problem that has arisen in their friendship (Duck & Wright, 1993).

What does intimacy in a friendship mean to men and women? To assess your own thoughts, try Demonstration 6.4 before reading further. Monsour (1992) posed this same open-ended question to undergraduates and then compared the responses supplied by males and females. Both women and men were most likely to say that an important component of intimacy is **self-disclosure,** or revealing information about yourself to someone else. Both women and men also emphasized emotional expressiveness, unconditional support, and trust. However, females also emphasized physical contact with the friend, whereas—no surprise—males mentioned this less often.

Other research suggests that women typically value self-disclosure somewhat more than men. Dindia and Allen (1992) conducted a meta-analysis of 205 studies (!), which reported on 23,702 people. The d was 0.18, a small effect size, with women disclosing somewhat more than men. More recent studies generally report that women are more self-disclosing (Foubert & Sholley, 1996; Veniegas & Peplau, 1997). However, one study showed that men were actually *more* self-disclosing than women when instructed to discuss an incident concerning their own family (Leaper et al., 1995).

Why should women tend to be more self-disclosing? Let's consider some reasons (Canary & Emmers-Sommer, 1997; Derlega et al., 1993; Fehr, 1996):

1. Women value talking about feelings more than men do; we've already discussed females' greater training in emotions.
2. North Americans have gender-related norms about self-disclosure; men are not *supposed* to discuss private feelings with other men.
3. The gender differences may be traceable to the use of the self-report measure, rather than other operational definitions. Men may be reluctant to say that they share intimate feelings with other men, especially if they are guided by our culture's homophobic messages.
4. Our expectations about self-disclosure lead us to perceive that men are uncomfortable in conversations about personal feelings; as a result, people are less likely to initiate personal conversations with a man.

Friendships Between Women.   As Pat O'Connor (1992) emphasizes, we must not take a simplistic approach to women's friendships. Friendships with other women can bring joys and satisfactions, but also costs and disappointments. The nature of a friendship may depend on women's age, life stage, social class, ethnicity, and marital status. For example, students in my Psychology of Women class often observe that their relationships with women friends change when these friends marry. Their friends' priorities shift, and husbands may even express jealousy, an observation supported by the research (F. Johnson, 1996). However, women often report that friendships are a vitally important source of support, affirmation, and pleasure (Block & Greenberg, 1985; F. Johnson, 1996).

One particularly interesting topic is women's friendships with members of another ethnic group. Sadly, Rose (1996) concludes that mutually satisfying cross-race friendships are rare. They are more likely if both women have thought extensively about their own ethnic identity and if their friends and family are supportive of their friendship. Otherwise, as one Black woman in Rose's study commented, the friendship will be held together "by a very weak glue" (S. Rose, 1996, p. 224).

SECTION SUMMARY   *Characteristics Related to Helping and Caring*

1. **Overall gender differences in helpfulness are not strong; men are more likely to help on dangerous tasks and on tasks requiring expertise in masculine areas. Males may be somewhat more likely to offer unsolicited help.**

2. **In general, women and men do not differ in nurturance or in responsiveness to babies.**

3. **In general, women and men do not differ in empathy; gender similarities are found for physiological and nonverbal measures, but women are more empathic on self-report measures.**

4. **Theorists at the Stone Center have proposed a relational model that emphasizes growth through our relationships with other people, with women being especially concerned about interpersonal connections. Carol Gilligan (1982), also from the differences perspective, has suggested that men favor a justice perspective, whereas women emphasize a care perspective.**

5. **Most research supports a similarities perspective, especially when making moral judgments about the same kind of situation and when considering the values of cultures other than European American groups.**

6. **Men and women have similar friendship patterns in terms of what friends do when they get together; women are slightly more self-disclosing than men; women's friendships vary widely in their emotional nature, but cross-race friendships are relatively rare.**

CHARACTERISTICS RELATED TO AGGRESSION AND POWER

We have seen that the research on helping and caring does not allow a simple, straightforward conclusion about gender differences. The situation is similar for attributes associated with aggression and power.

The previous section focused on characteristics that are stereotypically associated with females; this section focuses on characteristics stereotypically associated with males. Perhaps the central topic in this cluster is **aggression,** which we'll define as any behavior directed toward either another person or that person's property, with the intention of doing harm (J. White & Kowalski, 1994).

Let's begin by considering some issues raised by social constructionists about the nature of aggression. Then we'll examine the research on aggression, assertiveness, and leadership. The last two topics in this chapter—persuasion and influenceability—are interrelated. Specifically, persuasion uses power to convince others, and influenceability focuses on being convinced by others.

Gender and Aggression: The Social Constructionists' Concerns

As we saw in the introduction to this chapter, the social constructionists argue that we humans actively construct our views of the world. This point holds true for people trying to make sense out of their daily experiences, and for theorists and researchers trying to make sense out of human behavior. As a result, a group of researchers who are studying aggression will be guided by the way North American scholars have constructed the categories (Fry & Gabriel, 1994). The cultural lenses they wear restrict their vision.

In particular, researchers have constructed aggression so that it is considered a *male* characteristic. To appreciate this point, reread the definition of aggression in the first paragraph of this section. What kinds of aggression do you visualize—hitting, shooting, and other kinds of physical violence? As J. White and Kowalski (1994) point out, aggression can be verbal as well as physical. If you are a typical college student, you are much more likely to experience verbal aggression—instead of physical aggression—in your everyday life (Howard & Hollander, 1997). Aggression can also be passive (rather than active) and indirect (rather than direct). However, our cultural lenses do not encourage us to "see" the kinds of aggression that might be more common in females.

Social constructionists point out that each culture devises its own set of lenses. Peplau and her coauthors (Peplau, Veniegas, et al., 1998) argue that each culture shapes a different construction of social behaviors such as aggression. Lepowsky (1998) reports on an egalitarian culture on the island of Vanatinai, a remote island near New Guinea in the South Pacific. In this remarkable culture, both girls and boys are socialized to be self-confident but not aggressive. During Lepowski's 10 years of research, she heard about only five acts of physical violence—and women were the aggressors in four of these incidents. In a culture that discourages aggression, gender differences may disappear.

Closer to home, Harris (1994) reported on female members of Mexican American gangs in the Los Angeles area. The young women she interviewed stated that they had joined the gang for group support—but also because of a need for revenge. Commenting on the physical violence, a gang member named Maryann reported, "It's not that you like to fight. You have to fight. But I like fighting" (p. 296). Reselda emphasized, "Most of us in our gangs always carry weapons. Guns, knives, bats, crowbars, any kind. . . . Whatever we can get hold of that we know can hurt, then we'll have it" (p. 297). In a subculture that admires aggression, gender differences may disappear as both females and males adopt aggressive tactics.

Throughout this section, keep in mind the cultural lenses that we wear. Also, remember that the way we ask questions has an important influence on the answers we obtain.

Aggression

Eleanor Maccoby and Carol Jacklin's (1974) classic book on gender comparisons concluded that gender differences in aggression are fairly well established. Our examination of this topic will reveal that males are *often* more aggressive than females. (Chapter 13 presents further evidence of male aggressiveness in sexual harassment, rape, and domestic violence.) We cannot ignore the major consequences of men's violence to individuals and to society. However, the many exceptions to the stereotype of the aggressive male force us to conclude that men and women are similar in some less physical kinds of aggression (Burn, 1996).

A breakthrough in our understanding of gender and aggression came from a superb review of previous research, conducted by Ann Frodi and her colleagues (1977), who found that males were often more aggressive. However, 61% of these studies did *not* show males being more aggressive than females for all the research conditions.

The analysis by Frodi and her colleagues has now been joined by additional research and meta-analyses (e.g., Baron & Richardson, 1994; Bettencourt & Miller, 1996; Hyde, 1986; Knight et al., 1996). This section will discuss five major conclusions from the research.

1. *Gender differences are relatively large when we study aggression in children.* During childhood, boys are often more aggressive than girls. Gender similarities are more common when we consider adults (Geen, 1998; Hyde, 1984).

2. *Gender differences are relatively large when we consider physical aggression.* For example, men are more likely than women to report having physically aggressive dreams (Bursik, 1998).

Let's examine the research on gender comparisons in a very important index of physical aggression—crime rates, a topic that has attracted substantial attention from the media. The data on crime show that men are consistently more likely than women to be the offenders in every category of criminal behavior (Knight et al., 1996; U.S. Bureau of the Census, 1997). For example, in 1996, about 1,300 men murdered their "intimate partner," whereas about 500 women murdered their "intimate partner" (Greenfeld et al., 1998; in this study, intimate partners included spouses, ex-spouses, girlfriends, and boyfriends). We'll return to this topic in Chapter 13, when we consider domestic violence.

As you have probably heard, however, the number of women in prison has been rapidly rising. The media reports may not mention that drug-related offenses are the major reason for the increase in women in prison (Murphy & Cleeton, 2000; T. Snell & Morton, 1994). Still, the media correctly report that women are increasingly likely to be arrested for violent crimes (Murphy & Cleeton, 2000; U.S. Bureau of the Census, 1997). For example, between 1991 and 1995, men's arrests for violent crimes actually decreased by 1%, whereas women's arrests for violent crimes increased by 28%. Keep in mind, though, that crime rates are still much lower for women than for men. In 1995, for example, men committed 91% of all murders and 82% of all aggravated assaults (U.S. Bureau of the Census, 1997).

What can we conclude from these data on criminal behavior? Women are clearly capable of committing atrociously violent murders (Pearson, 1998). They are also somewhat more likely to commit violent crimes now than in earlier eras. Still, the bottom line is that gender differences in physical aggression remain relatively large.

When we assess other, nonphysical kinds of aggression, we see that gender similarities are more common. Consider verbal attacks, for example. Cross-cultural research in Scandinavia, Tonga (a Polynesian society), and Argentina suggest that females are as likely as males to use verbal, indirect aggression, such as excluding people from one's group or gossiping. Women may even be *more* aggressive on these measures (Björkqvist, 1994; N. Hines & Fry, 1994; E. Olson, 1994).

In emphasizing gender similarities in verbal violence, we must not lose sight of the harmful consequences of men's physical violence. No one would argue that a woman's gossiping is equivalent to a man's breaking someone's arm.

3. Gender differences are relatively large when aggression is measured in terms of self-report. As we have seen throughout this chapter, people move in the direction of gender stereotypes when they report about themselves. For example, a study by A. Buss and Perry (1992) asked people to rate themselves on a variety of scales, such as those in Demonstration 6.5. Buss and Perry found that college men had much higher scores than women did on questions that assessed physical aggression. Men were slightly higher on both verbal aggression and hostility. However, no gender differences were reported for anger. Harris and Knight-Bohnhoff (1996) reported similar results when they tested men and women working on a military base. Another study—this time with 4th- and 5th-grade children—also found no gender differences in self-reported anger (Buntaine &

DEMONSTRATION 6.5

Assessing Aggression with the Self-Report Method

Complete the following questionnaire, rating every item on a scale where 1 = "very uncharacteristic of me" and 5 = "extremely characteristic of me." Then check the end of the chapter to help you interpret your answers.

_____ 1. I often disagree with other people.

_____ 2. If someone hits me, I'm likely to hit back.

_____ 3. I have trouble controlling my temper.

_____ 4. I sometimes become so mad that I break things.

_____ 5. I know that so-called friends talk about me behind my back.

_____ 6. When I'm frustrated, I let my irritation show.

_____ 7. When people annoy me, I often tell them what I think about them.

_____ 8. When people act especially nice to me, I often wonder what they want.

_____ 9. I am sometimes eaten up with jealousy.

_____ 10. If I have to resort to violence to protect my rights, I will.

_____ 11. When I disagree with my friends, I tell them directly.

_____ 12. Sometimes I'll explode with anger for no good reason.

(Based on A. Buss & Perry, 1992.)

Costenbader, 1997). Notice that these studies demonstrate not only gender differences in self-reported aggression, but also the importance of our operational definition of aggression. If we were to define aggression in terms of *anger,* we wouldn't find evidence for gender differences.

4. *Gender differences are relatively small when people's aggression has been provoked.* When people have been insulted, both men and women are likely to respond aggressively. Gender differences are larger for unprovoked aggression (Bettencourt & Miller, 1996). In other words, men are somewhat more likely than women to show spontaneous aggression.

5. *Gender differences are relatively small when either the perpetrator or the victim of aggression is anonymous.* For example, in a study by Lightdale and

Prentice (1994), participants played a video game in which they dropped bombs on their competitor's target. When the participants had briefly met before the game began, men played the game significantly more aggressively than women did. When they had not met beforehand, no gender differences were observed.

Keep in mind the general principle that responses of males and females are likely to overlap. For example, several studies have examined the scores that young boys and girls receive on measures of observed physical aggression (DiPietro, 1981; Favreau, 1993; Frey & Hoppe-Graff, 1994). Gender differences should be relatively large in these studies, because they assess children and they measure physical violence. Still, most of the boys and girls were similarly unaggressive, and the gender differences could be traced to a small number of aggressive boys.

Reviews of the literature have located few consistent, robust gender differences in aggression. Situational factors and socialization are probably the major determinants of gender differences (Burbank, 1994; J. White, 1983). Furthermore, our social construction of aggression has led psychologists to emphasize the kinds of aggression that are stereotypically masculine. They seldom explore those domains in which women may be more aggressive.

The myth of the nonaggressive female has several disadvantages for North American society:

1. If women see themselves as weak and nonaggressive, they may believe that they cannot defend themselves against men's aggression (J. White & Kowalski, 1994).

2. Because competitiveness is associated with aggression, women may be denied access to professions that value competition.

3. Aggressive men may be seen as normal, and men may choose not to inhibit their aggressive tendencies.

4. The criminal justice system has a double standard for punishment; men often receive much harsher sentences than women do (Murphy & Cleeton, 2000; Pearson, 1998).

In short, both women and men suffer when we hold stereotyped views of the gender differences in aggression.

Assertiveness

Assertiveness is the ability to stand up for one's own rights, without denying the rights of others. According to the popular stereotype, men are appropriately assertive; they insist on their rights when someone tries to take advantage of them. The stereotype also suggests that women's behavior matches the assertiveness of a doormat.

In general, these stereotypes are not supported by the research, which shows many inconsistencies (M. Crawford, 1988, 1995). In a review of the research,

Feingold (1994) found that half of the studies reported no gender differences; the overall effect size showed males were *not* more assertive ($d = 0.08$).

For many years, self-proclaimed experts argued that the answer to women's problems was that women were simply not assertive enough. (Notice the "blame-the-woman" flavor of this argument.) If women would just sign up for assertiveness training workshops, all their problems could be surmounted (M. Crawford, 1995). These "experts" neglected a basic problem: Many people do not respond positively to assertive women. In fact, M. Crawford (1988) demonstrated that adult males often dislike assertive females—an observation that is consistent with the analysis of gender bias in Chapter 2. Assertiveness is another example of our general principle that gender as a stimulus variable is typically more influential than gender as a subject variable.

Leadership

If you attend a college that has both female and male students, notice the gender of the student council leaders. If your college is typical, the leaders are predominantly men, even if most students are women. In general, research shows that male leaders emerge from mixed-gender groups, even when the members of the groups are presumably equal in ability (Eagly & Karau, 1991; Sapp et al., 1996). What are the personal characteristics of women leaders, and how do women perform as leaders?

Characteristics of Women Leaders.   Offermann and Beil (1992) compared women college leaders with other undergraduate college women. The women leaders were significantly higher in several components of achievement style. For example, leaders were more likely to give high ratings to statements such as "For me, the most gratifying thing is to have solved a tough problem" (p. 42). Women leaders were also less likely than other female undergraduates to express discomfort about using power.

In a second study, Offermann and Beil (1992) compared female student leaders with male student leaders. In general, the two groups were similar in their reactions about using power. They were also similar in most aspects of achievement motivation, except that males were more likely to enjoy achieving in competitive situations.

Cantor and Bernay (1992) interviewed 25 highly successful women in politics—Congresswomen, Senators, and other women whom female student leaders probably consider to be role models. These prominent women did not focus on the barriers that might have hindered their success. Instead, they emphasized a strong sense of their own competence and leadership ability. They also appreciated that strength and power could be effectively combined with the nurturance considered more typical of females.

Performance as Leaders.   You probably will not be surprised to learn that gender comparisons about leadership performance show a complex pattern. For example, when Eagly and Johnson (1990) analyzed laboratory research, they found that men are somewhat more concerned about getting the job done, whereas women are somewhat more concerned about the feelings of other group members. However, when they analyzed research on men and women who are actually employed as leaders in organizations, they found gender similarities. As noted at the beginning of this chapter, gender similarities are found when a role other than gender is prominent. In this case, the role of *executive* is prominent, and gender similarities are typical.

Another dimension of leadership style is whether the leader behaves democratically or autocratically. **Democratic leadership** allows subordinates to participate in making decisions. In contrast, **autocratic leadership** discourages subordinates from participating in decision making. For both laboratory and organizational studies, Eagly and Johnson (1990) found that the gender differences were small ($d = 0.22$). However, women were somewhat more likely to use democratic leadership, whereas men were somewhat more likely to use autocratic leadership.

Which gender is actually more effective in the leadership role? Eagly and her coauthors (1995) performed a meta-analysis on the ratings of leaders in laboratory research and in organizations. Overall, males and females are equally effective leaders ($d = 0.02$). However, men received more positive ratings than females when both genders were evaluated in a stereotypically masculine profession (e.g., military leadership). Women received more positive ratings than men in a stereotypically feminine profession (e.g., educational leadership). Furthermore, female raters were equally positive about male and female leaders. However, male raters were more positive about male leaders than female leaders. In other words, a female who is a military leader—supervising more men than women—will typically receive a low rating for her performance.

Other research by Eagly and her colleagues (1992) showed that female leaders were rated most negatively when their leadership style was autocratic. This finding is consistent with our earlier remarks about people's reactions to assertive females.

All this research on leadership ability has important implications for women and work, the topic of our next chapter. Unfortunately, however, few of the studies examine ethnic issues. We don't know, for example, whether Black men and women differ in their leadership style. We also don't know whether ethnicity has an influence on people's ratings of male and female leaders. Would people be especially likely to downgrade an Asian American or Latina woman if she held a leadership position in a traditionally masculine field?

Persuasion

Before you read further, be sure to try Demonstration 6.6 on persuasion strategies. Persuasion is one of the most basic components of power. A powerful person can persuade people to do something they would not ordinarily do.

DEMONSTRATION 6.6

Persuasion Techniques

Listed below are 8 of the 43 persuasion techniques that White and Roufail (1989) listed in their study. Rank order these techniques. Assign a 1 to the strategy that you would be most likely to use in persuading another person, and assign an 8 to the strategy you would be least likely to use. Use the numbers between 1 and 8 to assign intermediate ranks.

a. Make the other person miserable　　　　　　　　　————

b. Convince, persuade, and coax　　　　　　　　　　　————

c. Hint or suggest　　　　　　　　　　　　　　　　————

d. Threaten to use physical force　　　　　　　　　　————

e. Use reason and logic.　　　　　　　　　　　　　　————

f. Argue until the person changes his or her mind　　　————

g. Cry, pout, or sulk　　　　　　　　　　　　　　　————

h. Make others think the idea is theirs　　　　　　　　————

　　Now check, at the end of this chapter, the responses that White and Roufail's (1989) participants supplied.

What kind of strategy did you use most often in Demonstration 6.6? White and Roufail (1989) asked male and female undergraduates to rank a large number of strategies, including those listed in Demonstration 6.6. Their results showed that men and women typically used similar rankings. (Check page 232 at the end of the chapter to see the relative rankings supplied by White and Roufail's participants.) In general, the researchers found that people preferred verbal and rational appeals, and they avoided high-pressure strategies, such as the use of physical force.

What kind of communication style is most *persuasive* when a woman is trying to influence her conversational partner? Linda Carli (1990) found that men were most persuaded by women who used the kind of tentative language we discussed on page 199 (e.g., "I'm not sure"). They were not persuaded by women who used assertive language, a finding that was also reported by Buttner and McEnally (1996). Interestingly, though, *women* were more persuaded by a woman who used assertive language than by a woman who used tentative language (Carli, 1990). A female politician who plans to give a persuasive speech to voters therefore faces a dilemma: If she is too assertive, she'll lose the males, but if she is too tentative, she'll lose the females!

In another study, Carli and her coauthors (1995) shifted from verbal behavior to nonverbal behavior. One interesting analysis compared women who used a competent nonverbal style and men who used the same style. A competent nonverbal style includes a relatively rapid rate of speech, upright posture, calm hand gestures, and moderately high eye contact when speaking. A male audience was significantly more influenced by a man who used this competent style than by a woman who used this same style. Again, behavior associated with high status is not acceptable when used by a person with low status (Carli, 1991).

Linda Carli's research shows us that subtle sexism persists in social interactions. A competent woman finds herself in a double bind. If she speaks confidently and uses competent nonverbal behavior, she may not persuade the men with whom she interacts. But if she speaks tentatively and uses less competent nonverbal behavior, she will not live up to her own standards.

Influenceability

We have been examining persuasion strategies, as well as the verbal and nonverbal styles that are likely to persuade other people. But, for every person who persuades, another person is influenced and gives in to that persuasion. Let's now focus on the person who is influenced.

For many years, social psychologists maintained that women were far more influenceable than men. However, a meta-analysis by Eagly and Carli (1981) reported that the gender differences were small, though they were statistically significant. Females may be somewhat more easily influenced because traditional gender roles suggest that women should "give in"; they have been trained to preserve social harmony in interpersonal interactions (Eagly & Wood, 1985). In addition, women's lower status in most interactions suggests that the low-status individuals must yield to those with higher status and power.

Throughout this chapter, we have examined how women and men compare on a variety of social and personality characteristics. For example, we noted occasional gender differences in communication patterns, helpfulness, and aggression. However, gender similarities are typically more common, and every characteristic we discussed demonstrates a substantial overlap in the distribution of female and male scores. In summary, we have abundant evidence to argue against the claim that men and women are from different planets and have little in common. The title of John Gray's book, *Men Are From Mars, Women Are From Venus,* was certainly enticing enough to produce a best-seller. However, its message does not properly represent the research support for gender similarities.

 Section Summary *Characteristics Related to Aggression and Power*

1. **According to the social constructionist perspective, North American scholars emphasize the stereotypically masculine components of**

aggression, ignoring the kinds of aggression that might be more common in females. Some other cultures construct different "gender lenses" in which (a) neither women nor men are aggressive or (b) aggression in women is common.

2. Gender differences in aggression are inconsistent. These gender differences are relatively large (a) among children, rather than adults; (b) in physical aggression—for example, in the gender differences in the rate of violent crime—rather than in verbal aggression; and (c) when measured by self-report.

3. Gender differences in aggression are relatively small when people's aggression has been provoked and when the perpetrator and the victim do not know each other.

4. No consistent gender differences are found in assertiveness; assertiveness training for women may backfire because assertive women receive negative evaluations.

5. In general, males are more likely than females to emerge as group leaders; women are somewhat more likely to use a democratic leadership style, whereas men are somewhat more likely to use an autocratic style.

6. Males and females receive similar ratings in terms of leadership effectiveness, though each receives higher ratings when judged in a "gender-consistent" leadership position. Women are also likely to be downgraded by males (rather than females), especially if they use an autocratic leadership style.

7. Men and women generally use similar persuasion strategies, but women are less likely to persuade men when using a "feminine" style; women are slightly more influenceable than men are.

CHAPTER REVIEW QUESTIONS

1. The discussion of communication styles points out that men seem to take up more space than women, whether we use the word *space* to refer to physical space or—more figuratively—conversational space. Discuss this point, making as many gender comparisons as possible.

2. Turn back to Chapter 3 and review Bem's gender schema theory of gender typing (pages 95 to 97). Point out how this theory could explain each of the gender differences in verbal and nonverbal communication. Then explain how the power and social status explanation could account for most gender differences.

3. The section on facial expression points out that women's smiles often do not match their true emotions. However, women are more accurate than

men in decoding the emotions that underlie other people's facial expressions. Speculate how these two points might be related, and then list some practical implications of these two points.

4. The social constructionist perspective emphasizes that our cultural lenses shape the way we ask questions. In particular, these lenses influence our choice of issues to emphasize within each topic. Summarize the topics of helpfulness, aggression, assertiveness, leadership, and persuasion, pointing out how the nature of the results could be influenced by the kind of issues studied in each area (e.g., aggression in stereotypically masculine areas versus stereotypically feminine areas).

5. According to stereotypes, women care about interpersonal relationships, whereas men care about dominating other people. Like many stereotypes, this contrast contains a grain of truth. Discuss the grain of truth with respect to helping, friendship, aggression, leadership, and influenceability. Then point out the number of similarities shared by males and females.

6. What kinds of factors influence gender differences in aggression? Combining as many factors as possible, describe a situation in which gender differences are likely to be exaggerated, and a situation in which they are likely to be minimal.

7. Alice Eagly and her colleagues argue that gender differences are likely to emerge in areas in which men and women have had different amounts of practice or training. Using the chapter outline on page 195, point out how differential practice can account for many of the gender differences.

8. We noted that gender similarities are likely to be found in areas where other roles (e.g., work roles) are emphasized. Based on this argument, predict whether you would expect gender differences or similarities for the following pairs of individuals: (a) assertiveness shown by a male police officer and a female police officer when each is handing a ticket to a motorist caught speeding; (b) leadership qualities in a male college president and a female college president; (c) persuasion abilities of a male lawyer and a female lawyer in a courtroom; (d) influenceability of a male executive and a female office assistant.

9. Most of this chapter focused on the topic of "gender of the subject." However, "gender of the stimulus" was also discussed. How do people react to assertive women, to men and women leaders, and to females who are trying to influence other people?

10. To solidify your knowledge in preparation for the chapter on women and work (Chapter 7), think of a profession in which relatively few women are employed. Review each of the social and personality characteristics discussed in the current chapter. Note whether any of these factors provides a sufficient explanation for the relative absence of women in that profession.

NEW TERMS

social constructionist explanation (197)
nonverbal communication (198)
personal space (202)
dyads (203)
decoding ability (206)
altruism (212)
nurturance (214)
operational definitions (214)
empathy (214)
relational model (215)
self-in-relation theory (215)

differences perspective (216)
cultural feminism (216)
similarities perspective (216)
liberal feminism (216)
justice perspective (216)
care perspective (216)
self-disclosure (219)
aggression (221)
assertiveness (225)
democratic leadership (227)
autocratic leadership (227)

RECOMMENDED READINGS

Aries, E. (1996). *Men and women in interaction: Reconsidering the differences.* New York: Oxford University Press. Here's a wonderful book that examines the complexity of communication patterns in men and women; it explores leadership, conversation, and language style.

Canary, D. J., & Emmers-Sommer, T. M. (1997). *Sex and gender differences in personal relationships.* New York: Guilford. These authors present research in a way that can appeal to both professional psychologists and a more general audience. The book examines topics such as emotion, intimacy, and power.

Crawford, M. (1995). *Talking difference: On gender and language.* Thousand Oaks, CA: Sage. Mary Crawford's analysis of gender comparisons in language use is informed by feminist theory; her analysis of assertiveness-training workshops—designed for women—is also excellent.

Walsh, M. R. (Ed.). (1997). *Women, men, and gender: Ongoing debates.* New Haven, CT: Yale University Press. This wonderful book contains a series of paired debates on a variety of topics related to this chapter, such as conversational style, nonverbal communication, leadership, and relational theory.

ANSWERS TO THE DEMONSTRATIONS

Demonstration 6.5: These 12 scales assess four different components of aggression. For an informal index of your aggressiveness, add up the scores you assigned to each of the three questions assessing each dimension. Physical aggression—2, 4, 10; verbal aggression—1, 7, 11; anger—3, 6, 12; hostility—5, 8, 9.

Demonstration 6.6: The overall rankings supplied by the students in White and Roufail's (1989) study were: a. 7; b. 2; c. 3; d. 8; e. 1; f. 4; g. 6; h. 5.

ANSWERS TO THE
TRUE–FALSE QUESTIONS

1. True (p. 197); 2. False (p. 199); 3. False (p. 203); 4. True (p. 205); 5. False (p. 212); 6. False (p. 214); 7. False (p. 217); 8. False (p. 222); 9. False (p. 227); 10. True (p. 228).

*W*OMEN AND WORK

TRUE OR FALSE?

_____ 1. Compared to a woman who has not graduated from high school, a woman with at least four years of college is more than twice as likely to be employed.

_____ 2. The 1996 welfare reform policy has forced many women out of college programs in order to take low-level jobs.

_____ 3. Although women earn lower incomes than men, the discrepancy can be explained by different occupations, different amounts of work experience, and different numbers of hours worked each week.

_____ 4. Between 15% and 20% of the top U.S. corporations are now headed by women.

_____ 5. A woman making clothes in a U.S. sweatshop (a factory that violates labor laws) will typically earn about $10,000 annually if she works 16-hour days.

_____ 6. Women and men in the same profession—such as medicine—are typically fairly similar in their personal characteristics.

_____ 7. Women in blue-collar jobs are not as satisfied with their work situation as are women who are clerks or secretaries.

_____ 8. Research in both the United States and Canada shows that women perform about two-thirds of the household chores.

_____ 9. Children of employed women have normal cognitive development, compared to children cared for at home by their mothers; however, they have substantially more social and emotional problems.

_____ 10. Because of their heavy responsibilities, employed women are more likely than nonemployed women to experience problems with their physical and psychological health.

CHAPTER 7

Background Factors Related to Women's Employment
Personal Characteristics Related to Women's Employment
Women and Welfare
Discrimination in Hiring Patterns

Discrimination in the Workplace
Salary Discrimination
Discrimination in Promotions
Other Kinds of Treatment Discrimination
Discrimination Against Lesbians in the Workplace
What to Do About Treatment Discrimination

Women's Experiences in Selected Occupations
Employment in Traditionally Female Occupations
Employment in Traditionally Male Professions
Employment in Blue-Collar Jobs
Why Are Women Scarce in Certain Occupations?
Homemakers

Coordinating Employment with Personal Life
Marriage
Children
Personal Adjustment

Maria, a Native American woman, was frequently asked to represent her department at professional meetings that had little to do with her position at work. When she complained to her supervisors that these meetings were time-consuming, they replied that she was the department's only person of color, and diversity was necessary at these meetings. After 6 months, however, her boss formally reprimanded her, warning that she wasn't productive enough at work (Comas-Diaz & Greene, 1994a).

Roberta Berrien (1992), a physician, was recently called into the office of a male colleague. He pointed to his desk, which displayed two partially clad "breasts" that he had made out of cake batter. Dr. Berrien reported that she often overhears the receptionist tell patients who call the office, "Dr. Berrien is a woman, but she is a good doctor" (p. 2616).

Susan is a department secretary at a prestigious university. She is expected to work overtime—without overtime pay. In addition to her secretarial work, she performs many administrative responsibilities. For example, she organized a large-scale conference for the department, and she is in charge of intersession courses. The department members always say, "We don't know what we'd do without you, Susan!" They'll soon find out, because she's decided to leave; her salary after 10 years on the job is $19,000.

Work is becoming an increasingly important part of women's lives. In the United States and Canada, about 60% of women over the age of 15 are currently employed (Office of Research and Media Reaction, 1994; U.S. Bureau of the Census, 1997).

To remove any confusion, we need to discuss some terms related to work. The general term **working women** refers to (1) women who work for pay outside the home and (2) women who receive no pay for working full time in the home. The first category—women who receive money for their work outside the home—will also be referred to as **employed women.** They may receive a salary, be self-employed, or be licensed professionals. The second category—women who are unpaid for their work—will also be referred to as

236   **nonemployed women.** They may work for their families, their homes, or

volunteer social or political organizations, but they receive no money for these services.

BACKGROUND FACTORS RELATED TO WOMEN'S EMPLOYMENT

In Chapter 4, which explored adolescent women's career aspirations, we saw how career counselors, teachers, and social forces can reduce many women's life goals.

On the bright side, in some fields that were once reserved for men, the number of women has increased dramatically. Well into the 20th century, women were barred from many medical schools. For years, Yale University Medical School clung to men-only admissions by arguing that the facilities did not include a women's bathroom (M. Walsh, 1990). As recently as 1976, only 16% of U.S. medical school graduates were women. Just two decades later, in 1996, 41% of medical school graduates were women (Barzansky et al., 1997). The numbers of women in law schools and veterinary schools have also increased dramatically. We'll be well into the 21st century before an equal number of *practicing* doctors, lawyers, and veterinarians are female. However, the large percentages of women currently in the professional "pipelines" are encouraging.

In this chapter, we will examine areas in which women have made progress in recent decades, as well as areas in which women still face disadvantages. We'll begin this first section by examining women's personal characteristics that are associated with employment. Then we'll briefly explore two issues that are critical for women: welfare, and discrimination in hiring.

Personal Characteristics Related to Women's Employment

What situations or characteristics predict whether a woman works outside the home? Several decades ago, one of the best predictors of a woman's employment was whether she had young children; mothers of preschoolers were seldom employed. Employed mothers are now the norm in the United States, although mothers of preschoolers (62% of employed women) are still less likely to hold a job than women whose children are between the ages of 6 and 17 years (77% of employed women; see Kleiman, 1998). The same pattern for mothers is also found in Canada (Almey, 1995).

One of the best predictors of women's employment is education. As you can see from Figure 7.1, women with at least four years of college are more than twice as likely as women with less than four years of high school to be employed outside the home (U.S. Department of Labor, 1994).

Figure 7.1 also illustrates that Black women and Latinas are more likely than European American women to work outside the home. Census surveys have indicated that Asian American women are also more likely than European American

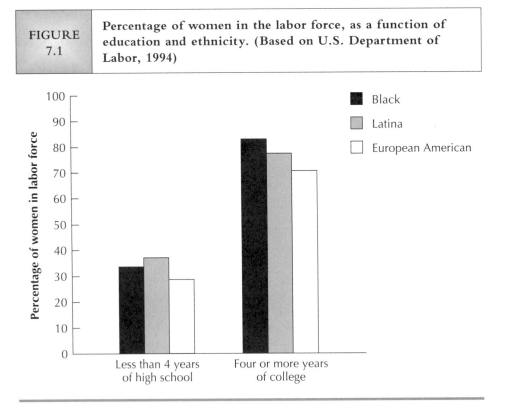

FIGURE 7.1   **Percentage of women in the labor force, as a function of education and ethnicity. (Based on U.S. Department of Labor, 1994)**

women to work outside the home. Compared to other ethnic groups, Native American women are slightly less likely to be employed (U.S. Bureau of the Census, 1993).

One category of female employees is receiving increased attention from researchers: immigrant women. They are often considered homogeneous by the media and the general public (Naidoo, 1990b). However, they differ widely in their country of origin, race, religion, language, education, and political beliefs.

Immigrant women in both the United States and Canada face a number of significant barriers. Many of these women are not fluent in the language of their new country. Their educational degrees, professional licenses, and work experience in another country may not be given full credit when they apply for a North American job (Chow, 1994; Naidoo, 1990a). Others face stereotypes. For example, a European American employer may believe that an Asian individual would be an excellent computer scientist, but not an insurance salesperson (Blank & Slipp, 1994; Leong & Hayes, 1990).

Immigrants from many countries are unusually well educated. Of the Asian Indians currently living in Ontario, Canada, 40% have had at least some university education, in contrast to only 20% in the general population (Rajagopal, 1990). Still, their salaries are lower than nonimmigrants with comparable training. Even well-educated immigrants must contend with negative or patronizing attitudes. One Asian Indian woman remarked:

> At lunch, in the Faculty Club, I am not charmed when colleagues compliment me for not having a "sing-song" accent. I am tired of being exotic, being complimented

---

DEMONSTRATION 7.1

A Quiz About Welfare

This quiz tests your knowledge about Aid to Families with Dependent Children (AFDC), a controversial policy in the United States that was abolished in 1996. Answer the questions below, and then check your accuracy by looking at the answers on page 274 at the end of the chapter. If possible, ask several friends to try the quiz, too, and note their accuracy. Can you determine any factors that are correlated with your friends' scores?

1. The average U.S. mother who received no benefits from AFDC had approximately two children. The average woman receiving AFDC had approximately how many children?

    (a) 1   (b) 2   (c) 3   (d) 4

2. In 1995, the federal poverty line for a family of 3 (one adult plus two children) was approximately:

    (a) $8,000   (b) $12,000   (c) $16,000   (d) $20,000

3. In 1995, the annual AFDC grant for a family of 3 averaged:

    (a) $4,500   (b) $6,000   (c) $8,500   (d) $10,000

4. The largest group of women receiving AFDC was

    (a) European American   (b) Latina   (c) Black   (d) Asian

5. Of all mothers who began receiving AFDC on a given date, what percentage were off AFDC one year later?

    (a) 10%   (b) 35%   (c) 50%   (d) 75%

6. Of daughters from families that received AFDC, what percentage went on to receive AFDC as adults?

    (a) 25%   (b) 40%   (c) 55%   (d) 70%

7. What percentage of people below the poverty line lived in public or subsidized housing?

    (a) 18%   (b) 27%   (c) 36%   (d) 45%

(Based on Belle, 1997.)

for qualities of voice, education, bearing, appearance, that are not extraordinary. (Naidoo, 1990b, p. 19)

In summary, a variety of personal characteristics are related to a woman's employment situation. They include parenting of young children, education, ethnic background, and immigrant status.

Women and Welfare

On the current political scene, one of the most heated debates focuses on women who receive welfare payments—specifically, whether these payments should be suspended if women do not find employment after an "appropriate" period of time. We need to address the myths about welfare, especially because policies have important effects on women's long-term prospects for employment.

The Aid to Families with Dependent Children (AFDC) program was created to provide welfare payments for children whose parents cannot provide economic support. From the intensity of the controversies, you might expect that a huge portion of the federal budget had been allocated to welfare. However, the actual amount spent on the AFDC program was only 1% in 1995 (Flanders, 1997). Before you read further, try Demonstration 7.1.

Some critics argue that economically poor women are eager to have more children because of the financial incentives of extra welfare benefits. It's difficult to test this hypothesis, but reviews of the research find no relationship for Blacks and Latinas. For European Americans, some studies show a weak relationship and some show none (Wilcox et al., 1996). The fact is that a mother on welfare received only about $90 a month in extra AFDC benefits if she had another child—certainly not enough to compensate for that child's food and clothing (Flanders, 1997).

In August 1996, President Clinton signed legislation that abolished AFDC. The current legislation includes many changes that will jeopardize economically poor women. For example, individuals can now remain on welfare for a lifetime maximum of 5 years. In addition, each of the 50 states is now allowed to decide which individuals are desperate enough to need financial assistance. Another provision with widespread consequences for women is that states are penalized if they do not force individuals into work programs (Albelda & Tilly, 1997).

The consequences of this last provision are enormous. For example, suppose that a college student who is a mother wants to escape from an abusive marriage. If she leaves the marriage and applies for welfare to support her children, she will be forced to leave college and earn a minimum wage in a low-level job (Madsen, 1998).

A Wisconsin woman was enrolled in a community college program so that she could become a police officer. Previous welfare policies allowed women to enroll in college programs that would make them more employable. However, Wisconsin's revised welfare policy forced her to drop out of college and take a $6.25-an-hour job as a clerk. As she said:

In class I was so confident and proud because I was going to do this. It's strange. I've gone from this positive, happy person to, I don't know, I'm just so sad." (D. Z. Jackson, 1998, p. 1)

You already know from Figure 7.1 that a woman's education is one of the best predictors of her employment. Compared to college graduates, women without college degrees are 10 times as likely to live in poverty (D. Z. Jackson, 1998). The current "welfare reform" is obviously short-sighted.

Discrimination in Hiring Patterns

In the 1960s, employers could legally refuse to hire a woman for a specific job simply because she was a woman (Clayton & Crosby, 1992). This overt discrimination is no longer legal, but subtle discrimination persists. The term **access discrimination** refers to discrimination used in hiring—for example, rejecting well-qualified women applicants, or offering them less attractive positions. Once they have been hired, women may face another kind of discrimination, called treatment discrimination, which we'll discuss later in this chapter.

When Does Access Discrimination Operate?   Several factors determine whether women face access discrimination when they apply for work.

1. *People who have strong gender-role stereotypes are more likely to demonstrate access discrimination.* For example, personnel administrators who were highly gender stereotyped were likely to be biased against women applying for a position as a sports reporter. In contrast, people who were less stereotyped were more likely to judge women fairly (D. Katz, 1987; Sharp & Post, 1980).

2. *Access discrimination is particularly likely to operate when people apply for a prestigious position.* For example, Kolpin and Singell (1996) studied the hiring patterns of economics departments in 181 U.S. universities. The departments that were ranked most prestigious were the least likely to hire female faculty members. You might wonder whether the women applicants were somehow less well qualified. However, the authors found that the women candidates were actually more productive than the male candidates; these well-qualified women experienced access discrimination.

3. *Access discrimination often operates for both women and men when they apply for "gender-inappropriate" jobs.* In general, employers select men for jobs when the majority of the current employees are male, and they select women when the majority are female (Clayton & Crosby, 1992; Konrad & Pfeffer, 1991; Lorber, 1994).

For example, Peter Glick (1991) mailed employment questionnaires to personnel officers and career placement consultants. He asked them to read the job applications and make judgments about the applicants' suitability for 35 specific jobs. Glick then calculated the respondents' preferences for female versus male applicants: positive numbers meant that the majority of respondents preferred a female for a job; negative numbers meant a male was preferred. Glick also consulted government statistics to determine the percentage of women currently employed in these jobs.

As Figure 7.2 shows, the respondents showed a clear preference for male applicants when 0% to 20% of the employees in an occupation were female (that is, most current employees were male). They showed weaker preferences for a male applicant when 20% to 60% of employees were female. When the clear majority (60% to 100%) of employees were female, the respondents actually preferred female applicants. These data suggest that employers tend to select a male for an executive position in a corporation, but they prefer a female as a worker in a day-care center. These two examples of discrimination are not really equivalent, however, because the position where the men experience bias pays less and is less prestigious.

4. *Access discrimination is particularly likely to operate when the applicant's qualifications are ambiguous.* For instance, employers will hire a man rather than a woman, when both candidates are not especially qualified for a job. In contrast, employers are less likely to discriminate against a woman if they have abundant information for evaluating a candidate, and if that information is directly relevant

FIGURE 7.2	**Hiring preferences for women versus men, as a function of the current percentage of women in the occupation being judged. (Based on Glick, 1991)**

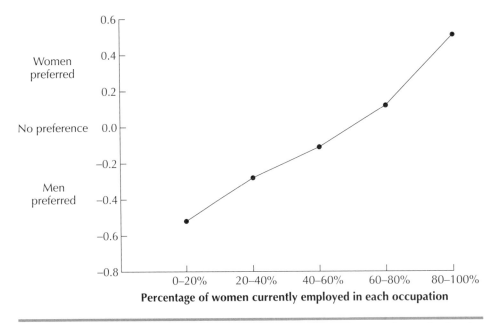

Note: Negative values indicate preference for males; positive values indicate preference for females.

to the proposed job (Larwood & Gutek, 1984; Martell, 1996a). A female applicant who has performed well for a company in a related position would
have a good chance of being hired. For example, research by Konrad and
Pfeffer (1991) showed that women were more likely to be hired for management positions in a university when they had already worked elsewhere in the
institution.

In summary, a woman is least likely to be considered for a job when the evaluators are stereotyped, when the position is prestigious, and when the job is
considered appropriate for males. She is also likely to face access discrimination
when information about her qualifications is insufficient or unclear.

How Does Access Discrimination Operate? People's stereotypes about
women may operate in several ways to produce access discrimination (Arvey,
1979; Martell, 1996a).

1. Employers may have negative stereotypes about women's abilities. An employer who believes that women are unmotivated and incompetent will probably react negatively to a specific woman candidate.

2. Employers may assume that the candidate must have certain stereotypically
   masculine characteristics in order to succeed on the job. Female candidates
   may be perceived as stereotypically feminine, even if they are truly assertive
   and independent. An employer may misperceive a woman as being deficient
   in these ideal characteristics.

3. Employers may pay attention to inappropriate characteristics when female
   candidates are being interviewed. The interviewer may judge a woman in
   terms of her physical appearance, secretarial skills, and personality, and gloss
   over the characteristics relevant to the executive position she is seeking.

Notice that, in each case, stereotypes encourage employers to conclude that a
woman would be unsuitable for a particular position.

Background Factors Related to Women's Employment

1. **Although many factors discourage women from entering stereotypically masculine fields, the percentage of women in some professions—such as medicine—has increased dramatically.**

2. **Women's employment status is influenced by factors such as parenting, education, ethnicity, and immigrant status.**

3. **Cutbacks in welfare have important consequences for women's lives;
   for example, women may be forced to leave a career-oriented college
   program in order to earn money in a low-level job.**

4. **Access discrimination is most likely to occur when the employer has
   strong stereotypes, when the position is prestigious, when a woman is**

applying for a stereotypically masculine position, and when her qualifications are ambiguous.

5. Stereotypes encourage access discrimination because (a) employers have negative stereotypes about women; (b) employers believe that women are lacking stereotypically masculine characteristics; and (c) employers may pay attention to characteristics that are irrelevant for the positions that women are seeking.

DISCRIMINATION IN THE WORKPLACE

So far, we've discussed one kind of discrimination against women—the access discrimination women face when they are applying for a job. A second problem, **treatment discrimination,** refers to the discrimination women face after they have obtained a job. We'll examine salary discrimination, promotion discrimination, other workplace biases, and the discrimination experienced by lesbians in the workplace. We'll also consider what people can do to combat workplace discrimination.

Salary Discrimination

The most obvious kind of treatment discrimination is that women earn less money than men. As of 1997, for example, U.S. women who worked full time earned only 74% of the median* annual salary of men (World Almanac, 1999). The comparable figure for Canada in 1993 was 72% (Statistics Canada, 1995).

The gender gap in salaries holds true for European Americans, Blacks, and Latinas/os (U.S. Bureau of the Census, 1997). As Figure 7.3 shows, European American males earn almost twice the annual salary of Latina females. (Unfortunately, the Census Bureau does not include Asian American and Native American workers in its calculations.)

The salary discrimination cannot be explained by gender differences in education. Women earn substantially lower salaries at *every* educational level—from those who have not attended high school to those who have completed some graduate work. One analysis showed that female *college* graduates made an average of only about $2,000 more per year than male *high school* graduates (U.S. Bureau of the Census, 1992).

One important reason for the discrepancy in salaries is that men enter jobs that pay more money. Engineers, who are usually male, earn about twice as much as elementary school teachers, who are usually female (Andriote, 1998).

---

*The *median* is the exact midpoint of a distribution; in this case, it is a dollar amount above which half of the men were receiving higher salaries and below which half were receiving lower salaries.

FIGURE 7.3	U.S. median annual salaries, as a function of ethnic group and gender. (Based on U.S. Bureau of the Census, 1997)

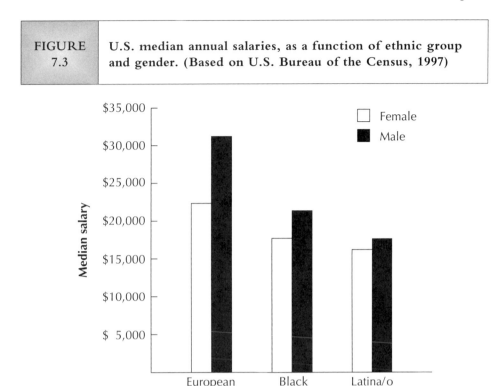

However, the choice of different kinds of jobs explains only part of the discrepancy. A number of carefully conducted studies clearly demonstrate that women are simply paid less than men, even when other factors are taken into account (P. England, 1992; Haslett et al., 1992; S. Kaplan et al., 1996; Thacker, 1995; Valian, 1998). Baker (1996) studied the salaries of male and female physicians in the United States. He statistically corrected for a variety of factors that could account for gender differences in salary, such as the physicians' specialty, ethnic group, type of medical school, and the income level of the community in which the physician practiced. The analysis showed that, for physicians with at least 10 years of experience, men still earned 17% more than women.

Looking at a wide variety of jobs, Dunn (1996) estimated that about 35% of the wage gap can be explained by the fact that men are more likely than women to enter occupations that pay well. An additional 15% of the wage gap can be explained by other factors, such as women taking time out to raise children. About 50% of the wage gap, Dunn estimated, may be attributed to discrimination.

Similar wage gaps are found in countries other than the United States and Canada (Benokraitis, 1997b). In Great Britain, Switzerland, and Germany, women earn between 66% and 76% of men's pay. In several countries, such as France, Iceland, and Australia, women earn close to 90% of men's pay (Reskin & Padavic, 1994). The salary gap is smaller in countries where the government has instituted a policy of pay equity.

Let's look at two more specific aspects of the salary gap: (1) the concept of comparable worth and (2) women's reactions to receiving lower pay.

Comparable Worth.   Most people are willing to acknowledge that a man and a woman with equivalent performance at the same job should receive the same salaries. That is, women and men should receive equal pay for equal work.

Comparable worth is more complicated. The concept of **comparable worth** argues that women and men should receive equal pay for *different* jobs when those different jobs are comparable (P. England, 1992; R. Stryker, 1996). People who favor comparable-worth legislation point out that much of the gender gap in wages can be attributed to **occupational segregation;** as we noted, men and women tend to choose different occupations. Specifically, people's wages reflect discrimination on the basis of the gender of the current job applicants. In other words, "women's jobs" (for example, as nurses, elementary-school teachers, and secretaries) pay less than "men's jobs" (for example, as auto mechanics, fire-fighters, and electricians) (R. Stryker, 1996). Theme 3 of this book states that women are devalued in our society. The work they do is also devalued in terms of the actual dollar value placed on their accomplishments.

Incidentally, the term *comparable worth* doesn't make much sense unless you see it in context. It is a shorthand term for "equal pay for jobs of comparable worth."

In general, occupations that are virtually all-male will pay about $1.00 more per hour than occupations that are virtually all-female (Lorber, 1994). One dollar per hour might not sound like much. However, if this discrepancy holds across people's lifetime of work, then those in "mostly male" occupations will earn almost $95,000 more than those in "mostly female" occupations.

In general, the strategy of comparable worth is to pay the same salaries for "men's jobs" and "women's jobs" that are matched in complexity, skill, or responsibility. The components of the job that must be considered are: education, training, previous experience, skills, dangerousness, dirtiness, and supervisory responsibilities (M. Barker, 1996; Lorber, 1994). By this reasoning, a woman with a bachelor's degree who works with children in a day-care center should earn more than a mechanic with a high school degree who works with air conditioners. Unfortunately, however, comparable-worth legislation has had only limited success in both the United States and Canada (M. Barker, 1996; Lorber, 1994; Statistics Canada, 1995).

Reactions to Lower Salaries.   How do women feel about their lower salaries? One answer to this question comes from research in which women and men decide how much they *ought* to receive for doing a particular job. In general, women choose lower salaries, suggesting that they are satisfied with less (Bylsma & Major, 1992; Major, 1989; Sumner & Brown, 1996). Now try Demonstration 7.2, to illustrate a study by Bylsma and Major (1992). These researchers found that male and female undergraduates who received no additional information gave very different salary requests. Specifically, men asked for an average of $6.30, whereas women asked for an average of $5.30. Women simply feel that they are entitled to less money!

How do women react to the gender gap in wages? Women are typically more concerned about women's lower wages than men are (Browne, 1997a)—a finding that should not be surprising. Men and women in the United States rank "good salary" second in a list of important job attributes, right behind "interesting or challenging work" (Browne, 1997b). Also, in a survey of employed women conducted by the AFL–CIO, 94% reported that equal pay for equal work was very important (E. Goodman, 1997).

Still, we have some evidence that women may not be as outraged as they should be (Clayton & Crosby, 1992; Crosby, 1982). Faye Crosby and her colleagues report that women often acknowledge that *women in general* are underpaid. However, women tend to show **denial of personal disadvantage;** they believe that they *personally* are not affected by injustices that harm the groups to which they belong (Crosby, 1993). Similarly, Roberts and Chonko (1994) found that women and men were equally satisfied with their salaries, even though men earned higher wages.

DEMONSTRATION 7.2

Gender Comparisons in Salary Requests

Ask a number of friends to participate in a very brief study. Ideally, you should recruit at least five males and five females. (Make sure that the two groups are roughly similar in average age and work experience.) Ask them the following question:

"I want you to imagine that you are an undergraduate who has been employed as a research assistant to Dr. Johnson, who is a professor of psychology. You will be working with him all summer, entering data that are being collected for a summer research project. What *hourly* salary do you believe would be appropriate for this summer job?"

When you have gathered all the data, calculate the average wage suggested by the males and the average wage suggested by the females. The text lists the salary requests that students provided in a study several years ago. Do you find a similar "wage gap" in the requests you gathered?

(Based on Bylsma & Major, 1992.)

> ### DEMONSTRATION 7.3
>
> ## *The Denial of Personal Disadvantage*
>
> Locate a number of employed women with whom you would feel comfortable discussing two questions about salary. Ask each woman these questions individually, in a setting where other people cannot easily eavesdrop:
>
> 1. Do you believe that women in general are the victims of gender discrimination, in terms of their work salaries?
> 2. Do you feel that you are presently a victim of gender discrimination, in terms of your salary at work?
>
> For each question, pursue your respondent's answer by asking her to provide more explanation, when necessary. If she seems uncomfortable or reluctant to provide information, change the subject immediately.
>
> (Based on Crosby, 1984.)

Why in the world should women be relatively happy about their salaries? Many women are honestly unaware that they receive a lower salary than comparable men. Furthermore, it's very difficult to detect discrimination by analyzing just a few cases at a time (Rutte et al., 1994). For these reasons, businesses and institutions must gather data on salaries; the pay inequities are more obvious with a large sample of men and women (Crosby, 1993).

Another reason that women do not acknowledge their disadvantage is that they want to believe that the world is a just and fair place in which people receive what they deserve (Clayton & Crosby, 1992). If a woman acknowledges that she is underpaid, then she must explain this inequity—and all of the explanations are unpleasant. Does she really want to conclude that her boss and the organization that employs her are villains? An unfortunate consequence is that, if she continues to deny her personal disadvantage, she is not likely to work for pay equity and other social justice issues. When you have the opportunity, try Demonstration 7.3 to discover whether the women you know tend to deny their personal disadvantage.

Discrimination in Promotions

Alice Huang came to the United States from China when she was 10 years old, a refugee with no money. And yet she earned a bachelor's degree from Wellesley, a doctorate from Johns Hopkins, and full-professor status from Harvard. She was also elected president of the American Society of Microbiologists. When she was being interviewed for a top-level job at a prestigious college, she realized that the interviewers did not seem enthusiastic about her qualifications. Huang recalled, "I told them that I doubted whether they were going to offer this job, at this time in the history of the institution, to an Asian-American woman" (S. Miller, 1992, p. 1224). Two of the interviewers actually nodded their heads, confirming her strong suspicions.

Alice Huang had bumped into the **glass ceiling,** a presumably invisible barrier that seems to block the advancement of women and people of color in many professional organizations (D. Kaufman, 1995). The *glass ceiling* metaphor may not be entirely accurate, however. Individuals who are experiencing advancement barriers report that the barriers are actually quite obvious and visible—not at all as transparent as glass (Quina et al., 1994).

The data persuasively confirm that women encounter glass ceilings in a variety of professions. Compared to men, women are less likely to be promoted to management positions in fields such as engineering, medicine, and business (Benokraitis, 1997a; Cox & Harquail, 1991; Tesch et al., 1995). The top 1,000 U.S. corporations are headed by 996 men and 4 women (Valian, 1998).

Labor theorists have constructed another metaphor to describe a related situation. The metaphor of the **sticky floor** describes the phenomenon that women are not promoted out of low-level jobs. One-third of all employed women perform some kind of office work. Women also work in service professions, as cashiers and waitresses. They are likely to remain in these jobs throughout their work life, never being considered for positions with greater responsibility (Headlee & Elfin, 1996).

A third metaphor describes another component of gender bias. According to the **glass escalator** phenomenon, when men enter fields often associated with women—becoming nurses, teachers, librarians, and social workers—they are often quickly promoted to management positions (Coleman, 1996; C. Williams, 1998). The glass escalator whisks them up to a more prestigious position. For example, a male teacher in elementary special education was asked whether his area was unusual for a man, compared to other areas of education. He replied, "Much more so. I am extremely marketable in special education. That's not why I got into the field. But I am extremely marketable because I am a man" (C. Williams, 1998, p. 288).

You may wonder whether women of color have experienced some kind of "double advantage" in recent years, when employers have been supposedly eager to hire underrepresented ethnic groups. We don't yet have much research on this topic. However, Black women and Black men seem to be promoted at similar rates (E. Bell et al., 1993; Nkomo & Cox, 1989). Furthermore, Black men and women who are professors do not experience any employment advantages, compared to European Americans (Murray, 1997).

In short, women generally face discrimination with respect to promotion. The three stereotypes that we mentioned on page 243, in connection with hiring patterns, also operate when women want to advance in their occupations (Martell et al., 1998). In addition, top executives (mostly male) are not likely to suggest that females might fill the other top positions (Burn, 1996). After reviewing a wide range of studies on treatment discrimination, Jerry Jacobs (1995a) concluded that females have a long way to go before they have the same status as men in the workplace. Specifically, "Women managers continue to trail their male counterparts in both earnings and authority" (p. 172).

Other Kinds of Treatment Discrimination

In addition to discrimination in salary and promotions, women experience treatment discrimination in other areas. For example, several studies show that women are likely to be evaluated more negatively than men. You'll recall from Chapter 2 that women sometimes (though not always) are downgraded for their performance. The research on evaluation in the workplace confirms a point we made throughout Chapter 6: Women are especially likely to be downgraded if they are seen as assertive, independent, and unfeminine (Fiske et al., 1993). Other analyses show that women are especially likely to receive negative workplace ratings (relative to men) when the rater is somewhat preoccupied with other tasks or when the rater makes a rating some time after observing the individual (Martell, 1991; Martell, 1996b). In the real world, executives frequently rate their employees under distracted or delayed conditions—with unfortunate consequences for women!

Negative evaluations are frequent among women working in stereotypically masculine fields (Yoder & Schleicher, 1996). Managers who have had little experience working with women are also especially likely to show discrimination (Eskilson & Wiley, 1996).

Other evidence of treatment discrimination comes from students' ratings of their professors. The results are not perfectly consistent. However, a review of the literature shows that male students are generally more likely than female students to give their female college professors poor ratings on their teaching performance (Basow, 1995).

Another form of treatment discrimination is **sexual harassment,** or "deliberate or repeated comments, gestures, or physical contacts of a sexual nature that are unwanted by the recipient" (American Psychological Association, 1990, p. 393). (We'll discuss sexual harassment in detail in Chapter 13.) Women frequently experience this kind of treatment discrimination on the job. Some harassers specifically tell women that sexual favors are a prerequisite for job advancement. Other harassers' messages are more subtle, though no less humiliating. One legal secretary recalled, for example, that her boss instructed one of his clients to ask her to get up and get him a cup of coffee so he could see what great legs she has (Pierce, 1995).

Another potential kind of treatment discrimination is less dramatic, though it has important implications. Specifically, coworkers may make negative, gender-related comments that convey the message that women are second-class citizens (I. Amato, 1992; St. Jean & Feagin, 1997). A Black female firefighter recalled her first encounter with her White male supervisor:

> The first day I came on, the first day I was in the field, the guy told me he didn't like me. And then he said: "I'm gonna tell you why I don't like you. Number one, I don't like you cuz you're Black. And number two, cuz you're a woman." And that was all he said. He walked away. (Yoder & Aniakudo, 1997)

You won't be surprised to learn, then, that women are often more likely than men to report negative interactions in the workplace (Kite & Balogh, 1997). Women may also be excluded from informal social interactions, both at work and after hours. They may not be part of informal conversations, lunches, golf games, and other social occasions. Business may be conducted at these events, and important information may be exchanged (Bronstein & Farnsworth, 1998; Karsten, 1994; Pierce, 1995). Furthermore, the friendships that are strengthened outside of work may provide access to prestigious assignments, useful hints, and other factors that could lead to career advancement. In addition to facing other forms of discrimination, women certainly do not have equal opportunities in informal social interactions.

Discrimination Against Lesbians in the Workplace

In Chapter 2, we noted that **heterosexism** is discrimination against lesbians, gay males, and bisexuals—any group that is not heterosexual. Lesbians frequently face heterosexism in the workplace. A lesbian mortgage broker remarked about the effects of heterosexism on her career:

> I was on the fast track in my company—I was on special committees, getting bonuses, the whole works. Somehow my employer found out that I had a female domestic partner and—*pow!*—it took no time before I was fired. Despite my not being out and being considered an attractive women, the mere fact of my being a lesbian was enough to get me fired. There was no law to protect me from this. (Blank & Slipp, 1994, p. 141)

Most students are surprised to learn that—in many cases—employers can fire employees for any reason they choose, including being a lesbian (Purcell & Hicks, 1996). As you can guess, many employers refuse to hire individuals who are known to be gay. For example, public schools discriminate against hiring lesbians, gays, and bisexuals as teachers. The unjustified argument is that these individuals may try to persuade young people to adopt a nonheterosexual orientation (Purcell & Hicks, 1996). Fortunately, as of 1994, 31 out of 50 large cities in the United States had adopted laws that protect lesbians, gays, and bisexuals from discrimination on the basis of sexual orientation (A. Leonard, 1994).

Unfortunately, that kind of protection does not yet apply to lesbians, gay men, and bisexuals in the U.S. military. Abundant research confirms that they have served as competently as have heterosexuals (Herek, 1993; Purcell & Hicks, 1996). Still, the policy has not changed substantially. Ironically, many military leaders argue that women in the military would be more likely to be sexually harassed if lesbians were openly welcomed into the military. As you might imagine, however, virtually all reported cases of sexual harassment involve heterosexual males' harassing of women (Herek, 1993).

The research suggests that people who are open and accepting of their gay identity are higher in self-esteem (Walters & Simoni, 1993). Sadly, many jobs seem to require that gay individuals remain in the closet (Diamant, 1993). In one study, for example, two-thirds of lesbian women had not discussed the issue with their employers (Eldridge & Gilbert, 1990). Many lesbians and gay men say they spend so much energy trying to hide their sexual orientation that their work is less productive (Blank & Slipp, 1994). Not surprisingly, lesbian women are more likely than heterosexual women to report dissatisfaction with their interactions with coworkers and employers (D. Peters & Cantrell, 1993).

Should lesbians, gay men, and bisexuals disclose their sexual orientation to potential employers? As Gonsiorek (1996) points out, openness makes sense for people who plan to be "out" in their work setting. However, he also remarks that it may be useful to receive the job offer first and then come out gradually to colleagues. As you know from this chapter, bias is less likely when people are already familiar with an employee's work.

What to Do About Treatment Discrimination

The title of this section is daunting: How can we possibly try to correct all the forces that encourage gender discrimination in the workplace? A few guidelines may be helpful, with respect to the actions of both individuals and institutions.

Individuals can have an impact on their own work experiences, as well as the experiences of other women:

1. Women should be aware of the conditions in which stereotypes are least likely to operate, for example, when the job applicant's qualifications are clear-cut, rather than ambiguous. Be sure to develop skills and experiences that are especially relevant to your occupation (Committee on Women in Psychology, 1998). You should also know your legal rights (S. Ross et al., 1993).

2. Join relevant organizations, use the Internet, and make connections with other supportive people (Benokraitis & Feagin, 1994; Sonnert, 1995). Feminist organizations may be especially helpful. Female psychology professors, in a study by Klonis and her coauthors (1997), reported that they experienced feminism as "a life raft in the choppy, frigid waters of gender discrimination" (p. 343).

3. Women who have "made it" in their professions must be attuned to less experienced colleagues, offering them support and advice (Bronstein & Farnsworth, 1998). Males who are feminists can also be helpful (Benokraitis & Feagin, 1994). And heterosexuals must work against heterosexism in the workplace, so that lesbians, gays, and bisexuals do not experience discrimination (Livingston, 1996).

In reality, however, individuals cannot overcome the entire problem of gender discrimination. Institutions must change. Many of you probably share my skepticism that government organizations and corporations would genuinely want to eliminate discrimination. However, one important component is already in place: Gender discrimination is legally prohibited (Sonnert, 1995). Organizations that are truly committed to change can take these precautions:

1. Understand Affirmative Action policies and take them seriously (Eberhardt & Fiske, 1998). Develop guidelines within the organization (Bronstein & Farnsworth, 1998).

2. Appoint a task force to examine gender issues within the organization, making it clear that its recommendations will be valued and carried out (Kite & Balogh, 1997). Diversity training workshops are also useful (Rynes & Rosen, 1995).

3. Invite women into the pool of candidates for hiring and promotions (Valian, 1998).

4. Train managers so that they can evaluate candidates fairly, reducing gender stereotypes (Facteau & Dobbins, 1996). Managers rating employees should be encouraged to ask themselves questions such as: "How would I evaluate this performance if the person were a man rather than a woman?" (Valian, 1998, p. 309).

Realistically, creating gender-fair work experience requires a massive transformation of our culture, beginning with nonsexist childrearing, awareness and acceptance of feminist concerns, and an appreciation of the value of women. A truly gender-fair work world would also provide a national child-care plan, and it would ensure that men would perform an equal share of child-care and housework responsibilities—a topic we'll examine at the end of this chapter (Cleveland, 1996; Sonnert, 1995).

 SECTION SUMMARY *Discrimination in the Workplace*

1. **Women earn less than men; research demonstrates that the wage gap remains, even when such factors as occupation, education, and experience are taken into account.**

2. **Comparable worth means that women and men should receive the same pay for jobs that require comparable complexity, skill, and responsibility.**

3. **Women typically report that a good salary is an important job attribute; however, they may fail to acknowledge that they are underpaid.**

4. **Women experience discrimination in terms of promotion; three interrelated kinds of discrimination are called the glass ceiling, the sticky floor, and (for men) the glass escalator.**

5. **Women experience other kinds of treatment discrimination, such as lower evaluations, negative job ratings, sexual harassment, and exclusion from social interactions.**

6. **Lesbians are especially likely to experience workplace discrimination; they may be fired because of their sexual orientation, and they may feel it necessary to hide their sexual orientation.**

7. **Treatment discrimination can be addressed through the actions of individuals and institutions, but the solution must depend on more widespread societal change.**

WOMEN'S EXPERIENCES IN SELECTED OCCUPATIONS

We have seen that women face access discrimination when they apply for work, as well as a variety of different treatment discriminations once they are employed. In this section, we will examine women's work experiences in several specific occupations.

On the news, we hear about women who are physicians, steel workers, and astronauts. Women who are nurses, cashiers, and cafeteria workers do not make headlines. Even though the majority of employed women may engage in traditional clerical and service occupations, their work is relatively invisible.

Let's begin by discussing several traditionally female occupations. Then we'll discuss two categories of nontraditional occupations, the professions and blue-collar work. After discussing why women are so scarce in nontraditional occupations, we'll consider homemakers, who are among the least visible female workers.

Employment in Traditionally Female Occupations

Table 7.1 lists some representative traditional occupations and shows the percentage of workers who are women. Close to half of all female professional or technical workers are in traditional areas such as nursing and precollege teaching. This observation does not imply that something is wrong with traditionally "female" occupations. In fact, our society's children would probably be better off if occupations such as child care and elementary school teaching were more highly valued. However, women in traditionally female jobs frequently confront real-world problems such as low income, underutilization of abilities, and lack of independence in decision making. Women in the traditional jobs listed in Table 7.1 also face the problem of being seen by men as sex objects (Kemp, 1994).

Similar employment patterns operate in Canada. Even though a large number of women have entered the labor force in recent years, 70% of all employed

TABLE 7.1	Percentage of Workers in Selected "Traditionally Female" Occupations Who Are Women (U.S. Bureau of the Census, 1997)

Occupation	Percentage of Workers Who Are Women
Secretaries	99%
Dental hygienists	98
Registered nurses	93
Elementary school teachers	83
Social workers	69

Canadian women work as teachers, nurses, and clerks, or in secretarial or service occupations (Statistics Canada, 1995).

Keep in mind, though, that the work considered traditional for women may be very different in developing countries. The majority of women in Western Europe work in service occupations, but throughout most of Africa, 75% of the women in the labor force work in agriculture (United Nations, 1995). We even see different work patterns within the same continent. For example, consider two African countries. In Sierra Leone, the men are responsible for the rice fields; in Senegal, the rice fields are managed by women (Burn, 1996).

Let's consider two traditionally female jobs that are relatively invisible: domestic work and work in the garment industry. In both, women are especially likely to be exploited.

Domestic Work. Immigrant women from the Caribbean and Latin America often come to the United States to live and work in private homes, doing domestic work until they can earn a "green card," which will allow them to find better jobs. Colen (1997) describes the lives of Caribbean domestic workers in New York City. These women are expected to work long hours for minimal pay. Many of the women describe the insults they receive from their employers, who treat them much like modern-day slaves. For example, one woman reports:

> I work hard. I don't mind working hard. But I want to be treated with some human affection, like a human being . . . I don't get any respect. . . . Since I came here this woman has never shown me one iota of . . . human affection as a human being. (P. 205)

Garment Work. Most of us wake up in the morning, button up a shirt, and do not consider the life of the person who made that shirt—most often, a woman. At present, half of all the clothes purchased in the United States have been made in another country, often under inhuman conditions (Zia, 1996). Many of our clothes are made in **sweatshops,** which are defined as factories that violate labor laws ("Factory Wages," 1997). For example, a woman working in a regulated factory in Honduras might earn $1.30 an hour—not a generous amount, but enough to live on. A woman working in a sweatshop would earn about $.35 an hour, certainly not enough to feed a family. A shirt with a prestigious label from a U.S. company might cost $50, yet the woman who made it receives only pennies for her labor.

Illegal sweatshops are operating in some North American cities. These sweatshops are hidden away so that inspectors cannot find them. They employ mostly Latina and Asian immigrants, many of whom are undocumented, so they know they cannot protest about the working conditions (Chinen, 1996; Zia, 1996). A woman may earn about $10,000 a year, working 16-hour days. Clothing manufacturers also hire women to work in their homes, where they are even less visible to inspectors looking for labor violations. These women are paid for each completed item, and they may not be aware that a legal factory would pay twice as much. In Toronto, an estimated 4,000 to 8,000 women work out of their homes (Bains, 1998).

The sweatshop issue cannot be addressed without looking at our economic system to discover who is making the greatest profits from our clothing industry. If this problem concerns you, call the National Labor Committee at (212) 242-3002 (or visit www.nicnet.org) to find out which companies pay women fairly and which ones have been charged for running sweatshops.

Employment in Traditionally Male Professions

Ironically, we have more information about the relatively small number of women working in "the male professions" than we have about the large number of women in traditionally female jobs. For example, in preparing this section, I found entire books on women in business and management (F. Harris, 1996; Moore & Buttner, 1997; Salmansohn, 1996), in college teaching (Caplan, 1993; Toth, 1997), in college president ranks (P. Mitchell, 1993), in engineering and science (McIlwee & Robinson, 1992; Sonnert, 1995), in medicine (Wear, 1997), and in law (Guinier et al., 1997).

Unfortunately, this emphasis on nontraditional professions creates an impression that employed women are more likely to be executives than clerical workers. A more accurate picture of reality is shown in Table 7.2, which lists the percentage of workers who are women in several prestigious occupations. You may want to glance back at Table 7.1 to compare the two groups.

Incidentally, you'll note that I used the phrase "prestigious occupations" to refer to the male-dominated professions. Glick and his colleagues (1995) asked college students to rate the prestigiousness of a variety of occupations. Those rated most prestigious were all professions in which more men are employed than women. This pattern suggests an interesting prediction. Some professions—such as veterinary medicine and psychology—once had far more males

TABLE 7.2	Percentage of Workers in Selected "Traditionally Male" Professions Who Are Female (U.S. Bureau of the Census, 1997)

Occupation	Percentage of Workers Who Are Women
Engineers	9%
Dentists	14
Architects	17
Physicians	26
Lawyers	30

than females. In the 1990s, however, the majority of students in vet schools and psychology graduate schools were females (Gose, 1998; Norcross et al., 1996; Pion et al., 1996). Will these two career choices become less prestigious as the number of women in these fields increases?

Let's consider some of the characteristics of these women in traditionally male professions. Then we'll examine the "climate" in which these women work.

Characteristics of Women in Traditionally Male Professions.   In general, the women who work in stereotypically masculine occupations are similar to the men in that area. To some extent, this similarity may occur because only those women with personal characteristics appropriate for that occupation would choose it for a career (S. Jenkins, 1994). For example, both men and women in managerial positions in business value characteristics such as "enterprising" and "powerful" more than characteristics such as "academic" (M. Hatcher, 1991; Ragins, 1989; Ragins & Sundstrom, 1989).

Some women rate even higher marks than their male colleagues in certain "masculine" characteristics. For instance, the research suggests that female psychologists are more likely than male psychologists to value achievement and risk (J. Holland, 1992; Nevill & Kruse, 1996).

In addition, women who work in a particular profession are likely to adopt the characteristics of others in that profession (who are mostly men) in order to succeed in the field. For example, as women physicians grow older, they grow stronger in leadership potential and self-control (Cartwright & Wink, 1994).

As we would expect, women and men in the same profession tend to be similar in cognitive skills. For example, corporate men and women receive similar scores on a test of critical thinking (M. Hatcher, 1991). Male and female medical students also receive almost identical scores on the examinations given during their final year of study (Case et al., 1993).

Other research shows that men and women are equally committed to their work. Specifically, a meta-analysis of 27 studies showed that male and female employees are similar in their belief in the organization, their acceptance of its goals, and their willingness to work hard for its benefit (Aven et al., 1993).

Naturally, men and women in the same occupation do not have *identical* styles. For example, female physicians spend more time talking with their patients than male physicians do. Women physicians also ask more questions and make more positive comments than do their male colleagues (Golub, 1995; J. Hall et al., 1994; Henderson, 1998).

We can therefore make a general statement that women in nontraditional jobs are similar to the men in these areas, consistent with Theme 1 of this book. However, one area in which gender differences are often found is self-confidence (Ragins & Sundstrom, 1989). This finding is not surprising. As Chapter 5 observed, men may be more self-confident than women in some achievement settings. Sandler (1992) pointed out that women faculty members must learn not to hide their achievement:

> If you don't tell anyone about a paper you published, they simply may not know about it. If you don't tell people about your ideas and achievements, they may begin to believe that you have none. To the extent that women are devalued, it is even more important for women than for men to display their achievements. (p. 7)

However, Sandler's advice makes me wonder. As we've discussed, people respond negatively to an assertive woman because she violates the stereotype of the passive female. I suspect that people's reactions would also be negative toward a woman who seems to be bragging—thus violating the stereotype of the modest, self-effacing female. This question would make an interesting research project!

The Workplace Climate for Women in Traditionally Male Professions.
In Chapter 4, we saw that young female students may face a chilly climate in their academic classrooms. For many women in the professions, the chilly climate continues. Earlier in this chapter, we noted several forms of treatment discrimination. Unfortunately, treatment discrimination has a clear effect on the professional environment.

Consider the case of Dr. Frances Conley, one of the first female neurosurgeons in a specialty that is still about 97% male. In 1991, Dr. Conley resigned from her prestigious position as a professor at Stanford University Medical School. Her letter testified:

> Those who administer my work environment at the present time have never been able to accept me as an equal person. Not because I lack professional competence, but because I use a different bathroom. I am minus the appropriate gender identification that permits full membership in the club. (Perrone, 1991, p. 5)

As Conley describes in her recent book, the male neurosurgeons would attempt to kiss her neck while she was scrubbing up, call her "honey" in front of patients, and brag about their sexual conquests (Conley, 1998). One neurosurgeon would sometimes invite her to go to bed with him, thrust his pelvis forward, look down at his genitals and directly ask his genitals whether they would like that experience.

Another problem for women in nontraditional professions is that men may treat them in a patronizing fashion. Older men are especially likely to treat women as sweet, helpless little girls (McIlwee & Robinson, 1992). A 38-year-old female engineer commented on this benevolent sexism:

> With the older engineers, they always treat you like you're their little daughter, which they don't do to the young male engineers. There's a protectiveness or there's a feeling there where they want to pat you on the head, and you want them to slap you on the back, not pat you on the head. (McIlwee & Robinson, 1992, p. 97)

Often, too, a woman in a nontraditional profession will not have a role model or mentor—someone who can offer her support and career advice. For example, a woman working on her doctorate in science or engineering may not meet women who have seniority in her field.

In short, women in nontraditional careers receive many messages that they are not really equal to their male colleagues. These messages come in the form of sexist comments, patronizing reactions, and a general absence of female colleagues.

Employment in Blue-Collar Jobs

Most of the information on working women describes the women in nontraditional professions. In contrast, the information on women in blue-collar jobs is quite scanty. Women are increasingly entering blue-collar fields. At present, women represent 17% of all blue-collar workers (O'Farrell, 1995). This figure translates into more than 5 million blue-collar jobs for women. Table 7.3 lists some representative employment rates for women in these jobs.

TABLE 7.3	Percentage of Workers in Selected "Traditionally Male" Blue-Collar Occupations Who Are Female (U.S. Bureau of the Census, 1997)

Occupation	Percentage of Workers Who Are Women
Automobile mechanics	1%
Carpenters	1
Firefighters	2
Truck drivers	5
Farm workers	19

A significant number of women are interested in blue-collar jobs, but they must first overcome important barriers. High schools and vocational schools encourage women into more traditional jobs, and employers resist hiring women for blue-collar work.

Women in blue-collar jobs report that they are often held to stricter standards than male coworkers. For example, a Black woman firefighter was forced by her White male supervisor to recertify after her vehicle skidded into a pole during an ice storm. In contrast, a male colleague received no penalty when his vehicle accidentally killed an elderly pedestrian crossing a street (Yoder & Aniakudo, 1997). Female cabdrivers in a Canadian study reported that they are frequently taunted on the job. Their male coworkers may shout "Woman driver!" as the women back the car into a cab pickup area (Boyd, 1997).

Sexual harassment is often common (F. Coffin, 1997; V. Smith, 1997). One woman cabdriver asked the dispatcher to call her for an early morning shift. Unfortunately, a male driver also heard her request. He called her at 3:40 A.M. and made sexually suggestive remarks (Boyd, 1997).

Blue-collar workers point out the financial advantages of their occupations, especially in contrast to traditionally feminine work as secretaries or waitresses (Bader, 1990; F. Coffin, 1997). As a female coal miner said about the economic advantages: "I can wash off coal black but I can't wash off those damn bill collectors" (Hammond & Mahoney, 1983, p. 19).

Other women mention additional advantages to blue-collar work, such as a sense of pride in their own strength, and satisfaction in doing a job well (Cull, 1997; Lunneborg, 1990). Others enjoy serving as a role model and encouraging young women to pursue work in nontraditional areas (F. Coffin, 1997).

High-paying blue-collar jobs clearly offer an attractive alternative to many of the traditional female occupations that have low salaries. For example, Cinthea Fiss, who is pictured in Figure 7.4, works as a stationary engineer in a 12-person crew that maintains a 52-story building. Describing the reactions she has received on the job, she wrote:

> I believe that the sexism I confront on my job is no greater than that which women face everywhere, except that it may be more blatant in a nontraditional blue-collar job. Sometimes, the sexism has been to my advantage. For instance, their [coworkers'] expectations of my abilities were so low that it was easy to astonish them with my competence. (Fiss, 1986, p. 108)

Why Are Women Scarce in Certain Occupations?

In a classic article, Riger and Galligan (1980) tackled the question of why so few women occupy managerial positions. Their argument is also relevant for women in the traditionally male professions, as well as for blue-collar working women.

Riger and Galligan (1980) identified two major classes of explanations for why men are so much more likely than women to have managerial positions.

| FIGURE 7.4 | Cinthea Fiss at work as a stationary engineer. |

According to **person-centered explanations,** female socialization encourages women to develop personality traits that are inappropriate to the requirements of the managerial role. One person-centered explanation is fear of success—the notion that women have negative reactions to successful achievement. However, Chapter 5 pointed out that research during recent years has found no gender differences in fear of success. Recall, also, that researchers have not found consistent gender differences in other areas related to achievement, such as attributions for one's own success or failure, or in personality characteristics.

Another person-centered explanation argues that women *behave* in a different manner from men in managerial positions, as a result of a difference in gender-role socialization (Hennig & Jardim, 1977). This explanation argues that little boys learn critical management skills by playing team sports. They learn to plan, to cooperate, and to compete. (But, keep in mind how our discussion on page 257 emphasized the similarity between men and women in the same occupations.)

Riger and Galligan (1980) preferred a second explanatory approach. According to **situation-centered explanations,** the characteristics of the organizational situation explain why women are rarely found in managerial and other important roles; personal skills or traits do not deserve the blame. For example, access discrimination may block women's opportunities. If women do manage to be hired, they face several kinds of treatment discrimination, such as the glass ceiling that blocks promotion. Young women are also unlikely to receive help from those at the top. Men may be unwilling to become mentors to aspiring women, and women at the top are in scarce supply.

Notice that the person-centered explanations and the situation-centered explanations suggest different strategies for improving women's employment conditions. The person-centered explanations propose that women should take courses in handling finances, conducting meetings, and assertiveness training.

In contrast, the situation-centered explanations propose strategies designed to change the *situation,* not the person. Programs should be instituted to train managers to use objective rating scales; Affirmative Action policies should be enforced; and women should be promoted into management positions (Riger & Galligan, 1980). Management personnel should be encouraged to listen more carefully to women and to take their views seriously (Schaller, 1991).

Although these suggestions sound excellent, they are not likely to occur spontaneously. To some extent, companies may realize that hiring competent women is in their own best interest. Also, as more women enter into nontraditional jobs, their coworkers may acknowledge their competence. Furthermore, with larger numbers of women engaged in an occupation, they will be more likely to push for fair treatment of women in the workplace. Now try Demonstration 7.4, if you haven't already.

DEMONSTRATION 7.4

Evaluating a Job Description

Based on the description below, decide whether you would be tempted to apply for this job.

Help Wanted

Requirements: Intelligence, energy, patience, social skills, good health. *Tasks:* At least 12 different occupations. *Hours:* About 100 hours per week. *Salary:* None. *Holidays:* None (must remain on standby 24 hours a day, 7 days a week). *Opportunities for Advancement:* None (future employees will not be impressed with your work on this job). *Job Security:* None (layoffs are likely as you approach middle age). *Fringe Benefits:* Food, clothing, and shelter generally provided, but any additional bonuses will depend on the financial standing and good nature of the employer. No pension plan.

(Based on Chesler, 1976, p. 97.)

Homemakers

You probably recognized that the unappealing job description in Demonstration 7.4 lists the duties of a wife and mother. A **homemaker** is defined as someone who works full time as an unpaid laborer in the home (Lindsey, 1996). Many women who are full-time homemakers may switch their focus at another time in their lives, when they seek part-time or full-time employment. Later in this chapter, we'll see that even women with full-time paying jobs continue to do far more than their share of housework and child care. Here, we will focus on the diversity of responsibilities performed by homemakers.

Little research has been conducted on homemakers or housework (Grana et al., 1993). As Theme 3 argues, topics associated almost exclusively with women tend to be invisible. Also, homemaking—by definition—is unpaid, and our culture undervalues work that does not earn money (Lindsey, 1996).

We do know that the variety of tasks included in homemaking is so extensive that any list will necessarily be incomplete. Here is just a fraction of the responsibilities: food shopping, meal preparation, washing dishes, household purchases, house cleaning, washing clothes, ironing, mending, gardening, care of the car, preparing children for school, transporting children, preparing children for bed, disciplining children, hiring child-care help, holiday planning, and finance management (Lindsey, 1996; St. John-Parsons, 1978). In financially conservative times, schools, businesses, and other organizations count on volunteers to donate time for activities such as acting as classroom aides and raising funds. Unpaid homemakers are most likely to volunteer their time for these tasks (Lindsey, 1996; Pearce, 1993).

We do not need to dwell on the obviously unpleasant nature of many tasks performed by homemakers. Any job is frustrating if it must be repeated just as soon as it is finished, or if it typically has no clear-cut standards of completion. (Is the kitchen floor ever really clean enough?)

How do homemakers view their responsibilities? According to one survey, 73% of American women and 69% of Canadian women agree that being a homemaker is "just as fulfilling as working for pay" (Office of Research and Media Reaction, 1994, p. 29). Grana and her colleagues (1993) found that homemakers rated their work as more physically demanding but less mentally demanding, compared to most paid workers' ratings of their jobs. However, women who work in janitorial and other service jobs are similar to homemakers in their evaluations of their work—as we might expect from the similarity of the responsibilities.

In short, our discussion of working women in this chapter must acknowledge the tremendous amount of time and effort women devote to housework. This work is diverse, extensive, repetitious, often frustrating, and low in prestige. However, it is work that someone must do.

Furthermore, as Demonstration 7.4 noted, the lack of job security places many women at risk for becoming displaced homemakers. A **displaced homemaker** is a woman who has lost her primary source of income because of divorce, widowhood, extended unemployment of her spouse, and similar reasons. For example, in 1994, the U.S. Department of Labor reported that nearly 16 million American women were displaced homemakers. When these women apply for jobs, they typically find that their years of experience in managing a home and a family will win little respect from potential employers. Some community programs try to address the problems faced by displaced homemakers by counseling in job-search strategies and by helping women develop employment-related skills. These programs can encourage women to make dramatic changes in their lives.

Women's Experiences in Selected Occupations

1. **The majority of employed women occupy traditional clerical and service jobs.**

2. **Women are especially likely to be exploited in two traditionally female jobs: domestic work and work in the garment industry.**

3. **Women who are employed in traditionally male professions are generally similar to the men in these professions, in terms of personal characteristics and cognitive skills, but the women may be lower in self-confidence.**

4. **Many women in traditionally male professions face sexual harassment, patronizing treatment, and a work environment that has few other women.**

5. **Women in blue-collar jobs may face poor treatment from the men on the job, but they value the pay and the sense of pride they gain from their work.**

6. **Person-centered explanations argue that women are absent from certain occupations because they lack the appropriate skills and personality characteristics. Situation-centered explanations account more adequately for the findings; they emphasize that the structure of organizations prevents women's success.**

7. **The work of homemakers is diverse, frustrating, and low in prestige; these women also face the risk of becoming displaced homemakers.**

COORDINATING EMPLOYMENT WITH PERSONAL LIFE

Most college women plan to combine a career with family life (Fitzgerald & Rounds, 1994; Hoffnung, 1993; Novack & Novack, 1996). Yet the popular media claim that the employed woman is a total wreck. As Barnett and Rivers (1996) describe the media's viewpoint:

[The employed woman is] so stressed out that she's going to drop dead of a heart attack right at her desk; she's probably chewing hundreds of Tums or thinking of sticking her head in the microwave because she's so prone to anxiety and depression. (p. 24)

Throughout this textbook, we've seen that reality is often different from the myth presented by the media. In this section, we'll see that employed women may find it challenging to combine their many roles, but they are *not* dropping out of their careers by the thousands, as magazine articles imply. Let's see how employment influences three components of a woman's personal life: (1) her marriage, (2) her children, and (3) her own well-being.

Marriage

In 1996, 55% of employed U.S. women were married and living with their husbands (U.S. Bureau of the Census, 1997). Most of the research on the personal lives of employed couples has focused on the relatively small portion of people in dual-career marriages. In a **dual-career marriage,** both the wife and the husband have high-status occupations, and both see their careers as central to

---

DEMONSTRATION 7.5

Division of Responsibility for Household Tasks

Think about a long-term heterosexual household with which you are familiar—it might be your parents, the parents of a close friend, or your own current relationship with someone of the other gender. For each task below, place a checkmark to indicate which member of the pair is *primarily* responsible. Is this pattern similar to the division of housework we are discussing in this chapter?

Task	Wife	Husband
Shopping for food		
Cooking		
Dishes		
Laundry		
Vacuuming		
Washing the car		
Gardening		
Taking out the trash		
Paying the bills		
Household repairs		

their self-concept (L. Gilbert, 1993). As you read about the research, keep in mind that the experiences of these elite couples may not be typical. Try Demonstration 7.5 before you read further, and then we'll consider three questions:

1. How do married people make decisions about jobs when faced by geographical constraints?
2. How do families divide their household responsibilities?
3. Does employment influence marital satisfaction?

Geographical Constraints Among Dual-Career Couples.   Many complications arise when two people who have trained for specific professions try to find employment in the same community. For example, two-thirds of the participants in Silberstein's (1992) study of dual-career families reported that geography was a major issue in their career decisions. Several couples in this study worked out specific plans in which they alternated who would make the decision to move. However, wives are more likely than husbands to move because of a spouse's job opportunities. Jane, a social scientist pursuing a post-PhD fellowship, made this remark:

> I think when we get to the next junction, it's more likely that we'll go where George wants to, because he has greater earning potential. So we would have to make decisions that are best for him. I mean, I love my work—and want to keep growing in it. But you have to think about the economic return, too. (Silberstein, 1992, p. 64)

Undergraduate students also anticipate this pattern of men's careers being considered more important when making decisions about where the couple should live. For example, Novack and Novack (1996) asked close to 1,000 students a variety of questions about career-related attitudes. According to the results, 47% of the women said they would be very likely to move because of a husband's career. Only 22% of the men said they would be very likely to move because of a wife's career.

Some couples decide to live apart because they are employed in different geographic regions. Arranging a commuting schedule requires extraordinary creativity and huge financial investments. Commuting also adds emotional strain. If they see each other only on weekends, should they remain brightly cheerful for the entire time? How can they resolve a fight if his plane leaves in 45 minutes? Love relationships are complicated enough when two people live together full-time. They are more stressful when the two people must continually become reacquainted, only to say goodbye again after several days.

Performing Household Tasks.   Throughout this chapter, we've often noted that women are treated unfairly in the world of work. When we consider how married couples divide the household tasks, we find additional evidence of unfairness.

Several studies in the United States suggest that women perform about two-thirds of the household tasks in two-job families (R. Kahn, 1991; Perkins & De-Meis, 1996; Silverstein, 1996). Research in Canada also shows that women do about two-thirds of the housework (Brayfield, 1992; Devereaux, 1993; Statistics Canada, 1995). Women are much more likely than men to do the cooking, cleaning, dishwashing, and shopping. The only chore that men are more likely to do is household repair (Galinsky & Bond, 1996; Starrels, 1994). Earlier in the chapter, we noted a wage gap between the salaries of employed men and women. Here, we notice a "leisure gap" for employed men and women (Headlee & Elfin, 1996).

A variety of factors influence the distribution of household tasks. For example, husbands who are androgynous or feminine on the Bem Sex-Role Inventory are more likely than masculine or undifferentiated men to perform cleaning and other housework tasks (N. Gunter & Gunter, 1990).

Are the household tasks shared more equally when the wife works outside the home, rather than being a full-time homemaker? Some research suggests they are (Risman, 1998; Spain & Bianchi, 1996). I found only one study focusing on the reverse question: What happens when the woman works outside the home and the husband is not employed? Davis and Chavez (1995) studied Latino/a families in which the wife was employed outside the home and was considered the primary wage earner in the household. Because the husbands were either unemployed or worked part-time, we might expect husbands to take on many household chores. The couples reported that both of them performed many of the tasks, but wives were still more likely than husbands to be responsible for the laundry, dishes, cooking, and cleaning. The "leisure gap" was therefore particularly striking in this sample; would it be equally large for European American househusbands?

Unfortunately, we do not have systematic research comparing how couples from different ethnic groups divide the housework. One study reported that housework is more evenly divided among French-Canadian couples than among English-Canadian couples (Brayfield, 1992). One nationwide study of more than 13,000 U.S. households concluded that women performed 67% of the housework in White households and 64% of the housework in Black households (D. John & Shelton, 1997). The figures are remarkably similar for these two ethnic groups.

As Spain and Bianchi (1996) observed, academic researchers seem to be more troubled by the unequal division of housework than are the women they interview. What's going on here? Nevill (1995) reported that college men and women have similar scores on a measure of commitment to home and family. Apparently, however, the men are not committed to housework, especially after they are married. How do the men explain their lack of responsibility for household tasks? Although many men may be more sensitive, one man explained, "People shouldn't do what they don't want to do. . . . And I don't want to do it" (Rhode, 1997, p. 150).

Surprisingly, women typically do not express anger toward their greater work in the home (Ferree, 1994). Instead, they tend to show the same "denial of personal disadvantage" that they show for the wage gap. Some employed women come home from work and feel guilty that they are not being "wifely" enough (Biernat & Wortman, 1991). Amy, who is employed full-time and has two daughters, feels guilty when she falls behind in doing the laundry:

> I'm so ashamed. If I'm behind, or there is something that [my husband] would really like and hasn't had for a week or so, like a flannel shirt, and hasn't seen it around, then he'll probably put a load of laundry in so he can get it. I'm pretty good—sometimes I just get bogged down, and he'll help out. (Hoffnung, 1992, p. 148)

Notice that the laundry is considered to be Amy's problem, and her husband simply "helps out." Furthermore, women downgrade their own performance on household tasks, whereas the husbands give their wives higher ratings (Wortman et al., 1991). If the women cannot negotiate a more equal division of housework, perhaps they should set lower standards for themselves.

Satisfaction with Marriage.   In general, a woman's employment status does not influence her marital satisfaction (Barling, 1990; Stoltz-Loike, 1992; Suitor, 1991). For example, Stacy Rogers (1996) analyzed data from a national sample of 1,323 women, all married continuously to the same man, and all with at least one child living at home. She found no statistically significant difference in the women's reports of marital quality, as a function of being employed or nonemployed.

However, marital satisfaction *is* related to other work-related factors. For example—no surprise!—women are less happy with their marriage if they are not satisfied with the division of housework (Suitor, 1991). Also, women are less happy with their marriage if they work outside the home for financial reasons and wish they could stay at home (Perry-Jenkins et al., 1992).

In summary, women who work outside the home may be busier than nonemployed women. However, they are not necessarily less satisfied with their marriages.

Children

About two-thirds of the mothers in the United States and Canada are employed outside the home (Statistics Canada, 1995; Wille, 1996a). This observation suggests two important questions concerning the children of employed women:

1. How are the child-care tasks divided in two-parent families?

2. Does a mother's employment influence children's psychological adjustment?

Taking Care of Children.   In the previous section, we saw that women perform more housework than men. Who's taking care of the children? The research suggests that fathers have substantially increased their child-care responsibilities since similar studies were conducted 25 to 30 years ago (L. Gilbert, 1994; Pleck, 1997; Silverstein, 1996). Still, researchers estimate that mothers perform between 60% and 90% of child-care tasks (Pleck, 1997; Silverstein, 1996).

No consistent ethnic differences have been reported in the proportion of child-care tasks that fathers perform (Pleck, 1997). Also, some research shows that fathers with nontraditional gender roles perform more child-care tasks than other fathers, but other research shows no differences (Deutsch et al., 1993; Mintz & Mahalik, 1996; Pleck, 1997).

Perhaps because they are less involved, fathers are less likely than mothers to say that they are happy with their relationship with their children (S. Rogers & White, 1998). However, mothers rate their husbands' caretaking abilities higher than fathers rate themselves (Wille, 1995).

Some related information should be better publicized. When fathers perform a high proportion of the child care, children show greater cognitive and social skills (Pleck, 1997; Silverstein, 1996). Apparently, children benefit from having two caring adults actively involved in their lives. Fathers who spend more time in child care are also healthier and more caring of other people than are uninvolved fathers (Barnett & Rivers, 1996; Pleck, 1997). In other words, both fathers and children seem to benefit from the time they spend together.

Many women have no husband who can—even theoretically—share in the care of the children. Mothers who are single, separated, divorced, or widowed must usually work outside the home for economic reasons. For these women, the logistic problems of arranging for child care and transporting children become even more complicated. In addition, unmarried mothers usually have sole responsibility for nurturing their children, helping them with homework, and disciplining them. Finally, these mothers must add the guilt of raising a "fatherless child" to the already substantial guilt arising from being an employed mother.

The Effects of Maternal Employment on Children.   College students tend to believe that a mother's employment has a negative impact on her children (Bridges & Etaugh, 1994, 1995, 1996). Sandra Scarr (1997) reported that a radio call-in audience ignored her discussion of the research on maternal employment. But the audience believed the anecdotal reports of another talk-show guest who speculated that children are emotionally harmed when their mothers are employed.

We need to emphasize that the topic of maternal employment and children's adjustment is complex. The nature of our conclusions depends on a wide variety of variables, such as the quality of the child-care program and the economic background of the family. As you'll see, however, the research is more optimistic than college students or talk-show audiences believe.

In general, the cognitive development of children who have been in a day-care center is similar to that of children cared for at home. For low-income families, day care may even provide cognitive advantages (Scarr, 1998; Scarr &

Eisenberg, 1993; Vandell & Ramanan, 1992). In addition, infants who spend time in a day-care center are just as securely attached to their mothers as are children whose mothers do not work outside the home (NICHD Early Child Care Research Network, 1997; Roggman et al., 1994).

The picture is mixed for other aspects of social development. Children who have participated in day care tend to be more cooperative and confident, and they are more skilled at taking another person's point of view. Some earlier studies suggested that children in day care may be more aggressive (Haskins, 1985; D. Phillips et al., 1987). However, this behavior may reflect independence rather than aggression (Clarke-Stewart, 1992).

Children whose mothers work outside the home do have one distinct advantage: Their mothers provide models of competent women who can achieve in the workplace (Coontz, 1997; Scarr, 1990). In general, the research shows that children of employed mothers are not as gender-stereotyped as children who are cared for in the home by their mothers (Etaugh, 1993a). Also, college students whose mothers were employed when these students were young are more supportive of maternal employment. These individuals may realize that their mothers' employment had a positive effect on their families when they were growing up (Willetts-Bloom & Nock, 1994).

In short, the overall picture suggests that children's development is not substantially affected by the family's choice of child-care arrangements. However, families in North America face a problem: High-quality child care at a reasonable price is not widely available (Coontz, 1997; Neft & Levine, 1997). We claim that children are a top priority, yet our governments do not subsidize child care. In France, Denmark, and Sweden, parents can enroll their children in a variety of programs at no cost or at a minimal charge (Neft & Levine, 1997). Will these programs be on the agenda for the United States and Canada in the near future?

Personal Adjustment

We have examined both the marriages and the children of employed women. What is the status of the women themselves? Do they experience role strain? How is their physical and mental health?

Role Strain. A female physician who directs an inner-city medical clinic for adolescents commented about her life:

> I don't know any professional women in her 40s who feels her life is balanced. At that age, we are all overcommitted. Perhaps we figure it out in our 50s. (Asch-Goodkin, 1994, p. 63)

This woman is describing **role strain,** which occurs when people have difficulty fulfilling all their different role obligations.

Employed women often experience role strain in the form of conflict between a job and family responsibilities. Several books have focused on this kind of role strain (e.g., Hays, 1996; Hochschild, 1997). However, the books also mention that employed women say they would miss their work identity if they stopped working outside the home. One mother, who is a well-paid professional, remarked:

> If I just stay at home, I'll kind of lose—I don't want to say my *sense* of identity—but I guess I'll lose my career identity. . . . My friend who stays at home, she had a career before she had her children, but I forget what it was. So that whole part of her, I can't even identify it now. (Hays, 1996, p. 142)

One answer might seem to be part-time work, especially when children are young. Women who are employed part-time report greater general satisfaction with their jobs and children, compared to women who are employed full-time (K. Barker, 1993). However, part-time employment brings role strain, and part-time employees feel that they are excluded from many professional opportunities. Unfortunately, then, part-time employment won't solve all the problems! Some organizations now offer flexible work-time arrangements and child-care centers in the workplace. We can look forward to learning whether these efforts can help solve the role-strain problem.

Physical Health. We might imagine that role strain could lead to poor physical health for employed women. However, the data suggest that employed women are—if anything—healthier than nonemployed women (Barnett & Rivers, 1996; Repetti et al., 1989; Waldron, 1991). Only one group of employed women has substantial health problems: women who have low-paying or unrewarding jobs, several children, and an unsupportive husband (Barnett & Rivers, 1996; Rushing & Schwabe, 1995).

Mental Health. After reading the earlier section about role strain, you may have a mental image of a bleary-eyed woman who arrives home from a grueling day at work just in time to feed the dog, change the baby's diapers, and set the dinner table. This woman, it would seem, has every right to be depressed and unhappy. However, as we'll see in this section, employed women are typically as happy as nonemployed women. In fact, many women are happier and better adjusted (Barnett & Rivers, 1996; Betz, 1993; S. Taylor, 1991). Many women are excited by the challenge of a difficult task and the enormous pleasure of successfully achieving a long-term occupational goal.

For many women, multiple roles provide a buffer effect (Barnett, 1997; Wille, 1996b). Specifically, employment acts as a buffer against the stress of family problems, and family life acts as a buffer against problems at work. The benefits of multiple roles seem to outweigh the disadvantages (Kirchmeyer, 1992, 1993).

Several studies have demonstrated that women's lives are enhanced by employment. For example, Hoffman and Hale-Benson (1987) studied Black, college-educated women who were married to professional men. Those who worked outside the home had significantly higher self-esteem than those who did not.

In one recent large-scale study, Barnett (1997) studied 300 married couples, all of whom worked outside the home. She found that women who had challenging and rewarding jobs coped well with problems at home, such as frustrating child-care issues. However, women who have low-status, unrewarding jobs report lower general life satisfaction and greater levels of distress (Noor, 1996). Another study demonstrated that French–Canadian women were significantly higher in self-esteem if their occupations gave them the opportunity to work independently and to feel accomplished. These characteristics of their jobs were more important than salary in determining self-esteem (Streit & Tanguay, 1994).

We cannot ignore the fact that employed women experience a leisure gap; their housework and child-care responsibilities are much greater than those of employed men (Hochschild, 1997). This problem cannot be solved by simple time-management techniques (Nevill & Calvert, 1996). Wise couples will negotiate more equitable sharing of the workload at home.

Most important, our society needs to acknowledge the reality of employed women. As Barnett and Rivers (1996) argue:

> The facts are clear: Women are working and will do so in even greater numbers in the near future. They are not going home. Paid employment has a positive impact on the physical and emotional health of women, and trying to get them to work part-time or relinquish their commitment to work will harm—not improve—their health. (p. 38)

 Section Summary *Coordinating Employment with Personal Life*

1. In most dual-career couples, the husband's employment is more important when making decisions about where the couple will live.

2. Among North American families, women do about two-thirds of the household tasks, though women typically do not express anger about their greater workload.

3. In general, a woman's satisfaction with her marriage is not influenced by whether she works outside the home.

4. North American women perform the clear majority of child-care tasks; fathers' time spent in child care is not clearly related to either ethnicity or the father's ideas about gender role.

5. In general, children of employed women do not experience major disadvantages with respect to cognitive abilities, attachment, or social development, and they may have advantages in gender-role development.

6. Employed women experience role strain from conflicting responsibilities.

7. Employed women are as healthy and as well adjusted psychologically as nonemployed women; women with satisfying jobs seem to be even healthier and better adjusted.

CHAPTER REVIEW QUESTIONS

1. Consider several women you know who are between the ages of 25 and 35. Think about the personal characteristics related to women's employment. Do these factors help explain which women are employed and which are nonemployed?

2. Where did you learn your previous information about women and welfare—from other classes, from the media, or from people you know? Which aspects of this chapter's discussion matched your previous information, and which aspects were new?

3. Based on this chapter's examination of access discrimination, describe a woman who is especially likely to face access discrimination when she applies for a job. What factors would make a woman *least* likely to face access discrimination?

4. What kinds of treatment discrimination might women face in the workplace? Discuss the research on this topic and supplement it with some of the factors mentioned in the section on women's experiences in selected occupations.

5. Suppose that a friend claims that the wage gap can be entirely explained by the fact that women are more likely than men to work part-time, to stop working while having children, and to have less education. How would you answer this claim, and how would you explain the concept of comparable worth?

6. Compare the experiences of employed women and employed men with respect to the glass ceiling, the sticky floor, the glass escalator, personality characteristics (of men and women in the same occupation), performance of household tasks, and performance of child-care responsibilities.

7. Outline the two general kinds of explanations that have been offered for women's underrepresentation in certain jobs. Review the section summaries in Chapters 5 and 6, and note which explanation is most supported by the evidence from cognitive and social gender comparisons.

8. Describe why homemakers must be included in the term *working women.* Then discuss the division of household tasks between husbands and wives. What factors influence that division, and what factors do not?

9. Imagine that you are a 25-year-old woman and you have decided to return to your former job after the birth of your first baby. A neighbor tells you that your child will probably develop psychological problems if you work outside the home. Cite evidence to defend your decision.

10. Imagine that you are part of a new task force in your state or province, and this task force has been instructed to make recommendations to improve the situation of women in the workplace. Based on the information in this chapter, make a list of 8 to 10 recommendations.

NEW TERMS

working women (236)

employed women (236)

nonemployed women (237)

access discrimination (241)

treatment discrimination (244)

comparable worth (246)

occupational segregation (246)

denial of personal disadvantage (247)

glass ceiling (249)

sticky floor (249)

glass escalator (249)

sexual harassment (250)

heterosexism (251)

sweatshops (256)

person-centered explanations (261)

situation-centered explanations (261)

homemaker (263)

displaced homemaker (263)

dual-career marriage (265)

role strain (270)

RECOMMENDED READINGS

Albeda, R., & Tilly, C. (1997). *Glass ceilings and bottomless pits: Women's work, women's poverty*. Boston, MA: South End Press. With all the media attention to women who have prestigious, fulfilling careers in traditionally male occupations, we really need to understand more about the relatively invisible women who face poverty. This ideal book gives useful information about the problems with welfare policy in the United States, and suggests how those problems can be addressed.

Barnett, R. C., & Rivers, C. (1996). *She works, he works*. San Francisco: Harper-SanFrancisco. This book, written for the general public, begins with a chapter titled "Ozzie and Harriet Are Dead," emphasizing that the "typical" family of the 1950s no longer exists. In addition to research, these authors provide in-depth case studies.

Dubeck, P. J., & Borman, K. (Eds.). (1996). *Women and work: A handbook*. New York: Garland. If your library can purchase just one book on women and work, I'd recommend this one. It includes dozens of short articles on all aspects of the topic, including patterns of employment, ethnicity issues, women in selected occupations, legal factors, and cross-cultural considerations.

Jacobs, J. A. (Ed.). (1995b). *Gender inequality at work*. Thousand Oaks, CA: Sage. This book contains 14 in-depth chapters on topics such as the gender gap in wages, women in managerial positions, occupational segregation, and women in public school teaching.

Martin, M. (Ed.). (1997). *Hard-hatted women: Life on the job*. Seattle: Seal Press. In this book, many women in blue-collar occupations speak for themselves. These women include welders, carpenters, steelworkers, police officers, truckers, and miners.

ANSWERS TO DEMONSTRATION 7.1

1. b; 2. b; 3. a; 4. a; 5. d; 6. a; 7. a

ANSWERS TO THE
TRUE–FALSE QUESTIONS

1. True (p. 237); 2. True (p. 240); 3. False (p. 245); 4. False (p. 249); 5. True (p. 256); 6. True (p. 257); 7. False (p. 260); 8. True (p. 267); 9. False (pp. 269–270); 10. False (pp. 271–272).

LOVE RELATIONSHIPS

CHAPTER 8

TRUE OR FALSE?

_____ 1. Men are more likely than women to emphasize attractiveness in a dating partner.

_____ 2. Several psychologists have argued that evolutionary forces can explain gender differences in characteristics of an ideal romantic partner; however, the evidence for this explanation is not strong.

_____ 3. In about half of current first marriages, the couples have lived together prior to marriage.

_____ 4. People's satisfaction with their marriage often drops during the first 20 years of marriage, but it often increases later in life.

_____ 5. Current research shows that most Latina/o marriages admire an ideal in which the man is clearly dominant and the woman is passive and long-suffering.

_____ 6. Women who are older and have been married for more years tend to have more adjustment problems following a divorce.

_____ 7. Lesbian and bisexual women who accept their identity tend to be better adjusted than those who have mixed feelings.

_____ 8. In general, bisexual women feel equal attraction to both women and men, at any given time period.

_____ 9. Researchers have now produced compelling evidence that a lesbian sexual orientation is biologically based.

_____ 10. Researchers have found that single women typically have many more psychological problems than married women.

Dating and Living Together
The Ideal Dating Partner
Explanations for Gender Differences in Preference Patterns
Characteristics of the Love Relationship
Living Together
Breaking Up

Marriage and Divorce
Getting Married
Marital Satisfaction
Responsibility and Power in Marriage
Marriage Patterns Among People of Color
Divorce

Lesbians and Bisexual Women
The Psychological Adjustment of Lesbians
Characteristics of Lesbian Relationships
Lesbian Women of Color
Bisexual Women
Theoretical Explanations About Sexual Orientation and Preference

Single Women
Characteristics of Single Women
Attitudes Toward Single Women
Advantages and Disadvantages of Being Single
Single Women of Color

$\mathbf{M}$y radio dial passes by Celine Dion's rendition of "Seduce Me" and then Hank Williams's classic "Your Cheatin' Heart" on the country music station. I'm searching for the classical music station and Donizetti's opera, *Lucia di Lammermoor*. Lucia is in love with Edgardo, but her family has arranged a marriage with the wealthy Arturo Bucklaw. Lucia is driven mad by the forced marriage, so she murders her husband and—following one of the most beautiful arias in opera—dies herself. In despair, Edgardo plunges a dagger into his own heart. Recently on the soap opera *The Young and the Restless,* Chris was trying to decide whether she should leave her husband Paul and return to her first husband Danny. And this spring, one of the most popular films is *Forces of Nature,* in which Ben Affleck falls in love with Sandra Bullock, although he had been traveling to meet his fiancée for their wedding.

No matter how many times we hear about "boy meets girl," we go back for more. You can probably think of a few songs, grand operas, soap operas, or movies that feature plots about power or danger or money. However, these are clearly outnumbered by themes about love. A chapter on love relationships is therefore essential for a book on the psychology of women. Our four major topics are (1) dating and living together, (2) marriage and divorce, (3) lesbians and bisexual women, and (4) single women.

DATING AND LIVING TOGETHER

Let's begin by talking about those heterosexual people whose thoughts and feelings are most visible—and audible—in the media. Incidentally, many heterosexuals report that they never thought much about their sexual orientation. When asked to describe their thoughts on the issue, students in one study often wrote comments such as "I never gave consideration to my sexual identity; it just came naturally" (Eliason, 1995, p. 826).

Let's consider how heterosexual individuals view the ideal dating partner, as well as two explanations for gender differences in this area. We'll then compare

The Ideal Partner

Below are excerpts from advertisements in the personals column of *City Newspaper*, Rochester, New York. Each excerpt describes the kind of person the writer of the ad is looking for. I have left out any mention of the gender of the ideal partner; otherwise, this portion of the ad is complete. In front of each description, put an F if you think the writer of the ad is female, and an M if you think the writer is male.

_____ 1. I am seeking a friend first and then maybe more. Warmth, intelligence, and sense of humor all pluses.

_____ 2. I'm looking for someone who is successful, but not a workaholic, with great sense of humor, healthy, honest, faithful, able to make commitment.

_____ 3. I am seeking a new best friend to laugh with. Interests include: movies, cards, antiques, the outdoors.

_____ 4. I'm looking for a 30-something nonsmoker. Trail-climbs and off-road bike by day, and share romantic cultured evenings. Friends first.

_____ 5. Looking for fun-loving single White Jewish [person] who enjoys dancing and dining.

_____ 6. I'm seeking a single White Protestant [person], 45–55 years old, who wants to share music, cooking, football Sundays, weekend trips, and holiday fun. Love of walking and biking a plus. Smoking will get you nowhere.

_____ 7. I'm seeking a single White [person] under 34 to share a life of kindness, togetherness, friendship and love.

_____ 8. . . . seeks single [person], 26–35, race unimportant. Must like dancing, dining, movies and cuddling, for exciting Fall romance. Will not be disappointed.

_____ 9. Looking for career-oriented self-confident individual who desires to share a variety of outdoor activities, including bicycling, skiing, back packing, gardening.

_____ 10. Seeking Black [person] 20's–40's who's honest, intelligent, positive, loving, caring and tender for a relationship.

Check the accuracy of your answers at the end of this chapter (page 320).

women and men with respect to several characteristics of the love relationship. Our final two topics will be couples who live together and couples who break up.

The Ideal Dating Partner

Before you read this section on ideal partners, try Demonstration 8.1. You may be convinced you can tell whether a man or a woman wrote these "personals," but be sure to check the answers. Let's first consider the North American research on this topic and then explore the studies from other cultures.

North American Studies.   What do women and men want in their romantic partner? The answer depends on whether they are discussing a sexual partner or a marriage partner. Regan and Berscheid (1997) asked undergraduates at a Midwestern university to rank a variety of personal characteristics in terms of their desirability for a partner for sexual activity and a partner for a long-term relationship such as marriage. Table 8.1 shows the five most important characteristics for each type of relationship, when females judged males and when males judged females.

As you can see, women and men both emphasized physical attractiveness when judging an ideal sexual partner. In addition, a statistical analysis showed that men were more likely than women to rank physical attractiveness as the most important characteristic.

Notice that the ideal characteristics shift when people judge an ideal marriage partner. However, gender differences are small, because both women and

TABLE 8.1	Characteristics That Males and Females Consider Most Important for a Sexual Partner and a Marriage Partner, Listed in Order of Importance (Source: Regan & Berscheid, 1997)	
	Females Judging Males	**Males Judging Females**
Sexual partner	Physically attractive	Physically attractive
	Healthy	Healthy
	Attentive to my needs	Overall personality
	Sense of humor	Attentive to my needs
	Overall personality	Self-confident
Marriage partner	Honest or trustworthy	Overall personality
	Sensitive	Honest or trustworthy
	Overall personality	Physically attractive
	Intelligent	Intelligent
	Attentive to my needs	Healthy

men value honesty, good personality, and intelligence. Notice, though, that men do mention physical attractiveness as the third most important characteristic.

Other research shows that physical appearance is extremely important when people first meet a potential romantic partner. Also, attractiveness is especially important when men are judging women (Feingold, 1992; Hatfield & Rapson, 1993; Nevid, 1984; Regan & Sprecher, 1995).

Perhaps you can anticipate a potential problem. If attractiveness is important when we first meet someone, we risk rejecting a person who does not meet our standards of physical appeal but could prove to be a good partner in a meaningful, long-term relationship. How much time do we require, to assess a person's attractiveness? According to Locher and his coauthors (1993), college students can make a rapid assessment of attractiveness—based on a 100-millisecond exposure—that is highly correlated with more leisurely assessments of attractiveness. A person who is not especially attractive can therefore be eliminated from consideration in about *one-tenth* of a second! This person may have a wonderful personality and may be honest, trustworthy, and intelligent—but how many of these qualities could he or she convey in a fraction of a second?

How accurate were you in guessing the gender of the people who wrote the personal ads in Demonstration 8.1? You probably hesitated because several of these ads could have been written by either a male or a female. In general, systematic studies of personal ads in both the United States and Canada confirm that men are more likely than women to emphasize physical attractiveness in a partner (S. Davis, 1990; Feingold, 1992; Rajecki et al., 1991). Men are more likely than women to describe their own financial status in an ad, but women are more likely to specify financial status in describing their ideal partner. However, both men and women tend to specify that an ideal partner should be warm, romantic, and sensitive—and also have a good sense of humor (Feingold, 1992; B. Green & Kenrick, 1994; Hatfield & Rapson, 1993).

You may have wondered what kind of personal ad attracts the greatest number of people calling for a date. Goode (1996) placed four advertisements in a variety of magazines and newspapers. An ad describing a beautiful waitress was about three times as likely to be answered as an ad for a successful, average-looking female lawyer. In contrast, an ad for a successful, average-looking male lawyer was about four times as likely to be answered as an ad for a handsome cabdriver. In this study, men were seeking physical attractiveness, whereas women were seeking a professionally successful person.

You may also have wondered whether women are looking for strong, dominant men or "nice guys." Jensen-Campbell and her colleagues (1995) arranged for female college students to listen to a conversation in which the target male showed either high or low levels of dominance and either high or low levels of altruism. The women did not rate the high-dominance men any more favorably than the low-dominance men. However, they rated the highly altruistic men as being more physically attractive, socially desirable, and preferable as dates, in comparison to less altruistic men. Desrochers (1995) found similar results. Any readers of this text who happen to be kind, thoughtful males—and are in search of a female partner—will be pleased to know that nice guys do *not* finish last.

Cross-Cultural Studies.   Because most of the participants in research on ideal partners have been European American men and women, the problems facing eligible marriage partners in other cultures are not fully appreciated. Individuals within immigrant communities are typically caught between the cultural traditions of their home country and those of their adopted country. Consider the predicament of women who have emigrated from India, where marriages are usually arranged by the couple's parents. These women now live in North America, where romantic love is supposed to be the basis for marriage (K. K. Dion & Dion, 1998; Hatfield & Rapson, 1996). Several decades ago, the immigrant Indian community developed an interesting alternative: The would-be husband—or the family of the would-be wife—places matrimonial advertisements in newspapers. One woman's family placed the following ad in *India Abroad:*

> Doctor brothers and well-established parents invite correspondence from highly qualified Jains [an Indian religion] for homeloving university-educated girl, 27, 5′1″. Canadian citizen, pure vegetarian, from traditional North Indian Jain family. (Luthra, 1989, pp. 340–341)

FIGURE 8.1	**Importance of financial prospects in a spouse, for women and men in three cultures. (Source: Hatfield & Sprecher, 1995)**

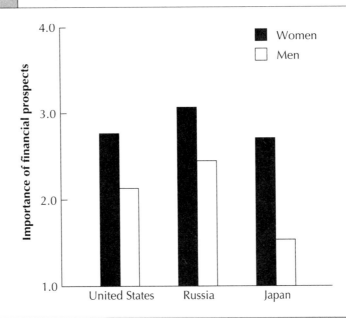

Note: 5 = most important

Different cultures value different characteristics in a marriage partner (Gibbons et al., 1996). In general, however, women are more likely than men to say that a partner should have good financial prospects. In contrast, men are more likely than women to say that a partner should be physically attractive (D. Buss & Schmitt, 1993; Sprecher et al., 1994; Winstead et al., 1997).

Hatfield and Sprecher (1995) asked college students in the United States, Russia, and Japan to rate a number of characteristics that might be important in selecting a marriage partner. Figure 8.1 shows that women in all three cultures are more likely than men to emphasize financial prospects in a spouse; Figure 8.2 shows that men in all three cultures are more likely than women to emphasize physical attractiveness.

Explanations for Gender Differences in Preference Patterns

One of the most controversial topics in the research on love relationships is whether evolutionary explanations can account for gender differences in romantic preferences. An approach called **evolutionary psychology** proposes that

FIGURE 8.2	Importance of physical attractiveness in a spouse, for women and men in three cultures. (Source: Hatfield & Sprecher, 1995)

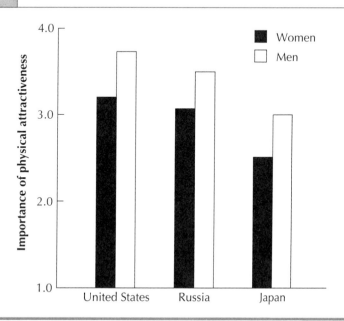

Note: 5 = most important

various species gradually change over the course of many generations in order to adapt better to their environment (Hayes, 1994). A basic principle of this approach is that both men and women have an evolutionary advantage if they succeed in passing on their genes to the next generation. David Buss (1994, 1995) argues that an evolutionary approach can explain why men and women have somewhat different views about ideal mates. Specifically, males are driven to prefer healthy-looking, attractive women because those women are most likely to be fertile—they will pass on the men's genes to the next generation.

Evolutionary psychologists also propose that women try to select a partner who will be committed to a long-term relationship. After all, women not only give birth to children, but they must make sure that the children are provided with financial resources. According to this argument, women look for men who have good incomes and are reliable (D. Buss, 1994).

Many feminist psychologists object to the evolutionary approach. They argue, for example, that the theory is highly speculative about evolutionary forces that operated many thousands of years ago (Eagly, 1997). In addition, the evolutionary approach argues that gender differences are both large and inevitable (G. Brooks, 1997; Hatfield & Rapson, 1996). As a result, some people may use this argument to justify why women *should* have lower status than men.

An explanation that sounds much more credible to me, and to most other feminists, emphasizes social factors. The **social learning approach** argues that men and women are socialized differently, and they experience different social opportunities and social costs (Hatfield & Sprecher, 1995). For example, women have more limited financial resources in our culture—as we saw in Chapter 7. As a result they are forced to focus on a partner's ability to earn money.

An important argument comes from social learning theorists. Gender differences in mate preferences, they say, are *not* inevitable. For example, if women's social status in our culture improves, women may place less emphasis on financial resources and more emphasis on factors such as physical attractiveness (Hatfield & Sprecher, 1995). A final point favoring the social learning approach is that the differences in mate preferences between the genders are much smaller than the differences in mate preferences between cultures (Hatfield & Sprecher, 1995).

Characteristics of the Love Relationship

We have looked at women's and men's ideal romantic partners. But how do women and men compare in an established love relationship? What factors predict satisfaction with a love relationship? Finally, how can we characterize the power distribution in a love relationship?

Gender Comparisons.   To some extent, women and men emphasize different aspects of love in their relationship. Sprecher and Sedikides (1993) examined some romantic couples in a university and some in the neighboring community. The results showed that women were significantly more likely to say that they experienced "companionate love," a relationship based on friendship. Women reported more liking, commitment, and satisfaction—all positive emotions. However, women also reported more sadness, depression, hurt, and loneliness. In other words, compared to men, women seemed to experience a wider range of both positive and negative emotions.

Research with a variety of ethnic groups shows that other cultures may place even greater emphasis on the friendship component of love. K. L. Dion and Dion (1993) studied students at the University of Toronto and found that Asian respondents were more likely than respondents from British and other European backgrounds to agree with statements such as "Love is really a deep

---

DEMONSTRATION 8.2

Friendship-Based Love

If you are currently in a love relationship, rate the following statements, based on that relationship. Alternately, rate a previous love relationship that you experienced, or a love relationship of a couple whom you know fairly well. In each case, use a scale in which 1 point = strongly disagree and 5 points = strongly agree. Then add up the total number of points. In general, high scores reflect a love relationship that is strongly based on friendship.

_____ 1. My love for my partner is based on a deep, long-lasting friendship.

_____ 2. I express my love for my partner through the activities and interests we enjoy together.

_____ 3. My love for my partner involves solid, deep affection.

_____ 4. An important factor in my love for my partner is that we often laugh together.

_____ 5. My partner is one of the most likable people I know.

_____ 6. The companionship I share with my partner is an important part of our love.

_____ 7. I feel I can really trust my partner.

_____ 8. I can count on my partner in times of need.

_____ 9. I feel relaxed and comfortable with my partner.

(Based on Grote & Frieze, 1994.)

friendship, not a mysterious, mystical emotion." However, in all ethnic groups, the gender differences were preserved: Females emphasized friendship more than males did. In research with deaf European Americans and people of African descent living in Jamaica, Nicotera (1997) confirmed the same pattern of gender differences.

In many other respects, however, the gender similarities are more striking. For example, men and women are both likely to say that the essential features of a love relationship are trust, caring, honesty, and respect (Rousar & Aron, 1990). As Hendrick and Hendrick (1996) concluded, women may emphasize friendship more than men do, but "the structure of women's and men's belief systems about love and relationships appears to be roughly similar" (p. 143).

Factors Related to Satisfaction with the Relationship.   Before you read further, try Demonstration 8.2, which is based on a demonstration by Grote and Frieze (1994). This questionnaire assesses the friendship dimension of a love relationship. We just examined gender differences in emphasizing friendship. Other research suggests that both men and women are more satisfied with their love relationships if they are based on friendship (Grote & Frieze, 1994). People who had friendship-based relationships also reported a greater degree of reciprocal understanding. In addition, relationships based on friendship lasted longer.

In Chapter 6, we saw that women are sometimes more likely than men to disclose personal information about themselves. In their romantic relationships, however, women and men have similar self-disclosure patterns (Hatfield & Rapson, 1993; Peplau, 1983). In addition both men and women are more satisfied with their love relationship if both partners are skilled at expressing their emotions (Lamke et al., 1994; Siavelis & Lamke, 1992). The strong, silent male or the mysteriously uncommunicative female may look appealing in the movies. However, people prefer a person with sensitivity and other interpersonal skills in real life.

Power in a Love Relationship.   Love songs emphasize sexuality, appearance, intimacy, affection, and caring. Have you ever heard a song about the division of *power* in a love relationship? Probably not, yet power is a critical aspect of romantic interactions (Peplau & Campbell, 1989).

College students say that they want an egalitarian balance of power in a relationship; both members should have equal input in making decisions. However, in studies of heterosexual couples, both men and women often report that the man is more powerful (Felmlee, 1994; Sprecher & Felmlee, 1997). Sprecher and Felmlee (1997), in a study of couples at a Midwestern university, asked which individual had more power in making decisions about activities the couple would do together. The results showed that 39% of the sample said that the man had more power, 34% said the power was equally divided, and 28% said that the woman had more power.

Power is unequally distributed even before the first date. Rose and Frieze (1993) asked students to describe the events that are part of a typical heterosexual couple's first date. The responses confirmed that the male holds the power; he asks for the date, plans it, and starts any sexual interaction. In contrast, the female is relatively powerless. Her role is to respond by accepting the date and reacting to the male's advances.

Couples obviously differ with respect to the distribution of power. What factors are related to egalitarian relationships? According to research on a sample of primarily White college students, people are more likely to report equal power in their romantic relationship if they trust their partner and if they are more concerned about their partner than about themselves. In addition, people who are highly committed to a relationship are most likely to report egalitarian interactions (Grauerholz, 1987). However, like many correlational studies, this one is difficult to interpret. For example, if a couple is highly committed to a relationship, they might try hard to balance the power. Alternatively, if a couple is initially equal in power and is pleased with this arrangement, they are highly committed to staying together on those terms.

Living Together

We don't have a good term for unmarried people who live together as wife and husband. Some of the legal terms are *cohabitants, unmarried-couple household,* and *common-law relationship*. All these terms sound more like a business arrangement than a love relationship! According to recent data, about 4 million heterosexual couples in the United States are now living together (Wingert & Joseph, 1998). Canadian studies report that about 7% of women over the age of 15 are living in a common-law relationship (Statistics Canada, 1995).

Just as there is no typical dating or marriage relationship, there is no "typical" pattern for living together. Some couples live together simply because it is convenient. About 70% engage in sexual activity only with their partner (Morris, 1997). Some couples choose to live together so that they can determine whether they should consider marriage.

In about half of first marriages, couples had lived together prior to marriage (Bumpass et al., 1991). Looking at a different issue, about 60% of all couples who live together will eventually decide to marry (Bumpass et al., 1991).

In one study, Bumpass and his colleagues (1991) asked couples who were living together to speculate how their lives would be different if they were to get married. On most items, both women and men replied that life would stay much the same, rather than becoming either better or worse. The largest gender difference occurred for the item, "freedom to do what you want." Thirty percent of the men said that life would be worse on this dimension if they were married, but only 17% of the women said their life would be worse.

Couples who live together before marriage are more likely to get divorced than those who have not lived together (Bennett et al., 1988; Morris, 1997; Newcomb,

1987). Does this mean that living together is a bad idea because it is likely to cause divorce? An alternative explanation is that people who are somewhat non-traditional are likely to live together before marriage, and they may also feel fewer constraints about seeking a divorce.

For some women, living together may provide an opportunity to have a close, continuous relationship with a man while still preserving the woman's sense of individuality. However, some couples who live together find that they adopt more traditional roles once they become married. As one woman reported:

> It seems that once the marriage contract was official, we began to expect each other to perform the roles of husband and wife rather than two people just wanting to love and live with each other. We didn't think that would happen to us. (Morris, 1997, p. 47)

Breaking Up

Two people named John and Cindy, have been dating for about a year. Then they break up. Who suffers more?

Choo and her coauthors (1996) remind us that any gender differences must be interpreted in the context of widespread gender similarities: "Men and women are more similar than different. In most things, it is not gender, but our shared humanity that seems to be important" (p. 144).

Choo and her colleagues (1996) studied a sample of students at the University of Hawaii. Unlike a typical sample from the continental United States, most of the participants were Asian Americans. The students were asked to think back on a romantic relationship that had broken up and to assess their emotional reactions immediately after the breakup. You may be surprised to learn that women felt more joy and relief following the breakup. However, men and women reported similar negative emotions (anxiety, sadness, and anger), as well as similar guilt.

Incidentally, these findings on emotional reactions echo a pattern in earlier research: We find gender differences in some areas, but gender similarities in other areas (Z. Rubin et al., 1981). For example, when V. C. Helgeson (1994) studied the emotions of the persons who had initiated the breakups, women and men reported similar emotions. However, when she studied the emotions of the persons whose partners had initiated the breakup, women reported more positive emotions than men did.

In addition to their emotional reactions, Choo and her colleagues (1996) asked the respondents to recall how they had coped with the breakup. Demonstration 8.3 shows some of the items. The researchers found that women and men were equally likely to blame themselves for the breakup (Questions 1 and 3 of Demonstration 8.3). They were also equally likely to take alcohol and drugs following the breakup (Question 2). However, women were somewhat more likely to blame their partner for the breakup (Questions 4 and 6), whereas men were more likely to try to distract themselves from thinking about the breakup (Questions 5 and 7).

DEMONSTRATION 8.3

Coping with a Breakup of a Love Relationship

Think about a person you once dated and felt passionate about, but then the two of you broke up. Read each of the items below, and place an X in front of each strategy you *frequently* used to cope with the breakup. (If you have not personally experienced a breakup, think of a close friend who has recently broken up with a romantic partner, and answer the questionnaire from that person's perspective.)

_____ 1. I tried to figure out what I might have done wrong.

_____ 2. I took alcohol or drugs.

_____ 3. I talked to my friends, trying to figure out if there was anything we could do to save the relationship.

_____ 4. I thought about how badly my partner had treated me.

_____ 5. I kept busy with my schoolwork or my job.

_____ 6. I told myself: "I'm lucky to have gotten out of that relationship."

_____ 7. I engaged in sports and other physical activities more than usual.

(Based on Choo et al., 1996.)

How can we explain the results? Several researchers (e.g., Choo et al., 1996) have reported that women are usually more sensitive to potential problems in a relationship. In other words, women may have anticipated the breakup and worried about some danger signs. As a result, they may be less shocked and more relieved when the breakup does occur. Why were women less likely than men to blame themselves for the breakup? Choo and her colleagues suggest one possibility: Women typically work harder than men do to maintain a relationship. When a breakup occurs, women realistically may not blame themselves for that outcome.

In short, we find many gender similarities and several modest gender differences with respect to the dating phase of the love relationship. For example, men are more likely to emphasize physical attractiveness in an ideal date, women are more likely to emphasize the friendship component of a love relationship, and men and women respond somewhat differently to a breakup. In our next section, we will also note both gender similarities and gender differences with respect to marriage and divorce.

> **SECTION SUMMARY** | *Dating and Living Together*

1. Women and men both value physical attractiveness as an important characteristic for an ideal sexual partner, but men emphasize it more; women and men both value characteristics such as honesty and intelligence in an ideal marriage partner, but men still emphasize attractiveness more than women do.

2. To explain why men emphasize physical attractiveness in a romantic partner—and women emphasize good financial prospects—evolutionary psychologists theorize that each gender emphasizes characteristics that are likely to ensure passing their genes on to their offspring. Social learning theory emphasizes that socialization, opportunities, and costs explain the differences; furthermore, the differences are not inevitable.

3. Women are somewhat more likely than men to emphasize friendship in a love relationship; gender differences are minimal in other features considered essential in a love relationship.

4. Relationships are more satisfying if they are based on friendship and if both partners can express their emotions.

5. College students say they want power to be equally divided in a relationship; however, the man is usually more powerful in a romantic relationship.

6. Couples decide to live together for a variety of reasons; many couples believe that their relationship would be similar if they decided to marry.

7. When couples break up, women are more likely than men to experience joy and relief, more likely to blame their partner for the breakup, and less likely to distract themselves from thinking about the breakup.

MARRIAGE AND DIVORCE

Our theme of individual differences in women's lives is especially important when we discuss women's experiences with marriage. For example, consider how two women describe their marriage.

In an interview, a woman named Linda compared her marriage with her previous dreams about marriage:

> Marriage is struggle, the two words are synonymous. But! We're not told that. I grew up with the lies that marriage is a sweet wonderful thing. . . . I was really brought up by TV and the movies, by advertisements, and the whole culture saying that you melted into each other's arms and had this love relationship that was

ever blossoming and growing but somehow never changed. . . . It's not that way at all. (Mayerson, 1996, pp. 29–30)

Contrast Linda's description with the observations of feminist author Letty Cottin Pogrebin (1997) about her own marriage. Recalling her parents' troubled marriage, she had originally vowed to remain single. However, she now describes being happily married for 34 years. As Pogrebin emphasizes, feminists must acknowledge that marriage can be a source of strength and joy; inequality and disappointment are *not* inevitable. She points out that she has no guiding philosophy:

> All I know is what I've had—34 years with a devoted partner who is my lover and closest friend. I know how it feels to live with someone whose touch excites, whose counsel calms, whose well-being matters as much as my own. I know that simple contentment is a kind of euphoria, that the familiar can be as intoxicating as the exotic, and that comfort and equality are, over the long haul, greater aphrodisiacs than romanticized power plays. I know how soul-satisfying it is to love someone well and deeply and to be loved for all the right reasons. I know how much more layered life is when everything is shared—sorrow and success, new enthusiasms, old stories, children, grandchildren, friends, memory. . . . We're what's called a good fit. (p. 37)

Let's begin our examination of marriage and divorce by first discussing several aspects of the transition to marriage. Then we'll look at marital satisfaction, the distribution of power in marriage, and marriage patterns among women of color. Our final topic in this section is the realities of divorce.

Getting Married

In the United States and Canada, the average ages for a first marriage are 26 years for women and 28 years for men (Neft & Levine, 1997). The majority of North Americans over the age of 17 are currently married. Figure 8.3 shows the percentages of married persons within the three major ethnic groups of U.S. residents. Unfortunately, the data did not include information about Asian Americans or Native Americans.

Ethnicity has an important impact because choice of a marriage partner is one of the most central traditions in a cultural community. For example, a study on marriages within the Korean community in Los Angeles found that only 8% involved someone who was not Korean by birth or descent (Min, 1993). Almost half of the Koreans studied married a partner who was also from Los Angeles, and 10% married Koreans from other U.S. cities. About one-third brought their marriage partners from Korea. Marriages between Korean Americans and people who have just emigrated from Korea are known to have many adjustment problems. For example, many Korean American men who have only a high school education bring in brides who have been college-educated in Korea, and the result is a significant gap in their relationship. Korean American women who bring in husbands from Korea are likely to find that their spouses have

| FIGURE 8.3 | **Percentages of married persons, 18 years and older, in three major ethnic groups of U.S. residents. (Based on data from U.S. Bureau of the Census, 1997)** |

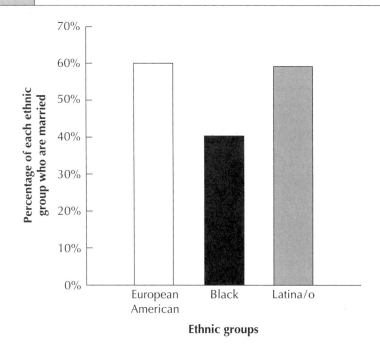

extremely traditional ideas about gender roles. Conflict between traditional customs in the home country and contemporary gender roles in North America undermines many marriages of recent immigrants from all of Asia, not only Korea (e.g., Naidoo & Davis, 1988).

For European Americans, the wedding itself is likely to be a major event that costs $19,000 or more (*Bride's* magazine, 1997). The bride's expenses alone may include a couple of thousand dollars for the wedding gown, as much as a thousand dollars for flowers, and many thousands of dollars for the reception. The United States is often called a country of excess, and this excess helps maintain the wedding industry's estimated income of $20 billion a year.

One final issue before we move on: What factors help determine whether a woman keeps her own name when she marries? Twenge (1997c) asked a sample of undergraduates in the Midwest whether they planned to take their future husband's name, if they were to marry; about 60% said they would. The remaining 40% planned some alternative, such as keeping their own name for all purposes, or hyphenating their name. Women who said they would keep some form of their current name tended to have more feminist attitudes. One woman who planned to take her husband's name for social purposes—but keep her own in professional settings—remarked:

> Socially, I would want to take my husband's name, but (hopefully) as a doctor I think it would be nice to have my own name since I worked so hard in school with that name. (p. 426)

Marital Satisfaction

How happy are women with their marriages? Let's see how marital satisfaction changes over time, how certain characteristics are associated with happy marriages, and how men and women compare in terms of marital satisfaction.

Satisfaction During Various Periods of Marriage.   Think of the words *newlywed* and *bride*. These words may suggest associations such as bliss, radiance, obliviousness to the rest of the world, and complete happiness. According to surveys, young married couples are perhaps the happiest people in any age group (Hatfield & Rapson, 1993; Orbuch et al., 1996).

Most research on marriage focuses on European American couples. However, Jean Oggins and her colleagues (1993) studied 199 Black and 174 White newlywed couples, all of whom were married for the first time. In general, the respondents were happiest if they felt that their partners valued them and showed this high regard through both words and behaviors.

Unfortunately, the early blissfulness of marriage may not last long. After several years, married people sometimes report being unhappy and dissatisfied (Hatfield & Rapson, 1993). Women are likely to resent that they perform more housework than their husbands, an inequity we emphasized in Chapter 7.

Marital satisfaction often drops steadily during the first 20 years of marriage (Hatfield & Rapson, 1993; Orbuch et al., 1996). During these two decades, intimacy, physical affection, and shared activities may decrease. Satisfaction seems to reach an all-time low point when children are in their late adolescence.

As Chapter 14 will show, women's lives begin to look up again, once their children have left home. Marital satisfaction generally improves as well (Koski & Shaver, 1997; Levenson et al., 1994; Orbuch et al., 1996). For example, Orbuch and her colleagues (1996) analyzed data from U.S. national surveys. They found that people who had been married 20 to 24 years were the least satisfied with their marriage, but satisfaction increased systematically for those who had been married 25 years or more. Couples who have been married at least 35 years also report relatively little conflict in their relationship (Levenson et al., 1994). The reasons for this increased satisfaction are not clear, but they may include factors such as reduced conflict over parenting issues after the children leave home, and an increase in economic resources.

Characteristics of Happy Marriages.   In a happy marriage, the wife and husband feel that their emotional needs are fulfilled, and each partner enriches the life of the other. Both people understand and respect each other—as noted in Pogrebin's (1997) comment at the beginning of this section. Each is concerned about the other's happiness and welfare.

Researchers have found that the following characteristics are correlated with happy, stable marriages (Karney & Bradbury, 1995; Kurdek, 1991a, 1993; Levenson et al., 1994; Markman et al., 1994; S. Rogers & Amato, 1997; Webster et al., 1995; Winstead et al., 1997):

1. High level of education;
2. Family economic resources;
3. Both individuals at least in their 20s at the time of marriage;
4. No premarital pregnancies;
5. Having parents who were happily married;
6. Good conflict-resolution skills;
7. Sexual satisfaction;
8. Positive behavior toward one another.

In general, happily married couples are likely to be skilled at interpreting each other's emotions. They consider their spouses to be their best friends. Also, each partner is fairly high in stereotypically feminine traits such as understanding, gentleness, and affection (Antill, 1983; Whitbourne & Ebmeyer, 1990).

Happily married couples even interpret their spouse's actions differently than unhappy couples do. For example, suppose that Jack gives a gift to his wife, Mary. If Mary is happily married, she is likely to think to herself, "How wonderful! Jack wanted to do something nice for me!" However, if Mary is unhappily married, she might think, "He's probably giving me these flowers just so he can spend money on himself." Unpleasant interactions can also be explained in both a positive or a negative light. These explanatory patterns could make a happy marriage even happier, but they could encourage more conflict in an unhappy marriage (Bradbury & Fincham, 1992; Fincham & Bradbury, 1990, 1992).

Gender Comparisons in Marital Satisfaction.   This topic is more complex than you might expect. The problem is that women report more extreme levels of emotion than men do. Specifically, women report more positive emotions (W. Wood et al., 1989). However, women are also more likely than men to experience major depression, as we'll see in Chapter 12.

Regarding satisfaction with marriage, some research shows that, compared to men, women are more sensitive to problems in their marital relationships (W. Wood et al., 1989). This sensitivity is consistent with our earlier observation that women are better than men at anticipating potential problems in a dating relationship.

Wendy Wood and her colleagues (1989) conducted a meta-analysis on the effects of gender and marital status on well-being. These authors found that both men and women were happier if they were married than if they were not. For men, the effect size, *d,* was 0.49; for women, it was 0.54. Therefore, in this analysis, men and women profited about equally from being married. Incidentally, both men and women are likely to live longer if they are married rather than divorced (H. Friedman et al., 1995).

Responsibility and Power in Marriage

Chapter 7 discussed how women are increasingly likely to work outside the home. Still, the responsibility of providing everyday services within the family home rests primarily with women.

What about the division of power within a family? Who makes the important decisions, and who is more influential? How does salary influence the balance of power, and what kinds of power distributions are found in North American marriages?

Salary and Power. My students are often skeptical about the influence of crass factors such as salary on intimate, romantic relationships. However, the research suggests that—at least to some extent—money *is* power (Blumstein & Schwartz, 1983; Steil, 1997).

According to a recent review of the literature, the more husbands earn—relative to their wives' salaries—the more power they have in decision making and the less domestic work they do. Wives who are employed have more power in decision making than nonemployed wives have. However, women who earn more than their husbands still do not have an equal voice in financial matters. In other words, these women bring the family more income than their husbands do, but their husbands still make most of the financial decisions (Steil, 1997).

Three Patterns of Power Distribution. We have emphasized individual differences throughout this book. The variation in marital roles is substantial. In a classic article, Peplau (1983) classified couples in terms of three patterns of marital roles: (1) a traditional marriage, (2) a modern marriage, and (3) an egalitarian marriage. Not every couple fits neatly into a single pattern. However, this classification system helps us appreciate the variety of relationships found in North American marriages.

In a **traditional marriage,** according to Peplau (1983), the husband is more dominant than the wife, and both partners maintain traditional gender roles. The wife is not employed, and the husband controls the money. The wife makes decisions about housework and child care, but the husband has the ultimate authority in family decisions. In 1998, the delegates to the Southern Baptist Convention passed a resolution stating that a wife should "submit graciously to her husband's leadership" (Wingert & Snow, 1998), providing a guideline for a traditional marriage.

In a **modern marriage,** husbands are less dominant. Modern couples say that husbands and wives should share equally in making decisions, yet husbands still tend to be more powerful. Traditional gender roles are modified somewhat. The husband may encourage his wife's employment, but her work is secondary to his. (For example, she will miss work if their child is ill.) The name *modern marriage* is appropriate. As we saw in Chapter 7, most married women do work outside the home, yet husbands and wives do not have similar power.

In an **egalitarian marriage,** the partners share power equally, without traditional gender roles. The wife and the husband have equal responsibility for housework, child care, finances, and decision making. Egalitarian marriages also emphasize companionship and sharing.

Sociologist Pepper Schwartz (1994) provides details about egalitarian marriages, which she calls peer marriages. She argues that peer marriages must be based on a true friendship in which both partners really understand and respect one another. They share many of the same interests, and they know how to resolve conflicts fairly; yet the two partners retain their unique styles and strengths. A husband who had been married 16 years remarked:

> I started out pretty traditional. But over the years it made sense to change. We both work, and so we had to help each other with the kids. . . . And we worked together at church, and we both went whole hog into the peace program. So that got shared. I don't know; you can't design these things. You play fair, and you do what needs doing, and pretty soon you find the old ways don't work and the new ways do. (p. 31)

Marriage Patterns Among People of Color

We do not have a large number of systematic studies about marriage patterns for people from ethnic groups that are not European American. However, some resources provide tentative hints.

Latinas.   One of the key concepts often discussed in connection with Latinas/os is *machismo*. Social scientists have traditionally defined **machismo** (pronounced "mah-*cheez*-mo") as the belief that men must show their manhood by being strong, sexual, and even violent—clearly dominant over women in relationships (Ybarra, 1995).

The parallel concept for women is *marianismo*. Social scientists have traditionally defined **marianismo** (pronounced "mah-ree-ah-*neez*-mo") as the belief that women must be passive and long-suffering, giving up their own needs to help their husbands and children (Chin, 1994; Ehlers, 1993). (As you might guess, *marianismo* is based on the Catholic representation of the Virgin Mary.) Fine and her colleagues (1999) describe how *machismo* and *marianismo* complement each other in a traditional Latina/o marriage:

> Love and honor your man—cook his meals, clean his house, be available and ready when he wants to have sex, have and care for his children, and look the other way at marital infidelities. . . . In return, he will agree to protect you and your children, work, pay the bills.

How well do *machismo* and *marianismo* capture the relationship between Latinos and Latinas in the current era? Castañeda (1996) concludes that the stereotype of the dominant husband and the submissive wife does not hold up. Fewer than half of Latinos and Latinas believe that marriages should adopt this pattern of inequity.

Leaper and Valin (1996) confirmed this changing pattern in a study of Mexican American married adults in central California. Some women and men did endorse traditional gender roles in marriage. However, egalitarian marriages were preferred by many people, especially those born in the United States, those who spoke only English at home, and those who were not Catholic. Ehlers (1993) also pointed out that the *marianismo* model fails to describe women's roles for the millions of economically poor Latinas who must take a job in order to survive. When women work in factories or picking crops, they cannot remain passive and totally focused on their husbands and children. In short, many Latinas and Latinos have created marital patterns that are very different from the models suggested by *marianismo* and *machismo* values.

Black Women.　If we look at the history of Blacks in the United States, we can see a system that encouraged the breakup of families. During much of the 19th century, slaves had no legal right to a family (Staples, 1995). Beginning in about 1925, a second force encouraged the breakup of southern Black families: Blacks' migration to northern cities. Poverty continues to be a disruptive factor in the current era.

As a result, Black women are less likely than European American women to be married, as we saw in Figure 8.3. In 1965, a government official named Daniel Patrick Moynihan brought attention to the Black family. (Ironically, Moynihan later became one of the most liberal members of the U.S. Senate.) In his early report, Moynihan argued that the Black community faced problems because 22% of all Black families were headed by women. In fact, Moynihan coined the term **Black matriarchy** to refer to women's domination in Black families (Staples, 1995). Women in Black families were supposed to be so dominant that they presumably emasculated Black men and encouraged other abnormalities in the family.

Much of the early research focused on the most economically poor Black families—typically, those without a husband/father living in the home (L. Johnson, 1997; McAdoo, 1993). The research then generalized from that selected sample to all Black families. Basically, Black women were being unfairly criticized for having the stamina to work outside the home and still be strong figures in their own homes (P. Collins, 1990; L. Johnson, 1997).

In contrast to the early studies, the current research does not support the idea of a Black matriarchy (Dodson, 1997; L. Johnson, 1997). For example, Oggins and her coauthors' (1993) study of newlyweds showed that both Black families and White families saw husbands as having slightly more power than wives.

In addition, Black men do not perceive themselves as having high levels of conflict with their wives (Gary, 1986). McAdoo (1993) specifically focused on decision-making power in a group of middle-income African American families living in the Baltimore area. The picture that emerged from this sample showed families that were close to the egalitarian model. The husband and wife contributed equally to decisions about what car to buy, what house to buy, children's curfews, and other similar issues. However, husbands had somewhat more power regarding the final decisions about what jobs they would take. In summary, the Black matriarchy is *not* a useful concept in explaining Black families in the 1990s.

Asian Women.   Research on marriage patterns in Latina/o families and Black families is scarce. Unfortunately, the research on marriage patterns in other ethnic groups is even rarer. In one study, Dhruvarajan (1992) examined the division of power among Hindu Asian Indians living in Winnipeg, Canada. These couples divide decision-making power along gender-stereotypical lines. Specifically, wives are primarily responsible for decisions concerning food, home decoration, and their own employment. In contrast, husbands are primarily responsible for decisions requiring large sums of money, such as buying a car and deciding where to live. Husbands in more highly religious families were especially likely to have greater decision-making power. Naturally, these results cannot be generalized to other Asian groups living in North America.

Divorce

So far, most of our discussion has focused on relatively upbeat topics such as dating, living together, and marriage. As you know, however, divorce has become more common in recent years. Between about 40% and 50% of first marriages currently taking place in the United States and Canada will end in divorce (Gorlick, 1995; Neft & Levine, 1997). In the United States, the divorce rates are fairly similar for European Americans, Blacks, and Latinas/os (Saluter, 1994).

Even though attitudes toward divorce are not as negative as they were several decades ago, the divorce experience is still traumatic for most people. Let's consider four aspects of divorce: (1) factors related to divorce, (2) the decision to divorce, (3) psychological effects, and (4) financial effects.

Factors Related to Divorce.   Earlier in this section, we discussed several factors related to a happy, stable marriage. Many of these factors are correlated with divorce. For example, divorce is more likely when a couple has a low level of education, a low family income, and premarital pregnancies (Kurdek, 1993).

Interpersonal factors are also important. For example, married couples who become less committed to the relationship and less dependent on one another are at risk for divorce (Kurdek, 1993). Other consistent predictors of divorce include jealousy, infidelity, spending money foolishly, frequent conflicts, and drinking or drug use (P. Amato & Rogers, 1997; McGonagle et al., 1993).

The Decision to Divorce.   Who is more likely to seek divorce, men or women? Folk wisdom might suggest that the men are most anxious to leave. However, you'll recall that women are more likely to foresee problems in a dating relationship. Similarly, women typically provide more complaints about the marriage than their husbands do (Amato & Rogers, 1997; Kitson, 1992). The data also show that wives initiate divorce more often than husbands do (Kitson, 1992). In some cases, women initiate divorce because of physical violence or psychological abuse; we'll discuss this problem in depth in Chapter 13.

Psychological Effects of Divorce.   Divorce is especially painful because it creates so many different kinds of separation, in addition to separation from a former spouse. When a woman is divorced, she may be separated from friends and relatives previously shared by the couple. She may also be separated from the home she has known and from her children. In addition, people are likely to judge a divorced woman negatively (Etaugh & Hoehn, 1995).

Divorce is one of the most stressful changes a person can experience (Bursik, 1991b). Depression and anger are often common responses, especially for women (Aseltine & Kessler, 1993; Kaganoff & Spano, 1995).

Another emotional reaction is called the **persistence of attachment;** although people may no longer love their ex-spouses, they may still feel a remaining bond. After all, the spouse was originally selected because he or she seemed like a good partner. People who are in the process of seeking a divorce may feel simultaneously glad to be out of the relationship and regretful about losing continuing bonds with that person (Kitson, 1992).

Divorce can sometimes lead to positive feelings. For example, mothers often report that they experience greater companionship with their children after a divorce (Gorlick, 1995). Women who felt constrained by an unhappy marriage may also feel relief. As one woman said, "For me, the divorce was not difficult. I had been living in loneliness for years by the time my marriage ended, so that being alone felt uplifting, free" (Hood, 1995, p. 132).

Many women also report that their divorce lets them know they are stronger than they had thought. Some of my own women friends seem to have grown more insightful and stronger after a divorce, and I had wondered whether this apparent strength might be a product of my own wishful thinking. Fortunately, this topic has been carefully examined by Krisanne Bursik (1991a, 1991b). Bursik studied 104 women in the Boston area who had been married at least 5 years and were separated from their spouses when the study began.

Surprisingly, those women who were older and married longer were *not* significantly lower on any measure of adjustment. Also, women with more children or with younger children did not report more problems. However, women who received higher scores on a test of "masculinity" were much more likely to be well adjusted, both at the beginning of the study and a year later. As we saw in Chapter 2, nontraditional women tend to be better adjusted. They also seem to be more resilient and competent in combating the stress of divorce.

In addition, Bursik assessed **ego development,** a kind of psychological growth in which a woman develops a more complex view of herself and of her relationships with other people (Bursik, 1991b). Most adults remain fairly stable in their ego development; they don't fully explore themselves. However, Bursik observed that many women who had been poorly adjusted at the beginning of the study were better adjusted and showed increased ego development one year later. For them, the disruptive effect of the divorce had actually been helpful. By forcing them to be introspective about their lives and their strengths, misfortune actually had a long-range positive effect.

Financial Effects of Divorce.   Despite the occasional positive effects of divorce, one consequence is painful: A woman's financial situation is usually worse following a divorce. In Canada, two-thirds of divorced single mothers and their children live in poverty (Gorlick, 1995). In the United States, about 40% of divorced fathers fail to pay child support (Neft & Levine, 1997).

Many women find that these economic difficulties affect their self-image as well as the more practical components of day-to-day life. One woman—a special education teacher and mother of two children—described how her divorce had completely changed her standard of living:

> I think it . . . has completely changed who I am, and to me that's so sad. Very sad. I've become a different person because I'm fearful. I'm less risk-taking. I'm depressed most of the time, and I used to not be that way. I used to have a lot of courage. It affects me at every level of my existence. I have to question whether I can afford going to movies or Doug [her son] needs orthodontia work. It's a very close budget. There were periods of time last year when we didn't have enough food. (Grella, 1990, p. 50)

In summary, divorce can provide an opportunity for women to appreciate their strength and independence. Unfortunately, however, many divorced women find that economic inequities create real-life emergencies for themselves and their children.

SECTION SUMMARY   *Marriage and Divorce*

1. **The majority of North Americans over the age of 17 are currently married; ethnicity has a moderate impact on marital status, and it also influences customs surrounding the marriage.**

2. **Marital satisfaction is high during the newlywed period; it typically drops during the first 20 years of marriage and then increases after the children have left the home.**

3. **Happy marriages are more common among people who are well educated, well situated financially, well acquainted prior to marriage, and interpersonally skilled.**

4. **Both men and women tend to be happier when married, rather than single.**

5. **Power within a marriage tends to be related to one's salary. Marriages can be categorized as traditional, modern, and egalitarian.**

6. Although some Latinas and Latinos emphasize *machismo* and *marianismo* in their marriages, a large percentage advocate more egalitarian marital patterns. Research with Black families does not support the concept of the Black matriarchy.

7. Interpersonal factors—such as decreased commitment, jealousy, and conflicts—are related to divorce. Women are more likely than men to complain about their marriage.

8. Divorce is almost always stressful, because it creates depression and anger. Some women experience positive effects, such as increased ego development. However, most divorced women experience financial problems that can have serious implications for their well-being.

LESBIANS AND BISEXUAL WOMEN

A **lesbian** is a woman who is psychologically, emotionally, and sexually attracted to other women. Most lesbians prefer the term *lesbian* to the term *homosexual*. They argue that the term *lesbian* acknowledges the emotional components of the relationship whereas *homosexual* focuses on sexuality. The term *lesbian*—like the term *gay*—is more proud, political, healthy, and positive (Kite, 1994).

Herek (1996) describes a common misunderstanding about sexual orientation:

> Sexual orientation is not simply about sex. Because sexual attraction and expression are important components of romantic relationships, sexual orientation is integrally linked to the close bonds that humans form with others to meet their personal needs for love, attachment, and intimacy. These bonds are not based only on specific sexual acts. They also encompass nonsexual physical affection, shared goals and values, mutual support, and ongoing commitment. (pp. 201–202)

In Chapter 1, we introduced the term **heterosexism,** or bias against lesbians, gay males, and bisexuals—groups that are not heterosexual. In North American culture, an important consequence of heterosexism is that we judge heterosexual relationships differently from lesbian, gay, and bisexual relationships. Try Demonstration 8.4 to appreciate how heterosexist thinking pervades our culture.

We cannot obtain accurate estimates of the number of women who consider themselves lesbians; researchers have been more diligent about estimating the number of gay men than the number of lesbian women. Some reviews suggest that 2% to 3% of women may be lesbian. However, social prejudice probably causes underreporting (Diamond, 1993; R. Friedman & Downey, 1994; S. Michaels, 1996). In addition, lesbian women constitute an invisible minority. As Barrett (1989) writes, "Many people insist that they do not know any lesbians, when one is, in fact, occupying the next desk at work, living in the house across the street, sitting around their own Christmas table" (pp. 19–20).

DEMONSTRATION 8.4

Heterosexist Thinking

Answer each of the questions below, and then explain why each question encourages us to question the heterosexist framework.

1. Suppose you are walking to class at your college, and you see a man and a woman kissing. Do you think, "Why are they flaunting their heterosexuality?"

2. Close your eyes and picture two women kissing each other. Does that kiss seem sexual or affectionate? Now close your eyes and imagine a woman and a man kissing each other. Does your evaluation of that kiss change?

3. Suppose that you have an appointment with a female professor. When you arrive in her office, you notice that she is wearing a wedding ring and has a photo of herself and a man smiling at each other. Do you say to yourself, "Why is she shoving her heterosexuality in my face?"

4. If you are heterosexual, has anyone asked you, "Don't you think that heterosexuality is just a phase you'll outgrow once you are older?"

5. In all the public debates you've heard about sexual orientation, have you ever heard anyone ask any of the following questions?

    a. The divorce rate among heterosexuals is now about 50%. Why don't heterosexuals have more stable love relationships?

    b. Why are heterosexual men so likely to sexually harass or rape women?

    c. What *really* causes heterosexuality?

(Based partly on Garnets, 1996, and Herek, 1996.)

The good news, however, is that people who care about women's issues no longer consider lesbians to be invisible. In fact, while preparing to update this section of the chapter, I accumulated 31 books and 68 articles published in the previous 3 years—and hundreds of additional resources were available.

Chapter 2 examined heterosexism and bias based on sexual orientation, Chapter 4 discussed the coming-out experience of adolescent lesbians, and Chapter 7 emphasized antilesbian prejudice in the workplace. Chapter 9 discusses sexuality issues among lesbians, and Chapter 10 will look at the research on lesbian mothers. In this section, we'll first discuss the psychological adjustment of lesbian women. Then we'll explore several characteristics of love relationships, specifically, equality, satisfaction, and the breakup of a relationship.

We'll also consider the experiences of lesbian women of color, as well as bisexual women. Our final topic will be potential explanations for sexual orientation.

The Psychological Adjustment of Lesbians

A large number of studies have shown that the average lesbian is as well adjusted as the average heterosexual woman (Gonsiorek, 1996). For example, Savin-Williams (1990) reviewed a large number of studies showing that lesbians are similar to heterosexual women in their self-esteem. In some studies, the lesbians had even higher self-esteem. In a representative study, Kurdek (1987) gave a test of psychological adjustment called the Symptom Checklist-90-R to lesbians and heterosexual women who lived together with their partners. The results showed that the two groups were equivalently well adjusted. However, lesbian women scored higher than heterosexual women on a measure called instrumentality, which reflected characteristics such as "acts like a leader" and "assertive."

Some studies suggest, however, that lesbian and gay male teenagers may be at somewhat greater risk for suicide. Also, some studies show that lesbians and gay men are more likely to have alcohol-related problems, but other research questions this finding (Gonsiorek, 1991, 1996; Hartstein, 1996; Herek, 1990). Both of these concerns deserve further research, and they should not be taken lightly.

Perhaps the most astonishing finding in the literature on gay adjustment is that so many gay males and lesbians score high on measures of psychological adjustment. In Chapter 2, our discussion of heterosexism emphasized that many gay people are victims of hate crimes. In light of these problems, we should be surprised that lesbians and gay men do *not* have high rates of psychological dysfunction (Garnets et al., 1992).

Lesbian Identity. Most lesbians are very comfortable with their identity (Herek et al., 1998; Strickland, 1995). For example, a 17-year-old lesbian explained:

> I was always different. I read a lot more than most kids. I played sports more than my girlfriends. All the things that made me feel different were also the things that made me feel good. When I started thinking I was gay it was just one more difference. (Schneider, 1989, p. 122)

Another young woman felt that being a lesbian had made her even stronger:

> I feel that I am the terrific person I am today because I'm a lesbian. I decided that I was gay when I was very young. After making that decision, which was the hardest thing I could ever face, I feel like I can do anything. (Schneider, 1989, p. 123)

Students in my classes often ask whether people who accept their lesbian or gay identity are better adjusted. The research shows a clear relationship. For instance, Walters and Simoni (1993) found that people who accepted their lesbian identity had higher self-esteem than those who had not accepted their lesbian identity. Also, lesbians who maintain relationships with other lesbians tend to have better psychological adjustment. Those who are politically active in the lesbian and gay community may also have better mental health (Evans & D'Augelli, 1996; Gonsiorek, 1996). Many lesbians create their own communities, and warm, supportive networks develop from the "families" they choose. These communities are especially helpful when lesbians are rejected by their birth families (Cruikshank, 1992; Esterberg, 1996).

Therapists' Views on Lesbian Adjustment.   For many years, therapists considered lesbian and gay individuals to be deviant. The list of "therapies" included forced heterosexual intercourse, castration, brain surgery, electroshock, and various drugs that cause nausea and vomiting (Clausen, 1997; R. Smith, 1979). Lesbians, gay men, and other concerned individuals began protesting about this biased treatment, and many influential therapists began raising questions about bias (Krajeski, 1996). As a result, on December 15, 1973, the American Psychiatric Association decided that homosexuality should no longer be listed as a disorder in their professional guidebook, the *Diagnostic and Statistical Manual.* This decision represented one of the most spectacular psychiatric "cures" ever accomplished! Overnight, millions of people were declared normal rather than deviant.

Within psychology, gay male and lesbian professionals—together with other supporters—have expressed their concern about sexual orientation issues. In 1984, for example, a new division of the American Psychological Association was formed: the Society for the Psychological Study of Lesbian, Gay, and Bisexual Issues. Naturally, some therapists still maintain homophobic attitudes. For example, one woman reported that a therapist had told her that she "wasn't really gay," but was simply acting out problems related to her father. Fortunately, she then sought a more enlightened therapist whose advice was more helpful (Garnets et al., 1991).

Characteristics of Lesbian Relationships

For most North Americans—lesbian, gay male, bisexual, or heterosexual—being in a love relationship is an important determinant of their overall happiness (Peplau et al., 1997). Surveys suggest that between 45% and 80% of lesbians are currently in a steady romantic relationship (Kurdek, 1995c). In other words, many lesbians consider being part of a couple to be an important part of their life.

According to Suzanna Rose and her colleagues (1994), most lesbian couples began their relationship as friends and then fell in love. An important hallmark of a strong friendship is emotional intimacy. In contrast, physical attractiveness is relatively unimportant as a basis for a lesbian love relationship. In fact, when lesbians place personal ads in newspapers, they rarely emphasize physical characteristics (S. Rose et al., 1994).

Let's now look more closely at several aspects of lesbian relationships. Specifically, how is equality emphasized in these relationships? How happy are lesbian couples? How do they respond when the relationship breaks up?

DEMONSTRATION 8.5

Assessing Commitment to a Relationship

Answer the following questions about a current love relationship or a previous love relationship. Or, if you prefer, think of a couple you know well, and answer the questionnaire from the perspective of one member of that couple. Use a rating scale where 1 = strongly disagree and 5 = strongly agree. These questions are based on a survey by Kurdek (1995a). This is a shorter version. Turn to page 320 at the end of this chapter to see which relationship dimensions are assessed by these items.

Rating	Question
_____	1. One advantage to my relationship is having someone to count on.
_____	2. I have to sacrifice a lot to be in my relationship.
_____	3. My current relationship comes close to matching what I would consider to be my ideal relationship.
_____	4. As an alternative to my current relationship, I would like to date someone else.
_____	5. I've put a lot of energy and effort into my relationship.
_____	6. It would be difficult to leave my partner because of the emotional pain involved.
_____	7. Overall, I derive a lot of rewards and advantages from being in my relationship.
_____	8. Overall, a lot of personal costs are involved in being in my relationship.
_____	9. My current relationship provides me with an ideal amount of equality.
_____	10. Overall, alternatives to being in my relationship are appealing.
_____	11. I have invested a part of myself in my relationship.
_____	12. It would be difficult to leave my partner because I would still feel attached to him or her.

Equality Among Lesbian Couples.   The balance of power is extremely important in lesbian relationships, and couples are happier if both members of the pair contribute equally to the decision making (Kurdek, 1995b; Peplau et al., 1982). We saw earlier that salary is an important determinant of power for heterosexual couples. However, salary isn't closely related to power among lesbian couples (Kurdek, 1995c). One possible explanation for this difference is that money is not as central to a woman's identity as it is to a man's identity.

In Chapter 7, we saw that women do most of the housework in heterosexual marriages, even when both the husband and the wife work full-time. As you might expect, lesbian couples are especially likely to emphasize that housework should be divided fairly (Kurdek, 1995c).

Satisfaction.   The research on lesbian couples shows that their satisfaction with their relationship is much the same as for heterosexual couples and gay male couples (Caldwell et al., 1981; Kurdek & Schmitt, 1986; Patterson, 1995b). Try Demonstration 8.5 before you read further.

Demonstration 8.5 contains some of the questions from a survey, designed by Lawrence Kurdek (1995a), to measure relationship commitment. On this survey, Kurdek's sample of lesbian couples had commitment scores that were similar to the scores of married couples. The results also showed that the lesbian couples were more committed to the relationship than were heterosexual dating couples who were not living together.

Are women in a lesbian relationship so emotionally close with their partner that each woman loses her sense of independence? Research by Schreurs and Buunk (1996) suggests that this potential issue is not a problem. Women who felt very intimate with their partner were often highly independent. Interestingly, women were most satisfied with a love relationship that was intimate but allowed both women to feel independent.

Breaking Up.   Although we do not have extensive information about how lesbian partners break up their love relationships, the general pattern seems to be similar to the heterosexual breakup pattern (Kurdek, 1995a). The common reasons for breaking up include: feeling emotionally distant from the partner, loneliness, relief from conflict, and differences in interests, background, and attitudes about sex (Kurdek, 1995b; Peplau et al., 1996).

The most common negative emotional reactions to breaking up included loneliness, confusion, anger, and guilt (Kurdek, 1991b). However, women who had broken up with a partner also reported positive emotions, such as relief from conflict and increased happiness. In general, these appear to be the same kinds of emotional reactions that heterosexual women feel when they break up with a partner.

However, the breakup of a lesbian relationship also differs from heterosexual breakups—especially the breakup of a marriage. For example, many factors keep heterosexual couples from splitting apart—the cost of divorce, or joint investments in children and property (Peplau & Amaro, 1982; Peplau et al., 1996).

These factors may be less significant for lesbian couples. In addition, lesbian couples are less likely to have support for their relationship from other family members—a factor that often keeps heterosexual couples together. Consider another point that lesbian friends have mentioned to me. Lesbians are likely to derive substantial emotional support from their partner, especially because they experience relatively little emotional support from heterosexuals. When their relationship breaks up, there are not many people with whom they can share their sorrow. In addition, their heterosexual friends often consider this loss to be less devastating than the breakup of a heterosexual relationship.

Lesbian Women of Color

Two Asian American lesbians decided to list as many U.S. lesbian writers as they could name. They lamented that they could easily rattle off the names of many women from different ethnic backgrounds, but not a single Asian American (Aguilar-San Juan, 1993). Although the situation is improving, almost all of the earlier professional articles and books focus on European American lesbians (Greene, 1996).

Leota Lone Dog (1991) echoes this concern about the invisibility of lesbians in many ethnic groups, based on her perspective as a lesbian Native American:

> There's a lot of fear about coming out in our Native American community. . . . It was bad enough to be an Indian—that was lonely enough. But to be gay and Indian, I ask myself, "Where would I ever find another one?" (p. 49)

As Aguilar-San Juan (1993) remarks, the lesbian community in both the United States and Canada is erroneously believed to be entirely White.

Lesbians of color often comment that they face a triple barrier in U.S. society—their ethnicity, their gender, and their sexual orientation (Greene, 1996). Espín (1996) adds that lesbians who have immigrated to North America from another country face even greater barriers. These women struggle with cultural differences, and the new culture may have different ideas about lesbianism than the country of origin.

Women of color may be more reluctant than European American women to "come out"—for example, in the workplace. A lesbian Puerto Rican social worker remarked:

> While some people who like me and are close to me might accept me and keep treating me the same way they did when they did not know I was a lesbian, I think the majority will react negatively. They might not say anything in front of me but in subtle ways they will use it against me. (Hidalgo, 1995, pp. 31–33)

Some lesbians of color face an extra barrier because their culture has even more traditional views of women than does the mainstream European American culture. As Alicia Gaspar de Alba (1993) pointed out, lesbian women do not fit into any of the traditional roles that are part of the stereotypical Latina framework—mother, wife, virgin, or prostitute. The lesbian woman doesn't propagate the race, and she doesn't serve men in either a domestic or a sexual capacity. As a result, she becomes marginalized both within and outside her own culture. Other cultures may also be more traditional than European American culture with respect to discussing sexuality. For example, Asian cultures typically believe that sexuality shouldn't be discussed even with a best friend (Chan, 1997).

Most of the resources that discuss lesbians of color describe how different ethnic groups react to lesbians. In contrast, Peplau and her colleagues (1997) examined how lesbians feel about their own relationships. Specifically, they sent questionnaires to 398 Black women throughout the United States who had said they were in a committed romantic relationship with another woman. Three-quarters of the women responded that they were "in love" and felt very close to their romantic partner. They also reported that they were quite satisfied with the relationship; the mean score was 5.3 on a scale where the maximum was 7.0.

In the current era, an increasing number of lesbian women of color can find organizations and community groups that provide support. However, these groups are much more likely in urban regions of North America. For example, Mi Ok Bruining (1995) describes the Asian Pacific lesbian organization to which she belongs. Mariana Romo-Carmona (1995) explains that Latina lesbians in the New York City area can watch a TV program featuring Latina lesbians, read brochures on health care written in Spanish by Latina lesbians, and march in the Puerto Rican Day parade with a contingent of lesbian and gay Latinas/os. Racism and heterosexism may still be present, but these groups can provide a shared sense of community.

Bisexual Women

Ann Fox (1991) recalled her first year in college, when she fell in love with her roommate:

> Since that time, I have loved other women. I have loved women in the same deep and romantic ways that I have loved some of the men in my life. I have loved them as friends, as lovers, and as possible life partners. For me, there has never been a question as to whether my feelings for women were more or less real than my emotional ties to men. They are simply (and complexly) different. I can no more deny the depth of my ability to love people of both genders than I could the fact of being, myself, a woman. (p. 29)

A **bisexual woman** is a woman who is psychologically, emotionally, and sexually attracted to both women and men (Firestein, 1996a). The word *bisexuality* is somewhat misleading because it suggests that a bisexual person is equally attracted to both men and woman at any given moment. As we'll see in the discussion of bisexual identity, an equal-attraction pattern is uncommon. We'll also see that bisexuality presents a dilemma for a culture that likes to construct clear-cut categories.

Identity Issues Among Bisexual Women. Most bisexual women report fluctuations in their romantic interests; they typically experience sequential relationships with women and men (Pope & Reynolds, 1991). For example, a woman with strong heterosexual attractions may—several years alter—find that she has equally strong attractions to women (Nichols, 1990).

Most bisexual women report that they felt attracted to men at an earlier age than they felt attracted to women (R. Fox, 1996; Weinberg et al., 1994). Weinberg and his colleagues believe that bisexuals actively work to make sense of their sexual interests—that is, to *construct* their bisexuality. Given the heterosexist bias in our culture, these individuals would certainly find it easier to make sense out of their heterosexual longings before they acknowledge any same-gender interests.

Bisexual women differ widely in their stories. Rust (1995) studied a group of bisexual women who attended conferences or social activities focusing on lesbian and bisexual issues. She found that 40% had been married to a man at some time, and 40% had been in a serious heterosexual relationship. She also found that 84% had identified themselves as lesbians at some point in their lives. Currently, 42% were involved in relationships with men, and 53% were involved in relationships with women. In short, bisexuality creates a fluid identity, rather than clear-cut life pathways (Garber, 1995).

Although little research has been conducted on the adjustment of bisexual women, they do not seem to have unusual difficulties (R. Fox, 1997; LaTorre & Wendenburg, 1983). Also, bisexual women typically, report that they are just as happy with their current sexual identity as lesbian women are (Rust, 1996b). In other words, bisexual women often contemplate their sexual identity—as we saw earlier—but they do not believe that this process is a painful struggle.

Bisexuals who come from a background of mixed ethnicity often find that their mixed heritage resonates comfortably with their bisexuality. After all, their experience with ethnicity has taught them from an early age that our culture constructs clear-cut ethnic categories. As a result, they are not surprised to encounter our culture's clear-cut categories of sexual orientation. For example, here's a quotation from a bisexual woman whose background includes Native American, Jewish, and British ancestors:

> Because I am of mixed ethnicity, I rotate between feeling "left out" of every group and feeling "secretly" qualified for several racial/cultural identities. I notice the same feeling regarding my sexual identity. (Rust, 1996a, pp. 69–70)

Attitudes Toward Bisexual Women. Bisexual women often report rejection by both the gay and the heterosexual communities. As Udis-Kessler (1991) remarked:

> The lesbian and gay reaction to bisexuals has tended to veer between "You don't exist" and "Go form your own community; you're not welcome in ours," while the heterosexual reaction has tended to veer between "You don't exist" and "I hate all you queers." (p. 350)

Paula Rust (1995) conducted an in-depth study that confirmed lesbians' skepticism about bisexual women. Many of the lesbian respondents argued that bisexuality doesn't really exist. Others thought that bisexuality was a transition phase that women might pass through on their journey to becoming lesbians. Still others claimed that bisexual women are really lesbians who want to retain "heterosexual privilege" by holding onto a romantic interest in men.

Chapter 2 emphasized that people like to have precise categories for males and females, fitting everyone neatly into one category or the other. Prejudice against lesbians and gay males can be partly traced to the fact that these people violate the accepted rules about categories: A person is not supposed to love someone who belongs to the same category. Bisexuals provide an additional frustration for people who like precise categories. After all, bisexuals cannot even be placed into the neat categories of lesbians or gay males—who *clearly* violate the categories. Bisexuals frustrate people who have a low tolerance for ambiguity!

Theoretical Explanations About Sexual Orientation and Preference

When we try to explain how lesbians develop their psychological, emotional, and sexual preference for women, we should reconsider a question raised earlier: How do *heterosexual* women develop their psychological, emotional, and sexual preference for men? Unfortunately, theorists rarely mention this question. Because of our culture's heterosexist bias, this preference is considered to be natural and normal. This assumption implies that lesbianism is considered unnatural and abnormal, and abnormalities require an explanation.

In reality, however, heterosexuality is more puzzling. After all, research from many branches of social psychology shows that we prefer people who resemble ourselves—not people who are different. On this basis, we should prefer those of our own gender.

I'm writing this section in 1998, surrounded by books and articles that proclaim how biological factors might explain the mystery of being lesbian or gay. However, it's clear that we do *not* have strong evidence for a biological explanation of lesbianism or bisexuality—despite the claims of the popular press. It's equally clear, however, that psychologists who favor sociocultural explanations have not devised appealing theories about the ways in which our cognitive processes, learning history, and social forces may shape our sexual orientations.

Let's begin by considering the biological explanations. Then we'll summarize the sociocultural explanations and the social constructionist perspective.

Biological Explanations.   To prepare this section on biological explanations, I reviewed dozens of articles and books. Surely, by 1998, we should have research confirming the importance of biological factors! In reality, however, researchers typically study gay men rather than lesbians. In addition, much of the research examines reproductive behavior in nonhuman species (L. Ellis & Ebertz, 1997) or sexual orientation in individuals exposed to abnormal levels of prenatal hormones (Meyer-Bahlburg et al., 1995). These research areas are too far removed to offer compelling explanations for lesbianism (Byne & Parsons, 1994; Tiefer, 1995a).

Other research examines normal humans in order to determine whether genetic factors, hormonal factors, or brain structures determine sexual orientation (e.g., J. Bailey & Pillard, 1991; Gladue, 1994; Halpern & Cass, 1994; LeVay, 1991, 1996). Some of the research suggests, for example, that a particular region on the X chromosome may contain genes for homosexuality. However, this research focuses almost exclusively on gay males, not lesbians or bisexuals (L. Ellis, 1996; Peplau, 1997). Many of these studies also have serious methodological flaws (e.g., Byne, 1994; Byne & Parsons, 1993; Marshall, 1995; Peplau et al., 1998).

Let's consider one of the few studies on genetic factors that studied lesbians rather than gay males. Bailey and his coauthors focused on lesbians who happened to be identical twins (Bailey, Pillard, et al., 1993). Of these lesbians, 48% had lesbian twin sisters. This is a remarkably high percentage. However, if genetic factors guarantee sexual orientation, why isn't that figure 100% (L. Ellis, 1996)? In addition, these twins grew up in the same environment and had numerous opportunities to discuss sexual orientation with each other. Social factors certainly had some influence on their sexual and romantic lives!

In a related study, Pattatucci and Hamer (1995) examined the sexual orientation of family members who were relatives of 358 heterosexual, bisexual, and lesbian women. Women who were lesbians were significantly more likely than heterosexual or bisexual women to have female relatives who were lesbian or bisexual. In one analysis, for example, 6% of lesbian women had lesbian sisters, in contrast to only 1% of heterosexual women. Fortunately, this article points out that environmental factors could be partially responsible for the results, although the authors favor a biological explanation.

In short, the research about the biological basis of sexual orientation is not compelling, especially because so few studies examine lesbians or bisexual women. However, the popular media convey an impression that the research clearly supports biological explanations. In addition, the individuals conducting the research often overemphasize the biological perspective. For example, Richard Pillard is known for his research on gay males who are identical twins (e.g., J. Bailey & Pillard, 1991). In a book review in the prestigious *New England Journal of Medicine*, Pillard (1997) wrote: "My own hunch is that biology will eventually prove to account for virtually all the variance in sexual orientation" (p. 646). Physicians throughout North America may well adopt that viewpoint, without questioning the flaws in the research and without realizing that so little research has been conducted on lesbians and bisexuals.

Sociocultural Explanations.   Unfortunately, as I've already noted, social scientists haven't rushed forward to propose alternative theories. Early theories are not very appealing. For example, I find Freud's approach even less attractive than the purely biological theories. Freud suggested that a lesbian is someone who failed to identify with her mother and also failed to move away from emphasizing the clitoris. Freud's followers continued to emphasize that lesbianism was a disturbance in the normal course of development, rather than simply a variation (Bohan, 1996).

Social learning theories are no more compelling (Bohan, 1996; L. Ellis, 1996). For example, some of these theories suggest that lesbians and bisexual women were sexually molested as children by adults who were lesbian and bisexuals. The factual data do not support this proposal.

Several more complex psychological theories have been recently proposed (e.g., D. J. Bem, 1996). However, these theories may misinterpret the relevant research, and they assume that the same exact theory holds true for both lesbians and gay males—even when no relevant research has been conducted with lesbians (Peplau et al., 1998).

Social Constructionist Explanations.   Several recent theorists have argued that sexual orientation is not a fundamental characteristic of individuals, nor is it a core aspect of their personality acquired either prenatally or in early childhood. In contrast to those essentialist explanations, the **social constructionist approach** argues that our culture creates sexual categories, which we use to organize our thoughts about our sexuality (Bohan, 1996; C. Kitzinger & Wilkinson, 1997). Based on their life experiences, most North Americans construct heterosexual identities for themselves. However, some women review their sexual and romantic experiences through the lenses of our culture and decide that they are either lesbian or bisexual.

The social constructionist approach argues that sexuality is both fluid and flexible, consistent with our earlier discussion of bisexuality. Women can therefore make a transition from being heterosexual to being lesbian, for example, by reevaluating their lives or by reconsidering their political values (C. Kitzinger & Wilkinson, 1997).

To examine the social constructionist approach, Celia Kitzinger and Sue Wilkinson (1997) interviewed 80 women who had strongly identified themselves as heterosexuals for at least 10 years and—at the time of the study—strongly identified themselves as lesbians. These women reported how they reevaluated their lives in making the transition. For example, one woman said:

> I was looking at myself in the mirror, and I thought, "That woman is a lesbian," and then I allowed myself to notice that it was me I was talking about. And when that happened, I felt whole for the first time, and also absolutely terrified. (p. 197)

However, quotations like this don't seem to offer clear-cut support for the social constructionist approach (Baumrind, 1995). For example, isn't it possible that the woman quoted above is really discovering her true sexual orientation for the first time? Golden (1996) interviewed lesbians and discovered that many felt their sexual orientation was truly beyond their conscious control. They had considered themselves to be different from other females at an early age—usually, in the range of 6 to 12 years. However, Golden pointed out that some respondents consciously chose their lesbian identity, consistent with social constructionist explanations.

In short, social constructionist explanations do acknowledge that the categories *heterosexual, bisexual,* and *lesbian* are fluid. These explanations may also explain how some women consciously choose their sexual category. However, these explanations may not adequately account for some women's experiences.

In reality, we do not have a satisfying comprehensive theory that considers the wide variety of women's sexual and romantic identities. To construct a theory, we need biological research focused on lesbians and bisexuals. The ideal theory may well identify a biological predisposition that encourages some women to become lesbian or bisexual. However, social experiences may determine which women will choose lesbian or bisexual identities and which women will choose heterosexual identities (Kauth & Kalichman, 1998). This theory would also specify that sexual categories are often fluid; some women arrive at their sexual identity by reviewing their lives and thinking through their alternatives.

 Section Summary *Lesbians and Bisexual Women*

1. **Lesbians are psychologically, emotionally, and sexually attracted to other women; however, in our culture, heterosexism leads us to judge heterosexual relationships differently from other romantic relationships.**

2. **Research demonstrates that the average lesbian and the average heterosexual woman are equally well adjusted.**

3. **Most lesbians are comfortable with their identity; those who accept their lesbian identity are higher in self-esteem.**

4. **The research shows that lesbian couples are happier when power is evenly divided; lesbian couples and heterosexual couples are equally satisfied with their relationships; the pattern of breaking up is fairly similar for lesbian couples and heterosexual couples.**

5. **Lesbian women of color may be more reluctant than European American lesbians to come out in their ethnic community, although some support groups have been organized for women of color.**

6. **Bisexual women illustrate that romantic attractions are often flexible; however, these women face rejection by both the lesbian and the heterosexual communities.**

7. **Biological research is designed to ascertain whether genetic factors, hormonal factors, and brain structures determine sexual orientation. However, the research seldom focuses on lesbians or bisexuals, and**

some research hints that biological factors may be partly responsible for sexual orientation.

8. **Sociocultural explanations and social constructionist explanations are also less than satisfying; the appropriate theory may include a biological predisposition combined with social experiences, with a social constructionist explanation accounting for some individuals.**

SINGLE WOMEN

The category called "single women" overlaps with many of the groups we have already considered. For example, women who are in dating or cohabiting relationships qualify as single. Women who are separated or divorced also qualify. So do lesbians and bisexual women who are not currently married. Widows, whom we will consider in Chapter 14, are also single. In addition, the category of single women includes those who have never married. When we consider all the different ways in which a woman can be single, 41% of U.S. women who are older than 17 years are single (U.S. Bureau of the Census, 1997). In Canada, 47% of women who are older than 15 years are single (Statistics Canada, 1995). The unifying characteristic that all these women share is that they are not currently living with a husband.

This section on single women focuses on women who have never married, because they are not considered elsewhere in the book. However, the other women mentioned above share some of the same advantages and disadvantages that belong to these never-married women, and many statements in this section apply to them as well.

Characteristics of Single Women

Little research has been conducted on single women, yet they constitute a large proportion of adult women. We know that they are generally well educated. In one study, for example, women who were never married had an average of 16 years of education, in contrast to 13 years for married women and 12 years for divorced and widowed women (Braito & Anderson, 1983). As you might imagine, single women are more likely than married women to work outside the home ("Facts on Working Women," 1998).

Research suggests that single, never-married women receive the same scores as married women on psychological tests measuring distress (Marks, 1996). Single women and married women are also similar in their life span, and both tend to live longer than divorced women (H. Friedman et al., 1995). Single women actually score higher than married women on measures of independence (Marks, 1996). However, single women score lower than married women on tests of self-acceptance (Marks, 1996).

What about the social relationships of single women? Apparently, there is no "typical single woman," just as there is no typical woman who is dating, living with a man, married, or lesbian. Researchers report that never-married women often belong to one of two very different categories (1) those who are socially isolated and (2) those who are very active socially (e.g., Braito & Anderson, 1983; Seccombe & Ishii-Kuntz, 1994). For example, Seccombe and Ishii-Kuntz found that 29% had social activities with friends at least once a week. However, 21% said they interacted with friends only monthly, 26% reported interactions only several times a year, and 25% replied that they never socialized with friends. Consistent with Theme 4 of this book, individual differences among women are very large.

How do single women feel about their romantic status? A polling firm sampled people living in New York City who were between the ages of 21 and 40 and were not currently in a serious romantic relationship (Penn & Schoen,

---

DEMONSTRATION 8.6

Attitudes Toward Single Women

Read the following paragraph:

> Susan Graham is 41 and married. She lives near Madison, Wisconsin. She has a master's degree from the University of Wisconsin, and she is a counseling psychologist.

Now take out a sheet of paper, and rate Susan on each of the following attributes, where 1 = not at all and 7 = very much. In each case, try to give your first impression.

1. competitive	6. happy	11. friendly
2. sociable	7. intelligent	12. relaxed
3. likable	8. attractive	13. talkative
4. influential	9. successful at work	14. reliable
5. stable	10. outgoing	15. secure

Now, set aside those answers so that you cannot see them, try to clear your head of the previous task, and read the following paragraph:

> Susan Graham is 41 and single. She lives near Madison, Wisconsin. She has a master's degree from the University of Wisconsin, and she is a counseling psychologist.

Take out a new sheet of paper, and rate Susan on the attributes listed above. Again, try to give your first impression. Then compare your responses in the two conditions.

(Based on Etaugh & Malstrom, 1981.)

1998). Of the women who identified themselves as heterosexual, 34% were happily single and dating, and 27% were happily single and *not* dating. In addition, 30% were looking for a romantic relationship, but only 5% described themselves as "panicking." In summary, single women are generally well adjusted and they may be quite satisfied with their single status.

Attitudes Toward Single Women

Think about the comments aimed at never-married women when you were growing up. If you are female, someone probably told you that if you weren't nicer to people (or smiled more, or were less of a tomboy, or whatever), then no one would want to marry you. Your family may have speculated that an unmarried aunt had been "too picky." At best, you may have been instructed never to refer to the fact that a relative was unmarried. My husband recalls being told as a small child to call a card game "Donkey"—rather than "Old Maid"—in the presence of a never-married aunt. Single women are often the objects of pity, if not outright scorn (Anderson & Stewart, 1994). Furthermore, single women are pitied and scorned more than single men are (Waehler, 1996).

Before you read further, try Demonstration 8.6, which is based on research by Etaugh and Malstrom (1981). These authors reworded the description of the individual in the demonstration so that this person was either male or female and was married, widowed, divorced, or never married; different participants rated each scenario. Let's look specifically at the results for the never-married person. This individual was perceived to be less sociable than divorced or married individuals; less attractive than divorced, widowed, or married individuals; and less reliable than married persons. In general, however, single women are typically judged to be as professionally competent as married women (Etaugh & Foresman, 1983; Etaugh & Riley, 1983). Apparently, single people are downgraded on socially relevant characteristics. However, their never-married status is not vitally important when we judge work performance.

Advantages and Disadvantages of Being Single

Among the advantages to being single, women most often mention "freedom" (K. Lewis & Moon, 1997). Single people are free to do what they want, according to their own preferences. As one never-married woman remarked:

> I had places to go and things to see. And I wasn't going to be stopped, nobody was going to stop me. It took me a long time to get going, but I made it. (K. Allen, 1994, p. 104)

Single women also mention that privacy is an advantage for them. They can be by themselves when they want, without the risk of offending someone. Many single women report that their status makes it easier to pursue career goals without compromise. In addition, they mention that they pursue a greater variety of friendships than would be available if they had married (K. Allen, 1989, 1994).

When women are asked about the disadvantages of being single, they frequently mention loneliness (K. Allen, 1994; Anderson & Stewart, 1994; Dalton, 1992). One woman reported:

> I am not a widow, but I'm the same as a widow. I'm a woman living alone, going home to an empty house. (K. Allen, 1994, p. 104)

Single people sometimes mention that they feel at a disadvantage in communities where couples predominate—a situation that some humorously call "the Noah's Ark Syndrome." Others report that they feel unsafe living alone in urban settings (Chasteen, 1994). Still others resent that they are the objects of pity, and they also resent that friends and relatives are overly concerned that they are not married (K. Lewis & Moon, 1997).

However, most single people create their own social networks of friends and relatives. Many of them have a housemate with whom they can share joys, sorrows, and frustrations. One woman described an advantage to her social world, in terms of "having friends that care for you as a person and not as part of a couple" (K. Lewis & Moon, 1997, p. 123). These social networks are often innovative. For example, one woman described a system that she called her "Ten Top People." These were individuals to whom she could feel free to turn for immediate help or for sharing happiness (M. Adams, 1976). In summary, single women frequently develop alternate support systems for caring and sharing.

Single Women of Color

We noted that little research has been conducted on single women. Sadly, single women of color are virtually invisible in the psychology research. This observation is especially ironic because 37% of Black women have never married, and 24% of Latina women have never married—in contrast to only 17% of European American women (U.S. Bureau of the Census, 1997).

Limited research has been conducted with Black women who are single. Supportive friendships often provide invaluable social interactions for single Black women. As Mays (1985) points out, Black women have been characterized throughout history by their close relationships with other women:

> Stories written by Black women about Black women abound in rich examples of the dynamics of diversity in same-sex close relationships among Black women. Common to these writings is the theme of survival. Relationships develop which cut across potential areas of divisive diversity to encompass Black women from different walks of life reaching out to other Black women out of a cultural heritage and herstory of female support. (pp. 67–68)

One study focused on the support networks of Black unmarried and married women in Richmond, Virginia (D. Brown & Gary, 1985). These women were asked about the number of friends and relatives with whom they maintained close contact. The unmarried respondents emphasized that other family members were extremely important in their lives; roughly two-thirds of the women mentioned kin as their closest relationship. About a quarter of the women mentioned female friends as their major close relationship. Only 6% cited male friends as their closest relationship.

One of the most interesting reports from the married women was that close to three-fourths of them did not mention husbands among their three closest relationships. (Comparable data from married women in other ethnic groups would be equally welcome.) Many married Black women found the same support among female friends and other relatives that was reported by the single Black women. The authors caution, however, that these findings may not be generalizable to Black women at all levels of education and income.

Single Black women also find supportive relationships in the workplace. For example, Denton's (1990) study of Black professional women uncovered many ways in which these friends could provide encouragement. For example, one woman remarked about her friend:

> She makes me feel good about the choices I make. I don't feel recognized or appreciated for my efforts on my job. I know I've done exemplary work . . . but I get no recognition for what I've done. [In this friendship] I get reinforced. She always lets me know I'm talented. (p. 455)

Researchers in past years have failed to provide a rich description of attitudes, social conditions, and behaviors of single women (Condra, 1991). In the next few decades, we may achieve a more complete understanding of the diversity of single women from all ethnic backgrounds.

 SECTION SUMMARY   *Single Women*

1. **Little research has been conducted on single women, even though they constitute a large proportion of the population; single women are fairly similar to married women in measures of adjustment.**

2. **Single women vary widely in their social activity.**

3. **People have somewhat negative attitudes toward the social characteristics of single people, but not toward their professional competence.**

4. **Single women value their freedom and their privacy, but they mention that loneliness is a disadvantage; most single women create alternate support systems.**

5. **Black single women emphasize the importance of family members and friends in providing close relationships and support, both socially and on the job.**

CHAPTER REVIEW
QUESTIONS

1. From time to time throughout this book, we have discussed the topic of attractiveness. How is attractiveness important in love relationships?

2. We discussed cross-cultural studies and research with women of color at several points in the chapter. Summarize this research with respect to the following topics: (1) the ideal romantic partner; (2) emphasis on friendship in a love relationship; (3) getting married; (4) marriage patterns; (5) lesbian women of color; and (6) Black single women.

3. What is evolutionary psychology, how does it explain women's and men's choices for an ideal romantic partner, and why is it inadequate in explaining romantic relationships as we enter into the 21st century? How can social learning theory account for that research? Finally, why would evolutionary psychology have difficulty accounting for gay and lesbian relationships?

4. The issue of power was discussed several times in this chapter. Summarize the relationship between money and power in marriage, the division of power in the three kinds of marriages, power in Black families, and the importance of balanced power in lesbian relationships.

5. Discuss how this chapter contains many examples of the theme that women differ widely from one another. Be sure to include topics such as patterns of living together, taking the husband's name during marriage, reactions to divorce, and the social relationships of single women.

6. Discuss gender similarities and differences that were noted throughout this chapter, including the ideal short-term romantic partner, the ideal long-term partner, reactions to breaking up, satisfaction with marriage, and the decision to divorce.

7. What factors determine satisfaction with relationships, or satisfaction with life, for married women, lesbians, and single women?

8. Lesbians, bisexuals, and single women all have lifestyles that differ from the norm. What are people's attitudes toward women in these three groups?

9. Imagine that you are having a conversation with a friend from your high school, whom you know well. This friend says that she thinks that lesbians have more psychological problems than heterosexual women do. She also thinks that lesbian couples are likely to have relationship problems. What information from this chapter could you provide, related to her concerns?

10. Suppose that you continue to talk with the high school friend mentioned in Question 9, and the conversation turns to people who have never married. She tells you she is worried about a mutual friend who doesn't seem to be interested in dating or finding a husband. How would you respond to your friend's concerns?

NEW TERMS

evolutionary psychology (283)

social learning approach (284)

traditional marriage (295)

modern marriage (295)

egalitarian marriage (296)

machismo (296)

marianismo (296)

Black matriarchy (297)

persistence of attachment (299)

ego development (299)

lesbian (301)

heterosexism (301)

bisexual woman (308)

social constructionist approach (312)

RECOMMENDED READINGS

Anderson, C. M., & Stewart, S. (1994). *Flying solo: Single women in midlife.* New York: W. W. Norton. This book provides an excellent blend of personal stories and information about single women.

Firestein, B. A. (Ed.). (1996b). *Bisexuality: The psychology and politics of an invisible minority.* Thousand Oaks, CA: Sage. I strongly recommend this book, which contains topics such as gender identity and bisexuality, bisexual women in therapy, and attitudes toward bisexuality.

Hatfield, E., & Rapson, R. L. (1996). *Love and sex: Cross-cultural perspectives.* Boston: Allyn & Bacon. If you are interested in love relationships beyond North America, this book will be of special interest. Some of my favorite sections focus on ideal romantic partners, passionate love in other countries, and falling in love.

Mandell, N., & Duffy, A. (Eds.). (1995). *Canadian families: Diversity, conflict, and change.* Toronto: Harcourt Brace Canada. This edited volume includes information on lesbians, divorce, and family violence, as well as a review of the literature on families.

Savin-Williams, R. C., & Cohen, K. (Eds.). (1996). *The lives of lesbians, gays, and bisexuals: Children to adults.* Fort Worth, TX: Harcourt Brace. This book should be in every college library; it contains remarkably well-written chapters on all aspects of lesbian, gay, and bisexual issues.

Winstead, B. A., Derlega, V. J., & Rose, S. (1997). *Gender and close relationships.* Thousand Oaks, CA: Sage. Here's a good overview of love relationships, with chapters on attraction and dating, maintaining a relationship, conflict, and violence.

ANSWERS TO THE DEMONSTRATIONS

Demonstration 8.1: 1. F; 2. F; 3. M; 4. M; 5. F; 6. F; 7. M; 8. F; 9. M; 10. M

Demonstration 8.5: Kurdek's (1995a) questionnaire is called the Multiple Determinants of Relationship Commitment Inventory, and it assesses six different components of love relationships. On the shortened version in this demonstration, each of six categories is represented with two questions: Rewards (#1 and #7); Costs (#2 and #8); Match to Ideal Comparison (#3 and #9); Alternatives (#4 and #10); Investments (#5 and #11); Barriers to Leaving the Relationship (#6 and #12). High relationship commitment was operationally defined in terms of high scores on Rewards, Match to Ideal, Investments, and Barriers to Leaving—and low scores on Costs and Alternatives.

ANSWERS TO THE TRUE–FALSE QUESTIONS

1. True (p. 281); 2. True (p. 284); 3. True (p. 287); 4. True (p. 293); 5. False (p. 297); 6. False (p. 299); 7. True (p. 303); 8. False (p. 309); 9. False (p. 311); 10. False (p. 314).

SEXUALITY

CHAPTER 9

TRUE OR FALSE?

_____ 1. Orgasm in women is caused primarily by stimulation of a small sexual organ called the clitoris.

_____ 2. Women are more likely than men to have several orgasms in sequence.

_____ 3. The majority of adults in the United States say that they learned about sexuality from their parents.

_____ 4. Most women recall that their first experience of sexual intercourse was pleasant.

_____ 5. People consistently judge a sexually active unmarried female more negatively than a sexually active unmarried male.

_____ 6. Surveys indicate that men and women are similar in their enjoyment of sexuality.

_____ 7. The most common sexual problems are typically caused by some kind of physical abnormality, rather than a psychological reason.

_____ 8. Researchers know more about male sexuality than about female sexuality.

_____ 9. More than half of all pregnancies in the United States were "accidents," rather than being planned.

_____ 10. When women with an unwanted pregnancy have an abortion, they typically do not experience serious psychological consequences.

Female Sexual Anatomy and Sexual Responses
External Sexual Organs
Sexual Responses
Theories About Orgasms
Gender Comparisons in Sexual Responses

Sexual Behavior and Attitudes
Sex Education
Adolescent Sexual Behavior
The Double Standard
Sexual Scripts
Sexual Activities
Communication About Sexuality
Sexuality Among Lesbians
Sexuality and Older Women

Sexual Problems
Disorders of Sexual Desire
Female Orgasmic Disorder
Painful Intercourse
How Gender Roles Contribute to Sexual Problems
Therapy for Sexual Problems

Birth Control and Abortion
Birth Control Methods
Who Uses Birth Control?
Obstacles to Using Birth Control
Family Planning in Developing Countries
Abortion

"The New Sexual Revolution" proclaims an article in a popular magazine. Is this *Glamour? Cosmopolitan? Mademoiselle?* No, it's *Ladies' Home Journal,* the magazine that fairly traditional women can usually count on for articles like "The Perfect Chocolate Pudding" and "Ten New Ideas for Christmas Tree-Trimming."

Sex sells. Several decades ago, American movie producers were not allowed to show a couple kissing for more than a few seconds—and their lips had to be dry, not moist (F. Walsh, 1996). Now, movie distributors regard a G rating as an invitation to financial failure. Sex also leaps out from the television screen—even in family sitcoms—and from fiction and nonfiction books. Sexual-advice books are also consistently popular, as you can see from examining the shelves of most bookstores (Tiefer, 1995b).

Our discussion of this passionate subject begins with a decidedly dispassionate topic—the biological components of sexuality. Other topics included in this chapter are sexual behavior and attitudes, sexual dysfunction in women, and birth control and abortion. (Chapter 11 discusses the related topic of sexually transmitted diseases.) Throughout this chapter, we will focus on the psychological components of sexuality, rather than the biological or reproductive aspects of sexuality.

FEMALE SEXUAL ANATOMY
AND SEXUAL RESPONSES
External Sexual Organs

Figure 9.1 shows the external sexual organs of an adult female. The specific shapes, sizes, and colors of these organs differ greatly from one woman to the next. Ordinarily, the labia are folded inward, so that they cover the vaginal opening. In this diagram, however, the labia are folded outward in order to show the locations of the urethral and vaginal openings.

FIGURE 9.1	Female external sexual organs.

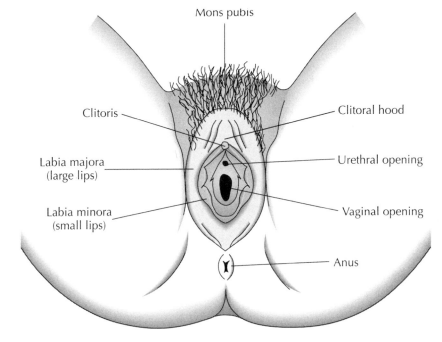

Mons pubis

Clitoris

Clitoral hood

Labia majora
(large lips)

Urethral opening

Labia minora
(small lips)

Vaginal opening

Anus

Mons pubis (pronounced "mons *pew*-biss") is a Latin phrase referring to the fatty tissue in front of the pubic bone. At puberty, the mons pubis becomes covered with pubic hair. The **labia majora** (pronounced "*lay*-bee-ah mah-*jore*-ah") are the "large lips" or folds of skin located just inside a woman's thighs. Located between the labia majora are the **labia minora** (pronounced "*lay*-bee-ah mih-*nore*-ah"), or "small lips."

Notice that the upper part of the labia region forms the **clitoral hood,** which covers the clitoris. As we will see later in this section, the **clitoris** (pronounced "*klih*-tuh-riss") is a small sensitive organ that is important in females' sexual response. The clitoris has a high density of nerve endings, possibly as many as a man has on his entire penis (Wade & Cirese, 1991). Because the clitoris is so sensitive, women often do not enjoy direct stimulation of the clitoris.

The urethral opening is the part of a woman's body through which urine passes; it is located near the clitoris. Notice that the vaginal opening is located between the urethral opening and the anus. The **vagina** is a flexible canal through which menstrual fluid passes. During heterosexual intercourse, the penis enters the vagina. The vagina also provides a passageway during the normal birth of an infant. At this point, you may wish to return to Figure 4.2, on page 127, to review several important internal organs that are relevant to sexual behavior.

Sexual Responses

During the 1960s, William Masters and Virginia Johnson (1966) wrote a book called *Human Sexual Response*. This book reported the results of their laboratory studies, emphasized the importance of the clitoris in women's sexual responses, and noted the similarity between women's and men's responses.

Contemporary researchers and theorists have criticized the Masters and Johnson approach. The critics argue that Masters and Johnson studied only individuals who readily experienced orgasms during sexual activity, but they claimed that the findings could be generalized to all people. As Leonore Tiefer (1995b) argues, we wouldn't expect to study human singing behavior by selecting and testing only accomplished recording artists! Other critics complain that sexuality shows much more variety than the neatly ordered sequence of events that Masters and Johnson described (McCormick, 1994). Still other theorists have proposed a sexual desire phase that occurs prior to the phases that Masters and Johnson proposed. The **sexual desire phase** emphasizes the importance of emotions and thoughts in arousing sexual interest and desire (H. Kaplan, 1979). Unfortunately, this psychologically interesting component of sexual responding receives relatively little attention, in comparison to the well-publicized components of the Masters and Johnson approach.

Masters and Johnson (1966) described four phases, each of which focuses on changes in the genitals. As you read about these phases, keep the critics' comments in mind. Also, as Wade and Cirese (1991) caution, "The stages are not like the cycles of an automatic washing machine; we are not programmed to move mechanically from one stage to another" (p. 140).

Masters and Johnson called the first phase the excitement phase. During the **excitement phase,** women become sexually aroused by touching, erotic thoughts, and suggestive pictures. During the excitement phase, blood rushes to the genital region, causing **vasocongestion** (pronounced "vas-owe-con-*jess*-chun"), or swelling due to the acculumation of blood. Vasocongestion causes the clitoris and the labia to grow as they fill with blood; it also produces droplets of moisture in the vagina. Heart rate, breathing rate, and muscle tension increase during the excitement phase.

During the **plateau phase,** the clitoris shortens in length and draws back under the clitoral hood. The clitoral region is now extremely sensitive. As a result, movement of the clitoral hood—produced either by thrusting of the penis or other touching—causes stimulation of the clitoris. The woman's heart rate, breathing rate, and muscle tension increase still further.

During the **orgasmic phase,** the uterus contracts strongly, at intervals roughly a second apart. (Figure 4.2, on page 127, shows the female internal organs, with the uterus located above the vagina.) A woman generally experiences between 3 and 15 of these contractions during an orgasm. Notice, then, that the orgasm—the topic of numerous popular articles, psychological theorizing, and private conversations—usually lasts only a fraction of a minute.

During the **resolution phase,** the sexual organs return to their earlier, unstimulated size. Breathing slows, muscles relax, and heart rate decreases. The resolution phase may last 30 minutes or more. However, females may have additional orgasms without going directly into the resolution phase.

Theories About Orgasms

Sigmund Freud had argued that women could have two different kinds of orgasms. He suggested that immature women, who had not resolved their "penis envy," could achieve only "clitoral orgasms," through stimulating the clitoral region. In contrast, Freud proposed that mature women could experience "vaginal orgasms," through intercourse. As McCormick (1994) points out, women in earlier decades spent countless hours with psychiatrists, trying to overcome their psychological immaturity in order to achieve the "correct" kind of orgasms.

The research of Masters and Johnson (1966), however, reached a different conclusion. According to their observations, an orgasm results from stimulation of the clitoris, either from direct touching in the clitoral area or from indirect pressure from a partner's thrusting penis. Women experience the same kind of orgasm, no matter what kind of stimulation is used.

Current researchers and theorists emphasize that women's views of sexuality do not focus simply on genitals and orgasms. As Naomi McCormick (1994) wrote:

> Cuddling, self-disclosing, even gazing into a partner's eyes are highly valued by women. A feminist vision of sexuality considers whole people, not just their genitals. Intellectual stimulation, the exchange of self-disclosures, and whole body sensuality may feel just as "sexy" as orgasms. (p. 186)

Gender Comparisons in Sexual Responses

The studies of Masters and Johnson and by more recent researchers allow us to draw a conclusion that would have been considered startling at the beginning of the 1900s: Women and men are reasonably similar in many aspects of their sexual responses. Notice that this conclusion echoes our more general thesis, throughout this book, that women and men are not as different as many people think. Let's look at three topics that illustrate similarities and two topics that illustrate differences.

Similarities

1. *Women and men experience similar phases in their sexual responses.* For example, both men and women experience vasocongestion, and their orgasms are physiologically similar.

DEMONSTRATION 9.1

Psychological Reactions to Orgasm

Try to guess whether a female or a male wrote each of the following descriptions of an orgasm. Place an F (female) or an M (male) in front of each passage. The answers can be found at the end of the chapter, on page 359.

_____ 1. A sudden feeling of lightheadedness followed by an intense feeling of relief and elation. A rush. Intense muscular spasms of the whole body. Sense of euphoria followed by deep peace and relaxation.

_____ 2. To me, an orgasmic experience is the most satisfying *pleasure* that I have experienced in relation to any other types of satisfaction or pleasure that I've had, which were nonsexually oriented.

_____ 3. It is like turning a water faucet on. You notice the oncoming flow but it can be turned on or off when desired. You feel the valves open and close and the fluid flow. An orgasm makes your head and body tingle.

_____ 4. A buildup of tension which starts to pulsate very fast, and there is a sudden release from the tension and desire to sleep.

_____ 5. It is a pleasant, tension-relieving muscular contraction. It relieves physical tension and mental anticipation.

_____ 6. A release of a very high level of tension, but ordinarily tension is unpleasant whereas the tension before orgasm is far from unpleasant.

_____ 7. On orgasm is a great release of tension with spasmodic reaction at the peak. This is exactly how it feels to me.

_____ 8. A building of tension, sometimes, and frustration until the climax. A *tightening* inside, palpitating rhythm, explosion, and warmth and peace.

(Based on Vance & Wagner, 1977, pp. 207–210.)

2. *Women and men have similar psychological reactions to orgasm.* Read Demonstration 9.1 and try to guess whether a man or a woman wrote each passage. Vance and Wagner (1977) asked people to guess which descriptions of orgasms were written by women and which were written by men. Most respondents were unable to guess at better than a chance level. Also, Wiest (1977) asked students to rate the word *orgasm* on 18 different scales such as "good–bad," "strong–weak," "hard–soft," and "sharp–dull." Male and female students provided almost identical ratings.

3. *Women can reach orgasm as quickly as men.* When a man and a woman are having intercourse, the man typically reaches orgasm more quickly than the woman. Because the woman's clitoris is the focus of her orgasmic response, the clitoris must be aroused by the relatively inefficient stimulation provided by the thrusting penis and its action on the clitoral hood. In contrast, the man's penis receives direct stimulation. However, when women are directly stimulated in the clitoral region, they experience a relatively rapid orgasm, typically within 3 minutes (Tavris & Wade, 1984). We need to emphasize, however, that "faster" isn't necessarily "better."

Differences

1. *Women are more likely than men to have multiple orgasms.* Masters and Johnson's (1966) discovery that women could have multiple orgasms brought some good news. Specifically, women could be viewed as sensual, active people. However, the discovery also brought bad news, because women were now required to reach a new standard. One orgasm was no longer good enough. The previous prudish standards were now replaced with extraordinary expectations for sexual performance. Incidentally, a survey of professional nurses concluded that about half of the respondents had experienced multiple orgasms at least once (Darling et al., 1991). Also, some men can apparently have multiple orgasms (M. Dunn & Trost, 1989; Hyde & DeLamater, 1997).

2. *Men ejaculate, and women do not.* During orgasm, men **ejaculate,** expelling semen from the penis. Despite some controversy, we have no convincing evidence that women have a comparable process.

In general, then, men and women are reasonably similar in these more internal, physiological components of sexuality (Kelley, 1987). In contrast, gender differences are larger in areas influenced by external factors such as culture. For example, we will see later in the chapter that men and women often hold different beliefs about a culturally transmitted value—whether sex is appropriate for two people who are not in a committed relationship.

 SECTION SUMMARY *Female Sexual Anatomy and Sexual Responses*

1. The external sexual organs in females include the mons pubis, labia majora, labia minora, clitoral hood, clitoris, and vaginal opening.

2. **Individual differences are large, and sexual responses do not follow a clear-cut sequence; a desire phase may precede genital changes; Masters and Johnson (1966) described four phases of sexual response: excitement, plateau, orgasm, and resolution.**

3. **Female orgasms are similar, whether they are produced by direct stimulation of the clitoris or by intercourse; current theorists emphasize views of sexuality that consider aspects of sexuality other than genitals and orgasms.**

4. **Women and men are similar in their sexual responses, their psychological reactions to orgasm, and—under certain conditions—their rate of reaching orgasm. However, women are more likely to have multiple orgasms, and men ejaculate during orgasm.**

SEXUAL BEHAVIOR
AND ATTITUDES

As we examined the biological side of sexuality, we discussed swelling genitals, contracting muscles, and racing heartbeats. Let's now turn to the humans who possess these organs. What are their behaviors, thoughts, and opinions about sexuality?

Sex Education

Take a moment to think about your early ideas, experiences, and attitudes about sexuality. Was sex a topic that produced half-suppressed giggles in the school cafeteria? Did you worry about whether you were too experienced, or not experienced enough? Sexuality is an important topic for adolescents—and many preadolescents. In this section, we will examine how children learn about sexuality, both at home and at school.

Parents and Sex Education.   A large-scale study of U.S. adults showed that only 25% of men and 40% of women reported learning about sex at home (Janus & Janus, 1993). Although young people frequently say they would prefer that their parents discuss sex education with them, only a minority report that parents are a major source of this information (S. White & DeBlassie, 1992).

Most parent–child conversations about sexuality take place between mothers and daughters (Murry, 1996). For example, Nolin and Petersen (1992) found that mothers and daughters had discussed roughly twice as many sexuality-related topics as had mothers and sons, fathers and daughters, or fathers and sons.

Researchers have discovered that individuals who have had a college course in human sexuality are more likely than other similar students to discuss sexuality with their children (B. King et al., 1993). They may feel more informed and more comfortable about discussing potentially embarrassing concepts. Kathryn

Wright (1997), a specialist in adolescent medicine, recommends that parents become well informed, even practicing saying words like *vagina* and *penis,* so that they can approach these conversations more positively.

Many women recall hearing only negative messages about sexuality from their parents. These women are especially likely to engage in risky sexual behavior (L. Ward & Wyatt, 1994). Other women recall hearing mixed messages such as "Sex is dirty," and "Save it for someone you love" (K. Wright, 1997).

Researchers are now studying parent–child communications among women of color. Latinas often report that sex is a forbidden topic with their parents (Fine, 1992; Murry, 1996; J. Taylor et al., 1995). One young woman responded to a teacher's advice to talk with her parents about sexuality:

> Not our parents! We tell them one little thing and they get crazy. My cousin got sent to Puerto Rico to live with her religious aunt, and my sister got beat 'cause my father thought she was with a boy. (p. 36)

Black mothers seem to feel more comfortable than Latina or European American mothers in speaking to their daughters about sexuality. For example, one Black adolescent reported discussing contraception with her mother. These conversations were helpful "because she was understanding, she was letting me know if there was anything I needed that she was there" (Taylor et al., 1995).

Schools and Sex Education.   What do our school systems say about sexuality? According to psychologists, the answer is not encouraging (Fine, 1992; Tiefer, 1995b). Teachers and school administrators may resent having to teach about the real-life problems related to sexuality. They may decide to leave out "objectionable" topics such as intercourse, contraception, abortion, and sexual orientation.

The typical sex education program in high school is 8 to 10 hours in length, and it focuses mostly on the reproductive system, or—as some have called it—an "organ recital" (Blau & Gullotta, 1993; Tiefer, 1995b). Students don't hear about the connections between sexuality and emotions. As a result, sex education in school often has little impact on students' sexual behavior.

In recent years, most schools have required teachers to discuss AIDS (acquired immunodeficiency syndrome). However, these programs often emphasize an oversimplified "Just Say No" approach (J. Stryker et al., 1995). Most current sex education programs are typically not effective in addressing the sexual issues that adolescents consider important or in reducing the incidence of AIDS and other sexually transmitted diseases.

However, some communities in the United States have developed more comprehensive programs. For example, more than 500 schools now feature health centers that focus on adolescent sexuality issues. Students can easily visit these centers—often located in the school itself—for information about sexuality as well as contraceptives and pregnancy tests (D. Kaplan, 1995).

Any comprehensive educational program must help students develop the skills and behaviors that encourage them to use the information they receive.

Teenagers may have the appropriate knowledge. However, the educational program will fail if they cannot think through the consequences of their own decisions (Blau & Gullotta, 1993). Furthermore, research on these comprehensive programs shows that, when contraception is available in the context of an educational program, the services do *not* promote greater sexual activity (Hardy & Zabin, 1991; K. Wright, 1997). This research should be reassuring to parents who are concerned about school programs on sexuality.

Adolescent Sexual Behavior

We do not have abundant information about teen sexual behavior (Gardner & Wilcox, 1993). However, research suggests that adolescent sexual experience is related to factors such as early puberty, poor academic performance, and poverty (Millstein & Halpern-Felsher, 1998).

Ethnicity is also related to adolescent sexual experience. For example, Black female adolescents are likely to have their first sexual experience 1 or 2 years before European American or Latina female adolescents (Hatfield & Rapson, 1996; Millstein & Halpern-Felsher, 1998). Asian American female adolescents are the least likely to have early sexual experiences.

Unfortunately, peer pressure encourages some teenagers to become sexually active (Kantrowitz, 1987; K. Martin, 1996). These teenagers risk unwanted pregnancies and sexually transmitted diseases—topics we'll examine later in this chapter and in Chapter 11.

For many adolescents, decisions about sexuality are critically important in defining their values. A student in one of my courses wrote about an ongoing conflict with her boyfriend.

> The major issue which has always caused conflict in our relationship is sex. He wants to, I don't: but it's not that simple . . . I just don't feel I am ready, there are things I want to do for myself first, before I get really deeply involved, and, never one to gamble, I don't want to chance anything. Besides, if something went wrong and if, for example, I got pregnant, I would be the one who was stuck. I have other reasons, though not so easily explained, it's a matter of self-esteem. I was raised in a very traditional environment, and I have my own dreams of how things will be. I want to wait until I am married. I know most people don't agree, they believe it is silly and prudish; but it is part of my moral code, something which I feel very strongly about, and something which is part of the many interwoven, inexplicable things which make up my identity.

Romance novels portray idyllic images of young women being blissfully transformed by their first sexual experience. However, most women do not have positive memories of their first intercourse (Mayerson, 1996; Nicolson, 1997; Tiefer & Kring, 1998). The experience may also be physically painful.

In addition, young women often report that they felt coerced. In fact, they frequently mention that the major reason they consented to intercourse was that they were afraid that their boyfriend would leave them otherwise (K. Martin,

1996). They are often confused and scared, as if they had lost a part of themselves. Martin (1996) summarized her interviews: "Girls see sex as boys taking something from them and not as a give-and-take or a two-way interaction that should be enjoyable for both people" (p. 87). Young women who expect a sexual experience to be loving may report disappointment if the romance doesn't continue (Lickona, 1994; Millstein & Halpern-Falsher, 1998).

A description provided by one woman provides a positive contrast to the stories about confusion and loss:

> I really feel blessed that I was introduced to sex in such a positive way, in such a loving way and still enjoy it and I have a wonderful relationship with my whole body . . . and it feels good. (Daniluk, 1993, p. 61)

In summary, young women's early introductions to sexuality are typically far from pleasant. As we have seen, parents and schools seldom help young people make informed decisions about sexuality. In addition, young women's early sexual experiences may not be as joyous as they had hoped.

The Double Standard

Prior to the 1950s and 1960s, North Americans held a **double standard;** they believed that premarital sex was inappropriate for women but excusable or even appropriate for men (Oliver & Sedikides, 1992). In the present era, the double standard has faded somewhat, and the situation is complicated. Specifically, the likelihood that people will endorse the double standard depends on characteristics of the people who are making the judgment, characteristics of the people

---

DEMONSTRATION 9.2

Judgments About Sexuality, as a Function of Gender

Suppose you heard about a 19-year-old named Jennifer Miller. Jennifer first had sexual intercourse at the age of 16, with a student from another high school whom she met that night at a party. Since then, she has had sex with eight other males, none of them in a long-term relationship. What would be your reaction to Jennifer? How do you think your friends would react to her story?

Now try to erase Jennifer from your mind. Concentrate instead on this scenario. A 19-year-old named Jason Moore first had sexual intercourse at the age of 16, with a student from another high school whom he met that night at a party. Since then, he has had sex with eight other females, none of them in a long-term relationship. What would be your reaction to Jason? How do you think your friends would react to his story?

being judged, details of the situation, and how the attitudes are assessed (Hatfield & Rapson, 1996; Sprecher & McKinney, 1993). Be sure you've tried Demonstration 9.2 before you read further.

The complex pattern of the double standard is illustrated in a study by Sprecher and Hatfield (summarized in Hatfield & Rapson, 1996). For example, one of the questions presented to college students was whether it was appropriate to have sex on a first date or in a casual relationship. The men demonstrated the double standard: They thought casual sex was fine for themselves, but not for women. However, the women did not demonstrate the double standard: They thought that casual sex was inappropriate for *both* men and women.

Sprecher and Hatfield also asked the students about the appropriateness of sex when two people were discussing marriage or were engaged to be married (Hatfield & Rapson, 1996). In this case, neither men nor women endorsed a double standard. Once people are seriously considering marriage, both genders believe that premarital intercourse is appropriate for both men and women.

The double standard is also more likely to emerge when people rate a person, rather than an action, and when that person could be considered promiscuous. For example, Sprecher and her coauthors (1987) found that females were evaluated more negatively than males for the situation described in Demonstration 9.2. People are also more likely to use the double standard when making judgments about teenagers, rather than older individuals.

In summary, we sometimes find evidence of the double standard, with more tolerant attitudes toward male sexuality. However, present-day North Americans often judge men and women by the same standards.

What about other cultures? Weinberg and his colleagues (1995) report that the double standard is even less evident in Sweden than in the United States. Sweden endorses gender equality in many areas of life, such as work and politics. Consistent with those values, Swedish students were even more likely than U.S. students to judge men and women by the same standards of sexual conduct.

In some cultures, however, the double standard is so strong that it has life-threatening consequences for women. For example, in some Middle Eastern and Latin American cultures, a man is expected to uphold the family honor by killing a daughter, a sister, or even a mother who is suspected of engaging in "inappropriate" sexual activities (Eisler, 1996). The same sexual activity would be ignored in a male family member.

Consider, for example, the autobiography of Princess Sultana of Saudi Arabia (Hatfield & Rapson, 1996; Sasson, 1992). At puberty, young women in Saudi Arabia are strictly controlled; they wear veils so that men cannot see their faces. However, Sultana and her teenage female friends rejected these values, and they met secretly to flirt with young men. When their fathers discovered these activities, they punished their daughters. For example, one father bound his daughter in chains and drowned her in a swimming pool. In contrast, teenage males are allowed to be sexually active. One time, for example, Sultana walked into a room and discovered that her brother was raping a terrified 8-year-old girl—a practice that is considered acceptable behavior for a Saudi male (Sasson, 1992).

Sexual Scripts

A script for a play specifies what people say and do. A **sexual script** is less detailed, but it provides a general description of "appropriate" behavior for women and men in sexual interactions (McCormick, 1994; Tiefer & Kring, 1998). As we enter the 21st century, the North American sexual script specifies that men are the initiators of sexual relationships. In contrast, women are expected either to resist or to comply passively with their partner's advances (Regan & Berscheid, 1995; S. Thompson, 1995).

People who have traditional values are likely to act according to these clear-cut scripts. For example, a traditional woman waits for her date to kiss her—she does not initiate kissing. Only one person is in charge in this kind of relationship. Even during marriage, sex is regulated according to the male's erotic schedule (P. Schwartz, 1994).

Some people are not bound by these sexual scripts. Schwartz (1994) describes several married couples who favor more egalitarian relationships. In these relationships, both individuals can initiate sexual activity, and they try to assess their partner's responsiveness. Also, both the man and the woman realize that they can feel free to say, "No, not tonight . . ." without offending their partner. In these egalitarian relationships, women feel more free about expressing their erotic interests.

In the traditional sexual script, an important consequence of the "male-as-initiator" concept is that women in a dating relationship require a more meaningful commitment before they will consent to further sexual activities (S. Thompson, 1995). Apparently, people apply the double standard to their own behavior in dating relationships. A meta-analysis conducted by Oliver and Hyde (1993) confirms the gender differences in this area. Specifically, men have significantly more permissive attitudes toward premarital sex; the d for this gender difference was a substantial 0.81. Interestingly, however, men and women seem to be similar in their *enjoyment* of sexuality. With respect to satisfaction with sexual activity—either within the current relationship or in general—the d was close to zero.

Unfortunately, however, men often violate the standard sexual script. They may continue to make sexual advances, ignoring their partner's indication that these advances are not welcome. The male may use coercion—for example, by saying that he will break off a relationship if his girlfriend doesn't have sex with him. The most coercive sexual interaction is **rape,** which is sexual intercourse that is forcibly committed, without consent. As Chapter 13 discusses, a woman can be raped by an acquaintance, a boyfriend, or even a husband—as well as by a stranger.

Sexual Activities

Any attempt to describe the frequency of various sexual activities inevitably runs into roadblocks. How can a survey manage to obtain a random sample of respondents who represent all geographic regions, ethnic groups, and income levels? Can we trust the self-reports of men and women, especially when they apply the double standard to their own sexual behavior? For example, one widely publicized survey of 3,000 U.S. adults reported that 39% of the men claimed to have had more than 30 sexual partners during their lifetime, in contrast to 16% of the women (Janus & Janus, 1993). Have the men really been that much more active? And where are all those women with whom they presumably had sex? The data suggest they couldn't have been represented in this survey!

Probably the most respected survey of sexual behavior was conducted by sociologist Edward Laumann and his colleagues (1994) at the National Opinion Research Center (NORC). The NORC survey interviewed a sample of 3,432 adults, who answered questions about a wide range of topics. The results showed, for example, that 17% of men claimed to have had more than 20 sexual partners during their lifetime, in contrast to 3% of women—definitely less sensational than the data reported by the Janus and Janus (1993) survey. Incidentally, a meta-analysis of 12 earlier studies confirmed a general trend for men to report a somewhat greater number of sexual partners, with a *d* of 0.25 (Oliver & Hyde, 1993).

Other researchers have focused on specific kinds of sexual activities. For example, in a study of sexual fantasies, Leitenberg and Henning (1995) found that about 95% of both men and women reported that they have had sexual fantasies. Murnen and Stockton (1997) conducted a meta-analysis of the research on sexual arousal in response to sexual stimuli (e.g., a sexually explicit photograph). Their analysis showed that men reported somewhat greater sexual arousal than did women (*d* = .31).

Interestingly, the sexual behavior that shows the greatest gender differences is masturbation (Oliver & Hyde, 1993). Here the *d* was 0.96, a figure that dwarfs most other gender differences we've discussed in this book. An example of the gender differences is reflected in the NORC suvey, which noted that 27% of men and 8% of women reported that they masturbated at least once a week (Laumann et al., 1994). Perhaps some of the gender differences can be traced to the more obvious prominence of the male genitals (Oliver & Hyde, 1993). The gender differences with respect to masturbation may well have some important theoretical significance, as well as practical implications for male and female sexuality.

Communication About Sexuality

One man in a traditional marriage reported, "I'm so sick of being nagged about being more romantic. . . . When she starts giving me instructions—less here, more there—who wants that?" (P. Schwartz, 1994, p. 75). Apparently, women may have a difficult time asking for what they want; in contrast, their male partners may have a difficult time appreciating the women's desires (E. Cole, cited in McCormick, 1994; Wyatt & Riederle, 1994). However, we currently know little about the way partners communicate their preferences (Metts et al., 1998).

Some college campuses, however, have begun to explore the topic of communication in sexual relationships. For example, Antioch College in Ohio was concerned about miscommunications that often occur in dating situations. For instance, a woman may believe she is communicating that she is enjoying kissing—but wants nothing further. Her partner may misinterpret her apparent enjoyment and assume that she is interested in intercourse. Antioch College tried to address this problem by adopting the policy that verbal consent is needed before all sexual contact. Furthermore, consent can be withdrawn at any time. Some complained that this controversial policy would remove all the passion from sexuality. However, one supporter replied that asking permission—

DEMONSTRATION 9.3

The Sexual Assertiveness Scale for Women

The items listed below were shown to women students at a large state university in the Northeast. They were asked to rate each item, using a scale where 1 = disagree strongly and 5 = agree strongly. Your task is to inspect each item and estimate the average rating that the women supplied for that item (e.g., 2.8). When you have finished, check page 359 to see how the women actually responded. [Note: This demonstration is based on Morokoff et al., 1997, but it contains only 6 of the 18 items; the validity of this short version has not been established.]

_____ 1. I let my partner know if I want my partner to touch my genitals.

_____ 2. I wait for my partner to touch my breasts instead of letting my partner know that's what I want.

_____ 3. I give in and kiss if my partner pressures me, even if I already said no.

_____ 4. I refuse to have sex if I don't want to, even if my partner insists.

_____ 5. I have sex without a condom or latex barrier if my partner doesn't like them, even if I want to use one.

_____ 6. I insist on using a condom or latex barrier if I want to, even if my partner doesn't.

for example, "May I kiss the hollow of your neck?"—can be very romantic (Pfister, 1994).

Another recent development in the area of sexual communication focuses on women's sexual assertiveness. Previous research had suggested that women may hesitate to say "No" to men's sexual advances because they don't want to hurt their partner's feelings. Therefore, Patricia Morokoff and her coauthors (Morokoff et al., 1997) developed a Sexual Assertiveness Scale for women. Try Demonstration 9.3, before you read further; it includes some of the questions from the Sexual Assertiveness Scale. Then check the answers at the end of the chapter. Were you fairly accurate in predicting the women's answers? Did this exercise provide any new insights about your own communication patterns with respect to sexual activity?

Sexuality Among Lesbians

Much of the previous discussion focused on heterosexual relationships. Is sexuality substantially different in lesbian relationships? We know that—at the physiological level—lesbians and heterosexual women are similar with respect to sexual arousal and orgasm (Peplau & Amaro, 1982; Reinisch, 1990).

The research suggests that lesbian couples value nongenital physical contact, such as hugging and cuddling (Klinger, 1996; McCormick, 1994). Our North American culture tends to define "sexual activity" in terms of genital stimulation and orgasm. Researchers with that operational definition of sexual activity might conclude that lesbian couples are less sexually active than heterosexual couples or gay male couples (Herbert, 1996; Klinger, 1996). This conclusion would be especially true for couples who have been together for many years (Hatfield & Rapson, 1996). Several informal reports suggest that some lesbian couples have not engaged in genital sexual activities during the past several years. Nevertheless, most long-standing lesbian couples report that they are satisfied with the sex in their relationship. These findings suggest that we should broaden our definition of "sexual activity" beyond its current focus on genitals.

Other research suggests that when lesbians do engage in genital sexual activity, they are more likely than heterosexual women to experience an orgasm. Some possible explanations for this difference are that lesbian couples may communicate more effectively and be more sensitive to each other's preferences. They may also engage in more kissing and caressing than heterosexual couples (Hatfield & Rapson, 1996; Herbert, 1996).

In summary, we can conclude that lesbians seem as satisfied as heterosexuals with their sexual interactions, and lesbians may be even more satisfied. We need to keep in mind, however, that our culture does not tolerate evidence of sexual affection between two women. I recall a lesbian friend commenting that she feels sad and resentful that she and her partner cannot hold hands or hug each other in public, and kissing would be unthinkable.

Sexuality and Older Women

Prior to the work of Masters and Johnson (1966), many people believed that any sexual responsiveness a young woman might have would be drained away by the time she reached age 50 or 60. This pessimistic view of older women was entirely consistent with the generally negative attitude toward older women that we will explore in Chapter 14. However, Masters and Johnson's research emphasized that women can remain sensual and sexually responsive long after their reproductive years have passed.

Women's reproductive systems do change somewhat as women grow older. Estrogen production drops rapidly at menopause. As a result, the vagina loses some of its elasticity and may also produce less moisture (Leiblum & Segraves, 1995; S. Levine, 1998). However, these problems can be at least partially corrected by using supplemental lubricants. Also, as we'll see in Chapter 14, many older women take hormonal supplements, which reduce the problem of moisture underproduction. Finally, women who have been sexually active throughout their lives may not experience a reduction in moisture production (Zeiss, 1998).

Researchers have consistently reported that the frequency of genital sexual activity declines in married couples as they grow older (Call et al., 1995; Laumann et al., 1994). In one study on sexuality in middle-aged women, about 15% reported that they enjoyed sex less than in the previous year (Mansfield et al., 1998). However, about 10% said that they enjoyed sex more. Also, 20% said that they desired more nongenital touching. Notice that this finding is consistent with our observation that sexuality must be defined broadly, beyond a focus on the genitals.

The women in this study of Mansfield and her coauthors (1998) also emphasized the importance of "sweet warmth and constant tenderness," and "physical closeness and intimacy." One woman wrote, "Touching, hugging, holding, become as or more important than the actual sex act" (p. 297).

Many older women maintain the physiological capability to experience an orgasm, as well as an enthusiastic interest in sexual relationships. However, they may no longer have a partner. Heterosexual women typically outlive their husbands, and some husbands may leave them for young women. Some older husbands may no longer be able to maintain an erection, and they may stop all caressing and sexual activities once intercourse is not possible (S. Levine, 1998; Morris, 1997). In fact, in the NORC survey that we described earlier, 41% of the women in the oldest age category (55–59) reported that they had been sexually inactive during the past year. In contrast, only 16% of the men in that age category reported sexual inactivity (Laumann et al., 1994).

A survey of lesbians over the age of 60 showed that fewer than half had been "physically sexual" with another woman during the previous year (Kehoe, 1989). In summary, a large number of elderly women—both heterosexuals and lesbians—do not experience either sexual relations or close physical contact (Bachmann, 1991).

Another problem is that people seem to think that older women should be asexual. Our culture has constructed images of grandmothers baking cookies in the kitchen, not cavorting around in the bedroom (Reinisch, 1990). College students believe that their parents have intercourse once a month or less. In fact, many students have great difficulty even filling out a questionnaire about their parents' sexuality (Pocs et al., 1983).

Sexuality seems to be condemned more in older women than in older men. People tolerate a sexually eager old man—with a smile or perhaps even with admiration. But they often view a sexually eager old woman with suspicion or disgust. A manufacturer of lingerie is combating that view with ads of older women in lacy underwear and quotes such as: "Time is a purification system that has made me wiser, freer, better, some say sexier. Are those the actions of an enemy?" Yes, I realize that this advertising strategy is not motivated by altruism or feminist convictions. Still, the ads may help to change views of women's sexuality in later life.

 **Sexual Behavior and Attitudes**

1. **Although young people often say they would like their parents to discuss sex education, many parents—particularly fathers—avoid these conversations; sex education programs in schools usually fail to explore the topics most relevant to adolescents, but many school-based health programs offer more comprehensive services.**

2. **Most women report that their first experience with intercourse was not positive.**

3. **The double standard about sexuality is no longer widespread in North America, but it is still found in some situations (e.g., men making judgments about women who engage in casual sex). In some Middle Eastern and Latin American cultures, a woman may be killed for suspected sexual activity, whereas a man is allowed sexual freedom.**

4. **Sexual scripts specify what women and men are supposed to do in sexual interactions; for example, men are supposed to take the initiative in sexual activity.**

5. **The research shows that men report more sexual partners, that men and women are equally likely to report having sexual fantasies, and that men are much more likely to report masturbating.**

6. **Couples seem to experience difficulty communicating about sexual issues; components of communication include verbal consent for sexual activity, as well as sexual assertiveness.**

7. **Lesbian couples typically report satisfaction with their sexual activity, perhaps more than heterosexual couples.**

8. **The modest changes in some aspects of sexual responding do not present a barrier to sexual relations as women grow older; in reality, lack of a partner is an important obstacle in older women's sexuality.**

SEXUAL PROBLEMS

Sexual problems or **sexual dysfunctions** are terms that indicate a disturbance in sexual desire or in sexual responding, causing distress and interpersonal difficulty (American Psychiatric Association, 1994). As you might guess, we have no reliable estimates of the incidence of sexual problems in women. However, one survey ranked sexual difficulties fourth among the major problems facing heterosexual North American couples—after problems with rapid social change, domestic abuse, and finances (Carlson et al., 1996).

This section first examines three kinds of sexual problems in women: (1) disorders of sexual desire, (2) female orgasmic disorder, and (3) painful intercourse. Then we will see how traditional gender roles are partially responsible for sexual problems. Finally, we'll discuss therapy for sexual problems.

Disorders of Sexual Desire

As the names suggest, **disorders of sexual desire** or **hypoactive sexual desire disorder** means a deficiency in desire for sexual activity (Hyde & DeLamater, 1997). Individuals with this problem are not interested in sexual activity, and they often avoid situations that may arouse sexual feelings.

Women who experience a sexual desire disorder tell a variety of life stories. One woman wrote, "I've been married for 15 years; for the last 10 I've had no sexual feeling for my husband. I love him but he just doesn't 'turn me on.' This is putting a strain on my marriage" (Reinisch, 1990, p. 174). Another woman had been happily married for 31 years, and she reported that her husband was a gentle and considerate lover. However, she remained entirely passive during lovemaking (Kaplan, 1995). In fact, she kept her mind busy creating menus and making shopping lists.

The disorders of sexual desire may be caused by a variety of psychological factors. For example, women with this problem may suffer from a more general disorder, such as depression. That is, they may generally fail to experience pleasure (Carlson et al., 1996). Women who are not satisfied with the quality of their romantic relationship may also experience low levels of sexual desire (Hyde & DeLamater, 1997). As you can imagine, pregnancy and other factors that affect the sexual organs may lead to a temporary reduction in sexual desire.

The disorders of sexual desire are not confined to heterosexual couples (Carlson et al., 1996). In fact, these disorders may be the most common sexual problem faced by lesbians. For example, a case study described two women whose relationship was harmonious, considerate, and physically affectionate. However, they had not had any genital sexual activity with each other for the last 7 of the 14 years they had been together. One of the two women had found her sexual desire dwindling, and the other woman had not wanted to appear selfish by pressuring her partner (Nichols, 1982). As we saw in Chapter 8, the power in lesbian relationships is reasonably well balanced. It seems likely that the more sexually interested member of a lesbian couple may be reluctant to pressure her less enthusiastic partner.

Female Orgasmic Disorder

Women with **female orgasmic disorder** are sexually responsive, and they experience sexual excitement; however, they do not reach orgasm (American Psychiatric Association, 1994). This diagnosis is made after establishing that the problem cannot be traced to a general medical condition or to the physiological effects of a medication.

Exactly what constitutes an orgasm problem? Some women want to have an orgasm every time they engage in sexual activity. Others are satisfied if they feel emotionally close to their partner during sexual activity. The diagnosis of female orgasmic disorder should not be applied if a woman is currently satisfied with her situation (M. Kelly et al., 1990). Furthermore, a diagnosis of orgasmic disorder would not be appropriate if a woman reaches orgasm through clitoral stimulation, but not during intercourse (Reinisch, 1990).

One common cause of female orgasmic disorder is that women who are accustomed to inhibiting their sexual impulses have difficulty overcoming their inhibitions—even in a relationship where sex is approved. Other women have orgasm problems because they are anxious about losing control over their feelings. They may be embarrassed about experiencing such intense pleasure. Still others are easily distracted during sexual activity. They may suddenly focus on a distant noise, rather than on the sexual sensations. And many women may not have orgasms because their partners do not provide appropriate sexual stimulation. Female orgasmic disorder is a relatively common sexual problem (Wincze & Carey, 1992).

Painful Intercourse

Painful intercourse or **dyspareunia** (pronounced "diss-pah-*roo*-nih-ah") involves pain in the vagina, pelvis, or abdomen during or after intercourse. Disorders of sexual desire and female orgasmic disorder are usually caused by psychological factors. In contrast, painful intercourse typically has a physical explanation (Hyde & DeLamater, 1997). Therefore, a physical examination is especially useful, because a vaginal infection, a structural problem, or an ovarian problem may be diagnosed (D. Kaplan, 1995). However, other factors may be more relevant. Women who experience painful intercourse frequently report that they feel anxious in sexual situations. A traumatic sexual experience is sometimes responsible for this disorder.

How Gender Roles Contribute to Sexual Problems

Sexual problems are extremely complex. Their origin may be physical. The problems may also be caused by trauma experienced many years earlier or by subtle problems in a couple's interactions. Psychological factors, such as low self-esteem, may also contribute to sexual problems.

Gender roles, stereotypes, and biases may also contribute to sexual problems. As Tiefer (1996) points out, a heterosexual marriage is typically an unequal playing field, with the man having more power.

Various authors have emphasized that gender roles can create or intensify sexual problems (G. Brooks, 1995; Carlson et al., 1996; Fredrickson & Roberts, 1997; Morokoff, 1998):

1. Women are supposed to be asexual and passive, whereas men are supposed to be sexual and aggressive; many people therefore believe that women shouldn't enjoy sexual activity.

2. The double standard still suggests that males can enjoy some kinds of casual-sex experiences, but females should "save themselves" for marriage.

3. Women are afraid to seem selfish by requesting the kind of sexual activity they enjoy, such as clitoral stimulation. Stereotypes suggest that women should give, rather than request.

4. Sexual relations typically emphasize male sexuality. As a consequence, research seldom focuses on female sexuality. For example, researchers know how physical illness and drugs affect male sexuality, but they know relatively little about their effects on female sexuality. Consistent with Theme 3 of this book, women are relatively invisible.

5. Male gender roles contribute to sexual problems. Our culture emphasizes the length, strength, and endurance of a man's penis. (I'm writing this chapter after a summer filled with jokes about Viagra as a solution to male sexual disorders.) When a man focuses on these issues, he probably won't be able to *find* the woman's clitoris. He certainly won't worry about whether he is stimulating the clitoris gently—though this concern should be important. In addition, the media emphasis on male sexual performance probably makes many men anxious during lovemaking.

6. Physical attractiveness is emphasized more for females than for males, as we saw in the discussions of adolescence and dating. (We'll encounter this theme again in the chapter on psychological disorders and in the chapter on older women.) Indeed, many men may prefer to think about women's bodies as they are airbrushed into perfection in a magazine like *Playboy,* rather than

the bodies that belong to the women they know (G. Brooks, 1995). Women who feel less than perfectly attractive—that is, almost all women—may worry about their physical appearance. Consequently, they won't be able to enjoy the sensations of sexual arousal.

Because of these factors, women often believe that they are not supposed to be actively enthusiastic, experienced, or selfish in the area of sexuality. Furthermore, the male penis is viewed as central in sexual interactions. As a result, women are ignored—both in the research and in women's sexual needs.

Therapy for Sexual Problems

Leonore Tiefer (1995b), one of the leading sex therapists with a feminist perspective, argues that sexual problems must be addressed from a broad social perspective. Rather than focusing on Masters and Johnson's (1966) sexual response cycle, Tiefer argues that therapists should emphasize intimacy, pleasure, and women's concerns:

> For every dollar devoted to perfecting the phallus, I would like to insist that a dollar be devoted to assisting women with their complaints about partner impairments in kissing, tenderness, talk, hygiene, and general eroticism. (Tiefer, 1995b, p. 170)

In 1970, Masters and Johnson introduced a kind of sex therapy called sensate focus. **Sensate focus** was designed as a technique to encourage couples to focus on their sensory experience during sexual activity. Partner touch and stroke in order to discover sensitive areas in their own body and their partner's body. Later in the therapy, clitoral masturbation is encouraged for female orgasmic problems. However, couples who focus on sexual sensations may ignore the loving, tender aspects of lovemaking (Tiefer, 1995b). Masters and Johnson's therapy emphasized that short-term therapy could correct sexual problems. It may sometimes be helpful, but it isn't a complete answer.

Numerous other techniques have been developed by sex therapists. For example, **cognitive-behavioral therapy** combines behavioral exercises (such as those suggested in 1970 by Masters and Johnson) with therapy techniques that emphasize thought patterns or cognitive factors. One common technique is called **cognitive restructuring;** with this technique, the therapist tries to change people's inappropriately negative thoughts about some aspect of sexuality.

Janice Irvine (1990) provides a feminist analysis of a variety of behavioral and cognitive therapies. She believes that techniques such as sensate focus are useful in therapy. However, as Irvine writes:

> [These techniques] don't touch the source of the most intractable sexual problems for heterosexuals: fear, anger, boredom, overwork and lack of time, inequality in the relationship, prior sexual assault on the woman, and differential socialization

and sexual scripts. If a theoretical analysis is to account for these issues, sexual politics are inescapable . . . . (p. 199)

So far, unfortunately, sex therapists have not devised a comprehensive program that addresses these inequalities in a relationship, while also correcting specific problems in sexual responding. An ideal comprehensive program would also emphasize that human sexuality is much more than swelling sex organs. Tenderness, sensitivity, and communication are also essential.

 Sexual Problems

1. **In the disorders of sexual desire, an interest in sexual activity is reduced; depression, other psychological problems, and relational issues contribute to this disorder.**

2. **A woman who has a female orgasmic disorder feels sexual excitement but does not experience orgasm; psychological factors (e.g., anxiety) and inadequate sexual stimulation are often responsible.**

3. **Painful intercourse is often caused by physical problems, but psychological factors may also be responsible.**

4. **Gender roles can contribute to sexual disorders in several ways: (a) women aren't supposed to be interested in sex; (b) the double standard still operates in some cases; (c) women are afraid to request sexual stimulation; (d) male sexuality is emphasized, both in the bedroom and in research; (e) male gender roles create problems; and (f) physical attractiveness is emphasized for females more than for males.**

5. **Masters and Johnson's sensate focus therapy may sometimes be helpful, and so may cognitive-behavioral therapy techniques such as cognitive restructuring. However, a feminist perspective emphasizes that these approaches are too narrow; instead, therapy should emphasize gender equality, tenderness, communication, and general eroticism.**

BIRTH CONTROL
AND ABORTION

Birth control and abortion are among the most politically controversial topics in this book. For women, decisions about using birth control and terminating a pregnancy are among the most important choices they will make in their lifetime.

The most publicized data about pregnancy in the United States typically focus on teenagers. The fact is, that 40% of all U.S. women will become pregnant at

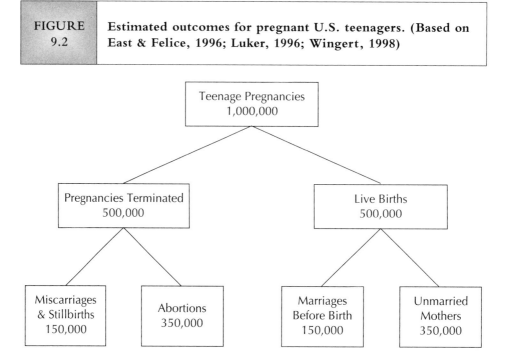

FIGURE 9.2   **Estimated outcomes for pregnant U.S. teenagers. (Based on East & Felice, 1996; Luker, 1996; Wingert, 1998)**

least once before reaching the age of 20 (Wingert, 1998). Figure 9.2 shows estimates of the outcomes for the approximately 1,000,000 teen pregnancies in the United States each year.* A young woman who does not experience a miscarriage or a stillbirth must make extremely important decisions: Should she carry the pregnancy to term, or should she seek an abortion? Should she choose marriage, or should she become a single mother? Should she give her baby up for adoption?

In this section, we will first discuss women's decisions about contraception, and then we'll look at some information about abortion. Because this is a psychology textbook, we will primarily focus on women's experiences. Still, we need to keep in mind that issues such as teen pregnancy have widespread political and economic consequences. For example, one source estimates that teen pregnancy costs the United States $7 billion a year in lost taxes and in costs

---

* Unfortunately, no comparable analysis is available for pregnant teenagers in Canada. However, we know that an average of 20,000 teens give birth each year in Canada (Colombo, 1997). Taking into account the difference in population between the two countries, a U.S. teenager is about three times as likely as a Canadian teenager to give birth.

such as public assistance (Wingert, 1998). Although these costs are noteworthy, we still need to keep them in perspective. For example, in the 1998 fiscal year, the United States spent $627 billion on military expenses—nearly 100 times its expenditure on teen pregnancy.

Birth Control Methods

Table 9.1 shows the major forms of birth control, together with some information about their use. You'll note that abstinence is listed as the only completely effective method of birth control. In earlier decades, people who recommended abstinence might have been considered prudish. However, in the current era, sexual intercourse presents not only a substantial risk of pregnancy for women, but also a significant risk of contracting a deadly disease. As Chapter 11 discusses, most of the birth control methods do not reduce the risk of AIDS. Even condoms cannot completely prevent the transmission of this disease. Yes, they make sex *safer,* but not completely safe.

Birth control methods other than abstinence are mostly intended for females, rather than males. Gender bias may encourage researchers to try to alter female fertility, rather than male fertility. Researchers are currently studying a male contraceptive that would suppress the production of sperm. However, the development of new contraceptives is financially risky, especially because drug companies are afraid of lawsuits (Service, 1994).

Incidentally, Table 9.1 does not list two behavioral birth control methods: (1) withdrawal (removal of the penis before ejaculation) and (2) the rhythm method, also known as natural family planning (intercourse only when a woman is least fertile). These methods are not listed because their effectiveness is unacceptably low—less than 80% (Ballagh, 1998).

However, examining birth control methods is not our primary concern. Instead, we'll focus on the psychological aspects of birth control. Let's consider the personal characteristics related to using birth control, the obstacles that prevent its use, and family planning in developing countries.

Who Uses Birth Control?

Many heterosexual women who are sexually active either use an unreliable birth control method—such as foam, withdrawal, or rhythm—or they use no contraception at all. Because sexually active heterosexual couples do not always use effective birth control methods, many women have unplanned pregnancies. We emphasized, for example, that approximately 1,000,000 teenagers become pregnant each year. Looking at the broader population of women in the United States, an estimated 57% of all pregnancies were unintended at the time of conception (S. Brown & Eisenberg, 1995). In other words, more than half of all U.S. pregnancies are "accidents." The comparable figure for Canada is 39% (Brown & Eisenberg, 1995).

TABLE 9.1	Major Birth Control Methods

Method	Effectiveness When Used Consistently	Possible Side Effects and Disadvantages
Abstinence	100% effective (assuming no sperm contact whatsoever)	No physical disadvantages; possible negative emotional reactions (e.g., from peer pressure)
Tubal ligation (severing of female's fallopian tubes)	99+% effective	Minor surgical risk; possible negative emotional reactions
Vasectomy (surgery to prevent passage of male's sperm)	99+% effective	Minor surgical risk; possible negative emotional reactions
Implants (e.g., Norplant) and injections (e.g., Depo-Provera)	99% effective	Menstrual irregularity; occasional surgical difficulty in removing implants; occasional weight gain
Birth control pills (synthetic hormones, taken by woman)	97–99% effective	Blood-clotting disorders, particularly for women over 35 and smokers; other medical side effects possible; must be taken regularly
Intrauterine device (plastic device placed in uterine cavity)	97% effective	Cramping, heavy bleeding, pelvic infections; may be expelled spontaneously
Condom (sheath placed on penis)	85–95% effective	Must be applied before intercourse; may decrease pleasure for male
Diaphragm (placed in vagina) and spermicidal foam or cream	80–95% effective	Must be applied before intercourse; may irritate genital area
Spermicidal foams creams, etc.	75–80% effective	Must be applied before intercourse; may irritate genital area

Note: For more information, consult Ballagh, 1988; K. Brewer, 1995; Carlson et al., 1996; Owen & Caudill, 1996.

Researchers have tried to identify what kinds of women use birth control, because this information could potentially help to decrease the number of unwanted pregnancies. Here are some relevant demographic factors that are related to women's contraceptive use:

1. *Social class.* Women from the middle and upper socioeconomic classes are more likely to use birth control (S. Brown & Eisenberg, 1995).

2. *Ethnicity.* European American women and Latina women are somewhat more likely than Black women to use birth control (Laumann et al., 1994). We do not have comparable data on other ethnic groups.

3. *Level of education.* Women who have had at least some college education are more likely than other women to use birth control. However, the NORC study showed that only 52% of women who had at least a master's degree reported that they consistently used contraception (Laumann et al., 1994). In other words, about half of these well-educated women could face an unwanted pregnancy.

Personality characteristics are also related to using birth control. For example, research on adolescents shows that young women are more likely to use contraceptives if they are high in self-efficacy (Schinke et al., 1996). **Self-efficacy** is the belief that you are competent and effective, and that you have the ability to alter your health habits.

Another important characteristic that is related to the use of birth control is a woman's emotional attitude toward sexuality. Specifically, some women are high in **sex guilt;** that is, they mentally punish themselves for being sexually active. These women are especially likely to use ineffective birth control methods or else no method at all (Gerrard et al., 1993). Apparently, their guilty emotions interfere with the ability to make rational decisions about contraception.

Obstacles to Using Birth Control

Why are more than half of all U.S. pregnancies "accidents"? The problem is that many barriers stand in the way of using effective birth control. A woman who avoids pregnancy must have adequate knowledge about contraception. She must also have access to it, and she must be willing to use it on a consistent basis. In more detail, here are some of the issues:

1. Parents and educators often avoid discussing sexuality with young people because they "don't want to give them any ideas." Even physicians avoid discussing sexuality with teenagers during an office visit (Beazley et al., 1996). Everyone is especially reluctant to discuss birth control with adolescents. As a result, many young people are misinformed or have gaps in their knowledge (Murry, 1996).

2. Contraceptive services are often unavailable to adolescents, so they cannot obtain the most reliable forms of birth control (S. Brown & Eisenberg, 1995;

M. Watson et al., 1996). Other women in the United States have no health insurance, which creates a problem in regions that do not have free family-planning clinics. Researchers estimate that every dollar spent on family planning services saves as much as $18 in health care and welfare costs that would need to be paid for unwanted pregnancies ("The Budget," 1996).

3. People may not think rationally about emotional issues connected with sexuality. For example, sexually inexperienced women often believe that they themselves are not likely to become pregnant during intercourse (Whitley & Hern, 1992). A Canadian study revealed other examples of irrational thinking. For example, 75% of adolescent males and females reported that they would always use condoms, yet only 42% of them said that they had used condoms during their last three episodes of sexual intercourse (H. Richardson et al., 1997).

4. Traditional women believe that if they were to obtain contraception, they would be admitting to themselves that they planned to have intercourse and are therefore not "nice girls" (Luker, 1996). In fact, college students downgrade a woman who is described as providing a condom prior to casual sex (Hynie et al., 1997).

5. All current contraceptives have some problems. However, women may overestimate the risk factors, which still compare favorably with the risks of childbirth (S. Brown & Eisenberg, 1995). Mothers and other adults may provide some of this misinformation. One young woman told this story:

> I think I was thirteen when I first started having sex. My best friend thought I was crazy 'cause I went to my mother and said, "Well, Mom, I like this boy and I might be doing something with him, and would you take me to get birth control?" And she said, "No, because once you start taking these pills, you'll become sterile." (Luker, 1996, pp. 147–148)

Unfortunately, this young girl sought help in a mature fashion. However, her mother did not have correct information.

6. People often believe that birth control devices will interrupt the lovemaking mood, because they are not considered very erotic or romantic (S. Campbell et al., 1992; Luker, 1996). Condoms and other contraceptives are seldom mentioned in movies, television, books, and magazines, as Demonstration 9.4 shows. Sexuality is often explicit in the media. We can see a woman and a man undressing, groping, groaning, and copulating. The one taboo topic seems to be contraception! Sexually active people do not see their heroines and heroes using contraceptives, so why should they themselves be concerned?

7. Many pregnant teenagers have experienced forced sexual intercourse, often with a much older man (Coley & Chase-Lansdale, 1998; Luker, 1996). When a 14-year-old female is raped by a 21-year-old male, she is unlikely to persuade him to wear a condom.

DEMONSTRATION 9.4

Contraception as a Taboo Topic

For the next two weeks, keep a record of the number of times you see couples in sexual relationships in the media. Monitor television programs, movies, stories in magazines, and books, as well as any other source that seems relevant. In each case, note whether contraceptives are mentioned, shown, or even hinted at.

Earlier in the chapter, we noted that schools must develop more comprehensive sex education programs. Simple "Just Say No" approaches are not effective (J. Stryker et al., 1995).

We also need to change people's attitudes toward contraception. People might use contraceptives more often if the women in soap operas were shown discussing birth control methods with their gynecologists and if the macho men of the movie screen carefully adjusted their condoms before the steamy love scenes.

Family Planning in Developing Countries

In the United States, 74% of couples who are of childbearing age use some kind of contraceptive. The percentage is almost identical for Canada: 73%. How about developing countries throughout the world? The data vary widely. Fewer than 5% of couples use contraceptives in Ethiopia, Angola, and other African countries. In China, however, 83% of couples use contraceptives. The Catholic Church strongly opposes the more reliable forms of birth control. Still, many countries that are predominantly Catholic have very high rates of contraceptive use (Neft & Levine, 1997). These countries include France (81%), Brazil (78%), and Italy (78%).

Some developing countries have instituted family planning programs. For example, during the 1960s and 1970s, Cuba began a health care campaign that offered free contraceptive devices; 70% of couples now use contraceptives (Neft & Levine, 1997; Stout & Dello Buono, 1996). Iran now requires couples to pass the nation's course in family planning before they can obtain a marriage license (R. Wright, 1998a). As a result, 65% of Iranian couples now use contraceptives. In neighboring Iraq, which is also a Muslim country, only 14% of couples use contraceptives (Neft & Levine, 1997).

One of the best predictors of contraceptive use in developing countries is the female literacy rate (Winter, 1996). When women are well educated, they are likely to take control of their lives and make plans for the future.

The use of contraceptives throughout the world has been rising steadily (Neft & Levine, 1997). Still, an estimated 120 million married couples throughout the world do not have access to family planning (García-Moreno & Türmen, 1995). When we consider the millions of *unmarried* couples who also have no available family planning, the numbers are staggering. Each of these couples must make choices about continuing with a pregnancy or considering adoption or abortion. Let's now explore the controversial topic of abortion and the alternatives.

Abortion

I am writing this chapter in 1998, 25 years after the Supreme Court's *Roe v. Wade* decision stated that women have the legal right to choose abortion. Before 1973, many abortions were performed illegally—often by untrained individuals in unsanitary conditions (Gorney, 1998; Risen & Thomas, 1998). In fact, an estimated 200,000 to 1.2 million illegal abortions were performed each year, and about 10,000 women died annually from these illegal abortions (Gorney, 1998).

Before 1973, countless women also attempted to end an unwanted pregnancy themselves. They douched themselves with Lysol and other powerful cleansers, they swallowed poisons such as turpentine, and they tried to stab knitting needles, coathangers, and other sharp objects through the cervix passage into their uterus (Gorney, 1998).

Legal decisions handed down in the late 1990s reduced the power of *Roe v. Wade*. Medicaid funding cannot be used for abortions for economically poor women. In some states, an abortion can be performed only after a specified waiting period or only in restricted situations (D. Miller, 1996). Another barrier is that many doctors are not trained to perform abortions; only 16% of the counties in the United States provide abortion services (Kissling, 1998; L. Phillips, 1998). Health care professionals who perform abortions may be harassed or even murdered by so-called "pro-life" groups, and abortion clinics may be bombed (Poppema, 1998). When I was preparing the current edition of this textbook, anti-abortionists murdered gynecologist Barnett Slepian in Amherst, New York, about an hour's drive from my home.

No one recommends abortion as a routine form of birth control. We need to provide more comprehensive education about sexuality, so that women do not need to consider the abortion alternative.

Table 9.2 describes the most common methods of abortion. In addition, a nonsurgical alternative has recently been tested in the United States. With this treatment, a drug called RU 486 is taken in conjunction with a hormone—under medical supervision—during the first 5 to 7 weeks of pregnancy. Some argue that the safety of RU 486 has not yet been established, and several visits to the doctor's office are required. However, others believe that the side effects are negligible and that RU 486 is cheaper and more convenient than surgical abortions (Carlson et al., 1996; D. Miller, 1996).

TABLE 9.2	Major Methods of Abortion

Method	When Used	Description
Vacuum aspiration	Before 14 weeks of pregnancy	A vacuum tube is inserted through the cervix, into the uterus; suction draws out the tissue.
Dilation and evacuation	13–24 weeks of pregnancy	The cervix is dilated in order to remove the larger volume of tissue; suction draws out the tissue.
Induced abortion	16–24 weeks of pregnancy	Saline or other chemical solution is injected into the amniotic sac around the fetus, inducing premature labor.

Note: For more information, consult Carlson et al., 1996; Hyde & DeLamater, 1997; D. Miller, 1996.

About one-quarter of all pregnancies in the United States are terminated via a legal abortion (S. Brown & Eisenberg, 1995; Russo, 1992). Compared to women who continue an unwanted pregnancy, pregnant women who seek abortions are more likely to be single women from middle-class or upper-class backgrounds (S. Brown & Eisenberg, 1995; L. Phillips, 1998).

Abortion may be a controversial issue, but one aspect of abortion is not controversial: its safety. A woman is about 25 times more likely to die as a result of childbirth than as a result of a legal abortion (D. Miller, 1996). As a general rule, abortions performed shortly after conception produce fewer complications and quicker recovery than later abortions (Hyde & DeLamater, 1997).

In contrast to this objective information about methods, numbers, and safety, we must now consider the more difficult topics, focusing on the psychological aspects of abortion.

Decisions About Abortions. Women who are considering an abortion typically struggle with their decision (N. Adler & Smith, 1998). After all, few other decisions in a woman's life are so final. If she decides to continue the pregnancy, the child will be a major part of her future life. If she decides to end this pregnancy, she might have other children in the future, but not this particular child.

Most women have made a decision about abortion before they even learn the results of their pregnancy tests (Cohan et al., 1993). Some women make the abortion decision with relatively little conflict. They realize that they do not want to have a child, and so they choose an abortion. For other women, however, the decision is not as clear-cut. One woman recalled her mixed reactions prior to her abortion:

> The rational part of me knew I needed to make some decision. But the emotional side of me overrode my logic, so all I did was beat myself up for becoming pregnant. I let myself get caught in a standing pool of shame and fear until it was almost too late. . . . (Kushner, 1997, p. 108)

Psychological Reactions to an Abortion.   Most women report that their primary reaction following an abortion is relief (N. Adler & Smith, 1998; D. Miller, 1996). However, individual differences are large, consistent with Theme 4 of this textbook (Major et al., 1998; D. Miller, 1996). Other studies show that the typical woman who has an abortion suffers no long-term effects such as problems with anxiety or self-esteem. Women who have had abortions are also no more likely to be admitted to psychiatric hospitals (N. Adler & Smith, 1998; Russo & Zierk, 1992).

Some women experience sadness, a sense of loss, or other negative feelings. However, these feelings are typically not very intense. Individuals who oppose legalized abortion have created a name—"post-abortion syndrome"—that is supposed to describe the depression and guilt that follow abortion. Although the name sounds like appropriately official psychological jargon, no scientific evidence has been found to support the presence of such a syndrome (D. Miller, 1996).

What are some of the factors related to psychological adjustment following an abortion? In general, women who cope most easily with an abortion tend to be older women and those who have the abortion early in their pregnancy (N. Adler et al., 1992). An important psychological factor related to adjustment is self-efficacy, or a woman's feeling that she is competent and effective (Cozzarelli, 1993; Major et al., 1998). Adjustment is also better if the woman's friends and relatives support her decision (N. Adler & Smith, 1998). A medical staff that is helpful and supportive during the abortion procedure contributes to adjustment. One woman recalls her experience:

> I elected to have it done with a local anesthetic. I was completely awake for the procedure, and it was gentle in every respect. The staff was really crackerjack, and there was a nurse with me at all times. The doctor was about as gentle as I could imagine him being. And all the follow-up was really nurturing. (De Puy & Dovitch, 1997, p. 56)

Some women report that the experience of becoming pregnant and having an abortion actually has an important side effect: It forces them to reevaluate their lives and choose new future directions. As one woman reported, "I concentrated on getting into a stable, monogamous relationship, I quit running around and sleeping around, and I worked really hard to get into a job where I feel valued and enjoy my work" (Kushner, 1997).

Follow-up counseling should be available to every woman who has had an abortion to help her sort through her emotions (R. Hatcher & Trussell, 1994; Kushner, 1997). The counseling should also focus on birth control options and on the steps that the woman will take to avoid future intercourse—if it is not in her best interest.

Children Born to Women Who Were Denied Abortions. In many cases, a woman wants to obtain an abortion, but circumstances—such as lack of money—prevent the abortion. As a result, many women will give birth to children who are not wanted. How do children develop psychologically in these circumstances? Some answers to this question come from a study conducted with 220 children whose mothers were denied abortions in Czechoslovakia (David et al., 1988). Each of these children was carefully matched with a child from a wanted pregnancy, so that the two groups were comparable.

The study showed that, by 9 years of age, the children born in unwanted pregnancies had fewer friends and responded poorly to stress, in comparison to children from wanted pregnancies. By age 23, the children born in unwanted pregnancies were more likely to report that their mothers were not interested in them and that they were receiving psychological treatment. They were also more likely to have marital difficulties, drug problems, conflicts at work, and trouble with the legal system. Other related research shows that many women who give birth to unwanted children continue to report negative feelings toward them many years later (Dagg, 1991). These implications for children's lives should be considered when governments try to make informed decisions about abortion policies.

Alternatives to Abortion. Unplanned pregnancies can be resolved by methods other than abortion. For example, people who oppose abortion often suggest adoption as an alternative. However, adoption is likely to create its own kind of trauma and pain. One woman who gave her son up for adoption 17 years earlier describes her experiences:

> I don't think there is a woman alive who has been through this, as I have, who doesn't wonder what happened to her child. It doesn't make any difference how many other children you have, they never take the place of that one you "put out" for adoption. I would like to know if my first boy is happy and healthy, and if he forgives me . . . I don't even know if he is alive or dead. (Russo, 1992, p. 620)

Another alternative is to deliver the baby and choose the motherhood option. An unwanted pregnancy can become a wanted baby by the time of delivery. However, thousands of babies are born each year to mothers who do not want them. This situation can be destructive for both the mother and the child. Some pregnant women choose to marry, a solution that may be helpful but often creates new problems (Leadbeater et al., 1996).

In the United States, the majority of adolescents who deliver a baby are currently choosing to become single mothers. The television soap operas portray single mothers who have good jobs and are well off financially (Larson, 1996). Reality is very different. For example, 86% of young single mothers in Canada live below the poverty line ("Looking for Solutions," 1993). Neither Canada nor the United States offers full social support and services for unmarried women who choose the motherhood option (R. Hatcher & Trussell, 1994). Currently, most unmarried teenage mothers encounter difficulties in completing school, finding employment, fighting poverty, and facing the biases that unmarried mothers often confront in our society.

We have seen that none of these alternatives—abortion, adoption, or motherhood—is free of problems. Instead, the answer that creates the least psychological pain appears to be pregnancy prevention, so that women do not have to choose among the less-than-optimal alternatives.

 **Section Summary**   *Birth Control and Abortion*

1. **Most forms of birth control are intended for the female, rather than the male; no method is completely problem-free.**

2. **Many sexually active women do not use reliable birth control methods. Female contraceptive use is related to social class, ethnicity, education, personality characteristics such as self-esteem, and emotional attitudes toward sexuality.**

3. **Couples avoid using birth control because of inadequate information, unavailable contraceptive services, irrational thinking, reluctance to admit they are sexually active, misinformation about the risks of contraceptives, and the feeling that birth control devices are not romantic. Many women had no choice about using birth control because they were raped.**

4. **Some developing countries have instituted family planning programs. Others—often similar with respect to geography and religion—do not support these programs. Literacy is highly correlated with women's contraceptive use.**

5. **Prior to *Roe v. Wade,* thousands of women died each year from illegal abortions; currently, legal abortions are much safer than childbirth.**

6. **Abortion decisions are often difficult, but women's primary psychological response to abortion is relief; women who have had an abortion are not at risk for long-term psychological problems.**

7. **Children born to women who have been denied an abortion are significantly more likely to experience difficulties than children from a wanted pregnancy.**

8. In general, adoption is not an emotionally satisfactory alternative to abortion, and women who choose the motherhood option face many difficulties. Pregnancy prevention is the preferable solution.

CHAPTER REVIEW QUESTIONS

1. At several points throughout this chapter, we have seen that sexuality has traditionally been male-centered. Address this issue, focusing on topics such as (a) theories about orgasms; (b) sexual scripts; and (c) sexual problems.

2. Many sections of this chapter discuss adolescent women. Describe the experiences a young woman might face as she discusses sexuality with her parents, has her first sexual experience, makes decisions about contraception, and tries to make a decision about an unwanted pregnancy.

3. How are gender roles relevant in (a) the initiation of sexual relationships; (b) sexual activity; (c) sexual problems; (d) therapy for sexual problems; and (e) decisions about contraception and abortion?

4. Review the material on gender comparisons in self-disclosure, which we examined in Chapter 6 (page 219). How might this information be relevant to the section on communication about sexuality in this chapter?

5. Describe the stages of sexual responding, pointing out gender similarities and differences; also discuss gender comparisons with respect to various sexual activities.

6. What information do we have about sexuality among lesbians, including sexual activity and sexual problems? Why would a male-centered approach to sexuality make it difficult to decide what "counts" as sexual activity in a lesbian relationship?

7. Describe each of the three sexual problems discussed in this chapter. Why might older women be especially likely to experience these problems? Also, summarize the kinds of therapeutic approaches currently used in treating sexual problems?

8. What are some of the stereotypes about women's sexuality? Which of these stereotypes have some basis in fact, and which do not?

9. Imagine that you have received a large grant to reduce the number of unwanted pregnancies in the region where you lived as a young teenager. What kinds of programs would you plan, to achieve both immediate and long-term effects?

10. What information do we have about the safety of abortion, the psychological consequences to the woman, and consequences for children whose mothers has been denied an abortion?

NEW TERMS

mons pubis (325)

labia majora (325)

labia minora (325)

clitoral hood (325)

clitoris (325)

vagina (325)

sexual desire phase (326)

excitement phase (326)

vasocongestion (326)

plateau phase (326)

orgasmic phase (326)

resolution phase (327)

ejaculate (329)

double standard (333)

sexual script (335)

rape (335)

sexual problems (341)

sexual dysfunctions (341)

disorders of sexual desire (341)

hypoactive sexual desire
  disorder (341)

female orgasmic disorder (342)

painful intercourse (342)

dyspareunia (342)

sensate focus (344)

cognitive-behavioral therapy (344)

cognitive restructuring (344)

self-efficacy (349)

sex guilt (349)

RECOMMENDED READINGS

Kushner, E. (1997). *Experiencing abortion: A weaving of women's words.* New York: Harrington Park Press. To prepare this book, Kushner interviewed 115 women who had abortions; the women's stories describe their decision processes, as well as the stress, anger, grieving, and acceptance that followed.

Laumann, E. O., Gagnon, J. H., Michael, R. T., & Michaels, R. T. (1994). *The social organization of sexuality: Sexual practices in the United States.* Chicago: University of Chicago Press. Here is a clear and thorough report on the respected NORC study of sexual behavior; it is impressively readable, and the charts are relatively easy to interpret.

Luker, K. (1996). *Dubious conceptions: The politics of teenage pregnancy.* Cambridge, MA: Harvard University Press. Luker's book traces the history of attitudes toward adolescent pregnancy, the current status of the problem, and how it can be addressed.

McCormick, N. B. (1994). *Sexual salvation: Affirming women's sexual rights and pleasures.* Westport, CT: Praeger. Don't let the unlikely title of this book keep you from reading it! McCormick provides an informative discussion of topics such as sexual pleasure, love, lesbian identity, and pornography.

Tiefer, L. (1995). *Sex is not a natural act and other essays.* Boulder, CO: Westview Press. Tiefer analyzes a variety of issues concerned with sexuality, using a feminist framework. The essays address topics such as Masters and Johnson's sexual response cycle, the nature of kissing, the feminist revolution and sexuality, and censorship of sexual material.

ANSWERS TO THE DEMONSTRATIONS

Demonstration 9.1: 1. F; 2. M; 3. F; 4. F; 5. M; 6. M; 7. M; 8. F.

Demonstration 9.3: 1. 2.7; 2. 2.7; 3. 4.2; 4. 4.1; 5. 4.6; 6. 4.4. (Note that a woman who is high in sexual assertiveness would provide high ratings for items 1, 4, and 6; she would provide low ratings for items 2, 3, and 5.)

ANSWERS TO THE TRUE–FALSE QUESTIONS

1. True (p. 325); 2. True (p. 329); 3. False (p. 330); 4. False (p. 332); 5. False (pp. 333–334); 6. True (p. 335); 7. False (pp. 341–342); 8. True (p. 343); 9. True (p. 347); 10. True (p. 354).

PREGNANCY, CHILDBIRTH, AND MOTHERHOOD

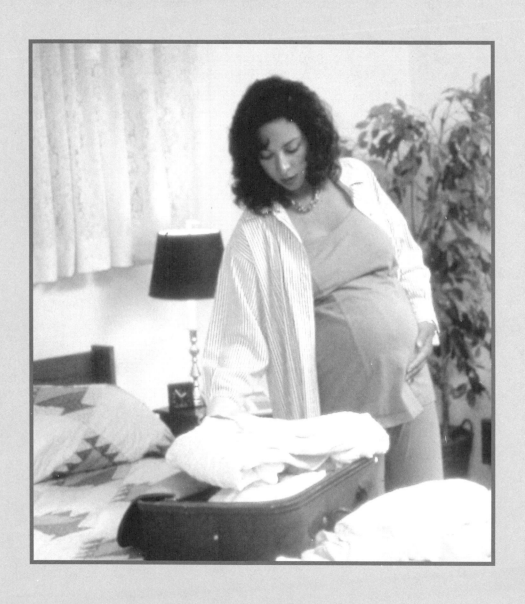

TRUE OR FALSE?

_____ 1. Psychologists have conducted little research on the psychological aspects of pregnancy and childbirth.

_____ 2. Pregnancy typically produces a wide range of positive and negative emotions for women.

_____ 3. Statistics gathered in North America show that fewer than 10% of pregnant women smoke during their pregnancy.

_____ 4. People typically avoid standing close to a pregnant woman.

_____ 5. Women who are employed more than 45 hours a week are significantly more likely than other women to have difficulties during pregnancy, as well a high rate of premature births.

_____ 6. Highly educated women have higher expectations about childbirth than do less educated women.

_____ 7. Prepared childbirth is a method of learning about breathing and other childbirth techniques, so that pain is eliminated during childbirth.

_____ 8. A mother's dominant emotional response during early motherhood is a feeling of hidden strength and exhilaration.

_____ 9. Approximately half of North American mothers experience postpartum blues within a few days after birth; common symptoms include crying, sadness, and irritability.

_____ 10. Current research shows that college students evaluate a woman positively if she chooses not to have children.

Pregnancy
    The Biology of Pregnancy
    Physical Reactions to Pregnancy
    Emotional Reactions to Pregnancy
    Attitudes Toward Pregnant Women
    Pregnant Women and Employment

Childbirth
    The Biology of Childbirth
    Expectations About Childbirth
    Emotional Reactions to Childbirth
    Alternative Models of Childbirth

Motherhood
    Stereotypes About Motherhood
    The Reality of Motherhood
    Motherhood and Women of Color
    Lesbian Mothers
    Postpartum Disturbances
    Breastfeeding
    Deciding Whether to Have Children
    Infertility

For many women, one of the most important sequences of life events is: pregnancy → childbirth → motherhood. Think how a woman's life will change once she discovers she is pregnant. Those 9 months of her life will focus on her changing body and on plans for the arrival of a new human being. Her thoughts will range from the very practical ("Where will the baby sleep?") to the very abstract ("What will motherhood mean to me?"). Childbirth will be an extremely intense experience—a combination of exhilaration, pain, and accomplishment. Few endeavors can match motherhood's intense blend of joys and difficulties. Pregnancy, childbirth, and motherhood are extremely emotional, intensely preoccupying, and very crucial phases in the lives of most women.

The world currently has more than 6 billion inhabitants, each of whom was produced by a woman's pregnancy. You might imagine that the sheer frequency of pregnancy would make it a popular topic for psychological research. However, the topic of pregnancy is almost ignored in psychology. Issues such as teen pregnancy, unwanted pregnancy, and infertility all attract modest interest. However, only a handful of studies on normal, intentional pregnancies are published each year.

The media also ignore the motherhood sequence. In Chapter 9, we saw that the theme of love dominates music, television, and entertainment. Sexuality is equally prominent. However, pregnancy and childbirth are virtually invisible—consistent with Theme 3—and motherhood is rarely explored in depth.

Let's examine these phases of reproduction in more detail. As you'll see, each phase has important psychological components.

PREGNANCY

What are the major biological components of pregnancy? How do women react to pregnancy, both emotionally and physically? Also, how do other people react to pregnant women? Finally, how do women combine pregnancy with their employment?

The Biology of Pregnancy

Typically, the egg and the sperm unite while the egg is traveling down a fallopian tube. Interestingly, even an act that seem as value-free as the joining of the egg and the sperm may be represented in a gender-biased fashion. Specifically, you probably learned in your high school biology textbook that the male sperm *penetrates* the female egg. However, this description is actually a myth, because the egg is much more active during the fertilization process:

> You can clearly see the egg reach out with a tentacle and draw the sperm into the inner area. Then the egg penetrates the top of the head of the sperm and blows it up. Then [the sperm's] genetic material is distributed throughout the egg. Thus, the two merge into one, but the egg's role is active, agentic. (Rabuzzi, 1994, p. 2)

The fertilized egg continues along the fallopian tube, floats around in the uterus for several days, and then may implant itself in the thick tissue that lines the uterus. If a fertilized egg does not implant itself, then this tissue is sloughed off as menstrual flow—the same menstrual flow that occurs when an egg has not been fertilized. However, if implantation does occur, this tissue provides an ideal environment in which a fertilized egg can develop into a baby.

Shortly after the fertilized egg has implanted itself, the placenta begins to develop. The **placenta,** which is connected to the growing embryo, is an organ that allows oxygen and nutrients to pass from the mother to the embryo. The placenta also helps transport the embryo's waste products back to the mother's system. This amazing organ also helps to manufacture enormous quantities of hormones. By the end of her pregnancy, a woman's estrogen and progesterone levels are much higher than before her pregnancy.

Typically, a woman first suspects she is pregnant when she has been sexually active and then misses a menstrual period. A pregnancy test can usually confirm her suspicion. Incidentally, if you try a home pregnancy test very early in a pregnancy, the result may be a "false negative." In about 20% of home pregnancy tests, a woman may really be pregnant, but her hormone levels are not yet high enough for the test to read positive (Carlson et al., 1996).

By tradition, pregnancy is divided into three trimesters. Each **trimester** is therefore about 3 months in length. Most women are pregnant for 37 to 42 weeks (Carlson et al., 1996). Let's now consider how women react both physically and emotionally during these months of pregnancy.

Physical Reactions to Pregnancy

Virtually every organ system in a woman's body is affected by pregnancy, although most of the consequences are relatively minor. Nausea is an especially common symptom during the first trimester. It is often called "morning sickness," even though it may occur at any time of the day. Surveys suggest that 50% to 70% of all pregnant women will experience nausea at some point in their pregnancy (Hofmeyr et al., 1990; Woollett & Marshall, 1997). Furthermore, 10%

to 20% experience nausea throughout the entire 9 months of pregnancy ("New Solutions," 1994).

Fortunately, the physiological basis of nausea is now widely acknowledged. In earlier eras, women's morning sickness was interpreted as a sign that they wanted to reject either the developing fetus or their husband.

Nausea is such a common symptom of pregnancy that women who do *not* experience nausea may feel unusual. One woman reported about her physical condition during pregnancy: "There were no problems. I've never had morning sickness. I didn't feel I was really pregnant" (Woollett & Marshall, 1997, p. 193).

Other common physical changes during pregnancy include weight gain and protrusion of the abdomen. Many women also report breast tenderness, frequent urination, and fatigue (Carlson et al., 1996).

Several decades ago, pregnancy was regarded as a 9-month sickness, and that view sometimes persists today (S. Myers & Grasmick, 1990; Woollett & Marshall, 1997). However, women are increasingly likely to believe that being pregnant is both normal and healthy—although occasionally somewhat uncomfortable and inconvenient.

Our general theme about the wide range of individual differences holds true with pregnancy as with other phases in women's lives. As we saw, some women never experience nausea, but others may be nearly immobilized by nausea and vomiting. Variability is also revealed in women's interest in sexual activity during pregnancy (Seegmiller, 1993). In one study, 60% of women reported less interest than usual, 20% reported no change, and another 20% actually reported *more* interest in sex (Hofmeyr et al., 1990). Part of this increased sexual arousal may be traced to an increased blood supply in the genital area (Leonhardt-Lupa, 1995).

Emotional Reactions to Pregnancy

All I seem to think about is the baby. . . . I'm so excited. I'd love to have the baby right now. Somehow this week I feel on top of the world. I love watching my whole tummy move. (Lederman, 1996, p. 35)

I think I, in a sense, have a prepartum depression—already! . . . Over Easter, when I was home from teaching, it just really hit me how I would be home like that all the time. . . . I was very depressed one day just kind of anticipating it and realizing how much of a change it was going to be, because I had been really active with my teaching, and it had been a pretty major part of my life now for four years. (Lederman, 1996, p. 39)

These quotes from two pregnant women illustrate how individual women respond differently to the same life event, consistent with Theme 4. In pregnancy, the situation is extremely unpredictable, because *each woman* may experience a wide variety of emotions during the 9 months of her pregnancy. For example, those two quotes—although very different in emotional tone—could have come from the same woman.

Positive Emotions.   For many women, the news that they are pregnant brings a rush of positive emotions, excitement, and anticipation. Many women report feeling wonder and awe at the thought of having a new, growing person inside their own bodies. Most married women also sense that other people approve of their pregnancy. After all, women are *supposed* to have children.

For many women, pregnancy represents a transition into adulthood. They may describe a sense of purpose and accomplishment about being pregnant (Leifer, 1980).

Another positive emotion is the growing sense of attachment that pregnant women feel toward the developing baby (Bergum, 1997; Condon & Corkindale, 1997). One woman reported:

> When I had my first scan, the man explained everything, like this is his leg, this is his foot, little hands, little head. I couldn't see his other leg and asked "Where's his other leg then?" Then they pushed him round and showed me his other leg. It was quite nice. That's when you realize you are having a baby, when you actually see it on the scan. (Woollett & Marshall, 1997, p. 189)

In addition, many pregnant women find pleasure in anticipating the jobs of motherhood and childrearing, which they believe will provide a tremendous source of satisfaction (Leifer, 1980). As we'll see in the section on motherhood, their expectations may be very different from reality.

Negative Emotions.   Unfortunately, many emotions that pregnant women feel are negative, often intensified by their physical reactions of nausea and fatigue. Many women report that their emotions are fragile and continually changing. Depressive feelings, fears, and anxieties are also common (Condon & Corkindale, 1997; O'Hara, 1995).

As we have often mentioned in earlier chapters, women are evaluated in terms of their attractiveness. Because North American culture values slimness, a woman's self-image may deteriorate as she watches her body grow bigger (Lederman, 1996; Mercer, 1995). Women often say that they feel fat and ugly during pregnancy. Interestingly, however, these women's romantic partners may feel otherwise. For example, Cowan and Cowan (1992) questioned married couples who were expecting a baby. They noted that most husbands responded positively:

> Most of the husbands were supportive, and some were truly proud of the changes in their wives' bodies as the pregnancy progressed. They were pleased by what they saw and by what their wives' full bodies signified. Eduardo [one of the fathers in the study] watches his wife maneuver gracefully into a chair during our interview. "The great painters," he says, "tried to show the beauty of a pregnant woman, but when I look at Sonia, I feel they didn't do it justice." (p. 59)

Fortunately, many women are able to overcome our culture's concern about weight. They are excited to see their abdomen swell, to feel the baby move, and to anticipate a healthy pregnancy.

Many women are worried about other physical problems. Some pregnant women are concerned about their health and bodily functions (C. Cowan & Cowan, 1992). These anxieties are heightened by the increasing evidence that alcohol, smoking, and a wide variety of drugs can harm the developing fetus (Field, 1998; Kline, 1996; Lemieux, 1996). Incidentally, studies in both the United States and Canada show that many pregnant women try to stop smoking cigarettes during their pregnancy, but it's difficult to break this addiction (Edwards & Sims-Jones, 1998; Groff et al., 1997; Ko & Schulken, 1998). In fact, an estimated 25% to 30% of women continue to use cigarettes throughout their pregnancy (Floyd et al., 1991; Vasta et al., 1995).

An important part of women's negative reactions to pregnancy is caused by the fact that other people begin to respond differently to them, as we will see in the next section. They are categorized as "pregnant women"—women who have no identity aside from being vessels to hold the growing baby (Rabuzzi, 1994). Women may also begin to see themselves in these terms.

In summary, a woman's emotional reaction to pregnancy can range from excitement and anticipation to worry and a loss of identity (Statham et al., 1997). Consistent with Theme 4 of this book, the individual differences can be enormous. For most women, pregnancy is a complex blend of both pleasant and unpleasant reactions.

Naturally, a woman's overall response to pregnancy depends on factors such as her physical reactions to pregnancy, whether the pregnancy was planned, her relationship with the baby's father, and her employment status (E. Kaplan, 1997; Ludtke, 1997; Seegmiller, 1993). We can understand predominantly negative emotions from an unmarried, pregnant 16-year-old whose boyfriend and family have rejected her, and who must work as a waitress to earn an income. We can also understand predominantly positive emotions from a happily married 26-year-old who has hoped for this pregnancy for 2 years and whose family income allows her to buy the stylish "executive" maternity clothes that she can wear to her interesting, fulfilling job.

Attitudes Toward Pregnant Women

Most women experience three major gynecological events: menarche, pregnancy, and menopause. Menarche and menopause are highly private events, to be discussed only with intimate acquaintances. In contrast, pregnancy is public, especially in the last trimester. Interestingly, even strangers will often invade the privacy of a pregnant woman. These strangers may feel free to pat the stomach of a pregnant woman and offer unsolicited advice to her (Bergum, 1997; Seegmiller, 1993). These same people would *never* take such liberties with a woman who was not pregnant!

Some classic research by Shelley Taylor and Ellen Langer (1977) reported that people tend to avoid standing close to a pregnant woman. For example, elevator passengers make great efforts to avoid standing near a pregnant woman. Other research suggests that people are especially likely to help a pregnant woman, for example, if she has dropped her keys (Walton et al., 1988). Unfortunately, we don't have recent research in this area. Do people still treat pregnant women differently than women who are not pregnant?

People also show a strong tendency to infantilize pregnant women. Until recently, a pregnant woman was expected to place herself in the complete care of an obstetrician, who would tell her what to eat and how to live her life. She might be scolded for gaining more than 10 or 15 pounds during pregnancy. Otherwise, she was told not to worry her pretty little head about all those complicated aspects of pregnancy, because her doctor would make all the important decisions (S. Kitzinger, 1995). This kind of treatment would certainly *not* encourage women to be confident, tough, and effective mothers. Theme 2 of this book states that people treat women and men differently. This differential treatment is heightened when a woman is pregnant.

In the current era, most obstetricians are more aware that pregnant women should be treated like intelligent adults who appreciate knowing relevant information. However, many health care professionals may withhold useful feedback. For example, an interviewer asked an Asian woman why her obstetrician had administered certain medical tests. The woman replied:

> Don't know why we had the tests. I never asked for the results. There probably wasn't anything wrong with me so they didn't tell me. They don't give you the results of the tests unless there is anything wrong: you have to ask. They could be

---

DEMONSTRATION 10.1

Attitudes Toward Pregnant Women, as Illustrated in Department Stores

Select several nearby stores that sell maternity clothes; try to obtain a sample of stores that vary in social status. Visit each store. (You may want to come prepared with a "shopping for a pregnant friend" cover story.) Record where the maternity clothes are placed. Are they near the lingerie, the clothes for overweight women, the uniforms, or someplace else?

Also notice the nature of the clothes themselves. In the 1970s, the clothes were infantile, with ruffles and bows. During the 1980s, the clothes sometimes emphasized a woman's pregnant status; for example, a label "BABY" would be accompanied by an arrow pointing to the bulging belly. Clothes are now more like clothing for nonpregnant women. Do the different kinds of stores feature different styles?

Finally, check on the price of the clothing. How much would a pregnant woman's wardrobe be likely to cost, assuming that she will need maternity clothes during the last six months of her pregnancy?

a bit more helpful . . . because some Asians there they don't know how to speak and they won't push for anything. (Woollett & Marshall, 1997)

Many people who infantilize a pregnant woman *mean* well. However, they may inadvertently increase her anxiety and make her question her decision-making capabilities. A more useful service would be to provide current information and allow her to make her own choices whenever possible. A pregnant woman who is encouraged to make informed decisions about her pregnancy will probably be more competent in making informed child-rearing decisions, once her baby is born.

Some years ago, Horgan (1983) reported another measure of people's attitudes toward pregnant women—by visiting department stores. The expensive, high-status stores placed maternity clothes near the lingerie and loungewear. This arrangement suggests an image of femininity, delicacy, luxury, and privacy. In contrast, the less expensive, low-status stores placed maternity clothes near the uniforms and the clothing for overweight women. Here, a pregnant woman is seen as fat, with a job to do. Try Demonstration 10.1, a modification of Horgan's study.

Pregnant Women and Employment

Until recently, European American women in the United States and Canada typically stopped working outside the home once they became pregnant. However, Black women have had different expectations. Being a good mother never meant that a woman should stay at home full-time (P. Collins, 1991). In developing countries, pregnant women are often expected to work in the fields or to perform other physically exhausting tasks—sometimes until labor begins (S. Kitzinger, 1995).

Title VII of the U.S. Civil Rights Act of 1964 prohibits discrimination against pregnant workers in terms of hiring, fringe benefits, and other work opportunities. At present, pregnant women often continue at their jobs until shortly before their due date (Berryman & Windridge, 1997). However, discrimination against pregnant women may still operate in the workplace (Lindgren & Taub, 1993; Seegmiller, 1993). For instance, people in one study rated a pregnant female as being less achievement-oriented than a nonpregnant female (Blasko et al., 1989).

Some physically demanding occupations may be challenging for pregnant women. For example, female doctors who are residents in pediatrics work long hours, and they must also see emergency cases about two nights a week. When a sample of pregnant residents was interviewed, roughly one-quarter said that combining work with pregnancy was pleasant. Half reported it was tolerable, and one-quarter found it miserable (Klevan et al., 1990).

Combining a demanding job with pregnancy may sometimes be unpleasant. However, it does not seem to damage the health of the pregnant woman or the baby. For example, a nationwide questionnaire was sent to all women who had graduated from medical school and were now working as residents. The questionnaire was also sent to wives of their male classmates, who served as a control group of women with less time-consuming occupations. The pregnant women who were residents worked about twice as many hours each week—an average of 70 hours, in contrast to 39 for the doctors' wives. However, the women residents were no more likely to have miscarriages, premature births, or low-birthweight babies (Klebanoff et al., 1990). In other words, both pregnant women and their babies are impressively resilient.

Pregnancy

1. **Pregnancy and childbirth receive little attention in psychological research and in the media.**

2. **At the beginning of pregnancy, the fertilized egg implants itself in the tissue lining the uterus, and the placenta develops shortly afterward.**

3. **Although individual differences are great, several common physical reactions to pregnancy include nausea, weight gain, and fatigue.**

4. **The variety of emotional reactions to pregnancy is large. Positive emotions include feelings of excitement and wonder, a sense of purpose, growing attachment, and the anticipated pleasure of motherhood.**

5. **Negative emotions include fragile emotional stability, concerns about physical appearance, health worries, and concern about the reactions received from others.**

6. **People may avoid standing near pregnant women or may invade their privacy; pregnant women may also be infantilized.**

7. **Discrimination against pregnant workers is illegal, but they may still be treated differently in the workplace. However, most women with challenging jobs feel comfortable about combining work with pregnancy, and employment during pregnancy does not endanger the health of the pregnant woman or the baby.**

CHILDBIRTH

Women in the United States have an average of 2.1 children, and Canadian women have an average of 1.9 children (Neft & Levine, 1997). In other words, childbirth is a relatively common event in North America. However, this important event is virtually ignored by psychologists. Interesting topics—such as women's emotional reactions to childbirth—are almost invisible. In fact, most of our information must be gathered from nursing journals. Let's consider the biology of childbirth, expectations about childbirth, and emotional reactions to childbirth. Then we'll consider some current practices that are likely to improve women's childbirth experiences.

The Biology of Childbirth

Childbirth begins when the uterus starts to contract strongly. These contractions may initially feel like menstrual cramps, and they become more painful as labor progresses (Carlson et al., 1996).

The labor period is divided into three stages. During the first stage, the cervix becomes dilated to about 10 cm (4 inches), a process that may last anywhere from a few hours to at least a day. The second stage of labor lasts from a few minutes to several hours. The contractions, aided by the mother's pushing, move the baby farther down the vagina. Women report feelings of strong pressure and stretching during this stage (McKay, 1993). The contractions often become extremely painful. Progesterone levels now begin to drop. The second stage ends when the baby is born.

The third stage of labor, which usually lasts less than 20 minutes, is clearly an anticlimax. The placenta separates from the uterine wall, and then is expelled along with some other tissue that had surrounded the fetus. Estrogen levels drop during this third stage, so that the levels of both major hormones become drastically lower than they were several hours earlier.

Social factors can have a profound effect on the biology of childbirth (N. Collins et al., 1993). For example, women in one study participated in a program that included customized childbirth classes and a nurse assigned to

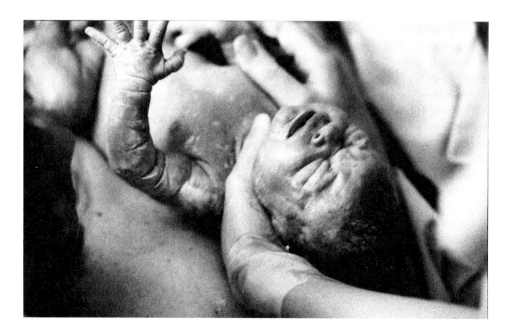

each woman for the entire childbirth experience (Frigoletto et al., 1995). Labor was 2.7 hours shorter for this group than for women who had the standard treatment.

Currently, about 20% to 25% of all deliveries in the United States and Canada are performed by cesarean section, or c-section. In a **cesarean section,** the physician makes an incision through the woman's abdomen and into the uterus, in order to deliver the baby (Carlson et al., 1996). Some cesarean sections are necessary because a vaginal delivery would be risky (for example, when a woman's uterine contractions are not strong enough or if the baby is too big). However, many health care critics argue that the rate of c-sections is high because they are more convenient or profitable for the medical staff (Curtin & Kozak, 1998; DiMatteo & Kahn, 1997; Goer, 1995).

In North America, childbirth is relatively safe. In developing countries, however, more than half a million women die each year from problems during pregnancy and childbirth (Nowak, 1995). Some of these countries have recently begun formal programs to train midwives in childbirth procedures. This training has reduced the death rate for both the pregnant women and their infants (Buckley, 1997).

Expectations About Childbirth

In one large-scale study, 82% of pregnant women said that it was important to them for childbirth to be a fulfilling experience (J. Green et al., 1990). However, this study did not find that a woman's educational level was correlated with her expectations. That is, women with little education were just as likely as well-educated women to have high expectations for childbirth and to want to avoid medication during childbirth.

Do women have a realistic expectation about the amount of pain experienced during labor and delivery? A study in England found that expectations corresponded fairly closely to reality (J. Green, 1993). However, research in the United States found that the experience was more painful than the women had anticipated (DiMatteo et al., 1993; Yarrow, 1992). Specifically, women in one U.S. sample reported that neither physicians nor family members had provided realistic information about the pain of childbirth (DiMatteo & Kahn, 1997). It's not clear whether some factor other than the nationality of the women in these samples can explain the difference in their experience.

Emotional Reactions to Childbirth

Women's emotional reactions to the birth of their child can vary as widely as their reactions to pregnancy (Wuitchik et al., 1990). For some women, childbirth can be a peak experience of feeling in tune with the birth. After giving birth, they may express intense joy. A woman in Hoffnung's (1992) study recalled, years later, her elation when her firstborn arrived:

I have never had such a high as after he was born! I guess it's the first child; you're so up for the whole thing. I think I could have flown if I had tried. . . . I have never felt that way about anything else at all: not getting married, not my other kids, nothing. (p. 17)

Many women's descriptions of childbirth emphasize the pain, but they may differ in their response to the pain. For example, one woman said:

I thought of the millions, literally billions of women who have experienced this pain, and if they could experience it, then I can too. That made me feel strong. (Bergum, 1997, p. 50)

Another woman found a different way to cope with the pain:

I don't think one should focus on the pain, that women should have to experience pain. But in the pain there is an experience of being inward and involved in feeling the pain—not enjoying it but taking hold, enduring, or whatever you do to handle it—and knowing that it is going to produce a child. (Bergum, 1997, p. 41)

Fathers who participate in the birth of their child may also experience intense joy, as in this description offered by a new father:

I couldn't have imagined the incredibly powerful feelings that engulfed me when I saw Kevin slip out of Tanya. I was right there, and this was my son! All the next day whenever he began to cry or nurse, I was in tears. I'm still transfixed watching him. It's the most amazing experience I ever had. (C. Cowan & Cowan, 1992)

Alternative Models of Childbirth

Many health care advocates suggest that the childbirth experience can be made more comfortable and emotionally satisfying for women. One of the most widely used programs, called **prepared childbirth,** features these elements (Hyde & DeLamater, 1997; Livingston, 1993):

1. Learning about pregnancy and childbirth in order to reduce fear;
2. Controlled breathing techniques, which distract attention away from the pain of the contractions;
3. Relaxation and social support from someone who has also attended classes, usually the baby's father or a close friend of the mother.

People who support prepared childbirth emphasize that this method does not *eliminate* pain; childbirth is still a stressful experience. However, women who have had a helpful coach present during childbirth are significantly more satisfied with the childbirth experience (Dannenbring et al., 1997). Prepared childbirth seems to provide a number of substantial benefits (Hyde & DeLamater, 1997; Wideman & Singer, 1984; D. Young, 1982). The mothers report more positive attitudes, less anxiety, and reduced pain. They also require less medication.

The technology of childbirth has made impressive advances during the past 50 years. Death rates are lower for both mothers and infants. An unfortunate side effect of this "high-tech" approach, however, is that births in hospitals may focus on expensive equipment, fetal monitoring, and sanitizing every part of the mother—rather than viewing childbirth as an exhilarating experience of warmth, joy, and sharing (S. Kitzinger, 1995; Peterson, 1996).

We've already noted that hospitals perform many cesarean sections for the benefit of the hospital staff, rather than the mother and the infant. As you can imagine, mothers are significantly more satisfied with the birth experience when they have had a normal, vaginal delivery, rather than a c-section (DiMatteo et al., 1996). Fortunately, some hospitals are now taking precautions to reduce the number of cesarean sections they perform (E. Nelson, 1996).

In contrast to the high-tech approach, the **family-centered approach** emphasizes that safe, high-quality health care can be delivered while simultaneously focusing on the woman's sense of individuality and autonomy, as well as the family's psychosocial needs (D. Young, 1982, 1993). The family-centered approach acknowledges that some high-risk pregnancies may require special technology. However, the vast majority of births are normal. Instead of focusing exclusively on the medical aspects of childbirth, the family-centered approach insists that professionals should realize that childbirth is an important psychological event in which a family is born and new relationships are formed.

Some of the changes that have been implemented include the following (Halldórsdóttir & Karlsdóttir, 1996; S. Kitzinger, 1995; D. Young, 1982, 1993):

1. Labor should not be artificially induced simply because it is more convenient for the physician.

2. Women should be encouraged to move around during labor and to sit upright when the child is being delivered, rather than lying flat on the delivery table with their feet in stirrups.

3. Hospital birth practices that have no health benefits should be modified. These include routine enemas, shaving the genital area, and forbidding any food during labor.

4. Anesthetics should not be used unless necessary or desired.

5. A supportive family member or friend should be present.

6. The birth experience is more pleasant when using special birthing rooms and out-of-hospital birth centers.

7. Health care providers must be caring individuals who can encourage women's sense of empowerment during childbirth.

The family-centered approach to childbirth emphasizes that the wishes of the mother should be taken seriously. This approach helps redistribute power, so that women in childbirth have more control over their own bodies. Women can make decisions about how they want to give birth, rather than being passive and infantilized.

DEMONSTRATION 10.2

Comparison of Childbirth Experiences

Locate women who had babies very recently, about 10 years ago, about 20 years ago, and in some year long before you were born. If possible, include your own mother or close relatives in your interview. Ask each of these women to describe her childbirth experience in as much detail as possible. After each women has finished, you may wish to ask some of the following questions, if they were not already answered:

1. Were you given any medication? If so, do you remember what kind?

2. How long did you stay in the hospital?

3. Did the baby stay with you in the room, or was she or he returned to the nursery after feedings?

4. Was a relative or friend allowed in the room while you were giving birth?

5. When you were in labor, were you encouraged to lie down?

6. Did you have "prepared childbirth"?

7. Do you recall any negative treatment from any of the hospital staff?

8. Were you treated like a competent adult?

9. Do you recall any positive treatment from any of the hospital staff?

10. If you could have changed any one thing about your childbirth experience, what would that have been?

Try Demonstration 10.2 to learn about the childbirth experiences of several women you know. Also, can you detect any changes in childbirth procedures for women with the most recent birth experiences?

 SECTION SUMMARY   *Childbirth*

1. **The three stages in labor are: (a) dilation of the cervix, (b) childbirth, and (c) expulsion of the placenta. Social factors can influence the duration of labor.**

2. **Women of all educational levels typically expect birth to be a fulfilling experience. In some studies, mothers' expectations match their childbirth experiences; in other studies, childbirth is more painful than expected.**

3. **Reactions to childbirth vary widely; some women report an intensely positive experience; others differ in their approaches to coping with pain.**

4. **Prepared childbirth emphasizes education, controlled breathing, relaxation, and social support; this approach generally produces more satisfying childbirth experiences.**

5. **The family-centered approach to childbirth focuses on the psychological importance of childbirth and discourages the unnecessary use of high-tech procedures.**

MOTHERHOOD

The word *motherhood* suggests some well-established stereotypes, which we'll consider in the first part of this section. Then we'll see how those stereotypes contrast with reality. We'll also examine the motherhood experience of two groups of women who are outside the mainstream of European American heterosexual mothers; specifically, we'll consider how both women of color and lesbian women experience motherhood. We'll then focus on two issues of concern to all women who have just given birth—postpartum depression and breastfeeding. The final topics in this chapter focus on the decision about whether to have children and the problem of infertility.

Stereotypes About Motherhood

For most people, the word *motherhood* brings forth a rich variety of pleasant emotions such as warmth, strength, protectiveness, nurturance, and self-sacrifice (Ganong & Coleman, 1995). You can easily generate other similar items to complete the list. In fact, you may find that the word *motherhood* creates positive images, even if you intend never to have children.

According to the stereotype, a pregnant woman is expected to be joyously upbeat, eagerly anticipating the blessed event (L. Brannon, 1994). Motherhood is portrayed as happy and fulfilling, an image perpetuated by the media (Hunter College, 1995). Furthermore, the stereotype of blissful motherhood specifies that the mother may require only a few moments of adjustment to the new baby, and then she will feel perfectly comfortable as her "natural" mothering skills take over (Hunter College, 1995). The motherhood stereotype emphasizes that a woman's ultimate fulfillment is achieved by becoming a mother (Hoffnung, 1995; Phoenix et al., 1991; Villani, 1997).

The popular stereotype about motherhood is also very narrowly defined (Phoenix et al., 1991). Think about the image of *motherhood* that you've been contemplating as you've read the last few paragraphs. Unless you are a person of color, this idealized woman is probably European American. She is also between the ages of about 20 and 35, she is heterosexual and married, her family income is comfortable, and she is slender and radiant.

However, much of North American culture is ambivalent about motherhood, though the negative aspects are generally less prominent. Mothers are sometimes portrayed as being overly concerned or domineering. Mothers nag more than fathers. It's the mother—not the father—who complains about Junior's messy room in the television sitcom. Also, the mother—not the father—gets blamed when children develop a psychological disorder (Phares, 1992; Phares & Compas, 1992). You'll recall from Chapter 2 that women in classical mythology and religion are sometimes virtuous and sometimes evil. Similarly, stereotypes about mothers contain contradictory messages of good and evil.

The Reality of Motherhood

Many lofty phrases are written in tribute to motherhood, but the role is actually accorded very low prestige (Hoffnung, 1995; Peterson, 1996). Our society values money, power, and achievement. However, not one of these rewards is associated with taking care of children. In reality, mothers do not receive the appreciation they deserve.

None of the stereotypes captures the rich variety of emotions that mothers actually experience. When one woman was asked what advice she wishes she had received before becoming a mother, she replied:

> I wish someone would have told me, "Motherhood can be very difficult, and there will be times when you wish you never had children. But there are also times when your children will give you such joy and pleasure, that all the bad things and feelings disappear as if they never existed. Focus on those times, and they will get you through anything." (Genevie & Margolies, 1987, p. 54)

Let's look in more detail at the reality of motherhood. We'll first consider a long list of negative factors and then examine the more abstract—but certainly intense—positive factors.

Negative Factors.   A newborn infant certainly creates pressures and stress for the mother. Here are some of the negative factors that women often mention:

1. Fathers help much less with child rearing than mothers had expected. As Chapter 7 noted, mothers take the major responsibility for their children (C. Grant et al., 1997).

2. Much of early motherhood is boring drudgery—diapering, washing, and feeding—much more work than mothers had expected (S. Kitzinger, 1995).

3. Child care is physically exhausting; fatigue is extremely common in the first weeks after childbirth. Sleep deprivation is also common (S. Kitzinger, 1994; Mercer, 1995). Because infant care takes so much time, new mothers often feel that they can accomplish very little other than taking care of the infant.

4. New mothers seldom have training for the tasks of motherhood; they often report feeling incompetent (Mercer, 1995).

5. Newborn babies seldom give positive reactions to their mothers until they are about 2 months old, when they begin smiling at their caretakers.

6. Because mothering is done at home, mothers of newborns have little contact with other adults (Hays, 1996). Friends and extended family may not be available to provide support. This kind of isolation further encourages the invisibility of women, already an important issue throughout this book.

7. Women who have been previously employed feel that others judge them negatively as "just a housewife"; they are deprived of other sources of identity (Villani, 1997).

8. Women often report that they feel tied down, because they cannot leave the house for more than a few minutes without making elaborate arrangements (Mercer, 1986).

9. For several days after childbirth, women report that they feel leaky and dirty, coping with after-birth discharges. They are also likely to feel pain in the vaginal area and in the uterus; their breasts may ache, and they may also experience pain and discomfort if they have had a cesarean section (S. Kitzinger, 1994).

10. Because the woman's attention has shifted to the newborn, her romantic partner may feel neglected. Many mothers comment that their husbands make them feel guilty about not being adequate, and the number of fights increases (Lerner, 1998).

11. Women feel disappointed in themselves because they do not match the standards of the Ideal Mother, the completely unselfish and perfect woman. She is our culture's stereotype of motherhood—but no one really lives up to that stereotype (Villani, 1997).

Positive Factors. Motherhood also has its positive side, though these qualities may not predominate early in motherhood. One positive feature often mentioned by women is that they feel a new connection between themselves and their own mothers (Hoffnung, 1988).

Some women discover that an important positive consequence of motherhood is a sense of their own strength. After all, they have successfully brought a child into this world. As one woman told me, "I discovered that I felt *very* empowered and confident, like, 'Don't mess with *me!* I've given birth!'" (Napper, 1998). Sadly, we often focus so much on childbirth's negative consequences for women that we fail to explore the life-enhancing consequences.

Another positive feature is the time that the mother and father can spend together, interacting with the infant. Interestingly, after a couple has a baby, they are more likely to pursue together some activities that the wife enjoys (D. Crawford & Huston, 1993). Parents often point out that children can be fun and interesting, especially when they can look at the world from a new viewpoint, through the eyes of a child.

But the major benefits for most mothers are the interactions with their children. One mother in Bergum's (1997) study captures the intensity of this loving interaction with her daughter, now three months old:

> She smiles at me. She looks me in the eye and smiles to light the world. Supreme harmony reigns as the light dapples through the apple trees.
>
> There must be traffic on 99th Street but I don't notice. Nothing seems to be going past on the avenue. Betsy and I are far away in this warm world. We are alone and connected and in love with each other.
>
> It is perhaps the most perfect time in my life. (p. 13)

A mother in Villani's (1997) study explained how her children developed an important part of her personality: "My kids have opened up emotions in me that I never knew were possible; they have slowed down my life happily" (p. 135). Many women point out that having children helped them to identify and develop their ability to nurture (Bergum, 1997).

Summarizing the comments of many mothers, Hoffnung (1995) wrote:

> The role of mother brings with it benefits as well as limitations. Children affect parents in ways that lead to personal growth, enable reworking of childhood conflicts, build flexibility and empathy, and provide intimate, loving human connections. . . . They expand their caretakers' worlds by their activity levels, their imaginations, and their inherently appealing natures. Although motherhood is not enough to fill an entire life, for most mothers, it is one of the most meaningful experiences in their lives. (p. 174)

If you were to ask a mother of an infant to list the positive and negative qualities of motherhood, the negative list would probably contain more items and more specific details. Most mothers find that the positive side of motherhood is more abstract, more difficult to describe, and yet more intense. The drudgery of dirty diapers is much easier to talk about than the near ecstasy of realizing that this complete human being was once part of her own body, and now this baby breathes and gurgles and hiccups without her help.

Also, shortly after birth, babies develop ways of communicating with other humans. The delights of a baby's first tentative smile are undeniable. An older baby can interact even more impressively with adults by making appropriate eye contact and conversational noises. Most mothers value the intimate, caring relationships they develop with their children. Motherhood has numerous joyous aspects. Unfortunately, our society has not devised creative ways to diminish the negative aspects so that we can appreciate the joys more completely.

Motherhood and Women of Color

Researchers are beginning to identify how the motherhood experiences of women of color often differ from the European American experience. However, mothers are still relatively invisible, even in the more comprehensive books about women of color. Interestingly, however, mothers are often prominent in fiction—for example, in the novels by African American women (E. Ross, 1995).

Sparks (1996) describes two major stereotypes about Black mothers. One stereotype, the Black welfare mother, is portrayed as being too lazy to work and having many babies in order to collect welfare payments. This stereotype fails to acknowledge the factors that produce poverty. A second stereotype, the Black superwoman, portrays a woman of incredible strength, who sacrifices her own needs for those of her children; in the current era, this stereotypical super-woman may also be highly career-focused in the workplace. This stereotype fails to acknowledge how racism may block the options available to Black women. Neither stereotype provides a realistic, positive role model for Black mothers in our culture.

Several theorists have pointed out the importance of extended families in Black culture. For example, P. Collins (1991) wrote:

> The centrality of women in African-American extended families is well known. Organized, resilient, women-centered networks of bloodmothers and othermothers are key in understanding this centrality. Grandmothers, sisters, aunts, or cousins acted as othermothers by taking on child care responsibilities for each other's children. When needed, temporary child care arrangements turned into long-term care or informal adoption. (p. 47)

Other authors confirm the stabilizing influence of the Black extended family (East & Felice, 1996; Staples & Johnson, 1993). These networks are especially important among economically poor mothers.

In Chapter 8, we saw the importance of *marianismo* for Latinas. **Marianismo** is the belief that women must be passive and long-suffering, giving up their own needs to help their husbands and children (Chin, 1994; Ehlers, 1993). Ginorio and her coauthors (1995) emphasize that real-life Latina mothers have typically been more active, holding substantial power within the family. These authors also emphasize that these real-life mothers are currently reshaping their roles and becoming more independent, especially as they enter the workforce in increasing numbers.

Some ethnic groups emphasize values in motherhood that would not be central for European American mothers. For example, many North American Indians emphasize the continuity of generations, with grandmothers being central when their daughters give birth (A. Adams, 1995). Consider Theresa, an Aboriginal woman living on the west coast of Canada. Theresa describes how her mother responded to the birth of Theresa's daughter:

> My mother came the day after she was born. She said, "I'm so proud of you. And I'm so happy that now you have a friend for yourself the way I have a friend for myself in you." And that really is how it is. My daughter's been a friend to me for a long time. (Morrison, 1987, p. 32)

In some Asian cultures, sons may have much more value than daughters. Here, a woman's reaction to motherhood may largely be determined by the gender of her newborn baby. The differing reactions to sons and daughters is captured in one early work of Chinese literature, *The Book of Poetry:*

When a son is born	When a daughter is born,
Let him sleep on the bed.	Let her sleep in the ground.
Clothe him with fine clothes.	Wrap her in common wrappings,
And give him jade to play with.	And give her broken tiles for
How lordly his cry is!	playthings.
May he grow up to wear crimson	May she have no faults, no merits of
And be the lord of the clan and the	her own.
tribe.	May she well attend to food and wine,
	And bring no discredit to her parents.

(Quoted in Croll, 1978, p. 23, and Hu, 1988, p. 121)

To the extent that these antifemale biases are shared by traditional Chinese American families today, mothers of daughters may feel they have disappointed their elders.

Many Asian cultures have customs and rituals for pregnant women and new mothers. For example, pregnant women in Cambodia are encouraged to eat the white meat of coconuts, so that their offspring will have light skin (Townsend & Rice, 1996). After giving birth, mothers stay for one month in a bed placed over a warm fire, in order to restore the body heat that is believed to be lost during childbirth.

Cultural beliefs may conflict with modern medicine when women from Asia migrate to the United States. For instance, Hmong women who have come to the United States from Southeast Asia are horrified at the prospect of being examined by a male obstetrician when they are pregnant. Other procedures—such as providing a urine sample or having their blood drawn—may seem terrifying to a Hmong woman, even if they seem routine to European Americans (Symonds, 1996).

As Collins (1994) points out, our knowledge about motherhood will not be helped by claiming that the experiences of women of color are more valid than the experiences of White, middle-class women. Instead, Collins emphasizes that examining motherhood "from multiple perspectives should uncover rich textures of differences. Shifting the center to accommodate this diversity promises to recontextualize motherhood and point us toward feminist theorizing that embraces differences as an essential part of commonality" (p. 73).

Lesbian Mothers

Researchers estimate that between 1 million and 5 million lesbian mothers are raising children in the United States (Patterson, 1996). Lesbian mothers are a diverse group. The largest number are women who had a child in a heterosexual relationship and subsequently identified as lesbian. Other lesbians decide to conceive by donor insemination or to acquire children by adoptions. Some lesbians are single parents; others live with a partner.

Many studies have compared the adjustment of children raised in lesbian households and children raised in heterosexual households. These studies show that the children are similar in characteristics such as intelligence, development,

Numerous studies demonstrate that children raised by lesbian mothers are similar in their psychosocial adjustment to children raised by heterosexual mothers.

moral judgments, self-concepts, psychological well-being, and social competence (American Psychological Association, 1995; Patterson, 1995a, 1996). Children raised by lesbians are also no more likely to be lesbian or gay than children raised by heterosexuals (Patterson, 1995b; Tasker & Golombok, 1995). One study compared young adults who had been reared as children by either lesbians or heterosexual women. The two groups were similar in measures of psychological health and feelings about their families (Tasker & Golombok, 1995).

Summarizing the research on lesbian parenting, one resource concludes:

> In summary, there is no evidence to suggest that lesbians and gay men are unfit to be parents or that psychosocial development among children of gay men or lesbians is compromised in any respect relative to that among offspring of heterosexual parents. Not a single study has found children of gay or lesbian parents to be disadvantaged in any significant respect relative to children of heterosexual parents. Indeed, the evidence to date suggests that home environments provided by gay and lesbian parents are as likely as those provided by heterosexual parents to support and enable children's psychological growth. (American Psychological Association, 1995)

Children raised by lesbian mothers may be well adjusted, but are they accepted by the wider community? Although some children feel uncomfortable talking about their mothers' sexual orientation, most are positive about their mothers' unconventional relationships (Tasker & Golombok, 1995). Furthermore, some psychologists have concluded that society is now more likely to accept gay and lesbian parenting, in comparison to earlier decades (Cavaliere, 1995).

Postpartum Disturbances

The stereotype about motherhood, as we noted earlier, portrays the new mother as being delighted with both her young infant and her maternal state. Unfortunately, a significant number of women develop psychological disturbances during the **postpartum period,** the weeks shortly after birth. Take a moment to glance back over the list of 11 negative factors on pages 376–377. Imagine that you are a new mother who is exhausted from childbirth, and you are experiencing most of these factors. Also, suppose that your infant is not yet old enough to smile delightfully. Under these stressful circumstances, you can easily imagine how emotional problems could arise.

Two different kinds of postpartum problems occur relatively often. The most common kind of problem is called **postpartum blues** or **maternity blues,** a short-lasting change in mood that usually begins within the first week after childbirth and lasts 2 to 4 days. Roughly half of new mothers experience postpartum blues, and it is found in many different cultures (Brockington, 1996; Gotlib, 1998; Misri, 1995). Common symptoms include tearfulness, sadness, insomnia, irritability, and feeling overwhelmed (O'Hara, 1995; Susman, 1996). Postpartum blues are probably a result of the emotional letdown following the excitement of childbirth, combined with the realistic life changes that a new baby brings (Brockington, 1996). The blues typically do not create any long-lasting problems, but it is important for women to be informed about this problem.

Postpartum depression is a more serious disorder, typically involving feelings of extreme sadness, fatigue, despair, loss of interest in enjoyable activities, and loss of interest in the baby. It affects about 10% to 15% of women who have given birth. Postpartum depression usually begins to develop 2 to 3 weeks after childbirth, and it may last for many months (O'Hara, 1995; Stanton & Danoff-Burg, 1995; Wessely, 1998). For example, a woman named Diana reported:

> When I came home from the hospital I had these strange feelings. I would be here during the day and would just vegetate and sometimes I would just lose control and weep. I felt like I didn't have a friend in the world. . . . I couldn't stop crying. (V. Taylor, 1996, p. 26)

Postpartum depression is similar to other kinds of depression that aren't associated with children. In fact, it may be the same as "regular" depression, which we'll explore in more detail in Chapter 12. However, the current edition of the major psychiatric resource—the *Diagnostic and Statistical Manual of Mental Disorders*—includes a separate discussion about depression that occurs after childbirth (American Psychiatric Association, 1994). As we'll also see in Chapter 12, most cases of depression can be successfully treated.

Women who have had previous episodes of depression or who have a family history of depression are at risk for postpartum depression (Gotlib, 1998; Susman, 1996). They are also more likely to experience postpartum depression with their first child, rather than with later-born children (Berthiaume et al., 1996). Women who lack social support from a partner, relatives, and friends are especially likely to develop postpartum depression (Logsdon et al., 1997; Neter et al., 1995). Stewart and Jambunathan (1996) found an unusually low rate of postpartum depression among Hmong women who had migrated from Laos to a community in Wisconsin. They speculate that the psychological health of these women can be traced to the high levels of support these women receive from their spouses and family members.

Professionals are beginning to explore the important benefits of social support in preventing postpartum depression. For example, Lavender and Walkinshaw (1998) conducted a well-controlled study with women who were predominantly European American. Half of the women who had just given birth received no special treatment, and half talked with a midwife who offered support and informal counseling. The midwives had no formal training in counseling, and the counseling session lasted between 30 minutes and 2 hours. Three weeks after giving birth, all women completed a standardized measure of depression. The results showed that 55% of the women in the control group received high scores on the depression scale, in contrast to only 9% in the group that had received counseling. If these results are replicated, then a program of supportive counseling should be a standard procedure following childbirth.

The origins of both postpartum blues and postpartum depression are controversial. We noted that the levels of progesterone and estrogen drop sharply during the last stages of childbirth. The levels of other hormones also change during the weeks following childbirth. However, the relationship between hormonal levels and postpartum disorders is inconsistent and not very strong (Kendall-Tackett & Kantor, 1993; O'Hara, 1995). Many of the stresses and sources of dissatisfaction following childbirth could contribute to the blues and depression (S. Kitzinger, 1995). However, we do not know which specific factors are most to blame—aside from one important factor: lack of social support.

Keep in mind that many women do not experience either the blues or depression following the birth of their baby. Earlier in this chapter, we noted that some women experience little discomfort and few psychological problems during pregnancy. Chapter 4 pointed out that many women do not have major premenstrual or menstrual symptoms, and we'll see in Chapter 14 that many women pass through menopause without any trauma. In short, women differ widely from one another. The various phases in a woman's reproductive life do not inevitably bring emotional or physical problems.

Breastfeeding

Currently, about 60% of North American mothers breastfeed their newborn infants, and 15% nurse their babies for a whole year (Schafer et al., 1998; Springen, 1998). Mothers who breastfeed are likely to be better educated and to have higher family incomes than mothers who bottlefeed (Schafer et al., 1998). Mothers who are in their 20s or older are also more likely than teenagers to breastfeed (Ineichen et al., 1997).

Ethnic differences in breastfeeding have sometimes been reported. For example, one study compared European Americans, Mexican Americans, and Blacks in Texas. Even though the groups were similar in socioeconomic class, 43% of European American mothers breastfed their infants, in contrast to 24% of Mexican American mothers and 9% of Black mothers (Baranowski et al., 1986). Employment patterns for mothers of newborns may partially explain these differences among ethnic groups; more recent data on this question would be very useful.

Some health care workers have devised programs in which low-income mothers receive guidance from women who have successfully breastfed their own infants (e.g., Ineichen et al., 1997; Schafer et al., 1998). For example, one Black woman described her feelings for her third child, whom she had breastfed with the help of a counselor:

> Yes, I love all my children and I'm close to them, but there's something special with me and him. It's like he's part of me, and he's still a part of me. I have what he needs. I give it to him, nobody makes it for me. I give it to him. I'm the reason that he's healthy. (Locklin & Naber, 1993, p. 33)

As this mother's remarks suggest, mothers who breastfeed are likely to believe that breastfeeding establishes a close bond between mother and baby. They typically report that nursing is a very pleasant experience of warmth, sharing, and openness (S. Kitzinger, 1994; Lawrence, 1998). Mothers who bottlefeed are more likely to argue that bottlefeeding is convenient and trouble-free.

The infant's father may also influence a mother's decision to breastfeed. For example, men whose partners expected to breastfeed are likely to believe that breastfeeding is better for babies. In contrast, men whose partners did not expect to breastfeed are likely to believe that breastfeeding makes a woman's breasts ugly. Some men may become somewhat jealous at the prospect of their partner's breastfeeding, because they think of breasts in erotic terms; the woman's breasts are intended for their own enjoyment, not for an infant (Hunter College, 1995).

Our culture does associate women's breasts with sexuality rather than infant nutrition. For this reason, we shun nursing in public places (Carter, 1995; I. Young, 1998). Think about it: How many women have you recently seen nursing in public?

The research demonstrates that human milk is better than cow's milk for human infants. After all, evolution has encouraged the development of a liquid that is ideally designed for efficient digestion. Breast milk also provides protection against infections, allergies, and other diseases (Lawrence, 1998; J. Newman, 1995). Breastfeeding also offers some health benefits for mothers, such as reducing the incidence of breast cancer and ovarian cancer (Lawrence, 1998).

Because of the health benefits, health professionals should try to encourage breast feeding. This precaution is especially valid in developing countries where sanitary conditions make bottle-feeding hazardous (Hunter College, 1995). However, the health professionals should not make mothers feel inadequate or guilty if they choose to bottlefeed their babies.

Deciding Whether to Have Children

As recently as 30 years ago, most married women did not need to make a conscious decision about whether to have a child. Almost all married women who were physically capable of having children did so, with little awareness that they really had a choice. However, attitudes have changed. In the United States, for example, 12% of married women between the ages of 40 and 44 do not have children. One survey showed that 9% of women between the ages of 18 and 34 say that they expect not to have children (U.S. Bureau of the Census, 1997). Some of these women may choose not to have children because they are unmarried. Other women may not have children because they, or their partners, are infertile.

Most women do include children in their life plans. For example, most college women say that they want to have children at some point in their lives (E. England & Manko, 1991; Wallach & Matlin, 1992).

In any event, we need to discuss the substantial number of women who prefer not to have children. Let's consider how these "child-free" women are viewed by others. We'll also explore some advantages and disadvantages of deciding not to have children.

Attitudes Toward Women Choosing Not to Have Children. A few decades ago, a young woman who did not plan to have children would have been viewed quite negatively. In contrast, research in the 1980s revealed that American college students were *not* especially biased against child-free women (Knaub et al., 1983; Shields & Cooper, 1983).

However, views of child-free women may have turned somewhat negative again in recent years. For example, Demonstration 10.3 is a modified version of a scenario tested by Mueller and Yoder (1997). These authors found statistically significant differences in the ratings of the women in the two scenarios on all three dimensions included in the demonstration. Table 10.1 shows their results obtained for college students in Wisconsin. I'd suspect that the ratings for the child-free woman would be somewhat more negative in a more general population that includes nonstudents. We clearly need additional systematic research, using a variety of measures, to determine current attitudes toward child-free women.

DEMONSTRATION 10.3

Attitudes Toward Child-Free Women

For this demonstration, you will need some volunteers—ideally, at least five persons for each of the two scenarios described below. Read the following paragraph aloud to half of the volunteers, either individually or in a group.

Kathy and Tom are an attractive couple in their mid-forties. They will be celebrating their twentieth wedding anniversary next year. They met in college and were married the summer after they received their undergraduate degrees. Tom is now a very successful attorney. Kathy, who earned her PhD in social psychology, is a full-time professor at the university. Kathy and Tom have no children. They are completely satisfied with their present family size, because they planned to have no children even before they were married. Because both have nearby relatives, they often have family get-togethers. Kathy and Tom also enjoy many activities and hobbies. Some of their favorites are biking, gardening, and taking small excursions to explore nearby towns and cities.

After reading this paragraph, pass out copies of the rating sheet below and ask volunteers to rate their impression of Kathy.

Follow the same procedure for the other half of the volunteers. However, for the sentence "Kathy and Tom have no children" and the following sentence, substitute this passage. "Kathy and Tom have two children. They are completely satisfied with their present family size, because they planned to have two children even before they were married." Compare the average responses of the two groups. Is Kathy considered to be more fulfilled? Does she have a happier and more rewarding life?

1	2	3	4	5
less fulfilled				more fulfilled

1	2	3	4	5
very unhappy				very happy

1	2	3	4	5
unrewarding life				rewarding life

(Based on Mueller & Yoder, 1997, p. 211.)

	Family Size in Scenario	
	Child-Free	**Two Children**
Fulfillment	4.0	4.4
Happiness	3.5	4.3
Rewarding life	3.5	4.2

TABLE 10.1 Ratings of a Child-Free Woman and a Woman with Two Children, on Three Different Characteristics (Based on Mueller & Yoder, 1997)

Note: 5 is the highest level of the attribute.

Advantages and Disadvantages of Being Child-Free. Here are some of the reasons that couples give for not wanting to have a child (Groat et al., 1997; Ireland, 1993; G. Michaels, 1988; Sunday & Lewin, 1985):

1. Parenthood is an irrevocable decision; you can't take children back to the store for a refund.

2. Children are expensive. By some estimates, it cost close to $1 million to raise a child in the United States from birth through college in the 1990s (C. Cowan & Cowan, 1992). The expense easily exceeds $1 million now. Also, a Canadian study emphasized the cost to women in terms of their own income; the average child-free woman earns about $4,700 more each year than the average woman with a child aged 2 to 5 years (Grindstaff, 1996).

3. Some women and men are afraid that they will not be good parents.

4. Some couples are reluctant to give up a satisfying and flexible lifestyle for a more child-focused orientation.

5. Children can interfere with educational and vocational plans.

6. Some couples do not want to bring children into a world threatened by nuclear war and other serious global problems.

Still, people who are enthusiastic about parenthood provide many reasons for having children (C. Cowan & Cowan, 1992; Gormly et al., 1987; McMahon, 1995):

1. Parenthood is challenging; it offers people the opportunity to learn what they can be.

2. Parenthood offers a relationship of love and nurturance with other human beings; children can enrich people's lives.

3. Parents have a unique chance to be responsible for someone's education and training. They can watch their child grow into an adult who may help the world become a better place.

4. Some people want to become parents in order to fulfill their relationship with their spouse.

5. Some people have children to "carry on the family line" or to ensure that some part of themselves continues into future generations.

6. Children can be a source of fun, pleasure, and pride.

Consider a representative study by Gormly and her coauthors (1987), who asked college women and men about their motivation for parenthood. Both women and men frequently responded either "to expand myself, have someone to follow me" or "to provide a family for myself." Close to half of the participants endorsed each of these options. However, a major gender difference emerged with respect to a third motivation for parenthood, "to achieve adult status or social identity." This response was chosen by 79% of the women, in contrast to only 21% of the men.

Several writers have pointed out how women in their childbearing years face a no-win situation (Ball, 1993; Hays, 1996). If a woman decides not to have children, people may say that she is cold and unfulfilled as a woman. If she has children and decides to work outside the home, she will be accused of either neglecting her children or being on the "mommy track" and not being serious about her work. If she has children and decides *not* to seek employment, some people will call her unproductive, an "intellectual lightweight." As Hays (1996) describes the situation, "A woman, in other words, can never fully do it right" (p. 133).

Jean Carter, a gynecologist, confirms this no-win situation with respect to the optimal number of children. The female clients in her practice say that they are told either, "Three children are too many" or "A single child will grow up lonely." As Carter says, "There's not much you can do to be considered normal and above reproach to everybody. But one of my desires is that we should all learn to accept one another's reproductive choices" (Ball, 1993, p. 52). These words sound like wise advice for all of us!

Infertility

Each of us knows several women who have wanted to have children, but pregnancy does not seem to be a possibility. One such woman wrote:

> I am someone who wanted to have children and a fairly traditional woman's life, but things did not work out that way for a variety of reasons and I have had to adjust my expectations. I am one of a growing number of women who face the spectre of infertility. We each have to work out our own creative solution to this problem. . . . Mine has been to abandon the dream of children and to opt for a professional life geared toward care-giving and a personal life geared toward learning. (Ireland, 1993, p. 22)

By the current definition, **infertility** is the failure to conceive after 1 year of sexual intercourse without using contraception (Garner, 1995; Stanton &

Danoff-Burg, 1995). An estimated 2.4 million couples in the United States meet that definition of infertility (Garner, 1995). The clear majority of these cases of infertility can be traced to a biological cause rather than a psychological explanation. According to estimates, 40% of infertility can be traced to problems in the male, 40% to problems in the female, and 20% to both (Carlson et al., 1996; Garner, 1995).

Some women, like the one whose words you just read, manage to refocus their interests. Other women, who had looked forward to children as a central part of their married lives, experience stress and a real sense of loss (Abbey et al., 1991). However, comparisons of fertile and infertile women show that the two groups do not differ in their marital satisfaction or self-esteem (Pasch & Dunkel-Schetter, 1997; Stanton & Danoff-Burg, 1995).

Still, the research does suggest that women who are infertile show higher levels of distress and anxiety than fertile women (Stanton & Danoff-Burg, 1995). Incidentally, theorists conclude that the infertility causes the distress and anxiety. Distress and anxiety do *not* cause infertility. Also, individual differences in psychological reactions to infertility are substantial, consistent with Theme 4 of this book.

One source of psychological strain for a couple that is facing infertility is that they may live with the constant hope, "Maybe next month . . ." (Greil, 1991). They may see themselves as "not yet pregnant," rather than permanently childless. As a result, they may feel unsettled, caught between hopefulness and mourning the child they will not have.

Women of color face an additional source of strain when they experience infertility. For example, Ceballo (1999) interviewed African American women who had tried to become pregnant for many years. These women often struggled with racist health care providers who seemed astonished that a Black woman should be infertile. As these women explained, everyone seems to believe that infertility is "a White thing," because they believe that Black women should be highly sexualized, promiscuous, and extremely fertile. One woman, Amanda, pointed out how she began to internalize these racist messages. As she said, she believed that she was "the only Black woman walking the face of the earth that cannot have a baby."

Many couples who are concerned about infertility decide to consult health care professionals for an "infertility workup," which will include a medical examination of both partners (Pasch & Dunkel-Schetter, 1997; Stanton & Danoff-Burg, 1995). About half of couples who seek medical treatment will eventually become parents, using one of several kinds of reproductive technologies (Giudice, 1998).

However, many women will not become pregnant—even after medical treatment—or they may experience miscarriages. Eventually, some will choose to adopt. Others will decide to pursue other interests. Ireland (1993) argues that feminism offers women an opportunity to appreciate their female identity, without the necessity of motherhood. A woman who might have focused on the regret of infertility in earlier eras can now shift her emphasis away from what is *not* in her life, so that she can fully appreciate the many positive options available in her future.

 Motherhood

1. The stereotypes about motherhood reveal our ambivalence about mothers: mothers are warm, nurturant, and happy, but mothers are also domineering nags.

2. Mothers of newborns have extensive responsibilities and more work than they expected; they may feel exhausted, incompetent, unrewarded, isolated, deprived of other sources of identity, tied down, and physically uncomfortable. In addition, their husbands may make them feel guilty.

3. Motherhood also has a strong positive side; the benefits include finding a new connection with one's own mother, spending time as a family, pleasurable interactions with the baby, and increased flexibility and empathy, as well as abstract, intense joys.

4. Compared to White women, women of color may have different motherhood experiences. Black mothers have to combat the stereotypes of the Black welfare mother and the Black superwoman; however, they have the benefit of the extended family; Latinas must combat the values implied by *marianismo;* North American Indians may emphasize the continuity of motherhood; mothers of female infants may be devalued in Asian cultures.

5. Research on lesbian mothers reveal that they do not differ from heterosexual mothers in their parenting skills or the adjustment of their children.

6. About half of new mothers experience the short-lasting depression called postpartum blues; between 10% and 15% experience the more severe postpartum depression.

7. Breastfeeding provides benefits for mother–infant bonding, as well as the health of both the infant and the mother.

8. At present, college students are somewhat negative about child-free women.

9. Child-free couples say that the disadvantages of parenthood include the irrevocability of the decision to have a child, the expense, and the interference with lifestyle and work.

10. Couples who want to have children cite advantages such as the challenge of parenthood, the opportunity to educate children, and the pleasurable aspects of children.

11. **Women face a no-win situation with respect to how they are judged for their decisions about motherhood and employment.**

12. **Women who are infertile are similar to women with children in terms of their marital satisfaction and self-esteem, but they may be more anxious; many women manage to refocus their lives when infertility seems likely.**

CHAPTER REVIEW QUESTIONS

1. At the beginning of the chapter, we emphasized that pregnancy and childbirth are ignored topics, particularly compared to topics such as love or sex. Based on the information in this textbook, why do you think that these topics have such low visibility?

2. This chapter emphasizes ambivalent feelings and thoughts more than any other chapter in the book. Address the issue of ambivalence with respect to five topics: (a) emotional reactions to pregnancy; (b) emotional reactions to childbirth; (c) the reality of motherhood; (d) the decision to have children; (e) reactions to infertility.

3. How do people react to pregnant women? How might these reactions contribute to women's emotional responses to pregnancy?

4. Contrast the high-tech approach to childbirth with the family-centered approach. Which characteristics would be likely to make women feel more in control of their experience during childbirth?

5. One of the themes of this book has been that stereotypes and reality about women do not always coincide. Address this issue with respect to some of the problems of motherhood.

6. A prominent theme throughout this book is that women react in a variety of ways to the same life event. Discuss this theme, focusing on individual differences in physical and emotional reactions to pregnancy, childbirth experiences, postpartum disturbances, and infertility.

7. What are the stereotypes about women of color who are mothers, and how is reality different from these stereotypes? What are the stereotypes and the reality for lesbian mothers?

8. Childbirth educators have made impressive changes in the way childbirth is now approached. However, the stresses of motherhood remain. Imagine that our society valued motherhood enough to fund programs aimed at decreasing the difficulties experienced during the early weeks after a baby is born. First, review those stresses. Then describe an ideal program that includes education, assistance, and social support.

9. Psychologists have conducted less research on pregnancy, childbirth, and motherhood than on any other topic in this book. Review this chapter and

suggest possible research projects that could clarify how women experience these three important events in their lives.

10. As this chapter pointed out, women in their child-bearing years face a no-win situation with respect to decisions about childbearing and employment. Consider the options for three categories of women: (a) married; (b) lesbian; and (c) single. What kinds of prejudices would be aimed at each category of women (e.g., a lesbian who decides to have children and to be employed full-time)? Can any of these women win the complete approval of society?

NEW TERMS

placenta (363)
trimester (363)
cesarean section (371)
prepared childbirth (372)
family-centered approach (373)
marianismo (379)

postpartum period (382)
postpartum blues (382)
maternity blues (382)
postpartum depression (382)
infertility (388)

RECOMMENDED READINGS

Birth: Issues in Perinatal Care. This quarterly journal provides an interdisciplinary perspective on topics that psychologists have generally ignored. The articles examine women's experiences during pregnancy, childbirth, and the postpartum period; it also discusses innovations such as the family-centered approach.

Bergum, V. (1997). *A child on her mind: The experience of becoming a mother.* Westport, CT: Bergin & Garvey. This welcome book interweaves women's stories with reviews of the literature; topics include childbirth, adoption from the perspective of the birth mother and the adoptive mother, and teenage mothers.

McMahon, M. (1995). *Engendering motherhood: Identity and self-transformation in women's lives.* New York: Guilford Press. I strongly recommend this book for its perspectives on the myths and realities of motherhood; it also focuses on the motherhood experiences in a sample of Canadian mothers.

Rice, P. L., & Manderson, L. (Eds.). (1996). *Maternity and reproductive health in Asian societies.* Amsterdam, Holland: Harwood Academic Publishers. Here's an excellent way to discover cross-cultural views of pregnancy, childbirth, and motherhood; the book emphasizes reports from Japan, Indonesia, Thailand, and the Philippines.

Villani, S. L. (1997). *Motherhood at the crossroads: Meeting the challenge of a changing role.* New York: Plenum Press. This wonderful book examines the myths of motherhood, the frustrations experienced by mothers, and how women resolve their conflicts about motherhood.

ANSWERS TO THE TRUE-FALSE QUESTIONS

1. True (p. 362); 2. True (p. 364); 3. False (p. 366); 4. True (p. 366); 5. False (p. 369); 6. False (p. 371); 7. False (p. 372); 8. False (pp. 376–377); 9. True (p. 382); 10. False (p. 385).

WOMEN AND PHYSICAL HEALTH

TRUE OR FALSE?

_____ 1. Because women often have unique health problems, researchers are more likely to use female participants than male participants.

_____ 2. Recent research suggests that men and women are treated similarly with respect to major health problems such as heart disease, and kidney disease.

_____ 3. Although the media have publicized the problem of female genital mutilation for young girls in Africa, the Middle East, and Asia, recent investigations have determined that only about 5,000 to 7,000 girls have been hurt by this ceremonial procedure.

_____ 4. When we consider U.S. residents who are in the upper income brackets, White women, White men, Black women, and Black men have fairly similar life expectancies.

_____ 5. Women are about 10 times as likely to die from heart disease as to die from breast cancer.

_____ 6. White men with disabilities are about twice as likely as White women with disabilities to participate in the labor force.

_____ 7. College students are highly accurate in judging which potential sexual partners are HIV positive and which are HIV negative.

_____ 8. Aside from AIDS, the other sexually transmitted diseases may be annoying or painful, but they cause no permanent health problems.

_____ 9. Alcohol kills more than five times as many people every year as all illegal drugs combined.

_____ 10. Black women are less likely than White women to smoke cigarettes and to try illegal drugs at some point in their lives.

The Health Care and Health Status of Women
Biases Against Women
Health Issues for Women in Developing Countries
Gender Differences in Life Expectancy
Gender Differences in Overall Health
Heart Disease, Breast Cancer, and Other Specific Health Problems

Women with Disabilities
Work Patterns of Women with Disabilities
Personal Relationships of Women with Disabilities

AIDS and Other Sexually Transmitted Diseases
Background Information on AIDS
Medical Aspects of AIDS
How AIDS Is Transmitted
Living with AIDS
Preventing AIDS
Other Sexually Transmitted Diseases

Women and Substance Abuse
Smoking
Alcohol Abuse
Other Substance-Abuse Problems

You may be somewhat puzzled by the title of this chapter, "Women and Physical Health." Why should women's health problems require special attention in a psychology course? This chapter will emphasize three major reasons that health issues are related to the psychology of women and gender.

1. *Gender makes a difference in the kinds of illness that people experience.* One theme of this book is that psychological gender differences are small. However, several *biological* gender differences have important consequences for women's health. Some consequences are obvious. For example, women may be diagnosed with cancer of the ovaries and the uterus, but need not worry about developing prostate cancer.

Some consequences are more subtle. For example, the female body has more fat and less fluid than the male body. As a result, toxic substances in the environment—which are especially likely to accumulate in fatty tissue—may have a more serious effect on women (Headlee & Elfin, 1996). This same gender difference with respect to fat and fluid also has important consequences for alcohol metabolism. Specifically, women's bodies have less fluid in which the alcohol can be distributed. So, even if a man and a woman are of identical weight, and both consume the same amount of alcohol, the woman will end up with a higher level of alcohol in her blood (J. Hamilton & Yonkers, 1996; Haseltine, 1997).

2. *Gender makes a difference in the way a disease is diagnosed and treated.* For example, we'll see that men are more likely than women to be treated for certain heart problems, consistent with Theme 2 of this book. Also, the disease symptoms that are found in males are considered to be normative or standard. In contrast, the same disease may cause a different set of symptoms in females; for example, AIDS can affect a woman's reproductive system. Ironically, these disease symptoms are considered to be deviations from the norm, consistent with our discussion of the normative male, on pages 65 to 66 (Stanton, 1995).

Gender also makes a difference in the way certain diseases are viewed. For example, researchers in previous decades rarely studied osteoporosis, a bone disease found predominantly in women. As Theme 3 emphasizes, topics important to women are often invisible.

However, one cluster of women's health problems *has* received abundant attention: women's reproductive systems (Stanton, 1995). A physician in the late 1800s captured this emphasis with his statement that "Woman is a pair of ovaries with a human being attached, where man is a human being furnished with a pair of testes" (cited in Fausto-Sterling, 1985, p. 90).

3. *Illness is an important part of many women's experience.* A textbook on the psychology of women must explore both gender differences and the life experiences of women. Sadly, health problems are a major concern for many women, and they become an increasingly central force as women grow older. Meyerowitz and Weidner (1998) estimate that more than 80% of women who are 55 or older experience at least one chronic health problem; more than 50% of this age group experience two or more problems.

Our focus on women's health in this chapter is part of a new field of psychology called health psychology. **Health psychology** attempts to understand how people stay healthy, why they engage in risky behavior, why they develop illnesses, and how they respond to illnesses (S. Taylor, 1995). Because of the increased interest in psychological factors associated with women's health, we now have many journals in the discipline. They include: *Journal of Women's Health, Health Care for Women International, Women's Health Issues, Women's Health,* and *Women & Health.*

This chapter will explore several important components of women's physical health. In the first section, we examine how gender is related to both health care and health status. The second section emphasizes the theme of variability among women, as we examine the lives of women with disabilities. The last two sections connected with women's health are sexually transmitted diseases and substance abuse. The topics in this chapter may initially seem unrelated. However, they all focus on the central issues: How does gender influence people's physical health, and how are women's lives influenced by their health?

THE HEALTH CARE AND HEALTH STATUS OF WOMEN

Theme 2 of this book states that women are treated differently from men. The biases against women in the health care system provide still further evidence for that theme, both in North America and in developing countries. This section also examines the gender differences in life expectancy and in general health, as well as several diseases that have an important impact on women's lives.

Biases Against Women

The medical profession has consistently been biased against women. Both women physicians and women patients have often been mistreated. A fascinating book by

Mary Roth Walsh (1977) features a title based on a 1946 newspaper advertisement: "DOCTORS WANTED: NO WOMEN NEED APPLY." The book documents the long history of attempts to keep women out of medical schools and medical practice.

These professional biases against female physicians still persist, as neurosurgeon Dr. Frances Conley (1998) reveals in a recent book. She describes how her male colleagues would try to grope her during a surgical operation, and how female medical students would be turned down for residency positions if they did not agree to have sex with influential male physicians. She also reports that male physicians known for their gender bias can sometimes rise to supervisory positions.

On the bright side, 43% of first-year U.S. medical students are now female, in contrast to only 9% in 1969 (Barzansky et al., 1997; Eisenberg et al., 1989). Now that women constitute such a large percentage, discrimination will probably decrease.

Nevertheless, the medical profession and the health care system show several biases against women patients. As you read about these biases, keep in mind three cautions: (1) not every doctor is biased against women; (2) not every female doctor is a feminist; and (3) some male doctors are feminists. What are these biases that operate in health care so that women patients become "second-class citizens"?

1. *Women are often neglected in medicine and medical research.* For example, one study analyzed all illustrations of men and women in medical textbooks, omitting those that focused on reproduction. Men were almost four times as likely as women to be pictured in these illustrations (Mendelsohn et al., 1994). In other words, the male body is normative, and it provides the standard. Without much analysis, medical experts assume that research conducted on males can be extended to females (Shumaker & Smith, 1994).

Furthermore, health care providers' decisions about women's health may be based on research that did not include women. For instance, one major study found that drinking 3 cups of coffee a day did not have an effect on the incidence of heart attacks. However, the 45,589 participants in the study were all men! (T. Adler, 1990). Women have been similarly ignored in research on heart disease and on AIDS (T. Johnson & Fee, 1997; Stanton, 1995).

Fortunately, this neglect of women has outraged health care consumers and some legislators. Medical educators are now encouraging medical schools to emphasize women's health as part of the regular curriculum (Wallis, 1998). In 1993, the U.S. National Institutes of Health began requiring that funded research must include both women and members of ethnic minorities (Meinert, 1995; Ruksznis, 1998; L. Sherman et al., 1995).

Some health care projects are specifically designed for women. For example, the Women's Health Initiative is currently studying health problems in older women, using a sample of 164,500 women over the age of 50 (Matthews et al., 1997). In addition, the Canadian Medical Research Council has established the

Canadian Committee for Women's Health Research (Gauthier, 1994). Thousands of women's health centers have also been established throughout North America ("Women's Health Centers," 1997).

None of these measures will instantly correct the neglect that health care professionals have, for centuries, shown toward women. However, women's health problems are now more visible. Health care is one area where feminist concerns have had a clear impact on women's lives.

2. *Gender stereotypes thrive in medicine.* Chapter 2 introduced many of the popular beliefs about men and women. The medical profession remains attached to many of these stereotypes. For example, consider how women are portrayed in the advertisements in medical journals (J. Hawkins & Aber, 1988, 1993). They are more likely than men to be shown without any clothes or with only part of their bodies represented. Also, women are much less likely to be shown in a work setting, and women of color are rarely seen. These misrepresentations encourage the physicians seeing these ads to think of women in a biased fashion.

Some health care policies also contribute to gender stereotypes. For example, consider the right of patients to refuse life-sustaining treatment—informally known as the "right to die." What happens when the patient is so ill that he or she cannot communicate with anyone? In 75% of the cases in which the patient was male, the physician tried to figure out what the individual wanted, based on previous conversations. The equivalent figure for female patients was 14%; instead, the physician typically consulted with women's husbands (S. Miles & August, 1990). According to these data, physicians believe that women are not as mature or as informed as men and therefore cannot make their own decisions.

3. *Medical care provided to women is often inadequate or irresponsible.* Women are sometimes given too much health care, but sometimes they are given too little (Livingston, 1999). Specifically, some surgical procedures are performed too often. We saw in Chapter 10 that cesarean sections are performed too often during childbirth, and we'll see later in this section that hysterectomies are also more common than they need to be. As we noted earlier, women's reproductive systems are emphasized by the medical profession.

However, when we consider diseases that affect both women and men, the women often receive too little health care. For example, women are less likely than men to receive surgical treatment for the same severity of coronary heart disease (Litt, 1998; Stanton, 1995). Women are also less likely than men to receive a kidney transplant, and they are less likely to receive treatment for drug and alcohol abuse (Landrine & Klonoff, 1997; Litt, 1998). The combination of "too much care" and "too little care" means that women often receive inappropriate treatment.

4. *Women are less likely than men in the United States to have adequate insurance.* Specifically, the current U.S. health care system offers the best health care to people who have private insurance provided by employers. Women are at a disadvantage, because they are less likely to be employed full time at the high-

income jobs that offer the best health insurance benefits (Litt, 1998; S. Miles & Parker, 1997). In contrast, women are more likely to have Medicaid insurance, which offers second-class benefits. For example, a large-scale study showed that patients with heart disease were twice as likely to receive bypass surgery if they had private insurance rather than Medicaid (Travis et al., 1995). In summary, the economic inequities we saw in connection with women's employment have widespread consequences. Realistically, health insurance sometimes makes a difference between life and death.

5. *The physician–patient relationship may exaggerate the subordinate status of women in society.* In Chapter 6, we saw that men often interrupt women in ordinary conversations. When the man is a physician and the woman is a patient in a medical setting, the inequity is sometimes worse. Here is a doctor's conversation with a patient who is nervous about the previous pain she had experienced with an intrauterine device (IUD):

Patient: It won't hurt, will it?
Doctor: Oh, I doubt it.
Patient: I'm taking your word [laugh].
Doctor: I haven't had anybody pass out from one yet.
Patient: The last time/
Doctor: [cuts patient off with a joke, both laugh]
Patient: The last time when I had that Lippes Loop, oh God/
Doctor: [interrupts patient] You won't even know what's going on, we'll just
            slip that in and you'll be so busy talking and you won't know it.

(Todd, 1989, p. 47)

By interrupting the patient twice, the doctor never learned that she was concerned about the pain that would persist after the IUD was in place, rather than the pain during insertion.

Some researchers have suggested that physicians' conversational styles may prevent female patients from conveying information and may also impair women's sense of control (Muller, 1990; Todd, 1989). However, one study suggested that patients actually interrupt doctors more than doctors interrupt patients (Irish & Hall, 1995). In addition, this study did not reveal a clear pattern of males interrupting females. We do not yet know what factors influence interruption patterns. However, doctors who interrupt patients may miss information that would be useful for diagnosis and treatment. In addition, inattentive doctors may mistakenly conclude that a physical disorder is a psychiatric condition, "all in the patient's head" (Klonoff & Landrine, 1997; Litt, 1997).

Health Issues for Women in Developing Countries

Many women in other countries do not need to be concerned that they will be treated in a biased fashion by health care professionals, because they will never even meet a physician, a nurse, or any person trained in health care. When resources are scarce, females are especially likely to suffer. In fact, about two-thirds of the women throughout the world live in poverty (Hunter College, 1995). In many developing countries, only the wealthiest women will have access to medical care.

Because women in developing countries usually have inadequate nutrition and health care, they face a relatively high chance of dying as a result of pregnancy or childbirth. For example, a woman living in either Mali or Sierra Leone—two countries in central Africa—stands a 1-in-10 chance of dying during pregnancy or childbirth. The comparable figure for the United States is 1 in about 4,000; for Canada, it's 1 in about 9,000 (Neft & Levine, 1997).

One of the most widely discussed issues related to women's health in developing countries is female genital mutilation. **Female genital mutilation** involves cutting or removing the female genitals. During this procedure, part or all of the clitoris is removed. In some cultures, the labia minora are also removed, and the labia majora are then stitched together. (See Figure 9.1 in Chapter 9.) This more drastic procedure leaves only a tiny opening—sometimes only ¼″ wide—to allow both urine and menstrual blood to pass out of the body (Neft & Levine, 1997; Toubia, 1995; A. Walker & Parmar, 1993).

Some people use the phrase "female circumcision" to refer to female genital mutilation. However, this term is misleading because it suggests a relatively minor operation similar to male circumcision (cutting off the foreskin from the tip of the penis, without damaging the penis). The male equivalent of the more drastic version of female genital mutilation would require removal of all the penis and part of the skin surrounding the testicles (Toubia, 1995).

Throughout the world, an estimated 80 to 114 million girls and women have experienced genital mutilation (Comas-Díaz & Jansen, 1995; Neft & Levine, 1997; Toubia, 1995). Most of these women live in Africa, but some live in the Middle East and Asia. Thousands of these women have emigrated to Canada, the United States, and Europe.

The operation is usually performed when the young girl is between the ages of 4 and puberty. The girl is typically held down by close female relatives. Meanwhile, an older woman from the village performs the operation, often using an unsterilized razor blade, a piece of glass, or a sharp rock (Neft & Levine, 1997). According to people in cultures that practice female genital mutilation, this procedure makes the genitals cleaner. They also believe that the operation reduces sexual activity outside of marriage; indeed, women's sexual pleasure will be reduced because the clitoris has been removed (Neft & Levine, 1997; Robertson, 1996). In countries such as Kenya, the young girls who undergo the mutilation ceremony at the same time are reported to form bonds of solidarity with one another. In other words, the ceremony is more complex than just preparing females for marriage (Robertson, 1996).

The operation is extremely painful. It can also cause severe blood loss and infections (often leading to death), damage to other organs, and difficulty in childbirth (Neft & Levine, 1997; Robertson, 1996; United Nations, 1995).

The World Health Organization and other prominent health groups have condemned the practice of female genital mutilation. The problem has received worldwide attention, and some countries have already reduced the percentage of females who experience genital mutilation (Lancaster, 1998; Robertson, 1996).

Gender Differences in Life Expectancy

Let's now shift our focus to a more general question: What is the life expectancy for women and for men? In the United States, the current average life expectancy is 80 years for women and 73 years for men. The comparable figures in Canada are 81 years for women and 76 years for men (Neft & Levine, 1997). This gender gap in life expectancy is found in all ethnic groups in the United States (Costello & Krimgold, 1998).

Interestingly, social class has a powerful effect on **mortality,** or death rate. For example, Figure 11.1 shows the likelihood of dying in any given year, for both males and females in the United States, who are either White or Black (Pappas et al., 1993). As you can see, males have higher mortality rates for both ethnic groups. However, at the higher income levels, mortality rates are quite similar for both genders and both ethnic groups. At the upper income levels, individuals from all four categories are less likely to live in unsafe environments and to work at risky jobs; they also receive better health care (N. Adler et al., 1994; N. Adler & Coriell, 1997). These data on social class analyzed only White and Black individuals. We don't yet know whether social class is similarly important for other ethnic groups.

If we look at mortality throughout the world, the gender gap is found in virtually every culture (Markides & Miranda, 1997; Neft & Levine, 1997). With remarkable consistency, women live longer than men.

But *why* do women live longer? Some researchers favor biological explanations. For example, females' second X chromosome may protect them from some health problems. Also, female hormones may offer premenopausal women some protection against several major diseases, including heart disease (Crose, 1997; S. Taylor, 1995).

However, research has focused more on gender differences in activities and lifestyles. For example, men are more likely to die from suicide, homicide, and motor vehicle accidents (Crose, 1997; Waldron, 1991). More men are exposed to dangerous substances at work, as in the case with coal miners (Travis et al., 1993). As we'll see later in the chapter, men are currently more likely to die of AIDS.

One important factor that clearly contributes to women's longevity is that women visit their health care providers more often than men do (Crose, 1997; Travis et al., 1993). We saw in earlier chapters that women are somewhat more attuned to emotions and to problems in a relationship. They may also be more sensitive to problems concerning their own health. In contrast, the male gender role encourages men to be physically "tough," rarely complaining about minor

FIGURE 11.1	Annual death rate for male and female Whites and Blacks (as a function of family income). (Source: Pappas et al., 1993)

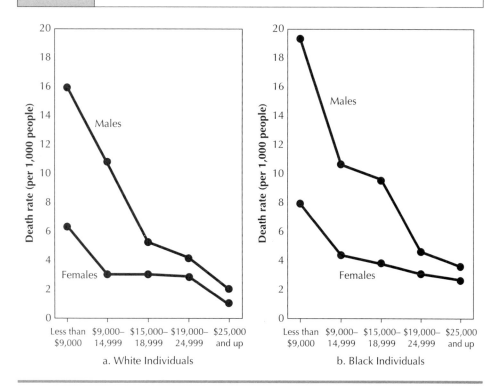

a. White Individuals   b. Black Individuals

symptoms (Leventhal, 1994). Women may be more likely to consult physicians during the early stages of a disease, before it becomes fatal.

Gender Differences in Overall Health

We have seen that women have an advantage with respect to mortality, or death rate. However, women have greater morbidity than men. **Morbidity** is defined as generalized poor health or illness. This means that women are more likely than men to have problems such as obesity, anemia, and respiratory illness. Women are also more likely to experience chronic or lifelong illnesses, headaches, and general fatigue (Furnham & Kirkcaldy, 1997; Morell, 1995b; Stanton, 1995).

Some of this gender difference is easy to explain: 80-year-old women are likely to have health problems related to their age, and most of the 80-year-old men have already died. Some of the difference can probably be traced to the fact that morbidity is usually assessed by self-report (Leventhal, 1994). A woman may be more likely than a man to report that she is bothered by her arthritis.

Some of women's health problems can also be traced to the fact that their incomes are lower than the incomes of men (Rodin & Ickovics, 1990). At least in the United States, economically poor women receive inadequate health care. Other explanations for the gender differences in morbidity are not so obvious. For example, women are the primary victims of rape, and women who have been raped are very likely to experience health problems during the years following the attack (Foa, 1998). In addition, an estimated 1.8 million U.S. women each year are victims of domestic violence (Blumenthal, 1995). In a variety of ways, then, women are more likely than men to experience illness and poor health.

Heart Disease, Breast Cancer, and Other Specific Health Problems

So far, we have seen that gender makes a difference for both mortality and morbidity. Women live longer, but they experience more illness during their lifetime. Let's now examine several specific diseases and health problems that are important in women's lives. The first problem, heart disease, affects women's lives because it is the most common cause of death—though it is also common in men. The other three problems—breast cancer, cancer of the reproductive system, and osteoporosis—are found either exclusively or more frequently in women. Therefore, these diseases need to be examined in our discussion of women's health.

Heart Disease.   Heart disease—also known as **cardiovascular disease**—includes numerous disorders involving the heart and its blood vessels. This year, heart disease will kill about 500,000 women in the United States and about 25,000 in Canada* (Normand, 1995b; Woods & Jacobson, 1997). Many people think that heart disease is a man's illness, but that myth is not correct. Men experience heart disease an average of 10 years earlier than women do, but women run the same risk by the time they reach 60 years of age (Woods & Jacobson, 1997).

What can people do to help prevent heart disease? Some precautions include a diet that is low in cholesterol and saturated fats, maintenance of a reasonable body weight, and regular exercise. As we'll discuss later in the chapter, women who smoke run a high risk of heart disease (Primomo, 1995; Stoney, 1998). In general, women who work outside the home are no more likely than other women to experience heart disease (Stoney, 1998).

---

*For comparison, it is helpful to know that the U.S. population is roughly nine times that of Canada. Notice that heart disease kills a higher proportion of women in the United States than in Canada.

Another more controversial precaution is for postmenopausal women to take hormone replacement therapy. As we'll see in Chapter 14, many women whose estrogen production has dropped may decide to take estrogen after menopause. Estrogen reduces the likelihood of heart problems, but many people argue that estrogen leads to other problems (e.g., an increase in cancer rates). In any event, a sensible diet, exercise, and avoidance of smoking are obvious behavioral precautions that do not have unfortunate side effects.

Breast Cancer.   At the beginning of this chapter, we noted that gender makes a difference in the way certain diseases are viewed. We've just seen that many people don't associate heart disease with women. The one disease in women that receives widespread publicity is breast cancer. Breast cancer is certainly an important problem that requires extensive medical research, and we all know women who have struggled with this disease. Still, health psychologists are uncertain why both medical researchers and the general public focus on breast cancer more than on other illnesses that are actually more dangerous for women (Meyerowitz & Hart, 1995). One likely possibility is that our culture tends to think that breasts are an essential part of being a woman. As a result, a woman

---

DEMONSTRATION 11.1

Thinking about Breast Cancer

Think about and answer the following questions concerned with breast cancer and its relevance in your life.

1. When was the last time you heard or saw a discussion of breast cancer? Was the discussion a general one, or did it provide specific information about how to conduct a breast self-examination or where to go for a mammogram?

2. Have you seen any notice about breast self-examination or mammograms (for example, in public buildings or at the student health service)?

3. If a woman in your home community wanted to have a mammogram, do you know where she would go? (If you don't, call the American Cancer Society at 800-227-2345 to find a nearby location.)

4. Think about several women over the age of 50 whom you value. Have you ever discussed breast cancer or mammograms with any of them? If not, try to figure out how you might raise these issues with them soon, or identify another person who could make certain that these women have had a recent mammogram.

who has had a breast removed—or partly removed—is viewed as being less female (Meyerowitz & Hart, 1995).

Approximately 180,000 women in the United States are diagnosed with breast cancer each year (Carlson et al., 1996; Keeley, 1996). Each year, about 46,000 U.S. women and 4,700 Canadian women will die from breast cancer (Carlson et al., 1996; Normand, 1995b). However, breast cancer is no longer the most deadly cancer for women. With the high rate of women smoking in the 1990s, it's no surprise that 59,000 U.S. women and 4,800 Canadian women die each year from lung cancer (Meyerowitz & Hart, 1995; Normand, 1995b).

Perhaps the most personally relevant statistic is that 1 in 8 women in the United States will develop breast cancer during the course of her lifetime (Travis et al., 1995). Before you read further, however, try Demonstration 11.1.

Regular, systematic breast self-examination seems to be the most important strategy for detecting cancer. Early detection of breast cancer is important because the chances of a cure are greater than 70% if the disease is diagnosed at an early stage (Rowland, 1998). If you are a woman, you should examine your breasts at least once a month, about a week after your menstrual period is over. (Breasts are likely to have normal lumps during menstruation.) Figure 11.2 provides instructions.

Many women are reluctant to examine their breasts, sometimes because they are afraid that they will discover a cancerous lump. In fact, only about 25% to 40% of U.S. women regularly examine their breasts (Keeley, 1996). We should emphasize, incidentally, that roughly 90% of the lumps detected by self-examination are benign (Alexander & LaRosa, 1994). Therefore, finding a lump does not necessarily mean bad news.

Breasts can also be examined using technological methods. For example, a **mammogram** is an X ray of the breast—a picture of breast tissue, taken while the breast tissue is flattened between plastic plates (Love, 1995). Women over the age of 50 should definitely have a screening mammogram every year or two in order to detect lumps that are too small to detect by self-examination. However, health care specialists disagree about screening for women *under* the age of 50 (Ganz, 1998; Mayer, 1998). Some American and Canadian medical organizations recommend a baseline mammogram prior to age 40, followed by regular screening for women between the ages of 40 and 50. However, other organizations advise women to wait until they are 50 (Mayer, 1998).

Unfortunately, most women over the age of 50 do not have regular mammograms, even though this screening procedure is clearly recommended. Women of color have especially low rates for mammogram screening (Royak-Schaler et al., 1997). For example, only about 50% of Asian American women in one study reported having had a mammogram, in contrast to 70% of European American women (Helstrom et al., 1998). Asian American women may be less likely to have mammograms for several reasons. Many do not speak English or do not have health insurance that would cover the cost of the procedure. But perhaps the major reason is that Asian American women are taught from an early age not to discuss topics related to sexuality, so breast cancer is an especially forbidden topic of conversation.

| FIGURE 11.2 | **Performing a breast self-exam (BSE).** **(From the American Cancer Society)** |

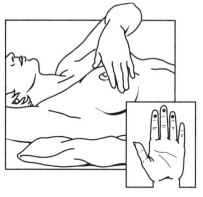

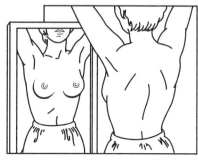

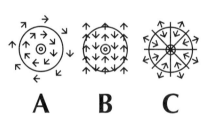

A   B   C

1. Lie down and put a pillow under your right shoulder. Place your right arm behind your head.
2. Use the finger pads of the three middle fingers on your left hand to feel for lumps or thickening. Your finger pads are the top third of each finger.
3. Press hard enough to know how your breast feels. If you're not sure how hard to press, ask your health care provider. Or try to copy the way your health care provider uses the finger pads during a breast exam. Learn what your breast feels like most of the time. A firm ridge in the lower curve of each breast is normal.
4. Move around the breast in a set way. You can choose either the circle (A), the up and down line (B), or the wedge (C). Do it the same way every time. It will help you to make sure that you've gone over the entire breast area, and to remember how your breast feels each month.
5. Now examine your left breast using right hand finger pads.

You might want to check your breasts while standing in front of a mirror right after you do your BSE each month. You might also want to do an extra BSE while you're in the shower. Your soapy hands will glide over the wet skin making it easy to check how your breasts feel.

What happens if breast cancer is detected, either through breast self-examination or a screening mammogram? The most common procedure is currently a **lumpectomy,** a surgical procedure that removes the cancerous lump and the immediately surrounding breast tissue. Radiation may also be used (B. Andersen, 1998).

Naturally, breast surgery causes some fear, grief, depression, and anger. As we noted earlier, women's breasts have special significance in our culture. The treatment cycle may also be both physically painful and difficult, and it is a socially lonely experience (Falco, 1998). As you might expect, women differ widely in their reactions to breast surgery (Royak-Schaler et al., 1997). In addition, women who have had breast surgery are likely to report major fluctuations in their emotions from day to day. For example, Kathlyn Conway (1997) described her reactions after surgery:

> Throughout January, I continue to fluctuate between normal life and desolation. Or perhaps, more accurately, I come to see that normal life holds happy days filled with family, work, and friends interspersed with days when I feel desolate and completely fearful of illness and death. (p. 237)

Fortunately, the majority of women cope well with the stress of surgery and the loss of breast tissue (Rowland, 1998; Schover, 1991). In one study of Black women who were only 2 months postsurgery, 38% reported low spirits or variable moods (Weaver, 1998). However, 62% reported that they were "in very good spirits."

Women often emphasize that the breast cancer experience forced them to clarify their values and to decide where to concentrate their future energies. For example, one woman reported after her surgery, "I'm going to be me. I'm not going to waste time by being someone other than my true self" (McCarthy & Loren, 1997, p. 195). Another commented on her personal transformation, "When you are diagnosed with breast cancer, you become an elder, no matter what your age. Through the events that occur, the decisions you make, the reevaluating and refocusing, you acquire wisdom and strength" (p. 195).

A relatively recent procedure is raising some new issues. As you may have heard, some women with a strong family history of breast cancer have chosen to have both breasts surgically removed in their 30s and 40s, to avoid developing breast cancer at a later time. This procedure does greatly reduce the incidence of breast cancer (Hartmann et al., 1999). However, we know little about the psychological consequences of this surgery. Do these women feel a sense of relief? Do they experience a personal transformation that resembles the reports of the women who have actually experienced breast cancer? We can expect to learn more answers during the next decade; we may also learn whether the genetic basis of breast cancer might have been overstated.

Reproductive System Cancer and Hysterectomies.   Several kinds of cancer often affect women's reproductive systems. These include cancer of the cervix and cancer of the endometrium. Turn back to Figure 4.2, on page 127, to see these structures.

In North America, the death rate from diseases like uterine cancer has dropped sharply in recent years. A major reason is the effectiveness of a screening test called the Pap smear (Cannistra & Niloff, 1996). The **Pap smear test** involves taking a sample of cells from the cervix to see whether they are precancerous or cancerous (Alexander & LaRosa, 1994; Falco, 1998). Gynecologists recommend that all women who are sexually active or who have reached the age of 18 should have an annual Pap smear. These deadly diseases are not limited to older women!

Most European American women have routine Pap smears. However, cancer of the cervix is much more deadly among women of color, who are less likely to have had this screening test. For example, one survey showed that only 55% of all Chinese American women had a Pap smear at some point in their lives, in contrast to an overall rate of 95% for all ethnic groups (Helstrom et al., 1998). Throughout the world, cancer of the cervix is one of the major causes of death, especially because women in developing countries do not have access to Pap smears (Cannistra & Niloff, 1996).

We noted at the beginning of the chapter that gender influences the way a disease is treated and that women's reproductive systems receive more attention than other health concerns. The best example of this principle is the high rate of hysterectomies in North America. A **hysterectomy** is the surgical removal of a woman's uterus (C. Ross, 1996). Some hysterectomies are advisable—for example, when advanced cancer cannot be treated by more limited surgery. However, many surgeons remove a woman's uterus when other less drastic treatments would be effective. As a result, about one-third of all U.S. women can expect to have a hysterectomy at some point in their lifetime (C. Ross, 1996). Women need appropriate information about the alternatives, before making decisions about whether they should have a hysterectomy (Clift, 1994).

The medical profession's casual attitude toward hysterectomies has had tragic consequences for millions of women. Betty J. Smith (personal communication, 1991) wrote about her own surgery in 1977. She had been assured that she needed a hysterectomy because she had solid—but benign—tumors in her uterus. Smith reported:

> What bothers me very much is that prior to my surgery when I questioned my gynecologist about any negative effects a hysterectomy would cause, he assured me that "There's nothing it can do but make you feel a lot better," even though I had told him I felt great.

In fact, the gynecologist removed not only her uterus, but also her healthy ovaries—a common medical procedure. The operation did *not* make her feel better; instead, it led to additional health complications.

Some hysterectomies are medically necessary, and some women who have had hysterectomies experience only minimal psychological or physical symptoms, consistent with our theme of individual differences. However, the medical community needs to examine its policies on this widespread operation. Any woman considering a hysterectomy—or any other surgery—should seek a second opinion.

Another disorder of the reproductive system has not received the attention it deserves. Cancer of the ovaries has the highest rate of death of all gynecological cancers (Falco, 1998). Unfortunately, there is no reliable screening test for this disorder. As a result, 80% of ovarian cancers are not discovered until they are in an advanced stage, and the cancer has spread to other parts of the body (Falco, 1998). Although women's health issues now receive greater attention than in earlier decades, ovarian cancer is one major disease that requires much more research.

Osteoporosis.   In the disorder called **osteoporosis** (pronounced "oss-tee-owe-poe-*roe*-siss"), the bones become increasingly porous and brittle. Women are twice as likely as men to develop this disorder (T. Johnson & Fee, 1997). Osteoporosis is very common among older women, especially postmenopausal women. For example, about half of all women over the age of 45 show some signs of osteoporosis (Fogel & Woods, 1995).

The most common cause of osteoporosis is loss of bone mass following menopause. Osteoporosis makes fractures much more likely, even from just tripping and falling in the kitchen. Hip fractures resulting from osteoporosis create major problems, especially because they are likely to cause a long-term disability (Alexander & LaRosa, 1994).

Because of the dangerous consequences of osteoporosis, women should be encouraged to do regular weight-bearing exercises, such as walking or jogging. Even young women should be certain to take adequate calcium and vitamin D in order to build strong bones, and then to continue this precaution throughout their lives (H. Nelson, 1998).

Some researchers recommend taking medicines (raloxifene, for example) that are designed to prevent osteoporosis (Delmas et al., 1997; Hosking et al., 1998). Others recommend estrogen replacement therapy for postmenopausal women. Estrogen clearly helps the body use calcium to maintain bone density (Delmas et al., 1997)—and it also decreases the risk of heart disease. However, estrogen replacement therapy has drawbacks, as well as advantages. We'll discuss this controversial issue in Chapter 14, in connection with menopause. Still, exercise and good nutrition are precautions that are easy to implement. They offer only advantages—and no drawbacks—in improving women's health.

 The Health Care and Health Status of Women

1. **The psychology of women must include an examination of health issues because women experience different illnesses than men, because gender influences the way a disease is treated, and because illness is an important factor in women's lives.**

2. **Biases against women include the neglect of women in medicine, the prevalence of gender stereotypes, inadequate or irresponsible medical**

`care, inadequate health insurance, and problems in the physician–patient relationship.

3. Women in developing countries often experience inadequate nutrition and health care. Female genital mutilation has jeopardized the health of millions of girls and women.

4. Women in all ethnic groups live longer than men. However, women report more health problems during their lives, so their morbidity is higher.

5. Heart disease is the most common cause of death in women; precautions such as diet and exercise are important.

6. In the United States, about 1 woman in 8 will develop breast cancer in her lifetime, but the chances for survival are high if the cancer is detected soon enough; most women cope surprisingly well with breast cancer.

7. Pap smears are effective in detecting early uterine cancer; hysterectomies may be advisable in some cases, but many are performed without sufficient medical justification. Ovarian cancer is an especially deadly disease.

8. Osteoporosis often leads to bone fractures in postmenopausal women.

WOMEN WITH DISABILITIES

We have seen that gender influences people's health, with respect to both health care and specific diseases. Now let's consider how gender is relevant when we consider individuals with disabilities.

One important theme of this book is that women vary widely from one another. We have already examined some factors that create variability; among them are ethnicity, country of residence, social class, and sexual orientation. Another factor that creates variability is disability.

Disability is defined as a restriction or lack of ability to perform an activity in the manner considered normal (Wendell, 1997). In general, the term "person with a disability" is preferable to "disabled person" (Humes et al., 1995). "Person with a disability" emphasizes someone's individuality first and the disability second. In addition, *disability* is generally preferable to *handicap*, which is a more negative term (Wendell, 1997).

By some estimates, 16% of women in the United States and Canada have disabilities (Bergob, 1995; Wendell, 1997). However, the variation within the disability category is tremendous. As Asch and Fine (1992) pointed out, the term "women with disabilities" is simply a social construct that links together unrelated conditions. In reality, life experiences may be very different for a woman who is blind, a woman who is missing an arm, and a woman who is recovering from a stroke. Still, many people judge individuals with a disability primarily in terms of their disability. As Y. King (1997) remarks, the popular culture assumes that being disabled is what these individuals *do* and *are:* "She's the one in the wheelchair."

The research and writing on disabilities have increased at a rapid rate, so that we now have several books that focus on women with disabilities (e.g., Blackford et al., 1993; L. Davis, 1997; Driedger et al., 1996; D. Dunn, 1994; Epstein, 1997; Ingstad & Whyte, 1995). In addition, the Society for Disability Studies is an organization that takes a multidisciplinary approach toward this growing field (Monaghan, 1998).

When we consider the topic of disabilities, we need to remind ourselves about a unity between women with disabilities and women without disabilities. Many of us do not currently live with a disability. However, every one of us could become disabled in a matter of seconds through an accident, a stroke, or a disease.

Theorists often note that women typically live on the margins of a world in which men occupy the central territory. In many ways, women with disabilities live on the margins of those margins (J. Rubin, 1988; Wendell, 1997). Women of color who have disabilities experience a triple threat, in which they constantly face sexism, racism, and **ableism** (discrimination on the basis of disability). As one woman pointed out, "I am Asian, disabled, and a woman. It's like a triangle. Depending on the issue, one side is up" (K. Martinez & O'Toole, 1991).

But how are disabilities related to gender? Why would the life of a woman with a disability be different from the life of a man with a disability? We will see in the following explorations of work and social experiences that disabilities tend to exaggerate the extent to which women and men are treated differently.

Work Patterns of Women with Disabilities

From an early age, women with disabilities face barriers in preparing for a career. For example, many women recall being shortchanged during childhood. Maria, age 15, reports, "My brother has the same hearing problem as I do. Growing up, he was encouraged in school, sports, and to learn to work. I was protected and kept at home" (Asch & Fine, 1992, p. 146). As Chapter 3 discussed, parents show some tendency to overprotect their daughters. They are even more likely to overprotect daughters with disabilities.

Women with disabilities must overcome additional barriers as they pursue an education. On college campuses, for example, they may be unable to find sign-language interpreters, wheelchair-friendly sidewalks, and other support services (Holcomb & Giesen, 1995). These barriers may keep women with disabilities from pursuing further education. Among Canadian women between the ages of 35 and 54, for example, women with disabilities are only half as likely to have a university degree, compared with women without disabilities (Bergob, 1995).

In both the United States and Canada, men with disabilities are much more likely than women with disabilities to be employed outside the home (Asch & Fine, 1992; Bergob, 1995). Figure 11.3, which is based on U.S. data, shows that the contrast is especially strong in the case of White men with disabilities.

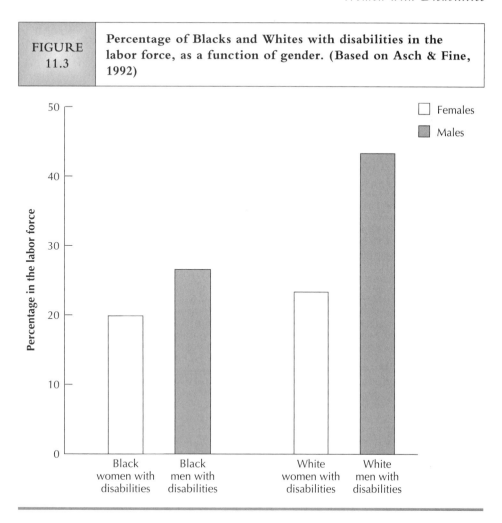

| FIGURE 11.3 | Percentage of Blacks and Whites with disabilities in the labor force, as a function of gender. (Based on Asch & Fine, 1992) |

Notice that they are nearly twice as likely as White women with disabilities to participate in the labor force. Part of the problem is that people with disabilities are likely to face discrimination very early in the hiring process, beginning at the job interview (Marchioro & Bartels, 1994).

Gender and disability combine in unique ways to form barriers against women with disabilities. Consider Mary Runté, for example, who is unable to use her hands. Her boss had not selected her for a project that interested her. (Only male employees had been selected.) She decided to tell her boss that her skills would be useful to the project team:

"I don't know," he said, "it wouldn't be fair to the others on the team to have to compensate for you not being able to perform all the assigned tasks. Besides," he added, "it would be embarrassing for you to have to explain to these people that you can't write. . . ." When I challenged this manager on the blatant fact that the only "task" I couldn't perform would be taking minutes, and that this task was only assigned to one group member, the recorder, he stated he had assumed this would be the role which the other team members would expect me to fill—"the guys hate taking notes."

As I am a woman, it was assumed I would perform the stereotypical role of secretary if assigned to this team. . . . The glass ceiling for a disabled woman turns her office into a crawl space. (Runté, 1998, p. 102)

As you might imagine, women with disabilities often encounter economic difficulties. For example, women with disabilities have average incomes that are only half of the income of men with disabilities (Holcomb & Giesen, 1995). As we noted at the beginning of this discussion, disabilities tend to exaggerate the differential treatment of women and men. Specifically, disabilities increase the male–female wage gap.

These economic difficulties may increase as women grow older. People with low-paying jobs—the clear majority of all women with disabilities—are unlikely to receive adequate retirement benefits. Chapter 14 examines the economic problems of elderly women. These problems are especially severe for elderly women who have disabilities.

In Chapter 7, we discussed the dilemma faced by lesbians in the workplace: Should they come out of the closet and risk discrimination? Should they try to pass, even though this option requires them to hide an important part of their identity? Women with invisible disabilities face a similar dilemma (Hillyer, 1993; Wendell, 1992). For instance, a woman with multiple sclerosis may not look disabled, but she may tire easily or experience numbness or memory problems. Should she tell her boss and risk patronizing comments or job discrimination? Or should she try to hide her disability, risking exhaustion or criticism for being lazy? Chapter 7 examined many biases that employed women face; these problems are intensified for women with disabilities.

Personal Relationships of Women with Disabilities

Throughout the book, we have emphasized how women are judged by their physical attractiveness. By the narrowly rigid standards of attractiveness in North America today, many women with disabilities may be viewed as unattractive (Wendell, 1997). As a consequence, they are likely to be excluded from the social world as well as the employment world (Rintala et al., 1997). Heterosexual women are less likely to date and to marry. Even less is known about the love relationships of lesbian women with disabilities (Asch & Fine, 1992).

Ynestra King (1997) describes an interesting example of this bias against women with disabilities, with respect to romantic relationships. When she is sitting down, her disability is invisible; when she stands up, it's obvious she has difficulty walking. She comments on the reactions in social interactions:

It is especially noticeable when another individual is flirting and flattering, and has an abrupt change in affect when I stand up. I always make sure that I walk around in front of someone before I accept a date, just to save face for both of us. Once the other person perceives the disability, the switch on the sexual circuit breaker often pops off—the connection is broken. "Chemistry" is over. I have a lifetime of such experiences, and so does every other disabled woman I know. (p. 107)

Many people consider women with disabilities to be asexual (Y. King, 1997). As McCormick (1994) points out, "In our culture, sex is viewed as belonging to healthy people who have perfect bodies" (p. 210). Women with disabilities often complain that they do not receive adequate counseling on sexuality (McCormick, 1994).

Furthermore, women's own sexual desires are likely to be ignored. A woman who has a spinal disorder described a conversation she had with a gynecologist prior to her adolescence. She asked whether she would be able to have satisfying sexual relations with a man. He replied, "Don't worry, honey, your vagina will be tight enough to satisfy any man" (Asch & Fine, 1992, p. 160). Apparently, he did not even consider her own sexual satisfaction!

Nonromantic friendships are also difficult. As one woman said, "You're going to have to go more than halfway to make friends" (Fisher & Galler, 1988, p. 176). People without disabilities often feel awkward, not knowing when to help someone who is disabled.

Women who have friends with disabilities will often avoid certain topics of discussion. These censored areas are likely to include sexuality, dating, and childbearing. One woman recalls, for example, how hurt she felt when her best friend in high school—who was not disabled—hid the fact that she had a boyfriend (Fisher & Galler, 1988). Some women with disabilities point out that their friends seem to avoid trying to understand what it's like to live with a disability (Wendell, 1997).

Throughout this book, we have examined how biases can have harmful effects for individuals in a less-favored social group. In addition to women, we have seen how people may be mistreated on the basis of ethnic group and sexual orientation. As disability activists increase their publicity, we will become more informed about this additional kind of discrimination.

SECTION SUMMARY *Women with Disabilities*

1. **Women with disabilities are diverse, yet they share similar discrimination in a society that is both sexist and ableist. Disabilities tend to exaggerate the differential treatment of women and men.**

2. **Women with disabilities may face barriers in education, difficulty in obtaining employment, discrimination on the job, and economic problems.**

3. **Women with invisible disabilities face a dilemma about whether to reveal their disabilities in the workplace.**

4. **Women with disabilities are often excluded from the social world of love relationships, sexuality, and friendships.**

AIDS AND OTHER SEXUALLY TRANSMITTED DISEASES

Any discussion of women's health must examine sexually transmitted diseases. As recently as the 1980s, most people believed that women were unlikely to get the deadly AIDS disease through sexual activity. We now know that thousands of women acquire AIDS each year from their sexual partners. This section will emphasize AIDS, but we will also look at five other sexually transmitted diseases—(1) chlamydia, (2) genital herpes, (3) genital warts, (4) gonorrhea, and (5) syphilis—that have important consequences for the lives of women.

Sexually transmitted diseases are more common than most people believe. For example, an estimated 6 million U.S. women contract a sexually transmitted disease every year. Half of these women are still in their teens (T. Johnson & Fee, 1997). Furthermore, in any given year, almost as many women report a sexually transmitted disease as report that they had been pregnant (Michael et al., 1994).

Women are more vulnerable than men, with respect to sexually transmitted diseases. For example, a woman who has sexual intercourse with an infected man is more than twice as likely to contract any sexually transmitted disease, in comparison with a man who has sexual intercourse with an infected woman (Michael et al., 1994).

Background Information on AIDS

Acquired immunodeficiency syndrome, or **AIDS,** is a viral disease that is spread by infected blood, semen, or vaginal secretions. As of June 1998, an estimated 401,000 U.S. residents had died of AIDS (Centers for Disease Control, 1998). The outlook is even more grim when we consider the situation worldwide. By the year 2000, an estimated 40 million people throughout the world will be HIV-positive (Freiberg, 1998). (For current data and other information related to AIDS, you can call the Centers for Disease Control's National AIDS Hotline at 1-800-342-2437.)

Figure 11.4 shows the increasing number of AIDS deaths among U.S. women since 1991. Ethnicity is also related to the likelihood of an AIDS diagnosis. Specifically, the incidence of AIDS is relatively high among Black women, somewhat lower among Latinas, and equally low among Asian American, Native American, and European American women (Morokoff, Mays, et al., 1997).

Researchers are now using some culturally sensitive interviewing techniques to discover why ethnicity is related to the incidence of AIDS. For example, earlier

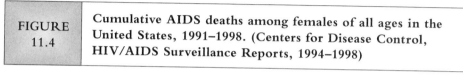

FIGURE 11.4 — **Cumulative AIDS deaths among females of all ages in the United States, 1991–1998. (Centers for Disease Control, HIV/AIDS Surveillance Reports, 1994–1998)**

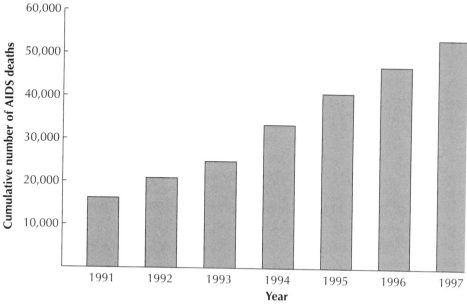

research with Latinas showed that they are well informed about AIDS (Landrine, 1995a). So why should they be more likely than European American women to become infected? Arguello interviewed young, unmarried Latinas in Los Angeles (cited in Landrine, 1995b). She found that these women—especially those who belonged to gangs—were engaging in anal intercourse so that they could still be considered virgins when they would marry several years later. Their Latino boyfriends demanded intercourse, yet Latino men also demand virgins when they marry. Latinas chose anal intercourse as a way to solve the dilemma. Also, the couples did not use condoms during anal intercourse, because condoms were perceived as a birth-control method, not a method for preventing AIDS. This research illustrates the importance of cultural context when we examine issues in the psychology of women.

Let's now consider the medical aspects of AIDS and how the disease is transmitted. Then we'll explore what it's like to live with AIDS and how the disease can be prevented.

Medical Aspects of AIDS

AIDS is caused by a virus called **human immunodeficiency virus (HIV),** which has the potential to destroy part of the immune system. In particular, HIV invades white blood cells and replicates itself. HIV then destroys those white blood cells—the very cells that coordinate the immune system's ability to fight infectious diseases (Kalichman, 1996).

Many HIV-positive individuals have no symptoms at first, and so they do not realize that they are infected. Others develop symptoms such as swollen lymph glands, fatigue, unexplained fevers, and diarrhea (Kalichman, 1996). Both men and women may have these symptoms if they are HIV positive. However, health care providers are more likely to suspect AIDS in males with these symptoms, so men are more likely to receive early treatment. In addition, women who are HIV positive are likely to develop vaginal yeast infections and cervical cancer. However, because the medical community tends to operate from a male-as-normative model, these two gynecological symptoms were not listed among the diagnostic signs of AIDS until recently (Lorber, 1997). As a result, many women did not receive early treatment.

People who are HIV positive are very contagious during the initial stages of the infection, even if they have no symptoms (J. Coffin, 1995; M. Hoffman, 1996). As a result, HIV-positive individuals are likely to spread the disease to other people, without realizing they are doing so.

AIDS is actually the end stage of the HIV infection. AIDS is the illness that occurs when the individual becomes seriously ill because other infections have taken advantage of a severely weakened immune system (Kalichman, 1996). In particular, women are likely to develop cancer and pneumonia (Carlson et al., 1996). These infections can be particularly deadly for people with AIDS, because their immune system no longer works properly. Tragically, once the AIDS diagnosis is established, the life expectancy may be only 2 years (Kalichman, 1996). However, this life-expectancy information is frequently changing for those individuals who can afford the new "drug cocktails." As we saw in Figure 11.1, social class has an important effect on an individual's health.

How AIDS Is Transmitted

Anyone who engages in risky behavior with an infected person can get AIDS. College students report in surveys that they believe they can judge which sexual partners look like they might have HIV infection (S. Williams et al., 1992). Unfortunately, *it is impossible to tell whether a person is infected.* Therefore, any contact with blood, semen, or vaginal secretions is potentially dangerous.

Most women are infected with HIV through using injected drugs or by having vaginal or anal intercourse with a man who is infected (Amaro, 1995). Gay and bisexual men who have had anal intercourse with men without condom protection are at high risk for becoming infected. However, women who have sex only with women—and do not use injected drugs—are at relatively low risk for becoming infected (Mays, 1996).

Living with AIDS

As you might imagine, HIV-positive individuals are likely to experience depression. Anxiety, anger, guilt, and fear are also common (Kalichman & Sikkema, 1994). One woman living with AIDS described her emotions: "I think I live in a state of numb terror. I'm just scared witless" (Huston, 1997, p. 71).

Some people respond to a diagnosis of AIDS with denial (M. Hoffman, 1996). These people are likely to spread the disease even further (S. Taylor et al., 1992).

Many women experience a new perspective on life that is both more hopeful and more tragic. Alicia McWilliams is 36, and she became HIV positive through unprotected sex. She comments:

> I enjoy the simple things in life. I can see the beauty in the sky and the trees. Sometimes I think, "When is my time going to come?" Especially when other people die. Last week I buried a friend. I let people know I'm afraid. Being sick is one of my greatest fears. I know this illness takes people out slow and painfully. (Huston, 1997, p. 17)

People living with AIDS often report that they are stunned by insensitive reactions from other people. For example, doctors may inform patients in an unfeeling way. Karri Stokely recalls how her physician looked down at the floor and told her, "Your HIV test came back positive" (Huston, 1997, p. 46). He instructed her to return to her infectious disease specialist and then ushered her out of the door—without any words of compassion.

However, some women are surprised by the messages of support. For example, Runions (1996) describes how she had left a fundamentalist Christian church some years earlier, when her religious beliefs took her in a different direction. When she went public with her personal story about AIDS, many church members wrote to her. "The letters were warm and accepting and forgiving. Bridges that I thought had been damaged beyond repair appeared to have been strengthened by the shock of my illness" (p. 67).

Preventing AIDS

At present, we have no cure for AIDS, so the only available alternative is to prevent it. Unfortunately, AIDS prevention is difficult, at both the individual and the global levels. An additional problem is that most studies on AIDS-prevention programs do not include women in their sample (Sikkema, 1998).

One problem with AIDS prevention is that most people think, "It can't happen to me!" (Seppa, 1997a). Many people also believe that you can eliminate the possibility of AIDS by asking a potential sexual partner about his or her HIV status. However, a study of HIV-positive individuals revealed that 40% of them had not disclosed their HIV status to their sexual partners (M. Stein et al., 1998). You can probably anticipate another problem. Many people are HIV positive, and they don't know it. So a woman may be having sex with a man who doesn't realize he is HIV positive, or who may not realize that he had sex with an HIV-positive individual two months before. Basically, if a woman decides to have sex, her sexual partner is not only that individual, but all of that individual's former partners . . . and their partners!

DEMONSTRATION 11.2

Strategies for Influencing a Partner to Use a Condom

Below are six strategies that an individual might use to persuade a sexual partner to use a condom. De Bro and her coauthors (1994) asked students to rate how effective each of these persuasion strategies would be, using a 9-point scale. Try to guess the rating assigned to each item by the women in the study (1 = "not at all effective"; 9 = "very effective"). Then repeat the exercise, this time guessing the rating assigned by the men in the study. The answers appear at the end of the chapter.

Rating by Women	Rating by Men	
_____	_____	1. "I would inform my partner that the number of cases of AIDS among heterosexual college students is increasing, so it makes sense to use a condom."
_____	_____	2. "Even though I want to use a condom because I'm worried about sexually transmitted diseases, I'd make up a different reason to tell my partner."
_____	_____	3. "I would just tell my partner that I will make love only if we use a condom."
_____	_____	4. "I would emphasize that my partner's respect for my feelings about using a condom would really enhance our relationship."
_____	_____	5. "I would let my partner know that I would be upset and angry at (him/her) for not wanting to use a condom."
_____	_____	6. "Before my partner had a chance to object to the use of a condom, I would get my partner so 'turned on' that (he/she) would forget about the condom."

(Based on De Bro et al., 1994.)

Condoms can help to limit the spread of the AIDS epidemic (Hein, 1998). However, surveys show that only 5% to 26% of women reported that they always used condoms during sexual intercourse (Morokoff et al., 1997). Some programs try to encourage high-risk female adolescents to urge their sexual partners to use condoms, but these have not been highly successful (Noell et al., 1997; Orr et al., 1996).

In general, college students believe that condoms are a reliable method of protection against pregnancy and sexually transmitted diseases but detract from sexual sensation (S. Campbell et al., 1992). Try Demonstration 11.2 to see how college women and men rated the effectiveness of various strategies for persuading a sexual partner to use a condom (De Bro et al., 1994). Then check page 431 to see whether your judgments were accurate, and which gender differences were significant. Do the results surprise you?

Even regular condom use does *not* guarantee protection against AIDS, because condoms can break or slip off. There is no perfectly safe sex, only *safer* sex. However, a condom is certainly better than no protection at all!

AIDS prevention at the national level must emphasize the use of condoms, even though their use cannot guarantee protection against AIDS. So far, the United States has lagged behind other industrialized countries in encouraging condom use and other AIDS-prevention programs (Hein, 1998).

Any AIDS-prevention program must be sensitive to the culture of the individuals served by the program (Sikkema, 1998). For example, Latino men are especially likely to control decisions about condom use during intercourse. A program designed only for Latina women may therefore be unsuccessful (Raffaelli & Suarez-Al-Adam, 1998). Most programs emphasize developing skills in problem solving and negotiation, as well as the details of condom use (Sikkema, 1998).

Other Sexually Transmitted Diseases

AIDS has attracted far more attention during the current era than all the other sexually transmitted diseases combined. These other diseases are especially important for the psychology of women, however, because women are more likely than men to be infected from a single sexual encounter. Sexually transmitted diseases also produce fewer detectable symptoms in women than in men (Kitasei, 1995). In addition, women also suffer the most severe long-term consequences of the sexually transmitted diseases (Fogel, 1995). For example, many women who do not seek early treatment for these diseases will become infertile (Morell, 1995a). Table 11.1 lists five of these diseases that have particularly important consequences for women's lives. They are **chlamydia** (pronounced, "klah-*mih*-dee-uh"), **genital herpes** ("her-pees"), **genital warts, gonorrhea** ("gon-uh-*ree*-uh"), and **syphilis** ("*siff*-ih-liss").

In the current era, women who are considering a sexual relationship need to worry not only about pregnancy, but also about the very real threat of sexually transmitted diseases. Some of these diseases may simply be uncomfortable or

TABLE 11.1	Sexually Transmitted Diseases (STDs) Other Than AIDS (Based on Fogel, 1995; Kitasei, 1995, Litt, 1997; Milburn & Brewer, 1995; Morell, 1995a)

Disease	Description (in Women)	Consequences
Chlamydia	Most common STD; often no symptoms, but sometimes burning urination and vaginal discharge; curable.	Can lead to infertility; can be passed on to newborn during delivery.
Genital herpes	Painful genital blisters, 5 to 8 attacks/year; can be treated, but not currently curable.	Can be passed on to newborn during delivery.
Genital warts	Caused by the human papilloma virus; small fleshy swellings in the genital area, but often painless; very common among college woman; can be treated, but not currently curable.	Can lead to cervical cancer, which may lead to death.
Gonorrhea	May produce vaginal discharge and pelvic pain, but may not have visible symptoms; usually curable.	Can lead to infertility.
Syphilis	Crater-shaped lesions; may be rash on the body, but may not have visible symptoms.	Can be passed on to newborn during delivery.

painful. However, other diseases may cause recurrent health problems for a woman or potential danger to an infant. Most tragically, a sexual relationship with an individual who has a sexually transmitted disease may literally be deadly.

 SECTION SUMMARY   *AIDS and Other Sexually Transmitted Diseases*

1. **Acquired immunodeficiency syndrome (AIDS) has killed hundreds of thousands of North Americans; the number of cases among women has risen dramatically in recent years.**

2. **AIDS is caused by the human immunodeficiency virus (HIV); people who are HIV positive may be very contagious, but because they may have no symptoms at first, they can be spreading the disease.**

3. **Most women are infected with HIV through using injected drugs or by having vaginal or anal intercourse with an infected man.**

4. **People living with AIDS are likely to be depressed, anxious, angry, guilty, and fearful.**

5. **Currently, AIDS cannot be cured; sexually active people should know that their partners may lie about their HIV status and that condoms do not offer complete protection. AIDS-prevention programs must be sensitive to the culture of the intended audience.**

6. **Other sexually transmitted diseases include chlamydia (which can cause infertility and can be passed on to a newborn), genital herpes (not curable and can be passed on to a newborn), genital warts (which can cause deadly cervical cancer), gonorrhea (which can lead to infertility), and syphilis (which can be passed on to a newborn).**

WOMEN AND SUBSTANCE ABUSE

Substance abuse is an important topic in the psychology of women for the three reasons mentioned at the beginning of the chapter. First, the pattern of substance abuse is somewhat different for women and men, as we'll see shortly. Second, substance abuse is treated differently in men and women. For example, physicians seem to be less effective in identifying problems with alcohol and illegal drugs when the patient is a woman. In addition, the screening tests that are used to identify these problems are based on male norms; they neglect common female problems, such as being a victim of sexual abuse (Wallen, 1998). The final reason that substance abuse is important is that these substances are a common cause of death in women.

Smoking

Cigarette smoking is the largest preventable cause of death in the United States. About 150,000 American women die each year from diseases related to smoking (Gallant & Keita, 1996; Husten, 1998). Lung cancer is the best-advertised consequence of cigarette smoking. As we mentioned earlier, each year, about 46,000 U.S. women and 4,700 Canadian women die from lung cancer (Carlson et al., 1996; Normand, 1995b). For reasons that are not clear, smoking increases the chance of lung cancer more for women than for men (Litt, 1997).

Women who smoke are also more likely than nonsmokers to die of other lung diseases such as emphysema, other cancers (e.g., cancer of the cervix), heart disease, and strokes (Litt, 1997; Pfau et al., 1996). Smoking also has gynecological consequences. Women who smoke run the risk of infertility, miscarriages, premature birth, and early menopause (Litt, 1997; Neft & Levine, 1997). Furthermore, babies born to smokers weigh less than babies born to nonsmokers (Litt, 1997). Older women who smoke also increase their chances of developing osteoporosis (Litt, 1997). You can see why some people say that the tobacco industry is the only business that kills its best customers!

Many nonsmoking women also suffer because of their husband's or partner's smoking habits. For example, women married to men who smoke are about 30% more likely to develop lung cancer than women married to nonsmokers (Fontham et al., 1994; Pfau et al., 1996). Women exposed to passive smoke are almost twice as likely as other women to develop heart disease (Kawachi et al., 1997).

About 24% of women and 28% of men in the United States smoke cigarettes (M. Gold, 1995; Shumaker & Smith, 1995). However, young women are often more likely to smoke than young men. In Canada, for instance, 30% of teenage females and 28% of teenage males are smokers ("Forget the Glamour," 1998). In North America, women will soon be just as likely as men to smoke cigarettes.

Ethnicity has a major effect on smoking rates. According to one estimate, for example, the rates were 33% for Native Americans, 25% for White women, 22% for Black women, 15% for Latina women, and only 8% for Asian American women (Husten, 1998).

Why would young women want to start smoking, given the serious problems associated with smoking? Teenage females often report that they take up smoking in order to control their weight and keep slim (Killen, 1998; L. Phillips, 1998). Interestingly, only 4% of Black females who are seniors in high school are cigarette smokers (Husten, 1998). This impressively low smoking rate may be partly due to the observation that Black female teenagers are less likely than White female teenagers to be obsessed with their weight and physical

---

DEMONSTRATION 11.3

Women in the Cigarette Ads

Between now and the end of the academic term, try to analyze the way that women are represented in the cigarette advertisements. Specifically, can you locate even one advertisement showing a woman who is not slender? Are the women in these ads young or old? What ethnic groups are represented? What are they doing in these ads? What message do these ads present about how cigarettes can improve your social life or your enjoyment of life? During 1998, the ads for Virginia Slims showed women engaged in very gender-stereotypical behavior (e.g., trying to cram piles of clothing into a suitcase), and they all carried the slogan "It's a Woman Thing!"—though they probably don't refer to the death rate from cigarettes. Can you identify any similar themes in the ads you inspect?

appearance (Landrine, 1995b). Young White women are also likely to smoke because they think that smoking makes them look more mature and sophisticated. In contrast, consider a comment from Edwena, a 15-year-old who describes herself as "a together Black woman":

> Smoking's stupid. People be thinking it looks really cool, but me and my friends just think it's stupid. I play basketball and I sing in the chorus, and so I need to be in good shape, and I need to have a clear voice. That's more important to me than looking so-called cool. Nothing cool about killing yourself. (L. Phillips, 1998, p. 25)

In Chapter 2, we saw that advertisers help perpetuate gender stereotypes, and Chapter 12 will show how advertisers also contribute to eating disorders in women. Tragically, cigarette advertisers contribute to the deaths of hundreds of thousands of women by appealing to women's interests in staying slim and looking glamorous. Demonstration 11.3 asks you to analyze the current cigarette ads.

Alcohol Abuse

A 30-year-old woman, reflecting about her life, wrote the following passage:

> I knew I couldn't be an alcoholic. I had a good job and I drank only wine. I certainly don't look like an alcoholic, whatever that look is. It took a long time for me to admit that I really was dependent on that wine. I needed it every day just to dull the world. (Alexander & LaRosa, 1994, p. 67)

In the section on smoking, we saw that women are rapidly catching up with men. However, men are still more likely than women to be diagnosed with alcohol abuse. **Alcohol abuse** is defined as a pattern of alcohol use that leads to significant distress or impairment (O'Connor & Schottenfeld, 1998). Impairment includes missing work or school, arrests for alcohol-related crimes, or family problems. According to U.S. estimates, about 4% of women and 13% of men are alcohol abusers (Blume, 1998).

One symptom of alcohol abuse is **blackouts,** or temporary loss of consciousness. A survey of high school juniors and seniors showed that 26% of females and 33% of males had experienced one or more blackouts (Windle et al., 1996). Ironically, well-educated women are more likely to be moderate or heavy drinkers, in comparison to women who have had less than an eighth-grade education (Alexander & LaRosa, 1994).

Problems Caused by Alcohol.   Alcohol directly affects women's health. For example, women who consume at least two drinks a day seem to double their chances of breast cancer, in contrast to nondrinkers (Wilsnack, 1995). Other health consequences of alcohol include liver problems, ulcers, brain damage, high blood pressure, and various cancers (Thun et al., 1997; Vogeltanz & Wilsnack, 1997). Children born to alcoholic mothers are likely to have **fetal alcohol syndrome,** which is characterized by facial abnormalities, retarded physical growth, and mental retardation (M. Jenkins & Culbertson, 1996).

Alcohol also has indirect effects on women's health. For example, alcohol is a contributing factor in about 19,000 U.S. automobile fatalities each year. Alcohol abuse also increases the number of deaths from drowning, fires, violent crimes, and suicide (Brake, 1994; Rivers, 1994). In fact, alcohol kills more than five times as many people every year as all illegal drugs combined (Royce & Scratchley, 1996).

Gender and Alcohol.   Most people think that alcoholism is a male problem (Vogeltanz & Wilsnack, 1997). In this case, the stereotype is partially correct in the United States, where men are about three times more likely than women to be alcohol abusers (Blume, 1998).

Studies on college campuses also reveal more males than females who abuse alcohol, though the gender difference is not enormous. For example, Wechsler and his coauthors (1994) collected survey data from 17,592 students at 140 representative colleges throughout the United States. One of the most striking findings was the large percentage of students who engaged in **binge drinking**—defined as four or more drinks in a row for females, and five or more drinks in a row for males—during the preceding two weeks. (The researchers specified fewer drinks for women because their body weight is generally lower.) The results showed that 50% of the males and 39% of the females could be categorized as binge drinkers. In addition, binge drinking was less common at women's colleges and at historically Black institutions. Now answer the questions in Demonstration 11.4.

Wechsler and his colleagues (1994) also included items that assessed the behavioral consequences of drinking. Specifically, those who frequently binged were likely to report doing something they later regretted, or engaging in unplanned sexual activity.

As we have seen from general surveys, males report greater problems with alcohol abuse. Males are also more likely than females to report that they consumed alcohol at some point during their lives (Windle et al., 1996). However, ethnicity has an impact on the size of this gender difference. For example, among European Americans and Native Americans, gender differences are small. In contrast, men are significantly more likely than women to consume alcohol among Blacks, Latinas/os and Asian Americans (Windle et al., 1996). Cultural norms in some ethnic groups specify that women should not consumer much alcohol (McCaul, 1998).

In discussing gender and alcohol, we need to expand on a topic mentioned at the beginning of this chapter. Research shows that, when a male and a female with the same body weight consume the same amount of alcohol, the woman will have a significantly higher blood alcohol level (J. Hamilton & Yonkers, 1996; Haseltine, 1997). This means that a 150-pound woman who drinks 2 ounces of whiskey will have a higher blood alcohol level than a 150-pound male

DEMONSTRATION 11.4

Alcohol Consumption and Its Behavioral Consequences

Answer each of the following questions as accurately as possible.

1. Think about your behavior during the last two weeks. How many times have you had four or more drinks in a row if you are female, or five or more drinks in a row if you are male? (The operational definition of a "drink" is 12 ounces of beer or a wine cooler, 4 ounces of wine, or 1.25 ounces of liquor.) _____

2. Since the beginning of this school year, how many times have you personally experienced each of the following problems as a consequence of drinking alcohol?

_____ a. Had a hangover

_____ b. Missed a class

_____ c. Fallen behind in schoolwork

_____ d. Done something you later regretted

_____ e. Forgotten what you did

_____ f. Argued with friends

_____ g. Had unplanned sexual activity

_____ h. Failed to use protection when you had sex

_____ i. Damaged property

_____ j. Gotten into trouble with campus or local police

_____ k. Got injured or hurt

_____ l. Required medical treatment for an alcohol overdose

(Based on Wechsler et al., 1994.)

friend who drinks 2 ounces of the same whiskey. In other words, women need to be more careful than men about limiting their alcohol consumption.

Gender differences are also relevant when people seek treatment for alcohol problems. Families are more likely to deny that female family members have a problem with alcohol (Blume, 1998; Vogeltanz & Wilsnack, 1997). Physicians are also more likely to identify problem drinking in male patients than in female patients (Wilsnack, 1995). In addition, society disapproves more strongly if a woman—rather than a man—gets drunk at a party. Women may therefore be more reluctant to admit they have a drinking problem (Vogeltanz & Wilsnack, 1997). Consistent with Theme 2, people react differently to male alcohol abusers than to female alcohol abusers.

Other Substance-Abuse Problems

Smoking and alcohol abuse are the two most common forms of substance abuse, but women also abuse other substances—prescription medicines, for example. Women are more likely than men to use sedatives and tranquilizers (Carlson et al., 1996; McCaul, 1998). These drugs are socially acceptable—after all, a doctor prescribes them! On page 399, for example, we noted that health professionals often give women too much medical attention. In this case, they may be prescribing mind-altering medication to women who don't really need these drugs.

When we consider illicit drugs, however, the picture changes, because men are more likely to use these drugs. For example, a U.S. nationwide survey showed that 42% of men and 32% of women reported using an illegal drug at some time in their life (McCaul, 1998). These drugs included marijuana, cocaine, crack, heroin, and LSD. Men are also about twice as likely as women to abuse cocaine and heroin (Greenfield, 1996).

Consider some recent trends in the use of illegal drugs. For example, the National Center on Addiction and Substance Abuse (1996) reviewed more than 1,700 studies on drug use and concluded that females between the ages of 12 and 18 are just as likely as males to use illegal drugs. In other words, substances such as cocaine and heroin are quickly becoming "equal opportunity destroyers."

Another trend that would surprise many people is that European American women are more likely than Black or Latina women to have tried illegal drugs at some point in their lives (McCaul, 1998). Also, high school students are more likely to have tried illegal drugs if they are enrolled in private schools, rather than public schools, and if their parents have either college or graduate degrees, rather than being less educated (Alderman & Friedman, 1995). In contrast to the typical stereotype, then, a young woman who is experimenting with drugs is likely to be a young European American female from a relatively wealthy family.

In addition to the direct medical consequences of these illegal drugs for women, we much consider the medical problems of babies born to pregnant drug users (Gallant & Keita, 1996). Furthermore, women who use heroin or other injectable drugs increase the risk of AIDS.

Women may also metabolize illegal drugs differently than men do, but little research has been conducted on this topic. In addition, few substance-abuse programs are designed to help women (Chrisler & Hemstreet, 1995; S. Hall, 1998; Litt, 1997). Once again, women at risk for health problems are considered to be invisible, and their health needs are ignored.

In this chapter, we have examined several health issues that are central in women's lives. We began by considering general health care issues, showing that women are often second-class citizens in the United States. Women in developing countries face the risks of poor health care, complications during pregnancy, and female genital mutilation. We also saw that women with disabilities face exaggerated discrimination. Finally, women in the current era are increasingly likely to contract AIDS and other sexually transmitted diseases, and to have problems with smoking, alcohol, and illegal substances. Feminist concerns have increased the visibility of women's health problems. Meanwhile, however, many of women's health concerns receive little attention.

 **Women and Substance Abuse**

1. **In the current era, women are almost as likely as men to smoke cigarettes, a problem that has widespread consequences for the women's health.**

2. **Women are still less likely than men to be alcohol abusers, but female abusers face the risks of health problems for themselves and fetal alcohol syndrome for their children.**

3. **People are more likely to ignore alcohol problems in females than in males.**

4. **Women are more likely than men to use prescription drugs. In general, men are more likely than women to use illegal drugs, but drug-use patterns are similar among male and female adolescents.**

CHAPTER REVIEW QUESTIONS

1. The beginning of this chapter examined gender comparisons in mortality, morbidity, and use of the health care system. Summarize this information and describe how these factors may be interrelated.

2. One of the themes of this book is that men and women are treated differently. How can this theme be applied to the information in the sections on biases against women in health care, on women with disabilities, and with respect to identifying specific diseases?

3. What are some of the specific health problems that women are likely to face, and how can women reduce the chances of developing these life-threatening diseases? What are other serious problems for women who smoke or abuse alcohol?

4. What is a disability, and how do women with disabilities differ from one another? In what ways does the life of a woman with a disability differ from the life of a woman who is not disabled?

5. What is AIDS, how is it transmitted, and why should sexually active women be concerned about this disease? Name and describe five other sexually transmitted diseases.

6. Alexander and LaRosa (1994) point out that the sexually transmitted diseases are biologically sexist. What do they mean by this statement? How does this statement also apply in substance abuse?

7. Imagine that you are counseling a high school female about preventing AIDS, avoiding smoking, and preventing alcohol abuse. What arguments would you use?

8. How is social class relevant when we consider health care, mortality, the life expectancy for people with AIDS, and substance abuse? How is ethnicity relevant when we consider women in developing countries, women's life expectancy, AIDS, and substance abuse?

9. Explain why gender comparisons are complicated when we consider the topic of substance abuse. Prior to reading the section on substance abuse, what did you believe about gender comparisons in this area?

10. One theme of this book is that women are relatively invisible. Relate this theme to topics such as the general research on women's health, as well as specific research on women with disabilities and on women with substance-abuse problems. In what areas are women unusually *visible?*

NEW TERMS

health psychology (397)
female genital mutilation (401)
mortality (402)
morbidity (403)
cardiovascular disease (404)
mammogram (406)
lumpectomy (408)
Pap smear test (409)
hysterectomy (409)
osteoporosis (410)
disability (411)
ableism (412)
acquired immunodeficiency syndrome
  (AIDS) (416)

human immunodeficiency
  virus (HIV) (418)
chlamydia (421)
genital herpes (421)
genital warts (421)
gonorrhea (421)
syphilis (421)
alcohol abuse (425)
blackouts (425)
fetal alcohol syndrome (425)
binge drinking (426)

RECOMMENDED READINGS

Blechman, E. A., & Brownell, K. D. (Eds.). (1998). *Behavioral medicine and women: A comprehensive handbook.* New York: Guilford. I'm extremely enthusiastic about this handbook, which contains 141 short chapters on topics such as gender bias, disease prevention, specific diseases common among women, and substance abuse.

Carlson, K. J., Eisenstat, S. A., & Ziporyn, T. (1996). *The Harvard guide to women's health.* Cambridge: Harvard University Press. I'd recommend this guide to any woman who wants a professional—but readable—resource to consult regarding her personal health.

Davis, L. J. (Ed.). (1997). *The disability studies reader*. New York: Routledge. Here's an excellent introduction to the interdisciplinary area of disability studies, with essays from historical, biological, psychological, and literary perspectives.

Gallant, S. J., Keita, G. P., & Royak-Schaler, R. (Eds.). (1997). *Health care for women: Psychological, social, and behavioral influences*. Washington, DC: American Psychological Association. I strongly recommend this volume, which contains chapters on women's general health, specific diseases, sexually transmitted diseases, and substance abuse.

Huston, R. (1997). *A positive life: Portraits of women living with HIV*. Philadelphia: Running Press. This book introduces us to women from many ethnic groups and economic backgrounds who are HIV positive. The photos of these women in their homes—often surrounded by family members—make this book especially moving.

ANSWERS TO
DEMONSTRATION 11.2

For each item, the average rating supplied by women is listed first, and the average rating supplied by men is listed second: 1. 7.0, 5.9; 2. 6.6, 6.6; 3. 7.6, 6.5; 4. 6.2, 5.7; 5. 4.5, 4.4; 6. 4.8, 6.1.

Also, the gender differences were significant for items 1, 3, 4, and 6.

ANSWERS TO THE
TRUE–FALSE QUESTIONS

1. False (p. 398); 2. False (p. 399); 3. False (p. 401); 4. True (pp. 402–403); 5. True (p. 404, p. 406); 6. True (p. 413); 7. False (p. 418); 8. False (p. 422); 9. True (p. 426); 10. True (p. 422, p. 428).

Women and Psychological Disorders

CHAPTER 12

Depression
Characteristics of Depression
Explanations for the Gender
Difference in Depression

Anxiety Disorders
Specific Phobias
Agoraphobia

**Eating Disorders and Related
Problems**
Anorexia Nervosa
Bulimia Nervosa
The Emphasis on Being Slim
Being Overweight and Dieting

**Treating Psychological
Disorders in Women**
Psychotherapy and Sexism
Psychotherapy with Women
of Color
Traditional Therapies and
Women
Gender-Sensitive Therapy

TRUE OR FALSE?

_____ 1. Men are more likely than women to experience a psychological disorder that is characterized by lying, aggressiveness, and other antisocial behavior.

_____ 2. Women in North America are two to three times more likely than men to suffer from major depression; in other cultures, the gender differences are minimal.

_____ 3. When a distressing event has happened, women are more likely than men to think about their emotions and about the causes and consequences of that event.

_____ 4. Women are about twice as likely as men to suffer from social phobias, or excessive fear of social situations.

_____ 5. Approximately 80% of people who have specific fears—such as a fear of the dark—are female.

_____ 6. People with anorexia nervosa are underweight, and they experience several physical problems; however, they are otherwise fairly well adjusted.

_____ 7. Contrary to popular opinion, media images do not seem to encourage eating disorders.

_____ 8. Black women are typically more satisfied with their bodies than are European American women.

_____ 9. People of color are less likely than European Americans to use mental health services.

_____ 10. Feminist therapy emphasizes that power should be fairly evenly distributed between the therapist and the client.

Individuals with **psychological disorders** have emotions, thoughts, and behaviors that are typically maladaptive, distressing to themselves, and different from the social norm. Consider the following self-description, which was provided by a woman experiencing major depression:

> I just feel sort of discouraged. . . . Nothing seems worthwhile any more. It seems as if all that was beautiful has lost its beauty. I guess I expected more than life has given. It just doesn't seem worthwhile going on. I can't seem to make up my mind about anything. . . . I am just no good. I am a failure. I was envious of other people. I didn't want them to have more than I had and when something bad happened to them I was glad . . . I am a miserable failure. . . . There is no hope for me. (Carson & Butcher, 1992, p. 390)

Many women throughout the world experience maladaptive, depressing thoughts like these. As we'll see in this chapter, women are more likely than men to suffer from depression, certain anxiety disorders, and eating disorders. They are also more likely to seek therapy for these problems.

Men are more likely than women to experience other problems. We saw in Chapter 11 that men are currently more likely than women to abuse alcohol and other drugs. Men are also more likely than women to have **antisocial personality disorder,** which is characterized by a variety of antisocial behaviors, including lying, impulsiveness, and aggressiveness (American Psychiatric Association, 1994). People with this disorder violate the rights of other people. They also believe that they are perfectly well adjusted and that the rest of the world has a problem.

If we compile overall tallies—and include all individuals with substance-abuse problems and antisocial personality disorder—then the incidence of psychological disorders in women and men is roughly similar (Russo & Green, 1993). Keep in mind, however, that the kinds of disorders may differ.

In this chapter, we will focus on three categories of disorders that are more common among women than men. Depression is our first topic because this disorder affects the largest number of women. We will also examine two other fairly common psychological problems: anxiety disorders and eating disorders. Finally, we will investigate both traditional and nontraditional approaches to treating psychological disorders.

DEPRESSION

The woman whose self-description appears in the introduction to this chapter is suffering from major depression. A person with **major depression** has frequent episodes of hopelessness and low self-esteem; this person seldom finds pleasure in any activities (American Psychiatric Association, 1994).

In North America, women are two to three times more likely than men to experience depression during their lifetime (Culbertson, 1997; R. Kessler et al., 1994; Weissman & Olfson, 1995). Interestingly, no consistent gender differences in depression are found among young children. However, around the time of puberty, females begin reporting more depressive symptoms than males. This gender difference continues throughout the life span (Nolen-Hoeksema & Girgus, 1995).

Gender differences in depression rates hold for White, Black, and Latina women in the United States (Russo & Green, 1993). Research in Canada shows gender differences for people from all ethnic backgrounds, including British, European, and Asian ethnicities (K. L. Dion & Giordano, 1990; Franks & Faux, 1990). Finally, cross-cultural studies report that women are more likely than men to experience depression in countries as varied as Sweden, Lebanon, Korea, Germany, Uganda, and New Zealand (Culbertson, 1997; Frodi & Ahnlund, 1995; Weissman & Olfson, 1995). Let's consider some of the characteristics of depression and then examine some explanations for the higher incidence of depression in women.

Characteristics of Depression

Depression is a disorder that includes emotional, cognitive, behavioral, and physical symptoms (American Psychiatric Association, 1994; Carlson et al., 1996):

1. *Emotional symptoms:* feeling sad, gloomy, tearful, guilty, apathetic, irritable, and unable to experience pleasure.

2. *Cognitive symptoms:* thoughts of inadequacy, worthlessness, helplessness, self-blame, and pessimism; these depressed thoughts interfere with normal functioning, so that the individual has trouble concentrating and making decisions.

3. *Behavioral symptoms:* decreased ability to do ordinary work, neglected personal appearance, decreased social contacts, and sleep disturbance. Many individuals attempt suicide. In general, women are more likely than men to attempt suicide, but men are more likely to die from suicide (Canetto & Lester, 1995a, 1995b).

4. *Physical symptoms:* illnesses such as indigestion, headaches, dizzy spells, fatigue, and generalized pain. Weight gain or weight loss is also common.

We should emphasize that most people have occasional episodes of extreme sadness. For example, this sadness is considered normal when a close friend or family member dies. However, these symptoms normally do not continue many years after the loss. Women with major depression struggle with persistent depression, without relief. They are also likely to have other problems discussed in this book, such as substance abuse, anxiety, and eating disorders (Craighead & Vajk, 1998; Joiner & Blalock, 1995). These additional problems, in turn, make the depression even more intense.

There is no "typical" depressed woman. However, some characteristics tend to be associated with depression. For example, a woman is more likely to be depressed if she has several young children in the home or if her income is low (Fishel, 1995; A. Olson & DiBrigida, 1994; Russo, 1990). As you might imagine, women who are unhappily married are more likely than happily married women to be depressed (Fincham et al., 1997).

Personality characteristics are also important. The following factors are especially likely to be correlated with depression: (1) low self-esteem; (2) low sense of personal accomplishment; (3) traditional feminine gender typing; (4) little sense of control over one's own life (L. Allen et al., 1996; Russo et al., 1993; Thornton & Leo, 1992).

Explanations for the Gender Difference in Depression

What are some of the explanations for the prevalence of depression among women? Let's begin with some explanations that were once thought to be important but no longer seem relevant. Then we will examine a much longer list of factors that do seem to contribute to the gender differences in depression.

Factors No Longer Considered Relevant.   Several decades ago, many theorists believed that gender differences in biological factors could explain why women are more likely than men to be depressed. For example, perhaps the gender differences could be traced to biochemical components, hormonal fluctuations, or some genetic factor combined with X chromosomes. However, careful reviews of the literature suggest that biological factors cannot explain the greater prevalence of depression in women (Fivush & Buckner, 1999; Sprock & Yoder, 1997).*

---

*Researchers have established that biological factors can predispose individuals to develop depression. However, males and females are similarly affected by these biological factors. For example, women are no more likely than men to have a genetic background associated with depression.

Maybe you've thought about another potential explanation. Chapter 11 pointed out that women are more likely than men to seek medical help. Is it possible that women and men are equally depressed, but women are simply more likely to seek help from a therapist? In answer, studies of the general population—rather than of people who consult therapists—show that women are indeed much more likely than men to be depressed (Gater et al., 1998; Sprock & Yoder, 1997).

Let's now consider some of the explanations that are currently thought to account for the gender differences in depression. As we frequently observe in psychology, human behavior is so complex that a single explanation is usually inadequate (Matlin, 1999). *All* of the following factors probably help to explain why the rate of depression is so much higher in women than in men.

Diagnostic Biases in Therapists.   The most recent summaries of the research suggest that therapists are somewhat likely to *overdiagnose* depression in women (Sprock & Yoder, 1997). That is, therapists are more likely to supply a diagnosis of major depression in women, compared to men with similar psychological symptoms. At the same time, therapists are somewhat likely to *underdiagnose* depression in men (Sprock & Yoder, 1997). That is, therapists are guided by their stereotypes about men being "tough," so they are reluctant to conclude that men have depression. In addition, men may try to disguise their depression by drinking excessively, so therapists may miss the appropriate diagnosis of depression ("Mood Disorders," 1998; Wolk & Weissman, 1995). Therapist bias is a greater problem than we had previously thought. However, a large number of other factors also contribute to the very real gender difference in depression.

General Discrimination Against Women.   Several forms of discrimination seem to increase the incidence of depression in women (Burt & Hendrick, 1997; Landrine & Klonoff, 1997; Nolen-Hoeksema & Girgus, 1995). In earlier chapters, we noted that women experience general discrimination and that their accomplishments are often devalued, relative to those of men. Furthermore, Chapter 7 showed that women are less likely to be hired and promoted in the workplace. In many cases, women's work is also less rewarding and prestigious.

Poverty.   People with economic problems are especially likely to have high levels of depression (Fishel, 1995; Woods et al., 1999). We can understand why an unemployed woman who is trying to support three young children—with no assistance from a husband who has deserted the family—should experience depression. In fact, the real question may be why so many women who have economic problems are *not* depressed!

Housework.   Women who choose a traditional role as a full-time homemaker are likely to find that their work is unstimulating and undervalued. On the other hand, women who work outside the home often have the equivalent of two jobs.

We saw in Chapter 7 that most women thrive when they are employed. However, some women who become overwhelmed with housework—in addition to a job—may develop depression (Nolen-Hoeksema, 1990; Wu & DeMaris, 1996).

To examine the relationship between housework and depression, Golding (1990) surveyed more than 1,000 Mexican American and European American women in the Los Angeles area. Among other items, she included questions about housework and depressive symptoms. For both groups of women, the amount of housework contributed to household strain, which in turn was re-

---

DEMONSTRATION 12.1

Responses to Depression

Suppose that a recent personal event has put you in a depressed mood (e.g., an unexpectedly low grade on an exam, the breakup of a love relationship, or a quarrel with a close friend or relative). Check which of the following activities you are likely to engage in when you are depressed.

_____ 1. Working on a hobby that takes concentration

_____ 2. Writing in a diary about how you are feeling

_____ 3. Getting away from everyone else to try to sort out your emotions

_____ 4. Doing something with your friends

_____ 5. Getting drunk

_____ 6. Telling friends about how depressed you are

_____ 7. Punching something

_____ 8. Engaging in sports

_____ 9. Writing a letter to someone describing your emotions

_____ 10. Engaging in reckless behavior (e.g., driving 10 miles over the speed limit)

_____ 11. Listening to music

_____ 12. Making a list of the reasons you are sad or depressed

When you have finished, count up how many of your responses fall into the first group: Items 2, 3, 6, 9, 11, and 12. Then count up the number that fall into the second group: Items 1, 4, 5, 7, 8, and 10. The results are discussed in the text.

(Based on Nolen-Hoeksema, 1990.)

lated to depressive symptoms. In short, gender inequities in housework may contribute to the higher rate of depression among women.

Emphasis on Physical Appearance.   Beginning in adolescence, some young women become excessively concerned about their physical appearance. As we'll see in the section on eating disorders, adolescent females often resent the weight they gain during puberty. They may find their changing body shape especially unappealing in an era when female fashion models are so painfully thin. This dissatisfaction may contribute to depression (Fredrickson & Roberts, 1997; Nolen-Hoeksema & Girgus, 1995). At this point, try Demonstration 12.1 before you read further.

Violence.   As Chapter 13 will emphasize, many women are the targets of violence. Women face sexual harassment at school and at work. They may be physically abused by their boyfriends or husbands. And a large number of women are raped, by men they know or by men who are strangers. The stress of violence clearly contributes to depression (Fishel, 1995; Nolen-Hoeksema, 1995). Unfortunately, however, this factor is often underemphasized in discussions of female depression and other psychological disorders.

An adolescent woman wrote the following account:

> I am fifteen years old, and last summer I was raped by the closest friend of my boyfriend. I did not consider it rape at the time, because I knew the guy relatively well, and I didn't think you were raped by your "friends." I felt like a whore and a piece of trash, but worse than that I felt used. I felt that I had no one to turn to for help, or even someone that I could tell. It was all because I felt I had done something to make him want to have sex with me. (Thom, 1987, p. 222)

Not surprisingly, women are likely to feel depressed and anxious during the months after they have been raped. Once again, the real question may be why so many women who are victims of violence manage to escape the symptoms of depression.

Women's Relationships.   Men are more likely than women to say that their spouses understand them and bring out their best qualities (McGrath et al., 1990). In other words, women typically give more social support than they receive in a marital relationship.

In addition, many women may become overly involved in the problems of their friends and family members. We saw in Chapter 5 that women sometimes have closer relationships with their friends than men do. Some theorists (e.g., Jordan, 1997) have argued that these intimate friendships are a source of empowerment and strength for women. However, other theorists and researchers have argued that women may become overinvolved with others' problems, so that they actually neglect their own needs (Fritz & Helgeson, 1998; V. S. Helgeson & Fritz, 1998; Westkott, 1997).

Responses to Depression.   So far, we have noted that a number of factors make depression more likely in women than in men. Therapists may overdiagnose depression in women. In addition, many factors—general discrimination, poverty, housework, concern about physical appearance, violence, and interpersonal relationships—predispose women toward depression.

Several researchers have pointed out one other factor that encourages depression: Women often respond differently than men when they are experiencing a depressed mood. Demonstration 12.1 focused on responses to depression.

Susan Nolen-Hoeksema is the major researcher on responses to depression. She proposed that when women are depressed, they are more likely than men to turn inward and focus on their symptoms. They contemplate the possible causes and consequences of their emotions, an approach called a **ruminative style** of response. Research confirms that women are significantly more likely than men to use ruminative strategies when they are depressed (Nolen-Hoeksema, 1990; Nolen-Hoeksema & Girgus, 1994).

Another approach to depression, called a **distracting style** of response, focuses on distracting oneself from sad emotions through some sort of activity. Nolen-Hoeksema (1990) had originally argued that men use this distracting style more often than women. However, more recent research suggests that men and women are equally likely to use distracting strategies (Nolen-Hoeksema et al., 1993; Strauss et al., 1997).

Furthermore, Nolen-Hoeksema proposes that rumination prolongs and intensifies a bad mood. Rumination tends to create a negative bias in people's thinking, so that predominantly pessimistic ideas come to mind. People are more likely to blame themselves and to feel helpless. This pessimistic style increases the likelihood of more long-term, serious depression. We also saw in the previous section that women often worry about other people's problems. Women who tend to ruminate about all these problems often make their depressed mood even worse.

Now look at your responses to Demonstration 12.1. Naturally, no 12-item questionnaire can provide an accurate assessment of your style of responding to depression. However, if you checked more items in the first group, you may tend to have a ruminative style. In contrast, if you checked more items in the second group, you may tend to have a distracting style. If you checked item 1, 4, or 8, your distracting style may help lift you out of a depressed mood. However, if you checked item 5 or 10, you should be concerned about maladaptive responses to depression. Those responses may not encourage depression, but your response style could endanger yourself and others.

Nolen-Hoeksema (1990) provides advice for those of you who have a ruminative style. The next time you are depressed, think briefly about the problem, and then do some activity that takes your mind away from your emotions. Wait until your depressed mood has lifted somewhat; only then, begin to analyze the situation that made you depressed. When you are less depressed, you will be able to think more clearly about the problem, and pessimistic ideas won't come to mind so readily. However, if your depression persists, you should seek help from a therapist.

Conclusions About Gender and Depression.   Therapists may be able to help women readjust their ruminative style, so that they can distract themselves temporarily from their depression. But look at the other sources of gender difference, such as poverty, workload, and violence. These problems of our society cannot be typically addressed by therapists working one-on-one with their clients. People who are genuinely concerned about depression in women must pressure elected officials and join organizations that are publicizing these issues. If social inequities created the depression problem, then we must work to change these inequities.

As Hare-Mustin and Marecek (1997) indicate, many current psychologists and psychiatrists place too much emphasis on biological factors that reside inside each person; they de-emphasize society's contributions. When they treat depression, they simply prescribe an antidepressant such as Prozac, rather than addressing the problems in society. This shifting focus parallels the ascendance of conservative politics in the United States. For example, we saw in Chapter 7 that the U.S. Government's policy on welfare has changed. Poverty is now the people's problem—in reality, women's own problem—rather than a societal problem that the government should try to correct. However, to address psychological problems, we must acknowledge that the problems occur in a social context and are intertwined with the other gender inequities discussed throughout this textbook.

 Depression

1. **Women are more likely than men to suffer from depression, certain anxiety disorders, and eating disorders; men are more likely to have problems with substance abuse and antisocial personality disorder.**

2. **Depression is two to three times more common in women than in men; this gender difference has been reported in a variety of ethnic groups in North America and also in many other countries.**

3. **Depression includes feelings of sadness and apathy, thoughts of inadequacy and pessimism, decreased performance, a potential for suicide attempts, and physical complaints.**

4. **Depression is more likely if a woman has young children in the home, a low income, an unhappy marriage, and personality characteristics such as low self-esteem.**

5. **The gender differences in depression cannot be explained by differences in biological predisposition or by women's being more likely to seek therapy.**

6. **Some likely explanations for gender differences in depression include therapists' diagnostic biases, general discrimination, poverty, housework, emphasis on physical appearance, violence, personal relationships, and ruminative responses to depression. Attempts to reduce depression in women must emphasize these societal problems.**

ANXIETY DISORDERS

A second category of psychological problems that occurs more often for women than for men is called anxiety disorders. Most of us feel anxious in certain situations. If you are facing a test for which you are unprepared, or if you are speaking in front of a large group of strangers, it's reasonable to feel anxious. However, a person with an **anxiety disorder** experiences persistent anxiety that causes intense suffering; also, the anxiety has no reasonable explanation.

Some anxiety disorders are not associated with major gender differences. For example, women are only slightly more likely than men to experience social phobias. A person with a **social phobia** has excessive fear of social situations, especially situations in which the person will be evaluated by others (Bach et al., 1998; Leary & Kowalski, 1995). We will focus instead on two anxiety problems that are much more common in women than in men: specific phobias and agoraphobia.

Specific Phobias

People who have **specific phobias** are afraid of one specific kind of situation or object. Typical specific phobias include a fear of snakes, a fear of the dark, and a fear of thunderstorms. Between 70% and 95% of people with specific phobias are female (American Psychiatric Association, 1994; R. Kessler et al., 1994).

One potential explanation for the gender difference is that our society is less tolerant of fear in males than in females. A boy who is afraid of snakes will be pushed to overcome his fear. In contrast, the female gender role encourages young girls to avoid feared objects, so that young girls remain fearful and vulnerable (Chambless, 1986; Kaschak, 1992).

Agoraphobia

Agoraphobia is a symptom associated with anxiety disorders; it is a fear of being in public places from which escape may be difficult. People with agoraphobia may be afraid to travel on public transportation or to attend a social activity that does not allow easy exit if the person becomes anxious. As a result, many people with agoraphobia are afraid to leave their homes (Bach et al., 1998; McHugh, 1996). Women are approximately three times as likely as men to experience agoraphobia (Bach et al., 1998).

Agoraphobia usually begins when a person is between the ages of 18 and 25 (McHugh et al., 1996). It often begins with a series of **panic attacks,** episodes of overwhelming anxiety that occur suddenly and unexpectedly. People who experience a panic attack may feel dizzy and nauseated, with chest pains, a sensation of being smothered, and a fear of dying (McHugh, 1996; Sherbourne et al., 1996). People who have had panic attacks are likely to worry about having future attacks in a place where they don't feel safe. This worry leads to agoraphobia.

Agoraphobia is disabling because many agoraphobics will not leave their homes. For example, McHugh (1996) described a woman with agoraphobia who would not leave her apartment. Relatives supplies her with groceries, because she could not shop for herself. In fact, great effort was required even to coax her to travel in an elevator to the ground floor of the apartment building. As you can imagine, people with agoraphobia are not likely to work outside their homes (Hafner & Minge, 1989; McHugh, 1996).

Why should women be more likely than men to experience agoraphobia? As we noted in connection with specific phobias, females in our culture are allowed to be fearful and vulnerable. Our culture also encourages women to focus on the interiors of their homes (McHugh, 1996). Women are expected to cook, clean, and decorate—as a glance at the traditional "women's magazines" will confirm. McHugh (1996) also points out that women may have realistic fears about traveling in potentially dangerous settings. Another factor will remind you of Nolen-Hoeksema's (1990) explanation of depression: Women may be more likely than men to ruminate about the possibility of a future panic attack (Lewinsohn et al., 1998).

Maureen McHugh (1996) points out that we must view agoraphobia in relation to the social treatment of women, rather than as a psychological disorder experienced by individuals. Rather than giving antianxiety medication to women, one at a time, we need to examine the social context of agoraphobia. How can we transform neighborhoods and public places so that they are safe for women traveling alone? How can we encourage young girls to develop appropriate self-confidence and a sense of adventure—rather than fear—in exploring destinations beyond their homes?

 SECTION SUMMARY *Anxiety Disorders*

1. **Specific phobias and agoraphobia are two anxiety-related problems that are much more common in women than in men.**

2. **People with specific phobias are afraid of a particular kind of object or situation. The female role encourages young girls to remain fearful.**

3. **Agoraphobia, a symptom often created by panic attacks, is a fear of being in a place from which escape is difficult. Agoraphobia in women is related to the feminine gender role, realistic fear of some public settings, and—possibly—gender differences in rumination.**

EATING DISORDERS AND RELATED PROBLEMS

Consider the following anecdote about a highly respected feminist scholar who was attending a reception in her honor. Several guests had been complimenting her on her most recent scholarly accomplishments, but she brushed aside these comments. Then one man remarked that she looked ravishing and much slimmer than when he had last seen her. The woman smiled broadly and replied, "That's the nicest compliment I have received all night" (Boskind-White & White, 1987, p. 13).

The truth is that this woman—and most women in North America—was preoccupied with her weight. Many women may not have one of the life-threatening disorders we will discuss shortly, but their thoughts are often drawn away from social pleasures and professional concerns and focused on their physical appearance and dieting. In fact, as Pike and Striegel-Moore (1997) emphasize, symptoms of disordered eating occur on a continuum of severity. Anorexia nervosa and bulimia nervosa are at the most extreme end of that continuum. However, many other females have varying degrees of body-image problems, so that their disorders correspond to locations within the less extreme portion of that continuum.

In this section, we'll first consider anorexia nervosa and bulimia nervosa, and then we'll address the more general question of our culture's emphasis on being slim. Our final topic will be the related issues of being overweight and dieting. We need to emphasize—in advance—that being overweight is *not* a psychological disorder. However, the emphasis on slimness and dieting, combined with the fear of being overweight, are major factors in creating eating disorders.

Anorexia Nervosa

A woman seeking treatment for anorexia nervosa described her food intake on the previous day:

> I had a grapefruit and black coffee for breakfast, and for dinner I had the normal salad I eat every night. I always skip lunch. I had promised myself that I would only eat three-quarters of the salad since I've been feeling stuffed after it lately— but I think I ate more than the three-quarters. I know it was just lettuce and broccoli, but I can't believe I did that. I was up all night worrying about getting fat. (M. Siegel et al., 1997)

A person with **anorexia nervosa** has an extreme fear of becoming obese and also refuses to maintain an adequate body weight, defined as 85% of expected weight (American Psychiatric Association, 1994; Sokol & Gray, 1998). People with this disorder typically overestimate their body weight. For example, one young women with anorexia nervosa weighed only 100 pounds, yet she said:

> I look in the mirror and see myself as grotesquely fat—a real blimp. My legs and arms are really fat and I can't stand what I see. I know that others say I am too

thin, but I can see myself and I have to deal with this my way. (Alexander & LaRosa, 1994, p. 25)

Between 90% and 95% of those with anorexia nervosa are female, and it strikes about 1% of adolescent females. The average age of onset is 17 years (American Psychiatric Association, 1994; Sokol & Gray, 1998), though concern about weight begins many years earlier.

Anorexia nervosa starts in a variety of ways. Some anorexics are initially slightly overweight. Then a comment from someone—or even a query as innocent as "Are you gaining weight?"—prompts them to begin a severe dieting program. Other anorexics trace the beginning of their disorder to a stressful life event, such as moving to a new school, or to a traumatic event such as sexual abuse (M. Siegel et al., 1997; Sokol & Gray, 1998). Many who develop this disorder tend to be overly perfectionistic (R. Rogers & Petrie, 1996).

One important medical consequence of anorexia nervosa is **amenorrhea,** or the cessation of menstrual periods. Other frequent medical consequences include heart, kidney, and gastrointestinal disorders. In fact, virtually every organ in the body is affected (Litt, 1997; Pike & Striegel-Moore, 1997). For example, researchers have recently reported changes in brain structures among young women with anorexia (Katzman et al., 1997). Another common problem is osteoporosis, the bone disorder we discussed in Chapter 11. Osteoporosis afflicts anorexics because of their low estrogen levels and inadequate nutrition (Pike & Striegel-Moore, 1997).

Anorexia nervosa is considered serious because between 5% and 10% of anorexics die (American Psychiatric Association, 1994; M. Siegel et al., 1997; Steinhausen, 1995). Unfortunately, treatment for this disorder is difficult, especially because many people with anorexia also meet the criteria for major depression. About 40% of anorexics will recover, and about 35% will show some improvement. Recovery is especially likely if treatment begins during the early stages of anorexia (Sokol & Gray, 1998; Steinhausen, 1995).

Anorexia nervosa illustrates the potentially life-threatening consequences of our culture's preoccupation with thinness. As one father told me about his anorexic daughter, "She'd rather be dead than fat."

Bulimia Nervosa

Bulimia nervosa is characterized by binge eating and by inappropriate methods used to prevent weight gain. Binge eating means consuming huge amounts of food, up to 60,000 calories at a time (Alexander & LaRosa, 1994; American Psychiatric Association, 1994). The binge-eating episodes are typically secretive. People with bulimia nervosa then try to compensate for this huge food intake by vomiting or using laxatives (Pike & Striegel-Moore, 1997). In between binges, they may diet or exercise excessively. Like anorexics, bulimics are obsessed about food, eating, and physical appearance. For example, a 20-year old college student with bulimia nervosa described her situation:

How did I get so weird? My life revolves around eating and ridding myself of food. My days are a waste. . . . There hasn't been a day when I haven't been tormented by the frustration I create for myself about where, when, and what I shall eat.

I have potential that if released could do amazing things. But it's trapped inside me. I am a suffering, driven, and depressed person. I remember myself as an involved, bright, laughing girl. . . . But somehow I began to change. That sparkly person disappeared. Who I was became how I looked. Finally, all that mattered was my weight.

Freedom for me is having no concern for how I look or what I eat. Probably the stupidest, most shallow definition of freedom ever written. (Pipher, 1995a, p. 39)

At least 90% of individuals with bulimia nervosa are female, and the disorder is especially common on college campuses. Between 1% and 3% of adolescent and young adult females develop bulimia (Heffernan, 1998; Pike & Striegel-Moore, 1997). However, recognizing the presence of bulimia is difficult because bulimics typically maintain a normal body weight (M. Siegel et al., 1997). They do not stand out in a crowd.

The medical consequences of bulimia nervosa include gastrointestinal, heart, and metabolism problems (J. Mitchell, 1995). Bulimics are also likely to have dental problems caused by the acid in the vomited material. Bulimia nervosa is typically not as life-threatening as anorexia nervosa. However, it is difficult to treat effectively and it is associated with serious medical and psychological problems (Pike & Striegel-Moore, 1997).

The Emphasis on Being Slim

We mentioned at the beginning of this section that most North America females are overly concerned about their physical appearance. Let's explore components of this issue in more detail, because it helps explain the behavior of those with anorexia and bulimia, as well as those with less extreme concerns about slimness. We'll explore media images, discrimination against overweight people, and women's general dissatisfaction with their bodies. Finally, we'll focus on how women of color view their bodies.

Media Images.   One research group explored an important media image of slimness, the popular Barbie® Doll. They calculated that if Barbie were as tall as adult women, only 1 in 100,000 real-life women would have a waistline or hips as slender as hers (Norton et al., 1996). Incidentally, Barbie's boyfriend, Ken, has a somewhat more realistic shape. If Ken were as tall as adult men, about 1 in 50 men would have his dimensions.

Women who have sought treatment for anorexia nervosa or bulimia nervosa frequently recall that the models in fashion magazines were an important motivational force in encouraging their pursuit of slimness (M. Levine & Smolak, 1996). Furthermore, the media have been featuring increasingly slender women in recent decades. Meanwhile, the male models in men's fashion magazines have remained the same size since the 1960s (Petrie et al., 1996; Polivy & McFarlane, 1998). In other words, media images of women are much less realistic than the media images of men—an observation that is consistent with the higher rates of eating disorders among women.

Other research on the media directly measures how these images influence women's views of their bodies. Specifically, women show increased anxiety about their bodies and decreased body-esteem after they have seen photographs of slender fashion models (Grogan et al., 1996; Thornton & Maurice, 1997). In contrast, women in a control group show no change in their body images after they have seen photographs of landscapes. In other words, viewing fashion models can be dangerous for women's mental health!

Discrimination Against Overweight Women.   Our society discriminates against women who are overweight. For example, most people would hesitate before making a racist comment, but they would not hesitate before making a comment about an overweight woman (Chrisler, 1994; Crandall, 1994). Women who are overweight also receive lower salaries, and they experience other forms of job discrimination. They are less likely to be viewed as sexually attractive and less likely to marry (W. Goodman, 1995; Regan, 1996; Wing & Klem, 1997).

Adults are not alone in downgrading overweight individuals. Even first graders report that they would prefer to be friends with a slender child, rather than a heavier one. Beginning at an early age, then, children may be biased against their overweight peers (Goldfield & Chrisler, 1995).

Females' Dissatisfaction with Their Bodies.   In our culture, where the ideal is the emaciated women who inhabit fashion magazines, it is not surprising that many females feel unhappy about their bodies. For instance, in one survey of 803 adult women from throughout the United States, roughly one-half were dissatisfied with their body weight, hips, and stomach (Cash & Henry, 1995). In addition, women are much less happy with their bodies than men are, and the gender gap in body dissatisfaction is increasing (Feingold & Mazzella, 1998; Muth & Cash, 1997). Research on children in elementary school now shows widespread concern about being fat and about dieting (Flannery-Schroeder & Chrisler, 1996).

Consider the consequences of this preoccupation with attractiveness and slenderness. A study of diaries written by American teenagers shows that young women 100 years ago wrote entries about trying to be more concerned about other people. In contrast, diaries written in the current era emphasize losing weight, getting a new haircut, and spending more time on makeup (Brumberg, 1997). Women's current dissatisfaction with their bodies produces unhappiness. It also focuses their attention on relatively superficial characteristics and on themselves, rather than on meaningful interactions with other people.

All females are not uniformly preoccupied with physical appearance. Compared to heterosexual women, lesbian women are generally more satisfied with their bodies (Beren et al., 1997; Bergeron & Senn, 1998). In addition, women who have feminist attitudes toward physical attractiveness or toward male–female relationships are typically happier with their bodies than women with more traditional values (Cash et al., 1997; Dionne et al., 1995). Also, lower-class European American women are less preoccupied with slimness than are European American women from other income brackets (Bowen et al., 1999). One further variable that is sometimes related to body dissatisfaction is ethnicity. Let's now turn our attention to the way that women of color regard these body-image issues.

Women of Color, Body Image, and Slimness.   Until recently, most of the research on body image and related topics has been conducted with European American populations or with populations in which the ethnic composition is not specified. However, several current studies have examined Black and Latina women.

In general, Black women are more satisfied with their body image than are European American women. Black women also believe that an average-weight woman is more attractive than a too-thin woman (Bowen et al., 1999; Cash & Henry, 1995; Hebl & Heatherton, 1998; L. Jackson & McGill, 1996). Interestingly, Black males also prefer average-weight women, whereas White males prefer thinner women (S. Thompson et al., 1996). A 34-year-old Black woman interviewed by Bowen and her colleagues (1999) commented:

> At work, where there are only a few of us Black women, I feel pretty fat. At home, with my friends, I don't think about it hardly at all. I guess it's because I'm closer to the middle of my Black friends' weight range. (p. 292)

Unfortunately, we do not yet have clear explanations for these important ethnic differences.

The research on Latina women is contradictory. Some research suggests that Latinas are less preoccupied with slimness, but other research reports that Latinas and European American women have similar levels of body dissatisfaction (Bowen et al., 1999; Cash & Henry, 1995). One reason for the inconclusive findings is the diversity within each ethnic group. For example, B. Thompson (1994) found in her interviews that women from the Dominican Republic did not value thinness. In contrast, a woman raised in an upper-class Argentinian family emphasized slimness more than most European American women. Factors such as social class, country of origin, and current place of residence undoubtedly influence how Latina women view their bodies. Another important factor is probably acculturation. Women who have adopted mainstream values while living in the United States and Canada tend to adopt our culture's ideas about slimness (Geller & Thomas, 1998; Lester & Petrie, 1995).

Researchers have now examined Black and Latina female populations in several studies. Unfortunately, however, the research on Asian and Native American women is not yet extensive enough to summarize (Bowen et al., 1999; Ponton, 1996). Any research with these two populations must be sensitive to the factors we have discussed, such as social class, if it is to explain the variety of viewpoints expressed within every ethnic group.

Being Overweight and Dieting

According to one commonly used definition, people are **overweight** or **obese** if they weigh at least 20% more than the recommended weights on standardized medical charts. Currently, about 35% of U.S. women and 31% of U.S. men are categorized as overweight (Wing & Klem, 1997). *Being overweight is not classified as a mental disorder.* However, we need to discuss the issue of being overweight because it is a central topic in many women's lives. In addition, the fear of becoming overweight is a major factor in the eating disorders described in this chapter.

Research demonstrates that people who eat foods that are high in fat—and people who do not exercise sufficiently—are likely to face greater health risks than other people. In addition, overweight people are more likely than other people to have high blood pressure and heart disease and to be at a greater risk for cancer (Manson et al., 1995; Wing & Klem, 1997). Earlier in this section, we pointed out that overweight people face another cluster of problems through social and professional discrimination.

Unfortunately, losing extra weight is a major challenge. Some people take up smoking in order to suppress their appetites, but, as we saw in Chapter 11, smoking has enormous health risks.

Approximately 40% of U.S. women (compared with 24% of men) are currently dieting to lose weight (Wing & Klem, 1997). According to one estimate, U.S. residents can now choose from more than 17,000 different diet plans and products (Hesse-Biber, 1998). However, these options are often expensive. In addition, many of them are ineffective because people regain the lost weight (Fraser, 1997b; Saltzberg & Chrisler, 1995). Think about this: If any of these programs were truly effective, why are there so many other programs on the market?

Ironically, dieting can often lead to weight gain. Dieting causes a change in metabolism. The dieter can survive on increasingly smaller portions of food. A "normal" food intake therefore causes weight gain. In addition, dieters may become so focused on food that they may be tempted to binge (Polivy & McFarlane, 1998). For these reasons, many clinicians suggest that clients should be encouraged to accept themselves and halt further dieting when they are only slightly overweight (Chrisler, 1994; Wilfley & Rodin, 1995).

We all need to focus less on weight issues, and we need to encourage the media not to show so many anorexic female actors and models. Something is clearly wrong when normal-weight women begin dieting! For people who are indeed overweight, modest weight loss with thoughtfully chosen, nutritious menus and appropriate exercise can produce some health benefits (Brownell & Rodin, 1994).

In this section, we have looked at three groups of people who are highly concerned about their weight. (1) Anorexics try to lose weight, and they succeed—sometimes with fatal consequences. (2) Bulimics fluctuate between gorging and dieting; their weight is usually normal, but their eating habits produce numerous other problems. (3) Overweight people may try to lose weight, typically

---

DEMONSTRATION 12.2

Analyzing the Media Approach to Eating and Weight Loss

Between now and the end of the term, try monitoring television, newspapers, and magazines. Look for advertisements and special features on food, eating, and weight loss. For example, I found an ad in *New York* magazine that showed a scoop of strawberry ice cream, a woman's face, and the text, "I pride myself on my level-headed approach to life. I never stay in the sun too long. But all it takes is one smooth taste of Häagen-Dazs® Strawberry ice cream and I find myself letting go. I savor every plump strawberry. I indulge myself in its creamy richness. I must do something about this Häagen-Dazs passion. Maybe I could organize it, structure it or control it . . . tomorrow." Doesn't this seem like it would encourage bingeing?

Pay attention not only to individual ads and features, but also to the irony of contradictory messages. Does your favorite magazine have articles on calorie-laden desserts right next to ads for weight-loss programs?

---

without success. Think how the guilt and anxiety that all three groups associate with eating might be reduced if more women were encouraged to accept and be content with their bodies.

Imagine, too, how much more positive we might feel if the women in the media had bodies that showed as much variety as the bodies we see in real life. And wouldn't it be wonderful to glance at the covers of magazines in the grocery story and *not* see guilt-inducing articles titled, "Finally—An Answer to Problem Thighs" or "How to Lose 15 Pounds in Just One Month"! Now that you are familiar with these issues related to eating, try Demonstration 12.2.

SECTION SUMMARY   *Eating Disorders and Related Problems*

1. **Many females have varying degrees of body-image problems. Anorexia nervosa and bulimia nervosa are at the extreme end of the continuum.**

2. **People with anorexia nervosa have an extreme fear of becoming obese, even when they weigh much less than their appropriate body weight. The problem is especially prominent among adolescent women; health problems are numerous, and the consequences may be fatal.**

3. **People with bulimia nervosa binge frequently, but their weight may be normal because they vomit or use other methods to prevent weight gain. Their health problems are numerous.**

4. **The media present images of inappropriate slimness, and these images make women anxious about their bodies; both adults and children downgrade overweight people.**

5. **A large number of women are dissatisfied with their bodies, though body dissatisfaction depends on factors such as feminist attitudes and ethnicity.**

6. **Obesity is not a psychological disorder, but it has potential health and social consequences; dieting can be both difficult and potentially dangerous.**

TREATING PSYCHOLOGICAL DISORDERS IN WOMEN

So far, we have discussed three categories of psychological disorders that are more common in women than in men: (1) depressive disorders, (2) anxiety disorders, and (3) eating disorders. If a woman seeks help for psychological problems like these, she will probably receive psychotherapy and/or drug treatment.

Psychotherapy is a process in which a therapist aims to treat psychological problems most often through verbal interactions. At present, professionals offer about 400 different kinds of psychotherapy (Garfield, 1995). Severely disturbed individuals who receive therapy are typically treated in hospitals or other psychiatric facilities. Others may receive psychotherapy for many years, but they can still function while living at home. Still others choose psychotherapy to help them during brief periods of stress in their lives.

Drug therapy treats psychological disorders via medication. In recent years, new drugs have been developed to help people cope with some psychological disorders. When used in conjunction with psychotherapy, these drugs may be useful. However, many drugs are prescribed inappropriately. We'll briefly discuss drug therapy in this section, though we'll emphasize psychotherapy as an approach to treating mental disorders.

We will first consider how sexism may influence psychotherapy, and then we will discuss psychotherapy for women of color. Our final two sections will examine traditional approaches to psychotherapy, as well as gender-sensitive therapy.

Psychotherapy and Sexism

Gender and Misdiagnosis.   Earlier in this chapter, we noted the potential for sexism in diagnosing psychological disorders. Specifically, therapists may overdiagnose depression in women and underdiagnose depression in men (Sprock & Yoder, 1997). Research about other psychological disorders shows a similar pattern in which gender stereotypes lead to misdiagnosis. For example, educators and therapists may overlook learning disabilities in girls (Caplan, 1999). They may not believe that academic achievement is crucial for females. As long as a girl is well behaved in class, they believe she does not need any special treatment.

Sexism also encourages another kind of misdiagnosis. We saw in Chapter 11 that many health care professionals respond less to medical problems in women than in men. A related concern is that a physical disorder may be misdiagnosed as a psychological problem. For example, an overactive thyroid gland often produces severe anxiety. Health care professionals, guided by the gender differences in anxiety disorders, may refer women who have this problem to a psychotherapist rather than a medical specialist (Klonoff & Landrine, 1997; Lerman, 1996).

The Treatment of Women in Therapy.   Gender bias may lead to misdiagnosis, but does gender bias lead to inappropriate treatment in therapy? The early research showed some evidence that it does. For example, therapists considered psychological symptoms in a male to be more serious than the same symptoms in a female (Hansen & Reekie, 1990). However, little additional research on gender bias has been conducted in recent years. One reason for this apparent neglect is that the original studies have been very well publicized. As a result, therapists know that they should not provide gender-biased responses when answering questionnaires (Atkinson & Hackett, 1995).

However, Gilbert and Scher's (1999) recent book on gender and psychotherapy points out several ways in which gender bias still operates. For example, therapists may view men as more competent than women in work settings. Therapists may also evaluate clients in terms of how well their behavior fits the gender stereotypes specified for women and men. In addition, therapists may blame women for events beyond their control. In treating a woman who has been sexually abused, for instance, they may ask her what she did to encourage the attack. In summary, therapists may be influenced by the same kinds of gender stereotypes and discrimination behavior that operate throughout our culture.

Sexual Relationships Between Therapists and Clients.   One of the principles of ethical conduct for psychologists states that therapists must not disrupt their professional relationships with clients by engaging in sexual intimacy with them. Nonetheless, some therapists break this rule. In fact, sexual misconduct is the major reason that therapists lose their professional licenses (American Psychiatric Association, 1990, 1996b; Gilbert & Scher, 1999). According to surveys, between 1% and 4% of male therapists and between 0.2% and 0.5% of female therapists have had sexual relationships with their clients (K. Pope, 1994; K. Pope & Vasquez, 1991).

Consider how a woman named Cathy experienced the devastating consequences of unethical behavior. She sought the help of a therapist because she was not experiencing orgasm during intercourse. As part of the "treatment," her therapist encouraged her to remove her blouse during the first therapy session.

After several sessions, the therapist initiated intercourse. That afternoon, Cathy committed suicide by jumping off the top of an office building (K. Pope & Bouhoutsos, 1986).

We need to emphasize that most psychotherapists are ethical people who understand that sexual relationships with clients are forbidden (Baur, 1997; L. Gilbert & Scher, 1999). Still, anyone who feels uneasy about a therapist's sexual advances should try to discuss the issue with the therapist. If this option is not possible, the client should seek a different therapist and consider reporting the offender to a licensing board (Gilbert & Scher, 1999).

Sexual relationships with clients are especially damaging because they demonstrate a violation of trust. They are also damaging because they represent situations in which a person with power takes advantage of someone who is relatively powerless and vulnerable. We examine similar power inequities in Chapter 13, where we'll discuss sexual harassment, rape, and battering.

Psychotherapy with Women of Color

The United States and Canada are rapidly becoming two of the most ethnically diverse countries in the world. For example, in the year 2000, an estimated one-third of the U.S. population are people of color. As a result, North American therapists need to be sensitive to ethnic-group differences in values and beliefs (C. Hall, 1997).

One basic problem is that people of color are not as likely as European Americans to use mental health services. Some of the reasons for this underusage include: (1) shame in talking about personal problems to strangers; (2) suspicion about therapists, especially European therapists; (3) language and economic barriers; (4) reluctance to recognize that help is necessary; and (5) culturally based preferences for other interventions such as prayer (Barney, 1994; Dinges & Cherry, 1995; Uba, 1994).

Some members of an ethnic group will be able to see a therapist from their own background. For example, Espín (1997) describes her own work as a Latina therapist, helping a Latina client who had experienced domestic violence. Espín's condemnation of this abuse was far more credible than if the same message had come from a European American therapist.

However, most members of ethnic minority groups will not be able to choose therapists from their own background. Only about 5% of therapists belong to ethnic minority groups (C. Hall, 1997; Daniel, 1994). As a result, most people of color must consult therapists whose life experiences may be very different from their own.

You can probably anticipate another advantage of clients' being matched with therapists from their own ethnic background. Most European American therapists are not fluent in a language other than English, so language can be a major barrier. To make the situation more vivid, if your own first language isn't Spanish, imagine describing your psychological problems to someone who speaks only Spanish. Your Spanish may be fluent enough to discuss the weather, but could you describe to a Latina therapist precisely how and why you feel depressed? Could you accurately capture the subtleties of your agoraphobia?

Let's consider some of the important issues that arise in therapy for women in four different ethnic groups. Then we'll discuss some general therapeutic issues for women of color.

Black Women. As several theorists emphasize, Black women suffer two second-class statuses in American society—being Black and being female (Adebimpe, 1997; L. Gilbert & Scher, 1999). This situation is likely to cause considerable stress. The nature of this stress is often qualitatively different from the stress experienced by middle-class European American women. Specifically, Black women may report stressful factors such as extreme poverty, inadequate housing, and neighborhood crime (Thomas & Miles, 1995).

However, Black women may have an advantage over European American women because their heterosexual relationships are often more evenly balanced with respect to power (McAdoo, 1993). Still, they are at a disadvantage if they seek help from a European American therapist who accepts the myth of the Black matriarchy (see Chapter 8). Therapists should also resist the myth that all Black women are strong and resilient (Greene, 1994). That perspective would encourage therapists to believe that their Black female clients do not really require care for themselves.

Latinas. In earlier chapters, we noted that Latina/o culture emphasizes gender roles in terms of *machismo* for men and *marianismo* for women. Mothers train daughters to remain virgins until marriage, when they must cater to their husband's sexual needs (Espín, 1997). Young girls also learn to play the role of "little wives" to the males in the family. Especially in working-class homes, women may learn that they are second-class citizens (L. Gilbert & Scher, 1999).

We noted earlier that someone whose original language is Spanish may have difficulty communicating in English. Women who locate Latina/o therapists may face other problems. For example, therapists who have been trained in Mexico are more likely than those trained in the United States to believe the stereotype that women are selfish (W. Snell et al., 1990). Therefore, a Hispanic therapist may indeed speak Spanish, but he or she may have negative ideas about women.

Furthermore, some Latinas have come to North America as refugees from a country besieged by war and turmoil. For example, government repression in El Salvador during the 1980s resulted in more than 75,000 deaths, as well as numerous rapes, tortures, "disappearances," and other human rights abuses. A woman who escaped from El Salvador may have seen her daughter raped and tortured, and her neighbors slaughtered (Bowen et al., 1992; Guarnaccia, 1997). Living through such traumatic circumstances often creates long-lasting stress-related disorders and other psychological problems. Well-meaning therapists—even if they are fluent in Spanish—may be unprepared to treat women who have lived through political upheaval.

Asian American Women. Although individual differences are substantial, many Asian American families are still strongly influenced by the idea that the male should be the powerful member of the household. These families expect women to play a passive, subordinate role. Younger, more educated women are likely to experience conflict when they sense that they have been unfairly treated by family members. These women are especially likely to have problems with parents and male partners who have very traditional orientations (True, 1990).

Like Latinas, women who are Asian American may not be fluent in English. For example, people from different Asian groups in the United States were surveyed about their fluency in English. Only 31% of Asian Indians answered that they did not speak English very well, but more than 60% of people from Southeast Asian countries said they did not speak English very well.

Therapists who are not familiar with an Asian culture may misinterpret some interactions. For example, they may believe that a quiet Asian woman is reserved because of her cultural values or her lack of fluency in English. However, she may actually be experiencing major depression (Uba, 1994).

Many researchers have tried to determine why Asian Americans are especially reluctant to use mental health services. They have concluded that Asian Americans are just as likely as European Americans to have mental health problems (Atkinson et al., 1993; Uba, 1994). However, an important cultural value in many Asian groups is to maintain the honor of the family, and to avoid any possibility of bringing shame to one's relatives. Psychological problems are judged especially harshly. As a result, a woman who enters psychotherapy is basically admitting that she has failed (Uba, 1994; Wang, 1994).

Several Asian American mental health centers are trying outreach programs, using culturally sensitive techniques. These centers have been reasonably successful in increasing the number of community residents who seek therapy (True, 1995).

Native Americans. Among Native American and Canadian aboriginal (Canadian Indian) women, two major mental health problems are the high rates of alcoholism and depression (LaFromboise et al., 1995; Waldram, 1997). Many theorists trace these problems to earlier governmental programs. For example, in Canada, many aboriginal children were taken from their families and placed in residential schools, where they were punished for speaking their own language. These programs encouraged children to assimilate into the European Canadian mainstream, at the same time that they undermined the influence of the tribal elders. Currently, unemployment and poverty are widespread in many native communities. The combination of all these factors is partly responsible for the high suicide rate. For example, the suicide rate among Canadian aboriginal women is 2.5 times higher than for other Canadian women (Waldram, 1997).

Eidell Wasserman (1994) is a European American therapist hired as a therapist for a reservation in Arizona. She reports that non-Natives working in a Native community are often seen as representative of the U.S. Government, which has had a history of harmful interactions. She found that one of her most powerful therapeutic tools was to enlist the support of community members. In addition, she helped train members of the Native community to work as mental health paraprofessionals.

General Strategies for Therapy with Women of Color.   Many therapists have suggested methods for European Americans who want to increase their skills in helping women of color. Many of these suggestions have been incorporated into graduate training programs (Aponte & Morrow, 1995; Bernal & Castro, 1994; Enns, 1997; Greene, 1994; C. Hall, 1997; Porter, 1995):

1. Search the client's history for strengths that can facilitate the counseling process. (As you'll see, many of these recommendations apply to *all* clients, not just women of color.)

2. Do not automatically assume that the client holds the values that are common in her culture.

3. Show empathy, caring, and appreciation for your client.

4. Learn about the history, experiences, religion, and cultural values of the client's ethnic group, but be aware of the diversity within any cultural group. Many graduate programs in clinical psychology now offer courses on cross-cultural psychology or on ethnic diversity.

5. Be aware that some immigrants and other people of color might want to become more acculturated into the European American mainstream, but others want to connect more strongly with their own culture.

6. Communicate to the client that racism may have played a significant role in her life; however, do not use racial oppression to explain all of a client's problems.

7. Hire bilingual staff members and paraprofessionals from the relevant ethnic communities; enlist other community professionals (e.g., school teachers) in helping to identify relevant problems in the community.

Traditional Therapies and Women

Therapists approach their work from a variety of theoretical viewpoints. A therapist's viewpoint influences both the techniques used in therapy and the goals of therapy. In addition, the therapist's theoretical viewpoint influences his or her ideas about women. We'll consider two traditional psychotherapy approaches:

(1) the psychodynamic approach and (2) the cognitive-behavioral approach. We'll also consider drug therapy in this section.

Psychodynamic Approach. **Psychodynamic therapy** refers to a variety of approaches descended from Freud's psychoanalytic theories. Like Freud, the psychodynamic therapists focus on childhood problems and unconscious conflict. However, psychodynamic therapists currently emphasize social interactions more than Freud did.

We mentioned the work of Sigmund Freud in the chapters on childhood (Chapter 3) and on sexuality (Chapter 9). Interestingly, Freud himself admitted that his theories about women were the weakest part of his work (Slipp, 1993).

We need to discuss Freud's theories once more, in connection with therapy because no other modern writer has influenced our culture's views on women as strongly as Freud did (Appignanesi & Forrester, 1992). Here are some components of Freud's approach that present problems for individuals who are concerned about women's mental health (Abel, 1995; Chodorow, 1994; Greenspan, 1993; Slipp, 1993):

1. In Freudian theory, the masculine—rather than the feminine—is the human norm.

2. Freud argues that women show **masochism** (pronounced "*mass*-owe-kism"), or pleasure derived from pain—a perspective that does not encourage modern-day therapists to treat battered women appropriately.

3. According to Freudian theory, women's lack of a penis leads them to experience more shame and envy than men, in addition to a less mature sense of justice.

4. Freud's approach argues that penis envy can be partially resolved by having a baby. The desire not to have children is therefore viewed as a sign of psychological disorders.

5. Mothers are the caretakers of young children. The Freudian approach blames mothers for the psychological problems that children experience, but it does not address the positive aspects of mothers' interactions with their children.

6. Freud did not address issues such as social class or ethnicity, although variables like these have an important impact on women's experiences.

A major part of psychodynamic therapy sessions focuses on childhood relationships and unconscious forces—factors that presumably help therapists understand current psychological problems. The emphasis on childhood and the unconscious is not inherently biased against women. However, most feminist critics argue that the six points we just discussed would not encourage women to become more positive about themselves or more psychologically healthy.

Many modern psychodynamic theorists have redefined some of the classic Freudian concepts. You may want to read more about these more feminist approaches (Chodorow, 1994, 1995; Jordan, 1998; J. Miller & Stiver, 1997).

Cognitive-Behavioral Approach.   The **cognitive-behavioral approach** traces psychological problems to inappropriate learning (behavioral factors) and to inappropriate thinking (cognitive factors). This approach encourages clients to try new behaviors. For example, a woman with a phobia may gradually expose herself to a feared object. The cognitive-behavioral approach also asks clients to question any irrational thought patterns they may have. For instance, suppose a woman is depressed because she has no boyfriend. A therapist may help the woman to see alternate viewpoints, such as "Just because I'm not in a love relationship right now doesn't mean I'm an unworthy person" (McGrath et al., 1990).

Cognitive-behavioral therapy is frequently used to treat eating disorders (e.g., Freedman, 1990; J. Grant & Cash, 1995). For example, a therapist may help a client develop behavioral strategies to reduce compulsive eating. The therapist may also work with the client to reword negative statements (e.g., "My thighs are disgusting") into more neutral forms (e.g., "My thighs are the heaviest part of me").

Many cognitive-behavioral principles can be combined with feminist therapy, which we will discuss shortly. However, most cognitive-behavioral therapists work to change client's own individual behaviors and thought problems (Enns, 1997). They typically do not discuss with the client the more general problem of society's widespread gender biases.

Drug Therapy.   As noted earlier, drug therapies treat psychological disorders by using medication. Our focus in this chapter is on psychotherapy, but other resources offer additional information about drug therapy (e.g., Gitlin, 1996).

Women are more likely than men to use sedatives and tranquilizers (Carlson et al., 1996; McCaul, 1998). However, women may be more likely than men to experience the kinds of psychological disorders for which these medications are appropriate. Unfortunately, we do not have current information about whether physicians may be overprescribing drugs for their female clients.

One recent study suggests an important factor that could influence physicians' ideas about gender and drug therapy. Specifically, Hansen and Osborne (1995) counted the number of advertisements for antidepressants in two well-known medical journals, and they noted the gender ratio in these ads. As you know, women are two to three times as likely as men to experience depression, so we might expect that about 65% to 75% of the ads would show women. However, these researchers found that women were featured in about 85% of the antidepressant ads in one journal, and 100% in the other journal. Their concern was that physicians who read these journals might overprescribe antidepressants for women and underprescribe them for men.

Drug therapy is an important component of treating serious psychological disorders in the current era. In many cases, drugs can allow severely disturbed clients to be more receptive to therapy. However, the drugs must be carefully prescribed, and their side effects must be monitored. Furthermore, therapists would strongly argue that any disorder serious enough to be treated with drug

---

DEMONSTRATION 12.3

Preferences About Therapists

Imagine that you have graduated from college and that a personal problem has developed for which you would like to consult a therapist. You feel that the problem is not a major one. However, you would like to sort out your thoughts and emotions on this particular problem by talking with a psychotherapist. The following list describes characteristics and approaches that therapists may have. Place a check mark in front of each characteristic that you would look for in a therapist. When you are done, check page 465 to see how to interpret your responses.

_____ 1. I want my therapist to avoid using sexist language.

_____ 2. I would like my therapist to help me think about forces in our society that might be contributing to my problem.

_____ 3. I would like my therapist to believe that the client and the therapist should have reasonably similar power in a therapy situation.

_____ 4. My therapist should avoid encouraging me to act in a more gender-stereotyped fashion.

_____ 5. I want my therapist to be well informed about the research on women and gender.

_____ 6. I think that therapists should reveal relevant information about their own experiences, if the situation is appropriate.

_____ 7. I want my therapist to address relevant issues other than gender in our therapy sessions—issues such as age, social class, ethnicity, disability, and sexual orientation.

_____ 8. My therapist should encourage me to develop male–female relationships in which the two individuals are fairly similar in their power.

_____ 9. I want my therapist to avoid interacting with me in a gender-stereotyped fashion.

(Based on Enns, 1997.)

therapy should receive psychotherapy as well. Before reading further, be sure to try Demonstration 12.3.

Gender–Sensitive Therapy

We have examined how the psychodynamic approach, the cognitive-behavioral approach, and drug therapy can be used in treating psychological disorders. However, the women's movement has created an awareness that psychotherapy must be sensitive to gender issues. Most therapists would probably endorse the principles of nonsexist therapy—even if they don't always act in a gender-fair fashion. Let's briefly describe this nonsexist approach, and then we'll consider feminist therapy in more detail.

Nonsexist Therapy.   According to the principles of **nonsexist therapy,** women and men should be treated similarly, rather than in a gender-stereotyped fashion (Worell & Remer, 1992). The nonsexist-therapy approach argues that therapists should be informed about the recent research on the psychology of women and about the pervasiveness of sexism in our society. Therapists should also avoid sexist language and gender-biased testing instruments (Enns, 1997; Rawlings & Carter, 1977).

Nonsexist therapists are also informed about the potential for misusing power when interacting with clients. For example, therapists should not use power as a tool to encourage more feminine behavior in women or to bias women's decisions about sexual orientation (Enns, 1997; Rawlings & Carter, 1977). However, nonsexist therapy does not specifically examine broader political issues such as social inequalities. In contrast, a major goal of feminist therapy is to address these social inequalities.

Feminist Therapy.   Feminist therapists agree that the principles of nonsexist treatment are essential in therapy; however, these principles are not sufficient. **Feminist therapy** has two important components: (1) social inequalities have been responsible for shaping women's behavior, so the personal is political; and (2) the distribution of power between the client and the therapist should be as egalitarian as possible (L. Gilbert & Scher, 1999; Greene, 1994).

In recent years, interest in feminist therapy has blossomed. Numerous books describe both the theory and practice of feminist psychotherapy (e.g., Burstow, 1992; Enns, 1997; L. Gilbert & Scher, 1999; E. Williams, 1995a; Worell & Johnson, 1997; Worell & Remer, 1992). Let's see how the two basic components of feminist therapy can be expanded into a number of major principles of feminist therapy.

The first six principles point out how social forces operate to devalue women (Albee, 1996; Enns, 1997; Fishel, 1995; Hare-Mustin & Marecek, 1997; L. Gilbert & Scher, 1999; E. Williams, 1995b). Let's examine these important principles:

1. Feminist therapists believe that women are less powerful than men in our culture, and so they have been assigned an inferior status. Women's major problems are not internal, personal deficiencies; instead, the problems are primarily societal ones such as sexism and racism.

2. Society should be changed to be less sexist; women should not be encouraged to adjust to a sexist society.

3. We must focus on women's strengths, not on characteristics that are presumed to be their deficits. Women can use these strengths to help define and solve problems.

4. We must work to change those institutions that devalue women, including governmental organizations, the justice system, educational systems, and the structure of the family.

5. Inequalities with respect to ethnicity, age, sexual orientation, social class, and disabilities should also be addressed; gender is not the only important inequality.

6. Women and men should have equal power in their personal relationships; furthermore, men can profit from feminist therapy.

The other component of feminist therapy focuses on power issues within the therapeutic relationship. As feminist theorists point out, some traditional psychotherapy sessions can be called the "power hour" because therapists have much more power than clients (Hare-Mustin & Marecek, 1997). In contrast, feminist therapy emphasizes more egalitarian interactions (Enns, 1997; Fadli, 1995; L. Gilbert & Scher, 1999; Hare-Mustin & Marecek, 1997; Simi & Mahalik, 1997; Wyche & Rice, 1997). Here are some of the ways that power is balanced in feminist therapy:

1. Whenever possible, the therapist should try to enhance the client's power in the therapeutic relationship. After all, if women clients are placed in subordinate roles in therapy, the situation simply mirrors women's inferior status in society.

2. Throughout therapy, clients are encouraged to become more self-confident and independent and to develop skills to help themselves; therapists are educators who help clients discover and enhance their own strengths.

3. The therapist believes that the client is her own best expert on herself; clients do not need to defer to the "authority" of the therapist.

4. When appropriate, feminist therapists may share information about their own life experiences, further reducing the power differential. However, a therapist's primary tasks are listening and thinking, rather than talking.

5. Group therapy is often used to emphasize clients' power and to minimize the therapist's power.

Feminist therapy sounds as if it could be a powerful tool in encouraging clients to analyze their psychological problems and to develop their personal strengths. However, we do not have current research that compares the outcomes of feminist therapy and more traditional therapy. Several studies, conducted by Carolyn Enns and her coauthors do reveal some relevant information. Specifically, these studies provided students with descriptions of several kinds of therapy sessions (Enns, 1997; Enns & Hackett, 1993; Hackett et al., 1992). In their evaluations of these sessions, students concluded that feminist therapists would be more likely than nonsexist therapists (1) to encourage women to focus on their own needs; (2) to encourage financial independence; and (3) to avoid encouraging traditional roles in a love relationship.

However, the research by Enns and her colleagues also suggests that feminist therapists may be more likely to ask their clients to do something that contradicts the clients' beliefs, whereas nonsexist therapists would be more likely to focus on the client's inner world. In some cases, feminist therapists may misuse their power and try to transform female clients into women they have no real desire to become. Good therapy should begin with the client's current situation, and it should evolve in a direction consistent with her own needs.

 Treating Psychological Disorders in Women

1. **Gender stereotypes may encourage some therapists to misdiagnose some psychological disorders, to misdiagnose some physical illnesses as psychological disorders, and to treat clients in a gender-biased fashion.**

2. **One clearly harmful violation of ethical conduct is a sexual relationship between a therapist and a client.**

3. **People of color are less likely than European Americans to use mental health services. Therapists must be aware of characteristics of diverse ethnic groups that may be relevant in therapy.**

4. **Therapists can increase their skills in helping women of color by a variety of methods, including searching the client's history for her personal strengths, being aware that the client may not share some of the values typically found in her culture, and learning more about the client's ethnic group.**

5. **Psychodynamic therapy is based on Freudian theory, an approach that emphasizes childhood experiences and unconscious conflict. This gender-biased approach considers women to be masochistic and less mature. Mothers are blamed for their children's psychological problems.**

6. **Cognitive-behavioral therapy emphasizes restructuring maladaptive thoughts and changing behaviors.**

7. **Drug therapy uses medication to treat psychological disorders; it may be helpful, but it must be used with caution.**

8. **Nonsexist therapy treats women and men similarly, and it attempts to avoid gender-stereotyped behavior.**

9. **Feminist therapy endorses the principles of nonsexist therapy, but it also argues that (a) social inequalities have helped shape women's behavior and (b) power should be more equally divided between the therapist and the client.**

CHAPTER REVIEW QUESTIONS

1. What are the characteristics of major depression, and what personality characteristics are most likely to be related to depression? Based on these characteristics, describe a woman who would be *unlikely* to experience depression.

2. What two factors are no longer considered relevant when we try to account for the fact that women are more likely than men to develop depression? What factors seem to be important in explaining this gender difference? In this second list, note which factors describe cultural and societal forces, rather than women's personal characteristics.

3. How would you define an anxiety disorder? Describe two kinds of anxiety problems that are found much more often in women than in men, and point out how gender roles may help explain the gender differences.

4. Discuss anorexia nervosa and bulimia nervosa. Describe typical characteristics of these eating disorders, as well as their medical consequences. How does our culture's emphasis on slimness contribute to these problems?

5. Discuss the information on ethnicity and body image. Then summarize the material on the unique concerns that women of color bring to a psychotherapy session. Why must therapists emphasize individual differences within every ethnic group?

6. Describe why the issue of obesity and dieting presents problems that are difficult to solve, with respect to the advisability of losing weight and the challenge of permanent weight loss.

7. Based on what you have read in this chapter, as well as the chapters on childhood and on sexuality, why does the classical approach of Sigmund Freud present major problems for those who favor a nonsexist or feminist approach to therapy?

8. Imagine that you are a feminist therapist, working with a female client who is severely depressed. Imagine someone who would fit this description and point out how you would use selected principles of feminist therapy to facilitate her recovery.

9. Many therapists favor an eclectic approach to the treatment of psychological disorders, in which they combine elements of several approaches. If you

were a therapist, how could you combine elements of cognitive-behavioral therapy, nonsexist therapy, and feminist therapy?

10. This chapter has emphasized psychological disorders. Some theorists point out that psychologists should place more emphasis on how individuals can achieve positive mental health—rather than on just avoiding disorders. Based on the information in this chapter, describe the characteristics of an individual who is mentally healthy.

NEW TERMS

psychological disorders (434)
antisocial personality disorder (434)
major depression (435)
ruminative style (440)
distracting style (440)
anxiety disorder (442)
social phobia (442)
specific phobias (442)
agoraphobia (442)
panic attacks (442)
anorexia nervosa (444)

amenorrhea (445)
bulimia nervosa (445)
overweight (449)
obese (449)
psychotherapy (451)
drug therapy (451)
psychodynamic therapy (457)
masochism (457)
cognitive-behavioral approach (458)
nonsexist therapy (460)
feminist therapy (460)

RECOMMENDED READINGS

Enns, C. Z. (1997). *Feminist theories and feminist psychotherapies.* New York: Haworth. This book provides an in-depth exploration of nonsexist therapy and various kinds of feminist therapy. It emphasizes how these therapies are related to different feminist approaches.

Gilbert, L. A., & Scher, M. (1999). *Gender and sex in counseling and psychotherapy.* Boston: Allyn & Bacon. I'd recommend this book to anyone considering a career in clinical or counseling psychology. It covers important topics such as gender bias in practice, gender-sensitive counseling, and ethical issues.

Goodman, W. C. (1995). *Confronting weight prejudice in America.* Carlsbad, CA: Gürze Books. Here's an excellent overview of issues such as the invisibility of overweight women, dieting in the media, how sexism influences weight prejudice, and positive responses to weight issues.

Siegel, M., Brisman, J., & Weinshel, M. (1997). *Surviving an eating disorder: Strategies for family and friends* (Rev. ed.). New York: HarperCollins. As the title suggests, this book is designed to advise people on helping a relative or friend who has an eating disorder. However, it also offers useful information for individuals who want to learn more about their own experiences with eating disorders.

Sprock, J., & Yoder, C. Y. (1997). Women and depression: An update on the report of the APA Task Force, *Psychology of Women Quarterly, 36,* 269–303. At present, no recent full-length book addresses the issue of women and depression; however, this article provides an excellent overview of the topic.

INTERPRETING DEMONSTRATION 12.3

Look at your answers to Demonstration 12.3, and count how many of the following items you endorsed: 1, 4, 5, and 9. If you checked most of these, you tend to appreciate a nonsexist-therapy approach. Now count how many of the following items you endorsed: 2, 3, 6, 7, and 8. If you checked most of these, you tend to appreciate a feminist-therapy approach. (Note that those who admire feminist therapy are also likely to prefer nonsexist therapy.)

ANSWERS TO THE TRUE–FALSE QUESTIONS

1. True (p. 434); 2. False (p. 435); 3. True (p. 440); 4. False (p. 442); 5. True (p. 442); 6. False (p. 445); 7. False (p. 447); 8. True (p. 448); 9. True (p. 453); 10. True (p. 461).

VIOLENCE AGAINST WOMEN

TRUE OR FALSE?

_____ 1. In order for a remark to be considered as sexual harassment, the person making the remark must specify that some sort of sexual favor is requested.

_____ 2. Surveys suggest that about 90% of women in the military say they had been sexually harassed.

_____ 3. People are currently much more sensitive about sexual harassment than they were in the 1980s.

_____ 4. An estimated 15% to 30% of North American women will be victims of a rape during their lifetime.

_____ 5. Women are not sufficiently concerned about the danger of rape; in fact, women and men are equally afraid of walking alone at night.

_____ 6. Many women report that the aftereffects of rape may last for years following the attack.

_____ 7. Only mentally unstable men would consider raping a woman.

_____ 8. The term "abuse of women" refers to psychological abuse as well as physical abuse.

_____ 9. Unemployment increases the likelihood of partner abuse.

_____ 10. Most abusive relationships improve spontaneously, but therapy is recommended when the abuse is severe or long-lasting.

Sexual Harassment
  Why Is Sexual Harassment an
    Important Issue?
  How Often Does Sexual
    Harassment Occur?
  Effects of Harassment on the
    Victim
  Attitudes Toward Sexual
    Harassment
  What to Do About Sexual
    Harassment

Rape
  Acquaintance Rape
  How Often Does Rape Occur?
  Fear of Rape
  Women's Reactions to Rape
  Attitudes Toward Rape
  Myths About Rape
  Child Sexual Abuse
  Marital Rape
  Rape Prevention

The Abuse of Women
  How Often Does the Abuse of
    Women Occur?
  The Dynamics of Abuse
  Women's Reactions to Abuse
  Characteristics of the Abusive
    Relationship
  Attitudes Toward the Abuse of
    Women
  Myths About the Abuse of
    Women
  How Abused Women Take
    Action
  Society's Response to the
    Problem of Abuse

Sexual harassment, rape, and the abuse of women may initially seem to have little in common. However, they share important similarities. For instance, all three involve some form of violence. Women who are sexually harassed may experience physical violence, though the violence is often more subtle. As we will emphasize, rape is a crime of violence, not an act of sexual passion. Finally, women who are abused are likely to experience both physical and psychological violence.

In all three situations, men have more power than women. When we consider sexual harassment, the harassers are usually persons with power in a work or academic setting. In rape, men have more physical power, and they often increase their power by threatening with a weapon. When women are abused, men again have more physical power, and their power is usually magnified because of power inequalities in marriage or in other intimate relationships.

In addition, a culture that values men more than women encourages some men to feel that they are entitled to certain "privileges" and activities (O'Neil & Harway, 1997; O'Neil & Nadeau, 1998). A high-ranking executive assumes he has the right to fondle his secretary. A male college student may feel little guilt about raping his girlfriend. A husband may believe that his wife is his property, so he has the right to batter her.

Furthermore, in all three victimizations, women are left feeling even less powerful after the violence. They have been forced to accept unwanted sexual attention, or their bodies have been violated or beaten. Powerlessness is yet another variation on one of the themes of this book: Women are treated differently than men.

Unfortunately, women seldom regain power by reporting the violence committed against them. Legal procedures are embarrassing and humiliating; they invade a woman's right to privacy even further. All these acts of violence make women more silent and more invisible. The relative invisibility of women is a theme we have mentioned repeatedly throughout this book.

Another similarity across all three situations is that people often blame the
victim. A woman is sexually harassed because "those tight pants invite it." A

DEMONSTRATION 13.1

Making Judgments About Sexual Harassment

Read each of the following four stories. If you believe that a story describes an incident of sexual harassment, write "yes" in front of the item number. If the story does not seem to describe sexual harassment, write "no." In addition, for each story, try to guess what percentage of students at a Northeastern urban university judged the story to represent sexual harassment. (The sample was 60% female.)

1. Dr. X, a male professor, approaches Mary after class and says the following: "Mary, I noticed your new haircut, and it really looks nice." Mary replies, "Thanks, Dr. X." Dr. X says, "No, I mean it *really* looks great . . . or maybe I mean that *you* look great." As she walks off to class, Mary says, "I really have to get to class now, Dr. X."

2. Jill is working with a man named Dr. Q on an independent study. Their work involves meeting together once a week. At their last meeting, the following conversation took place. Dr. Q said, "You know, Jill, we've been meeting for three weeks now, and I can't help but notice how nice you look in those jeans you wear to class. I was wondering why you don't wear them when we meet together. I thought you knew how much they turned me on." Jill did not verbally respond; she simply left the room.

3. Ann got on the elevator on her way to class. As usual, the elevator became crowded, and she was forced to move to the back. Feeling that the person next to her was staring at her, Ann looked up to see who it was. She recognized it was Dr. U from her morning class, and he was eyeing her body up and down and grinning. The elevator doors opened and Ann quickly got out.

4. Ellen is taking a class with Dr. Y. Dr. Y has repeatedly asked Ellen to meet him for coffee or lunch. Ellen has repeatedly declined all of his offers. Dr. Y called her at home last night and said, "Ellen, I know you keep refusing to have lunch with me, and I'm calling to find out why and hopefully to change your mind. I'm a nice guy, and all I want to do is spend some time with you so that we can get to know each other better." Ellen told him to stop calling her and hung up the phone.

These stories are based on the vignettes from a study by Dr. Krisanne Bursik (1992). Turn to the end of this chapter to compare the percentages you provided with the percentage of students in her study who judged each story as representing sexual harassment.

woman is raped because she "asked for it" by her seductive behavior. A woman is beaten because "she probably did something to provoke her husband." In contrast, the aggressor is often perceived as behaving "like any normal male." Although attitudes are changing, the aggressor may receive little blame for the violence.

Finally, all three kinds of violence have their origins in the customary gender-role socialization. Men are "supposed to be" aggressive, dominant, and controlling. Women are "supposed to be" unaggressive, submissive, and yielding. In a sense, sexual harassment, rape, and the abuse of women all represent a tragic exaggeration of traditional gender roles.

SEXUAL HARASSMENT

According to a general definition, **sexual harassment** involves "deliberate or repeated comments, gestures, or physical contacts of a sexual nature that are unwanted by the recipient" (American Psychological Association, 1990, p. 393). Most sexual harassment situations occur in either a work setting or a school setting.

The American legal system now prohibits two kinds of sexual harassment. In the first kind, called **quid pro quo harassment,** an individual with power in an organization makes it clear that someone with less power must submit to sexual advances in order to keep a job, get a good grade in a course, receive a promotion, and so forth. The Latin term *quid pro quo*, roughly translated, means "something for something." That is, the person with less power must give something in order to receive something else that should not be contingent on sexual interactions (Paludi & Barickman, 1998; Rhode, 1997).

The second kind of sexual harassment, called **hostile work environment,** applies to a situation where the atmosphere in a school or work setting is so intimidating and offensive that a student or an employee cannot work effectively (Paludi & Barickman, 1998). Before you read further, try Demonstration 13.1, an exercise designed to help you appreciate the characteristics of sexual harassment.

Let's consider several examples of sexual harassment in order to appreciate the variety of problems in this area.

1. *Quid pro quo sexual bribery.* A woman interested in a film contract was asked by a director to spend a weekend with him in order to talk about a proposed film. As she reported, "I didn't want to sleep with him, but he was holding it over my head and I was willing right then to sleep with him in order to get the job. I finally came to my senses" (NiCarthy et al., 1993, pp. 45–46). When she told him no, she never heard any more about the film contract.

2. *Hostile environment in the workplace.* In 1992, women working at the Mitsubishi Motor Company in Illinois began reporting a variety of harassing interactions. For example, men sometimes exposed themselves to the female workers, pretending to masturbate. Supervisors and coworkers called the women whores,

bitches, and sluts. Photos—displayed throughout the company—showed the managers at sex parties, licking whipped cream off women's breasts and sucking cherries from their vaginas (H. Brown, 1998).

3. *Hostile environment in an academic setting.* Psychologist Keri Heitner (1998) recalls her experience as a graduate student. As she walked down a hallway in the psychology building, one of her male professors approached her and asked, "After classes tonight, why don't you come to my apartment, so that I can make a nude drawing of you?" Fortunately, Heitner had the presence of mind to ask him to repeat the question and then replied, "That's what I thought you said, and if you ever ask me anything like that again, I'm going to the department chair" (p. 14).

Most of this section on sexual harassment examines how males sexually harass females they perceive to be heterosexual. Keep in mind, however, that lesbian women may be sexually harassed—for example, by males or by other lesbians in positions of power. Males can also be sexually harassed by women or by other men. However, in the most common situation, a male is harassing a female (Dziech & Hawkins, 1998).

You may read reports about females being harassed by their male classmates, beginning in elementary school and continuing through college (e.g., S. Houston & Hwang, 1996; Paludi & Barickman, 1998). Women are also harassed in public settings by whistles, cat calls, and sexually explicit comments. These forms of harassment are certainly worrisome. In this chapter, however, we will focus on two situations in which a female is being harassed by a male with higher status: (1) professors harassing students in college settings, and (2) supervisors harassing employees in work settings. Both situations raise particular problems because they involve power inequities and reasonably long-term relationships between the woman and the harasser.

Why Is Sexual Harassment an Important Issue?

The term "sexual harassment" did not even exist until the mid-1970s (MacKinnon, 1979). However, theorists quickly established that it was a feminist issue. Here are several reasons why sexual harassment is an important factor in gender relationships (Benokraitis, 1997b; Murray, 1998; L. Phillips, 1998; Zalk, 1996):

1. Sexual harassment is a form of violence against women.

2. Sexual harassment emphasizes that men typically have more power than women in our society.

3. Sexual demands are often coercive because women are offered economic or academic advantages if they comply, and harmful consequences if they say no.

4. Sexual harassment dehumanizes women; they are seen primarily as sexual beings, rather than as intelligent and skilled employees or students.

5. Women are often forced to be silent victims because of fear and the need to continue either in the workplace or at school.

6. If sexual harassment occurs in a public setting, without condemnation from supervisors, many onlookers will conclude that sexist behavior is acceptable.

How Often Does Sexual Harassment Occur?

It is extremely difficult to estimate how often sexual harassment occurs. The boundaries of sexual harassment are often unclear, and many cases go unreported (Arvey & Cavanaugh, 1995; Dziech & Hawkins, 1998). The 1991 Anita Hill/Clarence Thomas hearings brought sexual harassment into the national spotlight. This attention contributed to the dramatic rise in the number of sexual harassment complaints filed with the U.S. Equal Employment Opportunity Commission (EEOC): from 6,000 reported cases in 1990 to 15,300 in 1996 (Gratch, 1997; L. Kaufman, 1997).

Reports of sexual harassment on college campuses suggest that between 20% and 40% of undergraduate women have been harassed (Cochran et al., 1997; Rabinowitz, 1996; Sandler & Shoop, 1997). Women in graduate programs may be even more likely to experience sexual harassment. For example, a national survey revealed that 79% of female physicians reported being sexually harassed while in medical school (Dickstein, 1996).

The incidence of sexual harassment in the workplace varies widely, depending on the employment setting. Women employed in traditionally male occupations are especially likely to experience sexual harassment (Bondurant & White, 1996; Landrine & Klonoff, 1997; Murrell et al., 1995). For instance, women in the military frequently report sexual teasing, unwanted touching, and pressure for sexual favors. According to surveys, 90% of women in the military said that they had experienced sexual harassment (Newell et al., 1995; Rhode, 1997; Seppa, 1997b).

As you might imagine, sexual harassment is a major problem for women of color in blue-collar jobs (Brandenburg, 1997; Ragins & Scandura, 1995). For example, Yoder and Aniakudo (1996) interviewed Black female firefighters. More than 90% said that they had experienced unwanted sexual teasing, jokes, and remarks on the job. They also reported that their male coworkers played pranks such as pouring syrup into their firefighting boots and bursting in while they are using the toilet. Many also reported that their male coworkers created a "hostile work environment" by shunning them. One 40-year-old woman wrote:

. . . things are so subtle, as I said, because no one really talked to me. It was difficult the first, I'd say, six months, because I was basically alone. I'd walk in and everything would get quiet. I'd go to eat; everybody leaves the room. . . . As I've said, I've been on the job now seven years, and there's still guys that don't talk to me. (p. 260)

Sexual harassment is not limited to North America. Reports come from countries such as Israel, India, and China (S. Ellis et al., 1991; Pandey, 1992; Zhou, 1994). For example, about three-quarters of women in a Chinese survey admitted to having been sexually harassed (Zhou, 1994). These Chinese women's stories sound sadly familiar: a boss repeatedly comments on a woman's clothing and touches her body, or a restaurant owner insists on sexual relationships from women who want to keep their jobs.

Effects of Harassment on the Victim

Sexual harassment is not simply a minor inconvenience to women; it can change their lives. If a woman refuses her boss's sexual advances, she may receive a negative job evaluation, a demotion, or a transfer to another job. She may be fired or pressured into quitting (Paludi & Barickman, 1998; Studd, 1996). Women who have been harassed in an academic setting may drop out of school or miss classes taught by the harasser (Paludi & Barickman, 1998). However, the victims still suffer, as one student reported:

> The impact of this isolated incident on me has been enormous. It has changed my way of relating to the program. I used to think it could be a place of learning, mentoring, work and fun. Now, although there are still people there whom I trust and learn from, I am angry and insecure every time I'm in that building. (Paludi et al., 1995, p. 178)

How do women respond emotionally to sexual harassment? Most women experience anger, embarrassment, and depression. They may also feel ashamed, as if they were somehow responsible for the harassment (Paludi & Barickman, 1998; Quina, 1996; Rabinowitz, 1996). They may become less self-confident about their academic abilities (Satterfield & Muehlenhard, 1997). Common physical reactions include headaches, eating disorders, and sleep disturbances (Paludi & Barickman, 1998).

In part, a woman's reaction to sexual harassment depends on whether she decides to take any action against the harasser. If she does, she could be labeled a troublemaker. She may be scorned by some people, and she may find that employees will band together in defense of a colleague (Dziech & Weiner, 1990; Koss, 1990). If a woman takes legal action, her struggle will take time and savings. The emotional costs will also be high. All these problems will increase her feelings of helplessness and isolation. On the other hand, if she decides not to take any action against the harasser, she may feel even more powerless and victimized.

Attitudes Toward Sexual Harassment

Susan Bordo (1998) recalls her experience with sexual harassment when she was a graduate student. One of her professors had begun to express more than professional interest in her work. When she turned him down, he began to escalate the harassment. One day, he laughingly said, "It's time for class, dear," patting her on the rear as they stood in the open doorway of a classroom filled with other students. When she tried to explain to the professor how his actions had made her feel degraded, he replied that she should not be so sensitive. Then she described the episode to some of her close male friends. They acted similarly casual about the harassment. As they replied, "Well, what did you expect? You don't exactly dress like a nun!" (p. B6).

We noted earlier that women who have been sexually harassed respond with a variety of negative emotional responses. These negative emotions are further intensified when other people display casual attitudes toward the harassment, rather than offering the sympathy and understanding that the harassment victim deserves.

In the current era, people are more sensitive about sexual harassment than they were prior to the Hill/Thomas hearings (Jaschik-Herman & Fisk, 1995). Men are sometimes more accepting of sexual harassment than women are, at least in North American research (J.D. Johnson et al., 1997; Pryor et al., 1997; Saperstein et al., 1995). However, the characteristics of the situation are more important than the rater's gender in determining attitudes toward sexual harassment (Gutek & O'Connor, 1995). For example, Bursik (1992) found that male and female college students responded the same in classifying the stories you saw in Demonstration 13.1. Notice from the data on page 509 that Scenario 2 was most likely to be considered an example of sexual harassment. However, roughly half of the participants also thought that the other scenarios illustrated sexual harassment.

What to Do About Sexual Harassment

Individual Action.   What can an individual woman do when she has been sexually harassed? Here are some recommendations for students who are concerned about harassment in an academic setting (Alexander & LaRosa, 1994; Dziech & Weiner, 1990; Paludi & Barickman, 1998; Quina, 1996):

1. Become familiar with your campus's policy on sexual harassment, and know which officials are responsible for complaints.

2. If a professor's behavior seems questionable, review the situation objectively with someone you trust.

3. Sexual harassment frequently increases when the person being harassed simply tries to disregard it. If the problem persists, consider telling the harasser directly that his sexual harassment makes you feel uncomfortable. Another effective strategy is to send a typewritten letter to the harasser. Give a factual account of the events, describe your objections to the incident, and state clearly that you want the actions to stop (Paludi & Barickman, 1998). Sign your full name to the letter. Many harassment policies cannot be legally applied unless the harasser has been informed that the behavior is unwanted and inappropriate.

4. Keep records of all occurrences, and keep copies of all correspondence.

5. If the problem persists, report it to the appropriate officials on campus. An institution that takes no action is responsible if another act of harassment occurs after an incident is reported.

6. Join a feminist group on campus, or help to start one. A strong support group can encourage real empowerment and reduce the chances that other students will experience sexual harassment.

These six suggestions can also be adapted for the workplace; employed women can take similar steps to avoid and eliminate sexual harassment. If a harasser persists, threats of exposure to a superior may be necessary. Women who have been sexually harassed may also try to determine whether the harasser has approached their coworkers. They may need to file a formal complaint with a superior, a union official, or a personnel officer. Competent legal advice may also be necessary. Fortunately, a recent Supreme Court decision stated that employers are potentially liable when supervisors harass employees—even when the companies are not aware of the misconduct (Reibstein, 1998).

A woman who files a sexual harassment charge should be prepared for an unsympathetic response from college administrators or company officials. She is likely to be told that the event was simply a misunderstanding, or that the harasser is so competent and valuable that this "minor" incident should be forgotten. In many cases, the administrators—and even colleagues—will close ranks and treat the woman in a hostile fashion in order to protect the institution. Many women report feeling completely isolated and alienated during this experience.

Students in women's studies courses often protest that nothing about sexual harassment seems fair. This viewpoint is absolutely correct. A woman shouldn't have to suffer the pain and embarrassment of sexual harassment, see the quality of her work decline, and then—in many cases—find that administrators, supervisors, and the legal system do not support her.

How Men Can Help.   Men who care about women and women's issues can be part of the solution (Zalk, 1996). First, they themselves must avoid behaviors that might be perceived as sexual harassment. Langelan (1993) described some excellent methods that men can use to help correct the problem. Men should speak up when they see another man sexually harassing someone. Harassers may be more likely to stop if other males point out that they are offended by sexual harassment.

If you are a male reading this book, think what steps you might take if you hear that a woman is being sexually harassed by one of your male friends. It's difficult to tell a male friend that a woman may not enjoy his comments about her body. However, if you are silent, your silence may be interpreted as approval.

Society's Response to the Harassment Problem.   Individual women and men need to take action against sexual harassment. However, to stop sexual harassment more effectively, *institutions* must pay attention to the issue. Universities and corporations need to develop clear policies about sexual harassment (Biaggio & Brownell, 1996; Carothers & Richmond, 1997; Sandler, 1997). They should also publicize these policies and hold workshops—with top administrators in attendance—on sexual harassment issues. Students and employees should receive information about procedures to follow if they believe they have been sexually harassed.

Public opinion also needs to be changed. People must become more aware that sexual harassment limits the rights and opportunities of women in academic and work settings. Men need to realize that women often do not appreciate sexual attention. In addition, behavior that a man regards as flirtation may feel more like sexual harassment to a woman. Some men who harass may not be aware that they are creating a problem. Others may believe that they have a sanction to harass because of good-natured responses from other men. A change in public opinion can alter behavior, particularly because harassers often hold highly visible positions.

However, the real answer may lie in the unequal distribution of power between men and women (Langelan, 1993). If we really want to eliminate sexual harassment, we must go beyond the level of trying to convince individual harassers to alter their behavior. Instead, we need to change the uneven distribution of power that encourages sexual harassment.

 Sexual Harassment

1. **Sexual harassment, rape, and abuse of women all focus on violence and power inequalities—situations in which men feel entitled to certain privileges. All of these behaviors make women feel less powerful and less visible, and they are also related to gender-role socialization.**

2. **Two kinds of sexual harassment are (a) quid pro quo harassment and (b) harassment that creates a hostile work environment.**

3. **Sexual harassment is an important issue because (a) it emphasizes violence and gender inequalities; (b) it is coercive and dehumanizing; (c) it may force women to be silent victims; and (d) it may encourage onlookers to believe that sexist behavior is acceptable.**

4. **Sexual harassment occurs fairly often in academia and in the workplace, especially when women are employed in traditionally male occupations.**

5. **Women who have been sexually harassed often quit jobs or leave school; they may experience anger, embarrassment, depression, shame, and reduced self-confidence.**

6. **On some measures, men sometimes have more tolerant attitudes toward sexual harassment than women do; however, gender differences tend to be small.**

7. When we consider how to reduce sexual harassment, we must consider not only the individual actions of women and men, but also the policies of universities and corporations, as well as the more general issue of the unequal distribution of power in society.

RAPE

Rape can be defined as sexual penetration—without the individual's consent—obtained by force or by threat of physical harm, or when the victim is incapable of giving consent (T. Jackson & Petretic-Jackson, 1996; Koss, 1992; Ullman, 1996). A broader term, **sexual assault,** includes sexual touching and other forms of unwanted sexual contact, which may be accompanied by psychological pressure and coercion or by physical threats. For example, a man may say, "If you really loved me, you'd let me," or he may threaten to leave the relationship if the woman does not comply. The legal definition of rape may be used in a court case. However, the inclusiveness of the term *sexual assault* helps us understand the many ways in which men have power over women's lives.

Some rapes are committed by strangers. For example, a 25-year-old woman was attacked in a shopping-mall parking lot by a stranger who used a knife to force her into his car. He drove her to a deserted area, raped her, stabbed her, set the car on fire, and then left. Although she was severely injured, she survived (Koss & Harvey, 1991).

However, we'll emphasize in this section that a rapist is more likely to be an acquaintance than a stranger. For example, a 32-year-old nursing student heard loud knocking on her door. She looked out, and a man she knew slightly was sobbing and telling her he desperately needed to talk to someone. He explained that he had just learned that his mother was diagnosed with terminal cancer. She suggested several mutual friends who knew him better, but he replied that they were not available. Reluctantly, she let him in. After the door was closed, he immediately changed his demeanor. He shoved her against the wall and told her he would really hurt her if she did not keep quiet. He then proceeded to rape her in her living room. Nearly a year later, she commented, "It's terrible to live every day afraid to trust people" (Petretic-Jackson & Tobin, 1996, p. 94).

Tragically, rape is found in virtually every culture and in most civilizations throughout history (Biglan, 1996; Zillman, 1998). In recent years, invading soldiers have systematically raped women in countries such as Bangladesh, Peru, and Uganda (Neft & Levine, 1997). One of the most tragic reports described how Serbian forces in the former Yugoslavia raped countless thousands of Muslim women, in an attempt to drive Muslims from their homes (Kuzmanović, 1995; Stiglmayer, 1994).

Other examples of rape have been less publicized. Consider the young men at a coed boarding school in Kenya. The male students had called for a strike against the school's headmaster. When their female classmates refused to strike, the young men attacked, raping 71 young women and killing 19 others. The

---

DEMONSTRATION 13.2

Knowledge About Rape

Answer each of the following questions about rape by checking the space that represents your answer.

	Agree	Disagree
1. Women who have had sexual relationships with a man often try to protect their reputation by claiming they have been raped.	_____	_____
2. Women cannot always prevent being raped by resisting their attackers.	_____	_____
3. Men rape because they experience uncontrollable sexual urges.	_____	_____
4. Most women secretly desire to be raped.	_____	_____
5. Most rapes are not reported to the police.	_____	_____
6. A woman who is sexually experienced will not really be damaged by rape.	_____	_____
7. Women who dress in a sexually seductive way provoke rape.	_____	_____
8. Most reported sexual assaults actually were true cases of sexual assaults.	_____	_____
9. Sexual assaults usually occur away from a woman's home—in isolated areas.	_____	_____
10. A rapist cannot be identified by his appearance or general behavior.	_____	_____

(Based on Worell & Remer, 1992, pp. 195–196.)

---

deputy principal announced, "The boys never meant any harm against the girls. They just wanted to rape" (Heise, 1991, p. 23).

Before you read further, try Demonstration 13.2 to assess your knowledge about rape. Then you can check the answers at the end of the chapter.

Acquaintance Rape

Psychologists and other researchers are increasingly aware that a rapist is not likely to be a stranger attacking in a dark alley. Instead, a rapist may be your chemistry lab partner, your sister's boyfriend, a business acquaintance, or the proverbial "boy next door." **Acquaintance rape** can be defined as "unlawful sexual intercourse accomplished by force or fear with a person known to the victim who is not related by blood or marriage" (Wallace, 1999, p. 313). Let's consider some important aspects of acquaintance rape, as well as attitudes toward this kind of sexual assault.

Characteristics of Acquaintance Rape. Surveys suggest that about 15% of women will experience acquaintance rape. An additional 35% to 40% of women will experience some other form of sexual assault from an acquaintance (J. White & Kowalski, 1998).

Women who have been forced—against their will—to have sex with a person they know are often unsure whether they have been raped (Wallace, 1999). For example, a representative study conducted at a Canadian university focused on women who had been assaulted by an acquaintance and whose experience met the legal definition for rape. Among these women, only 40% classified the assault as rape (Shimp & Chartier, 1998). In other words, the majority of these women had indeed been raped, yet they did not apply that term to the assault.

Researchers have tried to determine the conditions associated with acquaintance rape. By some estimates, about half of rapes are associated with the use of alcohol by either the perpetrator or the victim (Abbey et al., 1994). You may also have read about a drug called Rohypnol, sometimes called "roofie" or "the date rape drug," which can be mixed with alcohol to increase the sensation of drunkenness (Lively, 1996; Wallace, 1999). Many cases have been reported in which a woman has passed out after Rohypnol has been slipped into her drink. The effect is like an alcohol blackout; the woman typically has no recall of any events that occurred after she passed out—even a rape attack. The drug has been banned in the United States, but it is available illegally. Incidentally, women who suspect they have been given Rohypnol can be tested up to about 60 hours afterward, to see whether traces of the drug are present.

Other researchers have tried to determine what kind of setting is associated with acquaintance rape. For example, Boswell and Spade (1999) found that certain conditions at fraternity parties increased the risk of rape. Specifically, rape was more common when the men attending the parties engaged in hostility and conversations that degraded women. For example, a man at one of these high-risk fraternity parties said, "Did you know that this week is Women's Awareness Week? I guess that means we get to abuse them more this week" (p. 273). Nudity and aggression were also common at these parties.

Some cases of acquaintance rape can probably be traced to a particular kind of miscommunication. Specifically, research by Antonia Abbey has demonstrated that men are more likely than women to perceive other people as being seductive (Abbey, 1982; Abbey & Harnish, 1995). For example, Saundra may smile pleasantly and maintain eye contact with Ted. To her, these are nonverbal gestures that she employs to convey platonic friendship. Nevertheless, Ted may interpret the gestures as a sexual invitation.

DEMONSTRATION 13.3

Assigning Responsibility for Rape

Read the first scenario below. Then decide who is responsible for the occurrence of the rape, John or Jane. If you believe that John is entirely responsible, assign a value of 100% to the John column and 0% to the Jane column. If they are both equally responsible, assign a value of 50% to each one. If Jane is entirely responsible, assign a value of 0% to the John column and 100% to the Jane column. Use any values between 0% and 100%, as long as the two values sum to 100. To make the situations comparable, assume that both John and Jane are college students in all five scenarios. After completing the first scenario, read and evaluate each subsequent one.

John   Jane

_____ _____ 1. Jane is walking back to her dorm from the library at 9 P.M., taking a route that everyone considers safe. As she passes the science building, John leaps out, knocks her down, drags her to an unlit area, and rapes her.

_____ _____ 2. Jane is at a party, where she meets a pleasant-looking student named John. After dancing for a while, he suggests they go outside to cool off. No one else is outside. John knocks her down, drags her to an unlit area, and rapes her.

_____ _____ 3. Jane is at a party, and she has had enough drinks that she is feeling somewhat dizzy. She meets a pleasant-looking student named John, who suggests they go outside to cool off. Once outside, she passes out. When she wakes up, she finds that John is on top of her and proceeding to rape her.

_____ _____ 4. Jane is on a first date with John, whom she knows slightly from her history class. After the movies, they go out for an elegant, late-night meal. Both decide to split the cost of both the movies and the meal. In the car on the way home, John stops in a secluded area. Jane tries to escape once she realizes what is happening, but John is much larger than she is, and he pins her down and rapes her.

_____ _____ 5. Jane is on a first date with John, whom she knows slightly from her history class. After the movies, they go out for an elegant, late-night meal. John pays for the cost of both the movies and the meal. In the car on the way home, John stops in a secluded area. Jane tries to escape once she realizes what is happening, but John is much larger than she is, and he pins her down and rapes her.

In general, research has confirmed the tendency for men to interpret behavior in a more sexual manner than women do (Edmondson & Conger, 1995; Patton & Mannison, 1995). Unfortunately, however, this research has often been misconstrued (M. Crawford, 1995). For example, the popular media often blame women for sending the wrong messages, rather than acknowledging that men misinterpret the messages.

The findings on miscommunication have practical implications for both women and men. First, women should be aware that their friendliness may be misperceived by men. Second, men must learn that friendly verbal and nonverbal messages from a woman may simply mean "I like you" or "I enjoy talking with you." A smile and extended eye contact do not necessarily mean "I want to have a sexual relationship with you."

Attitudes Toward Acquaintance Rape. Before you read further, try Demonstration 13.3, which examines how people assign responsibility for acquaintance rape.

People are much more likely to blame the rapist in a case of stranger rape, rather than acquaintance rape (Morris, 1997; Wallace, 1999). Compare your answers to the first and second scenario. In the first scenario, did you assign all (or almost all) of the blame to John? Did you shift the blame somewhat when Jane had known John for perhaps 30 minutes? Now concentrate on your response to the third scenario, in which Jane was drunk. Studies demonstrate that people are likely to hold a woman more responsible for a rape if she is intoxicated or "stoned" (Lundberg-Love & Geffner, 1989).

Now see whether your assignment of blame differed for Scenarios 4 and 5. Again, research shows that people are more likely to hold a woman responsible for a rape if the man paid for the date (Lundberg-Love & Geffner, 1989; Morris, 1997). Let's say that the evening cost $80. In Scenario 4, they therefore each paid $40. In Scenario 5, John paid $80. Does paying $40 extra give John the right to rape Jane?

Other research confirms something you may have suspected: People are reluctant to use the word "rape" when the two individuals know each other. Hannon and her colleagues (1996) constructed a vignette about two classmates on a date, in which intercourse occurred even though the woman resisted physically. Only 53% of the participants labeled the assault as rape.

Kelly McLendon and her coauthors (1994) discovered, however, that men and women may have fairly similar attitudes toward acquaintance rape. These researchers worked together with female and male students to create a scenario that described a forced sexual encounter between a dating couple. In each scenario, the incident was described from the viewpoint of both the man (John) and the woman (Joan).

College students from a university in the Southeast read the scenario and then made judgments about a number of statements concerning the incident. Figure 13.1 shows the results for several of these statements. As you can see, some items showed significant gender differences, but other items did not. In all

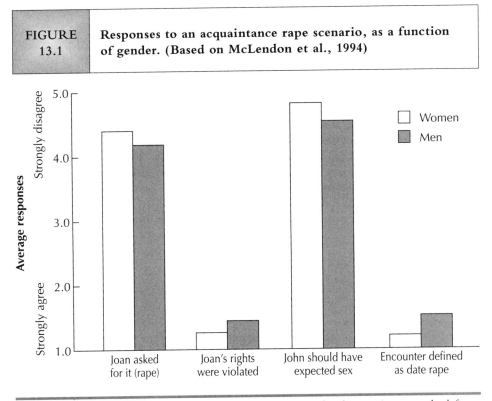

FIGURE 13.1 Responses to an acquaintance rape scenario, as a function of gender. (Based on McLendon et al., 1994)

Note: The gender differences were not statistically significant for the two items on the left, but they were significant for the two items on the right.

cases, however, the men's and women's ratings were within a half-point of each other, suggesting that the two genders do not live on separate planets. Keep in mind, that these results were obtained with college students. Do you think that the gender differences would be larger in a noncollege sample?

How Often Does Rape Occur?

As you can imagine, estimating the incidence of rape is difficult. One problem is that surveys differ in their definitions of rape and sexual assault. Another problem is that women are reluctant to indicate on a survey that they have been raped; they may be even more reluctant to report the crime to the police (Koss, 1992). However, current estimates in both the United States and Canada suggest that between 15% and 30% of women will be victims of rape at some point during their lives (Morris, 1997; Muehlenhard et al., 1997; Statistics Canada, 1993; L. Taylor, 1995; J. White & Bondurant, 1996). The data clearly demonstrate that rape is a real problem for women in North America (Koss, 1997).

Only a fraction of rape victims report the crime to the police. In the United States, an estimated 16% of victims report the rape (Boeschen et al., 1998). The percentage is even lower in other countries. In Korea, for example, fewer than 2% of rape victims contact the police (United Nations, 1995). Extremely low reporting is understandable in countries such as Pakistan, where a woman who has been raped may find herself charged with adultery. The judicial system can then impose unspeakably harsh sentences, such as death by stoning for illegal sexual relations (Neft & Levine, 1997).

What happens in the United States when a woman does decide to report to the police that she has been raped? Only 15% to 30% of reported rapes end up with the rapist being convicted. Furthermore, of those who are convicted, only half spend more than a year in jail (Fast & Fast, 1995; Rhode, 1997). By awarding light sentences, the justice system conveys the message that rape really isn't harmful to women.

Fear of Rape

The previous sections focused on women who had been raped. However, we also need to consider that all women suffer because of the threat of rape (Beneke, 1997). Young girls and elderly women can be raped, and many women are raped in the "safety" of their own homes. All women are vulnerable. One woman reported a routine that might sound familiar:

> When I get into the car, I always check the back seat to make sure that there is no one lurking around. I always have my keys in my hand, so that when I get to the car, I can stick the key into the door. . . . And I lock the doors right away. (Stanko, 1993, p. 159)

Surveys in both the United States and Canada confirm this fear of rape. Specifically, between 33% and 54% of women report that they feel unsafe when they are out alone at night. In contrast, only 10% to 17% of men report feeling unsafe (Gordon & Riger, 1989; M. Schwartz & DeKeseredy, 1997; Statistics Canada, 1995; L. Taylor, 1995).

Fear of rape controls women's behavior and restricts what they can do, no matter where they live. I teach at a college that is located in a small village in upstate New York farmland. Nevertheless, if they are alone at night, my female students cannot feel safe. Sadly, the fear of rape drastically reduces women's sense of freedom (Rozee, 1996).

A recent survey of women at a Midwestern university documented that they take many precautions to avoid being raped by a stranger. However, they take significantly fewer precautions to avoid being raped by an acquaintance—even though they correctly acknowledge that acquaintance rape is more common than stranger rape (Hickman & Muehlenhard, 1997).

We need to examine several important characteristics of rape: women's reactions to rape, attitudes and myths about rape, child sexual abuse, marital rape, and rape prevention.

Women's Reactions to Rape

Reactions During the Rape.   Women experience many diverse reactions during a rape attack. Naturally, a woman's responses may depend on the nature of the attack, whether she knows the assailant, the threat of danger, her stage in life, and other circumstances. However, almost all women who have been raped report that they were terrified, confused, overwhelmed, and anxious during the time they were being raped (Worell & Remer, 1992). A woman who feels that her life is in great danger may direct all her behavior toward staying alive.

Consider the case of Brenda, a 22-year-old college senior. One of her male classmates had been stopping by the library to visit her periodically, and she enjoyed their conversations together. One day, Brenda was shopping near her home and ran into her classmate. He asked if he could have a cup of coffee at her apartment and continue their conversation. After they had been in the apartment for about an hour, he startled her by suggesting that they go into her bedroom and have sex. Brenda felt a growing sense of panic, especially when he didn't listen to her increasingly anxious requests to leave her apartment. He then began playing with a knife that was lying on her kitchen counter. Fearing that he might stab her, Brenda decided to comply. He raped her and then left. She soon began to shake, and she felt so dirty that she scrubbed until her skin was raw and bleeding (Petretic-Jackson & Tobin, 1996).

Short-Term Adjustment.   A woman may experience a wide range of feelings during the first few weeks after a rape. Some women have an expressive style during the first few weeks after the attack. They show their feelings of fear, anger, and anxiety by crying and being restless and tense (Calhoun & Atkeson, 1991; Gordon & Riger, 1989; A. Kahn & Andreoli Mathie, 1999). Others have a controlled style; they hide their feelings with a calm, composed, and subdued external appearance.

Once again, we must emphasize our theme of individual differences. For example, Fine (1997) describes a 24-year-old mother who had just experienced a brutal gang rape. She showed little concern for her own physical and mental health and chose not to take legal action. As she told the staff members in the hospital emergency room:

> Prosecute? No, I just want to get home. While I'm pickin' some guy out of some line, who knows who's messin' around with my momma and my baby. (p. 152)

Among the early responses that most rape victims share, however, are feelings of helplessness and devaluation. Women frequently feel guilty as well, and they blame themselves for the rape (Allison & Wrightsman, 1993; A. Kahn & Andreoli Mathie, 1998). Consider the nursing student we discussed at the beginning of this section (p. 477). Her motives in letting her acquaintance into her home had been entirely altruistic; she was in no way responsible for her rape. Yet, after the rape, she blamed herself:

She said she felt "stupid" for being "taken in" the way she had, that "she should have known better." She did not tell anyone in her family about the assault since she believed they would think "less of her" for it. After all, she had acted carelessly in allowing her rapist into her home late at night. (Petretic-Jackson & Tobin, 1996, p. 94).

Self-blame is a particularly troublesome reaction because, in nearly all cases, the woman did nothing to precipitate the assault.

In the weeks following a rape, a woman may feel extremely vulnerable. She may realize that a tragedy has already struck—and another tragedy may strike in the future (Allison & Wrightsman, 1993; Janoff-Bulman, 1992). Most people who have not experienced a trauma believe that life is predictable, tragic events do not happen to good people, and strangers are trustworthy. Women who have been raped may feel that all these basic assumptions about humans are shattered. They may feel relatively defenseless in such an unpredictable world.

In addition to the psychological reactions that immediately follow a rape, a woman may have physical effects. She may be sore and bruised. She may experience gynecological symptoms, such as vaginal discharge, itching, and generalized pain. Realistically, a woman who has been raped needs to worry about whether her attacker infected her with AIDS and other sexually transmitted diseases—in addition to the possibility of pregnancy (Golding, 1996; Gostin et al., 1994). However, many women are too upset or too ashamed to seek medical attention.

A woman who has been raped must also decide whether to report the crime to the police. Women frequently decide not to make an official report because "it wouldn't do any good." They believe that the criminal justice system won't handle the case effectively, that officials won't believe them, that they might be embarrassed by the verifying procedure, and that the assailant might try to retaliate. Sadly, these fears may be realistic. The legal system often harasses and frightens women who have been raped—often blaming victims rather than supporting them (Allison & Wrightsman, 1993; Rhode, 1997).

Long-Term Adjustment. The effects of a rape do not disappear suddenly. The physical and mental aftereffects may last for years. Common physical health problems include pelvic pain, excessive menstrual bleeding, gastrointestinal problems, and neurological problems (Golding, 1996; Golding et al., 1997). Excessive weight loss and eating disorders are also common (Laws & Golding, 1996).

Many rape victims also meet the criteria for a psychological disorder called **posttraumatic stress disorder (PTSD),** a pattern of symptoms such as intense fear, heightened anxiety, and emotional numbing that follow a traumatic event (American Psychiatric Association, 1994; Foa, 1998; Koss et al., 1996). A woman experiencing PTSD following a rape may report that she keeps reexperiencing the rape, either in nightmares or in thoughts intruding during daily activities. Her memories of the rape may seem very vivid and emotionally intense. One large-scale study reported that 32% of rape victims met the criteria for posttraumatic stress disorder during the period following the rape. In addition, 12% still experienced PTSD at least one year afterward (Foa, 1998). Once again, however, individual differences are striking; many women experience a decrease in psychological symptoms within 3 months following the assault.

Many women seek professional psychotherapy to reduce persistent symptoms. Controlled studies have shown that several kinds of psychotherapy are effective. Many current approaches use components of the cognitive-behavioral approach (see p. 458 in Chapter 12). For example, the therapist may ask the client to gradually confront the painful memories, and the therapist helps her manage the anxieties that arise as she creates a mental image of the traumatic event (Foa, 1998).

Women who are raped can often manage to transform their terrifying experience in a way that makes them stronger, more determined, and more resilient. As Harney and Muehlenhard (1991) write, we need "to recognize the complexity with which women cope with, resist, and survive sexual assault" (p. 14).

Attitudes Toward Rape

Some writers have suggested that women who are raped are doubly victimized, first by the assailant and later by the attitudes of other people (Madigan & Gamble, 1991). The victim may find that her own family and friends, the court system, and society all tend to blame her and treat her negatively because of something that was not her fault. These responses are particularly damaging at a time when the victim needs compassion and help.

The legal system's treatment of rape is mostly beyond the scope of this book. However, we hear numerous reports of injustice and mistreatment. For example, a judge in Massachusetts explained why he had given a rapist a light sentence: "It's not like [the victim] was tortured or chopped up." A New York City judge recommended leniency for a man who had forcibly sodomized a retarded woman, because "there was no violence here" (Rhode, 1997, p. 122).

In general, the research on attitudes toward rape shows some gender differences. For example, men are more likely than women to blame rape victims for the assault (G. Cowan & Quinton, 1997; Kopper, 1996; Mori et al., 1995). In addition, people with traditional gender roles are more likely to blame rape victims for the assault (B. E. Johnson et al., 1997). Older adults are typically more likely than younger adults to blame the rape victim (C. Ward, 1995).

Myths About Rape

The attitudes toward rape that we have just examined are partially shaped by numerous myths about rape, rapists, and rape victims. As you might imagine, these rape myths can intensify the anguish of a woman who has been raped. Here are six of the more common myths.

Myth 1: Only deviant men would consider raping a woman. Many people believe the myth that only men with serious psychological disorders would think about raping someone (B. E. Johnson et al., 1997; C. Ward, 1995). This myth is not correct. For example, Osland and her colleagues (1996) gave a questionnaire about rape to undergraduate males at a small Midwestern college affiliated with a Protestant church. We might expect males at this kind of college to be especially repulsed by thoughts of sexual violence. However, 34% of them reported some likelihood to engage in rape or forced sex. These results do not imply that every college male is a potential rapist. However, the high percentage who would consider rape suggests that the inclination to rape is not limited to a few deviant men.

Myth 2: Rapists are strangers—people unknown to the victim. We don't know precisely what percentage of rapes is committed by strangers, especially because women would be less likely to report a rape that was committed by someone they know. As we'll see throughout this chapter, however, rapes are frequently committed by acquaintances and by relatives (C. Ward, 1995).

Myth 3: Women ask to be raped; they could avoid rape if they wanted to. Many people believe that women invite rape. According to one study, for example, 17% of undergraduates agreed with the statement, "Women provoke rapes" (B. E. Johnson et al., 1997, p. 697). Rape is the crime that is most likely to be blamed on the victim (J. White & Sorenson, 1992). In addition, prime-time TV dramas often set up the plot so that the rape victim "deserves" to be raped (Brinson, 1992).

Myth 4: Women routinely lie about rape. In a few rare cases, rape charges against a man are later found to be false. However, the percentage of false reports is very low. In the United States, for example, about 1% to 2% of reports of rapes are estimated to be false. In fact, the incidence of false reports of rape is about the same as for other violent crimes (C. Ward, 1995). *Under*reporting of rape is a much more worrisome problem than *over*reporting. However, the media widely publicize the isolated examples of false charges.

Myth 5: Only "bad" women are raped. The testimonies of rape victims demonstrate that any woman can be raped. In Singapore, for example, rape victims are 10 times more likely to be sexually naïve young female students, rather than women who work in nightclubs or in professions in which sexual experience might be likely (C. Ward, 1995). In North America and Great Britain, research shows that rape victims may be attractive or unattractive, slender or overweight, and ranging in age from 6 months to 93 years (Carroll & Jackson, 1996; C. Ward, 1995).

Myth 6: Pornography provides a "safety valve" or catharsis that makes men less likely to rape. According to this catharsis myth, rape would decrease if pornography were more widely available. However, researchers have discovered no support for this myth (R. Harris, 1994). Instead, pornography that emphasizes violence can indeed be harmful.

For example, consider a study by Malamuth (1998) in which men were asked whether they had ever been sexually aggressive toward a woman. Malamuth also assessed these men with respect to three risk factors, which he called hostile masculinity, promiscuity, and pornography consumption. The results showed that 72% of the men who were high in hostility, high in promiscuity, and high in pornography consumption reported at least one case of sexual aggression. In contrast, 44% of the men who were high in hostility, high in promiscuity, and *low* in pornography consumption reported sexual aggression. Although we need to be cautious about confounding variables, frequent exposure to pornography increased the risk of sexual aggression by about 64% in this sample. (Incidentally, "only" 11% of men who were low on all three variables reported sexual aggression.)

Pornography is clearly a complex social, moral, and legal issue (G. Cowan & Dunn, 1994). Many men can view pornography without behaving violently toward women. However, pornography is not simply an innocent entertainment. Also, no researcher has ever demonstrated that pornography makes men treat women more *positively*.

Now we will shift our focus away from attitudes toward rape and myths about rape. We'll consider two kinds of sexual abuse that raise additional concerns: child sexual abuse and marital rape. These two forms of abuse create unique problems because they typically occur in the context of an ongoing close relationship.

Child Sexual Abuse

Katherine Brady (1993), now a middle-aged woman, recalls how her father sexually abused her from the ages of 8 to 18. He showed her pornographic photos as "teaching tools," before engaging in fellatio and sexual intercourse. He also played sexual games with her, for example, pretending that he was wiring her breasts together. The issue of child sexual abuse reminds us that adult women are not the only victims of violence; even young children are vulnerable.

Child sexual abuse is particularly cruel because, in most cases, children are abused by relatives, neighbors, and caretakers. The irony is that the abusers are the very individuals who should be protecting them, nurturing them, and acting in their best interests.

Definitions of child sexual abuse vary. Some definitions specify physical contact between the perpetrator and the child, and some do not. However, a typical definition of **child sexual abuse** is "sexual exploitation or sexual activities with a child under circumstances which indicate that the child's health or welfare is harmed or threatened" (Wallace, 1999, p. 64).

The incidence of child sexual abuse depends on whether we use a broad or a limited definition of the term. Estimations are difficult because only a fraction of the cases are reported. Even so, estimates suggest that about 20% to 25% of all females have experienced child sexual abuse by the time they are 18 years old (L. Phillips, 1998; Wallace, 1999). Furthermore, girls are about twice as likely as boys to be sexually abused (Finkelhor & Dziuba-Leatherman, 1994).

Incest is a particular kind of child sexual abuse; again, definitions vary. One accepted definition is that **incest** refers to sexual relations between blood relatives (Wallace, 1999). Unfortunately, a large proportion of child sexual abuse incidents are committed by relatives. For example, one study of female rape victims under the age of 12 years showed that 46% of the perpetrators were family members (L. Phillips, 1998).

The Consequences of Child Sexual Abuse. Sexual abuse can have a profound impact on a child, both immediately and over the long term. For example, a woman may have lifelong problems with her reproductive system (Laws, 1998).

The immediate psychological consequences of child sexual abuse include fear, anger, depression, and guilt. Nightmares and other sleep disturbances are also common. As you might expect, many victims also stop trusting other people (Wallace, 1999). The long-term consequences of child sexual abuse include substance abuse, eating disorders, and risky sexual behavior (Laws, 1998; Wallace, 1999). As adults, incest survivors also show significantly more anger than other women (A. Newman & Peterson, 1996).

Ethnicity has an important impact on a child's reaction to sexual abuse (Fontes, 1995). For example, many Asian cultures emphasize loyalty to parents and to other adults, and sexual issues are not discussed (Okamura et al., 1995). As a result, child sexual abuse is seldom reported to authorities, and the child is often blamed for somehow attracting the adult's sexual attention.

The Recovered Memory/False Memory Controversy. The topic of child sexual abuse has created a major debate among psychologists: When children have been sexually abused, do they sometimes repress their memory of that experience, perhaps recovering that memory when a later event triggers recall (the **recovered memory perspective**)? Alternately, are many of these "recovered memories" actually false memories, or constructed stories about events that never really happened (the **false memory perspective**)? This controversy has generated hundreds of articles and books (e.g., Freyd, 1996; Pezdek & Banks, 1996; K. Pope & Brown, 1996).

One major problem is that we cannot easily determine whether a memory of childhood abuse is accurate. Children are abused in private settings, without witnesses. Also, psychologists cannot conduct the appropriate research to resolve the recovered memory/false memory controversy. We know from research on eyewitness testimony that people can be convinced to create a false memory for an event that never really happened. For example, researchers working with adults can plant a "memory" of a fictitious childhood event, such as spilling punch at a wedding. In follow-up interviews, these adults may claim that the event really did occur (Loftus, 1997). However, we cannot generalize from the creation of bland false memories such as these to the creation of traumatic memories about sexual abuse (L. Brown, 1996).

In the current era, psychologists in both the United States and Canada have begun to adopt a position that acknowledges the complexity of the issues. They argue that both the "recovered memory" and the "false memory" positions are at least partly correct (e.g., Kimball, 1999; Pezdek & Banks, 1996; Prout & Dobson, 1998). For example, here is part of a statement issued by the American Psychological Association (1996a):

- Controversies regarding adult recollections should not be allowed to obscure the fact that child sexual abuse is a complex and pervasive problem in America that has historically gone unacknowledged.
- Most people who were sexually abused as children remember all or part of what happened to them.
- It is possible for memories of abuse that have been forgotten for a long time to be remembered. . . .
- It is also possible to construct convincing pseudomemories for events that never occurred. . . .
- There are gaps in our knowledge about the processes that lead to accurate and inaccurate recollections of childhood abuse. (pp. 371–372)

This statement is especially important because it emphasizes that the ongoing debates should not distract us from our central concerns. Childhood sexual abuse is a critically important problem in our society because children are frequently betrayed by close caregivers who use power inappropriately (Freyd, 1996, 1997).

Marital Rape

A California state senator said to a group of women in 1979, "If you can't rape your wife, who can you rape?" According to some husbands, a marriage license apparently means that a man has complete freedom to do what he wants to his wife's body. (We'll see this attitude again in the section on the abuse of women.) Only 10 states have stringent laws against marital rape allowing a wife to charge her husband with marital rape, even when they are living in the same home. Those states are: Florida, Kansas, Maryland, Massachusetts, Nebraska, New York, Oregon, Rhode Island, Vermont, and Wisconsin (Fast & Fast, 1995).

Many cases of marital rape are so brutal that they include battering, as well as rape. The case of Mrs. Tompkins is probably typical. She is no longer living with her husband, but she reported that he had sexually assaulted her from 11 to 20 times over a period of 13 years. As she describes her experience:

He forced himself on me. He hit me, then pinned me down and had sex with me. Sometimes he would come home after drinking and he would wake me up and force himself on me. He would hold me down and take it. One time he came home after he had been out drinking and he wanted to go to bed with me and we had a fight about it. He started hitting on me and finally I stopped fighting. He had sex with me and then went to sleep. (D. Russell, 1990, p. 180)

By some estimates, between 10% and 15% of wives are raped by their husbands or ex-husbands (Morris, 1997). Some people mistakenly believe that marital rape is less traumatic for a woman than stranger rape. However, a woman who has been raped by her husband has had a long-standing emotional relationship with her rapist, and she must decide whether she will continue to live with this man. The woman may also be reluctant to report the rape if she is economically dependent on her husband (Hampton, 1995; Wallace, 1999).

Diana Russell (1990) wrote, in the concluding chapter of her book, *Rape in Marriage:*

> Wife rape is a much more serious problem than most people have realized. The fact that it is legal in . . . most countries not only perpetuates the problem but probably helps cause it, because it allows men and women alike to believe that wife rape is somehow acceptable. The first step toward reversing the destructive attitudes that lead to this destructive act is to make wife rape illegal; it must also be stripped of the stereotypes and myths that attach to it and be understood for what it is. (p. 357)

Rape Prevention

Rape prevention is an issue both for individual women and for society. Table 13.1, which lists some precautions that can be taken by individual women, is culled from much longer lists in several resources. Fischhoff (1992) counted more than 1,100 different rape-prevention strategies listed in resources like these. The advice is often confusing and conflicting (Corcoran & Mahlstedt, 1999; Fischhoff, 1992). Furthermore, no "magic formula" can prevent rape, though some strategies may reduce the dangers. Let's consider separately how women can help prevent rape by strangers and by acquaintances. Then we'll discuss how society can work to prevent rape.

Individuals' Prevention of Rape by Strangers.   Two major issues arise in connection with what individual women can do to avoid rape. The first issue can be called the "blame-the-victim" problem. Notice that many of the items in Table 13.1 will force women to limit their own freedom. Women should not hitchhike, walk in unlighted areas, or sit wherever they want on a bus. Why should women—the potential victims—be the ones who have to restrict their behavior? This complaint cannot be answered satisfactorily (Corcoran & Mahlstedt, 1999). The situation definitely *is* unjust. However, the reality is that women are less likely to be raped if they take these precautions. This injustice also emphasizes that the real solutions would require changes in society, rather than reliance on individual prevention techniques.

The second issue about rape prevention at the individual level is whether a woman should attempt to physically resist an attacker. The most systematic

TABLE 13.1	Safety Precautions to Avoid a Rape Confrontation with a Stranger (Based on Hull et al., 1992; C. Kelly, 1991; Ullman & Knight, 1993)

General Precautions

1. Make certain that your consumption of alcohol or other drugs does not endanger your alertness; women who use drugs or alcohol prior to a rape attack experience more severe sexual abuse and bodily injury.
2. Take a self-defense course; learn the vulnerable body parts of a potential attacker.
3. If you are attacked, do not be afraid to be rude and yell loudly; throw any available object at the attacker.

Precautions at Home

1. Make certain to use locks on doors and windows.
2. Ask repairmen and delivery men for identification before opening the door; do not let strangers in to use your phone.
3. Keep your curtains closed at night to avoid observation.
4. If you live in an apartment, don't enter the elevator with a strange man, and don't enter a deserted basement or laundry room; insist that the apartment manager keep hallways, entrances, and grounds well lit.

Precautions on the Street

1. Do not hitchhike. (Unfortunately, hitchhiking is notoriously dangerous.)
2. When you are walking, walk purposefully and assertively; be alert to your surroundings.
3. Avoid being alone on the streets or campus late at night; if you cannot avoid being alone, carry a police whistle (on a key chain, not around your neck), or a "practical" weapon such as an umbrella, a pen, or keys.
4. If you are being followed by a car, turn and then walk in the opposite direction to the nearest open store or neighbor.

Precautions in Cars and on Buses or Subways

1. Keep car doors locked, even when you are riding.
2. Check the back seat before getting into a car.
3. Keep your gas tank filled and the car in good working order. If you have car trouble, raise the hood; if a male offers to help, ask him to call the police.
4. If you are being followed, don't pull into your driveway; go to the nearest police or fire station and honk your horn.
5. At bus or subway stations, stay in well-lit sections, near change booths or a group of people.
6. If the bus is nearly empty, sit near the driver. If you are bothered by someone, inform the driver about the trouble.

studies now show that women reduce their chances of being raped when they try to block their assailants physically, push them, or incapacitate them (Fischhoff, 1992; Parrot, 1996). As one resource concludes, "Doing something is better than doing nothing" (Allison & Wrightsman, 1993). Notice, then, that the most effective techniques are those that are stereotypically masculine, rather than feminine (Parrot, 1996).

Resources on rape avoidance also recommend training in self-defense, especially because self-defense affords women greater empowerment and personal competence (Hammerle, 1997; Ozer & Bandura, 1990; Parrot, 1996). In a rape situation, women must quickly assess the specific situation, as well as their own physical strength, before deciding whether to resist. However, as Parrot points out, "even if a woman does not employ any of these prevention strategies and the result is rape, it is never the fault of the victim" (p. 224). The person who commits the rape is responsible; we must not blame the victim.

Individuals' Prevention of Acquaintance Rape. Women may feel comforted to think that they can protect themselves from rape by locking their doors and avoiding late-night walks in dangerous areas. But how will those precautions protect women from being raped by someone they know?

Unfortunately, women must use a different set of strategies to protect themselves from an acquaintance (Carroll & Jackson, 1996; Parrot, 1991, 1996). One precaution is to avoid a relationship with a man who talks negatively about women in general, or a man who insults you and ignores what you say. This man is likely to ignore your refusals if you say you do not want to have sex (Muehlenhard et al., 1989).

Some precautions on dating safety may sound obvious, but they can decrease the chances of acquaintance rape (Carroll & Jackson, 1996). When you are just getting to know someone, date in groups and go to public places. If possible, drive yourself to the location. Also, take some time to think how you would respond if a situation becomes threatening. What would your options be? Throughout a relationship, communicate with your dating partner about any sexual activities that seem appropriate or inappropriate.

In the previous section, we discussed effective ways of preventing rape by strangers. When the attacker is an acquaintance, he may respond to verbal assertiveness. For example, a woman may shout, "Stop it! What you are doing is rape!" (Parrot, 1996, p. 226). An attacker may also be responsive to crying, reasoning, and trying to appeal to him on a human level. Screaming or running away may be effective.

In an ideal world, women could trust their dates, their classmates, and their friends. In the real world, the clear majority of men would not rape an acquaintance. However, some do, and women must be prepared for this possibility.

Society's Prevention of Rape. An individual might be able to avoid being raped by following certain precautions. However, many rapists will simply seek another victim. In addition, solutions at the individual level mean that women will continue to live in fear about being raped. To prevent rape, we need to take a broader approach. We must acknowledge that a violent society—which often denies the value of women—will tend to encourage rape (Allison & Wrightsman, 1993; Corcoran & Mahlstedt, 1999; G. C. Hall & Barongan, 1997). Here are several important issues. The list starts with concrete suggestions and then considers some problems that require more fundamental changes (Allison & Wrightsman, 1993; Corcoran & Mahlstedt, 1999; DeKeseredy & Schwartz, 1998; G. C. Hall, 1996; M. Schwartz & DeKeseredy, 1997):

1. Hospitals and medical providers should be sensitive to the emotional and physical needs of women who have been raped.

2. Rape victims should be encouraged to report rape. Anonymous telephone counseling services and legal assistance should be easily available and widely publicized.

3. Laws must be reformed so that the legal process is less stressful and more supportive for the victims.

4. Professionals who work with children need to be alert for evidence of child sexual abuse; in some states, people who work with children are required to complete relevant training programs.

5. Education about rape needs to be improved, beginning in junior high or high school. Early exposure to the information is essential because students have already formed their attitudes toward rape by the time they reach college. Instructive programs must emphasize that men *can* control their sexual impulses and that women are not to be blamed for rape. The programs should also be a standard part of orientation for first-year college students, especially because a woman faces a very high risk of rape during the first weeks of college.

6. Men's groups must become more involved in rape prevention. On some college campuses, a fraternity will join together with campus women's groups to organize a rape awareness day or a "take-back-the-night rally." Unfortunately, however, this kind of collaborative activism is rare. Men and men's organizations need to remember the important quotation: "If you're not part of the solution, you're part of the problem."

7. Violence must be less glorified in the media. The violence in films and on television is widely recognized, yet the situation has not improved dramatically in recent years (Scharrer, 1998). We must emphasize that the representation of violence against women encourages aggression.

8. Ultimately, society must direct more attention toward the needs of women. As we've emphasized throughout this book, women are relatively underpaid, powerless, and invisible. Their needs are trivialized and disregarded. Every woman should be able to feel that her body is safe from attack and that she has the same freedom of movement that men have.

 *Rape*

1. Frequently, women who have been raped by an acquaintance will not consider the assault to be a "real" rape. Acquaintance rape is associated with alcohol and other drugs, and with a setting that is hostile toward women. Some instances of acquaintance rape can be traced to misinterpretations of sexual interest. People are more likely to blame the rapist in a case of stranger rape than in a case of acquaintance rape.

2. Between 15% and 30% of women in the United States and Canada will become victims of rape during their lifetime; in addition, the threat of rape keeps women afraid.

3. Women who have been raped report that, during the assault, they felt terrified, confused, and anxious. Afterward, victims often feel helpless and devalued; they may also blame themselves for the rape.

4. Long-term consequences for a rape victim may include posttraumatic stress disorder, though individual differences are prominent.

5. A woman who has been raped may be blamed by her family, the court system, and the general public; attitudes depend on factors such as gender and gender-role beliefs.

6. Some myths about rape that are not based on fact include the following: Only deviant men would consider rape; rapists are strangers; women ask to be raped; women lie about rape; only bad women are raped; and pornography reduces the incidence of rape.

7. Child sexual abuse has both immediate and long-term effects on mental and physical health; many psychologists maintain that some memories of child sexual abuse can be forgotten and then recovered, but many argue that adults can construct false memories of abuse that did not occur.

8. Many women are victims of marital rape, which can be a traumatic experience.

9. Safety precautions that prevent rape by a stranger typically limit women's freedom at home and in public places; it is important not to blame the victim of a rape attack.

10. Safety precautions for avoiding rape by an acquaintance include avoiding men who downgrade women; dating in groups at the beginning of a relationship; being verbally assertive; and appealing to acquaintances on a human level.

11. Ultimately, the number of rapes can be reduced only by greater societal attention to women's needs. The issues include reforming the

medical, counseling, legal, and educational resources of rape victims. Violence must be less glorified in the media, and women's issues should receive more attention.

THE ABUSE OF WOMEN

Dr. Christine Dotterer, a successful family physician, described how her husband abused her over a period of 19 years:

> In some ways my situation was classic. He would hit and punch me, and then would want to make up, usually with sex. There were stretches of time when things seemed pretty good, and the fact that he had bruised me two months earlier seemed to vanish. It's true that he actively discouraged my having friends—he didn't want me even to talk on the phone. But I thought that I just wasn't good at making friends, not that he might want me to be isolated. (Dotterer, 1992, p. 49)

Dr. Dotterer finally left this abusive relationship, after she saw her husband beat up her son. As in many other cases of domestic violence, this couple was European American, well educated, and middle class. The abuse of women is found in every social group on our continent.

I will use the term "abuse of women" to include the kind of aggression that Christine Dotterer experienced from her husband. In contrast, the term "domestic violence" implies that the man and the woman are living together. Therefore, this term seems to exclude the kind of violence often found in dating relationships—even among high school students (DeKeseredy & Schwartz, 1998; L. Phillips, 1998). The term "domestic violence" also implies *physical* abuse, yet women who have been abused often report that the psychological abuse is the most destructive component of the abusive experience.

The **abuse of women** includes intentional acts that injure a woman; these acts may be physical, psychological, or sexual. (We explored sexual abuse in the discussions of acquaintance rape and marital rape, in the previous section). Typically, *abuse* refers to injury that occurs in an ongoing relationship (Wallace, 1999; J. White & Kowalski, 1998).

Physical abuse can include hitting, kicking, burning, pushing, choking, and threatening with a weapon. Emotional abuse can include humiliation, name calling, degradation, intimidation, and refusing to speak (L. Goodman et al., 1993; Wallace, 1999). Another form of emotional abuse focuses on finances—for example, when a man withholds money or takes money away from his wife.

Because of space limitations, this section focuses on male violence against females. The research demonstrates that females may abuse males (e.g., Pearson, 1998; Wallace, 1999). However, the evidence is clear that women experience much more severe abuse from their male partners than men do from their female partners (DeKeseredy & Schwartz, 1998; White & Kowalski, 1998). As one resource summarized the research:

Male violence does much more damage than female violence: Women are much more likely to be injured, much more likely to enter the hospital after being assaulted by their partner, and much more likely to be in need of medical care. Wives are much more likely to be killed by their male partner than by all other types of perpetrators combined. (Jacobson & Gottman, 1998, p. 35)

Because of space limitations, we will not examine abuse in lesbian relationships; this topic is discussed in other resources (e.g., Renzetti, 1997; J. White & Bondurant, 1996). Before you read further, however, try Demonstration 13.4.

DEMONSTRATION 13.4

Attitudes Toward the Abuse of Women

Public opinion polls were conducted in the United States between 1992 and 1994. The focus of the polls was domestic violence, and the interviewers conducted the surveys on the telephone. Try to guess the percentage of people who responded in the specified way to the questions below. The results of the polls are shown on page 509.

1. If a male friend of yours complained about his wife screaming and hitting on him to the point where he said he had to slap her to calm her down, would you tell him that he should have walked away rather than hit her?

   What percentage said "yes"? _____

2. People worry about different things. Are you very worried, worried, or not worried about the growth in family violence?

   What percentage of women responded "very worried"? _____

   What percentage of men responded "very worried"? _____

3. People may say it is wrong to hit women. However, the constant pictures of women getting beaten, raped, or terrorized on television and in movies provides a message that this violence is acceptable.

   What percentage said "strongly agree" or "agree"? _____

4. Would you call the police if you saw a man beating his wife or girlfriend?

   What percentage said "yes"? _____

5. Would you support legislation to increase funding for battered women's programs?

   What percentage said "yes"? _____

(Based on Klein et al., 1997, pp. 7, 8, 121, 137, 144, 145.)

How Often Does the Abuse of Women Occur?

Earlier in this chapter, we discussed the difficulty of estimating how many women experience sexual harassment and rape. The traditional taboo about discussing the abuse of women also prevents us from obtaining accurate data about violence in intimate relationships. According to some estimates, between 20% and 35% of women in the United States will experience abuse during their lifetime (Koss et al., 1997; White & Kowalski, 1998). Looking at the statistics another way, between 2,000,000 and 4,000,000 U.S. women are abused each year (Birns, 1999; Klein et al., 1997). The data for women in Canada are similar; about 25% to 30% of married or formerly married women reported that they had been abused (Statistics Canada, 1993; L. Taylor, 1995).

Furthermore, about 30% to 40% of women who are seen in U.S. hospital emergency departments have symptoms related to domestic violence (Bonanni, 1993; Litt, 1997). Even pregnancy does not protect women from abuse. According to one survey, 17% of women seen at prenatal clinics reported either physical or sexual abuse during pregnancy (McFarlane et al., 1992).

As we mentioned at the beginning of this section, abuse is also common in dating relationships. For example, DeKeseredy and Schwartz (1998) reported the results from a large-scale survey of Canadian university students. The survey revealed that 31% of the women had been pushed, grabbed, or shoved by someone they were dating, 11% had been slapped, and 5% had been choked. Psychological abuse was even more common; 65% of the women said they had been degraded in front of friends or family, and 65% had experienced insults or swearing.

The problem of partner abuse is not limited to North America. The rate of abuse in European countries is similar to the North American rate (Neft & Levine, 1997; United Nations, 1995). Data gathered in Asia, Latin America, and Africa reveal even higher rates of abuse: More than half of adult women reported that they had been physically assaulted by a partner. For example, an interviewer asked a man in South Korea if he had beaten his wife. He replied:

> I was married at 28, and I'm 52 now. How could I have been married all these years and not beaten my wife? . . . For me, it's better to release that anger and get it over with. Otherwise, I just get sick inside. (Kristof, 1996, p. 17A)

Notice, however, that this man never considered whether the abuse was also better for his wife.

The Dynamics of Abuse

Most women are not abused continually. Instead, a cyclical pattern of abuse is more common, though certainly not universal (Schuller & Vidmar, 1992; Wallace, 1999). This **abuse cycle** typically has three phases: (1) tension building, (2) acute battering, and (3) the loving phase (L. E. Walker, 1979, 1989; Wallace, 1999).

In the tension building phase, the physical abuse is relatively minor, but verbal outbursts and threats increase the tension. The woman often tries to calm her partner. She may try to keep his abuse from escalating by anticipating his whims. However, tension keeps building.

When tension builds too high, the abuser responds with an acute battering incident, the hallmark of the second phase. The woman may experience extreme physical abuse.

In the third phase, the tension from the first two phases is gone, and the batterer becomes charming and loving. He apologizes and promises that he will never be violent again. He begs for forgiveness and makes the woman feel guilty if she is considering leaving the relationship. This may be a pleasant and flattering—though confusing—phase of the relationship. In fact, the woman may be encouraged to forget the tension, uncertainty, and pain of the earlier two phases. Indeed, the man may be genuinely repentant at this point in the cycle. Unfortunately, the cycle usually repeats itself, often with increased severity.

Women's Reactions to Abuse

As you might expect, fear and terror are common reactions to abuse. Women who have been abused may be hyperalert, searching for signs that their partner may be ready to strike again (Wallace, 1999). Women may alter their own behavior, in the hope of preventing future outbursts. However, these adjustments are often ineffective. The abuser will simply find another reason to be violent.

Women who have been abused may feel anxious. More than half of abused women develop depression. An estimated 25% to 40% of women may attempt suicide after experiencing abuse (L. Goodman et al., 1993; Litt, 1997).

Abused women also experience many problems with their physical health. They may suffer from bruises, cuts, burns, and broken bones as a direct result of an assault. Many months afterward, they may still experience headaches, abdominal pain, pelvic pain, gynecological problems, and other chronic disorders (Koss & Heslet, 1992; Litt, 1997). Naturally, these physical problems may intensify their psychological problems.

Characteristics of the Abusive Relationship

Researchers have identified several factors related to the abuse of women. For example, some family characteristics may be associated with abuse. In addition, certain personal attributes are especially common among men who abuse their partners.

Family Variables Associated with Abuse.   Abuse of women is somewhat more common among low-income families, though the relationship between abuse and social class is complex (Koss et al., 1998). For example, police may receive more domestic violence calls from the poorer areas of a city. However, middle-class and upper-class women may simply be less likely to call for police help. Also, remember that women on university campuses are likely to experience physical violence, even though most students come from families with relatively high incomes (DeKeseredy & Schwartz, 1998). In other words, no social class is immune (Schuller & Vidmar, 1992).

Even wealthy and influential men abuse their partners. For example, during his presidency, Ronald Reagan had said that he would pay increased attention to family violence. Reagan was apparently unaware that one of his high-ranking appointed officials—John Fedders—had been abusing his wife, Charlotte. Then *The Wall Street Journal* featured an article in which Charlotte Fedders described how she had been a victim of domestic violence. John Fedders resigned on the day her story was reported (Ferrato, 1991).

The relationship between ethnicity and family violence is also complex. Many analyses do not take social class into account, and we have just seen that social class is somewhat related to patterns of abuse. Furthermore, researchers have not conducted extensive research about family violence in various ethnic groups (Koss et al., 1997).

The limited research on abuse among Black couples reveals mixed feelings. That is, some studies report a higher abuse rate among Black couples—in comparison to White couples—but other studies report similar abuse rates (Joseph, 1997; Kanuha, 1994; Klein et al., 1997).

Research suggests that Latinas/os have different attitudes toward domestic abuse, in contrast to European Americans. For example, Latina women were less likely to say that verbal abuse should be categorized as domestic violence. However, the two groups are similar in the severity and frequency of the abuse they actually experience (Klein et al., 1997).

Some recent studies have focused on the abuse of women in Asian American communities. One survey showed that only 20% of Asian American women said that they were "very worried" about the growth of domestic violence. In contrast, between 41% and 44% of women from other ethnic groups supplied a "very worried" response (Klein et al., 1997). The number of *reported* cases of domestic abuse is relatively low in Asian American communities. One reason may be that Asian American families are extremely reluctant to let anyone outside the immediate family know about domestic problems (Ho, 1997). Many Asian cultures believe that women should accept their suffering and endure their hardships, and this value system discourages women from reporting domestic violence (Ho, 1997).

We noted earlier that domestic violence is relatively high in Asian countries. As a consequence, Asian immigrants who come to North America may have relatively high rates of abuse. One researcher examined attitudes toward domestic violence among Hmong people who had immigrated to Seattle from Laos. At a large picnic gathering, one man told a joke: "When we get on the plane to go back to Laos, the first thing we will do is beat up the women" (Donnelly, 1994, p. 74). The men laughed uproariously. The women joined in, too, because Hmong women are expected to laugh at the jokes their husbands make.

In summary, then, ethnic groups may vary in their beliefs about domestic violence. However, the data on the incidence of domestic violence are not consistent or valid enough to draw firm conclusions.

Personal Characteristics of Male Abusers.   One of the most commonly reported characteristics of male abusers is that they feel they are entitled to hurt their partners. From their egocentric perspective, their own needs come first (Birns, 1999). A good example of this "male entitlement" perspective is the Korean man who felt he was better off releasing his anger by beating his wife (p. 498). Abusers are also likely to believe that the male should be the head of the family—along with other traditional concepts about gender roles (Wallace, 1999). Not surprisingly, abusers have more positive attitudes toward physical and verbal aggression, in comparison with men who are not abusers (Bookwala et al., 1992).

Batterers are often described as being charming con artists. Their apparent sincerity can often fool unsuspecting people: "How could such a delightful, devoted husband possibly beat his wife?" In fact, a relatively large number of batterers meet the psychiatric diagnosis of antisocial personality disorder (Wallace, 1999). People with **antisocial personality disorder** have complete disregard for the lives of other people; they also display a variety of antisocial behaviors, including lying, impulsiveness, and aggressiveness (American Psychiatric Association, 1994). Men with this disorder show little concern for the welfare of others. However, they may appear charming to people who know them only superficially.

Situational factors also increase the likelihood of partner abuse. For example, men who are unemployed have a relatively high rate of domestic violence (Klein et al., 1997). Men whose friends endorse the abuse of women are also more likely to be aggressive (DeKeseredy & Schwartz, 1998).

Research also suggests that males who have a drinking problem are more likely to abuse women physically (Jacobson & Gottman, 1998; Wallace, 1999). It's possible that alcohol plays an important role because of its biochemical effects in altering judgment. However, many men simply use alcohol as an excuse for their violence. A typical explanation may be, "I don't know what got into me . . . it must have been the alcohol."

Attitudes Toward the Abuse of Women

The research on attitudes toward partner abuse suggests that we can be cautiously optimistic. An increasing number of North Americans believe that domestic violence is a serious crime. In the United States, for example, all 50 states have passed statutes to protect abused women (A. Roberts, 1996b). As feminists, we should not be premature in claiming that the problem is nearly solved. The abuse of women is a problem that is still extremely important. However, we should be pleased with feminist educational efforts combine with the media and legal reform to change societal attitudes (A. Roberts, 1996b).

In a representative series of surveys, Straus and his colleagues (1997) reported that 20% of their U.S. sample gathered in 1968 approved of a husband's slapping his wife's face. By 1994, when the survey was repeated, that percentage had dropped to 10%. However, we still need to wonder why 1 in 10 U.S. residents still believes that a man has the right to slap his wife's face!

In earlier chapters, we pointed out the negative impact that the media can have on issues such as gender stereotypes and body images. In contrast, the media had a generally positive impact on knowledge about domestic violence in the mid-1990s, during the coverage of the O. J. Simpson trial. For example, 93% of U.S. residents in a nationwide survey said that they had learned from the media coverage that domestic violence is a serious problem. Furthermore, 91% reported that family and friends should learn more about how to help victims of domestic violence (Klein et al., 1997).

In general, women have more negative attitudes toward abuse than men do (Klein et al., 1997; Straus et al., 1997). Gender roles also have an important impact on attitudes. Specifically, people with traditional attitudes toward women are likely to sympathize with a man who has abused his wife. In contrast, people with nontraditional attitudes are likely to blame the man (Kristiansen & Giulietti, 1990; Willis et al., 1996).

In this section on attitudes, we've noted that the public is more likely than in previous eras to condemn the abuse of women. However, we still have a long distance to cover before the abuse of women is treated with sufficient seriousness. For example, LaFrance (1998) points out that a man who is convicted of domestic violence in Wyoming can expect up to a 2-year jail sentence and a $2,000 fine. In contrast, a man who is convicted of "livestock rustling"—stealing a horse, for example—can expect up to a 10-year jail sentence and a $10,000 fine.

Myths About the Abuse of Women

We have already discussed the evidence against several commonly accepted myths about the abuse of women. For example, we have considered research that contradicts the following myths:

1. Abuse is relatively rare;
2. Men experience as much abuse as women;
3. Abuse is limited to the lower social classes;
4. Abuse is much more common among ethnic minority groups.

Let's examine some other myths. In each case, think about how the myth leads people to blame women for being battered.

Myth 1: Abused women are masochists. A person who obtains gratification—often sexual—from the pain of being beaten or tortured is called a **masochist** (pronounced "*mass*-uh-kist"). Early theorists reasoned that women who remain in violent relationships enjoy the trauma of being abused. A portion of the general population still holds this belief (Klein et al., 1997). However, we have no evidence for this myth (A. Roberts, 1996a). Women do not enjoy being abused, just as women do not enjoy being raped.

Myth 2: Abused women ask to be beaten. According to this myth, when a woman oversteps the boundaries of a proper wife, she deserves a beating. In other words, the blame for this abuse lies in the woman's behavior, not in the man's response. A student in my psychology of women course related an incident in which she had described a wife-abuse case to a group of friends. Specifically, a man had seriously injured his wife because dinner was not ready as soon as he came home from work. A male friend in this student's group—whom my student had previously considered enlightened—responded, "Yes, but she really should have prepared dinner on time."

Myth 3: Abused women could easily leave, if they really wanted to. This myth ignores both the interpersonal and the practical factors that prevent a woman from leaving. She may feel some love for the abusing man, because he is often decent. Also, as we noted earlier, many abusers become generous and kind during the days following a violent episode. An abused woman may sincerely believe that her husband is basically a good man who can be reformed.

Many abused women also face practical barriers. A woman may have no place to go, no money, and no way of escaping (McHugh et al., 1993). Another practical concern is that an abusing husband often becomes even more violent once a woman decides to leave (Birns, 1999; Jacobson & Gottman, 1998). In fact, a woman is at greater risk of being killed or seriously injured during the 2 years after a separation than she was during the years the couple lived in the same home.

How Abused Women Take Action

An abused woman may remain in the relationship or, like the majority of abused women, she may decide to pursue one of several options. Consider the case of 18-year-old Felicia, who decided to confide in her social worker at the health clinic. Felicia explained why she decided to take this important step:

> I told her because she always listened. She didn't blame me—for being pregnant or for him beating on me. It was a relief, because no one else believed it was happening. I told her because I was sick of it. But it was hard. It hurt a lot to talk about it. It made it real. But deep down inside, I was a really hurt person. When I told her, she believed it. What helped was a lot of counseling and a lot of friends telling me I was not a bad person. I had to hear it a lot of times, LOTS OF TIMES, but then I heard it. (B. Levy, 1993, p. 82)

To some extent, women's strategies for handling abuse may depend on their ethnic background. For example, Asian American family values typically emphasize acceptance of fate, persevering in unpleasant situations, and hiding domestic problems (Ho, 1997). These women may therefore be less likely than European American women to try to escape from an abusive relationship.

Let's discuss several options for women who have been abused. They can seek therapy, they can leave, or they can go to a battered women's shelter.

Therapy.   An abusive relationship seldom improves spontaneously. In fact, as we noted earlier, violence frequently escalates in a relationship. Women often seek the services of therapists. In earlier eras, therapists frequently adopted a "blame the victim" approach. Fortunately, therapists are becoming better educated about society's role in encouraging the abuse of women.

As one resource emphasizes, therapy for abused women should address three goals: "increasing the client's personal safety; increasing her sense of empowerment, esteem, and control; and reducing the psychological trauma resulting from the violence" (Petretic-Jackson & Jackson, 1996, p. 189).

Consider, for example, the feminist therapy approach that Rinfret-Raynor and Cantin (1997) used in working with abused women who were French Canadian. They informed the women about their legal rights, helped them explore community resources, and conducted both individual and group therapy. A major message throughout therapy was that the abuser is responsible for the violence—not the victim. The therapists also worked to increase the women's self-esteem and sense of independence. Compared to women who had received standard, nonsexist therapy, the women who had received feminist therapy experienced a greater decrease in physical violence.

Therapists are beginning to report some success with couples therapy, in which the husband and the wife attend therapy together. In general, the participants in these studies are couples who decided on their own to pursue therapy. As a result, these husbands are probably more receptive to change than "typical" abusing husbands (P. Brown & O'Leary, 1997).

Many theorists believe that a man and woman in an abusive relationship must not enter couples therapy until violence has stopped for at least 6 months. Until that time, they should attend therapy separately. For example, the early therapy with an abusive husband may focus on encouraging him to realize that the abuse is his personal responsibility; he also learns alternative methods to resolve arguments. Meanwhile, a woman who has been abused may receive feminist therapy with the goal of self-empowerment and greater understanding of domestic-violence issues (Philpot et al., 1997).

Deciding to Leave a Relationship.   Many women decide that abuse is too high a price to pay for the advantages of remaining in a relationship. Many women reach a crisis point after a particularly violent episode. Consider the following example:

> With Virginia, the day of reckoning came while James was cleaning his gun. It had no bullets in it, but when he pointed it at her after it was clean, she did not know it was empty. He said, "Do you realize how easy it would be for me to

accidentally use this on you some day?" He was in a relatively good mood, or so it seemed. Somehow, his concrete threat, said in a joking manner, crystallized the danger she was in, better than all the serious threats he had made in a bad mood. She took those earlier threats seriously, but she remembers thinking, "Even when he's happy, he still likes to torment me." At the moment he pointed the gun at her, Virginia began her countdown to escape. (Jacobson & Gottman, 1998, p. 139)

Other women begin planning to leave after they have been attacked in front of their children, after their partner breaks a promise about stopping the abuse, or after talking with a supportive friend (Giles-Sims, 1983; Jacobson & Gottman, 1998).

Unfortunately, people are so intrigued by the question, "Why do battered women stay?" that they forget to ask the real questions (Hoff, 1990). Some of these questions include: "Why are men violent?" and "Why are violent men *allowed* to stay?"

Shelters for Battered Women.   Shelters offer a place where an abused woman can go for safety, support, and information about social services available in the community. Many shelters also offer support groups for battered women, as well as counseling services. Staff members may also help women make their own decisions about their future options (Birns, 1999; Roche & Sandoski, 1996). In these shelters, many women become aware that the abuse problem is a social issue, and that victims must not be blamed for the abuse (Whalen, 1996).

The United States currently has more than 1,800 programs that address the issue of domestic violence (Klein et al., 1997). In Canada, approximately 100,000 women and children are admitted to battered women's shelters each year (L. Taylor, 1995).

Unfortunately, these shelters operate on extremely limited budgets. We need hundreds of additional shelters throughout North America. Thousands of women are turned away each year from shelters that are filled to capacity. The women must return to their homes, where they risk being beaten once again. Ironically, in the early 1990s, the U.S. Government did not hesitate to spend billions of dollars, ostensibly to protect the rights of citizens in Kuwait, which has a population of roughly 2 million people. Meanwhile, every year in the United States, the rights of perhaps twice that many women are violated when they are battered by their husbands. However, the federal government contributes very little to the support of battered women's shelters.

Society's Response to the Problem of Abuse

In recent years, the criminal justice system and the general public have become much more aware that abuse is a serious problem. Still, government policy has no consistent plan for providing shelters, services, and assistance for abused women or requiring counseling for the men who abuse them. Government

officials and agencies must publicize the fact that abuse of any kind is unac-
ceptable. This publicity should be just as vigorous as the antidrug and anti-
drunk-driving campaigns (Gondolf, 1988; Koshland, 1994). Police training must
also be improved. For example, police officers should be required to complete
training about domestic violence issues. Program directors of battered women's
shelters should be invited to provide additional information about the abuse of
women (A. Roberts, 1996b).

Community organizations are often silent about the issue of abused women.
Imagine what could happen if church groups, parent–teacher associations, and
service organizations—such as Rotary and the Kiwanis—were to sponsor a program on domestic violence. These organizations often set the moral tone for a
community, and they could send a strong message that domestic abuse should
not be tolerated.

One optimistic sign comes from the increased attention that medical organizations are giving to the issue of domestic violence. Earlier research demonstrated that health care providers who see battered women in the emergency
department seldom ask whether they are experiencing domestic violence
(J. Campbell & Landenburger, 1995; Litt, 1997). Several years ago, however, the
New York Department of Health began sending posters to all physicians in the
state. These posters provide excellent advice on recognizing and treating victims
of domestic violence. Beginning in 1995, a company called Audio-Digest began
developing audiotapes aimed at informing physicians about domestic violence
issues. Physicians should be much less likely to ignore the evidence about
abuse, now that a new norm of concern has been established.

Concern about domestic violence is emerging more slowly in developing
countries, but some of the efforts are encouraging. For example, a friend recently sent me a booklet on the abuse of women, developed for church groups
in Nicaragua (West & Fernández, 1997). Parts of the brochure debunked common myths such as: women deserve to be mistreated, abuse is God's will, and
abuse is limited to the lower class. The first shelter for battered women is now
being built in Nicaragua, with the aid of a group based in Wisconsin.

Ultimately, however, any attempt at solving the problem of abuse must acknowledge that the power imbalance in intimate relationships reflects the
power imbalance in our society (Whalen, 1996). As Jacobson and Gottman
(1998) point out, men who abuse women have been socialized to expect to
have power over women. In addition, the culture trains some men to control
their intimate partners through physical and emotional abuse. Television programs, music videos, and other media reinforce the images of men's violence
toward women (Rich et al., 1998). We can help to counteract these attitudes
by encouraging the media to provide less violent entertainment. We can
also encourage schools to address the issue of abuse at an early age, beginning in elementary school (DeKeseredy & Schwartz, 1998). As Mollie Whalen
(1996) points out, we must envision a world in which violence is not directed
at women as a group, in order to keep them powerless. Instead, intimate relationships would be based on "social equality, mutual trust, and caring"
(p. 112).

**SECTION
SUMMARY**   *The Abuse of Women*

1. About one-quarter of women in the United States and Canada will experience abuse during their lifetime; abuse is also common in dating relationships; abuse is even more likely in some other countries.

2. The abuse cycle often begins with verbal comments and moderate physical abuse; tension builds toward an acute battering incident; a period of calm and repentance follows.

3. Women who have been abused may feel anxious and depressed, and they experience many physical health problems.

4. Abuse is weakly correlated with social class, and its relationship with ethnicity is complex; male abusers have a sense of entitlement, and they are often charming con artists; unemployment is often a risk factor.

5. People treat domestic violence as a more serious issue than they did before the 1990s; gender and gender roles are both related to attitudes about domestic violence.

6. Myths about abused women that are not supported by the research are: (a) abused women are masochists who ask to be beaten, and (b) they could easily leave the relationship.

7. Therapy for an abused woman focuses on safety, empowerment, and trauma reduction; women often decide to leave an abusive relationship after reaching a specific crisis point; shelters are helpful, but they are poorly funded and temporary.

8. Government policy has no uniform provisions about shelters or services for abused women; health care providers now have better training about abuse issues.

9. As in other issues of violence, the problem of battered women cannot be resolved without seeking social equality at the societal level.

CHAPTER REVIEW
QUESTIONS

1. Throughout this chapter, we emphasized that people often "blame the victims" for events that are beyond their control. Describe how this process operates in sexual harassment, rape, and the abuse of women.

2. As noted in the introduction to this chapter, a culture that values men more than women encourages some men to feel they are entitled to certain privileges. Explain how this sense of entitlement is relevant in sexual harassment, rape, and the abuse of women.

3. How do women react to sexual harassment? Contrast these reactions with women's reactions to rape and abuse. Account for some of the similarities and differences.

4. This chapter examined attitudes about sexual harassment, rape, and abuse. Identify any similarities that apply to all three topics. Also, comment on gender comparisons in these attitudes.

5. What are the two general categories of sexual harassment? Name at least one example for each category, based on the recent media or on reports from friends. How do these examples illustrate why sexual harassment is an important issue? (Consult pp. 471–472 if necessary.)

6. Summarize the information about acquaintance rape, child sexual abuse, and marital rape. What does this information tell us about the balance of power and sexual violence in close personal relationships?

7. What are some of the common myths about sexual harassment, rape, and battering? What do all these myths reveal about society's attitudes toward men and women?

8. Imagine that you have been appointed to a national committee to address the problems of sexual harassment, rape, and abuse. What recommendations would you make for government policy, the legal system, universities, business institutions, the media, and educational programs? Feel free to list items other than those mentioned in this chapter.

9. The introduction to this chapter pointed out that sexual harassment, rape, and battering can all be related to the issue of men having more power than women. Now that you have read the chapter, address this issue in more detail, pointing out how violence makes women even less powerful.

10. Think about a high school female whom you know well. Imagine that she is about to go off to college. What kind of information can you supply from this chapter that would be helpful for her to know, with respect to violence against women? Now think about a high school male whom you know. If he were preparing to go to college, what information would you provide—both with respect to his avoiding violence against women and his role in supporting women who have experienced violence? (Better still, figure out how you can have an actual conversation about these topics with those individuals!)

NEW TERMS

sexual harassment (470)
quid pro quo harassment (470)
hostile work environment (470)
rape (477)
sexual assault (477)
acquaintance rape (479)
posttraumatic stress disorder
  (PTSD) (485)

child sexual abuse (488)
incest (489)
recovered memory perspective (489)
false memory perspective (489)
abuse of women (496)
abuse cycle (498)
antisocial personality disorder (501)
masochist (502)

RECOMMENDED READINGS

DeKeseredy, W. S., & Schwartz, M. D. (1998). *Woman abuse on campus: Results from the Canadian National Survey.* Thousand Oaks, CA: Sage. These authors summarize the results of a large-scale Canadian survey. The book clearly describes the research, as well as its implications for public policy.

Klein, E., Campbell, J., Soler, E., & Ghez, M. (1997). *Ending domestic violence: Changing public perceptions/Halting the epidemic.* Thousand Oaks, CA: Sage. This book summarizes the research on attitudes toward the abuse of women. I was relieved to see evidence that the media can have a positive impact on issues relevant to women.

Paludi, M. A. (Ed.). (1996). *Sexual harassment on college campuses: Abusing the ivory power.* Albany: State University of New York Press. The chapters in this book provide an excellent overview of the theoretical and practical aspects of academic sexual harassment.

Ward, C. A. (1995). *Attitudes toward rape: Feminist and social psychological perspectives.* London: Sage. In the third edition of this textbook, I lamented that our discipline did not have recent research about attitudes toward rape. This volume nicely answers my wishes, especially because it includes a cross-cultural perspective.

ANSWERS TO THE DEMONSTRATIONS

Demonstration 13.1: The percentages of students who considered each scenario to be sexual harassment were: 1. 52%; 2. 90%; 3. 40%; 4. 42%.

Demonstration 13.2: 1. Disagree; 2. Agree; 3. Disagree; 4. Disagree; 5. Agree; 6. Disagree; 7. Disagree; 8. Agree; 9. Disagree; 10. Agree.

Demonstration 13.4: 1. 83%; 2. 43% of women, 25% of men; 3. 48%; 4. 91%; 5. 88%.

ANSWERS TO THE TRUE–FALSE QUESTIONS

1. False (p. 470); 2. True (p. 472); 3. True (p. 474); 4. True (p. 482); 5. False (p. 483); 6. True (p. 485); 7. False (p. 487); 8. True (p. 496); 9. True (p. 501); 10. False (p. 504).

Women and Older Adulthood

TRUE OR FALSE?

_____ 1. Because most researchers are middle-aged or older, we have at least twice as much research on this period as on childhood and adolescence combined.

_____ 2. Most adults have stereotypes about elderly women; however, psychotherapists do not have strong stereotypes about this group.

_____ 3. Elderly women in North America have much more power than in any other culture.

_____ 4. Women typically have fewer retirement problems than men do.

_____ 5. According to recent data, retired men are about twice as likely as retired women to receive benefits from a retirement plan.

_____ 6. Most medical researchers agree that the risks of hormone replacement therapy during menopause far outweigh the benefits.

_____ 7. Because of hormonal changes, menopause often produces psychological symptoms such as depression and irritability.

_____ 8. Most women experience moderate depression when their children leave home.

_____ 9. Black, Latina, and Native American grandmothers are likely to take an active role in the lives of their grandchildren.

_____ 10. Because of a variety of health and social problems, elderly women are typically less satisfied with their lives, in comparison with younger women.

Attitudes Toward Older Women
The Media
The Double Standard of Aging
Cross-Cultural Views of Older Women

Older Women, Retirement, and Economic Issues
Planning for Retirement
Adjusting to Retirement
Economic Issues

Menopause
Physical Symptoms
Hormone Replacement Therapy
Psychological Reactions
Attitudes Toward Menopause

Social Aspects of Older Women's Lives
Family Relationships
Widowhood and the Death of Life Partners
Older Women of Color
Satisfaction with Life
Rewriting Our Life Stories
Final Words

Throughout this book, we have emphasized the contrast between people's stereotypes about women and the reality of women's lives. This contrast is also obvious when we examine the lives of older women. Consider the lives of elderly Black women, for example. We seldom see media coverage of this group (more evidence for our theme of invisible women). Still, those rare media images of elderly Black women convey the message that they are powerless and unproductive.

Contrast that view with the findings in a study by Leavitt and Saegert (1990), who examined the success of a program in Harlem. This program allowed tenants to cooperatively manage some apartment complexes that had been abandoned by their landlords. Most of the leaders in this "urban homesteading" project turned out to be elderly, economically disadvantaged Black women. They had developed an extensive network of social support and community-building that included meetings, fund raisers, potlucks, and parties. One committee visited people who owed rent, to help them work out payments. Another committee arranged holiday parties and aided people who were sick.

Primarily organized by Black women between the ages of 50 and 80, these apartment complexes had become impressively caring communities. As Leavitt and Saegert (1990) comment, these Harlem residents had "managed to carve out a place of relative security and control in the midst of poverty" (p. 217). Throughout this chapter, we'll encounter other, similar examples of the strength of older women.

This chapter considers women in middle age and old age, two life periods that are not defined by any clear-cut age spans. However, one fairly standard guideline is that middle age begins at about 40 and old age begins at about 65 (Gormly, 1997).

For many years, psychological research ignored older people—especially older women, consistent with our "invisibility" theme (Carstensen & Pasupathi, 1993; Fodor & Franks, 1990; Holden, 1997). This neglect was especially shameful because the average life span for a woman is about 80 years (Neft & Levine, 1997). In other words, about half of a woman's life was largely ignored.

512

Looking at the problem another way, the absence of information is also regretful because North America has so many elderly women. In 1996, the United States had about 20.0 million women and 13.9 million men over the age of 65—roughly 45% more women than men (Day, 1996). The comparable figures for Canada were 2.1 million women and 1.5 million men over 65—or 36% more women than men (Colombo, 1997). As an increasing number of women live into their 70s, 80s, and older, we need to emphasize the issues of older women.

A further problem is that researchers and theorists explore only a small portion of women's lives. For example, a computer search of the psychology listings under the topic of "Women and retirement" showed only 116 articles and books since 1990. A similar search under the topic "Menopause" revealed 21,405 citations during the same time span. Most women probably spend more time planning and thinking about their retirement, yet this topic is relatively invisible.

Fortunately, both psychology and women's studies are increasingly concerned about the needs and experiences of older women. In our earlier chapters, Chapter 8 discussed long-lasting romantic relationships, and Chapter 9 looked at sexuality and aging. Chapter 11 explored some issues relevant to older women's health, including osteoporosis and breast cancer. In this chapter, we'll focus on four topics: (1) attitudes toward older women, (2) retirement and economic issues, (3) menopause, and (4) social aspects of older women's lives.

ATTITUDES TOWARD OLDER WOMEN

Ageism is a bias against elderly people. Common examples of ageism include negative attitudes, myths, stereotypes, discrimination, and attempts to avoid interacting with elderly people (J. Johnson & Bytheway, 1993; Palmore, 1997; Whitbourne & Hulicka, 1990). One example of ageism is that physicians spend less time with older patients than younger ones—even though older individuals are likely to have more complex problems (Sharpe, 1995).

We'll begin this section on attitudes by considering how the media treat older women. Then we'll examine whether women are more likely than men to experience ageism—"the double standard of aging." Finally, we'll see that elderly women may be treated more positively in some other cultures.

The Media

Try Demonstration 14.1, to illustrate how older women are represented on television. You'll probably discover that—when you finally find a TV show featuring older women—they will be more concerned about cookie recipes or aphids on their rose bushes than about issues of greater significance. We all know spirited, accomplished older women in real life. However, your inspection of television's older women may not reveal many women of that caliber. Many of you who are

---

DEMONSTRATION 14.1

Older Women on Television

Between now and the end of this academic term, keep a record of the way older women are portrayed on television. This record should include both middle-aged women and elderly women. Be sure to include several kinds of programs—soap operas, game shows, situation comedies, shows during prime time, and Saturday morning cartoons—as well as advertisements. Pay attention to the number of older women, as well as how they are shown. Are they working outside the home? Do they have interests, hobbies, and important concerns, or are they mainly busy being nurturant? Do they enjoy the friendship of other women—the way real older women do? Do they seem "real," or are they represented in a stereotypical fashion?

---

reading this book are older women, and you may have noticed that women like yourself are invisible in the media.

A glance through magazines reveals the same message: older women are essentially invisible. For example, Betty Friedan (1993) searched the illustrations of *Vogue, Vanity Fair,* and *Ladies' Home Journal.* She found only a dozen photos of women who appeared to be over 60 years of age—out of nearly 400 photos.

Or, consider the advertisements that warn women in their 30s to begin using "anti-aging" creams. The ads also make older women feel inadequate (Friedan, 1993; Whitbourne, 1996). To hide signs of age, the ads say, women should dye their hair and have face-lifts. One innovative surgical procedure removes fat from a woman's thighs or buttocks and injects it into her lips, to restore a youthful fullness (Banner, 1992). Just imagine! You could be the first on your block to wear your hips on your lips!

Do older women fare better in the movies? Markson and Taylor (1993) examined the list of men and women who had been nominated for the prestigious Academy Awards, during the period between 1927 and 1990. Women over the age of 39 accounted for only 27% of the Best Actor awards, whereas men over 39 accounted for 67% of the Best Actor awards. A similar analysis by Bazzini and her coauthors (1997) confirmed that older women are seldom visible in the movies. Furthermore, older women were more likely than younger women to be portrayed as unfriendly, evil, unattractive, and not very intelligent.

This pervasive bias against older women has not been limited to recent decades. Negative images have been common throughout Western literature and storytelling (Markson, 1997; S. Sherman, 1997). You've heard many mother-in-law jokes; how about *father*-in-law jokes? Children dress up as "wicked old witches" for Halloween, but have you ever seen a costume for a wicked old *man?* We shouldn't be surprised, then, when women come to resent the aging process and try to hide signs of their age (Healey, 1993; R. Jacobs, 1997).

The Double Standard of Aging

As we've seen, North Americans have negative views about the aging process. Some theorists have proposed that people judge elderly women even more harshly than elderly men, a discrepancy called the **double standard of aging.** For example, people tend to think that wrinkles in a man's face reveal character and maturity. However, wrinkles send a far different message from a woman's face. After all, the ideal woman's face should be unblemished and show no signs of previous experiences or emotions!

Does the research provide evidence for the double standard of aging? This is a difficult question to answer because our stereotypes about older men and women are extremely complicated. These stereotypes depend on factors such as the gender gap, age, and occupation of the individuals we are judging, the particular attribute we are judging, and how the judgments are measured (Kite, 1996; Pasupathi et al., 1995). Let's consider some of the general research on the double standard of aging, and then we'll consider the double standard in love relationships.

General Research.   A study by Mary Kite and her colleagues (1991) emphasized the complicated nature of the double standard of aging. In general, their results suggest that young adults are more ageist than sexist. That is, their age stereotypes are more exaggerated than their gender stereotypes. For example, the young adults in this study made a major distinction between their reactions to 35-year-olds and their reactions to 65-year-olds. However, they didn't consider 65-year-old women to be much different from 65-year-old men. The young adults in this study saw elderly women *and* elderly men to be generous, family-oriented, and friendly, but focused more on the past than on the future, and troubled by health problems.

Still, the participants in this study did make some distinctions between the elderly women and men. A 65-year-old man was more likely to be considered intelligent and wise. In contrast, a 65-year-old woman was more likely to be considered active in the community, a grandparent, and—consistent with our earlier discussion—wrinkled.

Research by Silvia Canetto and her colleagues (1995) reported a similar pattern of considering older men to be more intelligent than older women. But the participants in this study also saw the older women as being more nurturant and sensitive than older men. At first, this sounds like an advantage for older women. However, Canetto and her coauthors pointed out a potential problem: People expect older women to devote themselves to others. As a result, an older woman who cares passionately about her work or her hobbies might be downgraded.

Using a different method, Hummert and her coworkers (1997) found more clear-cut evidence of a generalized double standard of aging. These researchers carefully assembled photographs of men and women representing different age groups. Let's consider specifically the part of the study in which the photographs being judged (the targets) had neutral facial expressions and were of people in either their 60s or their 70s. The participants in this study included men and women whose ages ranged from 18 through 96. They were asked to place each photograph next to one of six cards that described either a positive stereotype (e.g., a person who was lively, sociable, and interesting) or a negative stereotype (e.g., a person who was depressed, afraid, and lonely).

Figure 14.1 shows the average number of positive stereotypes that the participants selected. (The participants' age did not have a major impact on judgments, so Figure 14.1 combines the judgments of all participants.) As you can see, they selected a far smaller number of positive stereotypes for the older group of women than for all of the other three groups.

Unfortunately, psychotherapists also hold negative stereotypes about older women. Turner and Turner (1990) asked psychotherapists to make judgments about a variety of individuals, who were described as either young or old. Their judgments revealed that they thought White females, Black females, and Black males were less assertive and less willing to take risks if they were old rather

FIGURE 14.1	**Average number of positive stereotypes selected, as a function of target age and target gender. (Based on Hummert et al., 1997)**

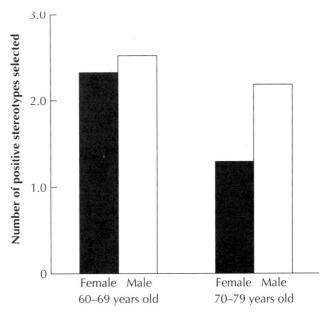

Note: Maximum positive score = 3.0

DEMONSTRATION 14.2

Relationships Between Older Women and Younger Men

Judge how likely you think it is that the relationship described below will succeed:

> Ann is a 40-year-old self-employed woman. She enjoys going to picnics in the park, dancing, reading, and listening to good music. She is originally from Chicago, where she graduated from business school before moving to California. Ann's father died a few years ago and her mother lives about 50 miles away. They have always been very close and have great respect for one another. About six months ago, Ann met a man named Jack at a party given by some mutual friends. Jack is a 22-year-old history teacher. He enjoys hiking, dancing, the movies, ceramics, and taking unusual courses at the local college. Jack is a native Californian, and his parents live in the same town. They have always had a very warm and caring relationship. Recently, Ann and Jack have been contemplating marriage. They both feel marriage is the best idea since they would not consider "just living together." (G. Cowan, 1984, p. 19)

Now read the passage over again, with Ann as the 22-year-old and Jack as the 40-year-old. Would your judgment about the success of the relationship be any different?

---

than young. However, they rated young White males and old White males as similar in assertiveness and risk taking. You can imagine how these biases might create problems. If therapists expect elderly women to be fairly passive, they may react negatively to *assertive* elderly women. They may also miss signs of depression if they believe older women should be inactive. Women who need psychotherapy must avoid not only therapists who are sexist, but also therapists who are ageist (R. Siegel & Sonderegger, 1990). Now try Demonstration 14.2, to prepare yourself for the next section.

Research on Love Relationships.   In general, people uphold a double standard of aging with respect to love relationships. Specifically, older men are considered to be appropriate romantic partners, but older women are not. Consistent with our earlier observations about movies, older women are rarely shown in romantic relationships. For example, as I'm writing this section, the major romantic movie is *The Horse Whisperer,* featuring 60-year-old Robert Redford. But his romantic partner, Kristin Scott Thomas, wouldn't be considered a "senior citizen." In fact, she's only 38.

People think that a marriage is not likely to succeed when a wife is much older than the husband. G. Cowan (1984) asked adolescents and adults to judge the potential success of various hypothetical romances, such as the two described in Demonstration 14.2. When the woman was 18 years older than the man, people were very pessimistic about the prospects for the marriage. However, when the man was 18 years older than the woman, people were much more optimistic.

Lesbians also report that people react negatively when one partner is much older than the other. A 41-year-old woman wrote:

> I set about telling my friends that I am a lesbian and, at the same time, that I love a 63-year-old woman. The questions, stated or implied: Am I looking for a mother? Is she looking for some security in her old age? Is lesbian love, then, really asexual? (Macdonald & Rich, 1983, p. 11)

The double standard of aging also applies to sexuality, because aging women are often dismissed as being undesirable sex partners (Blieszner, 1998; R. Jacobs, 1997). As we already noted in Chapter 9, people admire an old man's interest in sexuality, but they condemn the same interest shown by an old woman. Older women therefore face a particular disadvantage with respect to sexuality. Not only are they considered to look sexually unattractive and wrinkled, but they are also expected to show minimal interest in sexuality.

In this discussion, we've seen that the double standard of aging operates most powerfully when people judge two clusters of characteristics: (1) intelligence and competence, and (2) physical attractiveness and "romantic potential." Notice that the double standard of aging is, in fact, a variant of Theme 2 of this book. People react differently to women than they do to men. However, the differential treatment seems to increase as men and women grow older.

Cross-Cultural Views of Older Women

In general, this book has focused on women in North America. However, when we explore other cultures, we can find useful alternative models for viewing older women. In many of these cultures, a woman's power within the family increases as she grows older (Uba, 1994). For example, a young man living in the African country of Tanzania remarks that elderly women in his culture are considered to have special powers; elderly women and men are both valued for their knowledge of proverbs and traditions (Rich, 1994).

In some cultures, older women have direct power. For example, in many Latina/o cultures, elderly people are believed to have inner strength and a sense of mastery, so they can serve as a resource for younger people (Paz, 1993). In India, the elderly control family wealth and power, they arrange marriages, and they counsel younger people (Naidoo, 1990c).

Other cultures allow older women to exert pressure behind the scenes, even if they have little public power. For instance, an older woman in Taiwan who is displeased with her brother's behavior can discuss this problem with friends and relatives. The gossip network ultimately reaches the offending person, who is expected to improve his behavior (Grambs, 1989).

These positive attitudes in other cultures can certainly make older women feel valued. These attitudes also have important implications for cognitive functioning. For example, elderly women show little memory decline in cultures with positive attitudes toward the elderly, such as China (B. Levy & Langer, 1994). In contrast, people in the mainstream U.S. and Canadian cultures do not expect elderly women to be very intelligent. These expectations may indirectly cause elderly women to perform less well on a variety of cognitive tasks.

This section on attitudes toward elderly women may encourage you to introspect about the aging process. Do you hold any attitudes that are inappropriately negative? Think about the older women you admire—their wisdom, sense of humor, warmth, and competence. Try to incorporate these characteristics into your general viewpoint about older women. Can you think of specific ways in which your revised viewpoint can modify your response to the next older woman you meet?

 Attitudes Toward Older Women

1. **Ageism is a bias against elderly people.**

2. **The media underrepresent and misrepresent elderly women in magazines, advertisements, the movies, and popular culture.**

3. **The double standard of aging proposes that people judge older women more harshly than older men. The general research does not consistently support this concept, but it does typically show that people believe older men are more intelligent than older women.**

4. **The double standard of aging does seem to apply when people assess romantic relationships and sexual attractiveness.**

5. **In some cultures outside North America, older women's power increases as they grow older.**

OLDER WOMEN, RETIREMENT, AND ECONOMIC ISSUES

Think about the topic of women and retirement for a moment. Have you ever read a short story or a book about a woman retiring from her job? Have you seen a television show or a movie on this issue? Women are missing from the popular lore about retirement—and from the research (Carp, 1997; S. Phillips & Imhoff, 1997). Once again, we have evidence for the relative invisibility of women. However, this invisibility may change now that so many women are working outside the home. For example, in 1996, two-thirds of women between the ages of 45 and 64 were employed (U.S. Bureau of the Census, 1997). The media typically lag behind reality, but maybe we'll soon see a movie scene about a retirement party for a woman!

In contrast to retirement, the issue of poverty among elderly women has received some publicity, and we also hear women's personal stories. For example, a student in a psychology of women class recalled a conversation with two older women. They were wondering whether they would have enough money during retirement to buy cards and stamps, to stay in touch with friends who lived far away (Hoctor, 1993). Women with inadequate retirement funds must often struggle to pay for basic living expenses. Let's now consider these interrelated topics: retirement and economic issues.

Planning for Retirement

People retire for a number of reasons—health problems, mandatory retirement, and the lure of free time. Most research suggests that women retire earlier than men (Carp, 1997; Szinovacz, 1990). However, that generalization doesn't apply to all groups. For example, Black women and men tend to be the same age when they retire (Ralston, 1997). One reason that European American women retire early is to take care of a husband whose health is poor; Black women are less likely to retire for this reason (Carp, 1997; Hansson et al., 1997; Talaga & Beehr, 1995). Another reason that European American women are likely to retire early is because their husbands (typically, a few years older) have already retired (Carp, 1997; O'Rand et al., 1992).

One worrisome gender difference is that women are less likely than men to seek information about retirement benefits before they retire (Carp, 1997). The explanation isn't clear. Do women feel uncomfortable about finances? Do married women assume that their husbands will take care of "money matters"? Are they afraid they will learn discouraging information? This avoidance is a major problem because—as we'll soon see—they receive much lower retirement benefits than men do.

Adjusting to Retirement

Consistent with Theme 4 of this book, women have widely different reactions to retirement (Calasanti, 1996; Clair et al., 1993). However, most of the research suggests that women may experience more retirement problems than men. Women may also need more time to adapt to retirement (Clair et al., 1993; Etaugh, 1993b; Quick & Moen, 1998). One reason for these gender differences is that women have lower incomes, so they often have financial problems (S. Phillips & Imhoff, 1997). They may also miss their friends from work (Carp, 1997). Another reason is that retired women perform more housework than their retired husbands, and few women are inspired by housework (Antonucci et al., 1994; Dorfman, 1992).

As you can imagine, a woman's adjustment during retirement is influenced by her reasons for retirement. If a woman retires because she wants more time for herself, she will probably adjust well to retirement. In contrast, if a woman re- tires because she needs to care for a sick relative, she will probably not enjoy her retirement (Szinovacz, 1989). Significant life events—such as divorce or the death of family members—also influence a woman's adjustment to retirement. However, women who enjoy their retirement often become even happier with their marriage relationships (Higginbottom et al., 1993).

Many retired women enjoy volunteering for community or political projects after they have retired (Bergquist et al., 1993). For example, one 75-year-old woman remarked:

> I had to begin a whole new life! I tried several different things. I worked for a U.S. Senator, not for money. I never worked for money after I retired, because I didn't need to earn money. But I could not live without *work*. I cannot live my life without a purpose, a humanitarian purpose. (Doress & Siegal, 1987, p. 176)

We still have many unanswered questions about women and retirement. For example, how can we encourage women to learn more about their retirement benefits? What successful strategies do married women use to negotiate a more equal sharing of housework during retirement? How can women best maintain their social connections from work? And what kinds of volunteer activities are most likely to enhance a woman's satisfaction with retirement?

Economic Issues

At present, about one-quarter of elderly European American women in the United States live in poverty. Economic problems are even more widespread for women of color. For example, more than half of Black and Latina elderly women are living in poverty (Carstensen, 1998; Rubin, 1997). Poverty is also an issue for older Canadian women. In fact, elderly women who have no spouse are among the most impoverished groups in Canada (L. Taylor, 1994).

One of the major sources of income for elderly women in the United States is Social Security benefits. These benefits are based on a worker's lifetime earnings. Women have lower lifetime earnings because they have lower annual incomes and have typically worked fewer years (Carstensen, 1998; Hatch, 1995). Consequently, women often receive lower Social Security benefits than men do.

The other major source of income for elderly women is private pension plans. These are also based on earned income, and most women are not employed in jobs with pension plans. In fact, only 24% of retired women receive pension benefits, in contrast to 46% of men (Keller, 1997).

Here are some other reasons that women have lower incomes than men dur- ing old age (Barusch, 1994):

1. Women are not compensated for their unpaid work in the home.
2. Many women are displaced homemakers who worked in the home and then became divorced or widowed, which led to a substantial decrease in income.

3. Women are more likely to take early retirement, which reduces their retirement benefits.

4. Because employed women receive lower salaries than men, they are less likely to set aside retirement funds during their employment years.

5. Women live longer, so their savings are likely to become diminished.

6. As we saw in Chapter 11, women are more likely to have chronic illnesses, and the expense of treatment further decreases their usable income.

Naturally, we need to remind ourselves about individual differences. On the average, elderly women do indeed have lower incomes than elderly men. Still, many women have relatively high incomes. Furthermore, research with U.S. residents suggests that—beyond the income necessary to buy the essentials—extra income does not typically buy happiness (D. Myers & Diener, 1996). We cannot ignore the substantial number of women whose lives are altered by poverty. However, as we will see in the final section of this chapter, many elderly women lead lives that are satisfying and emotionally rich.

 SECTION SUMMARY *Older Women, Retirement, and Economic Issues*

1. **The issue of women's retirement is relatively invisible in both the media and the psychological research, although economic issues have received some attention.**

2. **European American women typically retire earlier than men, but gender differences are not found for African Americans; women are less likely than men to seek information about retirement.**

3. **Women are likely to experience more problems in retirement than men do, especially if they retire to care for a sick relative; many women enjoy volunteer activities after retirement.**

4. **A substantial number of elderly women in the United States live in poverty; they are likely to have lower incomes than men because of lower benefits from Social Security and private pension plans, as well as factors such as diminished savings and chronic illness.**

MENOPAUSE

So far, our study of older adulthood has examined two topics that are central in the life experiences of older women: (1) how other people react to them and represent them in the media, and (2) how older women experience retirement and economic issues. Let's turn our attention to the one topic that has generated the most media attention for older women: menopause. As we'll see, most older women do not consider the experience of menopause to be centrally important in their lives.

A woman enters **menopause** when she has stopped having menstrual periods for one year (Golub, 1992). Most women experience menopause between the ages of 42 and 58, with 51 being the most common age (Carlson et al., 1996). Some women find that their menstrual cycles stop abruptly. More often, the cycles become less and less regular, and the amount of flow decreases. In the current U.S. population, about 35 million women have entered menopause (Wise et al., 1996).

Two major factors cause menopause. (1) The aging ovaries no longer produce estrogen and progesterone at the previous rate, so the smooth sequence of the menstrual cycle is disrupted. Eventually, the hormone levels dip too low to produce shedding of the endometrial lining of the uterus. As a result, menstruation no longer occurs (Alexander & LaRosa, 1994). (2) The important brain structure called the hypothalamus may send a different pattern of messages to the hormonal system when a woman approaches 50 (Wise et al., 1996).

When I was writing the second edition of this textbook in the early 1990s, menopause was a taboo topic, invisible in books and magazines and on television. However, menopause became a popular topic by the late 1990s. Just as I began writing this chapter, for instance, actress Cybill Shepherd was featured in *People* magazine, discussing how she thinks that menopause deserves more public attention.

Frankly, I'm mystified by the increased popularity of menopause in the media. Why should we have so many books on menopause, yet only one book on women and retirement since the 1980s (Szinovacz et al., 1992)? Perhaps our culture's current fascination with the biological basis of behavior is partly responsible. The popularity of menopause issues may also reflect our culture's emphasis on women's reproductive roles. Finally, if we *really* paid attention to issues such as women's retirement, the problem would require costly, societally based remedies (DeCourville, 1999).

Let's consider four components of menopause. We'll begin with the physical symptoms, and then discuss hormone replacement therapy. We'll then consider psychological reactions to menopause, ending with a discussion of attitudes toward menopause.

Physical Symptoms

Several common physical symptoms accompany menopause. The best-known symptom is the **hot flash,** a sensation of heat coming from within the body and usually affecting the chest, neck, and head. For most women, hot flashes are accompanied by heavy perspiration, and severe hot flashes often disrupt sleep (Rowe & Devons, 1995). Surprisingly, the physiological mechanisms of hot flashes are not known, though they are related in a complex fashion to estrogen levels (Bee, 1998).

About 75% to 85% of women in the United States experience hot flashes during menopause. However, only 10% to 20% of women consider them bothersome enough to need treatment (Alexander & LaRosa, 1994; Carlson et al., 1996; Furman, 1995). In other words, hot flashes are common, but most women find that they don't disrupt their lives.

Other physical changes during menopause may include osteoporosis (which we discussed in Chapter 11), decreased vaginal secretions, thinning of the vaginal tissues, headaches, urinary symptoms, and fatigue (Alexander & LaRosa, 1994; Carlson et al., 1996; Whitbourne, 1996). This list of physical symptoms sounds frightening, but few women experience all symptoms. Throughout this book, we have emphasized individual differences in gynecological issues such as menarche, menstrual pain, premenstrual syndrome, pregnancy, and childbirth. Women's reactions to menopause show similar variation, providing additional evidence for Theme 4 of this book.

Hormone Replacement Therapy

Should women take hormones after menopause? This question may sound innocent, but it is perhaps the most confusing and controversial question about women's health in the current era (Alexander & LaRosa, 1994). The problem is that hormones certainly relieve many of the physical symptoms of menopause, and they offer additional health benefits. But they also have potential disadvantages. The question is especially important because most women in North America will be postmenopausal for about one-third of their lives (Davidson, 1995), so women need to make decisions that have long-term consequences.

Let me try to summarize the issues as of 1999, though the recommendations may change as results come in from ongoing research projects (Matthews et al., 1997). The original **estrogen replacement therapy** uses estrogen by itself, which effectively relieves symptoms such as hot flashes and genital changes; it also helps prevent osteoporosis. However, many women now use **hormone replacement therapy,** a term that usually refers to estrogen supplemented by progestin. Progestin is also a hormone, and it reduces the risk of endometrial cancer (Carlson et al., 1996). Physicians therefore usually recommend the estrogen-plus-progestin combination unless a woman has had her uterus removed ("Managing Menopause," 1998; Rosenbaum & Wexler, 1994).

Estrogen has an additional benefit for women's health, beyond relieving the symptoms of menopause. Specifically, estrogen reduces the incidence of coronary heart disease by about 50% (Cobleigh et al., 1994; Matthews et al., 1997). This is an important finding, because about one-third of all women who do not have estrogen replacement therapy will die from heart disease (Carlson et al., 1996). Women who use combined estrogen and progestin experience a similar reduction in coronary heart disease (Grodstein et al., 1996).

So, where's the catch? Probably the major drawback to hormone treatment is cancer. A woman increases her chances of developing endometrial cancer if she takes "unopposed estrogen"—estrogen without any progestin (O'Hanlan, 1998). However, endometrial cancer is unlikely with the combined hormone therapy. Still, regular gynecological examinations to detect potential cancer are recommended for both kinds of hormone therapy; in fact, they are an important precaution for *all* women. Furthermore, estrogen replacement therapy increases the risk of breast cancer by about 30%, and the combined hormone replacement therapy increases the risk by about 40% (Colditz et al., 1995). For this reason, women taking hormones should be especially careful to examine their breasts regularly (see page 407) and to have a mammogram at least every 2 years.

If you are keeping track, you'll see that hormone replacement therapy reduces the risk of coronary heart disease and osteoporosis, but it can increase the risk of endometrial cancer (unless a woman takes progestin) and breast cancer. How do these factors combine? One study examined the long-term effects of estrogen replacement therapy and combined hormone replacement therapy (Grodstein et al., 1997). Both kinds of treatment were associated with a lower risk of death. For example, women who were currently using combined hormone replacement therapy had a 64% reduction in their risk of death.

Ultimately, every woman approaching menopause must carefully weigh the advantages and disadvantages of hormone therapy. She should also discuss these issues with a health care provider whom she trusts (Alexander & LaRosa, 1994). Fortunately, some new large-scale studies have been launched to examine the long-term effects of hormones. The Women's Health Initiative, for example, is a 15-year project studying 164,500 women (Matthews et al., 1997). The picture should be much clearer by the time women now in their teens and 20s have reached menopause.

Psychological Reactions

Compared to the controversy surrounding hormone replacement therapy, the psychological reactions to menopause are clear-cut. Specifically, we have no evidence that menopause—by itself—causes psychological symptoms such as depression, irritability, and mood swings (Alexander & LaRosa, 1994; Carlson et al., 1996; Golub, 1992). This chapter has already pointed out a number of depressing factors in the lives of older women, including attitudes toward older women and women's economic status. Women also experience health problems, divorce, and death of relatives and friends. All these factors are more important than menopause in determining the psychological status of middle-aged women (Carlson et al., 1996).

This conclusion certainly differs from the negative images you have received from the popular media and general folklore. These sources suggest that a woman who is experiencing menopause is plagued by intense mood swings. According to this view, a menopausal woman's wildly fluctuating hormones force her to be grouchy, highly anxious, and depressed.

The problem is that the media often provide worst-case scenarios. For example, a director of a menopause clinic complained about the phone calls he receives from reporters. They typically ask him to describe the most severe menopausal symptoms, rather than the norm (Azar, 1994). As a consequence, the media contribute to the public's negative attitudes toward menopause. The

DEMONSTRATION 14.3

Attitudes Toward Menopause

Answer each of the following questions about menopause.

1. Within the past month, how often have you spontaneously thought about menopause? Were your thoughts positive or negative?

2. How often has another person talked to you about menopause within the past month? Was the tone of this conversation positive or negative?

3. How often have you seen something about menopause in newspapers and magazines, or on television, within the past month? How would you characterize the coverage of menopause?

4. As you analyze your own thoughts about menopause, what do you see as the advantages of menopause? What are the disadvantages?

5. If you have a romantic partner and you are female, what would you imagine this person's reaction would be when you are experiencing menopause? If you are male, how do you imagine you would respond to female friends or romantic partners during the time when they are experiencing menopause?

6. How comfortable would you be in initiating a conversation about menopause with an acquaintance from your own age group? How about a conversation with someone from another age group? (In fact, you might try this!)

media also perpetuate another related myth—that menopausal women are no longer interested in sexual activity. In Chapter 9, though, we noted that women who have sexual partners typically remain sexually active during old age.

Attitudes Toward Menopause

Before you read further, try Demonstration 14.3, to assess your own attitudes toward menopause. Menopause is no longer a taboo subject, but my students in their 20s report that they rarely discuss menopause with their friends.

Unfortunately, menopause has had a long history of being represented negatively. For example, a typical gynecology textbook from the 1960s included this passage:

> Emotional instability is another outstanding symptom of this phase of life. Nervousness and anxiety are extremely frequent. . . . She cries easily; she flares up at her family and friends; she is irritable and may have difficulty in composing her thoughts or her reactions. (J. Brewer & de Costa, 1967, p. 229)

FIGURE 14.2	Negative attitudes toward menopause, as a function of age and menopausal experience. (Based on Gannon & Ekstrom, 1993)

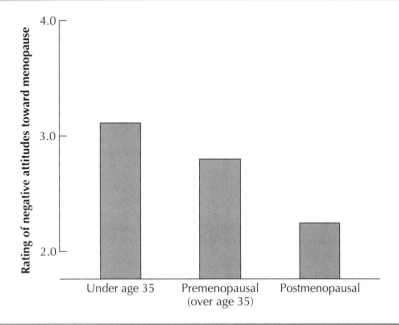

Note: 1 = neutral; 5 = most negative.

You can imagine how passages such as these shape the attitudes of physicians who treat menopausal women. For instance, a survey of physicians from one community revealed that 21% thought that menopause was a major health problem. In contrast, not one of the 120 menopausal women from that same community thought that menopause was a major health problem (DeLorey, 1992).

Interestingly, women who have actually gone through natural menopause have significantly *less* negative attitudes toward menopause than do younger women.* As part of a larger study, Gannon and Ekstrom (1993) asked women about their attitudes toward menopause in relation to their more general attitudes toward aging. Figure 14.2 shows the results for women who were postmenopausal; women who were premenopausal, but over the age of 35; and women under the age of 35. As you can see, women who have experienced

---

*The statements about physical and psychological reactions to menopause in this section refer to menopause that occurs naturally. As Chapter 11 described, women sometimes have negative reactions to the menopause that accompanies surgical removal of the ovaries.

menopause generally consider it to be mildly negative—not as negative as it was judged by two groups that had no personal knowledge of menopause.

Some researchers are beginning to explore how women of color experience menopause. For example, Mexican American women tend to have attitudes that are similar to those of the primarily European American population that Gannon and Ekstrom studied. Specifically, menopause is somewhat negative, but far from catastrophic (Kearns & Christopherson, 1992). Similarly, Black women experience some difficulty with hot flashes, sleep disturbances, and irritability. However, menopause does not cause them great distress (B. Jackson, 1992).

In Chapter 4, we explored the concept of "menstrual joy," or the idea that women can find some pleasure in menstruation. Some writers hint that women can have an experience that we could call "menopausal joy." For example, one woman described how her hot flashes could have a positive impact when she was teaching art:

> The sudden spurt of inner heat would send my head spinning. I had to sit back to steady myself. This could be in my studio, in the middle of a class. . . . But I felt a marvelous glow of individuality, that I was feeling something no one else in the room felt, and that this was a chapter in my biological history. (Apter, 1995, p. 213)

People from cultures outside North America may have similarly positive views. For example, George (1988) studied Sikh women who had left India and were currently living in Canada. Their Indian culture emphasizes that life has a time and a place for everything. Postmenopausal Sikh women have high status in their society. Not surprisingly, these women believe that menopause symbolizes a final cleansing event that makes them pure and free. They discuss menopausal experiences freely with other Sikh women, and none of them has reported depression or other psychological symptoms. Alternative viewpoints such as this one help us understand how each culture constructs menopause according to its own values. A cross-cultural perspective also provides us with some positive alternatives.

 SECTION SUMMARY   *Menopause*

1. **Menopause, or the cessation of menstrual periods, it now a relatively popular topic in the media.**

2. **Common physical symptoms include hot flashes, osteoporosis, genital changes, and headaches.**

3. **Hormone replacement therapy provides some benefits (lowered risk of coronary heart disease and osteoporosis) and some drawbacks (increased risk of endometrial cancer—unless progestin is taken—and breast cancer).**

4. **Contrary to folklore, menopause does not cause psychological symptoms such as depression and irritability.**

5. **Menopause has been represented very negatively, and women who are not yet menopausal are more negative about it than women who are postmenopausal. Mexican American and Black women have menopausal experiences resembling those of European Americans, but some cultures view menopause much more positively.**

SOCIAL ASPECTS OF OLDER WOMEN'S LIVES

We have considered how society views older women, as well as women's experiences as they pass through menopause and retire from the workforce. Now let's examine the changing social world of older women. How do their family relationships evolve as they grow older? How are women affected by the death of a spouse or other romantic partner? How do the experiences of women of color compare with the experiences of European American women? How happy are they with their lives—and how do they alter their lives if they are not satisfied?

Family Relationships

Chapter 8, on love relationships, explored one family role that is important for many women: being a wife. In that chapter, we examined some characteristics of happy, long-term relationships. We also looked at lesbian and bisexual relationships, which are central in the lives of many women. However, many adult women occupy other important family roles because they are mothers, daughters, and grandmothers.

Older Women as Mothers.   When many people think of a mother, they picture someone whose children range between infancy and the teenage years. Research on the mother–child relationship has neglected critical changes in this relationship once the child becomes an adult.

Much of the earlier research and theory on middle-aged women focused on the **empty-nest syndrome,** presumably a feeling of depression that results from children's leaving home. Notice that the name, *empty nest,* implies that a woman's role focuses completely on being a mother.

In reality, however, the research reveals the same wide variety of responses that our other discussions of women's lives have uncovered. As Grambs (1989) summarizes the studies, "Some mothers are devastated; others are delighted" (p. 126). In fact, the research confirms that middle-aged mothers whose children have left home tend to be about as happy as—or even slightly happier than—middle-aged mothers who have at least one child at home (Gee & Kimball, 1987; Grambs, 1989; V. Mitchell & Helson, 1990).

When researchers uncover individual differences in psychological reactions, they often ask what factors predict these reactions. In the case of the empty-nest syndrome, ethnicity seems to be an important factor. For example, European American middle-class women are more likely than Black or Latina women to experience depression (Borland, 1982; Facio, 1997). In addition, the empty-nest syndrome is more likely among women who were born in the 1920s and 1930s and who reached adulthood during the "Leave It to Beaver" era, when motherhood was emphasized. The empty-nest syndrome occurred less among women born in the 1900s and 1910s, who were encouraged to join the workforce during World War II (Adelmann et al., 1989). In other words, women whose entire identity was supposed to be wrapped up in their family were more likely to experience problems when their children moved away from home.

My college-age students are often dismayed to learn that their mothers may be somewhat happier after the children leave home. Please do not conclude that women are overjoyed with their children's departure. Mothers may indeed be saddened. However, serious depression is rare. Instead, mothers learn to reshape their lives around new interests and activities as their daughters and sons move into adulthood (Grambs, 1989).

Older Women as Daughters.   We usually think of adult women's roles as mothers and grandmothers. However, adult women are often daughters, as well.

Most of the research on the "daughter role" focuses on adult women who take care of elderly parents. The terms **sandwich generation** and **caught generation** refer to middle-aged people—especially women—who find themselves responsible for both their children and their parents. Daughters are more likely than sons to find themselves taking care of an elderly parent who is in poor health (Bould, 1997; Kimball, 1995; Lustbader & Hooyman, 1994). Most researchers estimate that daughters are about three times as likely as sons to become caretakers (Doress-Worters, 1994; Russo, 1990).

In a representative study of caregivers in Québec, women provided significantly more assistance than men did. However, women and men *perceived* the experience as equally burdensome (Jutras & Veilleux, 1991). The researchers explained these contradictory results:

> We suggest . . . that women do not experience a greater burden, in spite of their greater involvement, simply because they have been socialized to help others, or conversely that men experience a greater burden because for many of them it is the first time they have had to take care of someone else in such a direct and intimate manner. . . . (p. 16)

Because women spend much more time on these tasks than men do, taking care of the elderly is really a women's issue.

The resources on women's caretaking roles emphasize that the tasks are completely unpleasant and burdensome for middle-aged daughters. A colleague pointed out how this one-sided view is based on researchers' preconceived ideas. She commuted 800 miles each way to care for her severely ill mother—while working toward tenure at her university. Because of her experiences, she was invited to participate in a survey of women in similar situations. However, she was astonished to see that the questions tapped only negative experiences and feelings, with no indication of the positive emotions. Indeed, she had experienced incredible strain. On one occasion, in the Intensive Care Unit, she held her mother's hand with her right hand as her mother fought pneumonia. Simultaneously, with her left hand, this woman typed a psychology exam that was later faxed to a colleague teaching the course for her. The additional responsibilities did have an impact on her academic career. However, as she wrote,

> I considered myself blessed to have been able to give so much to my mother and to provide her hospice care in her home. She died in my arms. Yes it was stressful. Yes it was difficult. And, yes, I had these positive feelings—as well as negative feelings—at the time I was doing this. But I have no regrets and would do it again without thinking about it. (Skinner, 1999)

Ultimately, she decided to quit the study. The questions simply ignored the possibility that women could derive any enriching or pleasant experience from taking care of a beloved relative.

A small number of researchers have begun to explore other aspects of the relationship between grown children and their parents—beyond the caretaking role (C. L. Johnson & Barer, 1997; Josselson, 1996). One interesting observation is that middle-aged men and women are equally likely to think about their elderly parents, something we might not have expected from the data on caretaking (Troll, 1994). Unfortunately, however, the media generally ignore the social interactions between middle-aged people and their parents. Aside from an occasional brief reference, how often have you seen or read about a relationship between an adult woman and her mother in which they were interacting as adults?

Older Women as Grandmothers.   According to one of the traditional stereotypes, grandmothers are jolly, white-haired old ladies with glasses, who bestow cookies and affection on their grandchildren. According to another stereotype, grandmothers are frail and helpless (P. K. Smith, 1991). Neither of these stereotypes captures the wide variety of capabilities, interests, and personality characteristics that are typical of real grandmothers.

Most women are grandmothers for about half of their lives (Kivett, 1996). However—once again—we have little recent research on this role. In one study of individuals over the age of 85, only about 20% of the grandparents saw a grandchild more often than once a week (C. L. Johnson & Barer, 1997). In general, grandmothers and grandfathers seem to spend the same amount of time with grandchildren (M. S. Smith, 1991).

What do grandmothers do when they interact with their grandchildren? In terms of activities, they are likely to babysit and drop by for visits, often playing games, reading books, and enjoying conversations when they visit. They are also likely to impart advice to grandchildren about doing what is morally right and socially appropriate (Gee & Kimball, 1987; Scott, 1997; M. S. Smith, 1991). However, our theme of individual differences is evident in patterns of grandmothering: Some women feel it is their duty to advise, but others argue that good grandparents should not interfere with their grandchildren's upbringing (Korn-haber, 1996; Troll, 1982). Also, many grandmothers are actually functioning as parents to their grandchildren, especially in cases where the biological parents are teenagers.

Widowhood and the Death of Life Partners

For married women, the death of a spouse is typically the most traumatic and stressful event of their lives. This loss requires more readjustment than any other role transition (Bradsher, 1997; R. Jacobs, 1997; Mackie, 1991).

Women are more likely to become widows than men are to become widow-ers. The reasons for this discrepancy are: women live longer, they typically marry men older than themselves, and they are less likely to remarry (Bradsher, 1997; Etaugh, 1993b). As a result, the U.S. Census shows 4.4 times as many wid-ows as widowers over the age of 65 (U.S. Bureau of the Census, 1997). The ratio in Canada is not as extreme: 2.4 times as many widows as widowers (Colombo, 1997).

When her husband dies, a woman faces the pain, grief, and mourning that ac-company bereavement. Depending on her personal circumstances, she may ex-perience anger, and she may feel that nothing in life seems worthwhile. Loneliness is one of the major problems for widows (Bradsher, 1997). Many women have never before been alone in their homes; they went directly from the home of their parents into the home in which they lived with their hus-bands. Widows also report that they often feel awkward in social situations where most people are with a spouse.

Gender comparisons in bereavement patterns are highly inconsistent. Many studies show no gender differences, but some suggest that women suffer more, and others suggest that men suffer more (Bradsher, 1997; Stillion, 1984; Stroebe & Stroebe, 1983). To make sense of these gender comparisons, we would need to know a variety of factors, such as financial status and health problems. How-ever, both women and men are likely to experience stress, loneliness, and grief when a spouse dies.

We know relatively little about the grieving process for other life partners. For example, Shenk and Fullmer (1996) describe a lesbian couple in their 80s, who had lived together for 15 years in a small midwestern town. Hilda wrote about her bereavement after the death of her partner, Maurine:

> I sit to remember, to wish, and then to realize that life has to be different. I know life has to be different, and I am now picking up the happy thoughts from the past and going on. . . . (p. 85)

Unfortunately, our culture's heterosexism is likely to deny lesbians the kind of social support typically offered to women whose husbands have died.

We find enormous individual differences in bereavement, as in all important transitions in women's lives. Many women are resilient; others are still deeply depressed years later (Wortman & Silver, 1989). Many women discover a hidden strength that aids their recovery. One woman wrote, several months after the death of her husband:

> Each day I mourn a little less and feel a little more alive. I realize now that loving and honoring my husband does not require me to give up the possibility of happiness. . . . Now, more than ever, I understand that activities, interests, and doing things on my own behalf are essential. I have rediscovered the pleasure of my own company and that being alone doesn't mean I have to be lonely. (Adolph, 1993, p. 66)

Older Women of Color

Women of color are far more likely than European American women to face the economic difficulties we discussed earlier. We have noted that Black and Latina elderly women are twice as likely as European American elderly women to live in poverty (Carstensen, 1998; Rubin, 1997). Once again, however, the diversity theme is prominent. For example, researchers have noted that a significant number of elderly Black and Asian American women are fairly well-off financially (Kagawa-Singer et al., 1997; Ralston, 1997). Still, the majority of elderly women of color face a daily struggle in paying for housing, health care, transportation, and even enough food to eat.

Two different stereotypes are used to characterize elderly Black women (Ralston, 1997). One portrays them as victims of poverty and urban decay; the other portrays them as superhuman individuals who surmount obstacles through hard work and a good heart. Neither captures the complexity of their actual lives. In general, elderly Black women are likely to be very active in selected community organizations such as a church (Ralston, 1997).

In addition, Black women are often closely involved in the lives of their grandchildren (Kornhaber, 1996; Ralston, 1997). These women give their grandchildren social support by encouraging the young people to feel that they can talk with their grandmothers about anything. They may also monitor their grandchildren's activities, discipline them, and encourage them to achieve. However, many Black grandmothers report resentment about tackling the problems of grandchildren, especially if they only recently finished rearing their own children (Ovrebo & Minkler, 1993).

We have little research on Latinas (Facio, 1997). Like Black grandmothers, Latina grandmothers typically enjoy their social role. However, they often describe the role as "confining" or "limiting," especially if they are expected to take on child care responsibilities (Facio, 1997). A study of Puerto Rican women, currently living in the United States, emphasizes that elderly women are expected to provide help to children and grandchildren (Sánchez-Ayéndez, 1993). In return, elderly women are expected to *seek* help when they need it. As one elderly woman said:

> Of course I go to my children when I have a problem! To whom would I turn? I raised them and worked very hard to give them the little I could. Now that I am

old, they try to help me in whatever they can. . . . Good offspring should help their aged parents as much as they are able to. (p. 273)

When we look at elderly Asian American women, we see additional evidence of diversity within ethnic groups. For example, an elderly woman from India may be a retired physician. In contrast, fewer than 20% of elderly women from Laos have completed high school (Kagawa-Singer et al., 1997). In general, however, elderly Asians are more likely than elders in any other ethnic group to live with their children (Lubben & Becerra, 1987; Yee, 1997). Research with one specific population—Vietnamese refugees—concluded that elderly women who lived with their family had better social adjustment than those who lived in different households (Tran, 1991). However, we cannot draw any clear-cut conclusions that apply to the wide diversity of Asian American ethnic groups in North America.

Elderly Native American women are the least visible group in the psychology research. One important variable that determines the life patterns of these elderly women is whether they live in an urban or a rural setting. About half of elderly Native Americans live in cities, where they are dispersed throughout the general urban population. Very little is known about their experiences (R. John et al., 1997). The remaining half live in rural areas or on reservations, where elderly women typically assume the roles of grandmother, caregiver, educator, and wisdom keeper (R. John et al., 1997).

A study of Apache grandmothers living on a reservation in Arizona emphasized the strong bond between grandmothers and their grandchildren (Bahr, 1994). Apache children are more than three times as likely as European American children to live with their grandparents. The major reason is that the parents often seek employment off the reservation, in an urban setting. Most grandmothers in this study reported that they felt great satisfaction in caring for their grandchildren. These grandmothers are expected to be wise, energetic, and resourceful, especially in transmitting their cultural heritage to their grandchildren.

Throughout this chapter, we have discussed the invisibility of older women. Older women of color are even less visible. From the brief glimpses in the psychology literature, we typically lack the crucial information that would provide a clear picture of their lives and experiences.

Satisfaction with Life

If you glance through some of the topics discussed in this book, you'll see that many older women have every right to be unhappy. Chapter 11 examined physical problems such as breast cancer and osteoporosis, which are relatively common among older women. In this chapter, we have seen that women may be unhappy about retiring. Many worry about the health of their parents. Many will mourn the loss of a spouse or a close companion. Many older women, especially women of color, are likely to face economic crises. Even women who do not have any of these problems are likely to experience negative reactions from others because they live in a culture that rejects older women's wrinkles and other signs of age.

In reality, however, most middle-aged and elderly women are reasonably satisfied with their lives. For example, one study showed that women in their 50s believe that they are in their "prime of life." Mitchell and Helson (1990) asked 700 alumnae from a women's college to rate their current life satisfaction. Figure 14.3 shows the percentage of women in each age category who said that their lives were "first rate," in contrast to those who used the two most negative categories, "fair" and "not so good." As you can see, the older women were often more positive than some groups of younger women.

Most studies show that older women are just as happy as younger women—and perhaps even happier (C. L. Johnson & Barer, 1997; Keyes & Ryff, 1998). However, we need to keep in mind that studies are often conducted with people who are relatively well educated, as were the women in Mitchell and Helson's (1990) study. These women are not likely to face economic problems. The

FIGURE 14.3	Percentage of respondents who rated life as "first-rate" versus "fair" or "not so good," as a function of age. (Based on Mitchell & Helson, 1990)

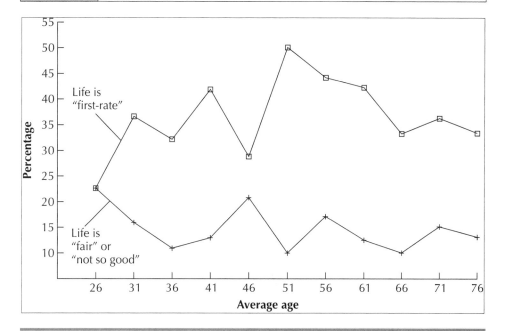

samples are also not likely to include very frail elderly people, whose poor health reduces their satisfaction with life (Atchley, 1991).

Remember the theme of individual variation, emphasized throughout this book. In particular, women vary in the ways they achieve happiness. Researchers have found that women do not share a ready-made blueprint for happiness (C. L. Johnson & Barer, 1997). One woman might find happiness through her husband and children, whereas another might be equally happy with a riskier, less traditional lifestyle.

Rewriting Our Life Stories

When they were young adults, many women may have thought they knew exactly where their lives were heading. Indeed, many women's lives reveal a pattern of continuity and predictability. However, many women find that their lives take an unexpected route. For example, Vickers and Thomas (1993) interviewed women between the ages of 40 and 60. Most denied having a "midlife crisis." However, the majority had begun to rethink parts of their lives. Many reported that they had begun to shape their own lives, taking responsibility for their future direction, rather than simply coping with their current situation.

Several books have explored the way women make choices and changes. Some titles capture how women can choose to pursue new life directions: *Secret Paths: Women in the New Midlife* (Apter, 1995); *Coming into Our Fullness: On Women Turning Forty* (Rountree, 1991); *On Women Turning 50: Celebrating Mid-Life Discoveries* (Rountree, 1993); and—my favorite title—*No More Frogs, No More Princes: Women Making Creative Choices at Midlife* (Vickers & Thomas, 1993).

The women interviewed in these books emphasize that, as women grow older, they can play by new rules. One woman reported:

> Something about turning forty gave me the freedom to say, "I don't care as much about what other people think. I don't have to prove anything to anybody anymore. I've proved it to myself. I'm comfortable with myself." (Vickers & Thomas, 1993)

Other women emphasized how older women can feel free about taking risks:

> Once women pass fifty, if they can avoid the temptations of the eternal youth purveyors, the sellers of unnatural thinness and cosmetic surgery, they may be able to tap into the feisty girls they once were. . . . They might, at fifty, be ready to take on risk, display a new-found vitality, and bid goodbye to conventional limitations. (C. Heilbrun, cited in Rountree, 1993, p. 1)

Final Words

To conclude this chapter, I asked a 69-year-old friend to reflect about her life and about old age. At the age of 58, Anne Hardy and her husband Duane decided to leave their comfortable community in Rochester, New York, to work in the South for several organizations that are concerned with civil rights and social justice. She wrote about this period in her life:

When our children were through college and on their own, our feeling was that it was time to close out the marketplace phase of our lives. We never had the empty-nest feeling. It was, instead, a kind of liberation, a time to move into a new phase. Just as marriage had been a new phase, followed by parenthood, this was another. The caring, the sharing of concerns, the readiness to be of help to each other when necessary, would continue with our children, unchanged by the fact that we were no longer living under one roof, but we were ready to move on, just as they were. We had both done a great deal of volunteer work in our free time for many years, and now we had the opportunity to do it full-time. Our needs are modest, we were able to accept subsistence salaries until we were able to "retire" on Social Security, at which time we continued to work full-time but no longer drew salaries.

. . . I am very conscious that my life hasn't been "typical," if there is such a thing. I've had many advantages denied to others. We have had fairly low income at times but were never really poor and certainly never hungry; my health has, for the most part, been good; we have loving, caring children; and best of all, I've had, in my husband, a superb companion and best friend. With today's economic stresses and disrupted families, I doubt it's a norm.

After 10 years of work in the South, Anne and her husband Duane retired and moved back north. Anne still continued to work for organizations such as Women's International League for Peace and Freedom, the Nuclear Freeze Campaign, and the U.S.–China People's Friendship Association. She commented on this transition:

"Retirement" has many advantages. It's possible to be involved in many activities, yet not be pressured by them. We set our own schedules. We're free of regimentation. If something interesting to do comes up, we can do that and shift other commitments around. It's a more flexible, less rigid, less scheduled life.

At the age of 69, I still don't feel "old," although chronologically, I'm not "young." I think one ages—given reasonable health—as one has been gradually aging in all the years before, very much depending on the quality of life one has built. My interests haven't changed, except that we have the added joy of six grandchildren in our lives. Elderly people are as diverse as young people. Differences between them remain; previous likes and dislikes remain, for the most part. I am still me, "old" or not, though I feel that I have become more understanding, less judgmental, more open to new experiences, still trying to grow as a person.

We have begun to experience the loss of relatives and friends, and chronic and serious illnesses are beginning to appear among our associates. It's sad, of course, but it has the positive side of drawing us closer to those of our families and friends who are still in our lives, makes us more loving, more willing to overlook small irritants, more giving. There is a heightened sense of importance of savoring today, since this is the only tomorrow we will ever have.

There are serious concerns and hopes about the future, naturally, both in regard to personal matters such as health and loss of close ones, and in regard to national and international events. What kind of world will our children and grandchildren inherit, if they inherit any world at all? What will the employment picture be for them? What will it be like when our children reach their later years, and when our grandchildren reach their employment years? I have lost much of my sense that we can influence the course of events; I have increasingly stronger conviction that we are in the hands of multinationals and conglomerates, of Eisenhower's "military-industrial complex." That feeling can be an immobilizing one. But to do nothing is to go along with what's happening. I know it's a cliché, but the future is *now.* This is the only world any of us has, and if we don't like it, or if we are worried about the direction it's going, we have to work to change it. "This is the way it is" is something we can't settle for. We have to work toward being able to say, "That is the way it *was,* and we have helped to improve it." I console myself a bit with the recollection that 40 years ago, when we debated whether we should bring children into the world, I had the same concerns—and we're all still here!

A Fundamentalist relative asked me recently what I felt about eternity. I answered that for me eternity is being created daily in what I do, how I live vis-à-vis other human beings, what kinds of values I gave and continue to give our children so that they in turn would have good values to pass on to their world and their children.

 ## Social Aspects of Older Women's Lives

1. **The empty-nest syndrome may affect some women, but most women are relatively happy after their children have left home.**

2. **During middle age, daughters are more likely than sons to become caretakers for elderly parents; the negative components of this caretaking role have been emphasized in the research, but many women may identify positive components.**

3. **Women differ widely in their grandmothering styles; for example, many believe they should give advice to grandchildren, but others feel that they should avoid interfering.**

4. **Most married women find that the death of a spouse is traumatic, and loneliness is a frequent problem. We know little about the grieving processes of lesbian couples.**

5. **Older women of color are especially likely to experience poverty. Elderly Black women are likely to be active in community organizations and to take responsibility for rearing grandchildren. Elderly Latinas are expected to help children and grandchildren, and to seek help when they need it. Elderly Asian women are more likely than women from other ethnic groups to live with their children. Elderly**

Native American women are expected to have close relationships with their grandchildren and to share their cultural heritage with these children.

6. **Older women seem to be as satisfied with their lives as other groups of people, despite health, financial, and personal problems.**

7. **Many women rethink their lives during middle age or later, and they make choices that take them in new directions.**

CHAPTER REVIEW
QUESTIONS

1. One of the themes of this book is that women tend to be relatively invisible, and this tendency is especially true for older women. Discuss this theme, pointing out how older women have not received enough attention in the following areas: (a) representation in the media; (b) research on retirement; and (c) the lives of elderly women of color. Then add to the list any other areas of older women's lives that seem important and were not covered in this chapter.

2. What is the double standard of aging? When does it seem most likely to operate, and when does it not apply?

3. From what you know about retirement, describe a woman who is likely to adjust well to retirement. Then describe a woman who is likely to adjust poorly to retirement.

4. Describe the economic situation of elderly women, and list as many factors as you can recall that account for the gender differences in income for elderly men and women.

5. Think about the women you know who have retired from their paid employment. How do their lives match the information on retirement that was discussed in this chapter, with respect to the timing of their retirement, their financial resources during later adulthood, and their adjustment to retirement?

6. What are some of the physical symptoms of menopause? Imagine that a middle-aged friend is now experiencing menopause, and she is considering hormone replacement therapy. How would you describe the pros and cons of both estrogen replacement and estrogen-plus-progestin replacement?

7. What psychological reactions do women have to menopause? How do the attitudes of premenopausal women compare with women's actual experiences?

8. Several aspects of older women's social lives receive attention, whereas other aspects are relatively invisible. Summarize what you know about older women as mothers, as daughters, and as widows. Then point out aspects of each topic for which we have little information.

9. Research in the psychology of women often focuses too heavily on the experiences of European American, middle-class women. What did you learn in this chapter about the lives of elderly women of color, economically disadvantaged women, and women in other cultures? The section on "Rewriting Our Life Stories" noted that a number of books describe how older women can make life changes and take risks. What groups of older women are *least* likely to have these options?

10. This chapter has discussed many legitimate reasons why older women might be dissatisfied with their lives. List as many of these as you can. Then suggest reasons why many older women are reasonably satisfied, adding your own insights to the information in this chapter.

NEW TERMS

ageism (513)

double standard of aging (515)

menopause (523)

hot flash (523)

estrogen replacement therapy (524)

hormone replacement therapy (524)

empty-nest syndrome (529)

sandwich generation (530)

caught generation (530)

RECOMMENDED READINGS

Carlson, K. J., Eisenstat, S. A., & Ziporyn, T. (1996). *The Harvard guide to women's health*. Cambridge, MA: Harvard University Press. This guidebook presents a clear and comprehensive overview of menopause and a variety of health issues relevant for older women.

Coyle, J. M. (Ed.). (1997). *Handbook on women and aging*. Westport, CT: Greenwood Press. This book contains 29 chapters that examine topics such as the double standard of aging, economic issues, women of color, and social relationships.

Roberto, K. A. (Ed.). (1996). *Relationships between women in later life*. Binghamton, NY: Haworth. Here's a book that specifically focuses on social relationships among older women, including issues such as older women and granddaughters, friendship in a nursing home, and relationships between sisters during old age.

Vickers, J. F., & Thomas, B. L. (1993). *No more frogs, no more princes: Women making creative choices at midlife*. Freedom, CA: Crossing Press. If I needed to buy a book to give a friend whose life is changing during middle age, this one remains my first choice. It describes how "ordinary" women negotiate their choices, and it includes women from a variety of ethnic backgrounds and life experiences.

Whitbourne, S. K. (1996). *The aging individual: Physical and psychological perspectives*. New York: Springer. I'd recommend this book for anyone who wants a general perspective on aging processes, including topics such as the nervous system, cognitive processes, and personality.

ANSWERS TO THE TRUE–FALSE QUESTIONS

1. False (p. 512); 2. False (p. 516); 3. False (p. 518); 4. False (p. 520); 5. True (p. 521); 6. False (p. 525); 7. False (p. 525); 8. False (p. 529); 9. True (p. 533); 10. False (p. 535).

Moving Onward . . .

CHAPTER 15

The Future of the Discipline of Psychology of Women
  The Increasing Number of
    Women Within Psychology
  Developing a More Inclusive
    Psychology of Women
  Specific Predictions About
    the Future of Psychology
    of Women

Feminism and Women of Color

The Men's Movement

Some Discouraging Trends
  The Rigid Interpretation of
    Feminism
  The Backlash Against Feminism

Some Helpful Trends
  Women's Studies Courses
  The Women's Movement in
    North America
  The Women's Movement
    Worldwide
  Helping to Change the Future:
    Becoming an Activist

TRUE OR FALSE?

_____ 1. According to a recent survey, the majority of men believe that the U.S. Congress would be better if it had a greater number of female members.

_____ 2. Most college courses in psychology of women were taught for the first time during the 1960s, during the rebirth of the women's movement.

_____ 3. Females now receive the majority of PhDs in psychology.

_____ 4. When women from some ethnic groups become feminist activists, they often complain that the men in their ethnic community feel that this activism is a threat to ethnic unity.

_____ 5. One of the basic beliefs of the Promise Keepers—and others who support the religious approach to the men's movement—is that men must take back their roles as family leaders and women should be followers.

_____ 6. Feminism has the reputation that its supporters must uphold a specific set of beliefs; however, most feminists acknowledge that people who call themselves feminists often disagree about important issues.

_____ 7. According to qualitative research, students say that their women's studies courses have increased their feminist identity; however, quantitative research shows that women's studies courses do not have a significant effect.

_____ 8. Between 70% and 80% of women in the United States say that they support political, economic, and social equality for women.

_____ 9. As of the late 1990s, women had been heads of state in more than 30 countries.

_____ 10. Feminist issues are not raised as often in developing countries as in North America and Europe; however, issues such as women's rights, violence against women, and lesbian concerns are now being considered.

You have now read 14 chapters about the lives of females, from their prenatal development through old age. As you struggle to assimilate all the diverse statistics, research studies, theories, and personal testimonies, you may be asking one central question: How are women doing as we move into the new millennium?

In trying to answer this question, let's consider some representative information—both uplifting and depressing—on the lives of women in the current era:

- Women now receive 40% of all PhD degrees in the United States ("The Nation," 1998).
- The current fundamentalist regime in Afghanistan has closed the schools for girls and prohibited women from working outside the home; if a woman appears with lipstick in public, her lips may be cut off with razor blades (Kirshenbaum, 1997).
- In Iran—the country just to the west of Afghanistan—about one-third of government employees are women, 40% of university students are women, and new laws have improved women's rights with respect to employment and family issues (R. Wright, 1998b).
- In a recent poll conducted by *TIME,* only 28% of women answered "Yes" to the question: "Is feminism relevant to you personally?" (Bellafante, 1998).
- According to the Women's Campaign Research Fund, 65% of men believe that "We'd have a better Congress if it had more women" (Rhode, 1997).

In other words, women's lives have improved considerably in some areas, yet the progress is often slow. In some countries, like Afghanistan, women's rights are much more restricted than they were a decade ago. In other countries, like Iran, the future looks relatively optimistic.

We'll begin this chapter by discussing the future of the discipline we call psychology of women. Then we'll examine how feminism is constructed for women of color. Our third section explores several different components of the men's movement. We'll then consider some discouraging trends—specifically, a perceived tendency to interpret feminism too rigidly, and a far more worrisome backlash against women's progress. Our final section examines some encouraging trends, such as women's studies courses, the women's movement, and activism.

THE FUTURE OF THE DISCIPLINE OF PSYCHOLOGY OF WOMEN

As we noted in Chapter 1, the discipline of psychology of women is relatively young. Most college courses with that title were offered for the first time in the 1970s or 1980s.

Most of us who teach courses in the psychology of women or the psychology of gender recall the strong connection we immediately felt with this emerging discipline. For example, here is why Letitia Anne Peplau—whose superb work in this field was emphasized in Chapter 8—found feminist psychology so compelling:

> I was attracted to feminism for fairly simple reasons. Feminist perspectives helped me understand my own life experiences and relationships in new and more insightful ways. Feminist analyses challenged traditional ideas and showed how patriarchal social arrangements constrain the life choices of women and men. Feminist activism sought to improve the lives of women and to work toward a more just society that places a high value on women as well as men. Feminist values have added a sense of passion and purpose to my research. I have found feminist scholarship nourishing when it has inspired me by examples of creative studies, raised new research questions, and offered provocative analyses and interpretations. (Peplau, 1994, p. 44)

Hundreds of professors throughout North America share this passion for teaching and studying the psychology of women. Three topics related to the future of our discipline are: (1) the increasing number of women entering psychology, (2) the issue of developing a more inclusive psychology of women, and (3) specific topics that will be emphasized during the coming years.

The Increasing Number of Women Within Psychology

As we noted in Chapter 12, the gender ratio has shifted within psychology, so that females now receive the majority of PhDs. In 1976, for example, only 33% of those receiving psychology PhDs were women. By 1994, 62% of psychology PhDs were earned by women (Ferdig et al., 1996). The majority of undergraduates in psychology—72%—are female (Pion et al., 1996). In the future, then, psychology will be largely a women's profession. Many feminists welcome the entry of so many new women into psychology. We should note, however, that some psychologists are dismayed that psychology is becoming a "women's profession"—and have even suggested that professional organizations should limit the number of women in our profession!

The increasing number of women in psychology does not necessarily *guarantee* a strong feminist discipline (Mednick, 1991). At present, for example, men still hold the positions of power as editors of psychology journals. In 1995, only 14% of these journal editors were female. Furthermore, as we have seen throughout this book, many women hold beliefs that are less feminist than the beliefs of many men. However, the increasing number of women entering psychology has certainly contributed to the growing support for feminist theory and research.

Developing a More Inclusive Psychology of Women

Traditional psychology, according to Edward Sampson (1993), "has been based on the point of view of primarily educated, heterosexual, White males from the more dominant social and economic classes" (p. 1225). In constructing the new discipline of psychology of women, we hoped to create a new perspective that values women's and men's lives equally. An ongoing problem, however, has been that psychology of women has typically focused on educated, heterosexual, middle-class White females (Espín, 1994; Yoder & Kahn, 1993).

Statistically, the psychologists who construct the theoretical frameworks for psychology of women are most likely to be middle-class European American women (Enns, 1997). In addition, researchers who conduct their studies in academic settings are likely to examine the women enrolled in their universities. These women are also likely to be educated, heterosexual, middle-class and European American.

In recent years, some scholars have moved away from the traditional population of European American females in order to examine other populations (e.g., Comas-Díaz & Greene, 1994b; Landrine, 1995a; Peplau et al., 1999; Uba, 1994). However, much of the current research on women of color, lesbian women, or lower-class women is limited to a comparison between the normative group and the "nonstandard" group. Like some of the work that compares women with men, this focus may lead to an exaggeration of differences. As Yoder and Kahn (1993) explain:

> This trap within psychology as a whole needs to be avoided by researchers within the psychology of women. Researchers of nonprivileged women need to be wary of calling for comparison groups without considering the potential pitfalls of comparative research. This may be difficult, given psychology's valuation of the experimental model. However, making comparisons of lower status women with privileged women as a comparative baseline can help to sustain a White privileged female norm. (p. 848)

In other words, a comparison-groups approach keeps European American women at the center. Every other group is then a "special case"—located out at the periphery (Morawski & Bayer, 1995). Another problem with a comparison-groups approach is that psychologists often select topics for research in which the ethnic group that is not European American is suspected to be deficient. For example, as I searched for studies on Native Americans and Canadian Aboriginals, I kept finding research on alcoholism and suicide. Why couldn't I find a similar abundance of research on topics such as romantic relationships during adolescence, or the experience of motherhood?

Unfortunately, too, psychologists seldom explore areas in which people of color successfully negotiate a problem. We could all learn from research such as the study by Leavitt and Saegert (1990). As the description on page 512 in Chapter 14 emphasized, economically poor, elderly Black women created caring communities within previously abandoned apartment buildings.

In summary, the psychology of women must not repeat the errors made by earlier generations of psychologists when they ignored women. Consistent with Theme 4, we need to appreciate—and, in fact, celebrate—the diversity of females included within the category called "women."

Specific Predictions About the Future of Psychology of Women

Several years ago, I spoke at York University, in Ontario, Canada, about the future of the psychology of women and gender in the 21st century (Matlin, 1993). In order to benefit from the wisdom of others in the discipline, I sent a questionnaire to members of the Canadian Psychological Association's Section on Women and Psychology, and also to individuals who had been awarded "fellow" status in the Division on the Psychology of Women of the American Psychological Association. The responses from these two groups were similar, so I'll consider them together.

In one question, respondents were asked to name the three topics in our discipline that they believed would become more important in the next 20 years. Three topics emerged as clear front-runners: (1) violence against women, (2) employment issues, and (3) physical health. Most respondents provided a context for their responses. For example, those who listed "violence" specified topics such as "Violence, especially connected to other forms of oppression" or "Violence against women as a human rights issue."

Another question asked respondents to name three topics that they believed would become *less* important in the next 20 years. Interestingly, 62% of the respondents failed to produce three topics. Those of us who focus on the psychology of women are reluctant to suggest that any topic should be ignored! However, one topic—research on gender differences—was predicted by two-thirds of the respondents to become less important.

A third question on the survey asked people to name three topics that clearly need more research but would probably still be underresearched in the next 20 years. The most commonly listed topics included: (1) physical health concerns, (2) women of color, (3) women in underdeveloped countries, and (4) women and poverty. Interestingly, then, many people mentioned the very topics we addressed in the discussion about creating a more inclusive psychology of women. People who are active in the psychology of women seem pessimistic that our discipline will soon become more inclusive.

A final question also produced an interesting response. The questionnaire asked, "Do you believe that the discipline of psychology of women/psychology of gender will be phased out as our information is integrated into other psychology courses, or will it remain intact?" Here, 79% answered that it would remain intact. This positive response reinforces the results of a survey of people teaching psychology of women courses. Virtually all respondents reported that they enjoyed teaching this course more than any other course (Matlin, 1989). In the 1970s, when many of us first taught the psychology of women, we often encountered resistance from other faculty members and administrators. They told us that women's studies was "trendy," a fad that wouldn't last 10 years. However, as we move into the 21st century, the discipline of psychology of women seems stronger than ever!

 SECTION SUMMARY   *The Future of the Discipline of Psychology of Women*

1. **Psychology of women is a relatively new discipline; most people in this area feel very committed to its continuation.**

2. **The percentage of women in psychology has been increasing markedly; however, women still do not hold many positions of power, and not all female psychologists are feminists. Still, this trend contributes to the support for feminist theory and research.**

3. **The discipline needs to explore the diversity of backgrounds that women represent, rather than centering on educated, heterosexual, middle-class, European American females.**

4. **According to a survey, those interested in psychology of women believe that several topics—violence against women, employment issues, and physical health—will become more important in the future, whereas research on gender differences will become less important.**

FEMINISM AND WOMEN OF COLOR

A Black feminist scholar, bell hooks, describes two contrasting experiences. On one occasion, she was lecturing in a crowded auditorium, describing how feminism had changed her life. A Black female student then rose to give an impassioned speech against feminism. She said that feminism only addressed the needs of White women—with whom she had nothing in common (hooks, 1994). At another gathering of scholars, bell hooks (1993) joined another Black woman and several Black men on a panel at Harvard University. The Black men basically ignored the two women in their interchanges, did not address the concerns of Black women, and stated that sexism was simply a White concern.

Like the student in hooks's audience, many Black women do not feel connected with feminism. Some Black women feel that their life experiences are too different from the life experiences of White women, who are more economically privileged (P. Collins, 1995). Black women also complain that they feel no connection with White women who are racist (hooks, 1989; Tong, 1998).

Other Black women have been hesitant to discuss how the Black community is sexist, because these complaints may be misinterpreted by European Americans as additional "evidence" that Black men are violent and overly sexual (Tong, 1998). This misinterpretation would ignore the fact that Black men have experienced racism from both European American men and women (S. Jackson, 1998).

Many Black women engage in feminist activities, yet they do not label themselves feminists—a tendency that probably describes women from all ethnic groups. Jackson (1998) interviewed Black women who were active in a variety of organizations in which Black women held leadership roles. One woman named Sandra saw herself as a feminist, which she defined as someone who "works on issues to promote the interests of women" (p. 41). However, Sandra correctly guessed that most of the other participants in the study would avoid calling themselves feminists. In fact, many participants were unclear of the definition of the term or had mixed feelings about feminism. As you can imagine, many women from other ethnic groups also share these perspectives.

Asian American women face different challenges in identifying with the feminist movement. In general, Asian cultures require women to be passive, invisible, and supportive of men (Root, 1995). An additional issue is an Asian set of core values—relevant for both women and men—that emphasizes fatalism and obedience. These values clearly discourage political activism (Root, 1995).

When Asian American women do begin to protest and to join the feminist movement, they are likely to be criticized by community members. These critics will accuse them of weakening the male ego, diluting the resources in the Asian American community, and destroying the working relationships between Asian women and men (Chow, 1991).

Many Asian American women are not familiar with the feminist movement. Pramila Aggarwal (1990) describes how she found a way to discuss feminist issues with Indian immigrant women in Canada. Aggarwal, a bilingual student, had been hired to teach English to Punjabi women in a garment factory in Toronto. During the course of the English classes, Aggarwal discovered that these women were very interested in women's issues, such as the division of labor in the home and sexual harassment in the workplace. From this experience, she concluded that feminist organizing requires being sensitive to the specific needs of women, rather than imposing one's own personal viewpoint.

Most U.S. students learn something about Black history and the civil rights movement in high school. Unless they live in the West, they are less likely to hear about the Chicano movement, which addresses the concerns of Mexican

Americans. As women began to participate in the Chicano movement during recent decades, they questioned their traditional roles. They also acknowledged that Chicana feminism would need to address both race and class, as well as gender (Garcia, 1991; Moraga, 1993). However, Chicano males have often misinterpreted the Chicana feminist movement as a threat to the political unity of the Chicano movement (Garcia, 1995). In fact, Chicano male activists may label them *vendidas,* or "sellouts." Chicana feminists may also be accused of "acting like a White woman" (Martínez, 1995).

Between the 1960s and the late 1990s, many colleges and universities have established programs in Chicano/Chicana studies, especially in Western and Southwestern states. In addition to courses in history and literature, some programs offer classes on Chicanas' role in the family, public policy, and the arts (Blea, 1997).

Nevertheless, European American feminists often pay too little attention to Chicanas and other Latina women. For example, a 1998 notice from National Organization for Women (NOW) announced its new brochure, "Juntas Podemos Cambiar El Mundo" ("Together We Can Change the World"). I'm pleased to see that this Spanish-language brochure is now available, but I'm dismayed that this important feminist organization waited until the late 1990s to publish it!

In summary, women of color may identify feminist issues in their lives. However, they are often reluctant to label themselves feminists. They may find it difficult to become feminist activists because activism is not consistent with their culture or because the males in their culture might believe that feminism would threaten the efforts to unify their ethnic group. In addition, they may feel that feminist groups that are organized by European Americans may not be sensitive to the concerns relevant to women of color.

 Feminism and Women of Color

1. **Many Black women do not feel connected with feminism, because their lives are too different from the lives of European American women and because European Americans do not understand racism.**

2. **Asian American women may find that feminist activism is not consistent with the traditional role of women in their culture; critics may accuse Asian feminists of undermining the unity in their community.**

3. **Similarly, Chicana feminists may be accused of undermining the Chicano movement; college courses are now being offered on Chicana issues.**

THE MEN'S MOVEMENT

Beginning in the mid-1970s, some men began examining the masculine gender role and its implications for men's lives. These investigations inspired a new academic field called men's studies. **Men's studies** is a collection of scholarly activities such as teaching courses and conducting research focused on men's lives (Doyle, 1995). Men's studies often focuses on gender-role socialization, gender-role conflict, and the issue of sexism (O'Neil et al., 1995). A variety of books present more details on men's studies (e.g., M. Kimmel, 1995, 1996; M. Kimmel & Messner, 1998; Levant, 1996; Levant & Pollack, 1995; Morris, 1997).

Within psychology, the group that focuses on men's studies is called the Society for the Psychological Study of Men and Masculinity (Division 51 of the American Psychological Association).* In 1998, for example, this division sponsored a variety of presentations at the annual meeting of the American Psychological Association. Several relevant topics included men in psychology graduate school, myths of boyhood culture, and masculinity among men of color.

So far, we have looked at men's studies—an academic approach to men's issues. Let's now focus on the political activist groups that are part of the men's movement. Just as there is no unitary "women's movement," we also can find no unitary, single-focus "men's movement" (Kilmartin, 1994). Four strands within the men's movement are commonly mentioned: (1) the profeminists, (2) the mythopoetic movement, (3) the religiously oriented approach, and (4) the men's rights approach.

The **profeminists** want to eliminate gender stereotypes, gender inequalities, and gender-related violence (Rhode, 1997). The profeminist movement is the strand of the men's movement that grew out of the feminist movement. Most people who teach men's studies in colleges and universities would probably call themselves profeminists (Rhode, 1997).

One of the major profeminist groups in the United States is the National Organization for Men Against Sexism (NOMAS) (1998). Its Statement of Principles begins:

> The National Organization for Men Against Sexism is an activist organization of men and women supporting positive changes for men. NOMAS advocates a perspective that is profeminist, gay-affirmative, and committed to justice on a broad range of social issues including race, class, age, religion, and physical abilities. (p. 591)

Groups such as NOMAS focus on making men more aware of sexism—with the ultimate goal of less discrimination against women (Schwalbe, 1995, p. 325). As you might expect, this group has lower membership than some of the other men's organizations we'll discuss shortly (Rhode, 1997). As R. Brannon (1997) points out, the "feel good" organizations have more popular appeal.

What kinds of actions have the profeminist men organized? In Toronto, the Metro Men Against Violence began wearing white ribbons after the murder of 14 women at École Polytechnique in Montreal in 1989, and they continued to

---

*You can visit the Website for the Society for the Psychological Study of Men and Masculinity on the World Wide Web at http//web.indstate.edu/spsmm.

hold meetings to examine issues related to male violence (Lees, 1992). A group called Black Men for the Eradication of Sexism brings young Black men in Atlanta together to examine gender issues (Rosado-Majors, 1998). Some psychologists hold gender-role workshops where men and women can discuss topics such as sexism while they explore their own gender roles (O'Neil, 1996a).

Men who favor the **mythopoetic approach** argue that modern men must develop new visions of masculinity in order to reclaim their "deep masculine" inner selves (Bliss, 1995; Doyle, 1995). To achieve this spiritual healing, men should join all-male gatherings in order to work through their psychological difficulties and gain a mature masculine quality. They feel that myths, poetry, and music can help men work together to achieve these goals. Books like Robert Bly's (1990) *Iron John* and Sam Keen's (1991) *Fire in the Belly* have become bestsellers, so these messages appeal to a large number of men.

Some men in the mythopoetic movement express fairly feminist views. For example, Shepherd Bliss (1995)—who created the term "mythopoetic"—specifically says, "We need New Masculinities which do not oppress women, men, or children" (p. 295). However, profeminists point out that the majority of the men at these all-male mythopoetic gatherings are middle-class, middle-aged, European American heterosexual men. They represent the most powerful cohort in North America, so they have the economic resources to address their concerns about masculinity issues (M. Kimmel & Kaufman, 1995).

The religiously oriented approach to the men's movement has become more visible during the current era. The **religious approach** argues that men should take back their roles as head of the household in order to become leaders in their family, church, and community (Rhode, 1997). As a result, women should accept the role of being followers. If these basic principles don't sound alarming, try replacing the sexism with racist equivalents: "Whites should take back their roles as masters, and Blacks should accept the role of being slaves."

Among the religious approaches, the most prominent is the Promise Keepers. This organization claims that close to 3 million men had attended its regional rallies by 1997 (Cose, 1997). At these huge rallies, men are told to be assertive about taking back their natural role, and the messages are strongly traditional. The founder of the Promise Keepers, Bill McCartney, has stated that homosexuality is "an abomination of almighty God" (Flanders, 1997, p. 166). The organization claims to support interracial harmony, but more than 95% of those who attend the rallies are European American (Flanders, 1997). It's not yet clear to me whether groups such as the Promise Keepers will continue to attract members; my current impression is that this movement has become less visible.

Another example of the religious approach was the Million-Man March, a gathering of Black men in Washington, DC, in 1995. The main organizer, Louis Farrakhan, is known for his sexist, homophobic, and anti-Jewish statements (Rhode, 1997). Women were explicitly banned from participating in the march; they were ordered to stay at home and pray. The Promise Keepers, the organizers of the Million-Man March, and other religiously based forms of the men's movement may voice some admirable statements, such as encouraging men to become more actively involved in their children's lives. However, we must carefully examine their principles, because these groups typically favor a reduction in the rights of women.

The final strand of the men's movement is not subtle about its message. Those who favor the **men's rights approach** argue that men—not women—are the real victims of sexism in the social and legal systems (Kilmartin, 1994; M. Kimmel, 1996). These men claim that women batter their husbands far more often than men batter their wives. The policies on sexual harassment and rape, they say, are written so that men are the true victims. They also argue that the divorce laws and child custody policies tend to favor women. Groups such as the Coalition for Free Men and Men Achieving Liberation and Equality (MALE) proclaim their commitment to ending sexism. To do so, they argue that they must fight against feminism—the major force that has reduced men's rights.

These four strands of the men's movement maintain such extremely different principles that they are not likely to join together (Doyle, 1995). Interestingly, college students appreciate the differences among the groups. Rickabaugh (1994) asked undergraduates at a California university to read descriptions of three men, each representing a different strand of the men's movement. (This study was conducted before the religious approach was visible at the national level.) Both men and women gave the highest rating to the profeminist man, the intermediate rating to the mythopoetic man, and the lowest rating to the men's rights advocate. The profeminist man was perceived as both nurturant and competent—a finding that should be encouraging to profeminist male students who are reading this book!

 The Men's Movement

1. **Men's studies include scholarly activities such as teaching courses and conducting research focused on men's lives.**

2. **The four major strands within the men's movement are (a) the profeminists, (b) the mythopoetic approach, (c) the religious approach, and (d) the men's rights approach.**

SOME DISCOURAGING TRENDS

The first section in this chapter focused on the future of psychology of women as a discipline—a topic that raises some optimism. Our discussions about women of color and the men's movement provided a mixture of optimism and pessimism. Now we'll turn to the bad news—two trends that have the potential to undermine feminism and the advancement of women in the current era. The first problem is a tendency toward a rigid interpretation of feminism. The second problem—a more worrisome attack by nonfeminists—is the backlash against feminism and women's issues.

The Rigid Interpretation of Feminism

Students, researchers, and the general public may sometimes perceive feminism as a set of rigid rules rather than a source of inspiration. Peplau (1994) noted that her undergraduate students at UCLA question her about whether feminists can wear makeup, or whether they can stay home full-time raising their young children. Unfortunately, many people have misunderstood feminism. They believe—erroneously—that feminism specifies a set of rigid regulations, and that women must obtain a perfect score on some kind of test in order to qualify as feminists. Feminist principles actually argue that we should respect women and their life choices and that we should also examine the societal forces influencing those choices.

Another issue concerns feminists' ideas about men. Most feminists feel quite positive about most men (Favreau, 1997a), although a few may feel that men have done too much harm to women to deserve positive feelings. However, the media suggest that all feminists are male-bashers (Rhode, 1997). Carol Tavris (1993) tells an anecdote about a British publisher's decision not to publish her excellent book, *The Mismeasure of Woman* (Tavris, 1992) in Great Britain. Specifically, the publisher feared that Tavris's book would not appeal to feminists because it was not a man-hating, woman-hating, or woman-loving book. In fact, the book does admire and celebrate women, but it also admires and celebrates men. This publisher underestimated the book's potential audience. Many feminists feel that men can help create the solution, rather than merely creating the problem.

How did feminism acquire the reputation of requiring its supporters to pass rigid tests and to display antagonism toward men? Indeed, a grain of truth may underlie these impressions. More important, as we described in Chapter 2, a stereotype can be created that distorts reality. The media help to exaggerate these views; as we saw from Tavris's anecdote, a publisher may even keep alternative perspectives from reaching the public.

As part of her study on views of feminism, Langer (1996) interviewed women from different regions of the United States. A happily married, 50-year-old mother in California described how the media have distorted the word *feminism:*

> I think women of all ages have trouble with the word "feminism" because it is defined for them by white males in positions of authority. . . . The connotations that feminists are strident, aggressive, dissatisfied, non-feminine women who want to deny safe, loving, secure homes to truly feminine women are advanced and embellished upon endlessly. . . . It is a fine scare tactic. (p. 246)

In reality, there is no single, unified version of feminism. Furthermore, feminism is never static. Instead, it continues to grow and evolve in many directions (Enns, 1997; Langer, 1996). For example, feminists disagree among themselves about a variety of important issues. Some of these issues include whether women should be encouraged to join the military, whether pornography should be regulated, and whether special career tracks should be designed for mothers of young children (Tobias, 1997).

Chapter 1 introduced several forms of feminism, and new varieties of feminism continue to develop. For example, ecofeminism is a kind of feminism that moves beyond humans' oppression of other humans (Tong, 1998; Winter, 1996). **Ecofeminists** oppose the way humans destroy other animals and natural resources, as well as each other.

One of the best ways to illustrate the diversity of views within feminism is to listen to the voices of women who call themselves feminists. For example, one of my personal heroines is Bella Abzug, a member of Congress who died in 1998. When asked for her views on feminism, she replied, "I'm proud to be a lifelong one. It's as natural as breathing, feeling, and thinking. Never go back, never apologize, and never forget we're half the human race" (Aronson, 1997, p. 43). Actor and producer Cybill Shepherd objects to women who "don't use the word 'feminist' when they are all benefiting from the great feminists who struggled and suffered and worked to give us everything women now enjoy—including the right to vote, to bring a lawsuit, the right to custody in divorce—everything. I feel it is my responsibility to use that word because of all the sacrifices women have made" (Aronson, 1997, p. 43).

When some women discuss feminism, they emphasize that it has served as a life raft. For example, a female psychologist wrote:

> Feminism has just helped me a lot. It's helped me feel a whole lot better about myself and . . . make sense of the world and a lot of things that didn't make sense before. I just made it a point to surround myself with people who facilitate that, and I don't have a whole lot of interest in spending much time with people who don't. . . . So, I guess I've kind of arranged my life around that. (Klonis et al., 1997, p. 340)

To complete this section on the diversity among feminists, try Demonstration 15.1.

DEMONSTRATION 15.1

Diversity of Views About Feminism

At the top of several pieces of paper, write these instructions: "Please define feminism in your own words, and describe how feminism is relevant or irrelevant in your life." Distribute one page to each of several friends, and ask them to provide a written reply. (You may wish to specify that they can omit their names from the sheets or use other precautions so that their replies are anonymous.) Among those who have positive views of feminism, can you identify a variety of perspectives? (You may want to check page 7 to remind yourself about various kinds of feminism.) Those who submit negative views can provide a viewpoint from which to understand the topic of the next section of this chapter: the backlash against feminism.

The Backlash Against Feminism

A stream of antifeminist articles continues to flow from popular magazines. For example, an article in *TIME* was titled, "Feminism: It's all about me!" (Bellafante, 1998). Using a strange kind of logic, the article claims that contemporary feminism is represented by such lightweights as the television character "Ally McBeal," whose primary preoccupation is the length of her miniskirts. Why does this article imply that this TV character represents feminism? And why is feminism to be blamed for the media ideas about what will appeal to the public?

Susan Faludi (1991, 1995) has documented the nature of the backlash against feminism. As she points out, the media and other aspects of popular culture give women messages that feminism has caused them dissatisfaction. The media often minimize women's accomplishments or ignore press conferences in which feminists discuss important issues (Dow, 1996; Gillespie, 1996). The net result, if not the intent, is to undercut the progress that the women's movement has made in recent years.

The media especially enjoy featuring women who claim that feminism has gone astray. Camille Paglia (1992) and Christina Hoff Sommers (1994) are two media favorites who like to criticize women's studies programs as being unscholarly.

The media also distorts the truth about related social trends. For example, colleges and universities are beginning to integrate the perspectives of women and people of color into the curriculum. With no data in hand, a well-known conservative writer claimed that "Alice Walker's *The Color Purple* is taught in more English departments today than all of Shakespeare's plays combined" (D'Souza, 1992, p. 68). Are "dead White males" really being deleted from the curriculum? A survey of actual curricula demonstrated that Shakespeare is still ahead of Walker by a ratio of 40 to 1 (Favreau, 1997a; Fish, 1994).

 SECTION SUMMARY   *Some Discouraging Trends*

1. **Some people believe that feminism consists of a set of rigid rules and that women must be antagonistic toward men; however, feminism really represents a diversity of viewpoints.**
2. **The popular media are filled with backlash messages, including attacks on women's studies and college curricula.**

SOME HELPFUL TRENDS

Despite the discouraging trends we have just examined, women's lives have been gradually improving in recent decades. The progress has been slower than many of us had naïvely imagined in the 1970s. We also notice a tendency to take two steps forward and then one step backward. However, this textbook has noted greater public awareness of issues such as the chilly classroom climate, women in the workplace, the distribution of housework, and violence against women. Three forces that have helped to improve women's lives are (1) women's studies courses, (2) the women's movement in North America, and (3) the women's movement at the international level. You can help to create a hopeful trend by continuing your interest in women's issues and by becoming an activist, a topic we'll explore in the final part of this section.

Women's Studies Courses

Thousands of women's studies courses are offered at colleges and universities throughout the United States and Canada. The National Women's Studies Association currently lists 725 women's studies programs in the United States, though the Association suspects this is an underestimate (National Women's Studies Association, 1999).

Students who have taken women's studies courses often comment on the new perspectives they have gained from them (Guy-Sheftall, 1996; Luebke & Reilly, 1995). For example, a student from Calgary commented on her women's studies courses:

> What have I taken away from the feminist classroom? Primarily a feeling of empowerment, a belief that I have the capacity to act, to implement change, to use my abilities to the fullest. . . . (Hashizume et al., 1994)

A graduate of San Diego State emphasized the importance of the knowledge she gained:

> My greatest reward for studying Women's Studies is that it has given credence to my convictions. It has given me a language/vocabulary to describe the many injustices I have felt as a woman. Before Women's Studies I knew that I didn't like the way I was treated; now I am able to define it. I was able to back up the many arguments I have found myself in with "facts" such as court cases, studies, and statistics. (Luebke & Reilly, 1995, p. 58)

For some individuals, women's studies courses are life-transforming. Consider these words from a graduate of the University of Colorado:

> Feminism is the lens through which I view and understand the world. It affects all aspects of my life and helps me to make sense out of it all. The people I have met, friends I have made, and experiences I have had through Women's Studies are invaluable. I wouldn't trade any of it for a traditional lifestyle. . . . I think my self-esteem/self-awareness/self-worth has been strongly supported/elevated by feminism. (Luebke & Reilly, 1995, p. 129)

Research using quantitative methods confirms that these courses have an important impact on students' lives. Specifically, women enrolled in women's studies courses are more likely than similar women enrolled in other courses to develop a strong feminist identity after taking the course (Bargad & Hyde, 1991; Gerstmann & Kramer, 1997). Other research has shown that women's studies courses were more likely than other courses to encourage activism related to women's issues (Stake et al., 1994; Stake & Rose, 1994).

In summary, students report that their women's studies courses are informative and thought-provoking. These courses also change students' perspectives, personal beliefs, and political actions.

The Women's Movement in North America

The first wave of the feminist movement in North America arose out of the antislavery movement of the 1830s. Women learned how to organize a political movement, and they saw clear links between freedom for slaves and freedom for women (M. Andersen, 1993). However, their efforts did not meet with immediate success. Women did not win the right to vote until August 26, 1920, when the Nineteenth Amendment was passed.

The current women's movement emerged out of the general discontent of the 1960s. Women were active in the civil rights movement and in protesting the war in Vietnam. As in the previous century, this focus on issues of social justice made women more aware that they were considered second-class citizens (Tobias, 1997). The National Organization for Women (NOW) was founded in 1966, a year that is often considered to be the beginning of the current feminist era in the United States (Tobias, 1997).

The scope of current feminist organizations is astonishing. Some groups, such as NOW, have a general focus that addresses issues like violence against women, reproductive rights, and workplace issues. Other groups emphasize a more specific issue, such as the abuse of women, antimilitarism, women's health, housing, welfare rights, urban schools, lesbian and bisexual concerns, immigration issues, or community problems (Ferree & Martin, 1995; Naples, 1998). At the same time, feminist communities have created a variety of feminist-run businesses. These include feminist bookstores, theater groups, vacation resorts, and spirituality groups.

So far, this discussion has focused on women who feel a clear connection with the feminist movement. The general population is more ambivalent about feminism. For example, according to a U.S. survey by *TIME*, 48% of women agreed that feminism today is relevant to most women (Bellafante, 1998). What happens when the surveys omit the word "feminism"—the word that the media have helped to discredit? When surveys ask women whether they support political, economic, and social equality for women, 70% to 80% agree (Rhode, 1997).

In summary, the feminist movement has grown and diversified considerably in recent decades. About half of the women surveyed believe that feminism is relevant to women's lives, and the clear majority agree with the goals of feminism.

The Women's Movement Worldwide

In New Zealand, women won the right to vote in 1893. Australia, Canada, and many European countries followed within the next three decades. As of 1999, women still could not vote in Kuwait. Women have been heads of state in more than 30 countries—among them, India, Haiti, Turkey, Iceland, Bolivia, and Canada—but not the United States (Neft & Levine, 1997).

Although women have been somewhat active in official government positions, their grass-roots actions have been more impressive. One of the bravest of these efforts was the Mothers of the Plaza, a group of women whose children had "disappeared" during the terrorist regime in Argentina during the 1970s. (Most of these young people had been secretly murdered because they had opposed the government.) The government had forbidden all public demonstrations, yet these mothers gathered at the Plaza de Mayo in Buenos Aires every Thursday, holding large photos of their missing children. Their bravery ultimately helped end that terrifying regime, and their actions inspired women in countries such as El Salvador and Guatemala to pursue similar actions (E. Kimmel & Kazanis, 1995).

Throughout the world, small groups of women are working to improve women's lives. We now have rich resources describing women's activism in individual countries such as Costa Rica and Russia (Leitinger, 1997; Racioppi & See, 1997) and regions such as Africa (Mikell, 1997). Other books trace the women's movement from a global perspective (e.g., Basu, 1995; Chow & Berheide, 1994; J. Peters & Wolper, 1995).

A superb group called The Global Fund for Women* provides small grants for women-led projects throughout the world. By 1998, it had donated about $9 million to more than a thousand groups in 125 countries (McCarten-Gibbs, 1998; Reaves, 1998). Here is just a small sample from a recent list of its projects:

- In Santa Cruz, Bolivia, for a radio show about women's rights.
- In Zabgreb, Croatia, for a group that maintains a lesbian helpline.
- In Yogyakatra, Indonesia, for a group that raises social awareness about violence against women.
- In Port-au-Prince, Haiti, to help women candidates run for elected office.
- In Mbale, Uganda, to a group of young women working to reduce the practice of female genital mutilation.

Women in developing countries share many of the same perspectives and concerns that women in North America and Europe express. However, women in these countries must also overcome basic survival problems. Some of the subtler points of North America feminism may seem irrelevant to a woman in India who knows that she must give her son more food than her daughter so that he can grow strong. These points may also seem irrelevant for a woman in Burma who must work under harsh conditions at 4 cents an hour, making sneakers for a prestigious American company (Selinger, 1998).

In 1995, the United Nations organized the Fourth World Conference on Women in Beijing, China. This event highlighted a wide variety of global issues

---

*The address for The Global Fund for Women is 425 Sherman Avenue, Suite 300, Palo Alto, CA 94306-1823. The phone number is 650-853-8305 and the Website is www.globalfundforwomen.org.

related to human rights for women. The official conference produced a document called the Beijing Platform for Action. This document, which was adopted by 189 government delegations, demands greater economic and political empowerment for women, as well as more active government intervention in achieving equality. Meanwhile, a parallel Non-Governmental Organization Forum gathered at a location 30 miles away. More than 20,000 individuals at this forum shared strategies and information with other, similar groups in different countries (Bunch & Fried, 1997; McCorduck & Ramsey, 1997; Stanley Foundation, 1997).

McCorduck and Ramsey (1997) point out how these two parallel meetings demonstrated that "Feminism once belonged almost exclusively to Western women, but women around the world have now seized it and made it their own" (p. 325). I recall the spirit of excitement that surrounded these Beijing meetings in 1995. However, I've seen little media coverage of the consequences of those meetings. Does global feminism have a chance in a world where women are given low priority?

Helping to Change the Future: Becoming an Activist

So far, this section on some hopeful trends in women's issues has examined women's studies courses, the women's movement in North America, and the women's movement worldwide. In most psychology courses, students remain passive as they read about the future of a discipline. This time it's different: *You* can be part of the hopeful trend—if you're not already involved—rather than assuming that the actions will be performed by other individuals. Here are just a few of the many options:

- Subscribe to a feminist magazine, such as *Ms. Magazine.* It will keep you informed about political activities, and the articles will help you keep thinking about feminist issues.
- Talk with friends and relatives about feminist issues. Remember, though, that it's often difficult to change other people's opinions.
- Help fight the backlash against women. When you see an advertisement that represents women negatively, write to the company and express your dissatisfaction. Similarly, when you see a positive ad, send a compliment to the company. You can obtain the company's address through the World Wide Web or through a resource such as *The Million Dollar Directory* (1999).
- Be a "critical consumer" when you read or listen to reports about women in the media. Review the research biases listed in Table 1.1, and ask yourself whether the conclusions in the report seem justified. If you'd like to express your discontent—or possibly your approval!—call in to a radio show or write a letter to the editor of a newspaper or magazine. Remember: You now have more information about women's lives than most other individuals, and you can help inform other people about these perspectives.

- Join a women's group on campus or in your community, or help to start one. Work with the group to make certain that diversity issues are an integral part of your mission.
- Consult other resources for other ideas. Some helpful ones include *The Feminist Dollar: The Wise Woman's Buying Guide* (P. Katz & Katz, 1997); *Women for a Change: A Grassroots Guide to Activism and Politics* (Zepatos & Kaufman, 1995); and *How to Make the World a Better Place for Women in Five Minutes a Day* (D. Jackson, 1992).

Remember that no one individual can attack all the problems that women face. Take comfort in small victories, and share these victories. Also, keep in mind a bumper sticker that quotes advice from anthropologist Margaret Mead: "Never doubt that a small group of thoughtful, committed citizens can change the world; indeed it's the only thing that ever has."

 SECTION SUMMARY *Some Helpful Trends*

1. **Qualitative and quantitative research on women's studies courses demonstrates that these courses provide new perspectives, help students develop a feminist identity, and encourage activism.**

2. **The first wave of the feminist movement in North America arose out of the antislavery movement and culminated in the passage of the Nineteenth Amendment.**

3. **The current feminist movement arose out of other social protests of the 1960s; the scope of feminist groups in the current era is extremely wide; the goals of the women's movement are endorsed by the clear majority of women.**

4. **Although women have achieved some positions of leadership throughout the world, the variety of grass-roots women's organizations is more impressive.**

5. **Students can become activists in order to help change women's lives.**

CHAPTER REVIEW QUESTIONS

1. What are the trends with respect to the gender ratio in psychology? What is the current gender ratio for psychology faculty and psychology majors at your own college or university? Why might the changing gender ratio help the women's movement, and why might it be less effective than expected?

2. People concerned about the psychology of women have emphasized that the discipline should be more inclusive. What developments have been made? Why does a problem arise if researchers use the comparison-groups approach?

3. When psychologists responded to a survey about the future of psychology of women, what areas did they expect to become more prominent, and what areas did they expect to become less prominent? Did any of these selections surprise you?

4. Why do women of color face special challenges in identifying with the feminist movement? Why would men of color be likely to oppose women from their ethnic group who would like to be active feminists?

5. Describe the four basic strands within the men's movement. Which would be likely to support the growth of the women's movement? Which would oppose it? Which might consider it to be irrelevant? Do you see any evidence of the men's movement in your community?

6. Describe the backlash against feminism and explain why this factor could help produce the rigid interpretation of feminism. What evidence of the backlash have you seen in the media in recent weeks?

7. Briefly trace the history of the women's movement in North America; what issues concerned the early activists? Then comment on the women's movement worldwide; what kinds of concerns have been addressed?

8. Several parts of this chapter addressed attitudes toward feminist issues. Why do we need to pay attention to the operational definitions of "attitudes toward feminist issues" in order to draw conclusions about this topic?

[These final two questions require you to review the entire textbook.]

9. This chapter focused on the positive and negative trends with respect to women and gender. To help yourself review this book, go back through the 15 chapters, noting which new developments are moving in a positive direction and which are moving in a negative direction.

10. You will need to set aside several hours for this final task: On separate pieces of paper, list each of the four themes of this book. Then skim through each of the 15 chapters, noting any mention of the themes on the appropriate piece of paper. (You can determine whether your lists are complete by checking the entries for Themes 1, 2, 3, and 4 in the subject index.) After you have completed that task, try to synthesize the material within each of the four themes.

NEW TERMS

men's studies (551)   religious approach (552)
profeminists (551)   men's rights approach (553)
mythopoetic approach (552)   ecofeminists (555)

RECOMMENDED READINGS

Kimmel, M. S. (1996). *Manhood in America: A cultural history.* New York: Free Press. Michael Kimmel is one of the major writers in men's studies; this book includes some interesting photos of the history of men's issues, and it explores such topics as masculinity, men in the workplace, and the men's movement.

Landrine, H. (Ed.). (1995a). *Bringing cultural diversity to feminist psychology: Theory, research, and practice.* Washington, DC: American Psychological Association. Landrine's book remains one of my favorites on the psychology of women of color; an especially useful feature is four chapters on the major ethnic minority groups.

Neft, N., & Levine, A. D. (1997). *Where women stand: An international report on the status of women in 140 countries 1997–1998.* New York: Random House. Here's an interesting and convenient guide to use when you are trying to locate data on global women's issues. Its topics include women's employment, health, education, family planning, and violence against women.

Rhode, D. L. (1997). *Speaking of sex: The denial of gender inequality.* Cambridge, MA: Harvard University Press. This is an excellent review of contemporary issues in gender discrimination. The chapters on the women's and men's movements and on the politics of feminism are especially relevant to the topics in our final chapter.

Tobias, S. (1997). *Faces of feminism: An activist's reflections on the women's movement.* Boulder, CO: Westview Press. Sheila Tobias provides an excellent history of feminism, with an emphasis on recent decades.

ANSWERS TO THE TRUE–FALSE QUESTIONS

1. True (p. 544); 2. False (p. 545); 3. True (p. 545); 4. True (p. 549); 5. True (p. 552); 6. True (p. 554); 7. False (p. 557); 8. True (p. 558); 9. True (p. 559); 10. True (p. 559).

References

AAUW Educational Foundation. (1992). *How schools shortchange girls.* Washington, DC: Author.

Abbey, A. (1982). Sex differences in attributions for friendly behavior: Do males misperceive females' friendliness? *Journal of Personality and Social Psychology, 42,* 830–838.

Abbey, A., Andrews, F. M., & Halman, L. J. (1991). Gender's role in responses to infertility. *Psychology of Women Quarterly, 15,* 295–316.

Abbey, A., & Harnish, R. J. (1995). Perception of sexual intent: The role of gender, alcohol consumption, and rape supportive attitudes. *Sex Roles, 32,* 298–313.

Abbey, A., Ross, L. T., & McDuffie, D. (1994). Alcohol's role in sexual assault. *Drug and Alcohol Reviews, 5,* 97–123.

Abel, E. (1995). Race, class, and psychoanalysis? Opening questions. In N. Tuana & R. Tong (Eds.), *Feminism and philosophy* (pp. 508–525). Boulder, CO: Westview Press.

Adams, A. (1995). Maternal bonds: Recent literature on mothering. *Signs, 20,* 414–427.

Adams, M. (1976). *Single blessedness.* New York: Basic Books.

Adams, S., Juebli, J., Boyle, P. A., & Fivush, R. (1995). Gender differences in parent-child conversations about past emotions: A longitudinal investigation. *Sex Roles, 33,* 309–323.

Adebimpe, V. R. (1997). Mental illness among African Americans. In I. Al-Issa & M. Tousignant (Eds.), *Ethnicity, immigration, and psychopathology* (pp. 95–118). New York: Plenum Press.

Adelmann, P. K., Antonucci, T. C., Crohan, S. E., & Coleman, L. M. (1989). Empty nest, cohort, and employment in the well-being of midlife women. *Sex Roles, 20,* 173–189.

Ader, D. N., & Johnson, S. B. (1994). Sample description, reporting, and analysis of sex in psychological research: A look at APA and APA division journals in 1990. *American Psychologist, 49,* 216–218.

Adler, N. E., & Coriell, M. (1997). Socioeconomic status and women's health. In S. J. Gallant, G. P. Keita, & R. Royak-Schaler (Eds.), *Health care for women: Psychological, social, and behavioral influences* (pp. 11–23). Washington, DC: American Psychological Association.

Adler, N. E., & Smith, L. B. (1998). Abortion. In E. A. Blechman & K. D. Brownell (Eds.), *Behavioral medicine and women: A comprehensive handbook* (pp. 510–514). New York: Guilford Press.

Adler, N. E., et al. (1992). Psychological factors in abortion: A review. *American Psychologist, 47,* 1194–1204.

Adler, N. E., et al. (1994). Socioeconomic status and health. *American Psychologist, 49,* 15–24.

Adler, T. (1990, December). NIH opens office on women's issues. *APA Monitor,* p. 5.

Adolph, M. R. (1993). The myth of the golden years: One older woman's perspective. In N. D. Davis, E. Cole, & E. D. Rothblum (Eds.), *Faces of women and aging* (pp. 55–66). Binghamton, NY: Haworth.

Aggarwal, P. (1990). English classes for immigrant women: A feminist organizing tool. *Fireweed, 30,* 95–100.

Aguilar-San Juan, K. (1993). Landmarks in literature by Asian American lesbians. *Signs, 18,* 936–943.

Aidoo, A. A. (1991). *The girl child: An investment in the future.* New York: United Nations Children's Fund.

Alagna, S. W., & Hamilton, J. A. (1986). Social stimulus perception and self-evaluation: Effects of menstrual cycle phase. *Psychology of Women Quarterly, 10,* 327–338.

Albee, G. W. (1996). The psychological origins of the White male patriarchy. *Journal of Primary Prevention, 17,* 75–97.

Albelda, R., & Tilly, C. (1997). *Glass ceilings and bottomless pits: Women's work, women's poverty.* Boston: South End Press.

Alderman, E. M., & Friedman, S. B. (1995). Behavioral problems of affluent youths. *Pediatric Annals, 24,* 186–191.

Alexander, L. L., & LaRosa, J. H. (1994). *New dimensions in women's health.* Boston: Jones and Bartlett.

Allen, B. P. (1995). Gender stereotypes are not accurate: A replication of Martin (1987) using diagnostic vs. self-report and behavioral criteria. *Sex Roles, 32,* 583–600.

Allen, K. R. (1989). *Single women/family ties: Life histories of older women.* Newbury Park, CA: Sage.

Allen, K. R. (1994). Feminist reflections on lifelong single women. In D. L. Sollie & L. A. Leslie (Eds.), *Gender, families, and close relationships: Feminist research journeys* (pp. 97–119). Thousand Oaks, CA: Sage.

Allen, L., et al. (1996). Acculturation and depression among Latina urban girls. In B. J. R. Lead-beater & N. Way (Eds.), *Urban girls: Resisting stereotypes, creating identities* (pp. 337–352). New York: New York University Press.

Allison, J. A., & Wrightsman, L. S. (1993). *Rape: The misunderstood crime.* Newbury Park, CA: Sage.

Almey, M. (1995). Labour force characteristics. In Statistics Canada (Ed.), *Women in Canada: A statistical report* (3rd ed.). Ottawa, Canada: Statistics Canada.

Amaro, H. (1995). Love, sex, and power: Considering women's realities in HIV prevention. *American Psychologist, 50,* 437–447.

Amato, I. (1992). Profile of a field: Women have extra hoops to jump through. *Science, 255,* 1372–1373.

Amato, P. R., & Rogers, S. J. (1997). A longitudinal study of marital problems and subsequent divorce. *Journal of Marriage and the Family, 59,* 612–624.

American Psychiatric Association. (1994). *Diagnostic and statistical manual of mental disorders* (4th ed.). Washington, DC: Author.

American Psychological Association. (1990). Ethical principles of psychologists. *American Psychologist, 45,* 390–395.

American Psychological Association. (1994). *Publication manual of the American Psychological Association* (4th ed.). Washington, DC: Author.

American Psychological Association. (1995). *Lesbian and gay parenting: A resource for psychologists.* Washington, DC: Author.

American Psychological Association. (1996a). Interim report of the working group on investigation of memories of childhood abuse. In K. Pezdek & W. P. Banks (Eds.), *The recovered memory/false memory debate* (pp. 371–372). San Diego: Academic Press.

American Psychological Association. (1996b). Report of the ethics committee, 1995. *American Psychologist, 51,* 1279–1286.

Andersen, B. L. (1998). Breast cancer: Biobehavioral aspects. In A. Blechman & K. D. Brownell (Eds.), *Behavioral medicine and women: A comprehensive handbook* (pp. 570–576). New York: Guilford Press.

Andersen, M. L. (1993). *Thinking about women: Sociological perspectives on sex and gender* (3rd ed.). New York: Macmillan.

Anderson, C. M., & Stewart, S. (1994). *Flying solo: Single women in midlife.* New York: Norton.

Andriote, J. (1998, February). The 1998 survey. *Working Woman,* pp. 24–45.

Antill, J. K. (1983). Sex role complementarity versus similarity in married couples. *Journal of Personality and Social Psychology, 45,* 145–155.

Antill, J. K., Goodnow, J. J., Russell, G., & Cotton, S. (1996). The influence of parents and family context on children's involvement in household tasks. *Sex Roles, 34,* 215–236.

Antonucci, T. C., Jackson, J. S., Gibson, R. C., & Herzog, A. R. (1994). Sex differences in age and racial influences on involvement in productive activities. In M. R. Stevenson (Ed.), *Gender roles through the life span* (pp. 259–282). Muncie, IN: Ball State.

Aponte, J. F., & Morrow, C. A. (1995). Community approaches with ethnic groups. In J. F. Aponte, R. Y. Rivers, & J. Wohl (Eds.) *Psychological interventions and cultural diversity* (pp. 128–144). Boston: Allyn & Bacon.

Appignanesi, L., & Forrester, J. (1992). *Freud's women.* New York: Basic Books.

Apter, T. (1995). *Secret paths: Women in the new midlife.* New York: Norton.

Archer, D., Iritani, B., Kimes, D. D., & Barrios, M. (1983). Face-ism: Five studies of sex differences in facial prominence. *Journal of Personality and Social Psychology, 45,* 725–735.

Archer, J. (1996). Comparing women and men: What is being compared and why? *American Psychologist, 51,* 153–154.

Aries, E. (1996). *Men and women in interaction: Reconsidering the differences.* New York: Oxford University Press.

Aries, E. (1998). Gender differences in interaction. In D. J. Canary & K. Dindia (Eds.), *Sex differences and similarities in communication* (pp. 65–81). Mahwah, NJ: Erlbaum.

Aries, E., & Johnson, F. L. (1983). Close friendship in adulthood: Conversational content between same-sex friends. *Sex Roles, 9,* 1183–1196.

Arnold, K. D., Noble, K. D., & Subotnik, R. F. (1996a). In K. D. Arnold, K. D. Noble, & R. F. Subotnik (Eds.), *Remarkable women: Perspectives on female talent development* (pp. 1–19). Cresskill, NJ: Hampton Press.

Arnold, K. D., Noble, K. D., & Subotnik, R. F. (1996b). *Remarkable women: Perspectives on female talent development.* Cresskill, NJ: Hampton Press.

Aronson, A. (1997, September/October). Yes I am a feminist and . . . *Ms. Magazine,* pp. 42–49.

Arvey, R. D. (1979). Unfair discrimination in the employment interview: Legal and psychological aspects. *Psychological Bulletin, 86,* 736–765.

Arvey, R. D., & Cavanaugh, M. A. (1995). Using surveys to assess the prevalence of sexual harassment: Some methodological problems. *Journal of Social Issues, 51,* 39–52.

Asch, A., & Fine, M. (1992). Beyond pedestals: Revisiting the lives of women with disabilities. In M. Fine (Ed.), *Disruptive voices: The possibilities of feminist research* (pp. 139–171). Ann Arbor: University of Michigan Press.

Asch-Goodkin, J. (1994, April). Women in pediatrics. *Contemporary Pediatrics,* pp. 54–67.

Aseltine, R. H., Jr., & Kessler, R. C. (1993). Marital disruption and depression in a community sample. *Journal of Health and Social Behavior, 34,* 237–251.

Ashton, E. (1983). Measures of play behavior: The influence of sex-role stereotyped children's books. *Sex Roles, 9,* 43–47.

Asso, D. (1987). Cyclical variations. In M. A. Baker (Ed.), *Sex differences in human performance* (pp. 55–80). New York: Wiley.

Atchley, R. (1991). The influence of aging or frailty on perceptions and expressions of the self: Theoretical and methodological issues. In J. E. Birren, J. E. Lubben, J. C. Rowe, & D. E. Deutchman (Eds.), *The concept and measurement of quality of life in the frail elderly* (pp. 207–225). San Diego: Academic Press.

Atkinson, D. R., & Hackett, G. (1995). *Counseling diverse populations.* Dubuque, IA: Brown & Benchmark.

Atkinson, D. R., Morten, G., & Sue, D. W. (1993). *Counseling American minorities: A cross-cultural perspective* (4th ed.). Dubuque, IA: Brown & Benchmark.

Aube, J., Koestner, R., Hodgins, H., & Craig, J. (1994). Masculine traits and reports of social functioning: Evidence for a positivity bias. *Sex Roles, 31,* 621–636.

Aven, F. F., Parker, B., & McEvoy, G. M. (1993). Gender and attitudinal commitment to organizations: A meta-analysis. *Journal of Business Research, 26,* 63–73.

Azar, B. (1994, May). Women are barraged by media on "the change." *APA Monitor,* pp. 24–25.

Bach, A. K., Weisberg, R. B., & Barlow, D. H. (1998). Anxiety disorders. In E. A. Blechman & K. D. Brownell (Eds.), *Behavioral medicine and women: A comprehensive handbook* (pp. 731–736). New York: Guilford Press.

Bachmann, G. A. (1991, February). Sexual dysfunction in the older woman. *Medical Aspects of Human Sexuality,* pp. 42–45.

Bader, E. J. (1990, July/August). Trade unions still sexist, racist. *New Directions for Women,* p. M1.

Bahr, K. S. (1994). The strengths of Apache grandmothers: Observations on commitment, culture and caretaking. *Journal of Comparative Family Studies, 25,* 233–248.

Bailey, B. A., & Nihlen, A. S. (1990). Effect of experience with nontraditional workers on psychological and social dimensions of occupational sex-role stereotyping by elementary school children. *Psychological Reports, 66,* 1273–1282.

Bailey, J. M., & Pillard, R. C. (1991). A genetic study of male sexual orientation. *Archives of General Psychiatry, 48,* 1089–1096.

Bailey, J. M., Pillard, R. C., Neale, M. C., & Agyei, Y. (1993). Heritable factors influence sexual orientation in women. *Archives of General Psychiatry, 50,* 217–223.

Bailey, K. R. (1993). *The girls are the ones with the pointy nails: An exploration of children's conceptions of gender.* London, Ontario: Althouse Press.

Bailey, S. M., et al. (1993). Girls, gender, and schools: *Excerpts from The AAUW report: How schools shortchange girls.* In S. Matteo (Ed.), *American women in the nineties* (pp. 274–305). Boston: Northeastern University Press.

Bains, A. (1998, February). Thirty-eight cents a shirt. *Toronto Life,* pp. 41–50.

Baker, L. C. (1996). Differences in earnings between male and female physicians. *New England Journal of Medicine, 334,* 960–964.

Ball, A. L. (1993, October 4). Childless by choice: Couples who sidestep the parent trap. *New York,* pp. 48–53.

Ballagh, S. A. (1998). Contraception. In E. A. Blechman & K. D. Brownell (Eds.), *Behavioral medicine & women* (pp. 506–514). New York: Guilford Press.

Ballara, M. (1992). *Women and literacy.* London: Zed Books.

Bank, B. J. (1995). Gendered accounts: Undergraduates explain why they seek their bachelor's degree. *Sex Roles, 32,* 527–544.

Banner, L. W. (1992). *In full flower: Aging women, power, and sexuality*. New York: Knopf.

Baranowski, T., et al. (1986). Attitudes toward breastfeeding. *Developmental and Behavioral Pediatrics, 7,* 367–372.

Barbee, A. P., et al. (1993). Effects of gender role expectations on the social support process. *Journal of Social Issues, 49,* 175–190.

Bardwell, J. R., Cochran, S. W., & Walker, S. (1986). Relationship of parental education, race, and gender to sex role stereotyping in five-year-old kindergartners. *Sex Roles, 15,* 275–281.

Bargad, A., & Hyde, J. S. (1991). Women's studies: A study of feminist identity development in women. *Psychology of Women Quarterly, 15,* 181–201.

Barker, K. (1993). Changing assumptions and contingent solutions: The costs and benefits of women working full- and part-time. *Sex Roles, 28,* 47–71.

Barker, M. A. (1996). Remedying gender-based wage discrimination: The comparable worth approach. In P. J. Dubeck & K. Borman (Eds.), *Women and work: A handbook* (pp. 375–382). New York: Garland.

Barling, J. (1990). *Employment, stress and family functioning.* Chichester, England: Wiley.

Barnett, R. C. (1997). How paradigms shape the stories we tell: Paradigm shifts in gender and health. *Journal of Social Issues, 53,* 351–368.

Barnett, R. C., & Rivers, C. (1996). *She works, he works.* San Francisco: HarperSanFrancisco.

Barney, D. D. (1994). Use of mental health services by American Indian and Alaska Native elders. *American Indian and Alaska Native Health Research, 5,* 1014.

Baron, R. A., & Richardson, D. R. (1994). *Human aggression* (2nd ed.). New York: Plenum Press.

Barone, D. F., Maddux, J. E., & Snyder, C. R. (1997). *Social cognitive psychology: History and current domains.* New York: Plenum Press.

Barrett, M. B. (1989). *Invisible lives.* New York: Morrow.

Barusch, A. S. (1994). *Older women in poverty: Private lives and public policies.* New York: Springer.

Barzansky, B., Jonas, H. S., & Etzel, S. I. (1997). Educational programs in U.S. medical schools, 1996–1997. *JAMA, 278,* 744–749.

Basow, S. A. (1995). Student evaluations of college professors: When gender matters. *Journal of Educational Psychology, 87,* 656–665.

Basu, A. (Ed.). (1995). *The challenge of local feminisms: Women's movements in global perspective.* Boulder, CO: Westview Press.

Bauer, P. A. (1993). Memory for gender consistent and inconsistent event sequences by 25-month-old children. *Child Development, 64,* 285–297.

Baumrind, D. (1995). Commentary on sexual orientation: Research and social policy implications. *Developmental Psychology, 31,* 130–136.

Baur, S. (1997). *The intimate hour: Love and sex in psychotherapy.* Boston: Houghton Mifflin.

Bazzini, D. G., et al. (1997). The aging woman in popular film: Underrepresented, unattractive, unfriendly, and unintelligent. *Sex Roles, 36,* 531–543.

Beal, C. R. (1994). *Boys and girls: The development of gender roles.* New York: McGraw Hill.

Beall, A. E. (1993). A social constructionist view of gender. In A. E. Beall & R. J. Sternberg (Eds.), *The psychology of gender* (pp. 127–147). New York: Guilford Press.

Beatty, W. W., & Bruellman, J. A. (1987). Absence of gender differences in memory for map learning. *Bulletin of the Psychonomic Society, 25,* 238–239.

Beazley, R. P., Langille, D. B., & Schmidt, K. M. (1996). Physicians as providers of reproductive health information to young women. *Canadian Journal of Human Sexuality, 5,* 1–6.

Bee, H. (1998). *Lifespan development* (2nd ed.). New York: Longman.

Begley, S. (1995, March 27). Gray matters. *Newsweek,* pp. 48–53.

Belansky, E. S., & Boggiano, A. K. (1994). Predicting helping behaviors: The role of gender and instrumental/expressive self-schemata. *Sex Roles, 30,* 647–661.

Belansky, E. S., Clements, P., & Eccles, J. S. (1992, March). *Adolescence: A crossroads for gender-role transcendence or gender-role intensification.* Paper presented at the meeting of the Society for Research on Adolescence, Washington, DC.

Belansky, E. S., Early, D. M., & Eccles, J. S. (1993, March). *The impact of mothers and peers on adolescents' gender role traditionality and plans for the future.* Paper presented at the meeting of the Society for Research on Child Development, New Orleans.

Belknap, P., & Leonard, W. M., II. (1991). A conceptual replication and extension of Erving Goffman's study of gender advertisements. *Sex Roles, 25,* 103–118.

Bell, A. R. (1990). Separate people: Speaking of Creek men and women. *American Anthropologist, 92,* 332–345.

Bell, D., & Klein, R. (1996). Foreword—Beware: Radical feminists speak, read, write, organise, enjoy life, and never forget. In R. Bell & R. Klein (Eds.), *Radically speaking: Feminism reclaimed* (pp. xvii–xxx). North Melbourne, Australia: Spinifex.

Bell, E. L., Denton, T. C., & Nkomo, S. (1993). Women of color in management: Toward an inclusive analysis. In E. A. Fagenson (Ed.), *Women in management: Trends, issues, and challenges in managerial diversity* (pp. 105–130). Newbury Park, CA: Sage.

Bellafante, G. (1998, June 29). Feminism: It's all about me! *Time Magazine,* pp. 54–62.

Belle, D. (1997, Summer). Poverty facts test. *Association for Women in Psychology Newsletter,* p. 1.

Bellinger, D. C., & Gleason, J. B. (1982). Sex differences in parental directives to young children. *Sex Roles, 8,* 1123–1139.

Bem, D. J. (1996). Exotic becomes erotic: A developmental theory of sexual orientation. *Psychological Review, 103,* 320–335.

Bem, S. L. (1974). The measurement of psychological androgyny. *Journal of Consulting and Clinical Psychology, 42,* 155–162.

Bem, S. L. (1975). Sex role adaptability: One consequence of psychological androgyny. *Journal of Personality and Social Psychology, 31,* 634–643.

Bem, S. L. (1977). On the utility of alternative procedures for assessing psychological androgyny. *Journal of Consulting and Clinical Psychology, 45,* 196–205.

Bem, S. L. (1981). Gender schema theory: A cognitive account of sex typing. *Psychological Review, 88,* 354–364.

Bem, S. L. (1983). Gender schema theory and its implications for child development: Raising gender-aschematic children in a gender-schematic society. *Signs, 8,* 598–616.

Bem, S. L. (1985). Androgyny and gender schema theory: A conceptual and empirical integration. In T. B. Sonderegger (Ed.), *Nebraska Symposium on Motivation, 1984: Psychology and gender* (pp. 179–226). Lincoln: University of Nebraska Press.

Bem, S. L. (1993). *The lenses of gender: Transforming the debate on sexual inequality.* New Haven, CT: Yale University Press.

Bem, S. L. (1995a). Dismantling gender polarization and compulsory heterosexuality: Should we turn the volume down or up? *Journal of Sex Research, 32,* 329–334.

Bem, S. L. (1995b). Working on gender as a gender-nonconformist. *Women & Therapy, 17,* 43–53.

Bem, S. L. (1996). Transforming the debate on sexual inequality: From biological difference to institutionalized androcentrism. In J. C. Chrisler, C. Golden & P. D. Rozee (Eds.), *Lectures on the psychology of women* (pp. 9–21). New York: McGraw-Hill.

Benbow, C. P. (1988). Sex differences in mathematical reasoning ability in intellectually talented preadolescents: Their nature, effects, and possible causes. *Behavioral and Brain Sciences, 11,* 169–232.

Benbow, C. P., & Stanley, J. C. (1980). Sex differences in mathematical ability: Fact or artifact? *Science, 210,* 1262–1264.

Beneke, T. (1997). Men on rape. In M. B. Zinn, P. Hondagneu-Sotelo, & Messner, M. A. (Eds.), *Through the prism of difference: Readings on sex and gender* (pp. 130–135). Boston: Allyn & Bacon.

Benjamin, L. T., Jr., & Shields, S. A. (1990). Foreword. In H. L. Hollingworth, *Leta Stetter Hollingworth: A biography* (pp. ix–xviii). Bolton, MA: Anker Publishing.

Bennett, N. G., Blanc, A. K., & Bloom, D. E. (1988). Commitment and the modern union: Assessing the link between premarital cohabitation and subsequent marital stability. *American Sociological Review, 53,* 127–138.

Benokraitis, N. V. (1997a). Sex discrimination in the 21st century. In N. V. Benokraitis (Ed.), *Subtle sexism: Current practice and prospects for change* (pp. 5–33). Thousand Oaks, CA: Sage.

Benokraitis, N. V. (1997b). *Subtle sexism: Current practice and prospects for change.* Thousand Oaks, CA: Sage.

Benokraitis, N. V., & Feagin, J. R. (1994). *Modern sexism: Blatant, subtle, and covert discrimination* (2nd ed.). Englewood Cliffs, NJ: Prentice Hall.

BenTsvi-Mayer, S., Hertz-Lazarowitz, R., & Safir, M. P. (1989). Teachers' selections of boys and girls as prominent pupils. *Sex Roles, 21,* 231–245.

Beren, S. E., et al. (1997). Body dissatisfaction among lesbian college students: The conflict of straddling mainstream and lesbian cultures. *Psychology of Women Quarterly, 21,* 431–445.

Berg, J. H., Stephen, W. G., & Dodson, M. (1981). Attributional modesty in women. *Psychology of Women Quarterly, 5,* 711–727.

Bergen, D. J., & Williams, J. E. (1991). Sex stereotypes in the United States revisited: 1972–1988. *Sex Roles, 24,* 413–424.

Bergeron, S. M., & Senn, C. Y. (1998). Body image and sociocultural norms: A comparison of heterosexual and lesbian women. *Psychology of Women Quarterly, 22,* 385–401.

Bergob, M. (1995). Women with disabilities. In Statistics Canada (Ed.), *Women in Canada, a statistical report* (3rd ed., pp. 163–166). Ottawa: Statistics Canada.

Bergquist, W. H., Greenberg, E. M., & Klaum, G. A. (1993). *In our fifties: Voices of men and women reinventing their lives.* San Francisco: Jossey-Bass.

Bergum, V. (1997). *A child on her mind: The experience of becoming a mother.* Westport, CT: Bergin & Garvey.

Berman, P. W. (1976). Social context as a determinant of sex differences in adults' attraction to infants. *Developmental Psychology, 12,* 365–366.

Berman, P. W. (1980). Are women more responsive than men to the young? A review of developmental and situational variables. *Psychological Bulletin, 88,* 668–695.

Bernal, M. E., & Castro, F. G. (1994). Are clinical psychologists prepared for service and research with ethnic minorities? *American Psychologist, 49,* 797–805.

Berndt, T. J. (1994). Intimacy and competition in the friendships of adolescent boys and girls. In M. R. Stevenson (Ed.), *Gender roles throughout the life span* (pp. 89–110). Muncie, IN: Ball State.

Berrien, R. (1992). Outside in. *JAMA, 268,* 2616.

Berryman, J. C., & Windridge, K. C. (1997). Maternal age and employment in pregnancy and after childbirth. *Journal of Reproductive and Infant Psychology, 15,* 287–302.

Berscheid, E. (1993). Foreword. In A. E. Beall & R. J. Sternberg (Eds.), *The psychology of gender* (pp. vii–xxi). New York: Guilford Press.

Berthiaume, M., David, H., Saucier, J., & Borgeat, F. (1996). Correlates of gender role orientation during pregnancy and the postpartum. *Sex Roles, 35,* 781–800.

Berzon, B. (1996). *Setting them straight.* New York: Penguin.

Best, D. L., & Williams, J. E. (1993). A cross-cultural viewpoint. In A. E. Beall & R. J. Sternberg (Eds.), *The psychology of gender* (pp. 215–248). New York: Guilford Press.

Bettencourt, B. A., & Miller, N. (1996). Gender differences in aggression as a function of provocation: A meta-analysis. *Psychological Bulletin, 119,* 422–447.

Betz, N. E. (1989). Implications of the null environment hypothesis for women's career development and for counseling psychology. *The Counseling Psychologist, 17,* 136–144.

Betz, N. E. (1993). Women's career development. In F. L. Denmark & M. A. Paludi (Eds.), *Psychology of women: A handbook of issues and theories* (pp. 627–684). Westport, CT: Greenwood Press.

Betz, N. E. (1994a). Basic issues and concepts in career counseling for women. In W. B. Walsh & S. H. Osipow (Eds.), *Career counseling for women* (pp. 1–41). Hillsdale, NJ: Erlbaum.

Betz, N. E. (1994b). Career counseling for women in the sciences and engineering. In W. B. Walsh & S. H. Osipow (Eds.), *Career counseling for women* (pp. 237–261). Hillsdale, NJ: Erlbaum.

Betz, N. E. (1997). What stops women and minorities from choosing and completing majors in science and engineering? In D. Johnson (Ed.), *Minorities and girls in school: Effects on achievement and performance* (pp. 105–140). Thousand Oaks, CA: Sage.

Betz, N. E., & Fitzgerald, L. F. (1987). *The career psychology of women.* Orlando, FL: Academic Press.

Biaggio, M., & Brownell, A. (1996). Addressing sexual harassment: Strategies for prevention and change. In M. A. Paludi (Ed.), *Sexual harassment on college campuses: Abusing the ivory power* (pp. 215–234). Albany: State University of New York Press.

Biernat, M., & Wortman, C. B. (1991). Sharing of home responsibilities between professionally employed women and their husbands. *Journal of Personality and Social Psychology, 60,* 844–860.

Biglan, A. (1996). Sexual coercion. In M. A. Mattaini & B. A. Thyer (Eds.), *Finding solutions to social problems: Behavioral strategies for change* (pp. 289–316). Washington, DC: American Psychological Association.

Bigler, R. S. (1995). The role of classification skill in moderating environmental influences on children's gender stereotyping: A study of the functional use of gender in the classroom. *Child Development, 66,* 1072–1087.

Binion, V. J. (1990). Psychological androgyny: A Black female perspective. *Sex Roles, 22,* 487–507.

Birns, B. (1999). Battered wives: Causes, effects, and social change. In C. Forden, A. E. Hunter, & B. Birns (Eds.), *Readings in the psychology of women: Dimensions of the female experience* (pp. 280–288). Boston: Allyn & Bacon.

Bischoping, K. (1993). Gender differences in conversation topics, 1922–1990. *Sex Roles, 28,* 1–18.

Bishop, E. G., Dickson, A. L., & Allen, M. T. (1990). Psychometric intelligence and performance on selective reminding. *The Clinical Neuropsychologist, 4,* 141–150.

Björkqvist, K. (1994). Sex differences in physical, verbal, and indirect aggression: A review of recent research. *Sex Roles, 30,* 177–188.

Blackford, K., Cutherbertson, C., Odette, F., & Ticoll, M. (Eds.). (1993). *Women and disability.* North York, Ontario: Inanna Publications.

Blank, R., & Slipp, S. (1994). *Voices of diversity: Real people talk about problems and solutions in a workplace where everyone is not alike.* New York: American Management Association.

Blasko, D. G., O'Brien, E. J., Huester, M. T., & O'Brien, J. P. (1989, August). *Sex differences in the effects of pregnancy status on perceptions of personality and business success.* Paper presented at the convention of the American Psychological Association, New Orleans.

Blau, G. M., & Gullotta, T. P. (1993). Promoting sexual responsibility in adolescence. In T. P. Gullotta, G. R. Adams, & R. Montemayor (Eds.), *Adolescent sexuality* (pp. 181–203). Newbury Park, CA: Sage.

Blea, I. I. (1997). *U.S. Chicanas and Latinas within a global context.* Westport, CT: Praeger.

Blechman, E. A., & Brownell, K. D. (Eds.). (1998). *Behavioral medicine and women: A comprehensive handbook.* New York: Guilford Press.

Bleier, R. (1991). Gender ideology and the brain: Sex differences research. In M. T. Notman & C. C. Nadelson (Eds.), *Women and men: New perspectives on gender differences* (pp. 63–73). Washington, DC: American Psychiatric Press.

Blieszner, R. (1998). *Feminist perspectives on old women's lives and ageism in society.* Paper presented at Virginia Polytechnic Institute.

Bliss, S. (1995). Mythopoetic men's movements. In M. S. Kimmel (Ed.), *The politics of manhood* (pp. 292–307). Philadelphia: Temple University Press.

Block, J. D., & Greenberg, D. (1985). *Women and friendship.* New York: Franklin Watts.

Blume, S. B. (1998, March). Alcoholism in women. *Harvard Mental Health Letter,* pp. 5–7.

Blumenthal, S. J. (1995). Improving women's mental and physical health: Federal initiative and programs. *Review of Psychiatry, 14,* 181–204.

Blumstein, P. W., & Schwartz, P. (1983). *American couples.* New York: Morrow.

Bly, R. (1990). *Iron John.* Reading, MA: Addison-Wesley.

Blyth, D. A., & Traeger, C. (1988). Adolescent self-esteem and perceived relationships with parents and peers. In S. Salinger, J. Antrobus, & M. Hammer (Eds.), *Social networks of children, adolescents, and college students* (pp. 171–194). Hillsdale, NJ: Erlbaum.

Boeschen, L. E., Sales, B. D., & Koss, M. P. (1998). Rape trauma experts in the courtroom. *Psychology and Law, 4,* 414–432.

Bohan, J. S. (1992). Prologue: Re-viewing psychology, re-placing women—an end searching for a means. In J. S. Bohan (Ed.), *Seldom seen, rarely heard: Women's place in psychology* (pp. 9–53). Boulder, CO: Westview Press.

Bohan, J. S. (1993). Regarding gender: Essentialism, constructionism, and feminist psychology. *Psychology of Women Quarterly, 17,* 5–21.

Bohan, J. S. (1996). *Psychology and sexual orientation: Coming to terms.* New York: Routledge.

Bohan, J. S. (1997, August). *The psychology of women, the women of psychology: Recurring questions, persistent themes.* Paper presented at the annual convention of the American Psychological Association, Chicago, IL.

Bonanni, P. P. (1993, January/February). Domestic violence: Don't turn away. *The Bulletin of the Monroe County Medical Society,* pp. 5–6.

Bondurant, B., & White, J. W. (1996). Men who sexually harass: An embedded perspective. In D. K. Shrier (Ed.), *Sexual harassment in the workplace and academia: Psychiatric Issues* (pp. 59–78). Washington, DC: American Psychiatric Press.

Bonebright, T. L., Thompson, J. L., & Leger, D. W. (1996). Gender stereotypes in the expression and perception of vocal affect. *Sex Roles, 34,* 429–445.

Bookwala, J., Frieze, I. H., Smith, C., & Ryan, K. (1992). Predictors of dating violence: A multivariate analysis. *Violence and Victims, 7,* 297–311.

Bordelon, K. W. (1985). Sexism in reading materials. *Reading Teacher, 38,* 792–797.

Bordo, S. (1998, May 1). Sexual harassment is about bullying, not sex. *Chronicle of Higher Education*, p. B6.

Borland, D. C. (1982). A cohort analysis approach to the empty-nest syndrome among three ethnic groups of women: A theoretical position. *Journal of Marriage and the Family, 44,* 117–129.

Boskind-White, M., & White, W. C. (1987). *Bulimarexia* (2nd ed.). New York: Norton.

Boston, M. B., & Levy, G. D. (1991). Changes and differences in preschoolers' understanding of gender scripts. *Cognitive Development, 6,* 417–432.

Boswell, A. A., & Spade, J. Z. (1999). Fraternities and collegiate rape culture: Why are some fraternities more dangerous places for women? In L. A. Peplau et al. (Eds.), *Gender, culture, and ethnicity: Current research about women and men* (pp. 269–283). Mountain View, CA: Mayfield.

Bould, S. (1997). Women and caregivers for the elderly. In J. M. Coyle (Ed.), *Handbook on women and aging* (pp. 430–442). Westport, CT: Greenwood Press.

Bowen, D. J., Carscadden, L., Beighle, K., & Fleming, I. (1992). Post-traumatic stress disorder among Salvadoran women: Empirical evidence and description of treatment. In E. Cole, O. M. Espin, & E. D. Rothblum (Eds.), *Refugee women and their mental health: Shattered societies, shattered lives* (pp. 267–280). New York: Haworth Press.

Bowen, D. J., Tomoyasu, N., & Cauce, A. M. (1999). The triple threat: A discussion of gender, class, and race differences in weight. In L. A. Peplau et al. (Eds.), *Gender, culture, and ethnicity: Current research about women and men* (pp. 291–306). Mountain View, CA: Mayfield.

Boyd, C. (1997). "Just like one of the boys": Tactics of women taxi drivers. In P. Greenhill & D. Tye (Eds.), *Undisciplined women: Tradition and culture in Canada* (pp. 213–222). Montreal: McGill-Queen's University Press.

Brabant, S., & Mooney, L. A. (1997). Sex role stereotyping in the Sunday comics: A twenty year update. *Sex Roles, 37,* 269–281.

Brabeck, M. M. (1996). The moral self, values, and circles of belonging. In K. F. Wyche & F. J. Crosby (Eds.), *Women's ethnicities: Journeys through psychology* (pp. 145–165). Boulder, CO: Westview Press.

Bradbury, T. N., & Fincham, F. D. (1992). Attributions and behavior in marital interaction. *Journal of Personality and Social Psychology, 63,* 613–628.

Bradsher, J. E. (1997). Older women and widowhood. In J. M. Coyle (Ed.), *Handbook on women and aging* (pp. 418–429). Westport, CT: Greenwood Press.

Brady, K. (1993). Testimony on pornography and incest. In D. E. H. Russell (Ed.), *Making violence sexy: Feminist views on pornography* (pp. 43–45). New York: Teachers College Press.

Braito, R., & Anderson, D. (1983). The ever-single elderly woman. In E. W. Markson (Ed.), *Older women* (pp. 195–225). Lexington, MA: Lexington Books.

Brake, M. (1994, March 14). Needed: A license to drink. *Newsweek,* p. 11.

Brandenburg, J. B. (1997). *Confronting sexual harassment: What schools and colleges can do.* New York: Teachers College Press.

Brannon, L. (1994). *Warning: Expectant parents—No unhappiness allowed.* Paper presented at the convention of the American Psychological Association, Los Angeles.

Brannon, R. (1997, August 16). *The birth of academic men's studies, in the context of feminism.* Paper presented at the annual meeting of the American Psychological Association, Chicago.

Brayfield, A. A. (1992). Employment resources and housework in Canada. *Journal of Marriage and the Family, 54,* 19–30.

Breedlove, S. M. (1994). Sexual differentiation of the human nervous system. *Annual Review of Psychology, 45,* 389–418.

Brewer, J. I., & de Costa, E. J. (1967). *Textbook of gynecology* (4th ed.). Baltimore: Williams & Wilkins.

Brewer, K. K. (1995). Contraception. In M. W. O'Hara et al. (Eds.), *Psychological aspects of women's reproductive health* (pp. 115–131). New York: Springer.

Bridge, M. J. (1993). *The news, as if all people mattered.* New York: Women, Men and Media.

Bridge, M. J. (1994). *Arriving on the scene: Women's growing presence in the news.* New York: Women, Men and Media.

Bridges, J. S. (1993). Pink or blue: Gender-stereotypic perceptions of infants as conveyed by birth congratulations cards. *Psychology of Women Quarterly, 17,* 193–205.

Bridges, J. S., & Etaugh, C. (1994). Black and White college women's perceptions of early maternal employment. *Psychology of Women Quarterly, 18,* 427–431.

Bridges, J. S., & Etaugh, C. (1995). College students' perceptions of mothers: Effects of maternal employment-childrearing pattern and motive for employment. *Sex Roles, 32,* 735–751.

Bridges, J. S., & Etaugh, C. (1996). Black and White college women's maternal employment outcome expectations and their desired timing of maternal employment. *Sex Roles, 35,* 543–562.

Briere, J., & Lanktree, C. (1983). Sex-role related effects of sex bias in language. *Sex Roles, 9,* 625–632.

Brinson, S. L. (1992). The use and opposition of rape myths in prime-time television dramas. *Sex Roles, 27,* 359–375.

Briton, N. J., & Hall, J. A. (1995). Beliefs about female and male nonverbal communication. *Sex Roles, 32,* 79–90.

Brockington, I. (1996). *Motherhood and mental health.* Oxford: Oxford University Press.

Brody, L. R., & Hall, J. A. (1993). Gender and emotion. In M. Lewis & J. M. Haviland (Eds.), *Handbook of emotions* (pp. 447–460). New York: Guilford Press.

Bronstein, P. A., Briones, M., Brooks, T., & Cowan, B. (1996). Gender and family factors as predictors of late adolescent emotional expressiveness and adjustment: A longitudinal study. *Sex Roles, 34,* 739–765.

Bronstein, P. A., & Farnsworth, L. (1998). Gender differences in faculty experiences of interpersonal climate and processes for advancement. *Research in Higher Education, 39,* 557–572.

Bronstein, P. A., & Quina, K. (1988). Perspectives on gender balance and cultural diversity in the teaching of psychology. In P. A. Bronstein & K. Quina (Eds.), *Teaching a psychology of people: Resources for gender and sociocultural awareness* (pp. 3–11). Washington, DC: American Psychological Association.

Brooks, C. I. (1987). Superiority of women in statistics achievement. *Teaching of Psychology, 14,* 45.

Brooks, G. R. (1995). *The centerfold syndrome: How men can overcome objectification and achieve intimacy with women.* San Francisco: Jossey-Bass.

Brooks, G. R. (1997, Spring). Our voice can make a difference. *Society for the Psychological Study of Men and Masculinity Bulletin,* pp. 1–3.

Brooks-Gunn, J., Gargiulo, J., & Warren, M. P. (1986). The menstrual cycle and athletic performance. In J. L. Puhl & C. H. Brown (Eds.), *The menstrual cycle and physical activity* (pp. 13–28). Champaign, IL: Human Kinetics.

Brooks-Gunn, J., & Matthews, W. S. (1979). *He and she: How children develop their sex-role identity.* Englewood Cliffs, NJ: Spectrum.

Brown, D. R., & Gary, L. E. (1985). Social support network differentials among married and nonmarried Black females. *Psychology of Women Quarterly, 9,* 229–241.

Brown, E. B. (1990). African-American women's quilting: A framework for conceptualizing and teaching African-American women's history. In M. M. Malson, E. Mudimbe-Boyi, J. F. O'Barr, & M. Wyer (Eds.), *Black women in America* (pp. 9–18). Chicago: University of Chicago Press.

Brown, H. (1998, September/October). After the suit, how do women fit in at Mitsubishi? *Ms. Magazine,* pp. 32–36.

Brown, L. M., & Gilligan, C. (1992). *Meeting at the crossroads: Women's psychology and girls' development.* Cambridge, MA: Harvard University Press.

Brown, L. S. (1996). On the construction of truth and falsity: Whose memory, whose history. In K. Pezdek & W. P. Banks (Eds.), *The recovered memory/false memory debate* (pp. 341–353). San Diego, CA: Academic Press.

Brown, P. D., & O'Leary, K. D. (1997). Wife abuse in intact couples. In G. K. Kantor & J. L. Jasinski (Eds.), *Out of the darkness: Contemporary perspectives on family violence* (pp. 194–207). Thousand Oaks, CA: Sage.

Brown, S. S., & Eisenberg, L. (1995). *The best intentions: Unintended pregnancy and the well-being of children and families.* Washington, DC: National Academy Press.

Browne, B. A. (1997a). Gender and beliefs about work force discrimination in the United States and Australia. *Journal of Social Psychology, 137,* 107–116.

Browne, B. A. (1997b). Gender and preference for job attributes: A cross-cultural comparison. *Sex Roles, 37,* 61–71.

Brownell, K. D., & Rodin, J. (1994). The dieting maelstrom: Is it possible and advisable to lose weight? *American Psychologist, 49,* 781–791.

Bruining, M. O. (1995). A few thoughts from a Korean, adopted, lesbian, writer/poet, and social worker. *Journal of Gay & Lesbian Social Services, 3,* 61–66.

Brumberg, J. J. (1997). *The body project: An intimate history of American girls.* New York: Random House.

Buckley, S. (1997, October 20). A matter of life and death. *Washington Post National Weekly Edition,* pp. 6–8.

Bumpass, L. L., Sweet, J. A., & Cherlin, A. (1991). The role of cohabitation in declining rates of marriage. *Journal of Marriage and the Family, 53,* 913–927.

Bunch, C., & Fried, S. (1997). Beijing '95: Moving women's human rights from margin to center. In R. Bredin (Ed.), *Perspectives: Women's studies* (pp. 152–154). Boulder, CO: Coursewise Publications.

Buntaine, R. L., & Costenbader, V. K. (1997). Self-reported differences in the experience and expression of anger between girls and boys. *Sex Roles, 36,* 625–637.

Burbank, V. K. (1994). Cross-cultural perspectives on aggression in women and girls: An introduction. *Sex Roles, 30,* 169–176.

Burn, S. M. (1996). *The social psychology of gender.* New York: McGraw-Hill.

Burnham, L. (1994). Race and gender: The limits of analogy. In E. Tobach & B. Rosoff (Eds.), *Challenging racism and sexism: Alternatives to genetic explanations* (pp. 143–162). New York: Feminist Press.

Bursik, K. (1991a). Adaptation to divorce and ego development in adult women. *Journal of Personality and Social Psychology, 60,* 300–306.

Bursik, K. (1991b). Correlations of women's adjustment during the separation and divorce process. *Journal of Divorce and Remarriage, 14,* 137–162.

Bursik, K. (1992). Perceptions of sexual harassment in an academic context. *Sex Roles, 27,* 401–412.

Bursik, K. (1995). Gender-related personality traits and ego development: Differential patterns for men and women. *Sex Roles, 32,* 601–615.

Bursik, K. (1997). *Personal communication.*

Bursik, K. (1998). Moving beyond gender differences: Gender role comparisons of manifest dream content. *Sex Roles, 38,* 203–214.

Burstow, B. (1992). *Radical feminist therapy: Working in the context of violence.* Newbury Park, CA: Sage.

Burt, V. V., & Hendrick, V. C. (1997). *Concise guide to women's mental health.* Washington, DC: American Psychiatric Press.

Buss, A. H., & Perry, M. (1992). The aggression questionnaire. *Journal of Personality and Social Psychology, 63,* 452–459.

Buss, D. M. (1994). *The evolution of desire: Strategies of human mating.* New York: Basic Books.

Buss, D. M. (1995). Psychological sex differences: Origins through sexual selection. *American Psychologist, 50,* 164–168.

Buss, D. M., & Schmitt, D. P. (1993). Sexual strategies theory: An evolutionary perspective on human mating. *Psychological Review, 100,* 204–232.

Buss, D. M., et al. (1990). International preferences in selecting mates: A study of 37 cultures. *Journal of Cross-Cultural Psychology, 21,* 5–47.

Buttner, E. H., & McEnally, M. (1996). The interactive effect of influence tactic, applicant gender, and type of job on hiring recommendations. *Sex Roles, 34,* 581–591.

Bylsma, W. H., & Major, B. (1992). Two routes to eliminating gender differences in personal entitlement: Social comparisons and performance evaluations. *Psychology of Women Quarterly, 16,* 193–200.

Byne, W. (1994, May). The biological evidence challenged. *Scientific American,* pp. 50–55.

Byne, W., & Parsons, B. (1993). Human sexual orientation: The biologic theories reappraised. *Archives of General Psychiatry, 50,* 228–239.

Byne, W., & Parsons, B. (1994, February). Biology and human sexual orientation. *Harvard Mental Health Newsletter,* pp. 5–7.

Cahan, S., & Ganor, Y. (1995). Cognitive gender differences among Israeli children. *Sex Roles, 32,* 469–484.

Calasanti, T. M. (1996). Gender and life satisfaction in retirement: An assessment of the male model. *Journal of Gerontology: Social Sciences, 51B,* 518–529.

Caldwell, M. A., Finn, S., & Marecek, J. (1981). Sex-role identity, sex-role behavior, and satisfaction in heterosexual, lesbian, and gay male couples. *Psychology of Women Quarterly, 5,* 488–494.

Calhoun, K. S., & Atkeson, B. M. (1991). *Treatment of rape victims: Facilitating psychosocial adjustment.* Elmsford, NY: Pergamon Press.

Call, V., Sprecher, S., & Schwartz, P. (1995). The incidence and frequency of marital sex in a national sample. *Journal of Marriage and the Family, 57,* 639–652.

Callahan, C. M., et al. (1996). Factors influencing recruitment, enrollment, and retention of young women in special secondary schools of mathematics, science, and technology. In K. Arnold, K. D. Noble, & R. F. Subotnik (Eds.), *Remarkable women: Perspectives on female talent development* (pp. 243–260). Cresskill, NJ: Hampton Press.

Cameron, D., McAlinden, F., & O'Leary, K. (1993). Lakoff in context: The social and linguistic functions of tag questions. In S. Jackson (Ed.), *Women's studies: Essential readings* (pp. 421–426). New York: New York University Press.

Campbell, J. C., & Landenburger, K. (1995). Violence against women. In C. I. Fogel & N. F. Woods (Eds.), *Women's health care: A comprehensive handbook* (pp. 407–425). Thousand Oaks, CA: Sage.

Campbell, S. M., Peplau, L. A., & De Bro, S. C. (1992). Women, men, and condoms: Attitudes and experiences of heterosexual college students. *Psychology of Women Quarterly, 16,* 273–288.

Canary, D. J., & Emmers-Sommer, T. M. (1997). *Sex and gender differences in personal relationships.* New York: Guilford Press.

Canetto, S. S., Kaminski, P. L., Felicio, D. M. (1995). Typical and optimal aging in women and men: Is there a double standard? *International Journal of Aging and Human Development, 40,* 187–207.

Canetto, S. S., & Lester, D. (1995a). Gender and the primary prevention of suicide mortality. *Suicide and Life-Threatening Behavior, 25,* 58–69.

Canetto, S. S., & Lester, D. (1995b). Women and suicidal behavior: Issues and dilemmas. In S. S. Canetto & D. Lester (Eds.), *Women and suicidal behavior* (pp. 3–8). New York: Springer.

Cann, A. (1993). Evaluative expectations and the gender schema: Is failed inconsistency better? *Sex Roles, 28,* 667–678.

Cann, A., & Vann, E. D. (1995). Implications of sex and gender differences for self: Perceived advantages and disadvantages of being the other gender. *Sex Roles, 33,* 481–491.

Cannistra, S. A., & Niloff, J. M. (1996). Cancer of the uterine cervix. *New England Journal of Medicine, 334,* 1030–1038.

Cantor, D. W., & Bernay, T. (1992). *Women in power: The secrets of leadership.* New York: Houghton Mifflin.

Caplan, P. J. (1993). *Lifting a ton of feathers: A woman's guide for surviving in the academic world.* Toronto: University of Toronto Press.

Caplan, P. J. (1999). Gender issues in the diagnosis of mental disorder. In C. Forden, A. E. Hunter, & B. Birns (Eds.), *Readings in the psychology of women: Dimensions of the female experience* (pp. 321–327). Boston: Allyn & Bacon.

Caplan, P. J., & Caplan, J. B. (1999). *Thinking critically about research on sex and gender* (2nd ed.). New York: Longman.

Caplan, P. J., Crawford, M., Hyde, J. S., & Richardson, J. T. E. (Eds.). (1997). *Gender differences in human cognition.* New York: Oxford University Press.

Caraway, N. (1991). *Segregated sisterhood: Racism and the politics of American feminism.* Knoxville: University of Tennessee Press.

Carli, L. L. (1990). Gender, language, and influence. *Journal of Personality and Social Psychology, 59,* 941–951.

Carli, L. L. (1991). Gender, status, and influence. *Advances in Group Processes, 8,* 89–113.

Carli, L. L., LaFleur, S. J., & Loeber, C. C. (1995). Nonverbal behavior, gender, and influence. *Journal of Personality and Social Psychology, 68,* 1030–1041.

Carlson, K. J., Eisenstat, S. A., & Ziporyn, T. (1996). *The Harvard guide to women's health.* Cambridge, MA: Harvard University Press.

Carmody, D. L. (1994). Today's Jewish women. In A. Sharma (Ed.), *Today's woman in world religions* (pp. 245–266). Albany: State University of New York Press.

Carothers, R. L., & Richmond, J. E. (1997). The role of the president in sexual harassment prevention. In B. R. Sandler & R. J. Shoop (Eds.), *Sexual harassment on campus: A guide for administrators, faculty, and students* (pp. 314–323). Boston: Allyn & Bacon.

Carp, F. M. (1997). Retirement and women. In J. M. Coyle (Ed.), *Handbook on women and aging* (pp. 112–128). Westport, CT: Greenwood Press.

Carr, P. G., Thomas, V. C., & Mednick, M. T. (1985). Evaluation of sex-typed tasks by Black men and women. *Sex Roles, 13,* 311–316.

Carroll, K., & Jackson, T. L. (1996). Rape education and prevention training. In T. L. Jackson (Ed.), *Acquaintance rape: Assessment, treatment and prevention* (pp. 177–213). Sarasota, FL: Professional Resource Press.

Carson, R. C., & Butcher, J. N. (1992). *Abnormal psychology and modern life* (9th ed.). New York: HarperCollins.

Carstensen, L. L. (1998, March/April). Everything old is new again. *Stanford Today,* pp. 46–50.

Carstensen, L. L., & Pasupathi, M. (1993). Women of a certain age. In S. Matteo (Ed.), *American women in the nineties: Today's critical issues* (pp. 66–78). Boston: Northeastern University Press.

Carter, J., Lane, C., & Kite, M. (1991). *Which sex is more likable? It depends on the subtype.* Paper presented at the meeting of the American Psychological Society, Washington, DC.

Carter, P. (1995). *Feminism, breasts and breast-feeding.* New York: St. Martin's Press.

Cartwright, L. K., & Wink, P. (1994). Personality change in women physicians from medical student years to mid-40s. *Psychology of Women Quarterly, 18,* 291–308.

Case, S. M., Becker, D. F., & Swanson, D. B. (1993). Performances of men and women on NBME Part I and Part II: The more things change . . . *Academic Medicine, 68*(Suppl.), pp. 525–527.

Casey, M. B. (1996). Understanding individual differences in spatial ability within females: A nature/nurture interactionist framework. *Developmental Review, 16,* 241–260.

Cash, T. F., Ancis, J. R., & Strachan, M. D. (1997). Gender attitudes, feminist identity, and body images among college women. *Sex Roles, 36,* 433–447.

Cash, T. F., & Henry, P. E. (1995). Women's body images: The results of a national survey in the U.S.A. *Sex Roles, 33,* 19–28.

Castañeda, D. (1996). Gender issues among Latinas. In J. C. Chrisler, C. Golden, & P. D. Rozee (Eds.), *Lectures on the psychology of women* (pp. 166–181). New York: McGraw-Hill.

Cate, R., & Sugawara, A. I. (1986). Sex role orientation and dimensions of self-esteem among middle adolescents. *Sex Roles, 15,* 145–158.

Catsambis, S. (1994). The path to math: Gender and racial-ethnic differences in mathematics participation from middle school to high school. *Sociology of Education, 67,* 199–215.

Cavaliere, F. (1995, July). Society appears more open to gay parenting. *APA Monitor,* p. 51.

Ceballo, R. (1999). The only Black woman walking the face of the earth who cannot have a baby? In M. Romero & A. Stewart (Eds.), *Women's untold stories: Outside the master narrative.* New York: Routledge.

Centers for Disease Control. (1998, June). *HIV/AIDS surveillance report.* Atlanta, GA: Author.

Centerwall, B. S. (1992). Television and violence: The scale of the problem and where to go from here. *JAMA, 267,* 3059–3063.

Chambless, D. L. (1986). Fears and anxiety. In C. Tavris (Ed.), *EveryWoman's emotional well-being* (pp. 416–436). Garden City, NY: Doubleday.

Chan, C. S. (1997). Don't ask, don't tell, don't know: The formation of a homosexual identity and sexual expression among Asian American lesbians. In B. Greene (Ed.), *Ethnic and cultural diversity among lesbians and gay men* (pp. 240–248). Thousand Oaks, CA: Sage.

Chasteen, A. L. (1994). "The world around me": The environment and single women. *Sex Roles, 31,* 309–328.

Chesler, P. (1976). *Women, money, and power.* New York: Bantam Books.

Chia, R. C., Allred, L. J., & Jerzak, P. A. (1997). Attitudes toward women in Taiwan and China. *Psychology of Women Quarterly, 21,* 137–150.

Chin, J. L. (1994). Psychodynamic approaches. In L. Comas-Díaz & B. Greene (Eds.), *Women of color* (pp. 194–222). New York: Guilford Press.

Chinen, J. N. (1996). Women in the garment industry. In P. J. Dubeck & K. Borman (Eds.), *Women and work: A handbook* (pp. 216–220). New York: Garland.

Chipman, S. F. (1996). Female participation in the study of mathematics: The U. S. situation. In G. Hanna (Ed.), *Towards gender equity in mathematics education: An ICMI study* (pp. 285–296). Norwell, MA: Kluwer.

Chipman, S. F., Krantz, D. H., & Silver, R. (1992). Mathematics anxiety and science careers among able college women. *Psychological Science, 3,* 292–295.

Chodorow, N. J. (1994). *Femininities, masculinities, sexualities: Freud and beyond.* Lexington: University Press of Kentucky.

Chodorow, N. J. (1995). Gender as a personal and cultural construction. *Signs, 20,* 516–544.

Choo, P., Levine, T., & Hatfield, E. (1996). Gender, love schemas, and reactions to romantic break-ups. *Journal of Social Behavior and Personality, 11,* 143–160.

Chow, E. N. (1991). The development of feminist consciousness among Asian American women. In J. Lorber & S. A. Farrell (Eds.), *The social construction of gender* (pp. 255–268). Newbury Park, CA: Sage.

Chow, E. N. (1994). Asian American women at work. In M. Baca Zinn, & B. T. Dill (Eds.), *Women of color in U.S. society* (pp. 203–227). Philadelphia: Temple University Press.

Chow, E. N., & Berheide, C. W. (Eds.). (1994). *Women, family, and policy: A global perspective.* Albany: State University of New York Press.

Chrisler, J. C. (1991). The effect of premenstrual symptoms on creative thinking. In D. L. Taylor & N. F. Woods (Eds.), *Menstruation, health, and illness* (pp. 73–83). New York: Hemisphere.

Chrisler, J. C. (1994). Reframing women's weight: Does thin equal healthy? In A. J. Dan (Ed.), *Reframing women's health* (pp. 330–338). Thousand Oaks, CA: Sage.

Chrisler, J. C. (1996). PMS as a culture-bound syndrome. In J. C. Chrisler, C. Golden, & P. D. Rozee (Eds.), *Lectures on the psychology of women* (pp. 106–121). New York: McGraw-Hill.

Chrisler, J. C., & Hemstreet, A. H. (1995). The diversity of women's health needs. In J. C. Chrisler & A. H. Hemstreet (Eds.), *Variations on a theme: Diversity and the psychology of women* (pp. 1–28). Albany: State University of New York Press.

Chrisler, J. C., Johnston, I. K., Champagne, N. M., & Preston, K. E. (1994). Menstrual joy: The construct and its consequences. *Psychology of Women Quarterly, 18,* 375–387.

Chrisler, J. C., & Levy, K. B. (1990). The media construct a menstrual monster: A content analysis of PMS articles in the popular press. *Women & Health, 16,* 89–104.

Clair, J. M., Karp, D. A., & Yoels, W. C. (1993). *Experiencing the life cycle: A social psychology of aging* (2nd ed.). Springfield, IL: Charles C. Thomas.

Clark, J., & Zehr, D. (1993). Other women can: Discrepant performance predictions for self and same-sex other. *Journal of College Student Development, 34,* 31–35.

Clark, R., Lennon, R., & Morris, L. (1993). Of Caldecotts and Kings: Gendered images in recent American children's books by Black and non-Black illustrators. *Gender & Society, 7,* 227–245.

Clark, R. A. (1993). Men's and women's self-confidence in persuasive, comforting, and justicatory communicative tasks. *Sex Roles, 28,* 553–567.

Clarke-Stewart, A. (1992). Consequences of child care—One more time: A rejoinder. In A. Booth (Ed.), *Child care in the 1990s: Trends and consequences* (pp. 116–124). Hillsdale, NJ: Erlbaum.

Clausen, J. (1997). *Beyond gay or straight: Understanding sexual orientation.* Philadelphia: Chelsea House.

Clayton, S. D., & Crosby, F. J. (1992). *Justice, gender, and affirmative action.* Ann Arbor: University of Michigan Press.

Cleveland, J. N. (1996). Persistent gender bias in personnel decisions. In P. J. Dubeck & K. Borman (Eds.) *Women and work: A handbook* (pp. 338–341). New York: Garland.

Clift, E. (1994, Spring). My uterus, myself: The good news about hysterectomy. *On the Issues,* pp. 32–33.

Clopton, N. A., & Sorell, G. T. (1993). Gender differences in moral reasoning: Stable or situational? *Psychology of Women Quarterly, 17,* 85–101.

Cobleigh, M. A., et al. (1994). Estrogen replacement therapy in breast cancer survivors. *JAMA, 272,* 540–545.

Cochran, C. C., Frazier, P. A., & Olson, A. M. (1997). Predictors of responses to unwanted sexual attention. *Psychology of Women Quarterly, 21,* 207–226.

Coffin, F. (1997). Drywall rocker and taper. In M. Martin (Ed.), *Hard-hatted women: Life on the job* (pp. 63–70). Seattle: Seal Press.

Coffin, J. M. (1995). HIV population dynamics in vivo: Implications for genetic variation, pathogenesis, and therapy. *Science, 267,* 483–489.

Cohan, C. L., Dunkel-Schetter, C., & Lydon, J. (1993). Pregnancy decision making: Predictors of early stress and adjustment. *Psychology of Women Quarterly, 17,* 223–239.

Cohen, J. (1969). *Statistical power analysis for the behavioral sciences.* New York: Academic Press.

Cohen, J., et al. (1996). *Girls in the middle: Working to succeed in school.* Washington, DC: American Association of University Women.

Colby, A., & Damon, W. (1983). Listening to a different voice: A review of Gilligan's *In a different voice. Merrill-Palmer Quarterly, 29,* 473–481.

Colditz, G. A., et al. (1995). The use of estrogens and progestins and the risk of breast cancer in postmenopausal women. *New England Journal of Medicine, 332,* 1589–1593.

Coleman, M. (1996). Barriers to career progress for women in education: The perceptions of female headteachers. *Educational Research, 38,* 317–332.

Colen, S. (1997). "With respect and feelings": Voices of West Indian child care and domestic workers in New York City. In M. Crawford & R. Unger (Eds.), *In our own words: Readings on the psychology of women and gender* (pp. 199–218). New York: McGraw-Hill.

Coley, R. L., & Chase-Lansdale, P. L. (1998). Adolescent pregnancy and parenthood. *American Psychologist, 53,* 152–166.

Collaer, M. L., & Hines, M. (1995). Human behavioral sex differences: A role for gonadal hormones during early development? *Psychological Bulletin, 118,* 55–107.

Collins, N. L., Dunkel-Schetter, C., Lobel, M., & Scrimshaw, S. C. M. (1993). Social support in pregnancy: Psychosocial correlates of birth outcomes and postpartum depression. *Journal of Personality and Social Psychology, 65,* 1243–1258.

Collins, P. H. (1990). *Black feminist thought: Knowledge, consciousness, and the politics of empowerment.* Boston: Unwin Hyman.

Collins, P. H. (1991). The meaning of motherhood in Black culture and Black mother/daughter relationships. In P. Bell-Scott, et al. (Eds.), *Double stitch: Black women write about mothers and daughters* (pp. 42–60). Boston: Beacon Press.

Collins, P. H. (1994). Shifting the center: Race, class, and feminist theorizing about motherhood. In D. Bassin, M. Honey, & M. M. Kaplan (Eds.), *Representations of motherhood* (pp. 56–74). New Haven, CT: Yale University Press.

Collins, P. H. (1995). The social construction of Black feminist thought. In N. Tuana & R. Tong (Eds.), *Feminism and philosophy* (pp. 526–547). Boulder, CO: Westview Press.

Colombo, J. R. (1997). *The 1998 Canadian global almanac.* Toronto: Macmillan Canada.

Comas-Díaz, L., & Greene, B. (1994a). Women of color with professional status. In L. Comas-Díaz & B. Greene (Eds.), *Women of color: Integrating ethnic and gender identities in psychotherapy* (pp. 347–388). New York: Guilford Press.

Comas-Díaz, L., & Greene, B. (Ed.). (1994b). *Women of color: Integrating ethnic and gender identities in psychotherapy.* New York: Guilford Press.

Comas-Díaz, L., & Jansen, M. A. (1995). Global conflict and violence against women. Peace and conflict: *Journal of Peace Psychology, 1,* 315–331.

Committee on Women in Psychology. (1998). *Surviving and thriving in academia: A guide for women and ethnic minorities.* Washington, DC: American Psychological Association.

Condon, J. T., & Corkindale, C. (1997). The correlates of antenatal attachment in pregnant women. *British Journal of Medical Psychology, 70,* 359–372.

Condra, M. B. (1991). The social environment of older, unmarried persons [Review of *The unmarried in later life*]. *Contemporary Psychology, 36,* 146–147.

Condry, J. C., & Condry, S. (1976). Sex differences: A study of the eye of the beholder. *Child Development, 47,* 812–819.

Conley, F. K. (1998). *Walking out on the boys.* New York: Farrar, Straus & Giroux.

Conway, K. (1997). *Ordinary life: A memoir of illness.* New York: Freeman.

Conway, M., Pizzamiglio, M. T., & Mount, L. (1996). Status, communality, and agency: Implications for stereotypes of gender and other groups. *Journal of Personality and Social Psychology, 71,* 25–38.

Coontz, S. (1997). *The way we really are: Coming to terms with America's changing families.* New York: BasicBooks.

Corcoran, C. B., & Mahlstedt, D. (1999). Preventing sexual assault on campus: A feminist perspective. In C. Forden, A. E. Hunter, & B. Birns (Eds.), *Readings in the psychology of women* (pp. 289–299). Boston: Allyn & Bacon.

Cortés, C. E. (1997). Chicanas in film: History of an image. In C. E. Rodríguez (Ed.), *Latin looks: Images of Latinas and Latinos in the U.S. media* (pp. 121–141). Boulder, CO: Westview.

Cose, E. (1997, October 13). Promises . . . promises. *Newsweek,* pp. 29–31.

Cossette, L., Malcuit, G., & Pomerleau, A. (1991). Sex differences in motor activity during early infancy. *Infant Behavior and Development, 14,* 175–186.

Cossette, L., Pomerleau, A., Malcuit, G., & Kaczorowski, J. (1996). Emotional expressions of female and male infants in a social and a nonsocial context. *Sex Roles, 35,* 693–709.

Costello, C., & Krimgold, B. K. (1998). *The American woman 1996–1997: Women and work.* New York: Norton.

Cota, A. A., Reid, A., & Dion, K. L. (1991). Construct validity of a diagnostic ratio measure of gender stereotypes. *Sex Roles, 25,* 225–235.

Côté, J. E. (1996). Identity: A multidimensional analysis. In G. R. Adams, R. Montemayor, & T. P. Gullotta (Eds.), *Psychosocial development during adolescence* (pp. 130–164). Thousand Oaks, CA: Sage.

Cowan, C. P., & Cowan, P. A. (1992). *When partners become parents: The big life change for couples.* New York: Basic Books.

Cowan, G. (1984). The double standard in age discrepant relationships. *Sex Roles, 11,* 17–24.

Cowan, G. (1995). Black and White (and blue): Ethnicity and pornography. In H. Landrine (Ed.), *Bringing cultural diversity to feminist psychology: Theory, research, and practice* (pp. 397–411). Washington, DC: American Psychological Association.

Cowan, G., & Dunn, K. F. (1994). What themes in pornography lead to perceptions of the degradation of women? *The Journal of Sex Research, 31,* 11–21.

Cowan, G., & Hoffman, C. D. (1986). Gender stereotyping in young children: Evidence to support a concept-learning approach. *Sex Roles, 14,* 11–22.

Cowan, G., & Quinton, W. J. (1997). Cognitive style and attitudinal correlates of the perceived causes of rape scale. *Psychology of Women Quarterly, 21,* 227–245.

Cox, T. H., & Harquail, C. V. (1991). Career paths and career success in the early career stages of male and female MBAs. *Journal of Vocational Behavior, 39,* 54–75.

Coyle, J. M. (Ed.). (1997). *Handbook on women and aging.* Westport, CT: Greenwood Press.

Cozzarelli, C. (1993). Personality and self-efficacy as predictors of coping with abortion. *Journal of Personality and Social Psychology, 65,* 1224–1236.

Crabb, P. B., & Bielawski, D. (1994). The social representation of material culture and gender in children's books. *Sex Roles, 30,* 69–79.

Craighead, W. E., & Vajk, F. C. (1998). Depression and comorbid disorders. In E. A. Blechman & K. D. Brownell (Eds.), *Behavioral medicine and women: A comprehensive handbook* (pp. 757–763). New York: Guilford Press.

Crandall, C. S. (1994). Prejudice against fat people: Ideology and self-interest. *Journal of Personality and Social Psychology, 66,* 882–894.

Crawford, D. W., & Huston, T. L. (1993). The impact of the transition to parenthood on marital leisure. *Personality and Social Psychology Bulletin, 19,* 39–46.

Crawford, M. (1984). *Personal communication.*

Crawford, M. (1988). Gender, age, and the social evaluation of assertion. *Behavior Modification, 12,* 549–564.

Crawford, M. (1989). Agreeing to differ: Feminist epistemologies and women's ways of knowing. In M. Crawford & M. Gentry (Eds.), *Gender and thought: Psychological perspectives* (pp. 128–145). New York: Springer-Verlag.

Crawford, M. (1995). *Talking difference: On gender and language.* Thousand Oaks, CA: Sage.

Crawford, M., & Chaffin, R. (1997). The meanings of difference: Cognition in social and cultural context. In P. J. Caplan, M. Crawford, J. S. Hyde, & J. T. E. Richardson (Eds.), *Gender differences in human cognition* (pp. 81–130). New York: Oxford University Press.

Crawford, M., Chaffin, R., & Fitton, L. (1995). Cognition in social context. *Learning and Individual Differences, 7,* 341–362.

Crawford, M., & MacLeod, M. (1990). Gender in the college classroom: An assessment of the "chilly climate" for women. *Sex Roles, 23,* 101–122.

Croll, E. (1978). *Feminism and socialism in China.* London: Routledge & Kegan Paul.

Crombie, G. (1983). Women's attribution patterns and their relation to achievement: An examination of within-sex differences. *Sex Roles, 9,* 1171–1182.

Cronin, C., & Jreisat, S. (1995). Effects of modeling on the use of nonsexist language among high school freshpersons and seniors. *Sex Roles, 33,* 819–830.

Crosby, F. J. (1982). *Relative deprivation and working women.* New York: Oxford University Press.

Crosby, F. J. (1984). The denial of personal discrimination. *American Behavioral Scientist, 27,* 371–386.

Crosby, F. J. (1993, December 15). Affirmative Action is worth it. *Chronicle of Higher Education,* pp. B1-B2.

Crose, R. (1997). *Why women live longer than men.* San Francisco: Jossey-Bass.

Cross, S. E., & Markus, H. R. (1993). Gender in thought, belief, and action: A cognitive approach. In A. E. Beall & R. J. Sternberg (Eds.), *The psychology of gender* (pp. 55–98). New York: Guilford Press.

Cruikshank, M. (1992). *The gay and lesbian liberation movement.* New York: Routledge.

Culbertson, F. M. (1997). Depression and gender: An international review. *American Psychologist, 52,* 25–31.

Cull, P. (1997). Carpenter. In M. Martin (Ed.), *Hard-hatted women: Life on the job* (pp. 45–54). Seattle: Seal Press.

Curtin, S. C., & Kozak, L. J. (1998). Decline in U.S. cesarean delivery appears to stall. *Birth, 25,* 259–262.

Dabul, A. J., & Russo, N. F. (1996). Rethinking psychological theory to encompass issues of gender and ethnicity: Focus on achievement. In K. F. Wyche & F. J. Crosby (Eds.), *Women's ethnicities* (pp. 183–199). Boulder, CO: Westview Press.

Dagg, P. K. B. (1991). The psychological sequelae of therapeutic abortions—denied and completed. *American Journal of Psychiatry, 148,* 578–585.

Dalton, S. T. (1992). Lived experience of never-married women. *Issues in Mental Health Nursing, 13,* 69–80.

Daniel, J. H. (1994, November/December). Snapshots. *Ms. Magazine,* p. 59.

Daniluk, J. C. (1993). The meaning and experience of female sexuality: A phenomenological analysis. *Psychology of Women Quarterly, 17,* 53–69.

Dannenbring, D., Stevens, M. J., & House, A. E. (1997). Predictors of childbirth pain and maternal satisfaction. *Journal of Behavioral Medicine, 20,* 127–142.

Darling, C. A., Davidson, J. K., Sr., & Jennings, D. A. (1991). The female sexual response revisited: Understanding the multiorgasmic experience in women. *Archives of Sexual Behavior, 20,* 527–540.

Daubman, K. A., Heatherington, L., & Ahn, A. (1992). Gender and the self-presentation of academic achievement. *Sex Roles, 27,* 187–204.

David, H. P., Dytrych, Z., Matějček, Z., & Schüller, V. (Eds.). (1988). *Born unwanted: Developmental effects of denied abortion.* New York: Springer.

Davidson, N. E. (1995). Hormone-replacement therapy—Breast versus heart versus bone. *New England Journal of Medicine, 332,* 1638–1639.

Davis, L. J. (Ed.). (1997). *The disability studies reader.* New York: Routledge.

Davis, S. (1990). Men as success objects and women as sex objects: A study of personal advertisements. *Sex Roles, 23,* 43–50.

Davis, S. K., & Chavez, V. (1995). Hispanic househusbands. In A. M. Padillo (Ed.), *Hispanic psychology: Critical issues in theory and research* (pp. 257–270). Thousand Oaks, CA: Sage.

Day, J. C. (1996). *Population projections of the United States by age, sex, race, and Hispanic origin: 1995–2050. U.S. Bureau of the Census.* Washington, DC: U.S. Government Printing Office.

Dayhoff, S. A. (1983). Sexist language and person perceptions: Evaluation of candidates from newspaper articles. *Sex Roles, 9,* 543–555.

Deaux, K. (1976). Sex: A perspective on the attribution process. In J. H. Harvey, W. J. Ickes, & R. F. Kidd (Eds.), *New directions in attribution research* (Vol. 1, pp. 335–352). Hillsdale, NJ: Erlbaum.

Deaux, K. (1979). Self-evaluation of male and female managers. *Sex Roles, 5,* 571–580.

Deaux, K. (1995). How basic can you be? The evolution of research on gender stereotypes. *Journal of Social Issues, 51,* 11–20.

Deaux, K., & Major, B. (1987). Putting gender into context: An interactive model of gender-related behavior. *Psychological Review, 94,* 369–389.

de Beauvoir, S. (1961). *The second sex.* New York: Bantam Books.

De Bro, S. C., Campbell, S. M., & Peplau, L. A. (1994). Influencing a partner to use a condom: A college student perspective. *Psychology of Women Quarterly, 18,* 165–182.

DeCourville, N. H. (1998). *Personal communication.*

DeKeseredy, W. S., & Schwartz, M. D. (1998). *Woman abuse on campus: Results from the Canadian National Survey.* Thousand Oaks, CA: Sage.

Delaney, J., Lupton, M. J., & Toth, E. (1988). *The curse: A cultural history of menstruation* (2nd ed.). Urbana: University of Illinois Press.

De León, B. (1995). Sex role identity among college students. In A. M. Padilla (Ed.), *Hispanic psychology: Critical issues in theory and research* (pp. 245–256). Thousand Oaks, CA: Sage.

Delk, J. L., Madden, R. B., Livingston, M., & Ryan, T. T. (1986). Adult perceptions of the infant as a function of gender labeling and observer gender. *Sex Roles, 15,* 527–534.

Delmas, P. D., et al. (1997). Effects of raloxifene on bone mineral density, serum cholesterol concentration, and uterine endometrium in postmenopausal women. *New England Journal of Medicine, 337,* 1641–1647.

DeLorey, C. (1992). Differing perspectives of menopause: An attribution theory approach. In A. J. Dan & L. L. Lewis (Eds.), *Menstrual health in women's lives* (pp. 198–205). Urbana: University of Illinois Press.

Demarest, J., & Glinos, F. (1992). Gender and sex-role differences in young adult reactions towards "newborns" in a pretend situation. *Psychological Reports, 71,* 727–737.

Denton, T. C. (1990). Bonding and supportive relationships among black professional women: Rituals of restoration. *Journal of Organizational Behavior, 11,* 447–457.

De Puy, C., & Dovitch, D. (1997). *The healing choice: Your guide to emotional recovery after an abortion.* New York: Simon & Schuster.

Derlega, V. J., Metts, S., Petronio, S., & Margulis, S. T. (1993). *Self-disclosure.* Newbury Park, CA: Sage.

Desrochers, S. (1995). What types of men are most attractive and most repulsive to women? *Sex Roles, 32,* 375–391.

Deutsch, F. M., Lussier, J. B., & Servis, L. J. (1993). Husbands at home: Predictors of paternal participation in childcare and housework. *Journal of Personality and Social Psychology, 65,* 1154–1166.

Devereaux, M. S. (1993, Autumn). Time use of Canadians in 1992. *Canadian Social Trends,* pp. 13–35.

Dhruvarajan, V. (1992). Conjugal power among first generation Hindu Asian Indians in a Canadian city. *International Journal of Sociology of the Family, 22,* 1–33.

Diamant, L. (Ed.). (1993). *Homosexual issues in the workplace.* Washington, DC: Taylor & Francis.

Diamond, M. (1993). Homosexuality and bisexuality in different populations. *Archives of Sexual Behavior, 22,* 291–310.

Diamond, M. (1996). Prenatal predisposition and the clinical management of some pediatric conditions. *Journal of Sex & Marital Therapy, 22,* 139–147.

Dickstein, L. J. (1996). Sexual harassment in medicine. In D. K. Shrier (Ed.), *Sexual harassment in the workplace and academia: Psychiatric issues* (pp. 223–243). Washington, DC: American Psychiatric Press.

Di Dio, L., Saragovi, C., Koestner, R., & Aubé, J. (1996). Linking personal values to gender. *Sex Roles, 34,* 621–636.

DiMatteo, M. R., & Kahn, K. L. (1997). Psychosocial aspects of childbirth. In S. J. Gallant, G. P. Keita, & R. Royak-Schaler (Eds.), *Health care for women: Psychological, social, and behavioral influences* (pp. 175–186). Washington, DC: American Psychological Association.

DiMatteo, M. R., Kahn, K. L., & Berry, S. H. (1993). Narratives of birth and the postpartum: Analysis of the focus group responses of new mothers. *Birth, 20,* 204–211.

DiMatteo, M. R., et al. (1996). Cesarian childbirth and psychosocial outcomes: A meta-analysis. *Health Psychology, 15,* 303–314.

Dindia, K., & Allen, M. (1992). Sex differences in self-disclosure: A meta-analysis. *Psychological Bulletin, 112,* 106–124.

Dinges, N. G., & Cherry, D. (1995). Symptom expression and the use of mental health services among American Ethnic Minorities. In J. F. Aponte, R. Y. Rivers, & J. Wohl (Eds.), *Psychological interventions and cultural diversity* (pp. 40–56). Boston: Allyn & Bacon.

Dion, K. K., & Dion, K. L. (1998). Individualistic and collectivistic perspectives on gender and the cultural context of love and intimacy. In D. L. Anselmi & A. L. Law (Eds.), *Questions of gender* (pp. 520–531). New York: McGraw-Hill.

Dion, K. L., & Dion, K. K. (1993). Gender and ethnocultural comparisons in styles of love. *Psychology of Women Quarterly, 17,* 463–473.

Dion, K. L., & Giordano, C. (1990). Ethnicity and sex as correlates of depression symptoms in a Canadian university sample. *International Journal of Social Psychiatry, 36,* 30–41.

Dionne, M., et al. (1995). Feminist ideology as a predictor of body dissatisfaction in women. *Sex Roles, 33,* 277–287.

DiPietro, J. A. (1981). Rough and tumble play: A function of gender. *Developmental Psychology, 17,* 50–58.

Dodson, J. E. (1997). Conceptualizations of African American families. In H. P. McAdoo (Ed.), *Black families* (3rd ed., 67–82). Thousand Oaks, CA: Sage.

Donnelly, N. D. (1994). *Changing lives of refugee Hmong women.* Seattle: University of Washington Press.

Doress, P. B., & Siegal, D. L. (1987). *Ourselves, growing older: Women aging with knowledge and power.* New York: Simon & Schuster.

Doress-Worters, P. B. (1994). Adding elder care to women's multiple roles: A critical review of the caregiver stress and multiple roles literatures. *Sex Roles, 31,* 597–616.

Dorfman, L. T. (1992). Couples in retirement: Division of household work. In M. Szinovacz, D. J. Ekerdt, & B. H. Vinick (Eds.), *Families and retirement* (pp. 159–173). Newbury Park, CA: Sage.

Dotterer, C. S. (1992, April 27). Physician tells of her struggle to leave abusive husband. *American Medical News*, p. 49.

Dovidio, J. F., et al. (1988). The relationship of social power to visual displays of dominance between men and women. *Journal of Personality and Social Psychology, 54*, 233–242.

Dow, B. J. (1996). *Prime-time feminism*. Philadelphia: University of Pennsylvania Press.

Doyle, J. A. (1995). *The male experience* (3rd ed.). Madison, WI: Brown & Benchmark.

Driedger, D., Feika, I., & Batres, E. G. (Eds.). (1996). *Across borders: Women with disabilities working together*. Charlottetown, Prince Edward Island: Gynergy Books.

D'Souza, D. (1992). *Illiberal education: The politics of race and sex on campus*. New York: Vintage Books.

Dubas, J. S., Graber, J. A., & Petersen, A. C. (1991). A longitudinal investigation of adolescents' changing perceptions of pubertal timing. *Developmental Psychology, 27*, 580–586.

Dubeck, P. J., & Borman, K. (Eds.). (1996). *Women and work: A handbook*. New York: Garland.

Duck, S., & Wright, P. H. (1993). Reexamining gender differences in same-gender friendships: A close look at two kinds of data. *Sex Roles, 28*, 709–727.

Dugger, K. (1996). Social location and gender-role attitudes: A comparison of Black and White women. In E. N. Chow, D. Wilkinson, & M. B. Zinn (Eds.), *Race, class, and gender: Common bonds, different voices* (pp. 32–51). Thousand Oaks, CA: Sage.

Dunn, D. (1996). Gender and earnings. In P. J. Dubeck & K. Borman (Eds.), *Women and work: A handbook* (pp. 61–63). New York: Garland.

Dunn, D. S. (Ed.). (1994). *Psychosocial perspectives on disability*. Corte Madera, CA: Select Press.

Dunn, M. E., & Trost, J. E. (1989). Male multiple orgasms: A descriptive study. *Archives of Sexual Behavior, 18*, 377–387.

Dusek, J. B., & Flaherty, J. F. (1981). The development of self-concept during the adolescent years. *Monographs of the Society for Research in Child Development, 46*, (4, Serial No. 191). Chicago: University of Chicago Press.

Dziech, B. W., & Hawkins, M. W. (1998). *Sexual harassment in higher education: Reflections and new perspectives*. New York: Garland.

Dziech, B. W., & Weiner, L. (1990). *The lecherous professor: Sexual harassment on campus* (2nd ed.). Urbana: University of Illinois Press.

Eagly, A. H. (1987). *Sex differences in social behavior: A social-role interpretation*. Hillsdale, NJ: Erlbaum.

Eagly, A. H. (1997). Sex differences in social behavior: Comparing social role theory and evolutionary psychology. *American Psychologist, 52*, 1380–1382.

Eagly, A. H., & Carli, L. L. (1981). Sex of researchers and sex-typed communications as determinants of sex differences in influenceability: A meta-analysis of social influence studies. *Psychological Bulletin, 90*, 1–20.

Eagly, A. H., & Crowley, M. (1986). Gender and helping behavior: A meta-analytic review of the social psychological literature. *Psychological Bulletin, 100*, 283–308.

Eagly, A. H., & Diekman, A. B. (1997). The accuracy of gender stereotypes: A dilemma for feminism. *Revue Internationale de Psychologie Sociale/International Review of Social Psychology*, in press.

Eagly, A. H., & Johnson, B. T. (1990). Gender and leadership style: A meta-analysis. *Psychological Bulletin, 108*, 233–256.

Eagly, A. H., & Karau, S. J. (1991). Gender and the emergence of leaders: A meta-analysis. *Journal of Personality and Social Psychology, 60*, 685–710.

Eagly, A. H., Karau, S. J., & Makhijani, M. G. (1995). Gender and the effectiveness of leaders: A meta-analysis. *Psychological Bulletin, 117*, 125–145.

Eagly, A. H., Makhijani, M. G., & Klonsky, B. G. (1992). Gender and the evaluation of leaders: A meta-analysis. *Psychological Bulletin, 111*, 3–22.

Eagly, A. H., & Mladinic, A. (1994). Are people prejudiced against women? Some answers from research on attitudes, gender stereotypes, and judgments of competence. In W. Stroebe & M. Hewstone (Eds.), *European Review of Social Psychology*. New York: Wiley.

Eagly, A. H., Mladinic, A., & Otto, S. (1991). Are women evaluated more favorably than men? An analysis of attitudes, beliefs, and emotions. *Psychology of Women Quarterly, 15*, 203–216.

Eagly, A. H., & Wood, W. (1985). Gender and influenceability: Stereotype versus behavior. In V. E. O'Leary, R. K. Unger, & B. S. Wallston (Eds.), *Women, gender, and social psychology* (pp. 225–256). Hillsdale, NJ: Erlbaum.

Eagly, A. H., & Wood, W. (1991). Explaining sex differences in social behavior: A meta-analytic perspective. *Personality and Social Psychology Bulletin, 17,* 306–315.

Eagly, A. H., Wood, W., & Diekman, A. (in press). Social role theory of sex differences and similarities: A current appraisal. In T. Eckes & H. M. Trautner (Eds.), *The developmental social psychology of gender.* Mahwah, NJ: Erlbaum.

East, P. L., & Felice, M. E. (1996). *Adolescent pregnancy and parenting: Findings from a racially diverse sample.* Mahwah, NJ: Erlbaum.

Eaton, W. O., & Enns, L. R. (1986). Sex differences in human motor activity level. *Psychological Bulletin, 100,* 19–28.

Eberhardt, J. L., & Fiske, S. T. (1998). Affirmative action in theory and practice: Issues of power, ambiguity, and gender versus race. In D. L. Anselmi & A. L. Law (Eds.), *Questions of gender: Perspectives and paradoxes* (pp. 629–641). New York: McGraw-Hill.

Eberts, E. H., & Lepper, M. R. (1975). Individual consistency in the proxemic behavior of preschool children. *Journal of Personality and Social Psychology, 32,* 841–849.

Eccles, J. S. (1987). Gender roles and women's achievement-related decisions. *Psychology of Women Quarterly, 11,* 135–172.

Eccles, J. S. (1989). Bringing young women to math and science. In M. Crawford & M. Gentry (Eds.), *Gender and thought: Psychological perspectives* (pp. 36–58). New York: Springer-Verlag.

Eccles, J. S. (1994). Understanding women's educational and occupational choices. *Psychology of Women Quarterly, 18,* 585–609.

Eccles, J. S. (1997). User-friendly science and mathematics: Can it interest girls and minorities in breaking through the middle school wall? In D. Johnson (Ed.), *Minorities and girls in school: Effects on achievement and performance* (pp. 65–104). Thousand Oaks, CA: Sage.

Eccles (Parsons), J. S., Adler, T. F., & Kaczala, C. M. (1982). Socialization of achievement attitudes and beliefs: Parental influences. *Child Development, 53,* 310–321.

Eccles, J. S., Adler, T., & Meece, J. L. (1984). Sex differences in achievement: A test of alternate theories. *Journal of Personality and Social Psychology, 46,* 26–43.

Eccles, J. S., Jacobs, J. E., & Harold, R. D. (1990). Gender-role stereotypes, expectancy effects, and parents' socialization of gender differences. *Journal of Social Issues, 46,* 183–201.

Eccles, J. S., et al. (1993). Parents and gender-role socialization during the middle childhood and adolescent years. In S. Oskamp & M. Costanzo (Eds.), *Gender issues in contemporary society* (pp. 59–83). Newbury Park, CA: Sage.

Eccles, J. S., Wigfield, A., & Schiefele, U. (1998). Motivation to succeed. In W. Damon (Series Ed.) & N. Eisenberg (Vol. Ed.), *Handbook of child psychology: Vol. 4: Social, emotional, and personality development* (pp. 1017–1095). New York: Wiley.

Edmondson, C. B., & Conger, J. C. (1995). The impact of mode of presentation on gender differences in social perception. *Sex Roles, 32,* 169–183.

Edwards, N., & Sims-Jones, N. (1998). Smoking and smoking relapse during pregnancy and postpartum: Results of a qualitative sutdy. *Birth, 25,* 94–100.

Ehlers, T. B. (1993). Debunking marianismo: Economic vulnerability and survival strategies among Guatemalan wives. In M. Womack & J. Martl (Eds.), *The other fifty percent* (pp. 303–319). Prospect Heights, IL: Waveland Press.

Eisenberg, N., Fabes, R., & Shea, C. (1989). Gender differences in empathy and prosocial moral reasoning: Empirical investigations. In M. M. Brabeck (Ed.), *Who cares? Theory, research, and educational implications of the ethic of care* (pp. 127–143). New York: Praeger.

Eisenberg, N., & Lennon, R. (1983). Sex differences in empathy and related capacities. *Psychological Bulletin, 94,* 100–131.

Eisenberg, N., Martin, C. L., & Fabes, R. A. (1996). Gender development and gender effects. In D. C. Berliner & R. C. Calfee (Eds.), *Handbook of educational psychology* (pp. 358–396). New York: Macmillan.

Eisler, R. (1996). *Sacred pleasure: Sex, myth, and the politics of the body.* New York: HarperCollins.

Eldridge, N. S., & Gilbert, L. A. (1990). Correlates of relationship satisfaction in lesbian couples. *Psychology of Women Quarterly, 14,* 43–62.

Eliason, M. J. (1995). Accounts of sexual identity formation in heterosexual students. *Sex Roles, 32,* 821–834.

Ellis, L. (1996). Theories of homosexuality. In R. C. Savin-Williams & K. Cohen (Eds.), *The lives of lesbians, gays, and bisexuals: Children to adults* (pp. 11–34). Fort Worth, TX: Harcourt Brace.

Ellis, L., & Ebertz, L. (Eds.). (1997). *Sexual orientation: Toward biological understanding.* Westport, CT: Praeger.

Ellis, S., Barak, Z., & Pinio, A. (1991). Moderating effects of personal cognitions on experienced and perceived sexual harassment of women at the workplace. *Journal of Applied Social Psychology, 21,* 1320–1337.

Emans, S. J. (1997). Menarche and beyond—do eating and exercise make a difference? *Pediatric Annals, 26,* S137–S141.

England, E. M., & Manko, W. (1991, April). *College student evaluations of stereotypic female subcategory members.* Paper presented at the meeting of the Eastern Psychological Association, New York.

England, P. (1992). *Comparable worth: Theories and evidence.* New York: Aldine de Gruyter.

Enns, C. Z. (1997). *Feminist theories and feminist psychotherapies.* New York: Haworth.

Enns, C. Z., & Hackett, G. (1993). A comparison of feminist and nonfeminist women's and men's reactions to nonsexist and feminist counseling: A replication and extension. *Journal of Counseling and Development, 71,* 499–509.

Epstein, S. (1997). *We can make it: Stories of disabled women in developing countries.* Geneva, Switzerland: International Labour Office.

Erkut, S., Fields, J. P., Sing, R., & Marx, F. (1996). Diversity in girls' experiences: Feeling good about who you are. In B. J. R. Leadbeater & N. Way (Eds.), *Urban girls: Resisting stereotypes, creating identities* (pp. 53–64). New York: New York University Press.

Eskilson, A., & Wiley, M. G. (1996). The best teacher: Mediating effects of experience with employed women on men managers' responses to subordinates' mistakes. *Sex Roles, 34,* 237–252.

Espín, O. M. (1994). Feminist approaches. In L. Comas-Díaz & B. Greene (Eds.), *Women of color: Integrating ethnic and gender identities in psychotherapy* (pp. 265–286). New York: Guilford Press.

Espín, O. M. (1996). Immigrant and refugee lesbians. In E. D. Rothblum & L. A. Bond (Eds.), *Preventing heterosexism and homophobia* (pp. 174–183). Thousand Oaks, CA: Sage.

Espín, O. M. (1997). *Latina realities: Essays on healing, migration, and sexuality.* Boulder, CO: Westview Press.

Espinosa, P. (1997, October 3). The rich tapestry of Hispanic America is virtually invisible on commercial TV. *Chronicle of Higher Education,* p. B7.

Esterberg, K. G. (1996). Gay cultures, gay communities: The social organization of lesbians, gay men, and bisexuals. In R. C. Savin-Williams & K. Cohen (Eds.), *The lives of lesbians, gays, and bisexuals: Children to adults* (pp. 375–392). Fort Worth, TX: Harcourt Brace.

Etaugh, C. (1993a). Maternal employment: Effects on children. In J. Frankel (Ed.), *Employed mothers and the family context* (pp. 68–88). New York: Springer.

Etaugh, C. (1993b). Women in the middle and later years. In F. L. Denmark & M. A. Paludi (Eds.), *Psychology of women: A handbook of issues and theories* (pp. 213–246). Westport, CT: Greenwood Press.

Etaugh, C., & Foresman, E. (1983). Evaluations of competence as a function of sex and marital status. *Sex Roles, 9,* 759–765.

Etaugh, C., & Hoehn, S. (1995). Perceiving women: Effects of marital, parental, and occupational sex-typing variables. *Perceptual and Motor Skills, 80,* 320–322.

Etaugh, C., Levine, D., & Mennella, A. (1984). Development of sex biases in children: 40 years later. *Sex Roles, 10,* 911–922.

Etaugh, C., & Liss, M. B. (1992). Home, school, and playroom: Training grounds for adult gender roles. *Sex Roles, 26,* 129–147.

Etaugh, C., & Malstrom, J. (1981). The effect of marital status on person perceptions. *Journal of Marriage and the Family, 43,* 801–805.

Etaugh, C., & Riley, S. (1983). Evaluating competence of women and men: Effects of marital and parental status and occupational sex-typing. *Sex Roles, 9,* 943–952.

Ethier, K., & Deaux, K. (1990). Hispanics in ivy: Assessing identity and perceived threat. *Sex Roles, 22,* 427–460.

Evans, N. J., & D'Augelli, A. R. (1996). Lesbians, gay men, and bisexual people in college. In R. C. Savin-Williams & K. Cohen (Eds.), *The lives of lesbians, gays, and bisexuals: Children to adults* (pp. 201–226). Fort Worth, TX: Harcourt Brace.

Facio, E. (1997). Chicanas and aging: Toward definitions of womanhood. In J. M. Coyle (Ed.), *Handbook on women and aging* (pp. 335–350). Westport, CT: Greenwood Press.

Facteau, J. D., & Dobbins, G. H. (1996). Sex bias in performance evaluations. In P. J. Dubeck & K. Borman (Eds.), *Women and work: A handbook* (pp. 334–338). New York: Garland.

Factory wages: Airing the dirty laundry. (1997, May/June). *Ms. Magazine*, p. 21.

Facts on working women. (1998). In R. Breden (Ed.), *Perspectives: Women's studies* (pp. 3–6). Boulder, CO: Coursewise.

Fadli, M. (1995). Feminist and multi-cultural therapy. In E. F. Williams (Ed.), *Voices of feminist therapy* (pp. 95–100). Luxembourg: Harwood.

Fagot, B. I. (1978). The influence of sex of child on parental reactions to toddler children. *Child Development, 49,* 462.

Fagot, B. I. (1995). Psychological and cognitive determinants of early gender-role development. *Annual Review of Sex Research, 6,* 1–31.

Fagot, B. I., & Leinbach, M. D. (1993). Gender-role development in young children: From discrimination to labeling. *Developmental Review, 13,* 203–224.

Fagot, B. I., & Leinbach, M. D. (1994). Gender-role development in young children. In M. R. Stevenson (Ed.), *Gender roles through the life span: A multidisciplinary perspective* (pp. 3–24). Muncie, IN: Ball State University Press.

Fagot, B. I., & Leinbach, M. D. (1995). Gender knowledge in egalitarian and traditional families. *Sex Roles, 32,* 513–526.

Fagot, B. I., Leinbach, M. D., Hort, B. E., & Strayer, J. (1997). Qualities underlying the definition of gender. *Sex Roles, 37,* 1–18.

Fagot, B. I., & Rodgers, C. (1998). Gender identity. In H. Friedman (Ed.) Encyclopedia of mental health (Vol. 2, pp. 267–276). San Diego, CA: Academic Press.

Falco, K. (1998). *Reclaiming our lives after breast and gynecologic cancer.* Northvale, NJ: Jason Aronson.

Faludi, S. (1991). *Backlash: The undeclared war against American women.* New York: Crown.

Faludi, S. (1995, March/April). "I'm not a feminist, but I play one on TV." *Ms. Magazine,* pp. 31–39.

Fantham, E., et al. (1994). *Women in the classical world.* New York: Oxford University Press.

Fast, T. H., & Fast, C. C. (1995). *The women's atlas of the United States* (Rev. Ed.). New York: Facts on File.

Fausto-Sterling, A. (1985). *Myths of gender: Biological theories about women and men.* New York: Basic Books.

Fausto-Sterling, A. (1992). *Myths of gender: Biological theories about women and men* (2nd ed.). New York: Basic Books.

Favreau, O. E. (1993). Do the Ns justify the means? Null hypothesis testing applied to sex and other differences. *Canadian Psychology/Psychologie Canadienne, 34,* 64–78.

Favreau, O. E. (1997a). Evaluating political correctness: Anecdotes vs. research. *Canadian Psychology/Psychologie Canadienne, 38,* 212–220.

Favreau, O. E. (1997b). Sex and gender comparisons: Does null hypothesis testing create a false dichotomy? *Feminism & Psychology, 7,* 63–81.

Favreau, O. E., & Everett, J. C. (1996). A tale of two tails. *American Psychologist, 51,* 268–269.

Fehr, B. (1996). *Friendship processes.* Thousand Oaks, CA: Sage.

Feingold, A. (1988). Cognitive gender differences are disappearing. *American Psychologist, 43,* 95–103.

Feingold, A. (1992). Gender differences in mate selection preferences: A test of the parental investment model. *Psychological Bulletin, 112,* 125–139.

Feingold, A. (1993). Cognitive gender differences: A developmental perspective. *Sex Roles, 29,* 91–112.

Feingold, A. (1994). Gender differences in personality: A meta-analysis. *Psychological Bulletin, 116,* 429–456.

Feingold, A., & Mazzella, R. (1998). Gender differences in body image are increasing. *Psychological Science, 9,* 190–195.

Feiring, C. (1996). Concepts of romance in 15-year-old adolescents. *Journal of Research on Adolescents, 6* 181–200.

Feiring, C. (1998). Gender identity and the development of romantic relationships in adolescence. In W. Furman, B. B. Brown, & C. Feiring (Eds.), *Contemporary perspectives in adolescent romantic relationships.* Cambridge, England: Cambridge University Press.

Feiring, C., & Lewis, M. (1991). The transition from middle childhood to early adolescence: Sex differences in the social network and perceived self-competence. *Sex Roles, 24,* 489–509.

Felmlee, D. H. (1994). Who's on top? Power in romantic relationships. *Sex Roles, 31,* 275–295.

Fennema, E. (1990). Teachers' beliefs and gender differences in mathematics. In E. Fennema & G. C. Leder (Eds.), *Mathematics and gender* (pp. 169–187). New York: Teachers College Press.

Ferdig, L. A., Kelleher, J., & Keita, G. (1996). *Women in the American Psychological Association, 1995*. Washington, DC: American Psychological Association.

Fernald, J. L. (1995). Interpersonal heterosexism. In B. Lott & D. Maluso (Eds.), *The social psychology of interpersonal discrimination* (pp. 80–117). New York: Guilford Press.

Ferrato, D. (1991). *Living with the enemy*. New York: Aperture.

Ferree, M. M. (1994). Negotiating household roles and responsibilities: Resistance, conflict, and change. In M. R. Stevenson (Ed.), *Gender roles through the life span* (pp. 203–221). Muncie, IN: Ball State University.

Ferree, M. M., & Martin, P. Y. (Eds.). (1995). *Feminist organizations*. Philadelphia: Temple University Press.

Field, T. (1998). Maternal cocaine use and fetal development. In E. A. Blechman & K. D. Brownell (Eds.), *Behavioral medicine and women: A comprehensive handbook* (pp. 27–30). New York: Guilford Press.

Figert, A. E. (1996). *Women and the ownership of PMS: The structuring of a psychiatric disorder*. New York: Aldine de Gruyter.

Fincham, F. D., & Bradbury, T. N. (1990). *The psychology of marriage: Basic issues and applications*. New York: Guilford Press.

Fincham, F. D., & Bradbury, T. N. (1992). Assessing attributions in marriage: The relationship attribution measure. *Journal of Personality and Social Psychology, 62,* 457–468.

Fincham, F. D., et al. (1997). Marital satisfaction and depression: Different causal relationships for men and women? *Psychological Science, 8,* 351–357.

Fine, M. (1992). Sexuality, schooling, and adolescent females: The missing discourse of desire. In M. Fine (Ed.), *Disruptive voices: The possibilities of feminist research* (pp. 31–59). Ann Arbor: The University of Michigan Press.

Fine, M. (1997). Coping with rape: Critical perspectives on consciousness. In M. Crawford & R. Unger (Ed.), *In our own words: Readings on the psychology of women and gender* (pp. 152–164). New York: McGraw-Hill.

Fine, M., & Bowers, C. (1984). Racial self-identification: The effects of social history and gender. *Journal of Applied Social Psychology, 14,* 136–146.

Fine, M., Roberts, R. A., & Weis, L. (1998). Refusing the betrayal: Latinas redefining gender, sexuality, family and home. *Manuscript under review.*

Finkelhor, D., & Dziuba-Leatherman, J. (1994). Victimization of children. *American Psychologist, 49,* 173–183.

Firestein, B. A. (Ed.). (1996a). *Bisexuality: The psychology and politics of an invisible minority*. Thousand Oaks, CA: Sage.

Firestein, B. A. (1996b). Introduction. In B. A. Firestein (Ed.), *Bisexuality: The psychology and politics of an invisible minority* (pp. xix–xxvi). Thousand Oaks, CA: Sage.

Fischhoff, B. (1992). Giving advice: Decision theory perspectives on sexual assault. *American Psychologist, 47,* 577–588.

Fish, S. (1994). *There's no such thing as free speech, and it's a good thing too*. Oxford: Oxford University Press.

Fishel, A. H. (1995). Mental health. In C. I. Fogel & N. F. Woods (Eds.), *Women's health care: A comprehensive handbook* (pp. 323–362). Thousand Oaks, CA: Sage.

Fisher, B., & Galler, R. (1988). Friendship and fairness: How disability affects friendship between women. In M. Fine & A. Asch (Eds.), *Women with disabilities* (pp. 172–194). Philadelphia: Temple University Press.

Fisher-Thompson, D. (1990). Adult sex-typing of children's toys. *Sex Roles, 23,* 291–303.

Fisher-Thompson, D. (1993). Adult toy purchases for children: Factors affecting sex-typed toy selection. *Journal of Applied Developmental Psychology, 14,* 385–406.

Fisher-Thompson, D., Sausa, A. D., & Wright, T. E. (1995). Toy selection for children: Personality and toy request influences. *Sex Roles, 33,* 239–255.

Fiske, S. T. (1993). Social cognition and social perception. *Annual Review of Psychology, 44,* 155–194.

Fiske, S. T., et al. (1991). Social science research on trial: Use of sex stereotyping research in *Price Waterhouse v. Hopkins*. *American Psychologist, 46,* 1049–1060.

Fiske, S. T., et al. (1993). Accuracy and objectivity on behalf of the APA. *American Psychologist, 48,* 55–56.

Fiske, S. T., & Stevens, L. E. (1993). What's so special about sex? Gender stereotyping and discrimination. In S. Oskamp & M. Costanzo (Eds.), *Gender issues in contemporary society* (pp. 173–196). Newbury Park, CA: Sage.

Fiss, C. (1986). Stationary engineer. In M. M. Michelson (Ed.), *Women & Work* (pp. 108–109). Pasadena, CA: New Sage Press.

Fitzgerald, L. F., & Rounds, J. (1994). Women and work: Theory encounters reality. In W. B. Walsh & S. H. Osipow (Eds.), *Career counseling for women* (pp. 327–353). Hillsdale, NJ: Erlbaum.

Fivush, R. (1989). Exploring sex differences in the emotional content of mother-child conversations about the past. *Sex Roles, 20,* 675–691.

Fivush, R. (1998). Gendered narratives: Elaboration, structure and emotion in parent-child reminiscing across the preschool years. In C. P. Thompson et al. (Eds.), *Autobiographical memory: Theoretical and applied perspectives* (pp. 79–103). Hillsdale, NJ: Erlbaum.

Fivush, R., & Buckner, J. P. (1999). Gender, sadness and depression: Socio-cultural and developmental perspectives. In A. H. Fischer (Ed.), *Gender and emotions.* New York: Cambridge University Press.

Flanders, L. (1997). *Real majority, media minority.* Monroe, ME: Common Courage Press.

Flannagan, D., Baker-Ward, L., & Graham, L. (1995). Talk about preschool: Patterns of topic discussion and elaboration related to gender and ethnicity. *Sex Roles, 32,* 1–15.

Flannery-Schroeder, E. C., & Chrisler, J. C. (1996). Body esteem, eating attitudes, and gender-role orientation in three age groups of children: *Current Psychology, 15,* 235–248.

Floyd, R. L., Zahniser, S. C., Gunter, E. P., & Kendrick, J. S. (1991). Smoking during pregnancy: Prevalence, effects, and intervention strategies. *Birth, 18,* 48–53.

Foa, E. B. (1998). Rape and posttraumatic stress disorder. In E. A. Blechman & K. D. Brownell (Eds.), *Behavioral medicine and women: A comprehensive handbook* (pp. 742–746). New York: Guilford Press.

Fodor, I. G., & Franks, V. (1990). Women in midlife and beyond: The new prime of life? *Psychology of Women Quarterly, 14,* 445–450.

Foertsch, J., & Gernsbacher, M. A. (1997). In search of gender neutrality: Is singular *they* a cognitively efficient substitute for generic *he? Psychological Science, 8,* 106–111.

Fogel, C. I. (1995). Sexually transmitted diseases. In C. I. Fogel & N. F. Woods (Eds.), *Women's health care* (pp. 571–609). Thousand Oaks, CA: Sage.

Fogel, C. I., & Woods, N. F. (1995). Midlife women's health. In C. I. Fogel & N. F. Woods (Eds.), *Women's health care: A comprehensive handbook* (pp. 79–100). Thousand Oaks, CA: Sage.

Fontes, L. A. (Ed.). (1995). *Sexual abuse in nine North American cultures.* Thousand Oaks, CA: Sage.

Fontham, T. H., Correa, P., Reynolds, P., Wu-Williams, A., Buffler, P. A., Greenberg, R. S., Chen, V. W., Alterman, T., Boyd, P., Austin, D. F., & Liff, J. (1994). Environmental tobacco smoke and lung cancer in nonsmoking women: A multicenter study. *JAMA, 271,* 1752–1759.

Fordham, S. (1988). Racelessness as a factor in black students' school success: Pragmatic strategy or pyrrhic victory. *Harvard Educational Review, 58,* 54–84.

Forget the glamour, this trend's deadly: Lung cancer. (1998, October 5). *Toronto Globe and Mail,* p. C8.

Foubert, J. D., & Sholley, B. K. (1996). Effects of gender role, and individualized trust on self-disclosure. *Journal of Social Behavior and Personality, 11,* 277–288.

Fox, A. (1991). Development of a bisexual identity: Understanding the process. In L. Hutchins & L. Kaahumanu (Eds.), *Bi any other name: Bisexual people speak out.* Boston: Alyson Publications.

Fox, R. C. (1996). Bisexuality in perspective: A review of theory and research. In B. A. Firestein (Ed.), *Bisexuality: The psychology and politics of an invisible minority* (pp. 3–50). Thousand Oaks, CA: Sage.

Fox, R. C. (1997). Understanding bisexuality. *Society for the Psychological Study of Men and Masculinity Bulletin, 2*(4), 13–14.

Frable, D. (1987). Sex-typed execution and perception of expressive movement. *Journal of Personality and Social Psychology, 53,* 391–396.

Frances, S. J. (1979). Sex differences in nonverbal behavior. *Sex Roles, 5,* 519–535.

Frank, A. (1972). *The diary of a young girl.* New York: Pocket Books.

Franks, F., & Faux, S. A. (1990). Depression, stress, mastery, and social resources in four ethnocultural women's groups. *Research in Nursing and Health, 13,* 283–292.

Fraser, L. (1997a, July/August). Fear of fat: Why images of overweight women are taboo. *Extra!*, pp. 22–23.

Fraser, L. (1997b). *Losing it: America's obsession with weight and the industry that feeds on it.* New York: Dutton.

Fredrickson, B. L., & Roberts, T. (1997). Objectification theory: Toward understanding women's lived experiences and mental health risks. *Psychology of Women Quarterly, 21,* 173–206.

Freedman, R. (1986). *Beauty bound.* Lexington, MA: Heath.

Freedman, R. (1990). Cognitive-behavioral perspectives on body-image change. In T. F. Cash & T. Pruzinsky (Eds.), *Body images: Development, deviance and change* (pp. 272–295). New York: Guilford Press.

Freeman, J. (1989). How to discriminate against women without really trying. In J. Freeman (Ed.), *Women: A feminist perspective* (4th ed.). Palo Alto, CA: Mayfield.

Freiberg, P. (1998, February). We know how to stop the spread of AIDS: So why can't we? *APA Monitor,* p. 32.

French, M. (1992). *The war against women.* New York: Summit Books.

Freud, S. (1965). *New introductory lectures on psychoanalysis.* New York: Norton. (Original work published 1933)

Frey, C., & Hoppe-Graff, S. (1994). Serious and playful aggression in Brazilian girls and boys. *Sex Roles, 30,* 249–268.

Freyd, J. J. (1996). *Betrayal trauma: The logic of forgetting childhood abuse.* Cambridge, MA: Harvard University Press.

Freyd, J. J. (1997). Violations of power, adaptive blindness and betrayal trauma theory. *Feminism & Psychology, 7,* 22–32.

Friedan, B. (1993). *The fountain of age.* New York: Simon & Schuster.

Friedman, H. S., et al. (1995). Psychosocial and behavioral predictors of longevity. *American Psychologist, 50,* 69–78.

Friedman, R. C., & Downey, J. I. (1994). Homosexuality. *New England Journal of Medicine, 331,* 923–930.

Frieze, I. H., & McHugh, M. C. (Eds.). (1997). Measuring beliefs about appropriate roles for women and men. [Special issue]. *Psychology of Women Quarterly, 21*(1).

Frieze, I. H., Sales, E., & Smith, C. (1991). Considering the social context in gender research: The impact of college students' life stage. *Psychology of Women Quarterly, 15,* 371–392.

Frieze, I. H., Whitley, B. E., Jr., Hanusa, B. H., & McHugh, M. C. (1982). Assessing the theoretical models for sex differences in causal attributions for success and failure. *Sex Roles, 8,* 333–343.

Frigoletto, F. D., Jr., et al. (1995). A clinical trial of active management of labor. *New England Journal of Medicine, 333,* 745–750.

Fritz, H. L., & Helgeson, V. S. (1998). Distinctions of unmitigated communion from communion: Self-neglect and overinvolvement with others. *Journal of Personality and Social Psychology, 75,* 121–140.

Frodi, A., & Ahnlund, K. (1995). *Gender differences in the vulnerability to depression.* Paper presented at the convention of the Eastern Psychological Association, Boston.

Frodi, A., Macaulay, J., & Thome, P. R. (1977). Are women always less aggressive than men? A review of the experimental literature. *Psychological Bulletin, 84,* 634–660.

Fry, D. P., & Gabriel, A. H. (1994). Preface: The cultural construction of gender and aggression. *Sex Roles, 30,* 165–176.

Funk, J. B., & Buchman, D. D. (1996). Children's perceptions of gender differences in social approval for playing electronic games. *Sex Roles, 35,* 219–231.

Furman, C. S. (1995). *Turning point: The myths and realities of menopause.* New York: Oxford University Press.

Furnham, A., Abramsky, S., & Gunter, B. (1997). A cross-cultural content analysis of children's television advertisements. *Sex Roles, 37,* 91–99.

Furnham, A., & Kirkcaldy, B. (1997). Age and sex differences in health beliefs and behaviours. *Psychological Reports, 80,* 63–66.

Furnham, A., & Rawles, R. (1995). Sex differences in the estimation of intelligence. *Journal of Social Behavior and Personality, 10,* 741–748.

Furnham, A., & Singh, A. (1986). Memory for information about sex differences. *Sex Roles, 15,* 479–486.

Furnham, A., & Skae, E. (1997). Changes in the stereotypical portrayal of men and women in British television advertisements. *European Psychologist, 2,* 44–51.

Furumoto, L. (1996, August). *Reflections on gender and the character of American psychology.* Paper presented at the Annual Convention of the American Psychological Association, Toronto, Canada.

Gaeddert, W. P. (1987). The relationship of gender, gender-related traits, and achievement orientation to achievement attributions: A study of subject-selected accomplishments. *Journal of Personality, 55,* 687–710.

Galea, L. A. M., & Kimura, D. (1993). Sex differences in route-learning. *Personality and Individual Differences, 14,* 53–65.

Galinsky, E., & Bond, J. T. (1996). Work and family: The experiences of mothers and fathers in the U.S. labor force. In C. Costello & B. K. Krimgold (Eds.), *The American woman, 1996–97: Women and work.* New York: W. W. Norton.

Gallaher, P. E. (1992). Individual differences in nonverbal behavior: Dimensions of style. *Journal of Personality and Social Psychology, 63,* 133–145.

Gallant, S. J., & Keita, G. P. (1996). *Research agenda for psychosocial and behavioral factors in women's health.* Washington, DC: American Psychological Association.

Gallant, S. J., Keita, G. P., & Royak-Schaler (Eds.). (1997). *Health care for women: Psychological, social, and behavioral influences.* Washington, DC: American Psychological Association.

Gallant, S. J., Popiel, D. A., Hoffman, D. M., Chakraborty, P. K., & Hamilton, J. A. (1992). Using daily ratings to confirm premenstrual syndrome/Late Luteal Phase Dysphoric Disorder: Part II. What makes a "real" difference. *Psychosomatic Medicine, 54,* 167–181.

Gannon, L., & Ekstrom, B. (1993). Attitudes toward menopause: The influence of sociocultural paradigms. *Psychology of Women Quarterly,* 275–288.

Ganong, L. H., & Coleman, M. (1995). The content of mother stereotypes. *Sex Roles, 32,* 495–512.

Ganz, P. A. (1998). Cancer: Medical aspects. In A. Blechman & K. D. Brownell (Eds.), *Behavioral medicine and women: A comprehensive handbook* (pp. 595–603). New York: Guilford Press.

Garbarino, J., & Kostelny, K. (1992). Cultural diversity and identity formation. In J. Garbarino (Ed.), *Children and families in the social environment* (pp. 179–199). New York: Walter de Gruyter.

Garber, M. (1995). *Vice versa: Bisexuality and the eroticism of everyday life.* New York: Simon & Schuster.

Garcia, A. M. (1991). The development of Chicana feminist discourse, 1970–1980. In J. Lorber & S. A. Farrell (Eds.), *The social construction of gender* (pp. 269–287). Newbury Park, CA: Sage.

Garcia, A. M. (1995). The development of Chicana feminist discourse, 1970–1980. In A. S. López (Ed.), *Latina issues* (pp. 359–380). New York: Garland.

García-Moreno, C., Türmen, T. (1995). International perspectives on women's reproductive health. *Science, 269,* 790–792.

Gardner, W., & Wilcox, B. L. (1993). Political intervention in scientific peer review: Research on adolescent sexual behavior. *American Psychologist, 48,* 972–983.

Garfield, S. L. (1995). *Psychotherapy: An eclectic-integrative approach* (2nd ed.). New York: Wiley.

Garner, C. (1995). Infertility. In C. I. Fogel & N. F. Woods (Eds.), *Women's health care: A comprehensive handbook* (pp. 611–628). Thousand Oaks, CA: Sage.

Garnets, L. (1996). Life as a lesbian: What does gender have to do with it? In J. C. Chrisler, C. Golden, & P. D. Rozee (Eds.), *Lectures on the psychology of women* (pp. 136–151). New York: McGraw-Hill.

Garnets, L., Hancock, K. A., Cochran, S. D., Goodchilds, J., & Peplau, L. A. (1991). Issues in psychotherapy with lesbians and gay men: A survey of psychologists. *American Psychologist, 46,* 964–972.

Garnets, L., Herek, G. M., & Levy, B. (1992). Violence and victimization of lesbians and gay men: Mental health consequences. In G. Herek & K. Berrill (Eds.), *Hate crimes: Confronting violence against lesbians and gay men* (pp. 207–226). Newbury Park, CA: Sage.

Garrod, A., Smulyan, L., Powers, S., & Kilkenny, R. (1992). *Adolescent portraits.* Boston: Allyn & Bacon.

Garst, J., & Bodenhausen, G. V. (1997). Advertising's effects on men's gender role attitudes. *Sex Roles, 36,* 551–572.

Gary, L. E. (1986). Predicting interpersonal conflict between men and women: The case of Black men. *American Behavioral Scientist, 29,* 635–646.

Gash, H., & Morgan, M. (1993). School-based modifications of children's gender-related beliefs. *Journal of Applied Developmental Psychology, 14,* 277–287.

Gaspar de Alba, A. (1993). Tortillerismo: Work by Chicana lesbians. *Signs, 18,* 956–963.

Gastil, J. (1990). Generic pronouns and sexist language: The oxymoronic character of masculine generics. *Sex Roles, 23,* 629–643.

Gater, R., et al. (1998). Sex differences in the prevalence and detection of depressive and anxiety disorders in general health care settings. *Archives of General Psychiatry, 55,* 405–413.

Gates, H. L., Jr. (1997, October 20). Dole 2000: The G.O.P.'s best hope for the White House is an un-Republican named Elizabeth Dole. *New Yorker,* pp. 228–237.

Gauthier, J. (1994, Fall). Women's health research. *Psynopsis,* p. 10.

Geary, D. C. (1995). Sexual selection and sex differences in spatial cognition. *Learning and Individual Differences, 7,* 289–301.

Gee, E. M., & Kimball, M. M. (1987). *Women and aging.* Toronto: Butterworths.

Geen, R. G. (1998). Processes and personal variables in affective aggression. In R. G. Geen & E. Donnerstein (Eds.), *Human aggression: Theories, research, and implications for social policy* (pp. 1–21). San Diego, CA: Academic.

Geis, F. L. (1993). Self-fulfilling prophecies: A social psychological view of gender. In A. E. Beall & R. J. Sternberg (Eds.), *The psychology of gender* (pp. 9–54). New York: Guilford Press.

Geller, G., & Thomas, C. D. (1998, May). *A review of eating disorders among immigrant women.* Paper presented at the annual convention of the Canadian Psychological Association, Edmonton, Alberta.

Gender affects educational learning styles, researchers confirm. (1995, October). *Women in Higher Education,* p. 7.

Gender-specific pain relief. (1993, July 11). *Los Angeles Daily News,* p. C1.

Genevie, L., & Margolies, E. (1987). *The motherhood report.* New York: Macmillan.

George, T. (1988). Canadian Sikh women and menopause: A different view. *International Journal of Sociology of the Family, 18,* 297–307.

Gerbner, G. (1997). Gender and age in prime-time television. In S. Kirschner & D. A. Kirschner (Eds.), Perspectives on psychology and the media (pp. 69–94). Washington, DC: American Psychological Association.

Gerrard, M., Gibbons, F. X., & McCoy, S. B. (1993). Emotional inhibition of effective contraception. *Anxiety, Stress, and Coping, 6,* 73–88.

Gerstmann, E. A., & Kramer, D. A. (1997). Feminist identity development: Psychometric analyses of two feminist identity scales. *Sex Roles, 36,* 327–348.

Gettys, L. D., & Cann, A. (1981). Children's perceptions of occupational sex stereotypes. *Sex Roles, 7,* 301–308.

Gibbons, J. L., Hamby, B. A., & Dennis, W. D. (1997). Researching gender-role ideologies internationally and cross-culturally. *Psychology of Women Quarterly, 21,* 151–170.

Gibbons, J. L., Richter, R. R., Wiley, D. C., & Stiles, D. A. (1996). Adolescents' opposite-sex ideal in four countries. *Journal of Social Psychology, 136,* 531–537.

Gibbons, J. L., Stiles, D. A., & Shkodriani, G. M. (1991). Adolescents' attitudes toward family and gender roles: An international comparison. *Sex Roles, 25,* 625–643.

Gibbons, J. L., et al. (1993). Matching future careers to possible selves. Adolescent girls' occupational alternatives in cross-national perspective. *Comenius, 52,* 390–409.

Gilbert, D. T., & Hixon, J. G. (1991). The trouble of thinking: Activation and application of stereotypic beliefs. *Journal of Personality and Social Psychology, 60,* 509–517.

Gilbert, L. A. (1993). *Two careers/one family: The promise of gender equality.* Newbury Park, CA: Sage.

Gilbert, L. A. (1994). Current perspectives on dual-career families. *Current Directions in Psychological Science, 3,* 101–105.

Gilbert, L. A., & Scher, M. (1999). *Gender and sex in counseling and psychotherapy.* Boston: Allyn & Bacon.

Gilbert, M. C. (1996). Attributional patterns and perceptions of math and science among fifth-grade through seventh-grade girls and boys. *Sex Roles, 35,* 489–506.

Giles-Sims, J. (1983). *Wife battering: A systems theory approach.* New York: Guilford Press.

Gillespie, M. (1996, January/February). A new day is coming. *Ms. Magazine,* p. 1.

Gilligan, C. (1982). *In a different voice.* Cambridge, MA: Harvard University Press.

Gilligan, C. (1990a). Preface. In C. Gilligan, N. P. Lyons, & T. J. Hanmer (Eds.), *Making connections* (pp. 6–29). Cambridge, MA: Harvard University Press.

Gilligan, C. (1990b). Prologue. In C. Gilligan, N. P. Lyons, & T. J. Hanmer (Eds.), *Making connections* (pp. 1–5). Cambridge, MA: Harvard University Press.

Gilligan, C., Lyons, N. P., & Hanmer, T. J. (Eds.). (1990). *Making connections.* Cambridge, MA: Harvard University Press.

Ginorio, A. B., Gutiérrez, L., Cauce, A. M., & Acosta, M. (1995). Psychological issues for Latinas. In H. Landrine (Ed.), *Bringing cultural diversity to feminist psychology: Theory, research, and practice* (pp. 241–263). Washington, DC: American Psychological Association.

Gitlin, M. J. (1996). *The psychotherapist's guide to psychopharmacology* (2nd ed.). New York: Basic.

Giudice, L. C. (1998). Reproductive technologies. In E. A. Blechman & K. D. Brownell (Eds.), *Behavioral medicine and women: A comprehensive handbook* (pp. 515–519). New York: Guilford Press.

Gladue, B. A. (1994). The biopsychology of sexual orientation. *Current Directions in Psychological Science, 3,* 150–154.

Glick, P. (1991). Trait-based and sex-based discrimination in occupational prestige, occupational salary, and hiring. *Sex Roles, 25,* 351–378.

Glick, P., Diebold, J., Bailey-Werner, B., & Zhu, L. (1997). The two faces of Adam: Ambivalent sexism and polarized attitudes toward women. *Personality and Social Psychology Bulletin, 23,* 1333–1344.

Glick, P., & Fiske, S. T. (1996). The Ambivalent Sexism Inventory: Differentiating hostile and benevolent sexism. *Journal of Personality and Social Psychology, 70,* 491–512.

Glick, P., & Fiske, S. T. (1997). Hostile and benevolent sexism: Measuring ambivalent sexist attitudes toward women. *Psychology of Women Quarterly, 21,* 119–135.

Glick, P., Wilk, K., & Perreault, M. (1995). Images of occupations: Components of gender and status in occupational stereotypes. *Sex Roles, 32,* 565–582.

Goer, H. (1995). *Obstetric myths versus research realities: A guide to the medical literature.* Westport, CT: Bergin & Garvey.

Gold, D., Crombie, G., & Noble, S. (1987). Relations between teachers' judgments of girls' and boys' compliance and intellectual competence. *Sex Roles, 16,* 351–358.

Gold, M. S. (1995). *Tobacco.* New York: Plenum Press.

Goldberg, P. A. (1968). Are women prejudiced against women? *Transaction, 5,* 28–30.

Goldberg, S., & Lewis, M. (1969). Play behavior in the year-old infant: Early sex differences. *Child Development, 40,* 21–31.

Golden, C. (1996). What's in a name? Sexual self-identification among women. In R. C. Savin-Williams & K. M. Cohen (Eds.), *The lives of lesbians, gays, and bisexuals* (pp. 229–249). Fort Worth, TX: Harcourt Brace.

Goldfield, A., & Chrisler, J. C. (1995). Body stereotyping and stigmatization of obese persons by first graders. *Perceptual and Motor Skills, 81,* 909–910.

Golding, J. M. (1990). Division of household labor, strain, and depressive symptoms among Mexican Americans and non-Hispanic Whites. *Psychology of Women Quarterly, 14,* 103–117.

Golding, J. M. (1996). Sexual assault history and women's reproductive and sexual health. *Psychology of Women Quarterly, 20,* 101–121.

Golding, J. M., Cooper, M. L., & George, L. K. (1997). Sexual assault history and health perceptions: Seven general population studies. *Health Psychology, 16,* 417–425.

Golombok, S., & Fivush, R. (1994). *Gender development.* New York: Cambridge University Press.

Golub, S. (1992). *Periods: From menarche to menopause.* Newbury Park, CA: Sage.

Golub, S. (1995). *Caring for women is different.* Paper presented at the British Virgin Islands Medical Conference, Tortola, British Virgin Islands.

Gondolf, E. W. (1988). *Battered women as survivors.* Lexington, MA: Lexington Books.

Gonsiorek, J. C. (1991). The empirical basis for the demise of the illness model of homosexuality. In J. C. Gonsiorek & J. D. Weinrich (Eds.), *Homosexuality: Research implications for public policy* (pp. 115–136). Newbury Park, CA: Sage.

Gonsiorek, J. C. (1996). Mental health and sexual orientation. In R. C. Savin-Williams & K. M. Cohen (Eds.), *The lives of lesbians, gays, and bisexuals: Children to adults* (pp. 462–478). Fort Worth, TX: Harcourt Brace.

Gonzalez, J. T. (1988). Dilemmas of the high-achieving Chicana: The double-bind factor in male/female relationships. *Sex Roles, 18,* 367–380.

Goode, E. (1996). Gender and courtship entitlement: Responses to personal ads. *Sex Roles, 34,* 141–169.

Goodman, E. (1997, September 12). Working women *still* want equal pay. *San Jose Mercury News,* p. A15.

Goodman, L. A., Koss, M. P., & Russo, N. F. (1993). Violence against women: Physical and mental health effects: Part I. Research findings. *Applied & Preventive Psychology, 2,* 79–89.

Goodman, W. C. (1995). *The invisible woman: Confronting weight prejudice in America.* Carlsbad, CA: Gürze Books.

Goodwin, B. J. (1996). The impact of popular culture on images of African American women. In J. C. Chrisler, C. Golden, & P. D. Rozee (Eds.), *Lectures on the psychology of women* (pp. 182–197). New York: McGraw-Hill.

Gordon, M. (1993, Fall). Sexual slang and gender. *Women and Language, 16,* 16–21.

Gordon, M. T., & Riger, S. (1989). *The female fear: The social cost of rape.* New York: Free Press.

Gorlick, C. A. (1995). Divorce: Options available, constraints forced, pathways taken. In N. Mandell & A. Duffy (Eds.), *Canadian families: Diversity, conflict and change* (pp. 211–234). Toronto: Harcourt Brace Canada.

Gormly, A. V. (1997). *Lifespan human development* (6th ed.). Fort Worth, TX: Harcourt Brace.

Gormly, A. V., Gormly, J. B., & Weiss, H. (1987). Motivations for parenthood among young adult college students. *Sex Roles, 16,* 31–39.

Gorney, C. (1998). *Articles of faith: A frontline history of the abortion wars.* New York: Simon & Schuster.

Gose, B. (1997, May 23). Minority enrollments rose in 1995, a study finds. *Chronicle of Higher Education,* p. A38.

Gose, B. (1998, April 24). The feminization of veterinary medicine. *Chronicle of Higher Education,* pp. A55–A56.

Gostin, L. O., Lazzarini, A., Alexander, D., Brandt, A. M., Mayer, K. H., & Silverman, D. C. (1994). HIV testing, counseling, and prophylaxis after sexual assault. *JAMA, 271,* 1436–1444.

Gotlib, I. H. (1998). Postpartum depression. In E. A. Blechman & K. D. Brownell (Eds.), *Behavioral medicine and women: A comprehensive handbook* (pp. 489–494). New York: Guilford Press.

Graham, S. (1994). Classroom motivation from an attributional perspective. In H. P. O'Neil, Jr., & M. Drillings (Eds.), *Motivation: Theory and research* (pp. 31–48). Hillsdale, NJ: Erlbaum.

Grambs, J. D. (1989). *Women over forty: Visions and realities* (rev. ed.). New York: Springer.

Grana, S. J., Moore, H. A., Wilson, J. K., & Miller, M. (1993). The contexts of housework and the paid labor force: Women's perceptions of the demand levels of their work. *Sex Roles, 28,* 295–315.

Grant, C. C., Duggan, A. K., Andrews, J. S., & Serwint, J. R. (1997). The father's role during infancy. *Archives of Pediatric and Adolescent Medicine, 151,* 705–711.

Grant, J. R., & Cash, T. F. (1995). Cognitive-behavioral body image therapy: Comparative efficacy of group and modest-contact treatments. *Behavior Therapy, 26,* 69–84.

Grant, L. (1994). Helpers, enforcers, and go-betweens: Black females in elementary school classrooms. In M. Baca Zinn & B. T. Dill (Eds.), *Women of color in U.S. society* (pp. 43–63). Philadelphia: Temple University Press.

Gratch, L. V. (1997). Recognizing sexual harassment. In B. R. Sandler & R. J. Shoop (Eds.), *Sexual harassment on campus: A guide for administrators, faculty, and students* (pp. 278–292). Boston: Allyn & Bacon.

Grauerholz, E. (1987). Balancing the power in dating relationships. *Sex Roles, 17,* 563–571.

Gray, J. (1992). *Men are from Mars, women are from Venus.* New York: HarperCollins.

Green, B. L., & Kenrick, D. T. (1994). The attractiveness of gender-typed traits at different relationship levels: Androgynous characteristics may be desirable after all. *Personality and Social Psychology Bulletin, 20,* 244–253.

Green, J. M. (1993). Expectations and experiences of pain in labor: Findings from a large prospective study. *Birth, 20,* 65–72.

Green, J. M., Coupland, V. A., & Kitzinger, J. V. (1990). Expectations, experiences, and psychological outcomes of childbirth: A prospective study of 825 women. *Birth, 17,* 15–24.

Greene, B. (1994). Diversity and difference: The issue of race in feminist therapy. In M. P. Mirkin (Ed.), *Women in context: Toward a feminist reconstruction of psychotherapy* (pp. 333–351). New York: Guilford Press.

Greene, B. (1996). Lesbians and gay men of color: The legacy of ethnosexual mythologies in heterosexism. In E. D. Rothblum & L. A. Bond (Eds.), *Preventing Heterosexism and homophobia* (pp. 59–70). Thousand Oaks, CA: Sage.

Greenfeld, L. A., et al. (1998). *Violence by intimates.* Washington, DC: U.S. Department of Justice.

Greenfield, S. F. (1996). Women and substance use disorders. In M. F. Jensvold, U. Halbreich, & J. A. Hamilton (Eds.), *Psychopharmacology and women: Sex, gender, and hormones* (pp. 299–321). Washington, DC: American Psychiatric Press.

Greenspan, M. (1993). *A new approach to women and therapy* (2nd ed.). Bradenton, FL: Human Services Institute.

Greil, A. L. (1991). *Not yet pregnant: Infertile couples in contemporary America.* New Brunswick, NJ: Rutgers University Press.

Grella, C. E. (1990). Irreconcilable differences: Women defining class after divorce and downward mobility. *Gender and Society, 4,* 41–55.

Grindstaff, C. F. (1996). The costs of having a first child for women aged 33–38, Canada 1991. *Sex Roles, 35,* 137–151.

Groat, H. T., et al. (1997). Attitudes toward childbearing among young parents. *Journal of Marriage and the Family, 59,* 568–581.

Grodstein, F., et al. (1996). Postmenopausal estrogen and progestin use and the risk of cardiovascular disease. *New England Journal of Medicine, 335,* 453–461.

Grodstein, F., et al. (1997). Postmenopausal hormone therapy and mortality. *New England Journal of Medicine, 336,* 1769–1775.

Groff, J. Y., Mullen, P. D., Mongoven, M., & Burau, K. (1997). Prenatal weight gain patterns and infant birthweight associated with maternal smoking. *Birth, 24,* 234–239.

Grogan, S., Williams, Z., & Conner, M. (1996). The effects of viewing same-gender photographic models on body-esteem. *Psychology of Women Quarterly, 20,* 569–575.

Grote, N. K., & Frieze, I. H. (1994). The measurement of friendship-based love in intimate relationships. *Personal Relationships, 1,* 275–300.

Grusec, J. E., & Lytton, H. (1988). *Social development.* New York: Springer-Verlag.

Guarnaccia, P. J. (1997). Social stress and psychological distress among Latinos in the United States. In I. Al-Issa & M. Tousignant (Eds.), *Ethnicity, immigration, and psychopathology* (pp. 71–94). New York: Plenum Press.

Guinier, L., Fine, M., & Balin, J. (1997). *Becoming gentlemen: Women, law school, and institutional change.* Boston: Beacon Press.

Gunnar, M. R., & Donahue, M. (1980). Sex differences in social responsiveness between six months and twelve months. *Child Development, 51,* 262–265.

Gunter, B., & McAleer, J. (1997). *Children and television* (2nd ed.). London: Routledge.

Gunter, N. C., & Gunter, B. G. (1990). Domestic division of labor among working couples: Does androgyny make a difference? *Psychology of Women Quarterly, 14,* 355–370.

Gur, R. C., et al. (1995). Sex differences in regional cerebral glucose metabolism during a resting state. *Science, 267,* 528–530.

Gutek, B. A., & O'Connor, M. (1995). The empirical basis for the reasonable woman standard. *Journal of Social Issues, 51,* 151–166.

Guthrie, R. V. (1998). *Even the rat was white: A historical view of psychology* (2nd ed.). Boston: Allyn & Bacon.

Guy-Sheftall, B. (1996). *Women's studies: A retrospective.* New York: Ford Foundation.

Hackett, G., Enns, C. Z., & Zetzer, H. A. (1992). Reactions of women to sexist and feminist counseling: Effects of counselor orientation and mode of information delivery. *Journal of Counseling Psychology, 39,* 321–330.

Haddock, G., & Zanna, M. P. (1994). Preferring "housewives" to "feminists": Categorization and the favorability of attitudes toward women. *Psychology of Women Quarterly, 18,* 25–52.

Hafner, R. J., & Minge, P. J. (1989). Sex role stereotyping in women with agoraphobia and their husbands. *Sex Roles, 20,* 705–711.

Hafter, D. M. (1979). An overview of women's history. In M. Richmond-Abbott (Ed.), *The American woman* (pp. 1–27). New York: Holt, Rinehart and Winston.

Halberstadt, A. G., & Saitta, M. B. (1987). Gender, nonverbal behavior, and perceived dominance: A test of the theory. *Journal of Personality and Social Psychology, 53,* 257–272.

Hall, C. C. I. (1997). Cultural malpractice: The growing obsolescence of psychology with the changing U.S. population. *American Psychologist, 52,* 642–651.

Hall, C. C. I., & Crum, M. J. (1994). Women and "body-isms" in television beer commercials. *Sex Roles, 31,* 329–337.

Hall, G. C. N. (1996). *Theory-based assessment, treatment, and prevention of sexual aggression.* New York: Oxford University Press.

Hall, G. C. N., & Barongan, C. (1997). Prevention of sexual aggression: Sociocultural risk and protective factors. *American Psychologist, 52,* 5–14.

Hall, G. S. (1906). The question of coeducation. *Munsey's Magazine,* 588–592.

Hall, J. A. (1984). *Nonverbal sex differences: Communication accuracy and expressive style.* Baltimore: Johns Hopkins University Press.

Hall, J. A. (1987). On explaining gender differences: The case of nonverbal communication. In P. Shaver & C. Hendrick (Eds.), *Sex and gender* (pp. 177–200). Newbury Park, CA: Sage.

Hall, J. A. (1996). Touch, status, and gender at professional meetings. *Journal of Nonverbal Behavior, 20,* 23–44.

Hall, J. A. (1998). How big are nonverbal sex differences? The case of smiling and sensitivity to nonverbal cues. In D. J. Canary & K. Dindia (Eds.), *Sex differences and similarities in communication* (pp. 155–177). Mahwah, NJ: Erlbaum.

Hall, J. A., & Halberstadt, A. G. (1986). Smiling and gazing. In J. S. Hyde & M. C. Linn (Eds.), *The psychology of gender: Advances through meta-analysis* (pp. 136–158). Baltimore: Johns Hopkins University Press.

Hall, J. A., & Halberstadt, A. G. (1994). "Subordination" and sensitivity to nonverbal cues: A study of working women. *Sex Roles, 31,* 149–165.

Hall, J. A., & Halberstadt, A. G. (1997). Subordination and nonverbal sensitivity: A hypothesis in search of support. In M. R. Walsh (Ed.), *Women, men, and gender: Ongoing debates* (pp. 120–133). New Haven, CT: Yale University Press.

Hall, J. A., Halberstadt, A. G., & O'Brien, C. E. (1997). "Subordination" and nonverbal sensitivity: A study and synthesis of findings based on trait measures. *Sex Roles, 37,* 295–317.

Hall, J. A., et al. (1994). Gender in medical encounters: An analysis of physician and patient communication in a primary care setting. *Health Psychology, 13,* 384–392.

Hall, J. A., & Veccia, E. M. (1990). More "touching" observations: New insights on men, women, and interpersonal touch. *Journal of Personality and Social Psychology, 59,* 1155–1162.

Hall, R. M., & Sandler, B. R. (1982). *The classroom climate: A chilly one for women?* Project on the Status and Education of Women. Washington, DC: Association of American Colleges.

Hall, S. (1998). Drug abuse treatment. In E. A. Blechman & K. D. Brownell (Eds.), *Behavioral medicine and women: A comprehensive handbook* (pp. 420–424). New York: Guilford Press.

Halldórsdóttir, S., & Karlsdóttir, S I. (1996). Empowerment or discouragement: Women's experience of caring and uncaring encounters during childbirth. *Health Care for Women International, 17,* 361–379.

Hallingby, L. (1993, January/February). "Sesame Street" still no kid treat. *New Directions for Women,* p. 13.

Halpern, D. F. (1985). The influence of sex-role stereotypes on prose recall. *Sex Roles, 12,* 363–375.

Halpern, D. F. (1992). *Sex differences in cognitive abilities* (2nd ed.). Hillsdale, NJ: Erlbaum.

Halpern, D. F. (1994). Stereotypes, science, censorship, and the study of sex differences. *Feminism and Psychology, 4,* 523–530.

Halpern, D. F. (1995). Cognitive gender differences: Why diversity is a critical research issue. In H. Landrine (Ed.), *Bringing cultural diversity to feminist psychology: Theory, research, and practice* (pp. 77–92). Washington, DC: American Psychological Association.

Halpern, D. F. (Ed.). (1995–1996). Psychological and psychobiological perspectives on sex differences in cognition [Two special issues]. *Learning and Individual Differences, 7*(4) and *8*(1).

Halpern, D. F. (1996). Sex, brains, hands, and spatial cognition. *Developmental Review, 16,* 261–270.

Halpern, D. F. (1997). Sex differences in intelligence: Implications for education. *American Psychologist, 52,* 1091–1102.

Halpern, D. F., & Cass, M. (1994). Laterality, sexual orientation, and immune system functioning: Is there a relationship? *International Journal of Neuroscience, 77,* 167–180.

Hamilton, D. L., & Sherman, J. W. (1994). Stereotypes. In R. S. Wyers, Jr., & T. K. Srull (Eds.), *Handbook of social cognition: Vol. 2* (2nd ed., pp. 1–68). Hillsdale, NJ: Erlbaum.

Hamilton, D. L., Sherman, S. J., & Ruvolo, C. M. (1990). Stereotype-based expectancies: Effects on information processing and social behavior. *Journal of Social Issues, 46,* 35–60.

Hamilton, J. A., & Yonkers, K. A. (1996). Sex differences in pharmacokinetics of psychotropic medication. In M. F. Jensvold, U. Habreich, & J. A. Hamilton (Eds.), *Psychopharmacology and women: Sex, gender, and hormones* (pp. 11–42).

Hamilton, M. C. (1988). Using masculine generics: Does generic *He* increase male bias in the user's imagery? *Sex Roles, 19,* 785–799.

Hamilton, M. C. (1991a). Masculine bias in the attribution of personhood: People = male, male = people. *Psychology of Women Quarterly, 15,* 393–402.

Hamilton, M. C. (1991b). *Preference for sons or daughters and the sex role characteristics of the potential parents.* Paper presented at the meeting of the Association for Women in Psychology, Hartford, CT.

Hammerle, G. (1997). Challenging sexual stereotypes: An interview with Charlene L. Muehlenhard. *Teaching of Psychology, 24,* 64–68.

Hammond, J. A., & Mahoney, C. W. (1983). Reward-cost balancing among women coal-miners. *Sex Roles, 9,* 17–29.

Hampton, H. L. (1995). Care of the woman who has been raped. *New England Journal of Medicine, 332,* 234–237.

Hannon, R., et al. (1996). College students' judgments regarding sexual aggression during a date. *Sex Roles, 35,* 765–780.

Hansen, F. J., & Osborne, D. (1995). Portrayal of women and elderly patients in psychotropic drug advertisements. *Women & Therapy, 16,* 129–141.

Hansen, F. J., & Reekie, L. J. (1990). Sex differences in clinical judgments of male and female therapists. *Sex Roles, 23,* 51–64.

Hansson, R. O., DeKoekkoek, P. D., Neece, W. M., & Patterson, D. W. (1997). Successful aging at work: Annual review, 1992–1996: The older worker and transitions to retirement. *Journal of Vocational Behavior, 51,* 202–233.

Hardie, E. A. (1997). Prevalence and predictors of cyclic and noncyclic affective change. *Psychology of Women Quarterly, 21,* 299–314.

Hardy, J. B., & Zabin, L. S. (1991). *Adolescent pregnancy in an urban environment: Issues, programs, and evaluation.* Washington, DC: Urban Institute Press.

Hare-Mustin, R. T., & Marecek, J. (1994). Asking the right questions: Feminist psychology and sex differences. *Feminism & Psychology, 4,* 531–537.

Hare-Mustin, R. T., & Marecek, J. (1997). Abnormal and clinical psychology: Some critical perspectives. In D. Fox & I. Prilleltensky (Eds.), *Abnormal and clinical psychology: Some critical perspectives* (pp. 105–120). London: Sage.

Hargreaves, D. J. (1977). Sex roles in divergent thinking. *British Journal of Educational Psychology, 47,* 25–32.

Harney, P. A., & Muehlenhard, C. L. (1991). Rape. In E. Grauerholz & M. A. Koralewski (Eds.), *Sexual coercion* (pp. 3–15). Lexington, MA: Lexington Books.

Harris, F. (1996). *About my sister's business: The Black woman's road map to successful entrepreneurship.* New York: Fireside.

Harris, M. B., & Knight-Bohnhoff, K. (1996). Gender and aggression II: Personal aggressiveness. *Sex Roles, 35,* 27–42.

Harris, M. G. (1994). Cholas, Mexican-American girls, and gangs. *Sex Roles, 30,* 289–301.

Harris, R. J. (1994). The impact of sexually explicit media. In J. Bryant & D. Zillmann (Eds.), *Media effects: Advances in theory and research* (pp. 247–272). Hillsdale, NJ: Erlbaum.

Hartmann, L. C., et al. (1999). Efficacy of bilateral prophylactic mastectomy in women with a family history of breast cancer. *The New England Journal of Medicine, 340,* 77–84.

Hartstein, N. B. (1996). Suicide risk in lesbian, gay, and bisexual youth. In R. P. Cabaj & T. S. Stein (Eds.), *Textbook of homosexuality and mental health* (pp. 819–837). Washington, DC: American Psychiatric Press.

Haseltine, F. P. (1997). Conclusion. In F. P. Haseltine & B. G. Jacobson (Eds.), *Women's health research: A medical and policy primer* (pp. 331–336). Washington, DC: Health Press.

Hashizume, L., Greggs, R., & Cairns, K. V. (1994). Feminist practice in counsellor education: Student and faculty experience. In J. Gallivan, S. D. Crozier, & V. M. Lalande (Eds.), *Women, girls, and achievement* (pp. 170–184). North York, Ontario: Captus University Publications.

Haskell, M. (1997). *Holding my own in no man's land: Women and men and film and feminists.* New York: Oxford University Press.

Haskins, R. (1985). Public aggression among children with varying day care experience. *Child Development, 56,* 689–703.

Haslett, B. J., Geis, F. L., & Carter, M. R. (1992). *The organizational woman: Power and paradox.* Norwood, NJ: ABLEX.

Hatch, L. R. (1995). Gray clouds and silver linings: Women's resources in later life. In J. Freeman (Ed.), *Women: A feminist perspective* (pp. 182–196). Mountain View, CA: Mayfield.

Hatcher, M. A. (1991). The corporate woman of the 1990s: Maverick or innovator? *Psychology of Women Quarterly, 15,* 251–259.

Hatcher, R. A., & Trussell, J. (1994). Contraceptive implants and teenage pregnancy. *New England Journal of Medicine, 331,* 1229–1230.

Hatfield, E., & Rapson, R. L. (1993). *Love, sex, and intimacy: Their psychology, biology, and history.* New York: HarperCollins.

Hatfield, E., & Rapson, R. L. (1996). *Love and sex: Cross-cultural perspectives.* Boston: Allyn & Bacon.

Hatfield, E., & Sprecher, S. (1995). Men's and women's preferences in marital partners in the United States, Russia, and Japan. *Journal of Cross-Cultural Psychology, 26,* 728–750.

Havens, B., & Swenson, I. (1988). Imagery associated with menstruation in advertising targeted to adolescent women. *Adolescence, 23,* 91–97.

Hawkins, B. D. (1994, November 3). An evening with Gwendolyn Brooks. *Black Issues in Higher Education,* pp. 16–21.

Hawkins, B. D. (1996, July 11). Gender gap. *Black Issues in Higher Education,* pp. 20–22.

Hawkins, J. W., & Aber, C. S. (1988). The content of advertisements in medical journals: Distorting the image of women. *Women & Health, 14,* 43–59.

Hawkins, J. W., & Aber, C. S. (1993). Women in advertisements in medical journals. *Sex Roles, 28,* 233–242.

Hayes, N. (1994). *Principles of comparative psychology.* Hillsdale, NJ: Erlbaum.

Hays, S. (1996). *The cultural contradictions of motherhood.* New Haven: Yale University Press.

Headlee, S., & Elfin, M. (1996). *The cost of being female.* New York: Praeger.

Healey, S. (1993). Confronting ageism: A MUST for mental health. *Women & Therapy, 14,* 41–54.

Heatherington, L. (1993). Two investigations of "female modesty" in achievement situations. *Sex Roles, 29,* 739–754.

Hebl, M. R., & Heatherton, T. F. (1998). The stigma of obesity in women: The difference is Black and White. *Personality and Social Psychology Bulletin, 24,* 417–426.

Hedges, L., & Nowell, A. (1995). Sex differences in mental test scores, variability, and numbers of high-scoring individuals. *Science, 269,* 41–45.

Hedley, M. (1994). The presentation of gendered conflict in popular movies: Affective stereotypes, cultural sentiments, and men's motivation. *Sex Roles, 31,* 721–740.

Heffernan, K. (1998). Bulimia nervosa. In E. A. Blechman & K. D. Brownell (Eds.), *Behavioral medicine and women: A comprehensive handbook* (pp. 358–363). New York: Guilford Press.

Heilbrun, A. B., & Mulqueen, C. M. (1987). The second androgyny: A proposed revision in adaptive priorities for college women. *Sex Roles, 17,* 187–207.

Hein, K. (1998). Aligning science with politics and policy in HIV prevention. *Science, 280,* 1905–1906.

Heise, L. (1991, December 16–22). Assaulted first by the rapist, then by societal response. *The Washington Post National Weekly Edition,* p. 23.

Heitner, K. (1998, Summer). Backtalk. *Division 35 Newsletter,* p. 14.

Helgeson, V. C. (1994). Long-distance romantic relationships: Sex differences in adjustment and breakup. *Personality and Social Psychology Bulletin, 20,* 254–265.

Helgeson, V. S., & Fritz, H. L. (1998). Distinctions of unmitigated communion from communion: Self-neglect and overinvolvement with others. *Personality and Social Psychology Review, 75,* 121–140.

Helstrom, A. W., Coffey, C., & Jorgannathan, P. (1998). Asian-American women's health. In A. Blechman & K. D. Brownell (Eds.), *Behavioral medicine and women: A comprehensive handbook* (pp. 826–832). New York: Guilford Press.

Henderson, N. (1998, February). Managed care is toughest on women doctors. *Medical Economics,* pp. 28–32.

Hendrick, C., & Hendrick, S. (1996). Gender and the experience of heterosexual love. In J. T. Wood (Ed.), *Gendered relationships* (pp. 131–148). Mountain View, CA: Mayfield.

Henley, N. M. (1977). *Body politics.* Englewood Cliffs, NJ: Prentice-Hall.

Henley, N. M. (1985). Psychology and gender. *Signs, 11,* 101–119.

Hennig, M., & Jardim, A. (1977). *The managerial woman.* New York: Pocket Books.

Henrie, R. L., Aron, R. H., Nelson, B. D., & Poole, D. A. (1997). Gender-related kowledge variations within geography. *Sex Roles, 36,* 605–623.

Henrion, C. (1997). *Women in mathematics: The addition of difference.* Bloomington: The University of Indiana Press.

Herbert, S. E. (1996). Lesbian sexuality. In R. P. Cabaj & T. S. Stein (Eds.), *Textbook of homosexuality and mental health* (pp. 723–742). Washington, DC: American Psychiatric Press.

Herek, G. M. (1990). Gay people and government security clearances: A social science perspective. *American Psychologist, 45,* 1035–1042.

Herek, G. M. (1993). Sexual orientation and military service: A social science perspective. *American Psychologist, 48,* 538–549.

Herek, G. M. (1994). Heterosexism, hate crimes, and the law. In M. Costanzo & S. Oskamp (Eds.), *Violence and the law* (pp. 89–112). Thousand Oaks, CA: Sage.

Herek, G. M. (1996). Why tell if you're not asked? Self-disclosure, intergroup contact, and heterosexuals' attitudes toward lesbians and gay men. In G. M. Herek, J. B. Jobe, & R. M. Carney (Eds.), *Out in force: Sexual orientation and the military* (pp. 197–225). Chicago: University of Chicago Press.

Herek, G. M., Cogan, J. C., Gillis, J. R., & Glunt, E. K. (1998). Correlates of internalized homophobia in a community sample of lesbians and gay men. *Journal of the Gay and Lesbian Medical Association, Vol. 2,* 17–25.

Herek, G. M., Kimmel, D. C., Amaro, H., & Melton, G. B. (1991). Avoiding heterosexist bias in psychological research. *American Psychologist, 46,* 957–963.

Herlitz, A., Nilsson, L., & Bäckman, L. (1997). Gender differences in episodic memory. *Memory & Cognition, 25,* 801–811.

Herman-Giddens, M. E., et al. (1997). Secondary sexual characteristics and menses in young girls seen in office practice: A study from the pediatric research in office settings network. *Pediatrics, 99,* 505–512.

Herrmann, D. J., Crawford, M., & Holdsworth, M. (1992). Gender-linked differences in everyday memory performance. *British Journal of Psychology, 83,* 221–231.

Hesse-Biber, S. (1998). Am I thin enough yet? In P. S. Rothenberg (Ed.), *Race, class, and gender in the United States: An integrated study* (4th ed., pp. 489–497). New York: St. Martin's Press.

Hickman, S. E., & Muehlenhard, C. L. (1997). College women's fears and precautionary behaviors relating to acquaintance rape and stranger rape. *Psychology of Women Quarterly, 21,* 527–547.

Hidalgo, H. (1995). The norms of conduct in social service agencies: A threat to the mental health of Puerto Rican lesbians. *Journal of Gay & Lesbian Social Services, 3,* 23–41.

Higginbotham, A. (1996, March/April). Teen mags: How to get a guy, drop 20 pounds, and lose your self-esteem. *Ms. Magazine,* pp. 84–87.

Higginbottom, S. F., Barling, J., & Kelloway, E. K. (1993). Linking retirement experiences and marital satisfaction: A mediational model. *Psychology and Aging, 8,* 508–516.

Hillyer, B. (1993). *Feminism and disability.* Norman: University of Oklahoma Press.

Hilton, J. L., & von Hippel, W. (1996). Stereotypes. *Annual Review of Psychology, 47,* 237–271.

Hines, M., & Kaufman, F. R. (1994). Androgen and the development of human sex-typical behavior: Rough-and-tumble play and sex of preferred playmates in children with congenital adrenal hyperplasia (CAH). *Child Development, 65,* 1042–1053.

Hines, N. J., & Fry, D. P. (1994). Indirect modes of aggression among women of Buenos Aires, Argentina. *Sex Roles, 30,* 213–236.

Ho, C. K. (1997). An analysis of domestic violence in Asian American Communities: A multicultural approach to counseling. In K. P. Monteiro (Ed.), *Ethnicity and psychology* (pp. 138–152). Dubuque, IA: Kendall/Hunt.

Hochschild, A. R. (1997). *The time bind.* New York: Henry Holt.

Hoctor, M. A. (1993). *Personal communication.*

Hoff, L. (1990). *Battered women as survivors.* London: Routledge.

Hoffman, L. W., & Kloska, D. D. (1995). Parents' gender-based attitudes toward marital roles and child rearing: Development and validation of new measures. *Sex Roles, 32,* 273–295.

Hoffman, M. A. (1996). *Counseling clients with HIV disease: Assessment, intervention, and prevention.* New York: Guilford Press.

Hoffman, P. H., & Hale-Benson, J. (1987). Self-esteem of Black middle-class women who choose to work inside or outside the home. *Journal of Multicultural Counseling and Development, 15,* 71–80.

Hoffnung, M. (1988). Teaching about motherhood: Close kin and the transition to motherhood. *Women's Studies Quarterly, 16,* 48–57.

Hoffnung, M. (1992). *What's a mother to do? Conversations on work and family.* Pasadena, CA: Trilogy.

Hoffnung, M. (1993). *College women's expectations for work and family.* Poster presented at the meeting of the Association for Women in Psychology, Atlanta, GA.

Hoffnung, M. (1995). Motherhood: Contemporary conflict for women. In J. Freeman (Ed.), *Women: A feminist perspective* (pp. 162–181). Mountain View, CA: Mayfield.

Hofmeyr, G. J., Marcos, E. F., & Butchart, A. M. (1990). Pregnant women's perceptions of themselves: A survey. *Birth, 17,* 205–206.

Holcomb, L. P., & Giesen, C. B. (1995). Coping with challenges: College experiences of older women and women with disabilities. In J. C. Chrisler & A. H. Hemstreet (Eds.), *Variations on a theme: Diversity and the psychology of women* (pp. 175–199). Albany: State University of New York Press.

Holden, S. L. (1997). *Older women in undergraduate introductory psychology textbooks.* Paper presented at the annual meeting of the American Psychological Association, Chicago.

Holland, D. C., & Eisenhart, M. A. (1990). *Educated in romance: Women, achievement, and college culture.* Chicago: University of Chicago Press.

Holland, J. L. (1992). *Making vocational choices: A theory of vocational personalities and work environments* (2nd ed.). Odessa, FL: Psychological Assessment Resources.

Hollingworth, L. S. (1914). Functional periodicity: An experimental study of mental and motor abilities of women during menstruation. *Teachers College, Columbia University. Contributions to Education, No. 69,* pp. *v*-14, 86–101.

Holms, V. L., & Esses, L. M. (1988). Factors influencing Canadian high school girls' career motivation. *Psychology of Women Quarterly, 12,* 313–328.

Hood, A. (1995). It's a wonderful divorce. In P. Kaganoff & S. Spano (Eds.), *Women and divorce* (pp. 119–133). New York: Harcourt Brace.

hooks, b. (1989). *Talking back: Thinking feminist, thinking Black.* Boston: South End.

hooks, b. (1993, October). Confronting sexism in Black life: The struggle continues. *Z Magazine,* pp. 36–39.

hooks, b. (1994, July 13). Black students who reject feminism. *Chronicle of Higher Education,* p. A44.

Horgan, D. (1983). The pregnant woman's place and where to find it. *Sex Roles, 9,* 333–339.

Horner, M. S. (1968). *Sex differences in achievement motivation and performance in competitive and non-competitive situations.* Unpublished doctoral dissertation, University of Michigan.

Horner, M. S. (1978). The measurement and behavioral implications of fear of success in women. In J. W. Atkinson & J. O. Raynor (Eds.), *Personality, motivation, and achievement* (pp. 41–70). Washington, DC: Hemisphere.

Hosking, D., et al. (1998). Prevention of bone loss with alendronate in postmenopausal women under 60 years of age. *New England Journal of Medicine, 338,* 485–491.

Hotaling, S. (1994). *A matter of equity: Gender role portrayals on network television commercials.* Unpublished manuscript, State University of New York at Geneseo.

Houser, B. B., & Garvey, C. (1985). Factors that affect nontraditional vocational enrollment among women. *Psychology of Women Quarterly, 9,* 105–117.

Houston, B. (1989). Prolegomena to future caring. In M. M. Brabeck (Ed.), *Who cares? Theory, research, and educational implications of the ethic of care* (pp. 84–100). New York: Praeger.

Houston, S., & Hwang, N. (1996). Correlates of the objective and subjective experiences of sexual harassment in high school. *Sex Roles, 34,* 189–204.

Howard, J. A., & Hollander, J. (1997). *Gendered situations, gendered selves.* Thousand Oaks, CA: Sage.

Hu, S. M. (1988). The Chinese family: Continuity and change. In B. Birns & D. F. Hay (Eds.), *The different faces of motherhood* (pp. 119–135). New York: Plenum Press.

Hull, D. B., Forrester, L., Hull, J. H., & Gaines, M. (1992). How to avoid date rape: College students' perceptions. In J. C. Chrisler & D. Howard (Eds.), *New directions in feminist psychology: Practice, theory, and research* (pp. 188–199). New York: Springer.

Humes, C. W., Szymanski, E. M., & Hohenshil, T. H. (1995). Roles of counseling in enabling persons with disabilities. In R. R. Atkinson & G. Hackett (Eds.), *Counseling diverse populations* (pp. 155–166). Madison, WI: Brown & Benchmark.

Humm, M. (1995). *The dictionary of feminist theory* (2nd ed.). Columbus, OH: Ohio State University.

Hummert, M. L., Garstka, T. A., & Shaner, J. L. (1997). Stereotyping of older adults: The role of target facial cues and perceiver characteristics. *Psychology and Aging, 12,* 107–114.

Hunter College Women's Studies Collective. (1995). *Women's realities, women's choices* (2nd ed.). New York: Oxford University Press.

Hurtz, W., & Durkin, K. (1997). Gender role stereotyping in Australian Radio commercials. *Sex Roles, 36,* 103–114.

Husten, C. G. (1998). Cigarette smoking. In E. A. Blechman & K. D. Brownell (Eds.), *Behavioral medicine and women: A comprehensive handbook* (pp. 425–430). New York: Guilford Press.

Huston, R. (1997). *A positive life: Portraits of women living with HIV.* Philadelphia: Running Press.

Huttenlocher, J., et al. (1991). Early vocabulary growth: Relation to language input and gender. *Developmental Psychology, 27,* 236–248.

Hyde, J. S. (1981). How large are cognitive gender differences? A meta-analysis using w^2 and d. *American Psychologist, 36,* 892–901.

Hyde, J. S. (1984). How large are gender differences in aggression? A developmental meta-analysis. *Developmental Psychology, 20,* 722–736.

Hyde, J. S. (1986). Gender differences in aggression. In J. S. Hyde & M. C. Linn (Eds.), *The psychology of gender: Advances through meta-analysis* (pp. 51–66). Baltimore: Johns Hopkins University Press.

Hyde, J. S. (1996a). Gender and cognition: A commentary on current research. *Learning and Individual Differences, 8,* 33–38.

Hyde, J. S. (1996b). Where are the gender differences? Where are the gender similarities? In D. M. Buss & Neil M. Malamuth (Eds.), *Sex, power, conflict: Evolutionary and feminist perspectives* (pp. 107–118). New York: Oxford University Press.

Hyde, J. S. (1997). Gender differences in math performance: Not big, not biological. In M. R. Walsh (Ed.), *Women, men, and gender: Ongoing debates* (pp. 283–287). New Haven, CT: Yale University Press.

Hyde, J. S., & DeLamater, J. (1997). *Understanding human sexuality* (6th ed.). New York: McGraw-Hill.

Hyde, J. S., Fennema, E., Ryan, M., Frost, L. A., & Hopp, C. (1990). Gender comparisons of mathematics attitudes and affect: A meta-analysis. *Psychology of Women Quarterly, 14,* 299–324.

Hyde, J. S., & Linn, M. C. (1988). Gender differences in verbal ability: A meta-analysis. *Psychological Bulletin, 104,* 53–69.

Hyde, J. S., & McKinley, N. M. (1997). Gender differences in cognition: Results from meta-analyses. In P. J. Caplan, M. Crawford, J. S. Hyde, & J. T. E. Richardson (Eds.), *Gender differences in human cognition* (pp. 30–51). New York: Oxford University Press.

Hyde, J. S., & Plant, E. A. (1995). Magnitude of psychological gender differences: Another side to the story. *American Psychologist, 50,* 159–161.

Hynie, M., Lydon, J. E., & Taradash, A. (1997). Commitment, intimacy, and women's perceptions of premarital sex and contraceptive readiness. *Psychology of Women Quarterly, 21,* 447–464.

Idle, T., Wood, E., & Desmarais, S. (1993). Gender role socialization in toy play situations: Mothers and fathers with their sons and daughters. *Sex Roles, 28,* 679–691.

Ineichen, B., Pierce, M., & Lawrenson, R. (1997). Teenage mothers as breastfeeders: Attitudes and behavior. *Journal of Adolescence, 20,* 505–509.

Ingstad, B., & Whyte, S. R. (Eds.). (1995). *Disability and culture.* Berkeley: Univesity of California Press.

Intons-Peterson, M. J., & Reddel, M. (1984). What do people ask about a neonate? *Developmental Psychology, 20,* 358–359.

Ireland, M. S. (1993). *Reconceiving women: Separating motherhood from female identity.* New York: Guilford Press.

Irish, J. T., & Hall, J. A. (1995). Interruptive patterns in medical visits: The effects of role, status and gender. *Social Science & Medicine, 41,* 873–881.

Irvine, J. M. (1990). *Disorders of desire: Sex and gender in modern American sexology.* Philadelphia: Temple University Press.

Ivins, M. (1997, September 27). Teen mothers lack good role models. *Liberal Opinion Week,* p. 12.

Ivy, D. K., et al. (1995). The lawyer, the babysitter, and the student: Inclusive language usage and instruction. *Women and Language, 18,* 13–21.

Jacklin, C. N. (1983). Methodological issues in the study of sex-related differences. In B. L. Richardson & J. Wirtenberg (Eds.), *Sex role research* (pp. 93–100). New York: Praeger.

Jacklin, C. N., & Baker, L. A. (1993). Early gender development. In S. Oskamp & M. Costanzo (Eds.), *Gender issues in contemporary society* (pp. 41–57). Newbury Park, CA: Sage.

Jacklin, C. N., DiPietro, J. A., & Maccoby, E. E. (1984). Sex-typing behavior and sex-typing pressure in child/parent interaction. *Archives of Sexual Behavior, 13,* 413–425.

Jacklin, C. N., & Maccoby, E. E. (1983). Issues of gender differentiation. In M. D. Levine, W. B. Carey, A. C. Crocker, & R. T. Gross (Eds.), *Developmental-behavioral pediatrics* (pp. 175–184). Philadelphia: Saunders.

Jacklin, C. N., & Reynolds, C. (1993). Gender and childhood socialization. In A. E. Beall & R. J. Sternberg (Eds.), *The psychology of gender* (pp. 197–214). New York: Guilford Press.

Jackson, B. B. (1992). Black women's responses to menarche and menopause. In A. J. Dan & L. L. Lewis (Eds.), *Menstrual health in women's lives* (pp. 178–190). Urbana: University of Illinois Press.

Jackson, D. (1992). *How to make the world a better place for women in five minutes a day.* New York: Hyperion.

Jackson, D. Z. (1998, April 27). Women on welfare need education—Why deny them? *Liberal Opinion,* p. 1.

Jackson, L. A., Fleury, R. E., Girvin, J. L., & Gerard, D. A. (1995). *Sex Roles, 33,* 559–568.

Jackson, L. A., Fleury, R. E., & Lewandowski, D. A. (1996). Feminism: Definition, support, and correlates of support among female and male college students. *Sex Roles, 34,* 687–693.

Jackson, L. A., Hodge, C. N., & Ingram, J. M. (1994). Gender and self-concept: A reexamination of stereotypic differences and the role of gender attitudes. *Sex Roles, 30,* 615–630.

Jackson, L. A., & McGill, O. D. (1996). Body type preferences and body characteristics associated with attractive and unattractive bodies by African Americans and Anglo Americans. *Sex Roles, 35,* 295–307.

Jackson, S. A. (1998). "Something about the word": African American women and feminism. In K. M. Blee (Ed.), *No middle ground: Women and radical protest* (pp. 38–50). New York: New York University Press.

Jackson, T. L., & Petretic-Jackson, P. A. (1996). Introduction: The definition, incidence, and scope of acquaintance rape and sexual assault. In T. L. Jackson (Ed.), *Acquaintance rape: Assessment, treatment, and prevention* (pp. 1–15). Sarasota, FL: Professional Resource Press.

Jacobs, J. A. (1995a). Women's entry into management: Trends in earnings, authority, and values among salaried managers. In J. A. Jacobs (Ed.), *Gender inequality at work* (pp. 152–177). Thousand Oaks, CA: Sage.

Jacobs, J. A. (1995b). *Gender inequality at work.* Thousand Oaks, CA: Sage.

Jacobs, R. H. (1997). *Be an outrageous older woman.* New York: HarperCollins.

Jacobson, N. S., & Gottman, J. M. (1998). *When men batter women.* New York: Simon & Schuster.

James, E. M. (1994). *Helen Thompson Woolley: Forgotten pioneer of the psychology of women.* Paper presented at the annual convention of the American Psychological Association, Los Angeles.

James, J. B. (1997). What are the social issues involved in focusing on *difference* in the study of gender? *Journal of Social Issues, 53,* 213–232.

Janoff-Bulman, R. (1992). *Shattered assumptions: Toward a new psychology of trauma.* New York: Free Press.

Janus, S. S., & Janus, C. L. (1993). *The Janus report on sexual behavior.* New York: Wiley.

Jaschik-Herman, M. L., & Fisk, A. (1995). Women's perceptions and labeling of sexual harassment in academia before and after the Hill-Thomas hearings. *Sex Roles, 33,* 439–446.

Jay, T. (1992). *Cursing in America.* Philadelphia: John Benjamins.

Jenkins, M. R., & Culbertson, J. L. (1996). Prenatal exposure to alcohol. In R. L. Adams et al. (Eds.), *Neuropsychology for clinical practice.* Washington, DC: American Psychological Association.

Jenkins, S. R. (1994). Need for power and women's careers over 14 years: Structural power, job satisfaction, and motive change. *Journal of Personality and Social Psychology, 66,* 155–165.

Jennings, J., Geis, L., & Brown, V. (1980). Influence of television commercials on women's self-confidence and independent judgments. *Journal of Personality and Social Psychology, 38,* 203–210.

Jensen-Campbell, L. A., Graziano, W. G., & West, S. G. (1995). Dominance, prosocial orientation, and female preferences: Do nice guys really finish last? *Journal of Personality and Social Psychology, 68,* 427–440.

John, D., & Shelton, B. A. (1997). The production of gender among Black and White women and men: The case of household labor. *Sex Roles, 36,* 171–193.

John, R., Blanchard, P. H., & Hennessy, C. H. (1997). Hidden lives: Aging and contemporary American Indian women. In J. M. Coyle (Ed.), *Handbook on women and aging* (pp. 290–315). Westport, CT: Greenwood Press.

Johnson, B. E., Kuck, D. L., & Schander, P. R. (1997). Rape myth acceptance and sociodemographic characteristics: A multidimensional analysis. *Sex Roles, 36,* 693–707.

Johnson, C. (1994). Gender, legitimate authority, and leader-subordinate conversations. *American Sociological Review, 59,* 122–135.

Johnson, C. L., & Barer, B. M. (1997). *Life beyond 85 years: The aura of survivorship.* New York: Springer.

Johnson, F. L. (1996). Friendships among women: Closeness in dialogue. In J. T. Wood (Ed.), *Gendered relationships* (pp. 79–94). Mountain View, CA: Mayfield.

Johnson, J., & Bytheway, B. (1993). Ageism: Concept and definition. In J. Johnson & R. Slater (Eds.), *Ageing and later life* (pp. 200–206). London: Sage.

Johnson, J. D., Adams, M. S., Ashburn, L., & Reed, W. (1995). Differential gender effects of exposure to rap music on African American adolescents' acceptance of teen dating violence. *Sex Roles, 33,* 597–605.

Johnson, J. D., et al. (1997). Perceptual ambiguity, gender, and target intoxication: Assessing the effects of factors that moderate perceptions of sexual harassment. *Journal of Applied Social Psychology, 27,* 1209–1221.

Johnson, L. B. (1997). Three decades of Black family empirical research: Challenges for the 21st century. In H. P. McAdoo (Ed.), *Black families* (3rd ed., pp. 94–113). Thousand Oaks, CA: Sage.

Johnson, M. E., & Dowling-Guyer, S. (1996). Effects of inclusive vs. exclusive language on evaluations of the counselor. *Sex Roles, 34,* 407–418.

Johnson, S. R. (1995). Menstruation. In M. W. O'Hara, et al. (Eds.). *Psychological aspects of women's reproductive health* (pp. 3–25). New York: Springer.

Johnson, T. L., & Fee, E. (1997). Women's health research: An introduction. In F. P. Haseltine & B. G. Jacobson (Eds.), *Women's health research: A medical and policy primer* (pp. 3–26). Washington, DC: Health Press International.

Joiner, T. E., Jr., & Blalock, J. A. (1995). Gender differences in depression: The role of anxiety and generalized negative affect. *Sex Roles, 33,* 91–108.

Jones, M. (1991). Gender stereotyping in advertisements. *Teaching of Psychology, 18,* 231–233.

Jordan, J. V. (1997). The relational model is a source of empowerment for women. In M. R. Walsh (Ed.), *Women, men, and gender: Ongoing debates* (pp. 373–379). New Haven, CT: Yale University Press.

Jordan, J. V. (1998). Empathy, mutuality, and therapeutic change: Clinical implications of a relational model. In B. M. Clinchy & J. K. Norem (Eds.), *The gender and psychology reader* (pp. 543–548). New York: New York University Press.

Joseph, J. (1997). Woman battering: A comparative analysis of Black and White women. In G. K. Kantor & J. L. Jasinski (Eds.), *Out of the darkness: Contemporary perspectives on family violence* (pp. 161–169). Thousand Oaks, CA: Sage.

Josselson, R. (1996). *Revising herself: The story of women's identity from college to midlife.* New York: Oxford University Press.

Jurgens, J. J., & Powers, B. A. (1991). An exploratory study of the menstrual euphemisms, beliefs, and taboos of Head Start mothers. In D. L. Taylor & N. F. Woods (Eds.), *Menstruation, health, and illness* (pp. 35–40). New York: Hemisphere.

Jutras, S., & Veilleux, F. (1991). Gender roles and care giving to the elderly: An empirical study. *Sex Roles, 25,* 1–18.

Kaganoff, P., & Spano, S. (Eds.). (1995). *Women and divorce.* New York: Harcourt Brace.

Kagawa-Singer, M., Hikoyeda, N., & Tanjasiri, S. P. (1997). Aging, chronic conditions, and physical disabilities in Asian and Pacific Islander Americans. In K. S. Markides & M. R. Miranda (Eds.), *Minorities, aging, and health* (pp. 149–180). Thousand Oaks, CA: Sage.

Kahn, A. S., & Andreoli Mathie, V. (1999). Sexuality, society, and feminism: Psychological perspectives on women. In C. B. Travis & J. W. White (Eds.), *Sexuality, society, and feminism: Psychological perspectives on women.* Washington, DC: American Psychological Association.

Kahn, A. S., & Yoder, J. D. (1989). The psychology of women and conservatism. *Psychology of Women Quarterly, 13,* 417–432.

Kahn, R. L. (1991). The forms of women's work. In M. Frankenhaeuser, U. Lundberg, & M. Chesney (Eds.), *Women, work, and health: Stress and opportunities* (pp. 65–83). New York: Plenum Press.

Kail, R. V., Jr., Carter, P., & Pellegrino, J. (1979). The locus of sex differences in spatial ability. *Perception & Psychophysics, 26,* 182–186.

Kalichman, S. C. (1989). The effects of stimulus context on paper-and-pencil spatial task performance. *Journal of General Psychology, 116,* 133–139.

Kalichman, S. C. (1996). *Answering your questions about AIDS.* Washington, DC: American Psychological Association.

Kalichman, S. C., & Sikkema, K. J. (1994). Psychological sequelae of HIV infection and AIDS: Review of empirical findings. *Clinical Psychology Review, 14,* 611–632.

Kantrowitz, B. (1987, February 16). Kids and contraceptives. *Newsweek,* pp. 54–65.

Kanuha, V. (1994). Women of color in battering relationships. In L. Comas-Díaz & B. Greene (Eds.), *Women of color* (pp. 428–454). New York: Guilford Press.

Kaplan, A. G., Gleason, N., Klein, R. (1991). Women's self development in late adolescence. In J. V. Jordan, A. G. Kaplan, J. B. Miller, I. P. Stiver, & J. L. Surrey (Eds.), *Women's growth in connection: Writings from the Stone Center* (pp. 122–140). New York: Guilford Press.

Kaplan, D. W. (1995, April). School-based health centers: Primary care in high school. *Pediatric Annals, 24,* 192–200.

Kaplan, E. B. (1997). *Not our kind of girl.* Berkeley: University of California Press.

Kaplan, H. (1979). *Disorders of sexual desire.* New York: Brunner/Mazel.

Kaplan, J., & Aronson, D. (1994, Spring). The numbers gap. *Teaching Tolerance,* pp. 21–27.

Kaplan, S. H., et al. (1996). Sex differences in academic advancement: Results of a national study of pediatricians. *New England Journal of Medicine, 335,* 1282–1289.

Karney, B. R., & Bradbury, T. N. (1995). The longitudinal course of marriage quality and stability: A review of theory, method, and research. *Psychological Bulletin, 118,* 3–34.

Karraker, K. H., Vogel, D. A., & Lake, M. A. (1995). Parents' gender-stereotyped perceptions of newborns: The eye of the beholder revisited. *Sex Roles, 33,* 687–701.

Karsten, M. F. (1994). *Management and gender: Issues and attitudes.* Westport, CT: Praeger.

Kaschak, E. (1992). *Engendered lives: A new psychology of women's experience.* New York: Basic Books.

Kastberg, S. M., & Miller, D. G. (1996). Of blue collars and ivory towers: Women from blue-collar backgrounds in higher education. In K. Arnold, K. D. Noble, & R. F. Subotnik (Eds.), *Remarkable women: Perspectives on female talent development* (pp. 49–67). Creskill, NJ: Hampton Press.

Katz, D. (1987). Sex discrimination in hiring: The influence of organizational climate and need for approval on decision making behavior. *Psychology of Women Quarterly, 11,* 11–20.

Katz, P. A. (1987). Variations in family constellation: Effects on gender schemata. In L. S. Liben & M. L. Signorella (Eds.), *Children's gender schemata* (pp. 39–56). San Francisco: Jossey-Bass.

Katz, P. A., Boggiano, A., & Silvern, L. (1993). Theories of female personality. In F. L. Denmark & M. A. Paludi (Eds.), *Psychology of women: A handbook of issues and theories* (pp. 247–280). Westport, CT: Greenwood Press.

Katz, P. A., & Katz, M. (1997). *The feminist dollar: The wise woman's buying guide.* New York: Plenum Press.

Katz, P. A., & Kofkin, J. A. (1997). Race, gender, and young children. In S. Luthar, J. A. Baruck, D. Cicchetti, & J. Weisz (Eds.), *Developmental psychopathology: Perspectives on adjustment, risk, and disorder* (pp. 51–74). New York: Cambridge University Press.

Katzman, D. K., et al. (1997). A longitudinal magnetic resonance imaging study of brain changes in adolescents with anorexia nervosa. *Archives of Pediatric and Adolescent Medicine, 151,* 793–797.

Kaufman, D. R. (1995). Professional women: How real are the recent gains? In J. Freeman (Ed.), *Women: A feminist perspective* (5th ed., pp. 287–305). Mountain View, CA: Mayfield.

Kaufman, L. (1997, January 13). A report from the front: Why it has gotten easier to sue for sexual harassment. *Newsweek,* p. 32.

Kauth, M. R., & Kalichman, S. C. (1998). Sexual orientation and development: An interactive approach. In D. L. Anselmi & A. L. Law (Eds.), *Questions of gender: Perspectives and paradoxes* (pp. 329–344). New York: McGraw-Hill.

Kawachi, I., et al. (1997). A prospective study of passive smoking and coronary heart disease. *Circulation, 95,* 2374–2379.

Kearns, J. R., & Christopherson, V. A. (1992). Mexican-American women's perceptions of menopause. In A. J. Dan & L. L. Lewis (Eds.), *Menstrual health in women's lives* (pp. 191–197). Urbana: University of Illinois Press.

Keeley, M. P. (1996). Social support and breast cancer: Why do we talk and to whom do we talk? In R. L. Parrott & C. M. Condit (Eds.), *Evaluating women's health messages* (pp. 293–306). Thousand Oaks, CA: Sage.

Keen, S. (1991). *Fire in the belly: On being a man.* New York: Bantam Books.

Kehoe, M. (1989). *Lesbians over 60 speak for themselves.* New York: Harrington Park Press.

Keller, C. (1997, Summer). Money talks: What women need to know. *AAUW Outlook,* pp. 16–17.

Kelley, K. (1987). Perspectives on females, males, and sexuality. In K. Kelley (Ed.), *Females, males, and sexuality* (pp. 1–12). Albany: State University of New York Press.

Kelly, C. (1991, March/April). Self-defense. *Ms. Magazine,* pp. 42–43.

Kelly, K., & Jordan, L. (1990). Effects of academic achievement and gender on academic and social self-concept: A replication study. *Journal of Counseling and Development, 69,* 173–177.

Kelly, M. P., Strassberg, D. S., & Kircher, J. R. (1990). Attitudinal and experiential correlates of anorgasmia. *Archives of Sexual Behavior, 19,* 165–177.

Kemp, A. A. (1994). *Women's work: Degraded and devalued.* Englewood Cliffs, NJ: Prentice-Hall.

Kendall-Tackett, K. A., & Kantor, G. K. (1993). *Postpartum depression: A comprehensive approach for nurses.* Newbury Park, CA: Sage.

Kerr, B. (1994). *Smart girls two: A new psychology of girls, women, and giftedness.* Dayton, OH: Ohio Psychology Press.

Kessler, R. C., et al. (1994). Lifetime and 12-month prevalence of DSM-III-R psychiatric disorders in the United States. *Archives of General Psychiatry, 51,* 8–19.

Kessler, S. J. (1998). *Lessons from the intersexed.* Piscataway, NJ: Rutgers University Press.

Keyes, C. L. M., & Ryff, C. D. (1998). Generativity in adult lives: Social structural contours and quality of life consequences. In D. P. McAdams & E. de St. Aubin (Eds.), *Generativity and adult development: How and why we care for the next generation* (pp. 227–263). Washington, DC: American Psychological Association.

Killen, J. D. (1998). Smoking prevention. In E. A. Blechman & K. D. Brownell (Eds.), *Behavioral medicine and women: A comprehensive handbook* (pp. 228–232). New York: Guilford Press.

Kilmartin, C. T. (1994). *The masculine self.* New York: Macmillan.

Kimball, M. M. (1989). A new perspective on women's math achievement. *Psychological Bulletin, 105,* 198–214.

Kimball, M. M. (1995). *Feminist visions of gender similarities and differences.* Binghamton, NY: Haworth.

Kimball, M. M. (1999). Acknowledging truth and fantasy: Freud and the recovered memory debate. In M. Rivera (Ed.), *Fragment by fragment: Feminist perspectives on memory and child sexual abuse* (pp. 21–42). Charlottetown, PEI, Canada: gynergy books.

Kimmel, E. B., & Kazanis, B. W. (1995). Explorations of the unrecognized spirituality of women's communion. *Women and Therapy, 6,* 215–227.

Kimmel, M. S. (Ed.). (1995). *The politics of manhood.* Philadelphia: Temple University Press.

Kimmel, M. S. (1996). *Manhood in America: A cultural history.* New York: Free Press.

Kimmel, M. S., & Kaufman, M. (1995). Weekend warriors: The new men's movement. In M. S. Kimmel (Ed.), *The politics of manhood* (pp. 15–43). Philadelphia: Temple University Press.

Kimmel, M. S., & Messner, M. A. (Eds.). (1998). *Men's lives* (4th ed.). Boston: Allyn & Bacon.

Kimura, D. (1987). Are men's and women's brains really different? *Canadian Psychology, 28,* 133–147.

Kimura, D. (1992, September). Sex differences in the brain. *Scientific American, 267,* 118–125.

Kimura, D., & Hampson, E. (1993). Neural and hormonal mechanisms mediating sex differences in cognition. In P. A. Vernon (Ed.), *Biological approaches to the study of human intelligence* (pp. 375–397). Norwood, NJ: ABLEX.

Kimura, D., & Hampson, E. (1994). Cognitive pattern in men and women is influenced by fluctuations in sex hormones. *Current Directions in Psychological Science, 3,* 57–61.

King, B. M., Parisi, L. S., & O'Dwyer, K. R. (1993). College sexuality education promotes future discussions about sexuality between former students and their children. *Journal of Sex Education and Therapy, 19,* 285–293.

King, Y. (1997). The other body: Reflections on difference, disability, and identity politics. In M. Crawford & R. Unger (Eds.), *In our own words: Readings on the psychology of women and gender* (pp. 107–111). New York: McGraw-Hill.

Kirchmeyer, C. (1992). Nonwork participation and work attitudes: A test of scarcity vs. expansion models of personal resources. *Human Relations, 45,* 775–795.

Kirchmeyer, C. (1993). Nonwork-to-work spillover: A more balanced view of the experiences and coping of professional women and men. *Sex Roles, 28,* 531–552.

Kirshenbaum, G. (1997, May/June). A fundamentalist regime cracks down on women. *Ms. Magazine,* pp. 12–18.

Kishwar, M. (1995). When daughters are unwanted: Sex determination tests in India. *Manushi, 86,* 15–22.

Kissling, F. (1998, January/February). *Roe v. Wade. Ms. Magazine,* p. 77.

Kitano, H. H. L., Shibusawa, T., & Kitano, K. J. (1997). Asian American elderly mental health. In K. S. Markides & M. R. Miranda (Eds.), *Minorities, aging, and health* (pp. 295–315). Thousand Oaks, CA: Sage.

Kitasei, H. H. (1995, March/April). STDs: What you don't know *can* hurt you. *Ms. Magazine,* pp. 24–28.

Kite, M. E. (1994). When perceptions meet reality: Individual differences in reactions to lesbians and gay men. In B. Greene & G. M. Herek (Eds.), *Contemporary perspectives on gay and lesbian psychology* (pp. 25–53). Newbury Park, CA: Sage.

Kite, M. E. (1996). Age, gender, and occupational label: A test of social role theory. *Psychology of Women Quarterly, 20,* 361–374.

Kite, M. E., & Balogh, D. W. (1997). Warming trends: Improving the chilly campus climate. In N. V. Benokraitis (Ed.), *Subtle sexism: Current practice and prospects for change* (pp. 264–278). Thousand Oaks, CA: Sage.

Kite, M. E., & Deaux, K. (1986). Attitudes toward homosexuality: Assessment and behavioral consequences. *Basic and Applied Social Psychology, 7,* 137–162.

Kite, M. E., Deaux, K., & Miele, M. (1991). Stereotypes of young and old: Does age outweigh gender? *Psychology and Aging, 6,* 19–27.

Kite, M. E., & Whitley, B. E., Jr. (1996). Sex differences in attitudes toward homosexual persons, behaviors, and civil rights: A meta-analysis. *Personality and Social Psychology Bulletin, 22,* 336–353.

Kite, M. E., & Whitley, B. E., Jr. (1998). Do Heterosexual women and men differ in their attitudes toward homosexuality? A conceptual and methodological analysis. In G. M. Herek (Ed.), *Stigma, prejudice, and violence against lesbians and gay men.* Thousand Oaks, CA: Sage.

Kitson, G. C. (1992). *Portrait of divorce: Adjustment to marital breakdown.* New York: Guilford Press.

Kitzinger, C., & Wilkinson, S. (1997). Transitions from heterosexuality to lesbianism: The discursive production of lesbian identities. In M. R. Walsh (Ed.), *Women, men, and gender: Ongoing debates* (pp. 188–203). New Haven: Yale University Press.

Kitzinger, S. (1994). *The year after childbirth: Surviving and enjoying the first year of motherhood.* New York: Scribner's.

Kitzinger, S. (1995). *Ourselves as mothers: The universal experience of motherhood.* Reading, MA: Addison-Wesley.

Kivett, V. R. (1996). The saliency of the grandmother-granddaughter relationship: Predictors of association. *Journal of Women & Aging, 8,* 25–39.

Klebanoff, M. A., Shiono, P. H., & Rhoads, G. G. (1990). Outcomes of pregnancy in a national sample of resident physicians. *New England Journal of Medicine, 323,* 1040–1045.

Klebanov, P. K., & Jemmott, J. B., III. (1992). Effects of expectations and bodily sensations on self-reports of premenstrual symptoms. *Psychology of Women Quarterly, 16,* 289–310.

Kleiman, C. (1998, April 26). Women in the workplace: A revolution that won't quit. *San Jose Mercury News,* p. PC1.

Klein, E., Campbell, J., Soler, E., & Ghez, M. (1997). *Ending domestic violence: Changing public perceptions/Halting the epidemic.* Thousand Oaks, CA: Sage.

Klevan, J. L., Weiss, J. C., & Dabrow, S. M. (1990). Pregnancy during pediatric residency. *American Journal of Diseases of Children, 144,* 767–777.

Kline, K. N. (1996). The drama of in utero drug exposure. In R. L. Parrott & C. M. Condit (Eds.), *Evaluating women's health messages* (pp. 61–75). Thousand Oaks, CA: Sage.

Klinger, R. L. (1996). Lesbian couples. In R. P. Cabaj & T. S. Stein (Eds.), *Textbook of homosexuality and mental health* (pp. 339–352). Washington, DC: American Psychiatric Press.

Klonis, S., Endo, J., Cosby, F., & Worell, J. (1997). Feminism as life raft. *Psychology of Women Quarterly, 21,* 333–345.

Klonoff, E. A., & Landrine, H. (1997). *Preventing misdiagnosis of women: A guide to physical disorders that have psychiatric symptoms.* Thousand Oaks, CA: Sage.

Knaub, P. K., Eversoll, D. B., & Voss, J. H. (1983). Is parenthood a desirable adult role? An assessment of attitudes held by contemporary women. *Sex Roles, 9,* 355–362.

Knight, G. P., Fabes, R. A., & Higgins, D. A. (1996). Concerns about drawing causal inferences from meta-analyses: An example in the study of gender differences in aggression. *Psychological Bulletin, 119,* 410–421.

Ko, M., & Schulken, E. D. (1998). Factors related to smoking cessation and relapse among pregnant smokers. *American Journal of Health Behavior, 22,* 83–89.

Kohlberg, L. (1966). A cognitive-developmental analysis of children's sex-role concepts and attitudes. In E. E. Maccoby (Ed.), *The development of sex differences* (pp. 82–173). Stanford, CA: Stanford University Press.

Kohlberg, L. (1981). *The philosophy of moral development: Essays on moral development* (Vols. I & II). San Francisco: Harper & Row.

Kohlberg, L. (1984). *Essays on moral development: Vol. 2, The psychology of moral development.* San Francisco: Freeman.

Kohlberg, L., & Ullian, D. Z. (1974). Stages in the development of psychosexual concepts and attitudes. In R. C. Friedman, R. M. Richart, & R. L. Van de Wiele (Eds.), *Sex differences in behavior* (pp. 209–222). New York: Wiley.

Kolbe, R. H., & Albanese, P. J. (1996). Man to man: A content analysis of sole-male images in male-audience magazines. *Journal of Advertising, 25,* 1–20.

Kolbe, R. H., & Albanese, P. J. (1997). The functional integration of sole-male images into magazine advertisements. *Sex Roles, 36,* 813–836.

Kolpin, V. W., & Singell, L. D., Jr. (1996). The gender composition and scholarly performance of economic departments: A test for employment discrimination. *Industrial and Labor Relations Review, 49,* 408–423.

Konrad, A. M., & Pfeffer, J. (1991). Understanding the hiring of women and minorities in educational institutions. *Sociology of Education, 64,* 141–157.

Kopper, B. A. (1996). Gender, gender identity, rape myth acceptance, and time of initial resistance on the perception of acquaintance rape blame and avoidability. *Sex Roles, 34,* 81–93.

Kornhaber, A. (1996). *Contemporary grandparenting.* Thousand Oaks, CA: Sage.

Kortenhaus, C. M., & Demarest, J. (1993). Gender role stereotyping in children's literature: An update. *Sex Roles, 28,* 219–232.

Koshland, D. E., Jr. (1994). The spousal abuse problem. *Science, 265,* 455.

Koski, L. R., & Shaver, P. R. (1997). Attachment and relationship satisfaction across the lifespan. In R. J. Sternberg & M. Hojjat (Eds.), *Satisfaction in close relationships* (pp. 26–55). New York: Guilford Press.

Koss, M. P. (1990). Changed lives: The psychological impact of sexual harassment. In M. A. Paludi (Ed.), *Ivory power: Sexual harassment on campus* (pp. 73–92). Albany: State University of New York Press.

Koss, M. P. (1992). The underdetection of rape: Methodological choices influence incidence estimates. *Journal of Social Issues, 48,* 61–75.

Koss, M. P. (1993). Rape: Scope, impact, interventions, and public policy responses. *American Psychologist, 48,* 1062–1069.

Koss, M. P. (1997). Dealing with date rape [Review of the book *Acquaintance rape: Assessment, treatment, and prevention*]. *Contemporary Psychology, 42,* 716.

Koss, M. P., & Harvey, M. R. (1991). *The rape victim: Clinical and community interventions* (2nd ed.). Newbury Park, CA: Sage.

Koss, M. P., & Heslet, L. (1992). Somatic consequences of violence against women. *Archives of Family Medicine, 1,* 53–59.

Koss, M. P., Ingram, M., & Pepper, S. (1997). Psychotherapists' role in the medical response to male partner violence. *Psychotherapy: Theory, Research, and Practice, 34,* 386–396.

Koss, M. P., et al. (1996). Traumatic memory characteristics: A cross-validated mediational model of response to rape among employed women. *Journal of Abnormal Psychology, 105,* 421–432.

Krajeski, J. (1996). Homosexuality and the mental health professions. In R. P. Cabaj & T. S. Stein (Eds.), *Textbook of homosexuality and mental health* (pp. 17–31). Washington, DC: American Psychiatric Press.

Krishnan, V. (1987). Preferences for sex of children: A multivariate analysis. *Journal of Biosocial Science, 9,* 367–376.

Kristiansen, C. M., & Giulietti, R. (1990). Perceptions of wife abuse. *Psychology of Women Quarterly, 14,* 177–189.

Kristof, N. D. (1996, December 9). Wife-beating still common practice in much of Korea. *San Jose Mercury News,* p. 17A.

Krueger, J., Rothbart, M., & Sriram, N. (1989). Category learning and change: Differences in sensitivity to information that enhances or reduces intercategory distinctions. *Journal of Personality and Social Psychology, 56,* 866–875.

Kuebli, J., & Fivush, R. (1992). Gender differences in parent-child conversations about past emotions. *Sex Roles, 27,* 683–698.

Kulkarni, V. (1997, November/December). Why they drop out: Reasons for lower literacy among girls. *Manushi,* pp. 32–33.

Kunda, Z., & Sherman-Williams, B. (1993). Stereotypes and the construal of individuating information. *Personality and Social Psychology Bulletin, 19,* 90–99.

Kurdek, L. A. (1987). Sex role self schema and psychological adjustment in coupled homosexual and heterosexual men and women. *Sex Roles, 17,* 549–562.

Kurdek, L. A. (1991a). Predictors of increases in marital distress in newlywed couples: A 3-year prospective longitudinal study. *Developmental Psychology, 27,* 627–636.

Kurdek, L. A. (1991b). The dissolution of gay and lesbian couples. *Journal of Social and Personal Relationships, 8,* 265–278.

Kurdek, L. A. (1993). Predicting marital dissolution: A 5-year prospective longitudinal study of newlywed couples. *Journal of Personality and Social Psychology, 64,* 221–242.

Kurdek, L. A. (1995a). Assessing multiple determinants of relationship commitment in cohabiting gay, cohabiting lesbian, dating heterosexual, and married heterosexual couples. *Family Relations, 44,* 261–266.

Kurdek, L. A. (1995b). Developmental changes in relationship quality in gay and lesbian cohabiting couples. *Developmental Psychology, 31,* 86–94.

Kurdek, L. A. (1995c). Lesbian and gay couples. In A. R. D'Augelli & C. J. Patterson (Eds.), *Lesbian, gay, and bisexual identities over the lifespan: Psychological perspectives* (pp. 243–261). New York: Oxford University Press.

Kurdek, L. A., & Schmitt, J. P. (1986). Relationship quality of partners in heterosexual married, heterosexual cohabiting, and gay and lesbian relationships. *Journal of Personality and Social Psychology, 51,* 711–720.

Kushner, E. (1997). *Experiencing abortion: A weaving of women's words.* New York: Harrington Park Press.

Kuzmanović, J. (1995). Legacies of invisibility: Past silence, present violence against women in the former Yugoslavia. In J. Peters & A. Wolper (Eds.), *Women's rights, human rights: International feminist perspectives* (pp. 57–61). New York: Routledge.

Kwa, L. (1994). Adolescent females' perceptions of competence: What is defined as healthy and achieving. In J. Gallivan, S. D. Crozier, & V. M. Lalande (Eds.), *Women, girls, and achievement* (pp. 121–132). North York, Ontario: Captus University Publications.

Labour Canada. (1986). *When I grow up: Career expectations and aspirations of Canadian schoolchildren.* Ottawa: Women's Bureau.

LaFrance, K. (1998, May 4). Livestock afforded more protection than an abused spouse. *Liberal Opinion,* p. 14.

LaFrance, M., & Carmen, B. (1980). The nonverbal display of psychological androgyny. *Journal of Personality and Social Psychology, 38,* 36–49.

LaFrance, M., & Henley, N. M. (1997). On oppressing hypotheses: Or, differences in nonverbal sensitivity revisited. In M. R. Walsh (Ed.), *Women, men, and gender: Ongoing debates* (pp. 104–119). New Haven, CT: Yale University Press.

LaFromboise, T. D. (1988). American Indian mental health policy. *American Psychologist, 43,* 388–397.

LaFromboise, T. D., Coleman, H. L. K., & Gerton, J. (1993). Psychological impact of biculturalism: Evidence and theory. *Psychological Bulletin, 114,* 395–412.

LaFromboise, T. D., Heyle, A. M., & Ozer, E. J. (1990). Changing and diverse roles of women in American Indian cultures. *Sex Roles, 22,* 455–476.

LaFromboise, T. D., et al. (1995). American Indian women and psychology. In H. Landrine (Ed.), *Bringing cultural diversity to feminist psychology: Theory, research, and practice* (pp. 197–239). Washington, DC: American Psychological Association.

Lakoff, R. T. (1990). *Talking power: The politics of language in our lives.* New York: Basic Books.

LaMar, L., & Kite, M. E. (1996). *Sex differences in attitudes toward gay men and lesbians: A multidimensional perspective.* Paper presented at the annual convention of the American Psychological Association, Toronto, Canada.

Lamke, L. K., Sollie, D. L., Durbin, R. G., & Fitzpatrick, J. A. (1994). Masculinity, femininity, and relationship satisfaction: The mediating role of interpersonal competence. *Journal of Social and Personal Relationships, 11,* 535–554.

Lancaster, J. (1998, July 3). Egyptian group reduces 'female circumcision.' *San Jose Mercury News,* pp. 8DD–9DD.

Landrine, H. (Ed.). (1995a). *Bringing cultural diversity to feminist psychology: Theory, research, and practice.* Washington, DC: American Psychological Association.

Landrine, H. (1995b). Introduction: Cultural diversity, contextualism, and feminist psychology. In H. Landrine (Ed.), *Bringing cultural diversity to feminist psychology: Theory, research, and practice* (pp. 1–20). Washington, DC: American Psychological Association.

Landrine, H., & Klonoff, E. A. (1997). *Discrimination against women: Prevalence, consequences, remedies.* Thousand Oaks, CA: Sage.

Landrine, H., Klonoff, E. A., & Brown-Collins, A. (1992). Cultural diversity and methodology in feminist psychology: Critique, proposal, empirical example. *Psychology of Women Quarterly, 16,* 145–163.

Langelan, M. J. (1993). *Back off! How to confront and stop sexual harassment and harassers.* New York: Simon & Schuster.

Langer, C. L. (1996). *A feminist critique: How feminism has changed American society, culture, and how we live from the 1940s to the present.* New York: HarperCollins.

Lanis, K., & Covell, K. (1995). Images of women in advertisements: Effects on attitudes related to sexual aggression. *Sex Roles, 32,* 639–649.

Larsen, K., & Long, E. (1988). Attitudes toward sex-roles: Traditional or egalitarian? *Sex Roles, 19,* 1–12.

Larson, M. S. (1996). Sex roles and soap operas: What adolescents learn about single motherhood. *Sex Roles, 35,* 97–109.

Larwood, L., & Gutek, B. A. (1984). Women at work in the USA. In M. J. Davidson & C. L. Cooper (Eds.), *Women at work* (pp. 237–267). Chichester, England: Wiley.

Latané, B., & Dabbs, J. M., Jr. (1975). Sex, group size and helping in three cities. *Sociometry, 38,* 180–194.

LaTorre, R. A., & Wendenburg, K. (1983). Psychological characteristics of bisexual, heterosexual and homosexual women. *Journal of Homosexuality, 9,* 87–97.

Laumann, E. O., Gagnon, J. H., Michael, R. T., & Michaels, S. (1994). *The social organization of sexuality: Sexual practices in the United States.* Chicago: The University of Chicago Press.

Lavender, T., & Walkinshaw, S. A. (1998). Can midwives reduce postpartum psychological morbidity? A randomized trial. *Birth, 25,* 215–219.

Lawrence, R. A. (1998). Breastfeeding. In E. A. Blechman & K. D. Brownell (Eds.), *Behavioral medicine and women: In comprehensive handbook* (pp. 495–500). New York: Guilford Press.

Laws, A. (1998). Sexual abuse. In E. A. Blechman & K. D. Brownell (Eds.), *Behavioral medicine and women: A comprehensive handbook* (pp. 470–474). New York: Guilford Press.

Laws, A., & Golding, J. M. (1996). Sexual assault history and eating disorder symptoms among White, Hispanic, and African-American women and men. *American Journal of Public Health, 86,* 579–582.

Lawton, C. A. (1996). Strategies for indoor wayfinding: The role of orientation. *Journal of Environmental Psychology, 16,* 137–145.

Lawton, C. A., Charleston, S. I., & Zieles, A. S. (1996). Individual and gender-related differences in indoor wayfinding. *Environment and Behavior, 28,* 204–219.

Leadbeater, B. J. R., & Way, N. (Eds.). (1996). *Urban girls: Resisting stereotypes, creating identities.* New York: New York University Press.

Leadbeater, B. J. R., Way, N., & Raden, A. (1996). *Why not marry your baby's father? Answers from African American and Hispanic adolescent mothers.* (pp. 193–209). New York: New York University Press.

Leaper, C., Leve, L., Strasser, T., & Schwartz, R. (1995). Mother-child communication sequences: Play activity, child gender, and marital status effects. *Merrill-Palmer Quarterly, 41,* 307–327.

Leaper, C., & Valin, D. (1996). Predictors of Mexican American mothers' and fathers' attitudes toward gender equality. *Hispanic Journal of Behavioral Sciences, 18,* 343–355.

Leaper, C., et al. (1995). Self-disclosure and listener verbal support in same-gender and cross-gender friends' conversations. *Sex Roles, 33,* 387–404.

Leary, M. R., & Kowalski, R. M. (1995). *Social anxiety.* New York: Guilford Press.

Leavitt, J., & Saegert, S. (1990). *From abandonment to hope: Community-households in Harlem.* New York: Columbia University Press.

Lederman, R. P. (1996). *Psychosocial adaptation in pregnancy* (2nd ed.). New York: Springer.

Lee, J., & Sasser-Coen, J. (1996). *Blood stories: Menarche and the politics of the female body in contemporary U.S. Society.* New York: Routledge.

Lees, D. (1992, December). The war against men. *Toronto Life,* pp. 45–104.

Leiblum, S. R., & Rosen, R. C. (Eds.). (1988). *Sexual desire disorders.* New York: Guilford Press.

Leiblum, S. R., & Segraves, R. T. (1995). Sex and aging. *Review of Psychiatry, 14,* 677–695.

Leifer, M. (1980). *Psychological effects of motherhood.* New York: Praeger.

Leinbach, M. D., & Fagot, B. I. (1993). Categorical habituation to male and female faces: Gender schematic processing in infancy. *Infant Behavior and Development, 16,* 317–332.

Leinbach, M. D., Hort, B. E., & Fagot, B. I. (1997). Bears are for boys: Metaphorical associations in young children's gender stereotypes. *Cognitive Development, 12,* 107–130.

Leitenberg, H., & Henning, K. (1995). Sexual fantasy. *Psychological Bulletin, 117,* 469–496.

Leitinger, I. A. (Ed.). (1997). *The Costa Rican women's movement: A reader.* Pittsburgh, PA: University of Pittsburgh Press.

Lemieux, R. (1996). Illicit drug use and the pregnant woman. In R. L. Parrott & C. M. Condit (Eds.), *Evaluating women's health messages* (pp. 49–60). Thousand Oaks, CA: Sage.

Lenney, E. (1977). Women's self-confidence in achievement settings. *Psychological Bulletin, 84,* 1–13.

Leonard, A. S. (1994, July 25). Fired for being gay. *The New Yorker,* p. 6.

Leonard, D. K., & Jiang, J. (1999). Gender bias and the college predictions of the SAT'S: A cry of despair. *Research in Higher Education, 40,* in press.

Leong, F. T. L., & Hayes, T. J. (1990). Occupational stereotyping of Asian Americans. *Career Development Quarterly, 39,* 143–154.

Leonhardt-Lupa, M. (1995). *A mother is born: Preparing for motherhood during pregnancy.* Westport, CT: Bergin & Garvey.

Lepowsky, M. (1998). Women, men, and aggression in an egalitarian society. In D. L. Anselmi & A. L. Law (Eds.), *Questions of gender* (pp. 170–179). New York: McGraw-Hill.

Lerman, H. (1996). *Pigeonholing women's misery.* New York: Basic Books.

Lerner, H. (1989). *Women in therapy.* New York: Harper & Row.

Lerner, H. (1998). *The mother dance.* New York: HarperCollins.

Lester, R., & Petrie, T. A. (1995). Personality and physical correlates of bulimic symptomatology among Mexican American female college students. *Journal of Counseling Psychology, 42,* 199–203.

Levant, R. F. (1996). *Masculinity reconstructed: Changing the rules of manhood.* New York: Plume.

Levant, R. F., & Pollack, W. S. (Eds.). (1995). *A new psychology of men.* New York: Basic Books.

LeVay, S. (1991). A difference in hypothalamic structure between heterosexual and homosexual men. *Science, 253,* 1034–1037.

LeVay, S. (1996). *The use and abuse of research into homosexuality.* Cambridge, MA: MIT Press.

Leve, L. D., & Fagot, B. I. (1997). Gender-role socialization and discipline processes in one- and two-parent families. *Sex Roles, 36,* 1–21.

Levenson, R. W., Carstensen, L. L., & Gottman, J. M. (1994). The influence of age and gender on affect, physiology, and their interrelations: A study of long-term marriages. *Journal of Personality and Social Psychology, 67,* 56–68.

Leventhal, E. A. (1994). Gender and aging: Women and their aging. In V. J. Adesso, D. M. Reddy, & R. Fleming (Eds.), *Psychological perspectives on women's health* (pp. 11–35). Washington, DC: Taylor & Francis.

Levering, M. (1994). Women, the state, and religion today in the People's Republic of China. In A. Sharma (Ed.), *Today's woman in world religions* (pp. 171–224). Albany: State University of New York Press.

Levin, J., & Arluke, A. (1985). An exploratory analysis of sex differences in gossip. *Sex Roles, 12,* 281–285.

Levine, F., & Le De Simone, L. (1991). The effects of experimenter gender on pain report in male and female subjects. *Pain, 44,* 69–72.

Levine, M. P., & Smolak, L. (1996). Media as a context for the development of disordered eating. In L. Smolak, M. P. Levine, & R. Striegel-Moore (Eds.), *The developmental psychopathology of eating disorders* (pp. 235–257). Mahwah, NJ: Erlbaum.

Levine, S. B. (1998). *Sexuality in mid-life.* New York: Plenum Press.

Levy, B. (1993). *In love and in danger.* Seattle, WA: Seal Press.

Levy, B., & Langer, E. (1994). Aging free from negative stereotypes: Successful memory in China and among the American Deaf. *Journal of Personality and Social Psychology, 66,* 989–997.

Levy, G. D., & Fivush, R. (1993). Scripts and gender: A new approach for examining gender-role development. *Developmental Review, 13,* 126–146.

Lewinsohn, P. M., et al. (1998). Gender differences in anxiety disorders and anxiety symptoms in adolescents. *Journal of Abnormal Psychology, 107,* 109–117.

Lewis, C., Scully, D., & Condor, S. (1992). Sex stereotyping of infants: A re-examination. *Journal of Reproductive and Infant Psychology, 10,* 53–63.

Lewis, K. G., & Moon, S. (1997). Always single and single again women: A qualitative study. *Journal of Marital and Family Therapy, 23,* 115–134.

Lickona, T. (1994, Summer). The neglected heart: The emotional dangers of premature sexual involvement. *American Educator,* pp. 34–39.

Lightdale, J. R., & Prentice, D. A. (1994). Rethinking sex differences in aggression: Aggressive behavior in the absence of social roles. *Personality and Social Psychology Bulletin, 20,* 34–44.

Lindgren, J. R., & Taub, N. (1993). *The law of sex discrimination* (2nd ed.). Minneapolis, MN: West Publishing.

Lindsey, L. L. (1996). Full-time homemaker as unpaid laborer. In P. J. Dubeck & K. Borman (Eds.), *Women and work: A handbook* (pp. 98–99). New York: Garland Press.

Linn, M. C., & Kessel, C. (1995, April). *Participation in mathematics courses and careers: Climate, grades, and entrance examination scores.* Paper presented at the AERA Annual Meeting, San Francisco.

Linn, M. C., & Petersen, A. C. (1985). Emergence and characterization of sex differences in spatial ability: A meta-analysis. *Child Development, 56,* 1479–1498.

Linn, M. C., & Petersen, A. C. (1986). A meta-analysis of gender differences in spatial ability: Implications for mathematics and science achievement. In J. S. Hyde & M. C. Linn (Eds.), *The psychology of gender: Advances through meta-analysis* (pp. 67–101). Baltimore: Johns Hopkins University Press.

Litt, I. F. (1997). *Taking our pulse: The health of America's women.* Stanford, CA: Stanford University Press.

Litt, I. F. (1998). Health issues for women in the 1990s. In D. L. Anselmi & A. L. Law (Eds.), *Questions of gender: Perspectives & paradoxes* (pp. 690–701). New York: McGraw-Hill.

Lively, K. (1996, June 28). The "date-rape drug." *Chronicle of Higher Education,* p. A29.

Livingston, J. A. (1996). Individual action and political strategies: Creating a future free of heterosexism. In E. D. Rothblum & L. A. Bond (Eds.), *Preventing heterosexism and homophobia* (pp. 253–265). Thousand Oaks, CA: Sage.

Livingston, M. (1993). Psychoprophylactic method (Lamaze). In B. L. Rothman (Ed.), *Encyclopedia of childbearing: Critical perspectives* (pp. 343–345). Phoenix: Oryx Press.

Livingston, M. (1999). How to think about women's health. In C. Forden, A. E. Hunter, & B. Birns (Eds.), *Readings in the psychology of women: Dimensions of the female experience* (pp. 244–253). Boston: Allyn & Bacon.

Locher, P., Unger, R., Sociedade, P., & Wahl, J. (1993). At first glance: Accessibility of the physical attractiveness stereotype. *Sex Roles, 28,* 729–743.

Locklin, M. P., & Naber, S. J. (1993). Does breastfeeding empower women? Insights from a select group of educated, low-income, minority women. *Birth, 20,* 30–35.

Loftus, E. F. (1997, September). Creating false memories. *Scientific American,* pp. 71–75.

Logsdon, M. C., Birkimer, J. C., & Barbee, A. P. (1997). Social support providers for postpartum women. *Journal of Social Behavior and Personality, 12,* 89–102.

Lone Dog, Leota. (1991). Coming out as a Native American. In B. Sang, J. Warshow, & A. J. Smith (Eds.), *Lesbians at midlife: The creative transition* (pp. 49–53). San Francisco: Spinsters, Ink.

Looking for solutions. (1993). *About Canada,* p. 4.

Lorber, J. (1994). *Paradoxes of gender.* New Haven, CT: Yale University Press.

Lorber, J. (1997). *Gender and the social construction of illness.* Thousand Oaks, CA: Sage.

Lott, B. (1987). Sexist discrimination as distancing behavior: I. A laboratory demonstration. *Psychology of Women Quarterly, 11,* 47–58.

Lott, B. (1989). Sexist discrimination as distancing behavior: II. Primetime television. *Psychology of Women Quarterly, 13,* 341–355.

Lott, B. (1996). Politics or science? The question of gender sameness/difference. *American Psychologist, 51,* 155–156.

Lott, B., Lott, A. J., & Fernald, J. L. (1990). Individual differences in distancing responses to women on a photo choice task. *Sex Roles, 22,* 97–110.

Lott, B., & Maluso, D. (1993). The social learning of gender. In A. E. Beall & R. J. Sternberg (Eds.), *The psychology of gender* (pp. 99–123). New York: Guilford Press.

Lott, B., & Maluso, D. (1995a). Introduction: Framing the questions. In B. Lott & D. Maluso (Eds.), *The social psychology of interpersonal discrimination* (pp. 1–11). New York: Guilford Press.

Lott, B., & Maluso, D. (Eds.). (1995b). *The social psychology of interpersonal discrimination.* New York: Guilford Press.

Lottes, I. L., & Kuriloff, P. J. (1994). The impact of college experiences on political and social attitudes. *Sex Roles, 31,* 31–54.

Love, S. M. (1995). *Dr. Susan Love's breast book* (2nd ed.). Reading, MA: Addison-Wesley.

Lubben, J. E., & Becerra, R. M. (1987). Social support among Black, Mexican, and Chinese elderly. In D. E. Gelfand & C. M. Barresi (Eds.), *Ethnic dimensions of aging* (pp. 130–144). New York: Springer.

Ludtke, M. (1997). *On our own: Unmarried motherhood in America.* New York: Random House.

Luebke, B. F., & Reilly, M. E. (1995). *Women's studies graduates: The first generation.* New York: Teachers College Press.

Luker, K. (1996). *Dubious conceptions: The politics of teenage pregnancy.* Cambridge, MA: Harvard University Press.

Lundberg-Love, P., & Geffner, R. (1989). Date rape: Prevalence, risk factors, and a proposed model. In M. A. Pirog-Good & J. E. Stets (Eds.), *Violence in dating relationships: Emerging social issues* (pp. 169–184). New York: Praeger.

Lunneborg, P. (1990). *Women changing work.* New York: Bergin & Garvey.

Lustbader, W., & Hooyman, N. R. (1994). *Taking care of aging family members: A practical guide.* New York: Free Press.

Luthra, R. (1989). Matchmaking in the classifieds of the immigrant Indian press. In Asian Women United of California (Eds.), *Making waves* (pp. 337–344). Boston: Beacon Press.

Lyons, N. P. (1990). Listening to voices we have not heard. In C. Gilligan, N. P. Lyons, & T. J. Hanmer (Eds.), *Making connections* (pp. 30–72). Cambridge, MA: Harvard University Press.

Lytton, H., & Romney, D. M. (1991). Parents' differential socialization of boys and girls: A meta-analysis. *Psychological Bulletin, 109,* 267–296.

Maccoby, E. E. (1998). *The two sexes: Growing up apart, coming together.* Cambridge, MA: Harvard University Press.

Maccoby, E. E., & Jacklin, C. N. (1974). *The psychology of sex differences.* Stanford, CA: Stanford University Press.

Macdonald, B., & Rich, C. (1983). *Look me in the eye: Old women, aging and ageism.* San Francisco: Spinsters, Ink.

MacDonald, K., & Parke, R. D. (1986). Parent-child physical play: The effects of sex and age of children and parents. *Sex Roles, 15,* 367–378.

MacKay, N. J., & Covell, K. (1997). The impact of women in advertisements on atitudes toward women. *Sex Roles, 36,* 573–583.

Mackie, M. (1991). *Gender relations in Canada: Further explorations.* Toronto: Butterworths.

MacKinnon, C. A. (1979). *Sexual harassment of working women.* New Haven, CT: Yale University Press.

Macrae, C. N., Hewstone, M., & Griffiths, R. J. (1993). Processing load and memory for stereotype-based information. *European Journal of Social Psychology, 23,* 77–87.

Macrae, C. N., Milne, A. B., & Bodenhausen, G. V. (1994). Stereotypes as energy-saving devices: A peek inside the cognitive toolbox. *Journal of Personality and Social Psychology, 66,* 37–47.

Madigan, L., & Gamble, N. (1991). *The second rape: Society's continued betrayal of the victim.* Lexington, MA: Lexington Books.

Madsen, S. S. (1998, July 31). A welfare mother in academe. *Chronicle of Higher Education,* p. A44.

Maggio, R. (1991). *Dictionary of bias-free usage.* Phoenix, AZ: Oryx Press.

Major, B. (1989). Gender differences in comparisons and entitlement: Implications for comparable worth. *Journal of Social Issues, 45,* 99–115.

Major, B., et al. (1998). Personal resilience, cognitive appraisals, and coping: An integrative model of adjustment to abortion. *Journal of Personality and Social Psychology, 74,* 735–752.

Malamuth, N. M. (1998). The confluence model as an organizing framework for research on sexually aggressive men: Risk moderators, imagined aggression, and pornography consumption. In R. G. Geen & E. Donnerstein (Eds.), *Human aggression: Theories, research, and implications for social policy* (pp. 229–245). San Diego: Academic Press.

Malveaux, J. (1997, March 20). An educational edge? A women's history month meditation. *Black Issues in Higher Education,* p. 36.

Managing menopause: An update. (1998, January). *Harvard Women's Health Watch,* pp. 2–3.

Mandell, N., & Duffy, A. (Eds.). (1995). *Canadian families: Diversity, conflict, and change.* Toronto: Harcourt Brace Canada.

Mansfield, P. K., Koch, P. B., & Voda, A. M. (1998). Qualities midlife women desire in their sexual relationships and their changing sexual response. *Psychology of Women Quarterly, 22,* 285–303.

Manson, J. E., et al. (1995). Body weight and mortality among women. *New England Journal of Medicine, 333,* 677–685.

Marchioro, C. A., & Bartels, L. K. (1994). Perceptions of a job interviewee with a disability. *Journal of Social Behavior and Personality, 9,* 383–394.

Markides, K. S., & Miranda, M. R. (Eds.). (1997). *Minorities, aging and health.* Thousand Oaks, CA: Sage.

Markman, H., Stanley, S., & Blumberg, S. L. (1994). *Fighting for your marriage: Positive steps for preventing divorce and preserving a lasting love.* San Francisco: Jossey-Bass.

Marks, N. F. (1996). Flying solo at midlife: Gender, marital status, and psychological well-being. *Journal of Marriage and the Family, 58,* 917–932.

Markson, E. W. (1997). Sagacious, sinful, or superfluous? The social construction of older women. In J. M. Coyle (Ed.), *Handbook on women and aging* (pp. 53–71). Westport, CT: Greenwood Press.

Markson, E. W., & Taylor, C. A. (1993). Real versus reel world: Older women and the academy awards. *Women & Therapy, 14,* 157–172.

Marshall, E. (1995). NIH's "gay gene" study questioned. *Science, 268,* 1841.

Marston, W. (1998, March). Seeing red, feeling blue? Cramps! Bloating! Breakouts! *Jump,* pp. 107–109.

Martell, R. F. (1991). Sex bias at work: The effects of attentional and memory demands on performance ratings of men and women. *Journal of Applied Social Psychology, 21,* 1939–1960.

Martell, R. F. (1996a). Sex discrimination at work. In P. J. Dubeck & K. Borman (Eds.), *Women and work: a handbook* (pp. 329–332). New York: Garland.

Martell, R. F. (1996b). What mediates gender bias in work behavior ratings? *Sex Roles, 35,* 153–169.

Martell, R. F., Parker, C., Emrich, C. G., & Crawford, M. S. (1998). Sex stereotyping in the executive suite: "Much ado about something." *Journal of Social Behavior and Personality, 13,* 127–138.

Marten, L. A., & Matlin, M. W. (1976). Does sexism in elementary readers still exist? *Reading Teacher, 29,* 764–767.

Martin, C. L. (1987). A ratio measure of sex stereotyping. *Journal of Personality and Social Psychology, 52,* 489–499.

Martin, C. L. (1990). Attitudes and expectations about children with nontraditional and traditional gender roles. *Sex Roles, 22,* 151–165.

Martin, K. A. (1996). *Puberty, sexuality, and the self: Boys and girls at adolescence.* New York: Routledge.

Martin, M. (Ed.). (1997). *Hard-hatted women: Life on the job.* Seattle, WA: Seal Press.

Martínez, E. (1995). In pursuit of Latina liberation. *Signs: Journal of Women in Culture and Society, 20,* 1019–1028.

Martínez, E. (1997, Spring). "Unite and overcome!" *Teaching Tolerance,* pp. 11–15.

Martinez, K., & O'Toole, C. J. (1991, January/February). Disabled women of color face triple threat. *New Directions for Women,* p. 4.

Marx, J. (1995). Snaring the genes that divide the sexes for mammals. *Science, 269,* 1824–1825.

Massoth, N. A. (1997). Editorial: It's not comical. *Society for the Psychological Study of Men and Masculinity Bulletin, 3*(1), p. 2.

Masters, W. H., & Johnson, V. E. (1966). *Human sexual response.* Boston: Little, Brown.

Masters, W. H., & Johnson, V. E. (1970). *Human sexual inadequacy.* Boston: Little, Brown.

Mathews, J. (1994, July 25). Different strokes for different genders. *The Washington Post National Weekly Edition,* p. 22.

Matlin, M. W. (1985). Current issues in psycholinguistics. In T. M. Schlechter & M. P. Toglia (Eds.), *New directions in cognitive science* (pp. 217–241). Norwood, NJ: ABLEX.

Matlin, M. W. (1989). Teaching psychology of women: A survey of instructors. *Psychology of Women Quarterly, 13,* 245–261.

Matlin, M. W. (1993). *Looking into the crystal ball: The psychology of women and gender in the 21st century.* Paper presented at a conference, "Psychology in the 21st Century," York University, Ontario, Canada.

Matlin, M. W. (1998). *Cognition* (4th ed.). Fort Worth, TX: Harcourt Brace.

Matlin, M. W. (1999). *Psychology* (3rd ed.). Fort Worth, TX: Harcourt Brace.

Matthews, K. A., et al. (1997). Women's Health Initiative: Why now? What is it? What's new? *American Psychologist, 52,* 101–116.

Mayer, J. A. (1998). Breast cancer screening: Improving adherence. In A. Blechman & K. D. Brownell (Eds.), *Behavioral medicine and women: A comprehensive handbook* (pp. 208–212). New York: Guilford Press.

Mayerson, C. (1996). *Goin' to the chapel: Dreams of love, realities of marriage.* New York: Basic Books.

Mays, V. M. (1985). Black women working together: Diversity in same-sex relationships. *Women's Studies International Forum, 8,* 67–71.

Mays, V. M. (Ed.). (1996). *The behavioral and social context of HIV infection risks in lesbians and women who have sex with women.* Mahwah, NJ: Erlbaum.

McAdoo, J. L. (1993). Decision making and marital satisfaction in African American families. In H. P. McAdoo (Ed.), *Family ethnicity: Strength in diversity* (pp. 109–119). Newbury Park, CA: Sage.

McArthur, L. Z., & Eisen, S. V. (1976). Achievements of male and female storybook characters as determinants of achievement behavior by boys and girls. *Journal of Personality and Social Psychology, 33,* 467–473.

McCarten-Gibbs, A. (1998). *Weaving and repairing the fabric of our communities: Annual Report 1997–1998.* Palo Alto, CA: Global Fund for Women.

McCarthy, P., & Loren, J. A. (1997). *Breast cancer? Let me check my schedule!* Boulder, CO: Westview.

McCaul, M. E. (1998). Drug abuse. In E. A. Blechman & K. D. Brownell (Eds.), *Behavioral medicine and women: A comprehensive handbook* (pp. 414–424). New York: Guilford Press.

McClintock, M. K., & Herdt, G. (1996). Rethinking puberty: The development of sexual attraction. *Current Directions in Psychological Science, 5,* 178–183.

McCorduck, P., & Ramsey, N. (1997). *The futures of women: Scenarios for the 21st century.* New York: Warner Books.

McCormick, N. B. (1994). *Sexual salvation: Affirming women's sexual rights and pleasures.* Westport, CT: Praeger.

McDonald, S. M. (1989). Sex bias in the representation of male and female characters in children's picture books. *Journal of Genetic Psychology, 150,* 389–401.

McFarlane, J., Parker, B., Soeken, K., & Bullock, L. (1992). Assessing for abuse during pregnancy. *JAMA, 267,* 3176–3178.

McFarlane, J. M., & Williams, T. M. (1994). Placing premenstrual syndrome in perspective. *Psychology of Women Quarterly, 18,* 339–373.

McGill, A. L. (1993). Selection of a causal background: Role of expectation versus feature mutability. *Journal of Personality and Social Psychology, 64,* 701–707.

McGonagle, K. A., Kessler, R. C., & Gotlib, I. H. (1993). The effects of marital disagreement style, frequency, and outcome on marital disruption. *Journal of Social and Personal Relationships, 10,* 385–404.

McGrath, E., Keita, G. P., Strickland, B. R., & Russo, N. F. (Eds.). (1990). *Women and depression.* Washington, DC: American Psychological Association.

McHugh, M. C. (1996). A feminist approach to agoraphobia: Challenging traditional views of women at home. In J. C. Chrisler, C. Golden, & P. D. Rozee (Eds.), *Lectures on the psychology of women* (pp. 339–357). New York: McGraw-Hill.

McHugh, M. C., Frieze, I. H., & Browne, A. (1993). Research on battered women and their assailants. In F. L. Denmark & M. A. Paludi (Eds.), *Psychology of women: A handbook of issues and theories* (pp. 513–552). Westport, CT: Greenwood Press.

McHugh, M. C., Koeske, R. D., & Frieze, I. H. (1986). Issues to consider in conducting nonsexist psychological research: A guide for researchers. *American Psychologist, 41,* 879–890.

McIlwee, J. S., & Robinson, J. G. (1992). *Women in engineering: Gender, power, and workplace culture.* Albany, NY: State University of New York Press.

McIntosh, P. (1998). White privilege: Unpacking the invisible knapsack. In P. S. Rothenberg (Ed.), *Race, class, and gender in the United States: An integrated study* (4th ed., pp. 165–169). New York: St. Martin's Press.

McKay, S. (1993). Labor: Overview. In B. K. Rothman (Ed.), *Encyclopedia of childbearing: Critical perspectives* (pp. 212–215). Phoenix: Oryx Press.

McLendon, K., et al. (1994). Male and female perceptions of date rape. *Journal of Social Behavior and Personality, 9,* 421–428.

McMahon, M. (1995). *Engendering motherhood: Identity and self-transformation in women's lives.* New York: Guilford Press.

Mednick, M. T. (1991). Currents and futures in American feminist psychology: State of the art revisited. *Psychology of Women Quarterly, 15,* 611–621.

Mednick, M. T., & Thomas, V. (1993). Women and the psychology of achievement: A view from the eighties. In F. L. Denmark & M. A. Paludi (Eds.), *Psychology of women: A handbook of issues and theories* (pp. 585–626). Westport, CT: Greenwood Press.

Meinert, C. L. (1995). The inclusion of women in clinical trials. *Science, 269,* 795–796.

Meinz, E. J., & Salthouse, T. A. (1998). Is age kinder to females than to males? *Psychonomic Bulletin & Review, 5,* 56–70.

Melpomene Institute. (1992). *Heroes: Growing up female and strong* [Film]. (Available from Melpomene Institute, 1010 University Avenue, St. Paul, MN, 55104)

Mendelsohn, K. D., et al. (1994). Sex and gender bias in anatomy and physical diagnosis text illustrations. *JAMA, 272,* 1267–1270.

Mercer, R. T. (1986). *First-time motherhood: Experiences from teens to forties.* New York: Springer.

Mercer, R. T. (1995). *Becoming a mother: Research on maternal identity from Rubin to the present.* New York: Springer.

Merritt, R. D., & Kok, C. J. (1995). Attribution of gender to a gender-unspecified individual: An evaluation of the people = male hypothesis. *Sex Roles, 33,* 145–157.

Metts, S., Sprecher, S., & Regan, P. C. (1998). Communication and sexual desire. In P. A. Andersen & L. K. Guerrero (Eds.), *Handbook of communication and emotion: Research, theory, applications, and contexts* (pp. 353–377). New York: Academic Press.

Meyer-Bahlburg, H. F. L., et al. (1995). Prenatal estrogens and the development of homosexual orientation. *Developmental Psychology, 31,* 12–21.

Meyerowitz, B. E., & Hart, S. (1995). Women and cancer: Have assumptions about women limited our research agenda? In A. L. Stanton & S. L. Gallant (Eds.), *The psychology of women's health: Progress and challenges in research and application* (pp. 51–84). Washington, DC: American Psychological Association.

Meyerowitz, B. E., & Weidner, G. (1998). Section editors' overview. In E. A. Blechman & K. D. Brownell (Eds.), *Behavioral medicine and women: a comprehensive handbook* (pp. 537–545). New York: Guilford Press.

Michael, R. T., Gagnon, J. H., Laumann, E. O., & Kolata, G. (1994). *Sex in America: A definitive survey.* Boston: Little, Brown.

Michaels, G. Y. (1988). Motivational factors in the decision and timing of pregnancy. In G. Y. Michaels & W. A. Goldberg (Eds.), *The transition to parenthood* (pp. 23–61). New York: Cambridge University Press.

Michaels, S. (1996). The prevalence of homosexuality in the United States. In R. P. Cabaj & T. S. Stein (Eds.), *Textbook of homosexuality and mental health* (pp. 43–63). Washington, DC: American Psychiatric Press.

Mikell, G. (Ed.). (1997). *African feminism: The politics of survival in Sub-Saharan Africa.* Philadelphia: University of Pennsylvania Press.

Milburn, A., & Brewer, K. K. (1995). Sexually transmitted diseases. In M. W. O'Hara et al. (Eds.), *Psychological aspects of women's reproductive health* (pp. 132–146). New York: Springer.

Miles, C. (1935). Sex in social psychology. In C. Murchinson (Ed.), *Handbook of social psychology* (pp. 699–704). Worcester, MA: Clark University Press.

Miles, S., & Parker, K. (1997). Men, women, and health insurance. *New England Journal of Medicine, 336,* 218–221.

Miles, S. H., & August, A. (1990, Spring/Summer). Courts, gender and "the right to die." *Law, Medicine, and Health Care, 18,* 85–95.

Miller, C., & Swift, K. (1988). *The handbook of nonsexist writing.* New York: Harper & Row.

Miller, C., Swift, K., & Maggio, R. (1997, September/October). *Ms. Magazine,* pp. 50–54.

Miller, D. H. (1996). A matter of consequence: Abortion rhetoric and media messages. In R. L. Parrott & C. M. Condit (Eds.), *Evaluating women's health messages: A resource book* (pp. 33–47). Thousand Oaks, CA: Sage.

Miller, D. T., Taylor, B., & Buck, M. L. (1991). Gender gaps: Who needs to be explained? *Journal of Personality and Social Psychology, 61,* 5–12.

Miller, J. B., & Stiver, I. P. (1997). *The healing connection: How women form relationships in therapy and life.* Boston: Beacon Press.

Miller, S. K. (1992). Asian-Americans bump against glass ceilings. *Science, 258,* 1224–1228.

Million Dollar Directory, The. (1999). Bethlehem, PA: Dun & Bradstreet.

Mills, J. (1984). Self-posed behavior of females and males in photographs. *Sex Roles, 10,* 633–637.

Mills, R. S. L., Pedersen, J., & Grusec, J. E. (1989). Sex differences in reasoning and emotion about altruism. *Sex Roles, 20,* 603–621.

Millstein, S. G., & Halpern-Felsher, B. L. (1998). Adolescent sexuality. In E. A. Blechman & K. D. Brownell (Eds.), *Behavioral medicine and women: A comprehensive handbook* (pp. 59–63). New York: Guilford Press.

Min, P. G. (1993). Korean immigrants' marital patterns and marital adjustment. In H. P. McAdoo (Ed.), *Family ethnicity: Strength in diversity* (pp. 287–299). Newbury Park, CA: Sage.

Mintz, R. D., & Mahalik, J. R. (1996). Gender role orientation and conflict as predictors of family roles for men. *Sex Roles, 34,* 805–821.

Mischel, W. (1966). A social-learning view of sex differences in behavior. In E. Maccoby (Ed.), *The development of sex differences* (pp. 56–81). Stanford, CA: Stanford University Press.

Mischel, W. (1970). Sex-typing and socialization. In P. Mussen (Ed.), *Carmichael's manual of child psychology (Vol. 2).* New York: Wiley.

Misri, S. (1995). *Shouldn't I be happy? Emotional problems of pregnant and postpartum women.* New York: Free Press.

Mitchell, E. S., et al. (1992). Methodological issues in the definition of premenstrual syndrome. In A. J. Dan & L. L. Lewis (Eds.), *Menstrual health in women's lives* (pp. 7–14). Urbana: University of Illinois Press.

Mitchell, J. E. (1995). Medical complications of bulimia nervosa. In K. D. Brownell & C. G. Fairburn (Eds.), *Eating disorders and obesity: A comprehensive handbook* (pp. 271–275). New York: Guilford Press.

Mitchell, P. T. (Ed.). (1993). *Cracking the wall: Women in higher education administration.* Washington, DC: College and University Personnel Association.

Mitchell, V., & Helson, R. (1990). Women's prime of life: Is it the 50s? *Psychology of Women Quarterly, 14,* 451–470.

Mogil J. S., Sternberg, W. F., Kest, B., Marek, P., & Liebeskind, J. C. (1993). Sex differences in the antagonism of swim stress-induced analgesia: Effects of gonadectomy and estrogen replacement. *Pain, 53,* 17–25.

Monaghan, P. (1998, January 23). Pioneering field of disability studies challenges established approaches and attitudes. *Chronicle of Higher Education,* pp. 15–16.

Money, J., & Ehrhardt, A. A. (1972). *Man and woman: Boy and girl.* Baltimore: Johns Hopkins University Press.

Monsour, M. (1992). Meanings of intimacy in cross- and same-sex friendships. *Journal of Social and Personal Relationships, 9,* 277–295.

Mood disorders: An overview—Part II. (1998, January). *Harvard Mental Health Letter,* pp. 1–5.

Moore, D. P., & Buttner, E. H. (1997). *Women entrepreneurs: Moving beyond the glass ceiling.* Thousand Oaks, CA: Sage.

Moraga, C. (1993). Women's subordination through the lens of sex/gender, sexuality, class, and race: Multicultural feminism. In A. M. Jaggar & P. S. Rothenberg (Eds.), *Feminist frameworks: Alternative theoretical accounts of the relations between women and men* (3rd ed., pp. 203–212). New York: McGraw-Hill.

Morawski, J. G. (1994). *Sex matters? The unending search for a valid psychology of sex differences.* Paper presented at the annual meeting of the History of Science Society, New Orleans.

Morawski, J. G., & Agronick, G. (1991). A restive legacy: The history of feminist work in experimental and cognitive psychology. *Psychology of Women Quarterly, 15,* 567–579.

Morawski, J. G., & Bayer, B. M. (1995). Stirring trouble and making theory. In H. Landrine (Ed.), *Bringing cultural diversity to feminist psychology: Theory, research, and practice* (pp. 113–137). Washington, DC: American Psychological Association.

Morell, V. (1995a). Attacking the causes of "silent" infertility. *Science, 269,* 775–777.

Morell, V. (1995b). Zeroing in on how hormones affect the immune system. *Science, 269,* 773–775.

Morgan, B. L. (1998). A three generational study of tomboy behavior. *Sex Roles, 39,* 787–800.

Mori, L., et al. (1995). Attitudes toward rape: Gender and ethnic differences across Asian and Caucasian college students. *Sex Roles, 32,* 457–467.

Morokoff, P. J. (1998). Sexual functioning. In E. A. Blechman & K. D. Brownell (Eds.), *Behavioral medicine and women: A comprehensive handbook* (pp. 440–446). New York: Guilford Press.

Morokoff, P. J., Mays, V. M., & Coons, H. L. (1997). HIV infection and AIDS. In S. J. Gallant, G. P. Keita, & R. Royak-Schaler (Eds.), *Health care for women: Psychological, social, and behavioral influences* (pp. 273–293). Washington, DC: American Psychological Association.

Morokoff, P. J., et al. (1997). Sexual Assertiveness Scale for women: Development and validation. *Journal of Personality and Social Psychology, 73,* 790–804.

Morris, L. A. (1997). *The male heterosexual.* Thousand Oaks, CA: Sage.

Morrison, D. (1987). *Being pregnant: Conversations with women.* Vancouver, British Columbia: New Star.

Moss, H. A. (1974). Early sex differences and mother-infant interaction. In R. C. Friedman, R. M. Richart, & R. L. Vande Wiele (Eds.), *Sex differences in behavior* (pp. 149–163). New York: Wiley.

Motowidlo, S. J. (1982). Sex role orientation and behavior in a work setting. *Journal of Personality and Social Psychology, 42,* 935–945.

Muehlenhard, C. L., Highby, B. J., Phelps, J. L., & Sympson, S. C. (1997). Rape statistics are not exaggerated. In M. R. Walsh (Ed.), *Women, men, & gender: Ongoing debates* (pp. 243–246). New Haven, CT: Yale University Press.

Muehlenhard, C. L., Julsonnet, S., Carlson, M. I., & Flarity-White, L. A. (1989). A cognitive-behavioral program for preventing sexual coercion. *The Behavior Therapist, 12,* pp. 211–214, 221.

Mueller, K. A., & Yoder, J. D. (1997). Gendered norms for family size, employment, and occupation: Are there personal costs for violating them? *Sex Roles, 36,* 207–220.

Muller, C. F. (1990). *Health care and gender.* New York: Russell Sage Foundation.

Murnen, S. K., & Stockton, M. (1997). Gender and self-reported sexual arousal in reponse to sexual stimuli: A meta-analytic review. *Sex Roles, 37,* 135–153.

Murphy, P. A., & Cleeton, E. C. (2000). *In the best interest of the child: Good mothers behaving badly and the law.* Philadelphia: Temple University Press.

Murray, B. (1997, January). Some schools are blind to hiring minority faculty. *APA Monitor,* p. 42.

Murray, B. (1998, July). Workplace harassment hurts everyone on the job. *APA Monitor,* p. 35.

Murrell, A. J., Olson, J. E., & Frieze, I. H. (1995). Sexual harassment and gender discrimination: A longitudinal study of women. *Journal of Social Issues, 51,* 139–149.

Murry, V. M. (1996). Inner-city girls of color: unmarried, sexually active nonmothers. In B. J. R. Leadbeater & N. Way (Eds.), *Urban girls: Resisting stereotypes, creating identities* (pp. 272–290). New York: New York University Press.

Muth, J. L., & Cash, T. F. (1997). Body-image attitudes: What difference does gender make? *Journal of Applied Social Psychology, 27,* 1438–1452.

Mwangi, M. W. (1996). Gender roles portrayed in Kenyan television commercials. *Sex Roles, 34,* 205–214.

Myers, D. G., & Diener, E. (1996, May). The pursuit of happiness. *Scientific American,* pp. 70–72.

Myers, S. T., & Grasmick, H. G. (1990). The social rights and responsibilities of pregnant women: An application of Parson's sick role model. *Journal of Applied Behavioral Science, 26,* 157–172.

Naidoo, J. C. (1990a). *Asian immigrant women in Canadian work settings: Identity challenges for the 90s.* Paper presented at the meetings of the International Association of Cross-Cultural Psychology, Nara, Japan.

Naidoo, J. C. (1990b). Immigrant women in Canada: Towards a new decade. *Currents, 6,* 18–21.

Naidoo, J. C. (1990c). *Multicultural and gender issues on aging in Canada.* Paper presented at the 22nd International Congress of Applied Psychology, Kyoto, Japan.

Naidoo, J. C., & Davis, J. C. (1988). Canadian South Asian women in transition: A dualistic view of life. *Journal of Comparative Family Studies, 19,* 311–327.

Napier, L. A. (1996). Nine native women: Pursuing the doctorate and aspiring to positions of leadership. In K. D. Arnold, K. D. Noble, & R. F. Subotnik (Eds.), *Remarkable women: Perspectives on female talent development* (pp. 133–148). Creeskill, NJ: Hampton Press.

Naples, N. A. (Ed.). (1998). *Community activism and feminist politics: Organizing across race, class, and gender.* New York: Routledge.

Napper, T. (1998). *Personal communication.*

Nash, H. C., & Chrisler, J. C. (1997). Is a little (psychiatric) knowledge a dangerous thing? *Psychology of Women Quarterly, 21,* 315–322.

National Center on Addiction and Substance Abuse. (1996). *Substance abuse and the American woman.* New York: Author.

National Foundation for Women Business Owners. (1994). *Styles of success: The thinking and management styles of women and men entrepreneurs.* Washington, DC: Author.

National Organization for Men Against Sexism. (1998). Statement of principles. In M. S. Kimmel & M. A. Messner (Eds.), *Men's lives* (4th ed., p. 591). Boston: Allyn & Bacon.

National Women's Studies Association. (1999). *Personal communication.*

Neft, N., & Levine, A. D. (1997). *Where women stand: An international report on the status of women in 140 countries.* New York: Random House.

Nelson, E. J. (1996). The American experience of childbirth: Toward a range of safe choices. In R. L. Parrott & C. M. Condit (Eds.), *Evaluating women's health messages: A resource book* (pp. 109–123). Thousand Oaks, CA: Sage.

Nelson, H. D. (1998). Osteoporosis prevention. In A. Blechman & K. D. Brownell (Eds.), *Behavioral medicine and women: A comprehensive handbook* (pp. 221–227). New York: Guilford Press.

Neter, E., Collins, N. L., Lobel, M., & Dunkel-Schetter, C. (1995). Psychosocial predictors of postpartum depressed mood in socioeconomically disadvantaged women. *Women's health: Research on gender, behavior, and policy, 1,* 51–75.

Nevid, J. S. (1984). Sex differences in factors of romantic attraction. *Sex Roles, 11,* 401–411.

Nevill, D. D. (1995). The work importance study in the United States. In D. E. Super & B. Šverko (Eds.), *Life roles, values, and careers: International findings of the work importance study* (pp. 204–221). San Francisco: Jossey-Bass.

Nevill, D. D., & Calvert, P. D. (1996). Career assessment and the salience inventory. *Journal of Career Assessment, 4,* 399–412.

Nevill, D. D., & Kruse, S. J. (1996). Career assessment and the values scale. *Journal of Career Assessment, 4,* 383–397.

Newcomb, M. D. (1987). Cohabitation and marriage: A quest for independence and relatedness. In S. Oskamp (Ed.), *Family processes and problems* (pp. 128–156). Newbury Park, CA: Sage.

Newell, C. E., Rosenfeld, P., & Culbertson, A. L. (1995). Sexual harassment experiences and equal opportunity perceptions of Navy women. *Sex Roles, 32,* 159–168.

Newman, A. L., & Peterson, C. (1996). Anger of women incest survivors. *Sex Roles, 34,* 463–474.

Newman, J. (1995, December). How breast milk protects newborns. *Scientific American,* pp. 76–79.

New solutions for morning sickness. (1994, January). *Tufts University Diet & Nutrition Letter,* pp. 6–7.

NiCarthy, G., Gottlieb, N., & Coffman, S. (1993). *You don't have to take it! A woman's guide to confronting emotional abuse at work.* Seattle: Seal Press.

NICHD Early Child Care Research Network. (1997). The effects of infant child care on infant-mother attachment security: Results of the NICHD Study of Early Child Care. *Child Development, 68,* 860–879.

Nicholls, J. G. (1975). Causal attribution and other achievement-related cognitions: Effects of task outcome, attainment value, and sex. *Journal of Personality and Social Psychology, 31,* 379–389.

Nichols, M. (1982). The treatment of inhibited sexual desire (ISD) in lesbian couples. *Women & Therapy, 1,* 49–66.

Nichols, M. (1990). Lesbian relationships: Implications for the study of sexuality and gender. In D. P. McWhirter, S. A. Sanders, & J. M. Reinisch (Eds.), *Homosexuality/Heterosexuality: Concepts of sexual orientation* (pp. 350–364). New York: Oxford University Press.

Nicholson, L. (1994). Interpreting *gender. Signs, 20,* 79–105.

Nicolson, P. (1997). *Against their will? Analysing women's accounts of first sexual intercourse.* Unpublished manuscript, Sheffield, England.

Nicotera, A. M. (1997). *The mate relationship: Cross-cultural applications of a rules theory.* Albany, NY: State University of New York Press.

Nielsen, L. (1996). *Adolescence: A contemporary view* (3rd ed.). Fort Worth, TX: Harcourt Brace.

Niemann, Y. F., Jennings, L., Rozelle, R. M., Baxter, J. C., & Sullivan, E. (1994). Use of free responses and cluster analysis to determine stereotypes of eight groups. *Personality and Social Psychology Bulletin, 20,* 379–390.

Nkomo, S. M., & Cox, T., Jr. (1989). Gender differences in the upward mobility of black managers: Double whammy or double advantage? *Sex Roles, 21,* 825–839.

Noell, J., Ary, D., & Duncan, T. (1997). Development and evaluation of a sexual decision-making and social skills program: "The choice is yours—preventing HIV/STDs." *Health Education & Behavior, 24,* 87–101.

Nolen-Hoeksema, S. (1990). *Sex differences in depression.* Stanford, CA: Stanford University Press.

Nolen-Hoeksema, S. (1995). Epidemiology and theories of gender differences in unipolar depression. In M. V. Seeman (Ed.), *Gender and psychopathology* (pp. 63–87). Washington, DC: American Psychiatric Press.

Nolen-Hoeksema, S., & Girgus, J. S. (1994). The emergence of gender differences in depression during adolescence. *Psychological Bulletin, 115,* 424–443.

Nolen-Hoeksema, S., & Girgus, J. S. (1995). Explanatory style and achievement, depression, and gender differences in childhood and early adolescence. In G. M. Buchanan & M. E. P. Seligman (Eds.), *Explanatory style* (pp. 57–70). Hillsdale, NJ: Erlbaum.

Nolen-Hoeksema, S., Morrow, J., & Fredrickson, B. L. (1993). Response styles and the duration of episodes of depressed mood. *Journal of Abnormal Psychology, 102,* 20–28.

Nolin, M. J., & Petersen, K. K. (1992). Gender differences in parent-child communication about sexuality: An exploratory study. *Journal of Adolescent Research, 7,* 59–79.

Noor, N. M. (1996). Some demographic, personality, and role variables as correlates of women's well-being. *Sex Roles, 34,* 603–620.

Norcross, J. C., Hanych, J. M., & Terranova, R. D. (1996). Graduate study in psychology: 1992–1993. *American Psychologist, 51,* 631–643.

Normand, J. (1995a). Education. In Minister of Industry (Ed.), *Women in Canada: A statistical report* (3rd ed., pp. 32–51). Ottawa: Statistics Canada.

Normand, J. (1995b). Health. In Minister of Industry (Ed.), *Women in Canada: A statistical report* (3rd. ed., pp. 32–51). Ottawa: Statistics Canada.

Norton, K. I., et al. (1996). Ken and Barbie at life size. *Sex Roles, 34,* 287–294.

Notman, M. T. (1991). Gender development. In M. T. Notman & C. C. Nadelson (Eds.), *Women and men: New perspectives on gender differences* (pp. 117–127). Washington, DC: American Psychiatric Press.

Novack, L. L., & Novack, D. R. (1996). Being female in the eighties and nineties: Conflicts between new opportunities and traditional expectations among White, middle class, heterosexual college women. *Sex Roles, 35,* 57–77.

Nowak, R. (1995). New push to reduce maternal mortality in poor countries. *Science, 269,* 780–782.

Obear, K. (1991). Homophobia. In N. J. Evans & V. A. Wall (Eds.), *Beyond tolerance: Gays, lesbians and bisexuals on campus* (pp. 39–66). Lanham, MD: American College Personnel Association.

Ochman, J. M. (1996). The effects of nongender-role stereotyped, same-sex role models in storybooks on the self-esteem of children in grade three. *Sex Roles, 35,* 711–735.

O'Connell, A. N., & Russo, N. F. (1983). *Models of achievement: Reflections of eminent women in psychology.* New York: Columbia University Press.

O'Connor, P. (1992). *Friendships between women: A critical review.* New York: Guilford Press.

O'Connor, P. G., & Schottenfeld, R. S. (1998). Patients with alcohol problems. *New England Journal of Medicine, 338,* 592–602.

O'Farrell, B. (1995). Women in blue-collar occupations: Traditional and nontraditional. In J. Freeman (Ed.), *Women: A feminist perspective* (5th ed., pp. 238–261). Mountain View, CA: Mayfield.

Offermann, L. R., & Beil, C. (1992). Achievement styles of women leaders and their peers. *Psychology of Women Quarterly, 16,* 37–56.

Office of Research and Media Reaction. (1994). *A world view of women.* Washington, DC: Author.

Oggins, J., Veroff, J., & Leber, D. (1993). Perceptions of marital interaction among Black and White newlyweds. *Journal of Personality and Social Psychology, 65,* 494–511.

O'Hanlan, K. A. (1998). Menopause. In E. A. Blechman & K. D. Brownell (Eds.), *Behavioral medicine and women: A comprehensive handbook* (pp. 520–527). New York: Guilford Press.

O'Hara, M. W. (1995). Childbearing. In M. W. O'Hara et al. (Eds.), *Psychological aspects of women's reproductive health* (pp. 26–48). New York: Springer.

Okamura, A., Heras, P., & Wong-Kerberg, L. (1995). Asian, Pacific Island, and Filipino Americans and sexual child abuse. In L. A. Fontes (Ed.), *Sexual abuse in nine North American cultures* (pp. 67–96). Thousand Oaks, CA: Sage.

Oliver, M. B., & Hyde, J. S. (1993). Gender differences in sexuality: A meta-analysis. *Psychological Bulletin, 114,* 29–51.

Oliver, M. B., & Sedikides, C. (1992). Effects of sexual permissiveness on desirability of partner as a function of low and high commitment to relationship. *Social Psychology Quarterly, 55,* 321–333.

Olsen, N. J., & Willemsen, E. (1978). Studying sex prejudice in children. *Journal of Genetic Psychology, 133,* 203–216.

Olson, A. L., & DiBrigida, L. A. (1994). Depressive symptoms and work role satisfaction in mothers of toddlers. *Pediatrics, 94,* 363–368.

Olson, E. (1994). Female voices of aggression in Tonga. *Sex Roles, 30,* 237–248.

O'Neil, J. M. (1996a). The gender role journey workshop: Exploring sexism and gender role conflict in a coeducational setting. In M. P. Andronico (Ed.), *Men in groups: Insights, interventions, and psychoeducational work* (pp. 193–213). Washington, DC: American Psychological Association.

O'Neil, J. M. (1996b). Men in groups: Insights, interventions, and psychoeducational work. In M. P. Andronico (Ed.), *Men in groups: Insights, interventions, and psychoeducational work* (pp. 193–213). Washington, DC: American Psychological Association.

O'Neil, J. M., & Egan, J. (1992). Men's and women's gender role journeys: A metaphor for healing, transition, and transformation. In B. R. Wainrib (Ed.), *Gender issues across the life cycle* (pp. 107–123). New York: Springer.

O'Neil, J. M., Good, G. E., & Holmes, S. (1995). Fifteen years of theory and research on men's gender role conflict: New Paradigms for empirical reseach. In R. Levant & W. Pollack (Eds.), *The new psychology of men* (pp. 164–206). New York: Basic Books.

O'Neil, J. M., & Harway, M. (1997). A multivariate model explaining men's violence toward women. *Violence Against Women, 3,* 182–203.

O'Neil, J. M., & Nadeau, R. A. (1998). Men's gender role conflict, defense mechanisms, and self-protective defensive strategies: Explaining men's violence against women from a gender role socialization perspective. In M. Harway & J. M. O'Neil (Eds.), *New perspectives on violence against women.* Thousand Oaks, CA: Sage.

O'Rand, A. M., Henretta, J. C., & Krecker, M. L. (1992). Family pathways to retirement. In M. Szinovacz, D. J. Ekerdt, & B. H. Vinick (Eds.), *Families and retirement* (pp. 81–98). Newbury Park, CA: Sage.

Orbuch, T. L., House, J. S., Mero, R. P., & Webster, P. S. (1996). Marital quality over the life course. *Social Psychology Quarterly, 59,* 162–171.

Orr, D. P., Langefeld, C. D., Katz, B. P., & Caine, V. A. (1996). Behavioral intervention to increase condom use among high-risk female adolescents. *Journal of Pediatrics, 128,* 288–295.

Osland, J. A., Fitch, M., & Willis, E. E. (1996). Likelihood to rape in college males. *Sex Roles, 35,* 171–183.

Ovrebo, B., & Minkler, M. (1993). The lives of older women: Perspectives from political economy and the humanities. In T. R. Cole, W. A. Achenbaum, P. L. Jakobi, & R. Kastenbaum (Eds.), *Voices and visions of aging: Toward a critical gerontology* (pp. 289–308). New York: Springer.

Owen, S. A., & Caudill, S. A. (1996). Contraception and clinical science: The place of women in reproductive technology. In R. L. Parrott & C. M. Condit (Eds.), *Evaluating women's health messages* (pp. 81–94). Thousand Oaks, CA: Sage.

Owens, R. E., Jr. (1998). *Queer kids: The challenges and promise for lesbian, gay, and bisexual youth.* Binghamton, NY: Haworth.

Ozer, E. M., & Bandura, A. (1990). Mechanisms governing empowerment effects: A self-efficacy analysis. *Journal of Personality and Social Psychology, 58,* 472–486.

Paglia, C. (1992). *Sex, art, and American culture.* New York: Vintage.

Palmore, E. B. (1997). Sexism and ageism. In J. M. Coyle (Ed.), *Handbook on women and aging* (pp. 3–13). Westport, CT: Greenwood Press.

Paludi, M. A. (1984). Psychometric properties and underlying assumptions of four objective measures of fear of success. *Sex Roles, 10,* 765–781.

Paludi, M. A. (Ed.). (1996). *Sexual harassment on college campuses: Abusing the ivory power.* Albany: State University of New York Press.

Paludi, M. A., & Barickman, R. B. (1998). *Sexual harassment, work, and education: A resource manual for prevention* (2nd ed.). Albany: State University of New York Press.

Paludi, M. A., & Gullo, D. F. (1987). The effect of sex labels on adults' knowledge of infant development. *Sex Roles, 16,* 19–30.

Paludi, M. A., et al. (1995). Academic sexual harassment: From theory and research to program implementation. In H. Landrine (Ed.), *Bringing cultural diversity to feminist psychology* (pp. 177–191). Washington, DC: American Psychological Association.

Pandey, A. (1992, January 31). Where victims are seen as villains: Dealing with sexual harassment. *India Abroad,* pp. 26–31.

Pappas, G., Queen, S., Hadden, W., & Fisher, G. (1993). The increasing disparity in mortality between socioeconomic groups in the United States, 1960 and 1986. *New England Journal of Medicine, 329,* 103–109.

Parrot, A. (1991). Institutional response: How can acquaintance rape be prevented? In A. Parrot & L. Bechhofer (Eds.), *Acquaintance rape: The hidden crime* (pp. 355–367). New York: Wiley.

Parrot, A. (1996). Sexually assertive communication training. In T. L. Jackson (Ed.), *Acquaintance rape: Assessment, treatment, and prevention* (pp. 215–242). Sarasota, FL: Professional Resource Press.

Pasch, L. A., & Dunkel-Schetter, C. (1997). Fertility problems: Complex issues faced by women and couples. In S. J. Gallant, G. P. Keita, & R. Royak-Schaler (Eds.), *Health care for women: Psychological, social, and behavioral influences* (pp. 187–201). Washington, DC: American Psychological Association.

Pasupathi, M., Carstensen, L. L., & Tsai, J. L. (1995). Ageism in interpersonal settings. In B. Lott & D. Maluso (Eds.), *The social psychology of interpersonal discrimination* (pp. 160–182). New York: Guilford Press.

Patrick, G. T. W. (1895). The psychology of women. *Popular Science Monthly, 47,* 209–225.

Pattatucci, A. M. L., & Hamer, D. H. (1995). Development and familiality of sexual orientation in females. *Behavior Genetics, 25,* 407–420.

Patterson, C. J. (1995a). Adoption of minor children by lesbian and gay adults: A social science perspective. *Duke Journal of Gender Law & Policy, 2,* 191–205.

Patterson, C. J. (1995b). Sexual orientation and human development: An overview. *Developmental Psychology, 31,* 3–11.

Patterson, C. J. (1996). Lesbian and gay parents and their children. In R. C. Savin-Williams & K. M. Cohen (Eds.), *The lives of lesbians, gays, and bisexuals: Children to adults* (pp. 274–304). Fort Worth, TX: Harcourt Brace.

Patton, W., & Mannison, M. (1995). Sexual coercion in high school dating. *Sex Roles, 33,* 447–456.

Paz, J. J. (1993). Support of Hispanic elderly. In H. P. McAdoo (Ed.), *Family ethnicity* (pp. 177–183). Newbury Park, CA: Sage.

Pearce, J. L. (1993). *Volunteers: The organizational behavior of unpaid workers.* London: Routledge.

Pearson, P. (1998). *When she was bad: Violent women and the myth of innocence.* New York: Viking.

Peirce, K. (1990). A feminist theoretical perspective on the socialization of teenage girls through *Seventeen* magazine. *Sex Roles, 23,* 491–500.

Peña, M. (1998). Class, gender, and machismo: The "treacherous-woman" folklore of Mexican male workers. In M. S. Kimmel & M. A. Messner (Eds.), *Men's lives* (4th ed., pp. 273–284). Boston: Allyn & Bacon.

Penelope, J. (1990). *Speaking freely: Unlearning the lies of the fathers' tongues.* Elmsford, NY: Pergamon Press.

Penn, M., & Schoen, D. (1998, March 30). The single files. *New York Magazine,* pp. 24–32.

Peplau, L. A. (1983). Roles and gender. In H. H. Kelley, E. Berscheid, A. Christensen, J. Harvey, & D. Peterson (Eds.), *Close relationships* (pp. 220–264). San Francisco: Freeman.

Peplau, L. A. (1994). Men and women in love. In D. L. Sollie & L. A. Leslie (Eds.), *Gender, families, and close relationships: Feminist research journeys* (pp. 19–49). Thousand Oaks, CA: Sage.

Peplau, L. A. (1997). *Personal communication.*

Peplau, L. A., & Amaro, H. (1982). Understanding lesbian relationships. In W. Paul, J. D. Weinrich, J. C. Gonsiorek, & M. E. Hotvedt (Eds.), *Homosexuality: Social, psychological, and biological issues* (pp. 233–247). Beverly Hills, CA: Sage.

Peplau, L. A., & Campbell, S. M. (1989). The balance of power in dating and marriage. In J. Freeman (Ed.), *Women: A feminist perspective* (4th ed., pp. 121–137). Mountain View, CA: Mayfield.

Peplau, L. A., Cochran, S. D., & Mays, V. M. (1997). *Ethnic and cultural diversity among lesbians and gay men* (pp. 11–38). Thousand Oaks, CA: Sage.

Peplau, L. A., DeBro, S. C., Veniegas, R. C., & Taylor, P. L. (1999). *Gender, culture, and ethnicity: Current research about women and men.* Mountain View, CA: Mayfield.

Peplau, L. A., Padesky, C., & Hamilton, M. (1982). Satisfaction in lesbian relationships. *Journal of Homosexuality, 8,* 23–35.

Peplau, L. A., Veniegas, R. C., & Campbell, S. M. (1996). Gay and lesbian relationships. In R. C. Savin-Williams & K. Cohen (Eds.), *The lives of lesbians, gays, and bisexuals: Children to adults* (pp. 250–273). Fort Worth, TX: Harcourt Brace.

Peplau, L. A., Veniegas, R. C., Taylor, P. L., & DeBro, S. C. (1998). Sociocultural perspectives on the lives of women and men. In L. A. Peplau, S. C. DeBro, R. C. Veniegas, & P. L. Taylor (Eds.), *Gender, culture, and ethnicity: Current research about women and men.* Mountain View, CA: Mayfield.

Peplau, L. A., et al. (1998). A critique of Bem's "exotic becomes erotic" theory of sexual orientation. *Psychological Review, 105,* 387–394.

Perkins, H. W., & DeMeis, D. K. (1996). Gender and family effects on the "second shift" domestic activity of college-educated young adults. *Gender & Society, 10,* 78–93.

Perrone, J. (1991, June 24). Sexism far from dead in medicine. *American Medical News,* p. 5.

Perry-Jenkins, M., Seery, B., & Crowter, A. C. (1992). Linkages between women's provider-role attitudes, psychological well-being, and family relationships. *Psychology of Women Quarterly, 16,* 311–329.

Peters, D. K., & Cantrell, P. J. (1993). Gender roles and role conflict in feminist lesbian and heterosexual women. *Sex Roles, 28,* 379–392.

Peters, J., & Wolper, A. (Eds.). (1995). *Women's rights, human rights: International feminist perspectives.* New York: Routledge.

Peterson, G. (1996). Childbirth: The ordinary miracle: Effects of devaluation of childbirth on women's self-esteem and family relationships. *Pre- and Perinatal Psychology Journal, 11,* 101–109.

Petretic-Jackson, P. A., & Jackson, T. (1996). Mental health interventions with battered women. In A. R. Roberts (Ed.), *Helping battered women* (pp. 188–221). New York: Oxford University Press.

Petretic-Jackson, P. A., & Tobin, S. (1996). The rape trauma syndrome: Symptoms, stages, and hidden victims. In T. L. Jackson (Ed.), *Acquaintance rape: Assessment, treatment, and prevention* (pp. 93–143). Sarasota, FL: Professional Resource Press.

Petrie, T. A., et al. (1996). Sociocultural expectations of attractiveness for males. *Sex Roles, 35,* 581–602.

Pezdek, K., & Banks, W. P. (Eds.). (1996). *The recovered memory/false memory debate.* San Diego, CA: Academic Press.

Pfau, M., Nelson, M. L., & Moster, M. (1996). Women and smoking: Consequences and solutions. In R. L. Parrott & C. M. Condit (Eds.), *Evaluating women's health messages: A resource book* (pp. 139–153). Thousand Oaks, CA: Sage.

Pfister, B. (1994, Spring). Swept awake! Negotiating passion on campus. *On the Issues,* pp. 12–16.

Phares, V. (1992). Where's Poppa? The relative lack of attention to the role of fathers in child and adolescent psychopathology. *American Psychologist, 47,* 656–664.

Phares, V., & Compas, B. E. (1992). The role of fathers in child and adolescent psychopathology: Make room for daddy. *Psychological Bulletin, 111,* 387–412.

Philbin, M., Meier, E., Hoffman, S., & Boverie, P. (1995). A survey of gender and learning styles. *Sex Roles, 32,* 485–494.

Phillips, D., McCartney, K., & Scarr, S. (1987). Child-care quality and children's social development. *Developmental Psychology, 23,* 537–543.

Phillips, L. (1998). *The girls report.* New York: National Council for Research on Women.

Phillips, S. D., & Imhoff, A. R. (1997). Women and career development: A decade of research. *Annual Review of Psychology, 48,* 31–59.

Philpot, C. L., Brooks, G. R., Lusterman, D. D., & Nutt, R. L. (1997). *Bridging separate gender worlds.* Washington, DC: American Psychological Association.

Phinney, J. S., & Alipuria, L. (1990). Ethnic identity in college students from four ethnic groups. *Journal of Adolescence, 13,* 171–183.

Phinney, J. S., & Rosenthal, D. A. (1992). Ethnic identity in adolescence: Process, context, and outcome. In G. R. Adams, T. P. Gullota, & R. Montemayor (Eds.), *Adolescent identity formation* (pp. 145–172). Newbury Park, CA: Sage.

Phoenix, A., Woollett, A., & Lloyd, E. (Eds.). (1991). *Motherhood: Meanings, practices and ideologies*. London: Sage.

Pierce, J. L. (1995). *Gender trials: Emotional lives in contemporary law firms*. Berkeley: University of California Press.

Pike, K. M., & Striegel-Moore, R. H. (1997). Disordered eating and eating disorders. In S. J. Gallant, G. P. Keita, & R. Royak-Schaler (Eds.), *Health care for women: Psychological, social, and behavioral influences* (pp. 97–114). Washington, DC: American Psychological Association.

Pilkington, N. W., & D'Augelli, A. R. (1995). Victimization of lesbian, gay, and bisexual youth in community settings. *Journal of Community Psychology, 23*, 34–56.

Pillard, R. (1997). [Review of the book *A natural history of homosexuality*]. *New England Journal of Medicine, 337*, 645–646.

Pion, G. M., et al. (1996). The shifting gender composition of psychology. *American Psychologist, 51*, 509–528.

Pipher, M. (1995a). *Hunger pains: The modern woman's tragic quest for thinness*. New York: Ballantine.

Pipher, M. (1995b). *Reviving Ophelia: Saving the selves of adolescent girls*. New York: Ballantine.

Pleck, J. H. (1997). Paternal involvement: Levels, sources, and consequences. In M. E. Lamb (Ed.), *The role of the father in child development* (pp. 66–103). New York: Wiley.

PMS: It's real. (1994, July). *Harvard Women's Health Watch*, pp. 2–3.

Pocs, O., Godow, A., Tolone, W. L., & Walsh, R. H. (1983). Is there sex after 40? In O. Pocs (Ed.), *Human sexuality 83/84* (pp. 190–192). Guilford, CT: Dushkin.

Pogrebin, L. C. (1997, September/October). Endless love. *Ms. Magazine*, pp. 36–37.

Polivy, J., & McFarlane, T. L. (1998). Dieting, exercise, and body weight. In E. A. Blechman & K. D. Brownell (Eds.), *Behavioral medicine and women: A comprehensive handbook* (pp. 369–373). New York: Guilford Press.

Pomerleau, A., Bolduc, D., Malcuit, G., & Cossette, L. (1990). Pink or blue: Environmental gender stereotypes in the first two years of life. *Sex Roles, 22*, 359–367.

Ponton, L. E. (1996). Disordered eating. In R. J. DiClemente, W. B. Hansen, & L. E. Ponton (Eds.), *Handbook of adolescent health risk behavior* (pp. 83–113). New York: Plenum Press.

Pooler, W. S. (1991). Sex of child preferences among college students. *Sex Roles, 25*, 569–576.

Pope, K. S. (1994, August). Sexual involvement between therapists and patients. *Harvard Mental Health Letter*, pp. 5–6.

Pope, K. S., & Bouhoutsos, J. C. (1986). *Sexual intimacy between therapists and patients*. New York: Praeger.

Pope, K. S., & Brown, S. (1996). *Recovered memories of abuse: Assessment, therapy, forensics*. Washington, DC: American Psychological Association.

Pope, K. S., & Vasquez, M. J. T. (1991). *Ethics in psychotherapy and counseling: A practical guide for psychologists*. San Francisco: Jossey-Bass.

Pope, R. L., & Reynolds, A. L. (1991). Including bisexuality: It's more than just a label. In N. J. Evans & V. A. Wall (Eds.), *Beyond tolerance: Gays, lesbians and bisexuals on campus* (pp. 205–221). Lanham, MD: American College Personnel Association.

Poppema, S. T. (1998, January/February). *Roe v. Wade*. *Ms. Magazine*, p. 76.

Porter, N. (1995). Supervision of psychotherapists: Integrating anti-racist, feminist, and multicultural perspectives. In H. Landrine (Ed.), *Bringing cultural diversity to feminist psychology: Theory, research, and practice* (pp. 163–175). Washington, DC: American Psychological Association.

Powlishta, K. K. (1995). Intergroup processes in childhood: Social categorization and sex role development. *Developmental Psychology, 31*, 781–788.

Price-Bonham, S., & Skeen, P. (1982). Black and white fathers' attitudes toward children's sex roles. *Psychological Reports, 50*, 1187–1190.

Primomo, J. (1995). Chronic illnesses and women. In C. I. Fogel & N. F. Woods (Eds.), *Women's health care: A comprehensive handbook* (pp. 651–671). Thousand Oaks, CA: Sage.

Prout, P. I., & Dobson, K. S. (1998). Recovered memories of childhood sexual abuse: Searching for the middle ground in clinical practice. *Canadian Psychology/Psychologie Canadienne, 39*, 275–265.

Pryor, J. B., et al. (1997). Gender differences in the interpretation of social-sexual behavior: A cross-cultural perspective on sexual harassment. *Journal of Cross-Cultural Psychology, 28*, 509–534.

Purcell, D. W., & Hicks, D. W. (1996). Institutional discrimination against lesbians, gay men, and bisexuals: The courts, legislature, and the military. In R. P. Cabaj & Terry S. Stein (Eds.), *Textbook of homosexuality and mental health* (pp. 763–782). Washington, DC: American Psychiatric Press.

Pyke, S. W. (1994). CPA achievements and weather trends in academe. *SWAP Newsletter, 21,* 12–15.

Pyke, S. W. (1998, June). *The inferior sex: Psychology's construction of gender.* Paper presented at the Canadian Psychological Association Annual Convention, Edmonton, Canada.

Quick, H. E., & Moen, P. (1998). Gender, employment, and retirement quality: A life course approach to the differential experiences of men and women. *Journal of Occupational Health Psychology, 3,* 44–64.

Quina, K. (1996). Sexual harassment and rape: A continuum of exploitation. In M. A. Paludi (Ed.), *Sexual harassment on college campuses: Abusing the ivory power* (pp. 183–197). Albany: State University of New York Press.

Quina, K., Romenesko, K., & Cotter, M. (1994). *Assessing the glass ceiling in higher education.* Paper presented at the meeting of the Eastern Psychological Association, Providence, RI.

Rabinowitz, V. C. (1996). Coping with sexual harassment. In M. A. Paludi (Ed.), *Sexual harassment on college campuses* (pp. 199–213). Albany: State University of New York Press.

Rabuzzi, K. A. (1994). *Mother with child.* Bloomington: Indiana University Press.

Racioppi, L., & See, K. O. (1997). *Women's activism in contemporary Russia.* Philadelphia: Temple University Press.

Raffaelli, M., & Suarez-Al-Adam, A. (1998). Reconsidering the HIV/AIDS prevention needs of Latina women in the United States. In N. L. Roth & L. K. Fuller (Eds.), *Women and AIDS: Negotiating safer practices, care, and representation* (pp. 7–41). New York: Haworth.

Ragan, J. M. (1982). Gender displays in portrait photographs. *Sex Roles, 8,* 33–43.

Ragins, B. R. (1989). Power and gender congruency effects in evaluations of male and female managers. *Journal of Management, 15,* 65–76.

Ragins, B. R., & Scandura, T. A. (1995). Antecedents and work-related correlates of reported sexual harassment: An empirical investigation of competing hypotheses. *Sex Roles, 32,* 429–455.

Ragins, B. R., & Sundstrom, E. (1989). Gender and power in organizations: A longitudinal perspective. *Psychological Bulletin, 105,* 51–88.

Rajagopal, I. (1990). The glass ceiling in the vertical mosaic: Indian immigrants in Canada. *Canadian Ethnic Studies, 22,* 96–101.

Rajbala. (1986, March-April). They called her a stone. *Manushi: A Journal about Women and Society, 33,* 2–3.

Rajecki, D. W., Bledsoe, S. B., & Rasmussen, J. L. (1991). Successful personal ads: Gender differences and similarities in offers, stipulations, and outcomes. *Basic and Applied Social Psychology, 12,* 457–469.

Rajecki, D. W., et al. (1993). Gender casting in television toy advertisements: Distributions, message content analysis, and evaluations. *Journal of Consumer Psychology, 2,* 307–327.

Ralston, P. A. (1997). Midlife and older Black women. In J. M. Coyle (Ed.), *Handbook on women and aging* (pp. 273–289). Westport, CT: Greenwood Press.

Rawlings, E., & Carter, D. K. (1977). Feminist and nonsexist psychotherapy. In E. Rawlings & D. Carter (Eds.), *Psychotherapy for women.* Springfield, IL: Charles C Thomas.

Reaves, J. (1998, July/August). Small grants, big deals. *Ms. Magazine,* p. 14.

Rebecca, M., Hefner, R., & Oleshansky, B. (1976). A model of sex-role transcendence. In A. G. Kaplan & J. P. Bean (Eds.), *Beyond sex-role stereotypes: Readings toward a psychology of androgyny* (pp. 90–97). Boston: Little, Brown.

Reeder, A. L., & Conger, R. D. (1984). Differential mother and father influences on the educational attainment of black and white women. *The Sociological Quarterly, 25,* 239–250.

Reeve, J. (1997). *Understanding motivation and emotion* (2nd ed.). Fort Worth, TX: Harcourt Brace.

Regan, P. C. (1996). Sexual outcasts: The perceived impact of body weight and gender on sexuality. *Journal of Applied Social Psychology, 26,* 1803–1815.

Regan, P. C., & Berscheid, E. (1995). Gender differences in beliefs about the causes of male and female sexual desire. *Personal Relationships, 2,* 345–358.

Regan, P. C., & Berscheid, E. (1997). Gender differences in characteristics desired in a potential sexual and marriage partner. *Journal of Psychology & Human Sexuality, 9,* 25–37.

Regan, P. C., & Sprecher, S. (1995). Gender differences in the value of contributions to intimate relationships: Egalitarian relationships are not always perceived to be equitable. *Sex Roles, 33,* 221–238.

Reibstein, L. (1998, July 6). The end of "See-No-Evil." *Newsweek,* pp. 36, 38.

Reid, P. T., Haritos, C., Kelly, E., & Holland, N. E. (1995). Socialization of girls: Issues of ethnicity in gender development. In H. Landrine (Ed.), *Bringing cultural diversity to feminist psychology: Theory, research, and practice* (pp. 93–111). Washington, DC: American Psychological Association.

Reid, P. T., & Kelly, E. (1994). Research on women of color: From ignorance to awareness. *Psychology of Women Quarterly, 18,* 477–486.

Reinisch, J. M. (1990). *The Kinsey Institute new report on sex: What you must know to be sexually literate.* New York: St. Martin's.

Reis, S. M., Callahan, C. M., & Goldsmith, D. (1996). Attitudes of adolescent gifted girls and boys toward education, achievement, and the future. In K. Arnold, K. D. Noble, & R. F. Subotnik (Eds.), *Remarkable women: Perspectives on female talent development* (pp. 209–224). Creskill, NJ: Hampton Press.

Renzetti, C. M. (1997). Violence in lesbian and gay relationships. In L. L. O'Toole & J. R. Schiffman (Eds.), *Gender violence: Interdisciplinary perspectives* (pp. 285–293). New York: New York University Press.

Repetti, R. L., Matthews, K. A., & Waldron, I. (1989). Employment and women's health. *American Psychologist, 44,* 1394–1401.

Reskin, B., & Padavic, I. (1994). *Women and men at work.* Thousand Oaks, CA: Pine Forge Press.

Rhode, D. L. (1997). *Speaking of sex: The denial of gender inequality.* Cambridge, MA: Harvard University Press.

Rice, P. L., & Manderson, L. (Eds.). (1996). *Maternity and reproductive health in Asian societies.* Amsterdam: Harwood Academic Publishers.

Rich, J. (1994, March). Growing old gracefully. *Maryknoll, 88,* 7–11.

Rich, M., et al. (1998). Aggressors or victims: Gender and race in music video violence. *Pediatrics, 101,* 669–674.

Richardson, H. R. L., Beazley, R. P., Delaney, M. E., & Langille, D. B. (1997). Factors influencing condom use among students attending high school in Nova Scotia. *Canadian Journal of Human Sexuality, 6,* 185–197.

Richardson, J. T. E. (1997a). Conclusions from the study of gender differences in cognition. In P. J. Caplan, M. Crawford, J. S. Hyde, & J. T. E. Richardson (Eds.), *Gender differences in human cognition* (pp. 131–169). New York: Oxford University Press.

Richardson, J. T. E. (1997b). Introduction to the study of gender differences in cognition. In P. J. Caplan, M. Crawford, J. S. Hyde, & J. T. E. Richardson (Eds.), *Gender differences in human cognition* (pp. 3–29). New York: Oxford University Press.

Richins, M. L. (1991). Social comparison and the idealized images of advertising. *Journal of Consumer Research, 18,* 71–83.

Rickabaugh, C. A. (1994). Just who is this guy, anyway? Stereotypes of the men's movement. *Sex Roles, 30,* 459–470.

Rickard, L. M. (1999). *A study of gender representation in television commercials.* Unpublished manuscript, SUNY Geneseo.

Riger, S., & Galligan, P. (1980). Women in management: An exploration of competing paradigms. *American Psychologist, 35,* 902–910.

Rinfret-Raynor, M., & Cantin, S. (1997). Feminist theray for battered women. In G. K. Kantor & J. L. Jasinski (Eds.), *Out of the darkness: Contemporary perspectives on family violence* (pp. 219–234). Thousand Oaks, CA: Sage.

Rintala, D. H., et al. (1997). Dating issues for women with physical disabilities. *Sexuality and Disability, 15,* 219–242.

Risen, J., & Thomas, J. L. (1998). *Wrath of angels: The American abortion war.* New York: Basic Books.

Risman, B. J. (1998). *Gender vertigo: American families in transition.* New Haven: Yale University Press.

Rivers, P. C. (1994). *Alcohol and human behavior: Theory, research, and practice.* Englewood Cliffs, NJ: Prentice Hall.

Roberto, K. A. (Ed.). (1996). *Relationships between women in later life.* Binghamton, NY: Haworth.

Roberts, A. R. (1996a). Introduction: Myths and realities regarding battered women. In A. R. Roberts (Ed.), *Helping battered women* (pp. 3–12). New York: Oxford University Press.

Roberts, A. R. (1996b). Police responses to battered women: Past, present, and future. In A. R. Roberts (Ed.), *Helping battered women* (pp. 85–95). New York: Oxford University Press.

Roberts, J. A., & Chonko, L. B. (1994). Sex differences in the effect of satisfaction with pay on sales force turnover. *Journal of Social Behavior and Personality, 9,* 507–516.

Roberts, T. (1991). Gender and the influence of evaluations on self-assessments in achievement settings. *Psychological Bulletin, 109,* 297–308.

Roberts, T., & Nolen-Hoeksema, S. (1989). Sex differences in reactions to evaluative feedback. *Sex Roles, 21,* 725–747.

Roberts, T., & Nolen-Hoeksema, S. (1994). Gender comparisons in responsiveness to others' evaluations in achievement settings. *Psychology of Women Quarterly, 18,* 221–240.

Robertson, C. (1996). Grassroots in Kenya: Women, genital mutilation, and collective action, 1920–1990. *Signs, 21,* 615–642.

Robinson, M. D., & Johnson, J. T. (1997). Is it emotion or is it stress? Gender stereotypes and the perception of subjective experience. *Sex Roles, 36,* 235–258.

Robinson, M. D., Johnson, J. T., & Shields, S. A. (1998). The gender heuristic and the database: Factors affecting the perception of gender-related differences in the experience and display of emotions. *Basic and Applied Psychology, 20,* 206–219.

Robinson, P. (1997). Puberty—Am I normal? *Pediatric Annals, 26,* S133–S136.

Roche, S. E., & Sandoski, P. J. (1996). Social action for battered women. In A. R. Roberts (Ed.), *Helping battered women* (pp. 13–30). New York: Oxford University Press.

Rodin, J., & Ickovics, J. R. (1990). Women's health. *American Psychologist, 45,* 1018–1034.

Rodríguez, C. E. (Ed.). (1997a). *Latin looks: Images of Latinas and Latinos in the U.S. media.* Boulder, CO: Westview Press.

Rodríguez, C. E. (1997b). The silver screen: Stories and stereotypes. In C. E. Rodríguez (Ed.), *Latin looks: Images of Latinas and Latinos in the U.S. media* (pp. 73–79). Boulder, CO: Westview.

Rogers, R. L., & Petrie, T. A. (1996). Personality correlates of anorexic symptomatology in female undergraduates. *Journal of Counseling and development, 75,* 138–144.

Rogers, S. J. (1996). Mothers' work hours and marital quality: Variations by family structure and family size. *Journal of Marriage and the Family, 58,* 606–617.

Rogers, S. J., & Amato, P. R. (1997). Is marital quality declining? The evidence from two generations. *Social Forces, 75,* 1089–1100.

Rogers, S. J., & White, L. K. (1998). Satisfaction with parenting: The role of marital happiness, family structure and parents' gender. *Journal of Marriage and the Family, 60,* 293–308.

Rogers, T. B., Kuiper, N. A., & Kirker, W. S. (1977). Self-reference and the encoding of personal information. *Journal of Personality and Social Psychology, 35,* 677–688.

Roggman, L. A., Langlois, J. H., Hubbs-Tait, L., & Rieser-Danner, L. A. (1994). Infant day care, attachment, and the "file drawer problem." *Child Development, 65,* 1429–1443.

Romer, N., & Cherry, D. (1980). Ethnic and social class differences in children's sex-role concepts. *Sex Roles, 6,* 245–263.

Romo-Carmona, M. (1995). Lesbian Latinas: Organizational efforts to end oppression. *Journal of Gay & Lesbian Social Services, 3,* 85–93.

Rongé, L. J. (1996, November). Keeping young female athletes on a healthy track. *American Academy of Pediatrics News,* pp. 14–15.

Roopnarine, J. L., & Mounts, N. S. (1987). Current theoretical issues in sex roles and sex typing. In D. B. Carter (Ed.), *Current conceptions of sex roles and sex typing* (pp. 7–31). New York: Praeger.

Root, M. P. P. (1995). The psychology of Asian American women. In H. Landrine (Ed.), *Bringing cultural diversity to feminist psychology: Theory, research, and practice* (pp. 265–301). Washington, DC: American Psychological Association.

Rosado-Majors, E. (1998, Summer). *Black men against sexism.* Hues, p. 45.

Rose, A. J., & Montemayor, R. (1994). The relationship between gender role orientation and perceived self-competency in male and female adolescents. *Sex Roles, 31,* 579–595.

Rose, S. (1996). Who to let in: Women's cross-race friendships. In J. C. Chrisler, C. Golden, & P. D. Rozee (Eds.), *Lectures on the psychology of women* (pp. 110–226). New York: McGraw-Hill.

Rose, S., & Frieze, I. H. (1993). Young singles' contemporary dating scripts. *Sex Roles, 28,* 499–509.

Rose, S., Zand, D., & Cini, M. A. (1994). Lesbian courtship scripts. In E. Rothblum & K. A. Behony (Eds.) *Boston marriages: Romantic but asexual relationships among contemporary lesbians* (pp. 70–85). Amherst, MA: University of Massachusetts Press.

Rosenbaum, A., & Wexler, L. F. (1994, December). Hormone replacement therapy: Does benefit outweigh risk? *IM,* pp. 23–28.

Rosenthal, R. (1976). *Experimenter effects in behavioral research* (enlarged ed.). New York: Halsted.

Rosenthal, R. (1993). Interpersonal expectations: Some antecedents and some consequences. In P. D. Blank (Ed.), *Interpersonal expectations: Theory, research, and applications* (pp. 3–24). New York: Cambridge University Press.

Rosenwasser, S. M., Lingenfelter, M., & Harrington, A. F. (1989). Nontraditional gender role portrayals on television and children's gender role perceptions. *Journal of Applied Developmental Psychology, 10,* 97–105.

Ross, C. S. (1996). Hysterectomies: Don't ask "Why not?" . . . Ask "Why?" In R. L. Parrott & C. M. Condit (Eds.), *Evaluating women's health messages: A resource book* (pp. 356–369). Thousand Oaks: Sage.

Ross, E. (1995). New thoughts on "The oldest vocation": Mothers and motherhood in recent feminist scholarship. *Signs, 20,* 397–413.

Ross, S. D., Pinzler, I. K., Ellis, D. A., & Moss, K. L. (1993). *The rights of women* (3rd ed.). Carbondale, IL: Southern Illinois University Press.

Rothbart, M. K. (1983). *Longitudinal observation of infant temperament.* Unpublished manuscript, University of Oregon, Department of Psychology, Eugene, Oregon.

Rotheram-Borus, M. J., Dopkins, S., & Sabate, N., & Lightfoot, M. (1996). Personal and ethnic identity, values, and self-esteem among Black and Latino adolescent girls. In B. J. R. Leadbeater & N. Way (Eds.), *Urban girls: Resisting stereotypes, creating identities* (pp. 35–52). New York: New York University Press.

Rotter, N. G., & Rotter, G. S. (1988). Sex differences in the encoding and decoding of negative facial emotions. *Journal of Nonverbal Behavior, 12,* 139–148.

Rountree, C. (1991). *Coming into our fullness: On women turning forty.* Freedom, CA: Crossing Press.

Rountree, C. (1993). *On women turning 50: Celebrating mid-life discoveries.* San Francisco: HarperCollins.

Rousar, E. E., III, & Aron, A. (1990, July). *Valuing, altruism, and the concept of love.* Paper presented at the Fifth International Conference on Personal Relationships, Oxford, England.

Rowe, J. W., & Devons, C. A. J. (1995). Physiological and clinical considerations of the geriatric patient. In E. W. Busse & D. G. Blazer (Eds.), *Textbook of geriatric psychiatry* (2nd ed., pp. 25–59). Washington, DC: American Psychiatric Press.

Rowland, J. H. (1998). Breast cancer: Psychosocial aspects. In E. A. Blechman & K. D. Brownell (Eds.), *Behavioral medicine and women: A comprehensive handbook* (pp. 577–587). New York: Guilford Press.

Royak-Schaler, R., Stanton, A. L., & Danoff-Burg, S. (1997). Breast cancer: Psychosocial factors influencing risk perception, screening, diagnosis, and treatment. In S. J. Gallant, G. P. Keita, & R. Royak-Schaler (Eds.), *Health care for women: Psychological, social, and behavioral influences* (pp. 295–314). Washington, DC: American Psychological Association.

Royce, J. E., & Scratchley D. (1996). *Alcoholism and other drug problems.* New York: Free Press.

Rozee, P. D. (1996). Freedom from fear of rape: The missing link in women's freedom. In J. C. Chrisler, C. Golden, & P. D. Rozee (Eds.), *Lectures on the psychology of women* (pp. 309–322). New York: McGraw-Hill.

Rubin, D. L., & Greene, K. (1992). Gender-typical style in written language. *Research in the Teaching of English, 26,* 7–40.

Rubin, D. L., & Greene, K. (1994). The suppressed voice hypothesis in women's writing: Effects of revision on gender-typical style. In D. L. Rubin (Ed.), *Composing social identity in written language* (pp. 133–149). Hillsdale, NJ: Erlbaum.

Rubin, J. Z. (1988). Foreword. In M. Fine & A. Asch (Eds.), *Women with disabilities* (pp. ix–x). Philadelphia: Temple University Press.

Rubin, R. M. (1997). The economic status of older women. In J. M. Coyle (Ed.), *Handbook on women and aging* (pp. 75–92). Westport, CT: Greenwood.

Rubin, Z., Peplau, L. A., & Hill, C. T. (1981). Loving and leaving: Sex differences in romantic attachments. *Sex Roles, 7,* 821–835.

Ruble, D. R., & Brooks-Gunn, J. (1982). A developmental analysis of menstrual distress in adolescence. In R. C. Friedman (Ed.), *Behavior and the menstrual cycle* (pp. 177–216). New York: Marcel Dekker.

Ruble, D. R., & Martin, C. L. (1998). Gender development. In W. Damon (Series Ed.) & N. Eisenberg (Vol. Ed.), *Handbook of child psychology: Vol. 4: Social, emotional, and personality development* (pp. 933–1016). New York: Wiley.

Ruble, T. L., Cohen, R., & Ruble, D. N. (1984). Sex stereotypes: Occupational barriers for women. *American Behavioral Scientist, 27,* 339–356.

Ruether, R. R. (1994). Christianity and women in the modern world. In A. Sharma (Ed.), *Today's woman in world religions* (pp. 267–301). Albany: State University of New York Press.

Ruksznis, E. (1998, January). Women's health research goes "where no man has gone before." *APS Observer,* pp. 14–15, 18.

Runions, D. (1996). HIV/AIDS: A personal perspective. In L. D. Long & E. M. Ankrah (Eds.), *Women's experiences with HIV/AIDS* (pp. 56–72). New York: Columbia University Press.

Runté, M. (1998). Women with disabilities: Alone on the playground. *Canadian Women Studies/les cahiers de la femme,* 18, 101–105.

Rushing, B., & Schwabe, A. (1995). The health effects of work and family role characteristics: Gender and race comparisons. *Sex Roles, 33,* 59–75.

Russell, D. E. H. (1990). *Rape in marriage* (rev. ed.). Bloomington: Indiana University Press.

Russo, N. F. (1990). Overview: Forging research priorities for women's mental health. *American Psychologist, 45,* 368–373.

Russo, N. F. (1992). Psychological aspects of unwanted pregnancy and its resolution. In J. D. Butler & D. F. Walbert (Eds.), *Abortion, medicine, and the law* (pp. 593–626). New York: Facts on File.

Russo, N. F., & Green, B. L. (1993). Women and mental health. In F. L. Denmark & M. A. Paludi (Eds.), *Psychology of women: A handbook of issues and theories* (pp. 379–436). Westport, CT: Greenwood Press.

Russo, N. F., Green, B. L., & Knight, G. (1993). The relationship of gender, self-esteem, and instrumentality to depressive symptomatology. *Journal of Social and Clinical Psychology, 12,* 218–236.

Russo, N. F., Kelly, R. M., & Deacon, M. (1991). Gender and success-related attributions: Beyond individualistic conceptions of achievement. *Sex Roles, 25,* 331–350.

Russo, N. F., & Zierk, K. L. (1992). Abortion, childbearing, and women's well-being. *Professional Psychology: Research and Practice, 23,* 269–280.

Rust, P. C. (1995). *Bisexuality and the challenge to lesbian politics: Sex, loyalty, and revolution.* New York: New York University Press.

Rust, P. C. (1996a). Managing multiple identities: Diversity among bisexual women and men. In B. A. Firestein (Ed.), *Bisexuality: The psychology and politics of an invisible minority* (pp. 53–83). Thousand Oaks, CA: Sage.

Rust, P. C. (1996b). Monogamy and polyamory: Relationship issues for bisexuals. In B. A. Firestein (Ed.), *Bisexuality: The psychology and politics of an invisible minority* (pp. 127–148). Thousand Oaks, CA: Sage.

Rutte, C. G., Diekmann, K. A., Polzer, J. T., Crosby, F. J., & Messick, D. M. (1994). Organization of information and the detection of gender discrimination. *Psychological Science, 5,* 226–231.

Rynes, S., & Rosen, B. (1995). A field survey of factors affecting the adoption and perceived success of diversity training. *Personnel Psychology, 48,* 247–270.

Saadawi, N. (1998). Nawal: "I had to find my own answer to the question." In M. C. Ward (Ed.), *A sounding of women: Autobiographies from unexpected places.* Boston: Allyn & Bacon.

Sadker, M., & Sadker, D. (1994). *Failing at fairness: How America's schools cheat girls.* New York: Scribner's.

Salmansohn, K. (1996). *How to succeed in business without a penis: Secrets and strategies for the working woman.* New York: Harmony Books.

Saltzberg, E. A., & Chrisler, J. C. (1995). Beauty is the beast: Psychological effects of the pursuit of the perfect female body. In J. Freeman (Ed.), *Women: A feminist perspective* (5th ed., pp. 306–315). Mountain View, CA: Mayfield.

Saluter, A. F. (1994). *Marital status and living arrangements: March 1993.* Washington, DC: U. S. Government Printing Office.

Sampson, E. E. (1993). Identity politics: Challenges to psychology's understanding. *American Psychologist, 48,* 1219–1230.

Sánchez-Ayéndez, M. (1993). Puerto Rican elderly women: Shared meanings and informal supportive networks. In L. Richardson & V. Taylor (Eds.), *Feminist frontiers III* (pp. 270–278). New York: McGraw-Hill.

Sandler, B. R. (1992). *Success and survival strategies for women faculty members.* Washington, DC: Association of American Colleges.

Sandler, B. R. (1997). Elements of a good policy. In B. R. Sandler & R. J. Shoop (Eds.), *Sexual harassment on campus: A guide for administrators, faculty, and students* (pp. 104–127). Boston: Allyn & Bacon.

Sandler, B. R., & Shoop, R. J. (1997). What is sexual harassment? In B. R. Sandler & R. J. Shoop (Eds.), *Sexual harassment on campus: A guide for administrators, faculty, and students* (pp. 1–21). Boston: Allyn & Bacon.

Saperstein, A., Triolo, B., & Heinzen, T. E. (1995). Ideology or experience: A study of sexual harassment. *Sex Roles, 32,* 835–842.

Sapp, S. G., Harrod, W. J., & Zhao, L. (1996). Leadership emergence in task groups with egalitarian gender-role expectations. *Sex Roles, 34,* 65–80.

Sasson, J. P. (1992). *Princess: A true story of life behind the veil in Saudi Arabia.* New York: William Morrow.

Satterfield, A. T., & Muehlenhard, C. L. (1997). Shaken confidence: The effects of an authority figure's flirtatiousness on women's and men's self-rated creativity. *Psychology of Women Quarterly, 21,* 395–416.

Savin-Williams, R. C. (1990). *Gay and lesbian youth: Expressions of identity.* New York: Hemisphere.

Savin-Williams, R. C., & Cohen, K. (Eds.). (1996). *The lives of lesbians, gays, and bisexuals: Children to adults.* Fort Worth, TX: Harcourt Brace.

Savin-Williams, R. C., & Dube, E. M. (1996). *Parental reactions to their child's disclosure of same-sex attractions.* Paper presented at the Annual Convention of the American Psychological Association, Toronto.

Scarborough, E. (1992). Women in the American Psychological Association. In R. B. Evans, V. S. Sexton, & T. C. Cadwallader (Eds.), *100 years: The American Psychological Association, a historical perspective* (pp. 303–325). Washington, DC: American Psychological Association.

Scarborough, E., & Furumoto, L. (1987). *Untold lives: The first generation of American women psychologists.* New York: Columbia University Press.

Scarr, S. (1990). Mother's proper place: Children's needs and women's rights. *Journal of Social Behavior and Personality, 5,* 507–515.

Scarr, S. (1997). Rules of evidence: A larger context for the statistical debate. *Psychological Science, 8,* 16–17.

Scarr, S. (1998). American child care today. *American Psychologist, 53,* 95–108.

Scarr, S., & Eisenberg, M. (1993). Child care research: Issues, perspectives, and results. *Annual Review of Psychology, 44,* 613–644.

Schafer, E., Vogel, M. K., Veigas, S., & Hausafus, C. (1998). *Birth, 25,* 101–106.

Schaller, J. G. (1991). Women and the future of academic pediatrics. *Journal of Pediatrics, 118,* 314–321.

Scharrer, E. (1998, December). *Men, muscles, machismo, and the media.* Department of Communication Research Colloquium, SUNY Geneseo, Geneseo, New York.

Schinke, S. P., Forgey, M. A., & Orlandi, M. (1996). Teenage sexuality. In M. A. Mattaini & B. A. Thyer (Eds.), *Finding solutions to social problems: Behavioral strategies for change* (pp. 267–288). Washington, DC: American Psychological Association.

Schmidt, P. J., et al. (1998). Differential behavioral effects of gonadal steroids in women with and in those without premenstrual syndrome. *New England Journal of Medicine, 338,* 209–216.

Schneider, M. (1989). Sappho was a right-on adolescent: Growing up lesbian. In G. Herdt (Ed.), *Gay and lesbian youth* (pp. 111–130). New York: Haworth Press.

Schover, L. R. (1991). The impact of breast cancer on sexuality, body image, and intimate relationships. *CA-A Cancer Journal for Clinicians, 41,* 112–125.

Schreurs, K. M. G., & Buunk, B. P. (1996). Closeness autonomy, equity, and relationship satisfaction in lesbian couples. *Psychology of Women Quarterly, 20,* 577–592.

Schroeder, D. A., Penner, L. A., Dovidio, J. F., & Piliavin, J. A. (1995). *The psychology of helping and altruism.* New York: McGraw-Hill.

Schuller, R. A., & Vidmar, N. (1992). Battered woman syndrome evidence in the courtroom: A review of the literature. *Law and Human Behavior, 16,* 273–291.

Schwalbe, M. (1995). Why mythopoetic men don't flock to NOMAS. In M. S. Kimmel (Ed.), *The politics of manhood* (pp. 323–332). Philadelphia: Temple University Press.

Schwartz, M. D., & DeKeseredy, W. S. (1997). *Sexual assault on the college campus: The role of male peer support.* Thousand Oaks, CA: Sage.

Schwartz, P. (1994). *Peer marriage: How love between equals really works.* New York: Free Press.

Scott, J. P. (1997). Family relationships of midlife and older women. In J. M. Coyle (Ed.), *Handbook on women and aging* (pp. 367–384). Westport, CT: Greenwood Press.

Seavey, C. A., Katz, P. A., & Zalk, S. R. (1975). Baby X: The effect of gender labels on adult responses to infants. *Sex Roles, 1,* 103–110.

Seccombe, K., & Ishii-Kuntz, M. (1994). Gender and social relationships among the never-married. *Sex Roles, 30,* 585–603.

Sedney, M. A. (1989). Conceptual and methodological sources of controversies about androgyny. In R. K. Unger (Ed.), *Representations: Social constructions of gender* (pp. 126–144). Amityville, NY: Baywood.

Seegmiller, B. (1993). Pregnancy. In F. L. Denmark & M. A. Paludi (Eds.), *Psychology of women: A handbook of issues and theories* (pp. 437–474). Westport, CT: Greenwood Press.

Selinger, M. (1998, November 18). Labor group charges harsh conditions persist. *Washington Times,* pp. B7–B8.

Selnow, G. W. (1985). Sex differences in uses and perceptions of profanity. *Sex Roles, 12,* 303–312.

Senneker, P., & Hendrick, C. (1983). Androgyny and helping behavior. *Journal of Personality and Social Psychology, 45,* 916–925.

Seppa, N. (1997a, January). Young adults and AIDS: "It can't happen to me." *APA Monitor,* p. 38.

Seppa, N. (1997b, May). Sexual harassment in the military lingers on. *APA Monitor,* pp. 40–41.

Serbin, L. A., & Sprafkin, C. (1986). The salience of gender and the process of sex typing in three- to seven-year-old children. *Child Development, 57,* 1188–1199.

Service, R. F. (1994). Contraceptive methods go back to the basics. *Science, 266,* 1480–1481.

Shafii, T. (1997, March). Resident's viewpoint: I'm not a nurse. *Pediatric News,* p. 5.

Sharp, C., & Post, R. (1980). Evaluation of male and female applications for sex-congruent and sex-incongruent jobs. *Sex Roles, 6,* 391–401.

Sharpe, P. A. (1995). Older women and health services: Moving from ageism toward empowerment. *Women & Health, 22,* 9–23.

Sharps, M. J., Price, J. L., & Williams, J. K. (1994). Spatial cognition and gender: Instructional and stimulus influences on mental image rotation performance. *Psychology of Women Quarterly, 18,* 413–425.

Sharps, M. J., Welton, A. L., & Price, J. L. (1993). Gender and task in the determination of spatial cognitive performance. *Psychology of Women Quarterly, 17,* 71–83.

Shaywitz, B. A., et al. (1995). Sex differences in the functional organization of the brain for language. *Nature, 373,* 607–609.

Shaywitz, S. E., Shaywitz, B. A., Fletcher, J. M., & Escobar, M. D. (1990). Prevalence of reading disability in boys and girls. *JAMA, 264,* 998–1002.

Shenk, D., & Fullmer, E. (1996). Significant relationships among older women: Cultural and personal constructions of lesbianism. *Journal of Women & Aging, 8,* 75–89.

Sherbourne, C. D., Wells, K. B., & Judd, L. L. (1996). Functioning and well-being of patients with panic disorder. *American Journal of Psychiatry, 153,* 213–218.

Sherman, L. A., Temple, R., & Merkatz, R. B. (1995). Women in clinical trials: An FDS perspective. *Science, 269,* 793–795.

Sherman, S. R. (1997). Images of middle-aged and older women: Historical, cultural, and personal. In J. M. Coyle (Ed.), *Handbook on women and aging* (pp. 14–28). Westport, CT: Greenwood Press.

Shields, S. A. (1975). Functionalism, Darwinism, and the psychology of women: A study in social myth. *American Psychologist, 30,* 739–754.

Shields, S. A. (1994). *Practicing social constructionism: Confessions of a feminist empiricist.* Paper presented at the annual meeting of the American Psychological Association, Los Angeles.

Shields, S. A. (1995). The role of emotion beliefs and values in gender development. In N. Eisenberg (Ed.), *Social development* (pp. 212–232). Thousand Oaks, CA: Sage.

Shields, S. A., & Cooper, P. E. (1983). Stereotypes of traditional and nontraditional childbearing roles. *Sex Roles, 9,* 363–376.

Shields, S. A., Steinke, P., & Koster, B. A. (1995). The double bind of caregiving: Representation of gendered emotion in American advice literature. *Sex Roles, 33,* 417–438.

Shimp, L., & Chartier, B. (1998, June). *Unacknowledged rape and sexual assault in a sample of university women.* Paper presented at the Annual Convention of the Canadian Psychological Association, Edmonton, Alberta.

Shumaker, S. A., & Smith, T. R. (1994). The politics of women's health. *Journal of Social Issues, 50,* 189–202.

Shumaker, S. A., & Smith, T. R. (1995). Women and coronary heart disease: A psychological perspective. In A. L. Stanton & S. Gallant (Eds.), *The psychology of women's health* (pp. 25–49). Washington, DC: American Psychological Association.

Siavelis, R. L., & Lamke, L. K. (1992). Instrumentalness and expressiveness: Predictors of heterosexual relationship satisfaction. *Sex Roles, 26,* 149–159.

Sidorowicz, L. S., & Lunney, G. S. (1980). Baby X revisited. *Sex Roles, 6,* 67–73.

Siegel, M., Brisman, J., & Weinshel, M. (1997). *Surviving an eating disorder: Strategies for family and friends* (Rev. ed.). New York: HarperCollins.

Siegel, R. J., Choldin, S., & Orost, J. H. (1995). The impact of three patriarchal religions on women. In J. C. Chrisler & A. H. Hemstreet (Eds.), *Variation on a theme: Diversity and the psychology of women* (pp. 107–144). Albany, NY: State University of New York Press.

Siegel, R. J., & Sonderegger, T. B. (1990). Ethical considerations in feminist psychotherapy with women over sixty. In H. Lerman & N. Porter (Eds.), *Feminist ethics in psychotherapy* (pp. 176–184). New York: Springer.

Signorella, M. L., Bigler, R. S., & Liben, L. S. (1993). Developmental differences in children's gender schemata about others: A meta-analytic review. *Developmental Review, 13,* 147–183.

Signorella, M. L., Bigler, R. S., & Liben, L. S. (1997). A meta-analysis of children's memories for own-sex and other-sex information. *Journal of Applied Developmental Psychology, 18,* 429–445.

Signorella, M. L., Frieze, I. H., & Hershey, S. W. (1996). Single-sex versus mixed-sex classes and gender schemata in children and adolescents. *Psychology of Women Quarterly, 20,* 599–607.

Signorielli, N. (1993). Television and adolescents' perceptions about work. *Youth and Society, 24,* 314–341.

Signorielli, N., & Lears, M. (1992). Children, television, and conceptions about chores: Attitudes and behaviors. *Sex Roles, 27,* 157–170.

Sikkema, K. J. (1998). HIV prevention. In E. A. Blechman & K. D. Brownell (Eds.), *Behavioral medicine & women: A comprehensive handbook* (pp. 198–202). New York: Guilford Press.

Silberstein, L. R. (1992). *Dual-career marriage: A system in transition.* Hillsdale, NJ: Erlbaum.

Silverstein, L. B. (1996). Fathering is a feminist issue. *Psychology of Women Quarterly, 20,* 3–37.

Simi, N. L., & Mahalik, J. R. (1997). Comparison of feminist versus psychoanalytic/dynamic and other therapists on self-disclosure. *Psychology of Women Quarterly, 21,* 465–483.

Singleton, C. H. (1987). Sex roles in cognition. In D. J. Hargreaves & A. M. Colley (Eds.), *The psychology of sex roles* (pp. 60–91). New York: Hemisphere.

Skinner, L. (1999). *Personal communication.*

Skinner, P. H., & Shelton, R. L. (1985). *Speech, language, and hearing: Normal processes and disorders* (2nd ed.). New York: Wiley.

Skowronski, J. J., & Thompson, C. P. (1990). Reconstructing the dates of personal events: Gender differences in accuracy. *Applied Cognitive Psychology, 4,* 371–381.

Skrypnek, B. J., & Snyder, M. (1982). On the self-perpetuating nature of stereotypes about women and men. *Journal of Experimental Social Psychology, 18,* 277–291.

Sleeper, L. A., & Nigro, G. N. (1987). It's not who you are but who you're with: Self-confidence in achievement settings. *Sex Roles, 16,* 57–69.

Slipp, S. (1993). *The Freudian mystique: Freud, women, and feminism.* New York: New York University Press.

Smetana, J. G. (1996, August). *Autonomy and authority in adolescent-parent relationships.* Paper presented at the International Society for the Study of Behavioral Development Conference, Quebec City.

Smith, B. J. (1991). *Personal communication.*

Smith, G. J. (1985). Facial and full-length ratings of attractiveness related to the social interactions of young children. *Sex Roles, 12,* 287–293.

Smith, M. S. (1991). An evolutionary perspective on grandparent-grandchild relationships. In P. K. Smith (Ed.), *The psychology of grandparenthood: An international perspective* (pp. 157–176). London: Routledge.

Smith, P. A., & Midlarsky, E. (1985). Empirically derived conceptions of femaleness and maleness: A current view. *Sex Roles, 12,* 313–328.

Smith, P. K. (1991). Introduction: The study of grandparenthood. In P. K. Smith (Ed.), *The psychology of grandparenthood: An international perspective* (pp. 1–16). London: Routledge.

Smith, R. W. (1979). A social psychologist looks at scientific research on homosexuality. In V. L. Bullough (Ed.), *The frontiers of sex research* (pp. 64–70). Buffalo, NY: Prometheus Books.

Smith, S. E., & Walker, W. J. (1988). Sex differences on New York state regents examinations: Support for the differential course-taking hypothesis. *Journal for Research in Mathematics Education, 19,* 81–85.

Smith, V. (1997). Sprinkler fitter. In M. Martin (Ed.), *Hard-hatted women: Life on the job* (pp. 143–149). Seattle: Seal Press.

Snell, T. L., & Morton, D. C. (1994). *Women in prison.* Washington, DC: U.S. Department of Justice.

Snell, W. E., Jr., et al. (1990). The influence of counseling orientation and culture on mental health standards for adult women and men. *International Journal of Intercultural Relations, 14,* 73–88.

Snyder, M., & Miene, P. (1994). On the functions of stereotypes and prejudice. In M. P. Zanna & J. M. Olson (Eds.), *The psychology of prejudice: The Ontario Symposium* (Vol. 7, pp. 33–54). Hillsdale, NJ: Erlbaum.

Söchting, I., Skoe, E. E., & Marcia, J. E. (1994). Care-oriented moral reasoning and prosocial behavior: A question of gender or sex role orientation. *Sex Roles, 31,* 131–147.

Sohn, D. (1982). Sex differences in achievement self-attributions: An effect-size analysis. *Sex Roles, 8,* 345–357.

Sokol, M. S., & Gray, N. S. (1998). Anorexia nervosa. In E. A. Blechman & K. D. Brownell (Eds.), *Behavioral medicine and women: A comprehensive handbook* (pp. 350–357). New York: Guilford Press.

Sommers, C. H. (1994). *Who stole feminism?* New York: Simon & Schuster.

Sommers-Flanagan, R., Sommers-Flanagan, J., & Davis, B. (1993). What's happening on music television? A gender role content analysis. *Sex Roles, 28,* 745–753.

Sonnert, G. (1995). *Who succeeds in science? The gender dimension.* New Brunswick, NJ: Rutgers University Press.

Spain, D., & Bianchi, S. M. (1996). *Balancing act: Motherhood, marriage, and employment among American women.* New York: Russell Sage Foundation.

Sparks, E. E. (1996). Overcoming stereotypes of mothers in the African American context. In K. F. Wyche & F. J. Crosby (Eds.), *Women's ethnicities: Journeys through psychology* (pp. 67–86). Boulder, CO: Westview Press.

Spence, J. T., & Hahn, E. D. (1997). The Attitudes Toward Women Scale and attitude change in college students. *Psychology of Women Quarterly, 21,* 17–34.

Spence, J. T., & Helmreich, R. L. (1983). Achievement-related motives and behaviors. In J. T. Spence (Ed.), *Achievement and achievement motives* (pp. 7–68). San Francisco, CA: Freeman.

Spender, D. (1989). *The writing or the sex.* New York: Pergamon Press.

Sprecher, S., & Felmlee, D. (1997). The balance of power in romantic heterosexual couples over time from "his" and "her" perspectives. *Sex Roles, 37,* 361–379.

Sprecher, S., & McKinney, K. (1993). *Sexuality.* Newbury Park, CA: Sage.

Sprecher, S., McKinney, K., & Orbuch, T. L. (1987). Has the double standard disappeared?: An experimental test. *Social Psychology Quarterly, 50,* 24–31.

Sprecher, S., & Sedikides, C. (1993). Gender differences in perceptions of emotionality: The case of close heterosexual relationships. *Sex Roles, 28,* 511–530.

Sprecher, S., Sullivan, Q., & Hatfield, E. (1994). Mate selection preferences: Gender differences examined in a national sample. *Journal of Personality and Social Psychology, 66,* 1074–1080.

Springen, K. (1998, June 1). The bountiful breast. *Newsweek,* p. 71.

Sprock, J., & Yoder, C. Y. (1997). Women and depression: An update on the report of the APA Task Force. *Sex Roles, 36,* 269–303.

Stack, C. B. (1994). Different voices, different visions: Gender, culture, and moral reasoning. In M. Baca Zinn & B. T. Dill (Eds.), *Women of color in U.S. society* (pp. 291–301). Philadelphia: Temple University Press.

Stagner, R. (1997, May). On the founding of SPSSI: "Reminiscences" from Dr. Stagner. *SpSSI Newsletter,* pp. 13–14.

Stake, J. E. (1997). Integrating expressiveness and instrumentality in real-life settings: A new perspective on the benefits of androgyny. *Sex Roles, 37,* 541–564.

Stake, J. E., et al. (1994). The women's studies experiences: Impetus for feminist activism. *Psychology of Women Quarterly, 18,* 17–24.

Stake, J. E., & Rose, S. (1994). The long-term impact of women's studies on students' personal lives and political activism. *Psychology of Women Quarterly, 18,* 403–412.

Stanko, E. A. (1993). Ordinary fear: Women, violence, and personal safety. In P. B. Bart & E. G. Moran (Eds.), *Violence against women: The bloody footprints* (pp. 155–165). Newbury Park, CA: Sage.

Stanley Foundation. (1997). *Building on Beijing: United States NGOs shape a women's national action agenda.* Muscatine, IA: Author.

Stanton, A. L. (1995). Psychology of women's health: Barriers and pathways to knowledge. In A. L. Stanton & S. J. Gallant (Eds.), *The psychology of women's health: Progress and challenges in research and application* (pp. 3–21). Washington, DC: American Psychological Association.

Stanton, A. L., & Danoff-Burg, S. (1995). Selected issues in women's reproductive health: Psychological perspectives. In A. L. Stanton & S. J. Gallant (Eds.), *The psychology of women's health* (pp. 261–305). Washington, DC: American Psychological Association.

Staples, R. (1995). Socio-cultural factors in Black family transformation: Toward a redefinition of family functions. In C. K. Jacobson (Ed.), *American families: Issues in race and ethnicity* (pp. 19–27). New York: Garland.

Staples, R., & Johnson, L. B. (1993). *Black families at the crossroads: Challenges and prospects.* San Francisco: Jossey-Bass.

Stapley, J. C., & Haviland, J. M. (1989). Beyond depression: Gender differences in normal adolescents' emotional experiences. *Sex Roles, 20,* 295–308.

Starr, T. (1991). *The "natural inferiority" of women: Outrageous pronouncements by misguided males.* New York: Poseidon Press.

Starrels, M. E. (1994). Husbands' involvement in female gender-typed household chores. *Sex Roles, 31,* 473–491.

Statham, H., Green, J. M., & Kafetsios, K. (1997). Who worries that something might be wrong with the baby? A prospective study of 1072 pregnant women. *Birth, 24,* 223–233.

Statistics Canada. (1993, November 18). The violence against women survey. *The Daily,* pp. 1–9.

Statistics Canada. (1995). *Women in Canada: A statistical report* (3rd ed.). Ottawa, Ontario: Author.

Steele, C. M. (1997). A threat in the air: How stereotypes shape intellectual identity and performance. *American Psychologist, 52,* 613–629.

Steele, J., & Barling, J. (1996). Influence of maternal gender-role beliefs and role satisfaction on daughters' vocational interests. *Sex Roles, 34,* 637–648.

Steil, J. M. (1997). *Marital equality: Its relationship to the well-being of husbands and wives.* Thousand Oaks, CA: Sage.

Stein, J. A., Newcomb, M. D., & Bentler, P. M. (1992). The effect of agency and communality on self-esteem: Gender differences in longitudinal data. *Sex Roles, 26,* 465–483.

Stein, M. D., et al. (1998). Sexual ethics: Disclosure of HIV-positive status to partners. *Archives of Internal Medicine, 158,* 253–257.

Steiner, M., et al. (1995). Fluoxetine in the treatment of premenstrual dysphoria. *New England Journal of Medicine, 332,* 1529–1534.

Steinhausen, H. (1995). The course and outcome of anorexia nervosa. In K. D. Brownell & C. G. Fairburn (Eds.), *Eating disorders and obesity: A comprehensive handbook* (pp. 234–237). New York: Guilford Press.

Stepnick, A., & Orcutt, J. D. (1996). Conflicting testimony: Judges' and attorneys' perceptions of gender bias in legal settings. *Sex Roles, 34,* 567–579.

Stern, M., & Karraker, M. K. (1989). Sex stereotyping of infants: A review of gender labeling studies. *Sex Roles, 20,* 501–522.

Stewart, A. J. (1994). Toward a feminist strategy for studying women's lives. In C. E. Franz & A. J. Stewart (Eds.), *Women creating lives: Identities, resilience, and resistance* (pp. 11–35). Boulder, CO: Westview Press.

Stewart, A. J., & Chester, N. L. (1982). Sex differences in human social motives: Achievement, affiliation, and power. In A. J. Stewart (Ed.), *Motivation and society* (pp. 172–218). San Francisco: Jossey-Bass.

Stewart, S., & Jambunathan, J. (1996). Hmong women and postpartum depression. *Health Care for Women International, 17,* 319–330.

Stiglmayer, A. (Ed.). (1994). *Mass rape: The war against women in Bosnia-Herzegovina.* Lincoln: University of Nebraska Press.

Stillion, J. M. (1984). *Death and the sexes.* Washington, DC: Hemisphere.

Stipek, D. J. (1984). Sex differences in children's attributions for success and failure on math and spelling tests. *Sex Roles, 11,* 969–981.

St. Jean, Y., & Feagin, J. R. (1997). Racial masques: Black women and subtle gendered racism. In N. V. Benokraitis (Ed.), *Subtle sexism* (pp. 179–205). Thousand Oaks, CA: Sage.

St. John-Parsons, D. (1978). Continuous dual-career families: A case study. *Psychology of Women Quarterly, 3,* 30–42.

Stoltz-Loike, M. (1992). *Dual career couples: New perspectives in counseling.* Alexandria, VA: American Association for Counseling and Development.

Stoney, C. M. (1998). Coronary heart disease. In E. A. Blechman & K. D. Brownell (Eds.), *Behavioral medicine and women: A comprehensive handbook* (pp. 609–614). New York: Guilford Press.

Stoppard, J. M., & Gruchy, C. D. G. (1993). Gender, context, and expression of positive emotion. *Personality and Social Psychology Bulletin, 19,* 143–150.

Stout, K., & Dello Buono, R. A. (1996). Birth control and development in three Latin American countries. In P. J. Dubeck & K. Borman (Eds.), *Women and work: A handbook* (pp. 505–509). New York: Garland.

Strasburger, V. C. (1991). Children, adolescents, and television. *Feelings and Their Medical Significance, 33*(1), 1–31.

Straus, M. A., Kantor, G. K., & Moore, D. W. (1997). Changes in cultural norms approving marital violence from 1968 to 1994. In G. K. Kantor & J. A. Jasinski (Eds.), *Out of the darkness: Contemporary perspectives on family violence* (pp. 3–16). Thousand Oaks, CA: Sage.

Strauss, J., et al. (1997). Response style theory revisited: Gender differences and stereotypes in rumination and distraction. *Sex Roles, 36,* 771–792.

Street, S., Kimmel, E. B., & Kromrey, J. D. (1995). Revisiting university student gender role perceptions. *Sex Roles, 33,* 183–201.

Street, S., Kromrey, J. D., & Kimmel, E. (1995). University faculty gender roles perceptions. *Sex Roles, 32,* 407–422.

Streit, U., & Tanguay, Y. (1994). Professional achievement, personality characteristics and professional women's self-esteem. In J. Gallivan, S. D. Crozier, & V. M. Lalande (Eds.), *Women, girls, and achievement* (pp. 63–75). North York, Ontario: Captus University Publications.

Streitmatter, J. (1994). *Toward gender equality in the classroom: Everyday teachers' beliefs and practices.* Albany: State University of New York Press.

Strickland, B. R. (1995). Research on sexual orientation and human development: A commentary. *Developmental Psychology, 31,* 137–140.

Stroebe, M. S., & Stroebe, W. (1983). Who suffers more? Sex differences in health risks of the widowed. *Psychological Bulletin, 93,* 279–301.

Stroeher, S. K. (1994). Sixteen kindergartners' gender-related views of careers. *Elementary School Journal, 95,* 95–103.

Stryker, J., et al. (1995). Prevention of HIV infection: Looking back, looking ahead. *JAMA, 275,* 1143–1148.

Stryker, R. (1996). Comparable worth and the labor market. In P. J. Dubeck & K. Borman (Eds.), *Women and work: A handbook* (pp. 74–77). New York: Garland.

Studd, M. V. (1996). Sexual harassment. In D. M. Buss & N. M. Malamuth (Eds.), *Sex, power, conflict* (pp. 54–89). New York: Oxford University Press.

Stumpf, H. (1995). Gender differences in performance on tests of cognitive abilities: experimental design issues and empirical results. *Learning and Individual Differences, 7,* 275–287.

Subrahmanyam, K., & Greenfield, P. M. (1994). Effect of video game practice on spatial skills in girls and boys. *Journal of Applied Developmental Psychology, 15,* 13–32.

Suitor, J. J. (1991). Marital quality and satisfaction with the division of household labor across the family life cycle. *Journal of Marriage and the Family, 53,* 221–230.

Sumner, K. E., & Brown, T. J. (1996). Men, women, and money: Exploring the role of gender, gender-linkage of college major and career-information sources in salary expectations. *Sex Roles, 34,* 823–839.

Sunday, S., & Lewin, M. (1985). *Integrating nuclear issues into the psychology curriculum.* Paper presented at the meeting of the Eastern Psychological Association.

Susman, J. L. (1996). Postpartum depressive disorders. *The Journal of Family Practice, 43,* S17–S24.

Sussman, N. M., & Rosenfeld, H. M. (1982). Influence of culture, language, and sex on conversational distance. *Journal of Personality and Social Psychology, 42,* 66–74.

Swim, J. K., Borgida, E., Maruyama, G., & Myers, D. G. (1989). Joan McKay versus John McKay: Do gender stereotypes bias evaluations? *Psychological Bulletin, 105,* 409–429.

Swim, J. K., & Sanna, L. J. (1996). He's skilled, she's lucky: A meta-analysis of observers' attributions for women's and men's successes and failures. *Personality and Social Psychology Bulletin, 22,* 507–519.

Switzer, J. Y. (1990). The impact of generic word choices: An empirical investigation of age- and sex-related differences. *Sex Roles, 22,* 69–82.

Symonds, P. V. (1996). Journey to the land of light: Birth among Hmong women. In P. L. Rice and L. Manderson (Eds.), *Maternity and reproductive health in Asian societies* (pp. 103–123). Amsterdam: Harwood Academic Publishers.

Szinovacz, M. (1989). Decision-making on retirement timing. In D. Brinberg & J. Jaccard (Eds.), *Dyadic decision-making* (pp. 286–310). New York: Springer.

Szinovacz, M. (1990). Women and retirement. In B. B. Hess & E. W. Markson (Eds.), *Growing old in America* (4th ed., pp. 293–303). New Brunswick, NJ: Transaction.

Szinovacz, M., Ekerdt, D. J., & Vinick, B. H. (Eds.). (1992). *Families and retirement.* Newbury Park, CA: Sage.

Talaga, J. A., & Beehr, T. A. (1995). Are there gender differences in predicting retirement decisions? *Journal of Applied Psychology, 80,* 16–28.

Tasker, F., & Golombok, S. (1995). Adults raised as children in lesbian families. *American Journal of Orthopsychiatry, 65,* 203–215.

Tatum, B. D. (1992, Spring). Talking about race, learning about racism: The application of racial identity development theory in the classroom. *Harvard Educational Review, 62,* 1–24.

Tavris, C. (1991). The mismeasure of woman: Paradoxes and perspectives in the study of gender. In J. D. Goodchilds (Ed.), *Psychological perspectives on human diversity in America* (pp. 89–136). Washington, DC: American Psychological Association.

Tavris, C. (1992). *The mismeasure of woman.* New York: Simon & Schuster.

Tavris, C. (1993). *Good intentions and wrong turns: A critique of modern feminism.* Paper presented at the annual meeting of the American Psychological Association, Toronto, Ontario, Canada.

Tavris, C., & Offir, C. (1977). *The longest war: Sex differences in perspective.* New York: Harcourt Brace Jovanovich.

Tavris, C., & Wade, C. (1984). *The longest war: Sex differences in perspective* (2nd ed.). New York: Harcourt Brace Jovanovich.

Taylor, J. M., Gilligan, C., & Sullivan, A. M. (1995). *Between voice and silence: Women and girls, race and relationships.* Cambridge, MA: Harvard University Press.

Taylor, L. E. (1994). The feminization of poverty. *Canada and the World, 60(2),* 16–18.

Taylor, L. E. (1995). Home brutal home. *Canada and the World, 60,* 24–28.

Taylor, S. E. (1991). *Health psychology* (2nd ed.). New York: McGraw-Hill.

Taylor, S. E. (1995). *Health psychology* (3rd ed.). New York: McGraw-Hill.

Taylor, S. E., et al. (1992). Optimism, coping, psychological distress, and high-risk sexual behavior among men at risk for acquired immunodeficiency syndrome (AIDS). *Journal of Personality and Social Psychology, 63,* 460–473.

Taylor, S. E., & Langer, E. J. (1977). Pregnancy: A social stigma? *Sex Roles, 3,* 27–35.

Taylor, V. (1996). *Rock-a-by baby: Feminism, self-help, and postpartum depression.* New York: Routledge.

Tenenbaum, H. R., & Leaper, C. (1997). Mothers' and fathers' questions to their child in Mexican-descent families: Moderators of cognitive demand during play. *Hispanic Journal of Behavioral Sciences, 19,* 318–332.

Tesch, B. J., Wood, H. M., Helwig, A. L., & Nattinger, A. B. (1995). Promotion of women physicians in academic medicine: Glass ceiling or sticky floor? *JAMA, 273,* 1022–1025.

Thacker, R. A. (1995). Gender, influence tactics, and job characteristics preferences: New insights into salary determination. *Sex Roles, 32,* 617–638.

The budget. (1996, February 12). *Family Planning Advocates Legislative Update,* p. 1.

The nation. (1998, August 28). *Chronicle of Higher Education Almanac,* pp. 5–43.

Thom, M. (Ed.). (1987). *Letters to Ms, 1972–1987.* New York: Holt.

Thomas, V. G., & Miles, S. E. (1995). Psychology of Black women: Past, present, and future. In H. Landrine (Ed.), *Bringing cultural diversity to feminist psychology* (pp. 303–330). Washington, DC: American Psychological Association.

Thompson, B. (1994). Food, bodies, and growing up female: Childhood lessons about culture, race, and class. In P. Fallon, M. A. Katzman, & S. C. Wooley (Eds.), *Feminist perspectives on eating disorders* (pp. 355–378). New York: Guilford Press.

Thompson, H. B. (1903). *The mental traits of sex.* Chicago: University of Chicago Press.

Thompson, S. (1995). *Going all the way: Teenage girls' tales of sex, romance, and pregnancy.* New York: Hill and Wang.

Thompson, S. H., Sargent, R. G., & Kemper, K. A. (1996). Black and White adolescent males' perceptions of ideal body size. *Sex Roles, 34,* 391–406.

Thompson, T. L., & Zerbinos, E. (1995). Gender roles in animated cartoons: Has the picture changed in 20 years? *Sex Roles, 32,* 651–673.

Thompson, T. L., & Zerbinos, E. (1997). Television cartoons: Do children notice it's a boy's world? *Sex Roles, 37,* 415–432.

Thorne, B. (1993). *Gender play: Girls and boys in school.* New Brunswick, NJ: Rutgers University Press.

Thornton, B., & Leo, R. (1992). Gender typing, importance of multiple roles, and mental health consequences for women. *Sex Roles, 27,* 307–317.

Thornton, B., & Maurice, J. (1997). Physique contrast effect: Adverse impact of idealized body images for women. *Sex Roles, 17,* 433–439.

Thun, M. J., et al. (1997). Alcohol Consumption and mortality among middle-aged and elderly U.S. adults. *New England Journal of Medicine, 337,* 1705–1714.

Tiefer, L. (1995a). [Review of the book *The sexual brain*] *Psychology of Women Quarterly, 18,* 440–441.

Tiefer, L. (1995b). *Sex is not a natural act and other essays.* Boulder, CO: Westview.

Tiefer, L. (1996). Towards a feminist sex therapy. *Women & Therapy, 19,* 53–64.

Tiefer, L., & Kring, B. (1998). Gender and the organization of sexual behavior. In D. L. Answelmi & A. L. Law (Eds.), *Questions of gender: Perspectives and paradoxes* (pp. 320–328). New York: McGraw-Hill.

Tobias, S. (1993). *Overcoming math anxiety* (rev. ed.). New York: Norton.

Tobias, S. (1997). *Faces of feminism: An activist's reflections on the women's movement.* Boulder, CO: Westview Press.

Todd, A. D. (1989). *Intimate adversaries: Cultural conflict between doctors and women patients.* Philadelphia: University of Pennsylvania Press.

Todoroff, M. (1994). Defining "achievement" in the lives of a generation of midlife single mothers. In J. Gallivan, S. D. Crozier, & V. M. Lalande (Eds.), *Women, girls, and achievement* (pp. 96–105). North York, Ontario: Captus University Publications.

Tong, R. P. (1998). *Feminist thought* (2nd ed.). Boulder, CO: Westview Press.

Toth, E. (1997). *Ms. Mentor's impeccable advice for women in academia.* Philadelphia: University of Pennsylvania Press.

Toubia, N. (1995). Female genital mutilation. In J. Peters & A. Wolper (Eds.), *Women's rights, human rights: International feminist perspectives* (pp. 224–237). New York: Routledge.

Townsend, K., & Rice, P. L. (1996). A baby is born in Site 2 camp: Pregnancy, birth and confinement among Cambodian refugee women. In P. L. Rice & L. Manderson (Eds.), *Maternity and reproductive health in Asian societies* (pp. 125–143). Amsterdam: Harwood Academic Publishers.

Tozzo, S. G., & Golub, S. (1990). Playing nurse and playing cop: Do they change children's perceptions of sex-role stereotypes? *Journal of Research in Childhood Education, 4,* 123–129.

Tran, T. V. (1991). Family living arrangement and social adjustment among three ethnic groups of elderly Indochinese refugees. *International Journal of Aging and Human Development, 32,* 91–102.

Travis, C. B. (1993). Women and health. In F. L. Denmark & M. A. Paludi (Eds.), *Psychology of women: A handbook of issues and theories* (pp. 283–323). Westport, CT: Greenwood Press.

Travis, C. B., Gressley, D. L., & Adams, P. L. (1995). Health care policy and practice for women's health. In A. L. Stanton & S. J. Gallant (Eds.), *The psychology of women's health: Progress and challenges in research and application* (pp. 531–565). Washington, DC: American Psychological Association.

Travis, C. B., Gressley, D. L., & Crumpler, C. A. (1991). Feminist contributions to health psychology. *Psychology of Women Quarterly, 15,* 557–566.

Travis, C. B., Gressley, D. L., & Phillippi, R. H. (1993). Medical decision making, gender, and coronary heart disease. *Journal of Women's Health, 2,* 269–279.

Troll, L. E. (1982). *Continuations: Adult development and aging.* Monterey, CA: Brooks/Cole.

Troll, L. E. (1994). Family connectedness of old women: Attachments in later life. In B. F. Turner & L. E. Troll (Eds.), *Women growing older: Psychological perspectives* (pp. 169–201). Thousand Oaks, CA: Sage.

True, R. H. (1990). Psychotherapeutic issues with Asian American women. *Sex Roles, 22,* 477–486.

True, R. H. (1995). Mental health issues of Asian/Pacific Island women. In D. L. Adams (Ed.), *Health issues for women of color: A cultural diversity perspective* (pp. 89–111). Thousand Oaks, CA: Sage.

Turner, B. F., & Turner, C. B. (1990). Through a glass, darkly: Gender stereotypes for men and women varying in age and race. In B. B. Hess & E. W. Markson (Eds.), *Growing old in America* (4th ed., pp. 137–150). New Brunswick, NJ: Transaction.

Twenge, J. M. (1997a). Attitudes toward women, 1970–1995. *Psychology of Women Quarterly, 21,* 35–51.

Twenge, J. M. (1997b). Changes in masculine and feminine traits over time: A meta-analysis. *Sex Roles, 36,* 305–325.

Twenge, J. M. (1997c). "Mrs. His name": Women's preferences for married names. *Psychology of Women Quarterly, 21,* 417–429.

Uba, L. (1994). *Asian Americans: Personality patterns, identity, and mental health.* New York: Guilford Press.

Udis-Kessler, A. (1991). Present tense: Biphobia as a crisis of meaning. In L. Hutchins & L. Kaahumanu (Eds.), *Bi any other name: Bisexual people speak out* (pp. 350–358). Boston: Alyson Publications.

Ullman, S. E. (1996). Social reactions, coping strategies, and self-blame attributions in adjustment to sexual assault. *Psychology of Women Quarterly, 20,* 505–526.

Ullman, S. E., & Knight, R. A. (1993). The efficacy of women's resistance strategies in rape situations. *Psychology of Women Quarterly, 17,* 23–38.

Unger, R. K. (1979). Toward a redefinition of sex and gender. *American Psychologist, 34,* 1085–1094.

Unger, R. K. (1981). Sex as a social reality: Field and laboratory research. *Psychology of Women Quarterly, 5,* 645–653.

Unger, R. K. (1983). Through the looking glass: No wonderland yet! (The reciprocal relationship between methodology and models of reality). *Psychology of Women Quarterly, 8,* 9–32.

Unger, R. K. (1988). Psychological, feminist, and personal epistemology: Transcending contradiction. In M. M. Gergen (Ed.), *Feminist thought and the structure of knowledge* (pp. 124–141). New York: New York University Press.

Unger, R. K., & Crawford, M. (1993). Commentary: Sex and gender—the troubled relationship between terms and concepts. *Psychological Science, 4,* 122–124.

United Nations. (1995). *The world's women, 1995: Trends and statistics.* New York: Author.

U.S. Bureau of the Census. (1992). *Statistical abstract of the United States 1992.* Washington, DC: U. S. Government Printing Office.

U.S. Bureau of the Census. (1993). *We the American . . . women.* Washington, DC: U.S. Government Printing Office.

U.S. Bureau of the Census. (1997). *Statistical abstract of the United States* (117th edition). Washington, DC: Author.

U.S. Department of Labor. (1994). *1993 Handbook on women workers: Trends and issues.* Washington, DC: U.S. Government Printing Office.

Valcarcel, C. L. (1994). Growing up Black in Puerto Rico. In E. Tobach & B. Rosoff (Eds.), *Challenging racism and sexism* (pp. 284–294). New York: Feminist Press.

Valian, V. (1998). *Why so slow: The advancement of women.* Cambridge, MA: MIT PRESS.

Vance, E. B., & Wagner, N. N. (1977). Written descriptions of orgasm: A study of sex differences. In D. Byrne & L. A. Byrne (Eds.), *Exploring human sexuality* (pp. 201–212). New York: Thomas Y. Crowell.

Vandell, D. L., & Ramanan, J. (1992). Effects of early and recent maternal employment on children from low-income families. *Child Development, 63,* 938–949.

Vasta, R., Haith, M. M., & Miller, S. A. (1995). *Child psychology: The modern science* (2nd ed.). New York: Wiley.

Vasta, R., Knott, J. A., & Gaze, C. E. (1996). Can spatial training erase the gender differences on the water-level task? *Psychology of Women Quarterly, 20,* 549–567.

Vázquez-Nuttall, E., & Romero-García, I. (1989). From home to school: Puerto Rican girls learn to be students in the United States. In C. T. García Coll & M. de Lourdes Mattei (Eds.), *The psychosocial development of Puerto Rican women* (pp. 60–83). New York: Praeger.

Veniegas, R. C., & Peplau, L. A. (1997). Power and the quality of same-sex friendships. *Psychology of Women Quarterly, 21,* 279–297.

Vickers, J. F., & Thomas, B. L. (1993). *No more frogs, no more princes: Women making creative choices at midlife.* Freedom, CA: Crossing Press.

Villani, S. L. (1997). *Motherhood at the crossroads: Meeting the challenge of a changing role.* New York: Plenum Press.

Vincent, P. C., Peplau, L. A., & Hill, C. T. (1998). A longitudinal application of the theory of reasoned action to women's career behavior. *Journal of Applied Social Psychology, 28,* 761–778.

Vitulli, W. F., & Holland, B. E. (1993). College students' attitudes toward relationships with their parents as a function of gender. *Psychological Reports, 72,* 744–746.

Vogeltanz, N. D., & Wilsnack, S. C. (1997). Alcohol problems in women: Risk factors, consequences, and treatment strategies. In S. J. Gallant, G. P. Keita, & R. Royak-Schaler (Eds.), *Health care for women: Psychological, social, and behavioral influences* (pp. 75–96). Washington, DC: American Psychological Association.

Voyer, D., Voyer, S., & Bryden, M. P. (1995). Magnitude of sex differences in spatial abilities: A meta-analysis and consideration of critical variables. *Psychological Bulletin, 117,* 250–270.

Wade, C., & Cirese, S. (1991). *Human sexuality* (2nd ed.). San Diego: Harcourt Brace Jovanovich.

Waehler, C. A. (1996). *Bachelors: The psychology of men who haven't married.* Westport, CT: Praeger.

Wainer, H., & Steinberg, L. S. (1992). Sex differences in performance on the mathematics section of the Scholastic Aptitude Test: A bidirectional validity study. *Harvard Educational Review, 62,* 323–336.

Waldram, J. B. (1997). The aboriginal peoples of Canada: Colonialism and mental health. In I. Al-Issa & M. Tousignant (Eds.), *Ethnicity, immigration, and psychopathology* (pp. 169–187). New York: Plenum Press.

Waldron, I. (1991). Effects of labor force participation on sex differences in mortality and morbidity. In M. Frankenhaeuser, U. Lundberg, & M. Chesney (Eds.), *Women, work, and health: Stress and opportunities* (pp. 17–38). New York: Springer.

Walker, A., & Parmar, P. (1993). *Warrior marks: Female genital mutilation and the sexual blinding of women.* New York: Harcourt Brace.

Walker, A. E. (1998). *The menstrual cycle.* New York: Routledge.

Walker, L. E. (1979). *The battered woman.* New York: Harper & Row.

Walker, L. E. (1989). Psychology and violence against women. *American Psychologist, 44,* 695–702.

Walker, L. J. (1984). Sex differences in the development of moral reasoning: A critical review. *Child Development, 55,* 677–691.

Walker, L. J. (1989). A longitudinal study of moral reasoning. *Child Development, 60,* 157–166.

Wallace, H. (1999). *Family violence: Legal, medical, and social perspectives* (2nd ed.). Boston: Allyn & Bacon.

Wallach, H. R., & Matlin, M. W. (1992). College women's expectations about pregnancy, childbirth, and infant care: A prospective study. *Birth: Issues in Perinatal Care, 19,* 202–207.

Wallen, J. (1998). Substance abuse and health care utilization. In E. A. Blechman & K. D. Brownell (Eds.), *Behavioral medicine and women: A comprehensive handbook* (pp. 309–312). New York: Guilford Press.

Wallis, L. A. (1998). Medical curricula and training. In E. A. Blechman & K. D. Brownell (Eds.), *Behavioral medicine & women: A comprehensive handbook* (pp. 303–308). New York: Guilford Press.

Walsh, F. (1996). *Sin and censorship: The Catholic Church and the motion picture industry.* New Haven: Yale University Press.

Walsh, M. R. (1977). *Doctors wanted: No women need apply.* New Haven, CT: Yale University Press.

Walsh, M. R. (1987). Introduction. In M. R. Walsh (Ed.), *The psychology of women: Ongoing debates* (pp. 1–15). New Haven, CT: Yale University Press.

Walsh, M. R. (1990). Women in medicine since Flexner. *New York State Journal of Medicine, 90,* 302–308.

Walsh, M. R. (Ed.). (1996). *The psychology of women: Ongoing debates* (2nd ed.). New Haven, CT: Yale University Press.

Walsh, M. R. (Ed.). (1997). *Women, men, and gender: Ongoing debates.* New Haven, CT: Yale University Press.

Walsh, W. B., & Osipow, S. H. (Eds.). (1994). *Career counseling for women.* Hillsdale, NJ: Erlbaum.

Walters, K. L., & Simoni, J. M. (1993). Lesbian and gay male group identity attitudes and self-esteem: Implications for counseling. *Journal of Counseling Psychology, 40,* 94–99.

Walton, M. D., et al. (1988). Physical stigma and the pregnancy role: Receiving help from strangers. *Sex Roles, 18,* 323–331.

Wang, N. (1994). Born Chinese and a woman in America. In J. Adleman & G. Enguídanos (Eds.), *Racism in the lives of women* (pp. 97–110). New York: Haworth.

Ward, C. A. (1995). *Attitudes toward rape: Feminist and social psychological perspectives.* London: Sage.

Ward, L. M., & Wyatt, G. E. (1994). The effects of childhood sexual messages on African-American and White women's adolescent sexual behavior. *Psychology of Women Quarterly, 18,* 183–201.

Ware, M. C., & Stuck, M. F. (1985). Sex-role messages vis-à-vis microcomputer use: A look at the pictures. *Sex Roles, 13,* 205–214.

Wasserman, E. B. (1994). Personal reflections of an Anglo therapist in Indian country. In J. Adleman & G. Enguídanos (Eds.), *Racism in the lives of women* (pp. 23–32). New York: Haworth.

Wasserman, G. A., & Lewis, M. (1985). Infant sex differences: Ecological effects. *Sex Roles, 12,* 665–675.

Waters, M. C. (1996). The intersection of gender, race, and ethnicity in identity development of Caribbean American teens. In B. J. R. Leadbeater & N. Way (Eds.), *Urban girls: Resisting stereotypes, creating identities* (pp. 65–81). New York: New York University Press.

Watson, M. S., Trasciatti, M. A., & King, C. P. (1996). Our bodies, our risk: Dilemmas in contraceptive information. In R. L. Parrott & C. M. Condit (Eds.), *Evaluating women's health messages: A resource book* (pp. 95–108). Thousand Oaks, CA: Sage.

Watson, P. J., Biderman, M. D., & Sawrie, S. M. (1994). Empathy, sex role orientation, and narcissism. *Sex Roles, 30,* 701–723.

Wear, D. (1997). *Privilege in the medical academy: A feminist examines gender, race, and power.* New York: Teachers College Press.

Weaver, G. D. (1998). *Emotional health of older African American women with breast cancer.* Paper presented at the annual convention of the American Psychological Association, San Francisco, CA.

Webster, P. S., Orbuch, T. L., & House, J. S. (1995). Effects of childhood family background on adult marital quality and perceived stability. *American Journal of Sociology, 101,* 404–432.

Wechsler, H., et al. (1994). Health and behavioral consequences of binge drinking in college: A national survey of students at 140 campuses. *JAMA, 272,* 1672–1677.

Weinberg, M. S., Lottes, I. L., & Shaver, F. M. (1995). Swedish or American heterosexual college youth: Who is more permissive? *Archives of Sexual Behavior, 24,* 409–437.

Weinberg, M. S., Williams, C. J., & Pryor, D. W. (1994). *Dual attraction: Understanding bisexuality.* New York: Oxford University Press.

Weisfeld, C. C., Weisfeld, G. E., & Callaghan, J. W. (1982). Female inhibition in mixed-sex competition among young adolescents. *Ethology and Sociobiology, 3,* 29–42.

Weisfeld, C. C., Weisfeld, G. E., Warren, R. A., & Freedman, D. G. (1983). The spelling bee: A naturalistic study of female inhibition in mixed-sex competition. *Adolescence, 18,* 695–708.

Weisner, T. S. (1992, February). *Parents' construction of activity settings: Parents' efforts to change their children's sex typing.* Paper presented at the meeting of the Society for Cross Cultural Research, Santa Fe, NM.

Weisner, T. S., Garnier, H., & Loucky, J. (1994). Domestic tasks, gender egalitarian values and children's gender typing in conventional and nonconventional families. *Sex Roles, 30,* 23–54.

Weissman, M. M., & Olfson, M. (1995). Depression in women: Implications for health care research. *Science, 269,* 799–801.

Wendell, S. (1992). Toward a feminist theory of disability. In H. B. Holmes & L. M. Purdy (Eds.), *Feminist perspectives in medical ethics* (pp. 63–81). Bloomington: Indiana University Press.

Wendell, S. (1997). Toward a feminist theory of disability. In L. J. Davis (Ed.), *The disability studies reader* (pp. 260–278). New York: Routledge.

Wessely, S. (1998). Commentary: Reducing distress after normal childbirth. *Birth, 25,* 220–221.

West, M., & Fernández, M. (1997). *Reflexion Cristiana: ¿Como ayudar a una mujer maltratada?* Managua, Nicaragua: Red de Mujeres contra la Violencia.

Wester, S. R., Crown, C. L., & Quatman, G. L., & Heesacker, M. (1997). The influence of sexually violent rap music on attitudes of men with little prior exposure. *Psychology of Women Quarterly, 21,* 497–508.

Westkott, M. C. (1997). On the new psychology of women: A cautionary view. In Walsh, M. R. (1997). *Women, men, and gender: Ongoing debates* (pp. 362–372). New Haven, CT: Yale University Press.

Whalen, M. (1996). *Counseling to end violence against women: A subversive model.* Thousand Oaks, CA: Sage.

Wheelan, S. A., & Verdi, A. F. (1992). Differences in male and female patterns of communication in groups: A methodological artifact? *Sex Roles, 27,* 1–15.

Wheeler, C. (1994, September/October). How much ink do women get? *Executive Female,* p. 51.

Whitbourne, S. K. (1996). *The aging individual: Physical and psychological perspectives.* New York: Springer.

Whitbourne, S. K. (1998). Identity and adaptation to the aging process. In C. Ryff & V. Marshall (Eds.), *Self and society in aging processes* (pp. 122–149). New York: Springer.

Whitbourne, S. K., & Ebmeyer, J. B. (1990). *Identity and intimacy in marriage.* New York: Springer-Verlag.

Whitbourne, S. K., & Hulicka, I. M. (1990). Ageism in undergraduate psychology texts. *American Psychologist, 45,* 1127–1136.

White, J. W. (1983). Sex and gender issues in aggression research. In R. G. Geen & E. I. Donnerstein (Eds.), *Aggression: Theoretical and empirical reviews* (Vol. 2, pp. 1–26). New York: Academic Press.

White, J. W., & Bondurant, B. (1996). Gendered violence in intimate relationships. In J. T. Wood (Ed.), *Gendered relationships* (pp. 197–210). Mountain View, CA: Mayfield.

White, J. W., & Kowalski, R. M. (1994). Reconstructing the myth of the non-aggressive woman: A feminist analysis. *Psychology of Women Quarterly, 18,* 487–508.

White, J. W., & Kowalski, R. M. (1998). Male violence toward women: An integrated perspective. In R. G. Geen & E. Donnerstein (Eds.), *Human aggression: Theories, research, and implications for social policy* (pp. 203–228). San Diego: Academic Press.

White, J. W., & Roufail, M. (1989). Gender and influence strategies of first choice and last resort. *Psychology of Women Quarterly, 13,* 175–189.

White, J. W., & Sorenson, S. B. (1992). A sociocultural view of sexual assault: From discrepancy to diversity. *Journal of Social Issues, 48,* 187–195.

White, S. D., & DeBlassie, R. R. (1992). Adolescent sexual behavior. *Adolescence, 27,* 183–191.

Whitley, B. E., Jr. (1985). Sex-role orientation and psychological well-being: Two meta-analyses. *Sex Roles, 12,* 207–225.

Whitley, B. E., Jr. (1988). Masculinity, femininity, and self-esteem: A multitrait–multimethod analysis. *Sex Roles, 18,* 419–431.

Whitley, B. E., Jr., & Hern, A. L. (1992). *Sexual experience, perceived invulnerability to pregnancy, and the use of effective contraception.* Paper presented at the meeting of the Eastern Psychological Association, Boston.

Whitley, B. E., Jr., McHugh, M. C., & Frieze, I. H. (1986). Assessing the theoretical models for sex differences in causal attributions of success and failure. In J. S. Hyde & M. C. Linn (Eds.), *The psychology of gender: Advances through meta-analysis* (pp. 102–135). Baltimore: Johns Hopkins University Press.

Widaman, K. F., et al. (1992). Differences in adolescents' self-concept as a function of academic level, ethnicity, and gender. *American Journal on Mental Retardation, 96,* 387–404.

Wideman, M. V., & Singer, J. E. (1984). The role of psychological mechanisms in preparation for childbirth. *American Psychologist, 39,* 1357–1371.

Wiest, W. M. (1977). Semantic differential profiles of orgasm and other experiences among men and women. *Sex Roles, 3,* 399–403.

Wilcox, B. L., Robbenmolt, J. K., O'Keeffe, J. E., & Pynchon, M. E. (1996). Teen nonmarital childbearing and welfare: The gap between research and political discourse. *Journal of Social Issues, 52,* 71–90.

Wilfley, D. E., & Rodin, J. (1995). Cultural influences on eating disorders. In K. D. Brownell & C. G. Fairburn (Eds.), *Eating disorders and obesity: a comprehensive handbook* (pp. 78–82). New York: Guilford Press.

Wille, D. E. (1995). The 1990s: Gender differences in parenting roles. *Sex Roles, 33,* 803–817.

Wille, D. E. (1996a). Employment and child care. In P. J. Dubeck & K. Borman (Eds.), *Women and work* (pp. 404–406). New York: Garland.

Wille, D. E. (1996b). Maternal role conflict. In P. J. Dubeck & K. Borman (Eds.), *Women and work* (pp. 408–409). New York: Garland.

Willetts-Bloom, M. C., & Nock, S. L. (1994). The influence of maternal employment on gender role attitudes of men and women. *Sex Roles, 30,* 371–389.

Williams, C. L. (1998). The glass escalator: Hidden advantages for men in the "female" positions. In M. S. Kimmel & M. A. Messner (Eds.), *Men's lives* (4th ed., pp. 285–299). Boston: Allyn & Bacon.

Williams, D. E., & D'Alessandro, J. D. (1994). A comparison of three measures of androgyny and their relationship to psychological adjustment. *Journal of Social Behavior and Personality, 9,* 469–480.

Williams, E. F. (1995a). Epilogue. In E. F. Williams (Ed.), *Voices of feminist therapy* (pp. 133–135). Luxembourg: Harwood Academic Publishers.

Williams, E. F. (Ed.). (1995b). *Voices of feminist therapy.* Luxembourg: Harwood Academic Publishers.

Williams, J. E., Bennett, S. M., & Best, D. (1975). Awareness and expression of sex stereotypes in young children. *Developmental Psychology, 11,* 635–642.

Williams, J. E., & Best, D. L. (1990). *Measuring sex stereotypes: A multinational study* (rev. ed.). Newbury Park, CA: Sage.

Williams, L. R. (1983). Beliefs and attitudes of young girls regarding menstruation. In S. Golub (Ed.), *Menarche* (pp. 139–148). Lexington, MA: Lexington Books.

Williams, S. S., et al. (1992). College students use implicit personality theory instead of safer sex. *Journal of Applied Social Psychology, 22,* 921–933.

Willingham, W. W., & Cole, N. S. (1997). *Gender and fair assessment.* Mahwah, NJ: Erlbaum.

Willis, C. E. (1997). The effect of sex role stereotype, victim and defendant rape, and prior relationship on rape culpability attributions. *Sex Roles, 26,* 213–226.

Willis, C. E., Hallinan, M. N., & Melby, J. (1996). Effects of sex role stereotyping among European American students on domestic violence culpability attributions. *Sex Roles, 34,* 475–491.

Willson, A., & Lloyd, B. (1990). Gender vs. power: Self-posed behavior revisited. *Sex Roles, 23,* 91–98.

Wilsnack, S. C. (1995). Alcohol use and alcohol problems in women. In A. L. Stanton & S. J. Gallant (Eds.), *The psychology of women's health: Progress and challenges in research and application* (pp. 381–443). Washington, DC: American Psychological Association.

Wilson, II, C. C., & Gutiérrez, F. (1995). *Race, multiculturalism, and the media: From mass to class communication.* Thousand Oaks, CA: Sage.

Wilson, E., & Ng, S. H. (1988). Sex bias in visual images evoked by generics: A New Zealand study. *Sex Roles, 18,* 159–168.

Wincze, J. P., & Carey, M. P. (1992). *Sexual dysfunction: A guide for assessment and treatment.* New York: Guilford Press.

Windle, M., Shope, J. T., & Bukstein, O. (1996). In R. J. DiClemente, W. B. Hansen, & L. E. Ponton (Eds.), *Handbook of adolescent health risk behavior* (pp. 115–159). New York: Plenum Press.

Winerip, M. (1994, February 16). Merit scholarship program faces sex bias complaint. *New York Times,* p. A18.

Wing, R. R., & Klem, M. L. (1997). Obesity. In S. J. Gallant, G. P. Keita, & R. Royak-Schaler (Eds.), *Health care for women: Psychological, social, and behavioral influences* (pp. 115–131). Washington, DC: American Psychological Association.

Wingert, P. (1998, May 11). The battle over falling birthrates. *Newsweek,* p. 40.

Wingert, P., & Joseph, N. (1998, November 2). I do, I do—Maybe. *Newsweek,* p. 58.

Wingert, P., & Snow, K. (1998, June 22). Using the bully pulpit? *Newsweek,* p. 69.

Winstead, B. A., Derlega, V. J., & Rose, S. (1997). *Gender and close relationships.* Thousand Oaks, CA: Sage.

Winter, D. D. (1996). *Ecological psychology: Healing the split between planet and self.* New York: HarperCollins.

Wise, P. M., Krajnak, K. M., & Kashon, M. L. (1996). Menopause: The aging of multiple pacemakers. *Science, 273,* 67–70.

Witelson, S. F., Glezer, I. I., & Kigar, D. L. (1995). Women have greater density of neurons in posterior temporal cortex. *Journal of Neuroscience, 15,* 3418–3428.

Wolf, N. (1991). *The beauty myth: How images of beauty are used against women.* New York: Doubleday.

Wolk, S. I., & Weissman, M. M. (1995). Women and depression: An update. *Review of Psychiatry, 14,* 227–259.

Women on Words & Images. (1972). *Dick and Jane as victims.* Princeton, NJ: Author.

Women's health centers. (1997, October). *Harvard Women's Health Watch,* p. 1.

Wood, J. T. (Ed.). (1996). *Gendered relationships.* Mountain View, CA: Mayfield.

Wood, W., Rhodes, N., & Whelan, M. (1989). Sex differences in positive well-being: A consideration of emotional style and marital status. *Psychological Bulletin, 106,* 249–264.

Woods, N. F., & Jacobson, B. G. (1997). Diseases that manifest differently in women and men. In F. P. Haseltine & B. G. Jacobson (Eds.), *Women's health research: A medical and policy primer* (pp. 159–187). Washington, DC: Health Press.

Woods, N. F., et al. (1999). Depressed mood and self-esteem in young Asian, Black, and White women in America. In C. Forden, A. E. Hunter, & B. Birns (Eds.), *Readings in the psychology of women* (pp. 328–339). Boston: Allyn & Bacon.

Woollett, A., & Marshall, H. (1997). Discourses of pregnancy and childbirth. In L. Yardley (Ed.), *Material discourses of health and illness* (pp. 176–198). London: Routledge.

Woolley, H. T. (1910). Psychological literature: A review of the recent literature on the psychology of sex. *Psychological Bulletin, 7,* 335–342.

Word, C. H., Zanna, M. P., & Cooper, J. (1974). The nonverbal mediation of self-fulfilling prophecies in interracial interaction. *Journal of Experimental Social Psychology, 10,* 109–120.

Worell, J. (1989). Sex roles in transition. In J. Worell & F. Danner (Eds.), *The adolescent as decision-maker: Applications to development and education* (pp. 245–280). San Diego: Academic Press.

Worell, J. (1996). Opening doors to feminist research. *Psychology of Women Quarterly, 20,* 469–485.

Worell, J., & Johnson, N. G. (Eds.). (1997). *Shaping the future of feminist psychology: Education, research, and practice.* Washington, DC: American Psychological Association.

Worell, J., & Remer, P. (1992). *Feminist perspectives in therapy: An empowerment model for women.* New York: Wiley.

Worell, J., & Robinson, D. (1994). Reinventing analogue methods for research with women. *Psychology of Women Quarterly, 18,* 463–476.

World almanac and book of facts, 1999. (1998). Mahwah, NJ: World Almanac Books.

Wortman, C. B., Biernat, M., & Lang, E. (1991). Coping with role overload. In M. Frankenhaeuser, U. Lundberg, & M. Chesney (Eds.), *Women, work, and health: Stress and opportunities* (pp. 85–110). New York: Plenum Press.

Wortman, C. B., & Silver, R. C. (1989). The myths of coping with loss. *Journal of Consulting and Clinical Psychology, 57,* 349–357.

Wosinska, W., Dabul, A. J., Whetstone-Dion, M. R., & Cialdini, R. B. (1996). Self-presentational responses to success in the organization: The costs and benefits of modesty. *Basic and Applied Social Psychology, 18,* 229–242.

Wright, K. (1997, February). Anticipatory guidance: Developing a healthy sexuality. *Pediatric Annals Supplement,* S142–C3.

Wright, R. (1998a, May 12). Iran a model of population control. *San Jose Mercury News,* p. A7.

Wright, R. (1998b, June 30). Iran's revolution within a revolution. *San Jose Mercury News,* p. 11A.

Wu, X., & DeMaris, A. (1996). Gender and marital status differences in depression: The effects of chronic strains. *Sex Roles, 34,* 299–319.

Wuitchik, M., Hesson, K., & Bakal, D. A. (1990). Perinatal predictors of pain and distress during labor. *Birth, 17,* 186–191.

Wyatt, G. E., & Riederle, M. H. (1994). Reconceptualizing issues that affect women's sexual decision-making and sexual functioning. *Psychology of Women Quarterly, 18,* 611–625.

Wyche, K. F., & Rice, J. K. (1997). Feminist therapy: From dialogue to tenets. In J. Worell & N. Johnson (Eds.), *Shaping the future of feminist psychology: Education, research, and practice* (pp. 57–71). Washington, DC: American Psychological Association.

Yarkin, K. L., Town, J. P., & Wallston, B. S. (1982). Blacks and women must try harder: Stimulus persons' race and sex attributions of causality. *Personality and Social Psychology Bulletin, 8,* 21–30.

Yarrow, L. (1992, November). Giving birth. *Parents Magazine,* pp. 148–159.

Ybarra, L. (1995). Marital decision-making and the role of *machismo* in the Chicano family. In A. S. López (Ed.), *Latina issues* (pp. 252–267). New York: Garland.

Yee, D. (1997). Issues and trends affecting Asian Americans, women, and aging. In J. M. Coyle (Ed.), *Handbook on women and aging* (pp. 316–334). Westport, CT: Greenwood Press.

Yoder, J. D., & Aniakudo, P. (1996). When pranks become harassment: The case of African American women firefighters. *Sex Roles, 35,* 253–270.

Yoder, J. D., & Aniakudo, P. (1997). "Outsider within" the firehouse: Subordination and difference in the social interactions of African American women firefighters. *Gender and Society, 11,* 324–341.

Yoder, J. D., & Kahn, A. S. (1993). Working toward an inclusive psychology of women. *American Psychologist, 48,* 846–850.

Yoder, J. D., & Schleicher, T. L. (1996). Undergraduates regard deviation from occupational gender stereotypes as costly for women. *Sex Roles, 34,* 171–188.

Young, D. (1982). *Changing childbirth: Family birth in the hospital.* Rochester, NY: Childbirth Graphics.

Young, D. (1993). Family-centered maternity care. In B. K. Rothman (Ed.), *Encyclopedia of childbearing: Critical perspectives* (pp. 140–141). Phoenix, AZ: Oryx Press.

Young, I. M. (1998). Breasted experience: The look and the feeling. In R. Weitz (Ed.), *The politics of women's bodies: Sexuality, appearance, and behavior* (pp. 125–136). New York: Oxford.

Zalk, S. R. (1996). Men in the academy: A psychological profile of harassers. In M. A. Paludi (Ed.), *Sexual harassment on college campuses* (pp. 81–113). Albany: State University of New York Press.

Zeiss, A. M. (1998). Sexuality and aging. In E. A. Blechman & K. D. Brownell (Eds.), *Behavioral medicine and women: A comprehensive handbook* (pp. 528–534). New York: Guilford Press.

Zepatos, T., & Kaufman, E. (1995). *Women for a change: A grassroots guide to activism and politics.* New York: Facts on File.

Zhou, M. (1994, June 10). China: Speaking out against sexual harassment. *Women's Feature Service.* Available via E-Mail: wfs@igc.apc.org.

Zia, H. (1996, January/February). Made in the U.S.A. *Ms. Magazine,* pp. 67–73.

Zillman, D. (1998). *Connections between sexuality and aggression* (2nd ed.). Mahwah, NJ: Lawrence Erlbaum.

Zimmerman, D. H., & West, C. (1975). Sex roles, interruptions and silences in conversation. In B. Thorne & N. Henley (Eds.), *Language and sex: Difference and dominance* (pp. 105–129). Rowley, MA: Newbury House.

Zucker, K. J., Wilson-Smith, D. N., Kurita, J. A., & Stern, A. (1995). Children's appraisals of sex-typed behavior in their peers. *Sex Roles, 33,* 703–725.

Zuckerman, M., & Wheeler, L. (1975). To dispel fantasies about the fantasy-based measure of fear of success. *Psychological Bulletin, 82,* 932–946.

Name Index

AAUW Educational
Foundation, 112
Abbey, A., 389, 479
Abel, E., 457
Aber, C. S., 399
Abzug, B., 555
Adams, A., 379
Adams, M., 317
Adams, S., 105
Adebimpe, V. R., 454
Adelmann, P. K., 530
Ader, D. N., 16
Adler, N. E., 353, 354, 402
Adler, T., 398
Adolph, M. R., 533
Affleck, B., 278
Aggarwal, P., 549
Agronick, G., 11
Aguilar-San Juan, K., 307
Ahnlund, K., 435
Aidoo, A. A., 113–114
Alagna, S. W., 130
Albeda, R., 274
Albee, G. W., 460
Albelda, G. W., 240
Albenese, P. J., 46, 47
Alderman, R., 428
Alexander, L. L., 406, 409,
    410, 425, 429, 445, 474,
    523, 524, 525
Alipuria, L., 139
Allen, B., 36, 65
Allen, K., 316–317
Allen, L., 436
Allen, M., 219
Allison, J. A., 484, 485, 493,
    494
Almey, M., 237
Amaro, H., 306, 338, 418
Amato, I., 250
Amato, P. R., 294, 298, 299
American Association of
    University Women
    (AAUW), 140, 142
American Psychiatric
    Association, 304, 341,
    342, 383, 434, 435, 442,
    444, 445, 452, 485, 501
American Psychological
    Association, 11, 42, 45,
    250, 304, 381, 470, 490,
    547–548, 551

Andersen, B. L., 408
Andersen, M., 558
Anderson, C. M., 316, 317,
    320
Anderson, D., 314, 315
Andriote, J., 244
Aniakudo, P., 251, 260, 472
Antill, J. K., 105, 294
Antonucci, T. C., 520
Aponte, J. F., 456
Appignanesi, L., 457
Apter, T., 528, 536
Aquinas, T., 39
Archer, D., 50
Archer, J., 163
Arguello, 417
Aries, E., 27, 197, 199, 201,
    232
Aristotle, 38
Arluke, A., 199
Armbrister, 55
Arnold, K., 142, 148, 158
Aron, A., 286
Aronson, A., 555
Aronson, D., 142, 143
Arvey, R. D., 243, 472
Asch, A., 411, 412, 413, 414,
    415
Asch-Goodkin, J., 270
Aseltine, R. H., Jr., 299
Ashton, E., 115
Asso, D., 133
Association for Women in
    Psychology, 11
Atchley, R., 536
Atkeson, B. M., 484
Atkinson, D. R., 452, 455
Aube, J., 74
August, A., 399
Aven, F. F., 258
Azar, B., 525

Bach, A. K., 442
Bachmann, G. A., 340
Bader, E. J., 260
Bahr, K. S., 534
Bailey, B. A., 114
Bailey, J. M., 311
Bailey, K. R., 115
Bailey, S. M., 112
Bains, A., 256
Baker, L. A., 107, 110

Baker, L. C., 245
Ball, A. L., 388
Ballagh, S. A., 347
Balogh, D. W., 251, 253
Bandura, A., 493
Bank, B. J., 143, 144
Banks, W. P., 489, 490
Banner, L. W., 514
Baranowski, T., 384
Barbee, A. P., 212
Bardwell, J. R., 103
Barer, B. M., 531, 535, 536
Bargad, A., 557
Barickman, R. B., 470, 471,
    473, 474
Barker, K., 271
Barker, M., 246
Barling, J., 146, 268
Barnett, R. C., 264–265, 269,
    271–272, 274
Barney, D. D., 453
Baron, R. A., 222
Barone, D. F., 65
Barongan, C., 494
Barrett, M. B., 301
Bartels, L. K., 413
Barusch, A. S., 521–522
Barzansky, B., 237, 398
Basow, S. A., 250
Basu, A., 559
Bauer, P. A., 101
Baumrind, D., 312
Baur, S., 453
Bayer, B. M., 546
Bazzini, D. G., 514
Beal, C. R., 86, 87, 121
Beall, A. E., 9, 197
Beatty, W. W., 174
Beazley, R. P., 349
Becerra, R. M., 534
Bee, H., 523
Beehr, T. A., 520
Begley, S., 162, 177
Beil, C., 226
Belansky, E. S., 146, 148, 213
Belknap, P., 48
Bell, A., 134
Bell, D., 7
Bell, E., 249
Bellafante, G., 544, 556, 558
Bellinger, D. C., 107
Bem, D. J., 312

641

Bem, S., 27, 28, 62, 64, 65, 70, 72, 73, 74, 76, 78, 82, 96, 98, 101, 116, 197
Benbow, C., 172
Beneke, T., 483
Benjamin, L. T., Jr., 11
Bennett, N. G., 287
Benokraitis, N. V., 4, 6, 41, 55, 245, 249, 252, 471
BenTsvi-Mayer, S., 113
Beren, S. E., 447
Berg, J. H., 189
Bergen, D. J., 52
Bergeron, S. M., 447
Bergob, M., 411, 412
Bergquiest, W. H., 521
Bergum, V., 365, 366, 372, 378, 392
Berheide, C. W., 559
Berman, P. W., 214, 215
Bernal, M. E., 456
Bernay, T., 226
Berndt, T. J., 152
Berrien, R., 236
Berryman, J. C., 368
Berscheid, E., 88, 280, 335
Berthiaume, M., 383
Berzon, B., 62
Best, D. L., 51, 54–55, 99, 100, 103
Bettencourt, B. A., 222, 224
Betz, N. E., 142–148, 271
Biaggio, M., 476
Bianchi, S. M., 267
Bielawski, D., 115
Biernat, M., 268
Biglan, A., 477
Bigler, R. S., 114
Birns, B., 498, 501, 503, 505
Bischoping, K., 199, 200
Bishop, E. G., 167
Björkqvist, K., 223
Blackford, K., 412
Blalock, J. A., 436
Blank, R., 238, 251, 252
Blasko, D. G., 368
Blau, G. M., 331, 332
Blea, I. I., 550
Blechman, E. A., 430
Bleier, R., 179
Blieszner, R., 518
Bliss, S., 552
Block, J. D., 220
Blume, S. B., 425, 426, 427
Blumenthal, S. J., 404
Blumstein, P. W., 295
Bly, R., 552
Blyth, D. A., 151, 152
Bodenhausen, G. V., 49
Boeschen, L. E., 483

Boggiano, A. K., 213
Bohan, J. S., 7, 9, 10, 312
Bonanni, P. P., 498
Bonaparte, N., 39
Bond, J. T., 267
Bondurant, B., 472, 482, 497
Bonebright, T. L., 207, 208
Bonhoutsos, J. C., 453
Bookwala, J., 501
Bordelon, K. W., 115
Bordo, S., 473
Borland, D. C., 530
Borman, K., 274
Boskind-White, M., 444
Boston, M. B., 102
Boswell, A. A., 479
Bould, S., 530
Bowen, D. J., 448, 454
Bowers, C., 139
Boyd, C., 260
Brabant, S., 47
Brabeck, M. M., 218
Bradbury, T. N., 294
Bradsher, J. E., 532
Brady, K., 488
Braito, R., 314, 315
Brake, M., 426
Brandenburg, J. B., 472
Brannon, L., 375
Brannon, R., 551
Branscombe, N. R., 58, 59
Brayfield, A. A., 267
Breedlove, S. M., 83, 85, 178
Brewer, J. I., 526
Brewer, K., 348, 422
Bridge, M. J., 46, 47
Bridges, J. S., 92, 269
Briere, J., 44
Brinson, S. L., 487
Brisman, J., 464
Briton, N. J., 201, 205, 206
Brockington, I., 382
Brody, L. R., 207, 210
Bronstein, P. A., 26, 151, 251, 252, 253
Brooks, C., 172
Brooks, G., 23, 284, 343, 344
Brooks-Gunn, J., 87, 129, 133
Brown, D. R., 317
Brown, E., 26
Brown, H., 471
Brown, L. M., 151, 490
Brown, P. D., 504
Brown, S. S., 347, 349, 350, 353, 489
Brown, T. J., 247
Browne, B. A., 247
Brownell, A., 476
Brownell, K. D., 430, 449
Bruellman, J. A., 174

Bruining, M. O., 308
Brumberg, J. J., 137, 447
Buchman, D. D., 108
Buckley, S., 371
Buckner, J. P., 436
Bullock, S., 278
Bumpass, L. L., 287
Bunch, C., 560
Buntaine, R. L., 223–224
Burbank, V. K., 225
Burn, S. M., 68, 69, 79, 222, 249, 255
Burnham, L., 6
Bursik, K., 74, 197, 222, 299–300, 469, 474
Burstow, B., 460
Burt, V. V., 437
Buss, A. H., 223, 224
Buss, D. M., 283, 284
Butcher, J. N., 434
Buttner, E. H., 228, 256
Buunk, B. P., 306
Bylsma, W. H., 247
Byne, W., 311
Bytheway, B., 513

Cahan, S., 168, 180
Calasanti, T. M., 520
Caldwell, M. A., 306
Calhoun, K. S., 484
Call, V., 339
Callahan, C. M., 144
Calvert, P. D., 272
Cameron, D., 199
Campbell, J. C., 506, 509
Campbell, S., 286, 350, 421
Canadian Committee for Women's Health Research, 399
Canadian Medical Research Council, 398–399
Canadian Psychological Association, 11, 547–548
Canary, D. J., 219, 232
Canetto, S., 435, 515
Cann, A., 56, 68, 101
Cannistra, S. A., 409
Cantin, S., 504
Cantor, D. W., 226
Cantrell, P. J., 252
Caplan, J. B., 14, 19, 33
Caplan, P. J., 14, 19, 33, 192, 256, 451
Caraway, N., 29
Carey, M. P., 342
Carli, L., 199, 228–229
Carlson, K. J., 341, 343, 348, 352, 353, 363, 364, 370, 371, 389, 406, 418, 423,

428, 430, 435, 458, 523, 524, 525, 540
Carmen, B., 207
Carmody, D. L., 39
Carothers, R. L., 476
Carp, F. M., 519, 520
Carr, P. G., 185
Carroll, K., 487, 493
Carson, R. C., 434
Carstensen, L. L., 512, 521, 533
Carter, D. K., 460
Carter, J., 388
Carter, P., 384
Cartwright, L. K., 257
Case, S. M., 257
Casey, M. B., 178
Cash, T. F., 447, 448, 458
Cass, M., 311
Castañeda, D., 296
Castro, F. G., 456
Cate, R., 140
Catsambis, S., 143
Caudill, S. A., 348
Cavaliere, F., 382
Cavanaugh, M. A., 472
Ceballo, R., 389
Centers for Disease Control and Prevention, 416–417
Centerwall, B. S., 116
Chaffin, R., 179
Chambless, D. L., 442
Chan, C. S., 308
Chartier, B., 479
Chase-Lansdale, P. L., 350
Chasteen, A. L., 317
Chavez, V., 267
Cherry, D., 102–103, 453
Chesler, P., 262
Chester, N. L., 183
Chia, R. C., 61
Chin, J. L., 296, 379
Chinen, J. N., 256
Chipman, S. F., 179, 180
Chodorow, N. J., 457
Chonko, L. B., 247
Choo, P., 288, 289
Chow, E. N., 25, 238, 549, 559
Chrisler, J. C., 129, 130, 131, 132, 133, 134, 428, 447, 449
Christopherson, V. A., 528
Cirese, S., 325, 326
Clair, J. M., 520
Clark, J., 185
Clark, R., 115, 190
Clarke-Stewart, A., 270
Clausen, J., 304
Clayton, S. D., 241, 247, 248

Cleeton, E. C., 223, 225
Cleveland, J. N., 253
Clift, E., 409
Clinton, B., 240
Clopton, N. A., 217
Coalition for Free Men, 553
Cobleigh, M. A., 524
Cochran, C. C., 472
Coffin, F., 260
Coffin, J., 418
Cohan, C. L., 354
Cohen, J., 142, 166
Cohen, K., 320
Colby, A., 217
Colditz, G. A., 525
Cole, E., 336–337
Cole, N. S., 169, 172, 173, 180
Coleman, M., 249, 375
Colen, S., 255
Coley, R. L., 350
Collaer, M. L., 83, 168
Collins, N., 370
Collins, P., 23, 297, 368, 379, 380, 549
Colombo, J. R., 24, 346, 513, 532
Comas-Díaz, L., 52, 236, 401, 546
Committee on Women in Psychology, 252
Compas, B. E., 376
Condon, J. T., 365
Condra, M. B., 318
Condry, J. C., 66, 91
Condry, S., 66, 91
Conger, J. C., 481
Conger, R. D., 144
Conley, F., 258–259, 398
Conway, K., 408
Conway, M., 209
Coontz, S., 270
Cooper, P. E., 385
Corcoran, C. B., 491, 494
Coriell, M., 402
Corkindale, C., 365
Cortés, C. E., 48
Cose, E., 552
Cossette, L., 86, 87
Costello, C., 402
Costenbader, V. K., 224
Cota, A. A., 51
Côté, J. E., 140
Covell, K., 49
Cowan, C. P., 365, 366, 372, 387
Cowan, G., 48, 99, 486, 488, 517
Cowan, P. A., 365, 366, 372, 387
Cox, T., Jr., 249

Coyle, J. M., 540
Cozzarelli, C., 354
Crabb, P. B., 115
Craighead, W. E., 436
Crandall, C. S., 447
Crawford, D., 377
Crawford, M., 6, 17, 19, 106, 145, 174, 179, 192, 199, 225, 226, 232, 481
Croll, E., 380
Crombie, G., 190
Cronin, C., 45
Crosby, F. J., 241, 247, 248
Crose, R., 402
Cross, S. E., 64
Crowley, M., 212
Cruikshank, M., 304
Crum, M. J., 48
Culbertson, F. M., 435
Culbertson, J. L., 426
Cull, P., 260
Curtin, S. C., 371

Dabbs, J. M., Jr., 213
Dabul, A. J., 182
Dagg, P. K. B., 355
D'Allessandro, J. D., 74
Dalton, S. T., 317
Damon, W., 217
Daniel, J. H., 453
Daniluk, J. C., 333
Dannenbring, D., 372
Danoff-Burg, S., 382, 389
Darling, C. A., 329
Daubman, K. A., 185
D'Augelli, A. R., 62, 304
David, H. P., 355
Davidson, N. E., 524
Davis, J. C., 292
Davis, L., 412, 431
Davis, S., 267, 281
Day, J. C., 24, 513
Dayhoff, S. A., 41
Deaux, K., 37, 52, 63, 139, 189, 213, 214
De Beauvoir, S., 37
DeBlassie, R. R., 330
De Bro, S. C., 420, 421
De Costa, E. J., 526
DeCourville, N. H., 523
DeKeseredy, W. S., 483, 494, 496, 498, 500, 501, 506, 509
DeLamater, J., 329, 341, 342, 353, 372
Delaney, J., 131, 134
De León, B., 75
Delk, J., 90–91
Dello Buono, R. A., 351
Delmas, P. D., 410

DeLorey, C., 527
Demarest, J., 91, 115
DeMaris, A., 438
DeMeis, D. K., 267
Denton, T. C., 318
De Puy, C., 354
Derlega, V. J., 219, 320
Desrochers, S., 281
Deutsch, F. M., 269
Devereaux, M. S., 267
Devons, C. A. J., 523
Dhruvarajan, V., 298
Diamant, L., 252
Diamond, M., 85, 86, 301
DiBrigida, L. A., 436
Dickstein, L. J., 472
Di Dio, L., 52
Diener, E., 522
DiMatteo, M. R., 371, 373
Dindia, K., 219
Dinges, N. G., 453
Dion, C., 278
Dion, K. K., 282, 285
Dion, K. L., 282, 285, 435
Dionne, M., 448
DiPietro, J. A., 225
Dobbins, G. H., 253
Dobson, K. S., 490
Dodson, J. E., 297
Donahue, M., 87
Donizetti, G., 278
Donnelly, N. D., 500
Doress, P. B., 521
Doress-Worters, P. B., 530
Dorfman, L. T., 520
Dotterer, C., 496
Dovidio, J. F., 205
Dovitch, D., 354
Dow, B. J., 556
Dowling-Guyer, S., 45
Downey, J. I., 301
Doyle, J. A., 551, 552, 553
Driedger, D., 412
D'Souza, D., 556
Dubas, J. S., 125
Dube, E. M., 155
Dubeck, P. J., 274
Duck, S., 219
Duffy, A, 320
Dugger, K., 54
Dunkel-Schetter, C., 389
Dunn, D., 245, 412
Dunn, K. F., 488
Dunn, M. E., 329
Durkin, K., 46
Dusek, J. B., 140
Dziech, B. W., 471, 472, 473, 474
Dziuba-Leatherman, J., 489

Eagly, A. H., 36, 58, 197, 212, 226, 227, 229, 284
East, P. L., 346, 379
Eaton, W. O., 86
Eberhardt, J. L., 253
Eberts, E. H., 201
Ebertz, L., 310
Ebmeyer, J. B., 294
Eccles, J. S., 67, 69, 112, 142, 143, 146, 147, 180, 185, 190, 192
Eccles (Parsons), J. A., 67
Edmondson, C. B., 481
Edwards, N., 366
Egan, J., 76
Ehlers, T. B., 296, 297, 379
Ehrhardt, A. A., 84, 85
Eisen, S. V., 115
Eisenberg, L., 347, 349, 350, 353
Eisenberg, M., 168, 213, 270
Eisenberg, N., 215, 398
Eisenhart, M. A., 148, 155, 156, 200
Eisenstat, S. A., 430, 540
Eisler, R., 334
Ekstrom, B., 527, 528
Eldridge, N. S., 252
Elfin, M., 249, 267, 396
Eliason, M. J., 278
Ellis, L., 310, 311, 312
Ellis, S., 473
Emans, S. J., 128
Emmers-Sommer, T. M., 219, 232
England, E. M., 385
England, P., 245, 246
Enns, C. Z., 7, 8, 456, 458, 459, 460, 461, 462, 464, 546, 554
Enns, L. R., 86
Epstein, S., 412
Equal Employment Opportunity Commission, 472
Erkut, S., 138
Eskilson, A., 250
Espín, O., 23, 25, 307, 453, 454, 546
Espinosa, P., 48
Esses, L. M., 147
Esterberg, K. G., 304
Etaugh, C., 101, 102, 109, 269, 270, 299, 315, 316, 520, 532
Ethier, K., 139
Evans, N. J., 304
Everett, J. C., 176

Facio, E., 530, 533
Facteau, J. D., 253
Fadli, M., 461
Fagot, B. I., 98, 99, 103, 104, 106, 107
Falco, K., 408, 409, 410
Faludi, S., 45, 556
Farnsworth, L., 251, 252, 253
Farrakhan, L., 552
Fast, C. C., 483, 490
Fast, T. H., 483, 490
Fausto-Sterling, A., 179, 397
Faux, S. A., 435
Favreau, O. E., 176, 177, 178, 225, 554, 556
Feagin, J. R., 41, 250, 252
Fedders, C., 500
Fedders, J., 500
Fee, E., 398, 410, 416
Fehr, B., 218, 219
Feingold, A., 167, 168, 169, 171, 174, 214, 226, 281, 447
Feiring, C., 140, 153, 154
Felice, M. E., 346, 379
Felmlee, D., 286
Fennema, E., 180
Ferdig, L. A., 545
Fernald, J. L., 62, 64
Fernández, M., 506
Ferrato, D., 500
Ferree, M. M., 268, 558
Field, T., 366
Figert, A. E., 129, 130–131
Fincham, F. D., 294, 436
Fine, M., 139, 296, 331, 411, 412, 413, 414, 415, 484
Finkelhor, D., 489
Firestein, B. A., 308, 320
Fischhoff, B., 491, 493
Fishel, A. H., 436, 437, 439, 460
Fisher, B., 415
Fisher-Thompson, D., 104, 105
Fisk, A., 474
Fiske, S. T., 58–59, 60, 61, 69, 250, 253
Fiss, C., 260–261
Fitzgerald, L. F., 146–147, 264
Fivush, R., 36, 85, 90, 92, 95, 99, 101, 105, 117, 118, 121, 124, 200, 207, 436
Flaherty, J. F., 140
Flanders, L., 46, 240, 552
Flannagan, D., 105
Flannery-Schroeder, E. C., 447

Floyd, R. L., 366
Foa, E. B., 404, 485, 486
Fodor, I. G., 512
Foertsch, J., 45
Fogel, C. I., 410, 421, 422
Fontes, L. A., 489
Fontham, T. H., 424
Fordham, S., 139
Foresman, E., 316
Forrester, J., 457
Foubert, J. D., 219
Fox, A., 308
Fox, R., 309
Frable, D., 203
Frances, S. J., 206
Franks, F., 435
Franks, V., 512
Fraser, L., 47, 449
Fredrickson, B. L., 125, 343,
    439
Freedman, R., 137, 203, 458
Freeman, J., 145
Freiberg, P., 416
French, M., 47
Freud, S., 14, 94–95,
    311–312, 327, 457
Frey, C., 225
Freyd, J. J., 489, 490
Fried, S., 560
Friedan, B., 514
Friedman, H., 295, 314
Friedman, R. C., 301
Friedman, S. B., 428
Frieze, I. H., 79, 185, 189,
    285, 286, 287
Frigoletto, F. D., Jr., 371
Fritz, H. L., 74, 439
Frodi, A., 222, 435
Fry, D. P., 221, 223
Fullmer, E., 532
Funk, J. B., 108
Furman, C. S., 524
Furnham, A., 46, 68, 117,
    185, 403
Furumoto, L., 10, 11, 12, 33

Gabriel, A. H., 221
Gaeddert, W. P., 189
Gagnon, J. H., 358
Galea, L. A. M., 174
Galinsky, E., 267
Gallaher, P. E., 207–208
Gallant, S. J., 130, 423, 428,
    431
Galler, R., 415
Galligan, P., 260–262
Gamble, N., 486
Gannon, L., 527, 528
Ganong, L. H., 375

Ganor, Y., 168, 180
Ganz, P. A., 406
Garbarino, J., 25
Garber, M., 309
Garcia, A. M., 550
García-Moreno, C., 352
Gardner, W., 332
Garfield, S. L., 451
Garner, C., 388, 389
Garnets, L., 302, 303, 304
Garrod, A., 25
Garst, J., 49
Garvey, C., 148
Gary, L. E., 297, 317
Gash, H., 114
Gaspar de Alba, A., 307
Gastil, J., 43, 44
Gater, R., 437
Gates, H. L., Jr., 210
Gauthier, J., 399
Geary, D. C., 174
Gee, E. M., 529, 531
Geen, R. G., 222
Geffner, R., 481
Geis, F. L., 64
Geller, G., 448
Genevie, L., 376
George, T., 528
Gerbner, G., 46
Gernsbacher, M. A., 45
Gerrard, M., 349
Gerstmann, E. A., 557
Gettys, L. D., 101
Ghez, M., 509
Gibbons, J. L., 54, 148, 151,
    283
Giesen, C. B., 412, 414
Gilbert, D., 67
Gilbert, L. A., 252, 266, 269,
    452, 453, 454, 460, 461,
    464
Gilbert, M., 181
Giles-Sims, J., 505
Gillespie, M., 556
Gilligan, C., 151, 152–153,
    215, 216–217, 218, 220
Ginorio, A. B., 379
Giordana, C., 435
Girgus, J. S., 435, 437, 439,
    440
Gitlin, M. J., 458
Giudice, L. C., 389
Giulietti, R., 502
Gladue, B. A., 311
Gleason, J. B., 107
Glick, P., 60, 61, 241–242,
    256
Glinos, F., 91
Global Fund for Women, 559

Goddard, M. K., 38
Gold, D., 113
Gold, M., 424
Goldberg, P., 57–58
Goldberg, S., 87
Golden, C., 312–313
Goldfield, A., 447
Golding, J. M., 438, 485
Golombok, S., 36, 85, 90, 92,
    99, 117, 118, 121, 124,
    381, 382
Golub, S., 114, 124, 128–129,
    132, 133, 258, 523, 525
Gondolf, E. W., 506
Gonsiorek, J. C., 252, 303,
    304
Gonzalez, J. T., 185
Goode, E., 281
Goodman, L., 496, 499
Goodman, W., 447, 464
Goodwin, B. J., 48
Gordon, M., 134, 483, 484
Gorlick, C. A., 298, 299, 300
Gormly, A. V., 387, 388, 512
Gorney, C., 352
Gose, B., 144, 145, 257
Gostin, L. O., 485
Gotlib, I. H., 382, 383
Gottman, J. M., 497, 501,
    503, 505, 506
Graham, S., 183
Grambs, J. D., 518, 529, 530
Grana, S. J., 263
Grant, C., 376
Grant, J. R., 458
Grant, L., 113
Grasmick, H. G., 364
Gratch, L. V., 472
Grauerholz, E., 287
Gray, J., 198, 229
Gray, N. S., 444, 445
Green, B. L., 281, 434, 435
Green, J., 371
Greenberg, D., 220
Greene, B., 52, 236, 307, 454,
    456, 460, 546
Greene, K., 199
Greenfeld, L. A., 223
Greenfield, P. M., 179
Greenfield, S. F., 428
Greenspan, M., 457
Greil, A. L., 389
Grella, C. E., 300
Grindstaff, C. F., 387
Groat, H. T., 387
Grodstein, F., 524, 525
Groff, J. Y., 366
Grogan, S., 447
Grote, N. K., 285, 286

Gruchy, C. D. G., 205
Grusec, J. E., 104, 107
Guarnaccia, P. J., 454
Guinier, L., 256
Gullo, D. F., 91
Gullotta, T. P., 331, 332
Gunnar, M. R., 87
Gunter, B., 117, 118, 121, 267
Gunter, N. C., 267
Gur, R. C., 179
Gutek, B. A., 243
Guthrie, R. V., 29
Gutiérrez, F., 48
Guy-Sheftall, B., 557

Hackett, G., 452, 462
Haddock, G., 59
Hafner, R. J., 443
Hafter, D. M., 38
Hahn, E. D., 53
Halberstadt, A., 205, 206, 209, 210
Hale-Benson, J., 271
Hall, C., 48, 453, 456
Hall, G. C. N., 494
Hall, G. S., 10
Hall, J., 199, 201, 202, 203, 204, 205, 206, 207, 209, 210, 211, 258, 400
Hall, R., 145
Hall, S., 428
Halldórsdóttir, S., 373
Hallingby, L., 117
Halpern, D. F., 19, 68, 162–163, 168, 169, 170, 174, 178, 192, 311
Halpern-Falsher, B. L., 332, 333
Hamer, D. H., 311
Hamilton, D., 64, 66, 68, 69
Hamilton, J. A., 130, 396, 426
Hamilton, M., 42, 65, 88
Hammerle, G., 493
Hammond, J. A., 260
Hampson, E., 133
Hampton, H. L., 491
Hannon, R., 481
Hansen, F. J., 452, 458
Hansson, R. O., 520
Hardie, E. A., 130–131
Hardy, A., 536–537
Hardy, D., 536–537
Hardy, J. B., 332
Hare-Mustin, R. T., 9, 197, 441, 460, 461
Hargreaves, D. J., 167
Harney, P. A., 486
Harnish, R. J., 479
Harquail, C. V., 249

Harris, F., 256
Harris, M. B., 223
Harris, M. G., 222
Harris, R. J., 487
Hart, S., 405, 406
Hartmann, L. C., 408
Hartstein, N. B., 303
Harvey, M. R., 477
Harway, M., 468
Haseltine, F. P., 396, 426
Hashizume, L., 557
Haskell, M., 47
Haskins, R., 270
Haslett, B. J., 57, 245
Hatch, L. R., 521
Hatcher, M., 257
Hatcher, R. A., 355, 356
Hatfield, E., 281, 282, 283, 284, 286, 293, 320, 332, 334, 338
Havens, B., 134
Haviland, J. M., 151
Hawkins, B., 23, 145
Hawkins, J. W., 399
Hawkins, M. W., 471, 472
Hayes, N., 284
Hayes, T. J., 238
Hays, S., 270, 271, 377, 388
Headlee, S., 249, 267, 396
Healey, S., 514
Heatherington, L., 185
Heatherton, T. F., 448
Hebl, M. R., 448
Hedges, L., 168, 169, 171, 174
Hedley, M., 153
Heffernan, K., 446
Heilbrun, A. B., 76
Heilbrun, C., 536
Hein, K., 421
Heise, L., 478
Heitner, K., 471
Helgeson, V. C., 288
Helgeson, V. S., 74, 439
Helmreich, R. L., 183
Helson, R., 529, 535
Helstrom, A. W., 406, 409
Hemstreet, A. H., 428
Henderson, N., 258
Hendrick, C., 74, 286
Hendrick, S., 286
Hendrick, V. C., 437
Henley, N. M., 12, 201, 207, 209, 210, 255
Hennig, M., 261
Henning, K., 336
Henrie, R. L., 174
Henrion, C., 180
Henry, P. E., 447, 448
Herbert, S. E., 338

Herdt, G., 124
Herek, G. M., 6, 17, 251, 252, 301, 302, 303
Herlitz, A., 167
Herman-Giddens, M. E., 125
Hern, A. L., 350
Herrmann, D. J., 167
Heslet, L., 499
Hesse-Biber, S., 449
Hickman, S. E., 483
Hicks, D. W., 251
Hidalgo, H., 307
Higginbotham, A., 137
Higginbottom, S. F., 521
Hill, A., 472
Hillyer, B., 414
Hilton, J. L., 68
Hines, M., 83, 85, 168
Hines, N. J., 223
Hixon, J. G., 67
Ho, C. K., 500, 504
Hochschild, A. R., 270, 272
Hoctor, M. A., 520
Hoehn, S., 299
Hoff, L., 505
Hoffman, C., 99
Hoffman, L. W., 107
Hoffman, M., 418, 419
Hoffman, P., 271
Hoffnung, M., 264, 268, 371–372, 375, 376, 377, 378
Hofmeyr, G. J., 363, 364
Holcomb, L. P., 412, 414
Holden, S. L., 512
Holland, B. E., 151
Holland, D., 148, 155, 156, 200
Holland, J., 257
Hollander, J., 5, 6, 9, 221
Hollingworth, L., 11, 133
Holms, V. L., 147
Hood, A., 299
hooks, b., 548–549
Hooyman, N. R., 530
Hopkins, A., 58, 65
Hoppe-Graff, S., 225
Horgan, D., 368
Horner, M., 184
Hosking, D., 410
Hotaling, S., 46
Houser, B. B., 148
Houston, B., 212
Houston, S., 471
Howard, J. A., 5, 6, 9, 221
Hu, S. M., 380
Huang, A., 248
Hulicka, I. M., 513
Hull, D. B., 492
Humes, C. W., 411

Humm, M., 7
Hummert, M. L., 515, 516
Hunter College, 375, 384, 385, 401
Hunter College Women's Studies Collective, 6, 7, 38, 39
Hurtz, W., 46
Husten, C. G., 423, 424
Huston, R., 419, 431
Huston, T. L., 377
Huttenlocher, J., 90, 168
Hwang, N., 471
Hyde, J. S., 9, 166, 168–169, 171–172, 176, 179, 180, 192, 222, 329, 335, 336, 341, 342, 353, 372, 557
Hynie, M., 350

Ickovics, J. R., 404
Idle, T., 104
Imhoff, A. R., 519, 520
Ineichen, B., 384
Ingstad, B., 412
Intons-Peterson, M. J., 87
Ireland, M. S., 387, 388, 389
Irish, J. T., 400
Irvine, J., 344–345
Ishii-Kuntz, M., 315
Ivins, M., 149
Ivy, D. K., 42

Jacklin, C. N., 11, 19, 87, 94, 104, 106, 107, 110, 167, 168, 222
Jackson, B., 528
Jackson, D., 561
Jackson, D. Z., 241
Jackson, L. A., 6, 7, 179, 180, 448
Jackson, S., 549
Jackson, T., 477, 487, 493, 504
Jacobs, J., 250, 274
Jacobs, R., 514, 518, 532
Jacobson, B. G., 404
Jacobson, N. S., 497, 501, 503, 505, 506
Jambunathan, J., 383
James, E., 11
James, J., 197
Janoff-Bulman, R., 485
Jansen, M. A., 401
Janus, C. L., 330, 336
Janus, S. S., 330, 336
Jardim, A., 261
Jaschik-Herman, M. L., 474
Jay, T., 199
Jemmott, J. B., III, 130
Jenkins, M. R., 426

Jenkins, S., 257
Jennings, J., 49
Jensen-Campbell, L. A., 281
Jiang, J., 173
John, D., 267
John, R., 534
Johnson, B. E., 486, 487
Johnson, B. T., 227
Johnson, C., 199, 531, 535, 536
Johnson, F., 220
Johnson, J., 513
Johnson, J. D., 49, 474
Johnson, J. T., 66
Johnson, L., 297, 379
Johnson, M. E., 45
Johnson, N. G., 460
Johnson, S., 16, 129, 130
Johnson, T. L., 398, 410, 416
Johnson, V., 326, 327, 329, 330, 339, 344, 345
Joiner, T. E., Jr., 436
Jones, M., 48
Jordan, J., 215, 439, 457
Jordan, L., 140
Joseph, J., 500
Joseph, N., 287
Josselson, R., 531
Jreisat, S., 45
Jurgens, J. J., 134
Jutras, S., 530

Kaganoff, P., 299
Kagawa-Singer, M., 533, 534
Kahn, A. S., 16, 181, 484, 546
Kahn, K. L., 371
Kahn, R., 267
Kail, R. V., Jr., 176, 177
Kalichman, S. C., 175, 313, 418, 419
Kang, 25
Kantor, G. K., 383
Kantrowitz, B., 332
Kanuha, V., 500
Kaplan, A., 151
Kaplan, D., 331, 341, 342
Kaplan, E., 366
Kaplan, H., 326
Kaplan, J., 142, 143
Kaplan, S., 245
Karau, S. J., 197, 226
Karlsdóttir, S. I., 373
Karney, B. R., 294
Karraker, K., 89, 92
Kaschak, E., 442
Kastberg, S. M., 146
Katz, D., 241
Katz, M., 561
Katz, P. A., 98, 102, 107, 109, 205, 561

Katzman, D. K., 445
Kaufman, D., 249
Kaufman, E., 561
Kaufman, F. R., 85
Kaufman, L., 472
Kaufman, M., 552
Kauth, M. R., 313
Kawachi, I., 424
Kazanis, B. W., 559
Kearns, J. R., 528
Keeley, M. P., 406
Keen, S., 552
Kehoe, M., 339
Keita, G. P., 423, 428, 431
Keller, C., 521
Kelley, K., 329
Kelly, C., 492
Kelly, E., 16, 19
Kelly, K., 140
Kelly, M., 342
Kemp, A. A., 254
Kendall-Tackett, K. A., 383
Kenrick, D. T., 281
Kerr, B., 142, 144
Kessel, C., 174
Kessler, R., 299, 435, 442
Kessler, S., 86
Keyes, C. L. M., 535
Killen, J. D., 424
Kilmartin, C. T., 6, 551, 553
Kimball, M. M., 7, 8, 9, 33, 165, 166, 169, 172, 173, 176, 180, 192–193, 217, 490, 529, 530, 531
Kimmel, E. B., 51, 52
Kimmel, M., 551, 552, 553, 559, 562–563
Kimura, D., 133, 167, 168, 174, 178
King, B., 330
King, Y., 411, 414, 415
Kion, K. L., 435
Kirchmeyer, C., 271
Kirkcaldy, B., 403
Kirshenbaum, G., 544
Kishwar, M., 88
Kissling, F., 352
Kitasei, H. H., 422
Kite, M. E., 52, 58, 59, 63, 64, 251, 253, 301, 515
Kitson, G. C., 299
Kitzinger, C., 312
Kitzinger, S., 367, 368, 373, 376, 377, 383, 384
Kivett, V. R., 531
Klebanov, P. K., 130, 369
Kleiman, C., 237
Klein, E., 497, 498, 500, 501, 502, 503, 505
Klein, R., 7

Klem, M. L., 447, 449
Klevan, J. L., 368
Kline, K. N., 366
Klinger, R. L., 338
Klonis, S., 252, 555
Klonoff, E., 56, 57, 399, 400, 437, 452, 472
Kloska, D. D., 107
Knaub, P. K., 385
Knight, G. P., 222, 223
Knight, R. A., 492
Knight-Bohnhoff, K., 223
Ko, M., 366
Kofkin, J. A., 98, 109
Kohlberg, L., 95–96, 99, 101, 216
Kok, C. J., 65
Kolbe, R. H., 46, 47
Kolpin, V. W., 241
Konrad, A. M., 241, 243
Kopper, B. A., 486
Kornhaber, A., 532, 533
Kortenhaus, C. M., 115
Koshland, D. E., Jr., 506
Koski, L. R., 293
Koss, M. P., 473, 477, 482, 485, 498, 499, 500
Kostelny, K., 25
Kowalski, R. M., 221, 225, 442, 479, 496, 498
Kozak, L. J., 371
Krajeski, J., 304
Kramer, D. A., 557
Krimgold, B. K., 402
Kring, B., 332, 335
Krishnan, V., 88
Kristiansen, C. M., 502
Kristof, N. D., 498
Kromrey, J. D., 52
Kruse, S. J., 257
Kuebli, J., 105, 200
Kulkarni, V., 113
Kunda, Z., 66
Kurdek, L., 294, 298, 303, 304, 305, 306
Kuriloff, P. J., 64
Kushner, E., 354, 355, 358
Kusmanović, J., 477
Kwa, L., 138

Labour Canada, 101
LaFrance, K., 502
LaFrance, M., 201, 207, 209, 255
LaFromboise, T., 25, 54, 455
Lakoff, R. T., 199
LaMar, L., 64
Lamke, L. K., 286
Lancaster, J., 402
Landenburger, K., 506

Landrine, H., 33, 56, 57, 75, 399, 400, 417, 425, 437, 452, 472, 546, 563
Langelan, M. J., 475, 476
Langer, C. L., 554
Langer, E., 366, 519
Lanis, K., 49
Lanktree, C., 44
LaRosa, J. H., 406, 409, 410, 425, 429, 445, 474, 523, 525
Larsen, K., 53
Larson, M. S., 356
Larwood, L., 243
Latané, B., 213
LaTorre, R. A., 309
Laumann, E. O., 336, 339, 349, 358
Lavender, T., 383
Lawrence, R. A., 384, 385
Laws, A., 489
Lawton, C. A., 174
Leadbeater, B. J. R., 158, 355
Leaper, C., 105, 107, 219, 297
Lears, M., 118
Leary, M. R., 442
Leavitt, J., 512, 547
Lederman, R. P., 364, 365
Le De Simone, L., 16
Lee, J., 125
Lees, D., 552
Leiblum, S. R., 339
Leifer, M., 365
Leinbach, M. D., 98, 99, 103
Leitenberg, H., 336
Leitinger, I. A., 559
Lemieux, R., 366
Lenney, E., 185
Lennon, R., 215
Leo, R., 436
Leonard, A., 251
Leonard, D. K., 173
Leonard, W. M. II, 48
Leong, F. T. L., 238
Leonhardt-Lupa, M., 364
Lepowsky, M., 221–222
Lepper, M. R., 201
Lerman, H., 452
Lerner, H., 217, 377
Lester, D., 435
Lester, R., 448
Levant, R. F., 6, 551
LeVay, S., 311
Leve, L. D., 105, 106
Levenson, R. W., 293, 294
Leventhal, E. A., 403, 404
Levering, M., 40
Levin, J., 199
Levine, A. D., 270, 291, 298, 300, 351, 352, 369, 401,

402, 424, 477, 483, 498, 512, 559, 563
Levine, F., 16
Levine, M. P., 446
Levine, S., 339
Levy, B., 503, 519
Levy, G. D., 95, 101, 102
Levy, K. B., 131
Lewin, M., 387
Lewinsohn, P. M., 443
Lewis, C., 91
Lewis, K. G., 316, 317
Lewis, M., 87, 140
Lickona, T., 333
Lightdale, J. R., 224–225
Lindgren, J. R., 368
Lindsey, L. L., 263
Linn, M. C., 168–169, 174, 176
Liss, M. B., 101, 102
Litt, I. F., 399, 400, 422, 423, 424, 428, 445, 498, 499, 506
Lively, K., 479
Livingston, J. A., 252
Livingston, M., 372, 399
Lloyd, B., 205
Locher, P., 281
Locklin, M. P., 384
Loftus, E. F., 490
Logsdon, M. C., 383
Lone Dog, L., 307
Long, E., 53
Lorber, J., 246, 418
Loren, J. A., 408
Lott, B., 5, 8, 37, 47, 55, 56, 79, 104, 165
Lottes, I. L., 64
Love, S. M., 406
Lubben, J. E., 534
Luebke, B. F., 557
Luker, K., 346, 350, 358
Lundberg-Love, P., 481
Lunneborg, P., 260
Lunney, G. S., 92
Lustbader, W., 530
Luthra, R., 282
Lyons, N. P., 152–153
Lytton, H., 104, 106, 107

Maccoby, E. E., 11, 87, 104, 109, 121, 167, 168, 222
Macdonald, B., 518
MacDonald, K., 105
MacKay, N. J., 49
Mackie, M., 40, 532
MacKinnon, C. A., 471
MacLeod, M., 145
Macrae, C. N., 64, 68
Madigan, L., 486

Madsen, S. S., 240
Maggio, R., 42, 45
Mahalik, J. R., 269, 461
Mahlstedt, D., 491, 494
Mahoney, C. W., 260
Major, B., 37, 214, 247, 354
Malamuth, N. M., 488
MALE. *See* Men Achieving
    Liberation and Equality
    (MALE)
Malstrom, J., 315, 316
Maluso, D., 5, 37, 47, 55, 79,
    104
Malveaux, J., 145
Mandell, N., 320
Manderson, L., 392
Manko, W., 385
Mannison, M., 481
Mansfield, P. K., 339
Manson, J. E., 449
Marchioro, C. A., 413
Marecek, J., 9, 197, 441, 460,
    461
Margolies, E., 376
Markides, K. S., 402
Markman, H., 294
Marks, N. F., 314
Markson, E. W., 514
Markus, H. R., 64
Marshall, E., 311
Marshall, H., 363, 364, 365,
    368
Marston, W., 135
Martell, R. T., 243, 249, 250
Marten, L. A., 115
Martin, C., 36, 65, 83, 85, 86,
    97, 99, 104, 105, 106, 121
Martin, K., 125, 332–333
Martin, M., 274
Martin, P. Y., 558
Martínez, E., 23, 24, 550
Martinez, K., 412
Marx, J., 83
Massoth, N. A., 47
Masters, W., 326, 327, 329,
    330, 339, 344, 345
Mathie, V., 484
Matlin, M. W., 30, 42, 115,
    385, 437, 547, 548
Matthews, W. S., 20, 87, 133,
    398, 524, 525
Maurice, J., 447
Mayer, J. A., 406
Mayerson, C., 291, 332
Mays, V. M., 317, 419
Mazzella, R., 447
McAdoo, J. L., 297, 454
McAleer, J., 117, 118, 121
McArthur, L. Z., 115
McCarten-Gibbs, A., 559

McCarthy, P., 408
McCartney, B., 552
McCaul, M. E., 426, 428, 458
McClintock, M. K., 124
McCorduck, P., 560
McCormick, N. B., 326, 327,
    335, 337, 338, 358, 415
McDonald, S. M., 115
McEnally, M., 228
McFarlane, J., 498
McFarlane, J. M., 130
McFarlane, T. L., 447, 449
McGill, A. L., 66
McGill, O. D., 448
McGonagle, K. A., 298
McGrath, E., 439, 458
McHugh, M. C., 19, 79, 442,
    443, 503
McIlwee, J. S., 256, 259
McIntosh, P., 22–23
McKay, S., 370
McKinley, N. M., 176
McKinney, K., 334
McLendon, K., 481, 482
McMahon, M., 387, 392
McWilliams, A., 419
Mead, M., 561
Mednick, M. T., 182, 183,
    184, 189, 546
Meinert, C. L., 398
Meinz, E. J., 167
Melpomene Institute, 137
Men Achieving Liberation
    and Equality (MALE),
    553
Mendelsohn, K. D., 398
Mercer, R. T., 365, 376, 377
Merritt, R. D., 65
Messner, M. A., 551
Metro Men Against Violence,
    551–552
Metts, S., 337
Meyer-Bahlburg, H. F. L.,
    310
Meyerowitz, B. E., 397, 405,
    406
Michael, R. T., 358, 416
Michaels, G., 387
Michaels, R. T., 358
Michaels, S., 301
Midlarsky, E., 54
Miene, P., 64
Mikell, G., 559
Milburn, A., 422
Miles, C., 38
Miles, S., 399, 400, 454
Mill, H. T., 39
Mill, J. S., 39
Miller, C., 42, 45
Miller, D., 352, 353, 354

Miller, D. G., 146
Miller, D. T., 66
Miller, J. B., 457
Miller, N., 222, 224
Miller, S., 249
Mills, J., 205
Mills, R., 213
Millstein, S. G., 332, 333
Min, P. G., 291
Minge, P. J., 443
Minkler, M., 533
Mintz, R. D., 269
Miranda, M. R., 402
Mischel, W., 96
Misri, S., 382
Mitchell, E., 129
Mitchell, J., 446
Mitchell, P., 256
Mitchell, V., 529, 535
Mladinic, A., 58
Moen, P., 520
Mogil, J. S., 20
Monaghan, P., 412
Money, J., 84, 85
Monsour, M., 218, 219
Montemayor, R., 140
Moon, S., 316, 317
Mooney, L. A., 47
Moore, D. P., 256
Moraga, C., 550
Morawski, J. G., 11, 546
Morell, V., 403, 421, 422
Morgan, B., 108
Morgan, M., 114
Mori, L., 486
Morokoff, P. K., 337, 338,
    343, 416, 421
Morris, L. A., 287, 288, 339,
    481, 482, 491, 551
Morrison, D., 379
Morrow, C. A., 456
Morton, D. C., 223
Moss, H. A., 90
Motowidlo, S. J., 74
Mounts, N. S., 94
Moynihan, D. P., 297
Muehlenhard, C. L., 473, 482,
    483, 486, 493
Mueller, K. A., 385, 386, 387
Muller, C. F., 400
Mulqueen, C. M., 76
Murnen, S. K., 336
Murphy, P. A., 223, 225
Murray, B., 249, 471
Murrell, A. J., 472
Murry, V. M., 330, 331, 349
Muth, J. L., 447
Mwangi, M. W., 47
Myers, D. G., 522
Myers, S. T., 364

Naber, S. J., 384
Nadeau, R. A., 6, 468
Naidoo, J. C., 238, 240, 292, 518
Napier, L. A., 146
Naples, N. A., 558
Napper, T., 377
Nash, H. C., 130
National Center on Addiction and Substance Abuse, 428
National Foundation for Women Business Owners, 20
National Labor Committee, 256
National Opinion Research Center (NORC), 336
National Organization for Men Against Sexism (NOMAS), 551
National Organization of Women (NOW), 550, 558
National Women's Studies Association, 557
Neft, N., 270, 291, 298, 300, 351, 352, 369, 401, 402, 424, 477, 483, 498, 512, 559, 563
Nelson, E., 373
Nelson, H., 410
Neter, E., 383
Nevid, J. S., 281
Nevill, D. D., 257, 267, 272
Newcomb, M. D., 287–288
Newell, C. E., 472
Newman, A. L., 489
Newman, J., 385
Ng, S. H., 42
NiCarthy, G., 470
NICHD Early Child Care Research Network, 270
Nicholls, J. G., 185
Nichols, M., 309, 342
Nicholson, L., 5
Nicolson, P., 332
Nicotera, A. M., 286
Nielsen, L., 137, 151
Niemann, Y., 52–53
Nigro, G. N., 185
Nihlen, A. S., 114
Niloff, J. M., 409
Nkomo, S. M., 249
Noble, K. D., 158
Nock, S. L., 270
Noell, J., 421
Nolen-Hoeksema, S., 105, 186–188, 435, 437–441, 443
Nolin, M. J., 330

Noor, N. M., 272
Norcross, J. C., 257
Normand, J., 144, 404, 406, 423
Norton, K. I., 446
Notman, M. T., 95
Novack, D. R., 264, 266
Novack, L. L., 264, 266
NOW. *See* National Organization of Women (NOW)
Nowak, R., 371
Nowell, A., 168, 169, 171, 174

Obear, K., 62
Ochman, J. M., 115
O'Connell, A. N., 12
O'Connor, P., 219, 425
O'Farrell, B., 259
Offermann, L. R., 226
Office of Research and Media Reaction, 236, 263
Offir, C., 95
Oggins, J., 293
O'Hanlan, K. A., 524
O'Hara, M. W., 365, 382, 383
Okamura, A., 489
O'Leary, K. D., 504
Olfson, M., 435
Oliver, M. B., 333, 335, 336
Olsen, N. J., 109
Olson, A. L., 436
Olson, E., 223
O'Neil, J. M., 6, 76, 468, 551, 552
O'Rand, A. M., 520
Orbuch, T. L., 293
Orcutt, J. D., 55
Orr, D. P., 421
Osborne, D., 458
Osipow, S. H., 158
Osland, J. A., 487
O'Toole, C. J., 412
Ovrebo, B., 533
Owen, S. A., 348
Owens, R. E., 62–63, 155
Ozer, E. M., 493

Padavic, I., 246
Paglia, C., 556
Palmore, E. B., 513
Paludi, M. A., 91, 184, 470, 471, 473, 474, 509
Pandey, A., 473
Pappas, G., 402, 403
Parke, R. D., 105
Parker, K., 400
Parmar, P., 401
Parrot, A., 493
Parsons, B., 311

Pasch, L. A., 389
Pasupathi, M., 512, 515
Patrick, G. T. W., 10
Pattatucci, A. M. L., 311
Patterson, C. J., 306, 380, 381
Patton, W., 481
Paul, Saint, 39
Paz, J. J., 518
Pearson, P., 223, 225, 496
Peirce, K., 47
Penelope, J., 41
Penn, M., 315–316
Peplau, L. A., 139, 140, 219, 221, 286, 295, 304, 306, 308, 311, 312, 338, 545, 546, 554
Perkins, H. W., 267
Perrone, J., 258–259
Perry, M., 223, 224
Perry-Jenkins, M., 268
Peters, D., 252
Peters, J., 559
Petersen, A. C., 174, 176
Petersen, K. K., 330
Peterson, C., 489
Peterson, G., 373, 376
Petretic-Jackson, P. A., 477, 484, 485, 504
Petrie, T. A., 445, 447, 448
Pezdek, K., 489, 490
Pfau, M., 423, 424
Pfeffer, J., 241, 243
Pfister, B., 338
Phares, V., 376
Philbin, M., 20
Phillips, D., 270
Phillips, L., 352, 353, 424, 425, 471, 489, 496
Phillips, S., 519, 520
Philpot, C. L., 504
Phinney, J. S., 139, 140
Phoenix, A., 375
Pierce, J. L., 250
Pike, K. M., 444, 445, 446
Pilkington, N. W., 62
Pillard, R. C., 311
Pion, G. M., 257, 545
Pipher, M., 137, 446
Plant, E. A., 166
Pleck, J. H., 269
Pocs, O., 340
Pogrebin, L. C., 291, 294
Polivy, J., 447, 449
Pollack, W. S., 6, 551
Pomerleau, A., 90
Ponton, L. E., 448
Pooler, W. S., 88
Pope, K. S., 452, 453, 489
Pope, R. L., 309
Poppema, S. T., 352

Porter, N., 456
Post, R., 241
Powers, B. A., 134
Powlishta, K. K., 109, 110
Prentice, D. A., 225
Price-Bonham, S., 107
Primomo, J., 404
Promise Keepers, 552–553
Prout, P. I., 490
Pryor, J. B., 474
Purcell, D. W., 251
Pyke, S. W., 10, 11

Quick, H. E., 520
Quina, K., 26, 249, 473, 474
Quinton, W. J., 486

Rabinowitz, V. C., 472, 473
Rabuzzi, K. A., 363, 366
Racioppi, L., 559
Raffaelli, M., 421
Ragan, J. M., 205
Ragins, B. R., 257, 258, 472
Rajagopal, I., 239
Rajbala, 61
Rajecki, D. W., 118, 281
Ralston, P. A., 520, 533
Ramanan, J., 270
Ramsey, N., 560
Rapson, R. L., 281, 282, 284,
    286, 293, 320, 332, 334,
    338
Rawles, R., 185
Rawlings, E., 460
Reagan, R., 500
Rebecca, M., 75
Reddel, M., 87
Redford, R., 517
Reeder, A. L., 144
Reekie, L. J., 452
Reeve, J., 183
Regan, P. C., 280, 281, 335,
    447
Reibstein, L., 475
Reid, P. T., 16, 19, 97
Reilly, M. E., 557
Reinisch, J. M., 338, 340, 341,
    342
Reis, S. M., 146
Remer, P., 460, 478, 484
Renzetti, C. M., 497
Repetti, R. L., 271
Reskin, B., 246
Reynolds, A. L., 309
Reynolds, C., 94
Rhode, D. L., 47, 113, 267,
    470, 472, 483, 485, 486,
    544, 551, 552, 554, 558,
    563
Rice, J. K., 461

Rice, P. L., 380, 392
Rich, C., 518
Rich, J., 506
Richabaugh, C. A., 553
Richardson, D. R., 222
Richardson, H., 350
Richardson, J., 170, 178, 179,
    192
Richins, M. L., 49
Richmond, J. E., 476
Riederle, M. H., 337
Riger, S., 260–262, 483, 484
Riley, S., 316
Rinfret-Raynor, M., 504
Rintala, D. H., 414
Risen, J., 352
Risman, B. J., 267
Rivers, C., 264–265, 269, 271,
    272, 274
Rivers, P. C., 426
Roberto, K. A., 540
Roberts, A., 501, 503, 506
Roberts, J. A., 247
Roberts, T., 125, 186, 343,
    439
Robertson, C., 401, 402
Robinson, D., 19
Robinson, J. G., 256, 259
Robinson, M. D., 66
Robinson, P., 125
Roche, S. E., 505
Rodgers, C., 103
Rodin, J., 404, 449
Rodríguez, C. E., 48, 79
Rogers, R. L., 445
Rogers, S. J., 268, 269, 294,
    298, 299
Rogers, T. B., 30
Roggman, L. A., 270
Romer, N., 102–103
Romero-García, I., 107–108
Romney, D. M., 104, 106, 107
Romo-Carmona, M., 308
Rongé, L. J., 138
Roopnarine, J. L., 94
Root, M. P. P., 25, 549
Rosado-Majors, E., 552
Rose, A. J., 140
Rose, S., 220, 287, 304, 320,
    558
Rosen, B., 253
Rosenbaum, A., 524
Rosenfeld, H. M., 201
Rosenthal, D. A., 140
Rosenthal, R., 17, 69
Rosenwasser, S. M., 118
Ross, C., 409
Ross, E., 378
Ross, S., 252
Rothbart, M. K., 87

Rotheram-Borus, M. J., 139
Rotter, G. S., 207
Rotter, N. G., 207
Roufail, M., 228
Rounds, J., 264
Rountree, C., 536
Rousar, E. E., III, 286
Rousseau, J. J., 38, 39
Rowe, J. W., 523
Rowland, J. H., 406, 408
Royak-Schaler, R., 406, 408,
    431
Royce, J. E., 426
Rozee, P. D., 483
Rubin, D. L., 199
Rubin, J., 412
Rubin, R. M., 521, 533
Rubin, Z., 288
Ruble, D., 83, 85, 86, 97, 99,
    104, 106, 121, 129
Ruble, T., 147
Ruether, R. R., 40
Ruksznis, E., 398
Runions, D., 419
Runté, M., 413, 414
Rushing, B., 271
Russell, D., 491
Russo, N. F., 12, 182, 189,
    353, 354, 355, 434, 435,
    436, 530
Rust, P. C., 309–310
Rutte, C. G., 248
Ryff, C. D., 535
Rynes, S., 253

Saadawi, N., 125
Sadker, D., 28, 112, 113, 121,
    140
Sadker, M., 28, 112, 113, 121,
    140
Saegert, S., 512, 547
St. Jean, Y., 250
St. John-Parsons, D., 263
Saitta, M. B., 205
Salmansohn, K., 256
Salthouse, T. A., 167
Saltzberg, E. A., 449
Saluter, A. F., 298
Sampson, E., 546
Sánchez-Ayéndez, M., 533
Sandler, B. R., 145, 258, 472,
    476
Sandoski, P. J., 505
Sanna, L. J., 67
Saperstein, A., 474
Sasser-Coen, J., 125
Sasson, J. P., 334
Satterfield, A. T., 473
Savin-Williams, R. C., 155,
    303, 320

Scandura, T. A., 472
Scarborough, E., 10, 11, 12, 33
Scarr, S., 21, 269–270
Schafer, E., 384
Schaller, J. G., 262
Scharrer, E., 47, 494
Scher, M., 452, 453, 454, 460, 461, 464
Schiefele, U., 192
Schinke, S. P., 349
Schliecher, T. L., 250
Schmidt, J. P., 306
Schmidt, P. J., 131
Schmitt, D. P., 283
Schneider, M., 303
Schoen, D., 315–316
Schottenfeld, R. S., 425
Schover, L. R., 408
Schreurs, K. M. G., 306
Schroeder, D. A., 212
Schulken, E. D., 366
Schuller, R. A., 498, 500
Schwabe, A., 271
Schwalbe, M., 551
Schwartz, M. D., 483, 494, 496, 498, 500, 501, 506, 509
Schwartz, P., 295, 296, 335, 336
Scott, J. P., 531
Scott Thomas, K., 517
Scratchley, D., 426
Seavey, C. A., 90
Seccombe, K., 315
Sedikides, C., 284, 333
Sedney, M. A., 76
See, K. O., 559
Seegmiller, B., 364, 366, 368
Segraves, R. T., 339
Selinger, M., 559
Selnow, G. W., 199
Senn, C. Y., 447
Senneker, P., 74
Seppa, N., 419, 472
Serbin, L. A., 101
Service, R. F., 347
Shafii, T., 36
Sharp, C., 241
Sharpe, P. A., 513
Sharps, M. J., 176
Shaver, P. R., 293
Shaywitz, B., 178
Shaywitz, S., 169–170
Shelton, B. A., 267
Shelton, R. L., 170
Shenk, D., 532
Shepherd, C., 523, 555
Sherbourne, C. D., 443
Sherman, J. W., 64, 68

Sherman, L., 398
Sherman, S., 514
Sherman-Williams, B., 66
Shields, S. A., 10, 11, 200, 206, 207, 214, 385
Shimp, L., 479
Sholley, B. K., 219
Shoop, R. J., 472
Shumaker, S. A., 398, 424
Siavelis, R. L., 286
Sidorowicz, L. S., 92
Siegal, D. L., 521
Siegel, M., 444, 445, 446, 464
Siegel, R. J., 517
Siegel, S., 39, 40
Signorella, M. L., 101, 103
Signorielli, N., 118, 146
Sikkema, K. J., 419, 421
Silberstein, L. R., 266
Silver, R. C., 532
Silverstein, L. B., 267, 269
Simi, N. L., 461
Simoni, J. M., 252, 303
Simpson, O. J., 502
Sims-Jones, N., 366
Singell, L. D., Jr., 241
Singer, J. E., 372
Singh, A., 68
Singleton, C. H., 167
Skae, E., 46
Skeen, P., 107
Skinner, L., 531
Skinner, P. H., 170
Skrypnek, B. J., 69
Sleeper, L. A., 185
Slepian, B., 352
Slipp, Samuel, 95, 457
Slipp, Sandra, 238, 251, 252
Smetana, J. G., 151
Smith, B. J., 409
Smith, L. B., 353, 354
Smith, M. S., 531
Smith, P. A., 54, 109–111
Smith, P. K., 531
Smith, R., 304
Smith, S. E., 172
Smith, T. R., 398, 424
Smith, V., 260
Smolak, L., 446
Snell, T., 223
Snell, W., 454
Snow, K., 295
Snyder, M., 64, 69
Söchting, I., 217
Society for the Psychological Study of Lesbian, Gay, and Bisexual Issues, 304
Society for the Psychological Study of Men and Masculinity, 551

Sohn, D., 189
Sokol, M. S., 444, 445
Soler, E., 509
Sommers, C. H., 556
Sommers-Flanagan, R., 46
Sonderegger, T. B., 517
Sonnert, G., 252, 253, 256
Sorell, G. T., 217
Sorenson, S. B., 487
Spade, J. Z., 479
Spain, D., 267
Spano, S., 299
Sparks, E. E., 379
Specter, A., 47
Spence, J. T., 53, 183
Spender, D., 199
Sprafkin, C., 101
Sprecher, S., 281, 282, 283, 284, 286, 334
Springen, K., 384
Sprock, J., 436, 437, 451, 465
Stack, C. B., 217
Stagner, R., 11
Stake, J. E., 76, 558
Stanko, E. A., 483
Stanley, J., 172
Stanley Foundation, 560
Stanton, A. L., 382, 388–389, 396–397, 398, 399, 403
Staples, R., 297, 379
Stapley, J. C., 151
Starr, T., 55
Starrels, M. E., 267
Statham, H., 366
Statistics Canada, 246, 255, 267, 268, 287, 314, 416, 482, 483, 498
Steele, C., 180
Steele, J., 146
Steil, J. M., 295
Stein, J., 140
Stein, M., 420
Steinberg, L. S., 173
Steiner, M., 132
Steinhausen, H., 445
Stepnick, A., 55
Stern, M., 92
Stevens, L. E., 58–59
Stewart, A. J., 12, 183
Stewart, S., 316, 317, 320, 383
Stiglmayer, A., 477
Stillion, J. M., 532
Stipek, D. J., 190
Stiver, I. P., 457
Stockton, M., 336
Stokely, K., 419
Stoltz-Loike, M., 268
Stoney, C. M., 404
Stoppard, J. M., 205

Stout, K., 351
Strasburger, V. C., 117
Straus, M. A., 502
Strauss, J., 440
Street, S., 51, 52
Streit, U., 272
Streitmatter, J., 114
Strickland, B. R., 303
Striegel-Moore, R. H., 444, 445, 446
Stroebe, M. S., 532
Stroebe, W., 532
Stroeher, S. K., 101
Stryker, J., 331, 351
Stryker, R., 246
Stuck, M. F., 180
Studd, M. V., 473
Stumpf, H., 167
Suarez-Al-Adam, A., 421
Subotnik, R. F., 158
Subrahmanyam, K., 179
Sugawara, A. I., 140
Suitor, J. J., 268
Sultana, Princess of Saudia Arabia, 334
Sumner, K. E., 247
Sunday, S., 387
Sundstrom, E., 257, 258
Susman, J. L., 382
Sussman, N. M., 201
Swenson, I., 134
Swift, K., 42
Swim, J., 57, 67
Switzer, J. Y., 42
Symonds, P. V., 380
Szinovacz, M., 520, 521, 523

Talaga, J. A., 520
Tanguay, Y., 272
Tasker, F., 381, 382
Tatum, B. D., 6, 139
Taub, N., 368
Tavris, C., 9, 65, 95, 177, 217, 329, 554
Taylor, C. A., 514
Taylor, J., 150, 151, 331
Taylor, L., 482, 483, 498, 505, 521
Taylor, S., 271, 366, 397, 402, 419
Taylor, V., 382
Tenenbaum, H. R., 107
Tesch, B. J., 249
Thacker, R. A., 245
Thom, M., 439
Thomas, B. L., 536, 540
Thomas, C., 448, 472
Thomas, J. L., 352
Thomas, V., 182, 183, 184, 189, 454

Thompson, B., 448
Thompson, H., 11
Thompson, S., 335, 448
Thompson, T., 117, 118
Thorne, B., 109
Thornton, B., 436, 447
Thun, M. J., 425
Tiefer, L., 311, 324, 326, 331, 332, 335, 343, 344, 358
Tilly, C., 240, 274
Tobias, S., 180, 554, 558, 563
Tobin, S., 477, 484, 485, 504
Todd, A. D., 400
Todoroff, M., 182
Tong, R. P., 7, 549, 555
Toth, E., 256
Toubia, N., 401
Townsend, K., 380
Tozzo, S. G., 114
Traeger, C., 151, 152
Tran, T. V., 534
Travis, C. B., 144, 184, 189, 400, 402, 406
Troll, L. E., 531, 532
Trost, J. E., 329
True, R. H., 25, 455
Trussell, J., 355, 356
Türmen, T., 352
Turner, B. F., 516
Turner, C. B., 516
Twenge, J. M., 53, 75, 292

Uba, L., 453, 455, 518, 546
Udis-Kessler, A., 309
Ullian, D. Z., 95
Ullman, S. E., 477, 492
Unger, R. K., 5–6, 12, 27, 28
United Nations, 46, 255, 401, 483, 498
U. S. Bureau of the Census, 223, 236, 238, 244, 245, 255, 257, 259, 265, 292, 314, 317, 385, 519, 532
U. S. Department of Labor, 112, 166, 237, 238, 264

Vajk, F. C., 436
Valcarcel, C. L., 138
Valian, V., 67, 86, 205, 245, 249, 253
Valin, D., 297
Vance, E. B., 328, 329
Vandell, D. L., 270
Vann, E. D., 56
Vasquez, M. J. T., 452
Vasta, R., 176, 366
Vázquez-Nuttall, E., 107–108
Veccia, E. M., 203, 204
Veilleux, F., 530

Veniegas, R. C., 139, 140, 219, 221
Verdi, A. F., 200–201
Vickers, J. F., 536, 540
Vidmar, N., 498, 500
Villani, S. L., 375, 377, 378, 392
Vincent, P. C., 148
Vitulli, W. F., 151
Vogeltanz, N. D., 425, 426, 427
Von Hippel, W., 68
Voyer, D., 174, 176

Wade, C., 325, 326, 329
Waehler, C. A., 316
Wagner, N. N., 328, 329
Wainer, H., 173
Waldram, J. B., 455, 456
Waldron, I., 271, 402
Walker, A., 128, 131, 132, 133, 134, 158, 401, 556
Walker, L. E., 498
Walker, L. J., 217
Walker, W. J., 172
Walkinshaw, S. A., 383
Wallace, H. R., 479, 481, 488, 489, 491, 496, 498, 499, 501
Wallach, H. R., 385
Wallis, L. A., 398
Walsh, F., 324
Walsh, M., 11, 33, 232, 237, 398
Walsh, W. B., 158
Walters, K. L., 252, 303
Walton, M. D., 367
Wang, N., 455
Ward, C., 486, 487, 509
Ward, L. M., 331
Ware, M. C., 180
Wasserman, E., 456
Wasserman, G., 87
Waters, M. C., 139
Watson, M., 350
Watson, P., 214
Way, N., 158
Wear, D., 256
Weaver, G. D., 408
Webster, P. S., 294
Wechsler, H., 426, 427
Weidner, G., 397
Weinberg, M. S., 309, 334
Weiner, L., 473, 474
Weinshel, M., 464
Weisfeld, C. C., 185
Weisner, T. S., 108
Weissman, M. M., 435, 437
Wendell, S., 411, 412, 414, 415

Wenderburg, K., 309
Wesseley, S., 382
West, C., 199
West, M., 506
Wester, S. R., 49
Westkott, M. C., 439
Wexler, L. F., 524
Whalen, M., 505, 506
Wheelan, S. A., 200–201
Wheeler, C., 46
Wheeler, L., 184
Whitbourne, S. K., 137, 294, 513, 514, 524, 540–541
White, J. W., 221, 225, 228, 472, 479, 482, 487, 496, 497, 498
White, L. K., 269
White, S. D., 330
White, W. C., 444
Whitley, B. E., Jr., 64, 74, 189, 350
Whyte, S. R., 412
Widaman, K. F., 140
Wideman, M. V., 372
Wiest, W. M., 329
Wigfield, A., 192
Wilcox, B. I., 332
Wilcox, B. L., 240
Wiley, M. G., 250
Wilfley, D. E., 449
Wilkinson, S., 312
Wille, D. E., 268, 269, 271
Willemsen, E., 109
Willetts-Bloom, M. C., 270
Williams, C., 249
Williams, D. E., 74
Williams, E., 460
Williams, H., 278
Williams, J., 51, 52, 54–55, 99, 100, 103
Williams, L., 134
Williams, S., 418

Williams, T. M., 130
Willingham, W. W., 169, 172, 173, 180
Willis, C. E., 502
Willson, A., 205
Wilsnack, S. C., 425, 426, 427
Wilson, C., 48
Wilson, E., 42
Wincze, J. P., 342
Windle, M., 425, 426
Windridge, K. C., 368
Winerip, M., 173
Wing, R. R., 447, 449
Wingert, P., 287, 295, 346, 347
Wink, P., 257
Winstead, B. A., 283, 294, 320
Winter, D. D., 351, 555
Wise, P. M., 523
Witelson, S. F., 179
Wolf, N., 49
Wolk, S. I., 437
Wolper, A., 559
Women on Words & Images, 115
Women's Campaign Research Fund, 544
Women's Health Initiative, 398, 525
Wood, J. T., 218
Wood, W., 212, 229, 294–295
Woods, N. F., 404, 410, 437
Woollett, A., 363, 364, 365, 368
Woolley, H. T., 10, 11
Word, C. H., 205
Worell, J., 12, 19, 140, 460, 478, 484
World Health Organization, 402

Wortman, C. B., 268, 532
Wosinska, W., 185
Wright, K., 331, 332
Wright, P. H., 219
Wright, R., 351, 544
Wrightsman, L. S., 484, 485, 493, 494
Wu, X., 438
Wuitchik, M., 371
Wyatt, G. E., 331, 337
Wyche, K. F., 461

Yarkin, K. L., 67
Yarrow, L., 371
Ybarra, L., 296
Yeakel, L., 47
Yee, D., 534
Yoder, C. Y., 436, 437, 451, 465
Yoder, J. D., 16, 181, 250, 251, 260, 385, 386, 387, 472, 546
Yonkers, K. A., 396, 426
Young, D., 372, 373
Young, I., 384

Zabin, L. S., 332
Zalk, S. R., 471, 475
Zanna, M. P., 59
Zehr, D., 185
Zeiss, A. M., 339
Zepatos, T., 561
Zerbinos, E., 117, 118
Zhou, M., 473
Zia, H., 256
Ziegler, Z., 142
Zierk, K. L., 354
Zillman, D., 477
Zimmerman, D. H., 199
Ziporyn, T., 430, 540
Zucker, K. J., 108
Zuckerman, M., 184

Subject Index

For names of both people and organizations, see the Name Index.

Ableism, 6, 412
Aboriginals. *See* Canadian Aboriginals
Abortion, 88, 352–355
Abstinence, as birth control, 348, 351
Abuse cycle, 498–499
Abuse of women. *See also* Child sexual abuse;
    Rape; Sexual harassment
  abusers' personal characteristics, 501
  actions to take, 503–505
  attitudes toward, 497, 501–502
  characteristics of abusive relationship,
    499–501
  compared with other forms of violence
    against women, 468, 470
  cross-cultural patterns, 498
  dating violence, 498
  decision to leave relationship, 503, 504–505
  definition of, 496
  depression and, 439, 499
  dynamics of, 498–499
  family variables associated with, 499–501
  frequency of, 498
  media's impact on, 502
  murder of battered women, 223
  myths about, 502–503
  during pregnancy, 498
  psychotherapy for abused women and
    abusers, 504
  shelters for battered women, 505
  society's response to, 505–506
  statistics on, 404, 498
  women's reactions to, 499
Access discrimination, 241–243
Accounting profession, 58
Achievement. *See* Competence; Educational
    achievement; Performance
Achievement motivation
  attributions for own success or failure,
    188–190
  confidence in own achievement and ability,
    185–188, 258
  definition of, 183
  exercises on, 183, 184, 186
  fear of success, 184–185
  tests of, 183–184
Acquaintance rape, 478–482, 493
Acquired immunodeficiency syndrome
    (AIDS), 347, 396, 402, 416–421, 428
Adjustment. *See* Personal adjustment

Adolescence
  alcohol abuse during, 425
  birth control during, 349–350
  body image and, 137–139
  career aspirations during, 146–149, 155
  definition of, 124
  education during, 141–146
  ethnic identity during, 139–140
  exercises about, 143, 147
  family during, 150–151
  friendship during, 152–153
  heterosexual relationships during, 153–155
  illegal drug use during, 428
  interpersonal relationships during, 140,
    150–156
  lesbian relationships during, 155–156
  peers during, 152–153
  pregnancy during, 345–347, 346n, 355–356,
    366
  puberty during, 124–28
  romantic relationships during, 148–149,
    153–156
  self-concept and identity during, 136–141
  self-esteem during, 140
  sexual behavior during, 332–333
  smoking during, 424–25
  verbal ability during, 168
  weight dissatisfaction during, 137
Adoption, 355
Advertising. *See also* Media
  body image and, 137–138, 446–447
  by cigarette companies, 425
  ethnicity and, 137–138
  gender stereotypes in, 45–49
  idealized White women in, 137–138
  in medical journals, 458
  on menstruation, 134
  older women's portrayal in, 340, 514
  sexuality in, 324, 340
  of toys, 118
  women's bodies versus men's bodies in,
    47–48, 50
AFDC, 239, 240–241
Affirmative action, 253, 262
Afghanistan, 544
Africa, 255, 351, 401, 477–478, 498, 518. *See
    also* specific countries
African Americans. *See also* Blacks
  as term, versus Blacks, 23

655

Ageism, 6, 513
Agency, definition of, 52
Aggression. *See also* Violence against women
  in children, 106–107, 110, 222, 270
  cross-cultural patterns in, 221–222, 223
  definition of, 221
  exercise about, 106
  gender comparisons, 106–107, 110,
      221–225
  among Mexican American gang members,
      222
  myth of nonaggressive female, 225
  physical versus verbal, 223
  self-report on, 223–224
  social constructionist explanation of,
      221–222
Aging. *See* Older women
Agoraphobia, 442–443
Aid to Families with Dependent Children
      (AFDC), 239, 240–241
AIDS, 347, 396, 402, 416–421, 428
Alcohol abuse, 303, 425–427, 501, 547
Altruism, 212–214
Ambivalent sexism, 60, 61
Ambivalent Sexism Inventory, 60, 61
Amenorrhea, 445
American Indians. *See* Native Americans
Androcentrism, 28, 65–66
Androgen, in prenatal development, 83
Androgen-insensitivity syndrome, 85
Androgynous people, 73
Androgyny
  blended androgyny, 76
  definition of, 71
  development of concept of, 71–74
  gender-role transcendence versus, 76
  and household task distribution, 267
  moving beyond androgyny, 75–76
  nonverbal behavior and, 207
  problems with, 75, 76
  research on, 74–75
  and self-esteem and adjustment, 74, 140
Anger. *See also* Abuse of women; Violence;
      Violence against women
  decoding from facial expressions, 207, 208
  family discussions about, 105, 151
  self-reports on, 223–224
Anglos. *See* Whites
Angola, 351
Anorexia nervosa, 137, 444–445
Antidepressants, 132, 441, 458
Antioch College, 337–338
Antisocial personality disorder, 434, 501
Anxiety disorders, 442–443
Architects, 257
Argentina, 223, 448, 559

Asian Americans
  abuse of women and, 500, 503–504
  advertising and, 137
  AIDS and, 416
  alcohol abuse by, 426
  androgyny of, 75
  body image and, 137
  breakup of love relationship, 288
  description of ethnic group, 25
  discrimination against, 25
  diversity among, 25, 54
  education of, 25
  ethnic identity during adolescence, 139
  feminism and, 549
  gender stereotypes about, 52, 53
  lesbian women of color, 307
  mammograms and, 406
  marriage of, 291–292
  motherhood of, 380
  older women, 534
  pap smears and, 409
  pregnancy and, 380
  promotions for, 248–249
  psychotherapy for, 455
  rape of, 483
  sexuality and, 308, 332, 406
  smoking and, 424
  statistics on, 24
  stereotypes of, 25
  sweatshops and, 256
Asian Indians, 25, 61, 88, 113, 148, 238–240,
      282, 298, 455, 528, 549
Asians. *See also* specific countries
  abuse of women and, 498, 500
  in Canada, 285–286
  child sexual abuse and, 489
  employment of, as immigrants, 256
  favoritism toward male infants, 88
  lesbian women of color, 308
  love relationships and, 285
  marriage of immigrants, 292
  motherhood and, 379–380
  older women, 518–519
  postpartum depression and, 383
  rape of, 487
  sexual harassment of, 473
  sexuality and, 308
  women's movement and, 559–560
Assertiveness, 12, 225–226, 337, 338
Athletics, 138–139
Attractiveness
  adolescence and, 137–139
  childhood and, 109–110, 137
  depression and emphasis on physical
      appearance, 439
  disabilities and, 414

in ideal dating and sexual partner, 280–281, 343
of infants, 214
lesbian relationships and, 304
in marriage partner, 281, 283–284
slimness and, 365, 439, 446–448
Attributions
definition of, 67, 188–189
gender stereotypes and, 67, 189
for own success or failure, 188–190
for success of ethnic groups, 67
for success of females versus males, 189–190
Atypical prenatal development, 85–86
Australia, 46, 246, 558
Autocratic leadership, 227

Babies. *See* Infancy
Bangladesh, 477
Barbie Doll, 446
Bates College, 173
Battering. *See* Abuse of women
Beauty. *See* Attractiveness
Beijing Platform for Action, 560
Beijing World Conference on Women, 559–560
Bem Sex-Role Inventory (BSRI), 72–75, 267
Benevolent sexism, 61
Bereavement, 532–533
Biases. *See also* Ableism; Ageism; Gender stereotypes; Homophobia; Racism; Sexism
in achievement motivation research, 182
in cognitive ability research, 163–166
heterosexist bias, 6, 62–64, 251–252, 301, 302
of medical profession, 396–400
in psychotherapy, 437, 451–453
in research, 14–22, 163, 182, 560
types of, 6
Binge drinking, 426
Binge eating, 445–446
Biological explanations
of depression, 436, 436n
of gender differences in cognitive abilities, 177–178
of sexual orientation, 310–311
Bipolar (scales), 71–72
Birth. *See* Childbirth
Birth control, 345–352
Birth control pills, 348
Bisexual women, 62, 251–252, 308–310
Black matriarchy, 297
Blackouts, 425
Blacks. *See also* Discrimination; Ethnicity; Racism
abuse of women and, 500
achievement motivation of, 183

advertising and, 137–138
AIDS and, 416
alcohol abuse by, 426
androgyny of, 75
attributions of success and, 67
birth control and, 349
Black matriarchy, 297
body image and, 137–138, 448
breast surgery and, 408
breastfeeding and, 384
career aspirations and romance during college, 148–149
childhood experiences of Black female, 23
children's books for, 115
children's gender stereotypes, 102–103
disabilities and, 412–413
discrimination against, 250–251, 260
divorce and, 298
empty-nest syndrome and, 530
ethnic identity of, 139–140
families of, 150, 297–298, 379
fear of success and, 184–185
feminism and, 548–549
gender stereotypes about, 52, 53, 54
gender typing and, 107
higher education and, 144, 145
illegal drugs and, 428
infertility and, 389
lesbian women of color, 308
marriage of, 292, 293, 297–298, 318
media's representation of, 48
menarche and, 124–125
menopause and, 528
moral reasoning by, 217–218
motherhood and, 378–379
older women, 512, 521, 533
picture book illustrators, 115
poverty of, 297, 521, 533
pregnancy and, 368
promotions for, 249
psychotherapy for, 454
puberty and, 124–125
retirement and, 520
salary discrimination and, 244, 245
self-esteem of, 271
sex education and, 331
sexuality and, 332
single women, 317–318
smoking and, 424, 425
statistics on, 23, 24
teachers' behaviors toward Black girls, 113
as term, versus African Americans, 23
welfare and, 240
women's friendships with members of other ethnic groups, 220

Blacks *(Continued)*
  work outside of home, 237–238, 250–251,
    260, 271, 368
"Blame-the-person" rationale, 12, 50, 184,
    190, 468, 470, 487, 491, 503
Blended androgyny, 76
Blue-collar jobs, 259–260
Body. *See also* Attractiveness; Body image;
    Slimness
  depression and emphasis on physical
    appearance, 439
  gender stereotypes about, 47–48
  Latinas' attitude toward, 151
  media portrayal of, 47–48, 50
Body image, 137–139, 447–448
Body posture, 202–203
Bolivia, 55, 55n, 559
Book of Poetry, 379–380
Books for children, 115–116
Borders crossers, 142
Box-score approach, 165
Brain
  cognitive abilities and, 178–179
  gender comparisons of, 10
  hypothalamus, 125–128
  lateralization of, 178–179
  menstruation and, 125–128
Brazil, 351
Breakup of love relationships, 288–289,
    306–307
Breast cancer, 405–408
Breast self-examination, 406, 407
Breastfeeding, 384–385
BSRI. *See* Bem Sex-Role Inventory (BSRI)
Bulimia nervosa, 445–446

Cambodia, 54, 380
Canada. *See also* Canadian Aboriginals;
    Canadian research
  comparable-worth legislation in, 246
  higher education in, 144
  immigrants in, 24, 238–241, 298, 528, 549
  older women in, 513, 519, 521
  population statistics for, 24, 404n
  profeminists in, 551–552
  psychology of women course of study, 11
  sexist ad in *Toronto Life,* 49
  shelters for battered women in, 505
  Sikh women in, 528
  women heads of state in, 559
  women's right to vote in, 558
  women's studies courses in, 557
Canadian Aboriginals, 25, 379, 455–456, 547
Canadian research
  abuse of women, 498
  AIDS, 416

attitudes toward "housewives" and
    "feminists," 59
  birth control, 350, 351
  body image, 448
  breast cancer, 406
  children's gender stereotypes, 103
  death from childbirth, 401
  disabilities, 411, 412
  divorce, 298, 300
  divorced women's income, 300
  gender stereotyping, 55
  heart disease, 404, 404n
  household task division, 267
  lesbians, 307
  life expectancy, 402
  living together, 287
  love relationships, 281, 285–286
  marriage, 291, 298
  menopause, 528
  motherhood of Native Canadians, 379
  number of children born per mother, 369
  poverty, 356
  preferences for males versus females as
    firstborn child, 88
  pregnancy, 346n, 347, 366
  rape, 482, 483
  salary discrimination, 244
  single mothers, 356
  single women, 314
  smoking, 366, 424
  teen pregnancies, 346n
  unintended pregnancies, 347
  women as invisible in newspapers, 46
  women clergy, 40
  women of color, 453
  women's caretaking role, 530
  women's employment, 236, 238–240,
    254–255, 256, 260, 268
  women's health, 399
Cancer
  breast cancer, 405–408
  cervical cancer, 408, 418, 423
  endometrial cancer, 408
  lung cancer, 406, 423, 424
  ovarian cancer, 410
  reproductive system cancer, 408–410
  uterine cancer, 409
Cardiovascular disease, 400, 402, 404–405,
    423, 424, 449
Care perspective, 216–218
Career aspirations, 146–149, 155. *See also*
    Work
Caribbean, 255
Caring. *See* Helping and caring
Castration complex, 94
Caught generation, 530–531

Cervical cancer, 408, 418, 423
Cesarean section, 371, 373, 399
Chicanas/os, 24, 54, 549–550. *See also*
        Latinas/os; Mexican Americans
Child care. *See* Day care
"Child-free" women, 385–388
Child sexual abuse, 312, 488–490
Childbirth. *See also* Infancy; Pregnancy
    biology of, 370–371
    cesarean section, 371, 373, 399
    emotional reactions to, 371–372
    exercise about, 374
    expectations about, 371
    family-centered approach to, 373
    and postpartum disturbances, 382–383
    prepared childbirth, 372–373
Childhood. *See also* Family; Infancy
    adjustment of children of lesbians, 380–382
    age as factor in gender stereotyping during,
        103
    aggression during, 106–107, 110, 222, 270
    attractiveness and, 109–110, 137
    of Black female, 23
    children born to women denied abortions,
        355
    day care, 269–270
    education during, 111–115
    emotions during, 105
    exercises about, 100, 106
    family's influence on gender typing during,
        103, 104–108
    gender constancy and, 98–99
    gender stereotypes about occupations and
        activities during, 101, 102, 114
    gender stereotypes about personality
        during, 99–101
    gender typing during, 104–119
    independence in, 107, 270
    knowledge about gender during, 98–103
    mothers' employment and, 269–270
    peers during, 108–111
    play during, 104–105
    psychoanalytic theory of, 94–95, 311–312,
        457
    school's influence gender typing during,
        111–115
    sexual abuse during, 312, 488–490
    television during, 116–119
Children's books, 115–116
Chilly classroom climate, 145
Chilly workplace climate, 258–259, 470–471
China, 88, 351, 379–380, 473, 519, 559–560
Chinese Americans, 25, 54, 380, 409. *See also*
        Asian Americans
Chlamydia, 421, 422
Cholesterol, 404

Christianity. *See* Religion
Cigarette smoking. *See* Smoking
Circumcision, 401
Civil Rights Act of 1964, 368
Class. *See* Social class
Classism, definition of, 6
Clitoral hood, 325
Clitoral orgasm, 327
Clitoris, 325, 343
Clothing, and body movements, 203
Cognitive abilities
    biological explanations for gender
        differences in, 177–179
    complex cognitive tasks, 167–168
    day care and, 269–270
    exercises on, 167, 175
    gender comparisons, 167–183
    general intelligence, 167
    genetics and, 178
    hormones and, 178
    mathematics ability, 16–17, 18, 142–144,
        171–174, 179–181
    memory, 167
    menstrual cycle and, 133
    with no gender differences, 167–168
    research biases on, 163–166
    social explanations for gender differences
        in, 179–181
    spatial ability, 166–167
    verbal ability, 168–170
Cognitive-behavioral approach, to
        psychotherapy, 344–345, 458
Cognitive developmental theory, 95–96
Cognitive restructuring, 344
Cohabitation, 287–288
Colleges. *See* Higher education
Coming into Our Fullness (Rountree), 536
Commercials. *See* Advertising
Common-law relationship, 287–288
Communication of research findings, 15,
        19–20
Communication patterns. *See also* Language;
        Verbal communication
    body posture, 202–203
    content of language, 199–201
    decoding ability, 206–207, 208, 209–210
    exercises about, 202, 206
    explanations for gender differences in,
        209–211
    facial expression, 205–206
    gaze, 204–205
    gender comparisons, 198–208
    language style, 199
    in love relationships, 294
    nonverbal communication, 198, 201–208
    personal space, 201–202, 209

Communication patterns *(Continued)*
  in persuasion, 228
  power and, 209
  social learning explanations for gender
    differences in, 209–210
  social status and, 209
  talkativeness, 199
  touch, 203–204
  verbal communication, 198–201
Communion, 52
Companionate love, 285–286
Comparable worth, 246
Comparison-groups research approach, 546–547
Competence. *See also* Performance
  attitudes toward women's competence,
    57–58
  and self-esteem during adolescence, 140
Conception, 363
Condoms, 348, 350, 420, 421
Confidence. *See* Self-confidence
Confounding variable, 16–17, 118
Congenital adrenal hyperplasia, 85
Contraception. *See* Birth control
Conversation. *See* Verbal communication
Coretta Scott King book awards, 115
Coronary heart disease, 400, 402, 404–405,
    423, 424, 449
Corpus luteum, 128
Costa Rica, 559
Couples therapy, for battered women and
    batterers, 504
Creativity, 167–168
Crime rates, 222–223
Critical thinking, 21–22
Croatia, 559
Cross-cultural patterns. *See also* specific
    countries
  abuse of women, 498
  aggression, 221–222, 223
  birth control, 351–352
  children's gender stereotypes, 103
  decoding ability, 207
  education, 113–114
  family relationships, 151
  gender stereotypes, 54–55
  marriage, 282–283
  menstruation, 134
  occupational choices of women, 148
  older women, 518–519
  postpartum blues and postpartum
    depression, 382, 383
  rape, 477–478, 483, 487
  salary discrimination, 245–246
  sexism, 61
  sexual harassment, 473
  sexuality, 308, 334

Cuba, 351
Cuban Americans. *See* Latinas/os
Cultural differences. *See* Cross-cultural
    patterns; Ethnicity; Social class
Cultural feminism, 7, 216
Czechoslovakia, 355, 477

Data interpretation, 15, 18–19
Dating. *See also* Love relationships; Sexuality
  abuse in, 498
  acquaintance rape and, 478–482, 493
  characteristics of love relationship, 284–287
  double standard and, 333–335
  gender comparisons, 283–284
  ideal dating partner, 279, 280–84
  personal ads and, 281
  power in love relationship, 286–287
  satisfaction with love relationship, 286
  self-disclosure in, 286
Day care, 269–270
Decoding ability, 206–207, 208, 209–210
Democratic leadership, 227
Denial of personal disadvantage, 247–248,
    268
Dentists, 257
Depo-Provera, 348
Depression
  of abused women, 439, 499
  biological factors in, 436, 436n
  characteristics of, 434, 435–436
  discrimination and, 437
  and emphasis on physical appearance, 439
  empty-nest syndrome and, 530
  explanations for prevalence of, among
    women, 436–441
  gender comparisons on, 436–441
  housework and, 437–439
  interpersonal relationships and, 439
  major depression, 434, 435–436
  postpartum depression, 382–383
  poverty and, 437
  responses to, 438, 440–441
  sexual harassment and, 473
  therapists' diagnostic biases for, 437
  violence and, 439, 499
Developing countries. *See also* specific
    countries
  cervical cancer in, 409
  death from childbirth in, 401
  education in, 113–114
  family planning in, 351–352
  female genital mutilation in, 401–402, 559
  health issues in, 400–402
  pregnancy and childbirth in, 371, 401
  women's movement in, 559–560
  women's occupational choices in, 148, 255

Diagnostic and Statistical Manual of Mental Disorders (American Psychiatric Association), 304, 383

Diaphragm, 348

Dieting, 449, 450

Differences perspective, 9, 197–198, 216. *See also* Gender comparisons

Differential treatment. *See* Ableism; Ageism; Discrimination; Homophobia; Racism; Sexism; Theme 2 (differential treatment)

Disabilities
  ableism and, 6, 412
  definition of, 411
  ethnicity and, 412–413
  personal relationships and, 414–415
  sexuality and, 415
  statistics on, 411
  work patterns and, 412–414

Discrimination. *See also* Ableism; Ageism; Gender stereotypes; Homophobia; Racism; Sexism; Sexual harassment; Theme 2 (differential treatment)
  access discrimination, 241–243
  against Asian Americans, 25
  against Blacks, 250–251, 260
  definition of, 37
  depression and, 437
  in evaluation in the workplace, 250
  guidelines for correction of, 252–253
  in hiring patterns, 241–243
  in interpersonal interactions, 55–57
  against lesbians and gay males, 62–64, 251–252
  against overweight people, 447, 449
  against pregnant workers, 368
  in promotions, 248–250
  salary discrimination, 236, 244–248
  in schools, 111–114, 142–144, 145
  in students' ratings of professors, 250
  treatment discrimination, 244–254
  in the workplace, 55–56, 58, 244–253

Diseases. *See* Physical health; and specific diseases

Disorders of sexual desire, 341–342

Displaced homemakers, 263–264

Distracting style, as response to depression, 440

Diversity among women. *See* Theme 4 (variability)

Divorce, 287–288, 298–300

Doctors. *See* Medical profession

Doing school, 142

Domestic work, 255

Dominican Republic, 448

Double standard of aging, 515–518

Double standard (of sexuality), 333–334, 343

Drug abuse. *See* Substance abuse

Drug therapies, 451, 458, 460

Dual-career marriages, 265–268

Dyads, 203–204

Dysmenorrhea, 128–129

Dyspareunia, 342–343

Eating disorders
  anorexia nervosa, 137, 444–445
  bulimia nervosa, 445–446
  and emphasis on slimness, 137, 445–448

Ecofeminists, 555

Economic issues. *See* Poverty; Salary

Educated in Romance: Women, Achievement, and College Culture (Holland and Eisenhart), 148–149

Education. *See also* Higher education
  during adolescence, 141–146
  of Asian Americans, 25
  borders crossers, 142
  changes in, 114–115, 143–144
  during childhood, 111–115
  chilly classroom climate, 145
  cross-cultural patterns in, 113–114
  doing school, 142
  exercise about, 143
  gender bias in schools, 111–114, 142–144, 145, 180
  gender stereotypes of girls in all-female versus coeducational schools, 103
  gender typing and, 111–115
  grades in mathematics courses, 172
  of immigrants, 238–240
  math and science education, 142–144, 172
  null academic environment, 145
  in romance, 148–149, 155
  school structure, 111–112
  sex education, 330–332, 349, 351
  sexual harassment in higher education, 471, 472, 473–474
  "silenced female" problem in, 112–113, 114
  welfare recipients and, 240–241

Educational achievement
  birth control and, 349, 351
  divorce and, 298
  happy marriages and, 294
  prediction of, 144
  salary based on, 244

Egalitarian love relationship, 286–287, 306

Egalitarian marriage, 296, 335

Egg, 83, 126, 128, 363

Ego development, 299–300

Egypt, 125

Ejaculate, 329

El Salvador, 454–455, 559

Elderly. *See* Older women

Embryo, 363
Emma Willard School, 152–153
Emotional disorders. *See* Psychological
    disorders
Emotions
    after abortion, 354
    during adolescence, 150–151
    at breakup of love relationship, 288
    breast surgery, 408
    during childbirth, 371–372
    during childhood, 105
    conversations about, 105
    decoding ability for, 207, 208, 209–210
    divorce and, 299–300
    expression of, and marital satisfaction, 294
    gender comparisons on, 197
    gender stereotypes of, 66
    about menarche, 125
    menopausal joy, 528
    menstrual joy, 131–132, 528
    parents' expression of, with children, 214
    PMS moods swings, 130–131
    during pregnancy, 364–366
    after rape, 484–486
    after sexual harassment, 473, 474
Empathy, 16, 214–215
Employed women, definition of, 236. *See also*
    Work
Empty-nest syndrome, 529–530
Endometrial cancer, 408
Endometrium, 126, 127, 128
Engineering, 166–167, 244, 257, 259, 260
England. *See* Great Britain
Essentialism, 9
Estrogen
    in childbirth, 383
    hormone replacement therapy for
        postmenopausal women, 405, 410,
        524–525
    in menstrual cycle, 125–128
    in prenatal development, 83
Estrogen replacement therapy, 524–525
Ethiopia, 351
Ethnicity. *See also* Social class; and specific
    ethnic groups
    abuse of women and, 500–501, 503–504
    AIDS and, 416–417
    alcohol abuse and, 426
    androgyny of women of color, 75
    athletics and, 138–139
    attributions of success and, 67
    birth control and, 349
    bisexual women and, 309
    Black matriarchy, 297
    body image and, 448
    breakup of love relationship, 288

breastfeeding and, 384
career aspirations and romance during
    college, 148–149
child care responsibilities of fathers versus
    mothers, 269
children's books for Blacks, 115
children's gender stereotypes, 102–103
disabilities and, 412–413
diversity within racial groups, 23–25, 54
divorce and, 298
empty-nest syndrome, 530
ethnic identity during adolescence,
    139–140
fear of success and, 184–185
feminism and, 548–550
gender stereotypes and, 48, 52–54, 56–57
gender typing and, 107–108
higher education and, 145–146
and idealized white women in advertising,
    137–138
leadership and, 227
lesbian women of color, 307–308
life expectancy and, 402
love relationships and, 286–287
mammograms and, 406
marriage and, 291–292, 293, 296–298, 318
media's representation of women of color,
    48
menopause and, 528
motherhood and, 378–380
older women, 512, 533–534
pap smears and, 409
poverty and, 297, 455–456, 521, 533
pregnancy and, 368
psychotherapy with women of color,
    453–456
puberty and, 124–125
retirement and, 520
self-esteem and, 271
sex education and, 331
sexuality and, 308, 332, 406
single women and, 317–318
slimness and, 448
smoking and, 424
statistics on, 24
teachers' behavior toward Black girls, 113
and Whites as norm, 16, 22, 26, 139, 546
women's friendships with members of
    other ethnic groups, 220
and work outside of home, 236–238,
    250–251, 255, 256, 260, 271, 368
Europe. *See* specific countries
European Americans. *See* Whites
Evolutionary psychology, 283–284
Excitement phase, of sexual response cycle,
    326

Exercise, 132, 410, 449
Expansiveness, 207–208
Experimenter expectancy, 17–18
Experiments. *See* Research

Faces
  decoding emotions from facial expressions,
    207, 208
  gender comparisons on facial expression,
    205–206
  men's versus women's faces in magazines
    and newspapers, 48, 50
  smiling, 87, 205–206, 210
Fallopian tubes, 126, 127
False memory perspective, 489–490
Family. *See also* Fathers; Marriage; Mothers;
    Parents
  abuse within, 488–491, 496–507
  of adolescents, 150–151
  Black families, 150, 297–298, 379
  child sexual abuse in, 312, 488–490
  children's gender stereotypes, 103
  cross-cultural patterns in, 151
  gender issues in, 151
  gender typing in, 104–108
  Hispanic families, 151
  household tasks shared in, 265, 266–268
  impact of mothers' employment on
    children, 269–270
  marital rape in, 490–491
  number of children in, 369
  older women's family relationships,
    529–534
  physical and emotional abuse within,
    496–507
Family-centered approach to childbirth, 373
Family planning. *See* Birth control
Family violence. *See* Abuse of women
Fathers. *See also* Family; Parents
  adolescents' feelings about, 151
  breastfeeding decision and, 384
  child care responsibilities of, 268–269, 376
  emotional expressiveness of, with children,
    214
  and gender-appropriate play of children,
    107
  moral reasoning by, 217
  sex education and, 330–331
Fears. *See also* Phobias
  accuracy in decoding, 207, 208
  family discussions of, 105, 151
  of rape, 483
  of success, 12, 184–185
Feedback, and self-confidence, 185–187
Feelings. *See* Emotions
Female genital mutilation, 401–402, 559

Female orgasmic disorder, 342
Feminine people, 73
Feminism
  ambivalence about term, 7, 558
  attitudes toward feminists, 59
  attitudes toward men and, 554
  backlash against, 556, 560
  becoming an activist, 560–561
  body image and feminist attitudes, 448
  cultural feminism, 7, 216
  definition of, 6–7
  ecofeminists, 555
  exercise about, 8
  first wave of, 558
  liberal feminism, 7, 216
  male feminists, 6–7, 551–552
  media portrayal of, 554, 556
  and nontraditional career choices, 148
  in North America, 558
  number of women identifying with, 544
  psychotherapy and, 460–462
  radical feminism, 7
  response to evolutionary psychology, 284
  rigid interpretation of, 554–555
  and women of color, 548–550
  women's movement and, 558–560
  women's studies courses and, 557–558
  worldwide women's movement, 558–560
Feminism & Psychology, 12
Feminist Dollar (Katz & Katz), 561
Feminist therapy, 460–462
Feminization of psychology, 11, 12, 256–257,
    545–546
Fertilization, 363
Fetal alcohol syndrome, 426
Filipinos, 25
Finland, 55
Fire in the Belly (Keen), 552
Follicle-stimulating hormone, 126, 127, 128
France, 103, 246, 351
Frequency distribution, 163–164
Freudian theory, 94–95, 311–312, 457
Friendship-based love, 285–286, 304
Friendships. *See also* Interpersonal
    relationships; Peers
  of adolescents, 152–153
  cross-race friendships, 220
  disabilities and, 414–415
  exercise about, 218
  gender comparisons in, 218–219
  love relationships based on, 285–286, 304
  of married women, 318
  overinvolvement in, and depression, 439
  self-disclosure in, 219, 286
  of single women, 315, 317–318
  between women, 219–220

Gangs, 222
Garment work, 255–256
Gay females. *See* Lesbians
Gay males, 62–63, 105, 251–252, 301, 303, 310–311
Gaze, 204–205
Gender. *See also* headings beginning with Themes; and other headings beginning with Gender
  definition of, 5
  distinction between sex and, 5–6
Gender as a stimulus variable, 28, 202
Gender as a subject variable, 27–28, 202
Gender comparisons. *See also* Theme 1 (gender similarities)
  aggression, 106–107, 110, 221–225
  alcohol abuse, 426–427
  altruism, 212–214
  assertiveness, 225–226
  attribution patterns, 189–190
  bereavement, 532
  brain, 10
  career aspirations during adolescence, 146
  caretaking role, 530–531
  cautions about research on, 163–165
  cognitive abilities, 166–181
  communication patterns, 198–211
  criminal behavior, 223
  depression, 436–441
  differences perspective on, 9, 216
  double standard of sexuality, 333–335
  drug therapy, 458
  early studies on, 10–11
  emotions, 197
  ethnic identity, 139
  friendships, 218–219
  health care and health status, 396–400, 403–404
  helping and caring, 212–220
  ideal dating partner, 280–284
  and "illusion of gender differences" during infancy, 86–87
  influenceability, 229
  intelligence, 11, 167
  leadership, 226–227
  life expectancy, 402–403
  love relationships, 284–287
  marital satisfaction, 294–295
  mate selection, 283–284
  mathematics ability, 16–17, 18, 142–144, 171–174
  media reports on, 20, 162, 178–179
  moral reasoning, 215–218
  nonverbal communication, 201–208
  persuasion, 227–229
  power, 286–287

  psychological disorders, 434, 442, 458
  reading disabilities, 169–170
  research on, 163–166
  science abilities, 142–144
  self-confidence, 65–66, 185–188, 258
  self-disclosure, 219, 286
  self-esteem during adolescence, 140
  sexual responses, 327, 329
  sexual role playing and sexual activities, 335–336
  similarities perspective on, 8–9, 216
  social behavior, 87
  social constructionist explanation of gender differences, 197–198
  spatial ability, 166–167, 174–177
  summarizing multiple studies, 165–166
  verbal ability, 168–170
  verbal communication, 198–201
  versus gender differences as term, 19
  widowhood, 532
Gender constancy, 98–99
Gender differences. *See also* Gender comparisons
  definition of differences perspective, 9
  emphasis of, by cultural feminists, 7, 216
  factors influencing size of, 197–198
  social constructionist explanation of, 197–198
  as term, 19
Gender identity, 95–96
Gender polarization, 65, 86
Gender prejudice, 109, 110
Gender-role transcendence, 76
Gender schema theory, 95–97, 101, 114
Gender segregation
  peers and, 109, 153
  within and among occupations, 246
Gender similarities, 8–9, 27–28, 167–168, 216. *See also* Theme 1 (gender similarities)
Gender stereotypes
  age stereotypes and, 514–519
  alternatives to, 70–77
  ambivalent sexism, 60, 61
  attributions and, 67
  biased judgments about women and men, 66–67
  of children, 99–103
  in children's books, 115–116
  of competence of women, 57–58
  complexity of contemporary sexism, 55–61
  content of, 51–55
  cross-cultural sexism, 61
  definition of, 36
  discrimination in interpersonal interactions, 55–57

effects of, 49–50
ethnicity and, 48, 52–54
exaggerating contrast between women and men, 65
exercises about, 43, 48, 51, 60, 63, 72, 100
gender as influence on, 53–54
gender polarization, 65
heterosexism, 6, 62–64, 251–252, 301, 302
in hiring, 241–243
historical perspectives on, 38–40
housework and, 47
invisibility of women in historical accounts, 38
in language, 40–45
in the media, 45–50, 115–119
in medicine, 396–400
memory for personal characteristics and, 68
"niceness" of women and girls, 58–59, 61, 113
normative male, 28, 65–66, 188
older women, 514–519
and people's responses to infant girls and boys, 66, 87–93
about personality, 36–37, 47, 99–101
in philosophy, 38–39
pleasantness of women and girls, 58–59, 61, 113
in religion and mythology, 39–40, 376
representation of women and men, 37–50
self-fulfilling prophecies and, 68–69
sexual problems and, 343–344
social cognitive approach to, 64–68
and violence against women, 470
on women's and men's bodies, 47–48
Gender typing
  aggression and, 106–107
  books and, 115–116
  cognitive developmental theory of, 95–96
  cross-cultural patterns in, 113–114
  definition of, 70–71, 82
  factors shaping, 107–108
  family's influence on, 104–108
  gender schema theory of, 95–97
  independence and, 107
  media and, 115–119
  peers and, 108–111
  and people's responses to infant girls and boys, 66, 87–93
  psychoanalytic theory of, 94–95
  schools and, 111–115
  sexual problems and, 343–344
  social learning theory of, 96–97
  teachers and, 112–115, 180
  television and, 116–119
  theoretical explanations of, 94–97

Genetic factors
  for depression, 436
  for sexual orientation, 311
  for spatial ability, 178
Genital herpes, 421, 422
Genital mutilation. *See* Female genital mutilation
Genital warts, 421, 422
Genitals
  female sexual anatomy, 324–26
  prenatal development of, 83–85
Germany, 55, 245–246
Glass ceiling, 249
Glass escalator, 249
Gonads, 83
Gonorrhea, 421, 422
Grandmothers, 531–534
Great Britain, 46, 245–246, 285, 487
Grieving process, 532–533
Guatemala, 559

Haiti, 559
Handicaps. *See also* Disabilities
  disabilities preferred as term, 411
Happiness
  ability to decode from facial expressions, 207, 208
  of employed women, 271
  of lesbian couples, 306
  in marriage, 293–295
  menopausal joy, 528
  menstrual joy, 131–32, 528
  of older women, 534–536
  of single women, 315–316
Harassment. *See* Sexual harassment
Harvard University, 248, 548–549
Health. *See* Medical profession; Personal adjustment; Physical health; Psychological disorders
Health Care for Women International, 397
Health insurance, 350, 399–400
Health psychology, 397. *See also* Physical health
Heart disease, 400, 402, 404–405, 423, 424, 449
Helping and caring
  altruism, 212–214
  empathy, 16, 214–215
  exercises about, 213, 218
  friendship, 218–220
  gender comparisons, 212–220
  moral judgments concerning other people, 215–218
  nurturance, 214
  for pregnant women, 366–367
Herpes, genital, 421, 422

Heterosexism, 6, 62–64, 251–252, 301, 302
Heterosexuality. *See* Love relationships;
    Sexuality
Higher education. *See also* specific
    universities
    ethnicity and, 144–146
    PhD degrees received by women, 544
    professors in, 250, 258
    reasons for seeking college degree, 143
    sexual harassment in, 471, 472, 473–474
    for welfare recipients, 240–241
Hiring patterns, 241–243. *See also* Work
Hispanics. *See also* Latinas/os
    as term, versus Latinas/os, 23–24
HIV, 418
Hmong people, 25, 380, 383, 500
Homemakers, 59, 262–264, 377, 437–439
Homophobia, 62, 304
Homosexuality. *See also* Gay males; Lesbians
    religion and, 552
    versus lesbian as term, 301
Hopi Indians, 184–185
Hormone replacement therapy, 405, 410,
    524–525
Hormones
    brain and, 125–128
    in childbirth, 383
    menopause and, 523
    menstruation and, 125–128
    postpartum disorders and, 383
    during pregnancy, 363
    premenstrual syndrome (PMS) and, 130,
        131
    in prenatal development, 83
    spatial abilities and, 178
Hostile sexism, 61
Hot flashes, 523–524
Housework. *See also* Homemakers
    attitudes toward housewives, 59, 377
    children's chores, 105
    depression and, 437–439
    division of responsibility for, 265
    gender stereotypes on, 47
    homemakers' view of, 263
    media portrayal of, 47
    variety of tasks, 263
*How to Make the World a Better Place for
    Women in Five Minutes a Day* (Jackson),
    561
HUES, 560
Human immunodeficiency virus (HIV), 418
Human Sexual Response (Masters and
    Johnson), 326
Hypoactive sexual desire disorder, 341–342
Hypothalamus, 125–128
Hypothesis formulation, 14–15
Hysterectomy, 409

Iceland, 246, 559
Identity
    of bisexual women, 308–309
    definition of, 137
    ethnic identity, 139–140
    lesbian identity, 303–304
Illnesses. *See* Physical health; and specific
    illnesses
Immigrants. *See also* specific ethnic groups
    abuse of women and, 500
    body image and, 448
    in Canada, 24, 238–241, 298, 528, 549
    diversity among, 238
    domestic work by, 255
    education of, 238–240
    ideal dating partner and, 282
    marriage of, 291–292, 298
    motherhood and, 380
    older women refugees, 534
    postpartum depression and, 383
    pregnancy of, 380
    psychotherapy for refugees, 454–455
    in sweatshops, 256
    work outside of home, 238–240, 255, 256
Implants, as birth control method, 348
In a Different Voice (Gilligan), 216
Incest, 489
Income. *See* Poverty; Salary
Independence
    in children, 107, 270
    in lesbian couples, 306
India, 61, 88, 113, 148, 282, 473, 559. *See also*
    Asian Indians
Indians. *See* Asian Indians; Native Americans
Individual differences. *See* Theme 4
    (variability)
Indonesia, 559
Infancy. *See also* Childbirth
    attractiveness of infants, 214
    breastfeeding of infants, 384–385
    day care during, 270
    definition of, 82
    exercise about, 88
    gender comparisons during, 86–87
    gender knowledge of infants, 98
    gender stereotypes of infants' behavior, 66
    mothers and infants, 214, 376–378
    parents' behavior toward infants, 89–90,
        104, 214
    people's responses to infant girls and boys,
        87–93
    physical development during, 86–87
    preferences for males versus females as
        firstborn child, 88
    social behavior during, 87
    strangers' responses to infants, 90–93
    temperament during, 86–87

Infanticide, 88
Infertility, 388–390
Influenceability, 229
Injections, as birth control method, 348
Instrumentality, 140, 142
Intelligence, 11, 167
Interaction patterns. *See* Interpersonal
  relationships
Intercourse. *See* Sexuality
International patterns. *See* Cross-cultural
  patterns; and specific countries
Interpersonal relationships. *See also*
  Friendships; Love relationships; Marriage
  during adolescence, 140, 150–156
  depression and, 439
  disabilities and, 414–415
  romantic relationships during adolescence,
    148–149, 153–156
  self-in-relation theory, 215–216
  sexism in interpersonal interactions, 55–57
Intersexuals, 86
Intimacy. *See* Friendships; Love relationships;
  Marriage; Sexuality
Intrauterine device (IUD), 348, 400
Invisibility. *See* Theme 3 (invisibility)
IQ. *See* Intelligence
Iran, 351, 544
Iraq, 351
Iron John (Bly), 552
Israel, 473
Italy, 351
IUD. *See* Intrauterine device

Japan, 103
Japanese Americans, 25
Jobs. *See* Work
Johns Hopkins, 248
Journal of Women's Health, 397
Judaism. *See* Religion
Jump, 134–135, 138
Justice perspective, 216–218

Kenya, 401, 477–478
Klamath, 54
Korea, 88, 483
Korean Americans, 291–292. *See also* Asian
  Americans
Kuwait, 505, 559

Labia majora, 325, 401
Labia minora, 325, 401
Labor and delivery. *See* Childbirth
Ladies' Home Journal, 514
Language. *See also* Communication patterns;
  Verbal communication
  content of, in verbal communication,
    199–201

  exercises about, 43
  masculine generic, 41–45
  nonsexist language, 45
  sexist language, 40–45
Laos, 383, 500, 534
Laotians, 25
Lateralization, 178–179
Latin America, 255, 334, 448, 498, 559. *See
  also* specific countries
Latinas/os
  abuse of women and, 500
  aggression by Mexican American females,
    222
  AIDS and, 416–417
  AIDS prevention and, 421
  alcohol abuse by, 426
  androgyny of, 75
  birth control and, 349
  body image and, 448
  breastfeeding and, 384
  children's gender stereotypes, 103
  condom use by, 421
  depression and, 438–439
  description of ethnic group, 23–25
  diversity among, 24–25, 54
  divorce and, 298
  empty-nest syndrome and, 530
  ethnic identity during adolescence, 139
  families of, 151
  fear of success and, 184–185
  feminism and, 549–550
  gender stereotypes and, 52, 56–57, 151
  gender typing and, 107–108
  higher education and, 145–146
  Hispanics as term versus, 23–24
  illegal drugs and, 428
  immigrant experience of, 24–25
  lesbian women of color, 308
  machismo and marianismo, 296–297, 379,
    454
  marriage of, 292, 296–297
  media's representation of, 48
  menopause and, 528
  motherhood and, 379
  older women, 518, 521, 533–534
  poverty of, 521, 533
  psychotherapy for, 454–455
  salary discrimination and, 244, 245
  sex education and, 331
  sexuality and, 332
  single women, 317
  smoking and, 424
  statistics on, 24
  sweatshops and, 256
  welfare and, 240
  work outside of home, 237–238, 255, 256
Lawyers. *See* Legal profession

Leadership, 226–227
Legal profession, 55–56, 257
"Leisure gap," 267, 272
Lesbians
    abuse in lesbian relationships, 497
    during adolescence, 155–156
    and age difference between partners, 518
    attitude toward bisexual women, 309–310
    attitudes toward, 62–64, 155
    bereavement at death of partner, 532
    biological explanations for sexual
        orientation, 310–311
    body image and, 447
    breakup of love relationship, 306–307
    characteristics of lesbian relationships,
        304–307
    children of, 380–382
    coming-out and, 155–156, 307
    definition of, 62, 301
    discrimination against, 62–64, 251–252
    equality among lesbian couples, 306
    exercise about, 63
    identity of, 303–304
    in the military, 251–252
    as mothers, 380–382
    psychological adjustment of, 303–304
    satisfaction of lesbian couples, 306
    self-esteem of, 252, 303
    sexual problems of, 342
    sexuality of, 338
    social constructionist explanations of
        sexual orientation, 312–313
    sociocultural explanations of sexual
        orientation, 311–312
    statistics on, 301
    theoretical explanations about sexual
        orientation and preference, 310–313
    therapists' views on adjustment of, 304
    women of color as, 307–308
    workplace experiences of, 251–252
Liberal feminism, 7, 216
Life expectancy, 402–403
Living together, 287–288
Love relationships. *See also* Gay males;
        Lesbians; Marriage; Sexuality
    during adolescence, 148–149, 153–156
    and age difference between partners, 517,
        518
    bisexual women, 308–310
    breakup of, 288–289, 306–307
    and career aspirations during college,
        148–149, 155
    characteristics of, 284–287
    companionate love, 285–286
    dating, 278–287
    disabilities and, 414–415

divorce, 298–300
    egalitarian balance of power in, 286–287,
        306
    exercises about, 154, 285, 289, 305
    friendship-based love, 285–286, 304
    gender comparisons, 284–287
    ideal partner for, 280–284
    of lesbians, 304–307, 518
    living together, 287–288
    marriage, 290–298
    media portrayal of, 153, 278
    of older women, 517–518
    power in, 286–287
    satisfaction with, 286, 306
    self-disclosure in, 286
Lumpectomy, 408
Lung cancer, 406, 423, 424
Luteinizing hormone, 126, 128

Machismo, 296–297, 454
Magazines. *See* Media; and specific titles
Major depression, 434, 435–436. *See also*
        Depression
Males. *See* Men; and headings beginning with
        Gender
Mali, 401
Mammogram, 406
Managerial positions, 243, 249–50, 260–262
Marianismo, 296–297, 379, 454
Marital rape, 490–491
Marriage. *See also* Family
    abuse of spouse in, 496–507
    age at first marriage, 291
    and age difference between partners, 518
    attractiveness in marriage partner, 281,
        283–284
    characteristics important for marriage
        partner, 280–284
    cross-cultural patterns for, 282–283
    decision not to have children, 385–388
    divorce following, 287–288, 298–300
    dual-career marriages, 265–268
    egalitarian marriage, 296, 335
    ethnicity and, 291–292, 293, 296–298, 318
    friendships of married women, 318
    gender comparisons in marital satisfaction,
        294–295
    getting married, 291–293
    household tasks shared in, 265, 266–268
    individual differences in, 290–291
    infertility and, 388–390
    living together prior to, 287–288
    modern marriage, 295–296
    power in, 295–296
    rape in, 490–491
    responsibility and power in, 295–296

salary and power in, 295
satisfaction with, 268, 293–295
sexuality in, 294, 335
traditional marriage, 295
woman keeping her own name after, 292–293
work and, 265–263
Masculine generic, 41–45
Masculine people, 73
Masochism/masochist, 14, 457, 502–503
Massachusetts Institute of Technology (MIT), 173
Masturbation, 336
Maternity blues, 382
Mathematics ability
  attitudes toward mathematics, 180
  experiences related to, 142–144
  gender comparisons, 16–17, 18, 142–144, 171–174
  grades in mathematics courses, 172
  parents' influence on, 180
  research biases on, 16–17, 18
  research on, 171–172
  SAT and, 172–174
  school experiences and, 142–144, 172, 180–181
  social explanations for gender differences in, 179–180
Media. *See also* Advertising; Television
  abuse of women and, 502
  antifeminist messages in, 554, 556
  body image and, 137, 138, 446–447
  crime rates in, 222–223
  employment of women outside home, 21, 46–47, 265
  exercises about, 20, 48
  fear of success in, 184
  gender comparisons in, 20, 162, 178–179
  gender stereotypes in, 45–50
  gender typing and, 115–119
  impact of, 49–50
  invisibility of women in, 46
  love relationships in, 153, 278
  menopause in, 523, 525–526
  menstruation and, 134–135
  older women in, 513–514
  personal ads, 281
  radio talk shows, 46
  rape in, 487
  romance novels, 332
  sexuality in, 324, 332, 340
  on "silenced female" problem in schools, 114
  single mothers in, 356
  slimness emphasized in, 446–447
  smoking and, 425

violence against women on, 49–50, 494
women's and men's bodies in, 47–48
Median, definition of, 244n
Medical profession. *See also* Physical health
  advertising in medical journals, 458
  attitude toward menopause, 527
  biases against women and, 396–400, 527
  medical research and, 398–400
  medical textbooks and, 398
  pregnancy of women residents, 369
  role strain of women physicians, 270
  sexual harassment in, 236, 258–259
  wage gap in, 245
  women in, 148, 236, 237, 245, 257–259, 270, 369
Memory, 68, 167
Men. *See also* headings beginning with Gender
  abuse of, by women, 496–497
  abusers' personal characteristics, 501
  actions to take against sexual harassment, 475, 476
  circumcision of, 401
  contraceptives for, 347
  feminist attitudes toward, 554
  as feminists, 6–7, 551–552
  masculine generic in language, 41–45
  men's movement and, 550–553
  normative male, 28, 65–66, 188, 398, 418, 457
  rape prevention and, 494
Men Are From Mars, Women Are From Venus (Gray), 198, 229
Menarche, 124–125
Menopausal joy, 528
Menopause
  attitudes toward, 526–528
  definition of, 523
  hormone replacement therapy and, 405, 410, 524–525
  hot flashes, 523–524
  media portrayal of, 523, 525–526
  physical symptoms of, 523–524
  premature menopause accompanying surgical removal of ovaries, 409–410, 527n
  psychological reactions to, 525–526
Men's movement, 550–553
Men's rights approach, 553
Men's studies, 551
Menstrual Distress Questionnaire, 130
Menstrual joy, 131–32, 528
Menstrual Joy Questionnaire, 131–132
Menstrual pain, 128–129
Menstruation
  advertising on, 134
  age at menarche, 124–125

Menstruation *(Continued)*
  anorexia nervosa and, 445
  attitudes toward, 125, 133–136
  biological aspects of menstrual cycle,
    125–28
  blood loss during, 128
  cognitive abilities and menstrual cycle, 133
  euphemisms for, 134–135
  events during menstrual cycle, 127–128
  exercise about, 135
  media portrayal of, 134–135
  menstrual pain, 128–129
  myths and taboos about, 134
  number of cycles during lifetime, 125
  performance and menstrual cycle, 133
  physical abilities and menstrual cycle, 133
  positive images of, 135–136
  positive symptoms of, 131–132
  premenstrual syndrome (PMS), 129–133
  structures and substances involved in,
    125–127
Mental disorders. *See* Psychological disorders
Mental health. *See* Personal adjustment;
    Psychological disorders; Psychotherapy
Mental rotation, 176–177
Meta-analysis, 165–166, 168–169, 189, 212,
    294–295, 335
Mexican Americans. *See also* Chicanas/os;
    Latinas/os
  aggression by Mexican American females,
    222
  breastfeeding and, 384
  Chicanas/os as term for, 24
  depression and, 438–439
  differences between other Latinas/os and,
    54
  fear of success and, 184–185
  feminism and, 549–550
  in gangs, 222
  gender stereotypes and, 52, 107
  marriage of, 297
  menopause and, 528
Middle age, 534–536. *See also* Empty-nest
    syndrome; Menopause
Middle East, 334, 351
Middlebury College, 173
Military, 251–252
Million Dollar Directory, 560
Million-man march, 552
Minority people. *See* Ethnicity
Mismeasure of Woman, The (Tavris), 554
MIT. *See* Massachusetts Institute of
    Technology (MIT)
Modeling, 97
Modern marriage, 295–296
Mons pubis, 325
Moral reasoning, 215–218

Morbidity, 403
Morning sickness, 363–364
Mortality, 402, 403
Mothers. *See also* Family; Parents
  adolescents' feelings about, 151
  blame of, when children develop
    psychological disorder, 457
  breastfeeding and, 384–385
  child care responsibilities of, 268–269,
    376–378
  and children born to women denied
    abortions, 355
  children's adjustment and maternal
    employment, 269–270
  decision not to become mother, 385–388
  emotional expressiveness of, with children,
    214
  employment of, 14, 21, 237
  ethnicity and motherhood, 378–380
  infant care by, 376–378
  infertility and, 388–390
  lesbian mothers, 380–382
  moral reasoning by, 217
  negative factors of motherhood, 376–377
  number of children born to, 369
  older women as, 529–530
  positive factors of motherhood, 377–378
  postpartum disturbances and, 382–383
  reality of motherhood, 376–378
  sex education and, 330–331, 350
  single mothers, 269, 355–356
  stereotypes about motherhood, 375–376
  work outside of home, 268–270
Mothers of the Plaza, 559
Motivation. *See* Achievement motivation
Ms. Magazine, 560
Müllerian ducts, 83
Multiple orgasms, 329
Murder, 223, 402
Music videos, 46, 50
Mythology, gender stereotypes in, 39–40, 376
Mythopoetic approach, 552

Native Americans
  AIDS and, 416
  alcohol abuse by, 426, 547
  as bisexual women, 309
  differences between Canadian Aboriginals
    and, 25
  diversity among, 25, 54
  ethnic identity of, 25
  fear of success and, 184–185
  gender stereotypes about, 52
  higher education and, 145, 146
  lesbian women of color, 307
  menstruation, 134
  motherhood and, 379

older women, 534
  psychotherapy for, 455–456
  research biases on, 15
  smoking and, 424
  statistics on, 24
  work outside of home, 236, 238
Native Canadians. *See* Canadian Aboriginals
Natural family planning, 347
Netherlands, 55
Never-married women. *See* Single women
New Guinea, 134, 221
New Moon, 116, 117
New Zealand, 103, 558
Newborns. *See* Infancy
"Niceness," 58–59, 61, 113
Nineteenth Amendment, 588
No More Frogs, No More Princes (Vickers &
  Thomas), 536
Nonemployed women. *See also* Housework
  definition of, 236–237
Non-Governmental Organization Forum, 560
Nonsexist language, 45
Nonsexist therapy, 460
Nontraditional employment, 143–144,
  147–148, 256–260
Nonverbal communication
  body posture, 202–203
  decoding ability, 206–207, 208, 209–210
  definition of, 198
  exercises about, 202, 206
  expansiveness, 207–208
  facial expression, 205–206
  gaze, 204–205
  gender comparisons, 201–208
  individual differences in, 207–208
  personal space, 201–202, 209
  persuasion and, 229
  touch, 203–204
Normative male, 28, 65–66, 188, 398, 418,
  457
Normative Whites, 16, 22, 26, 139, 546
Norplant, 348
Norway, 55, 55n
Null academic environment, 145
Nurses, 255
Nurturance, 214

Obese, 449
Occupational segregation, 246
Occupations. *See* Work
Older women
  ageism against, 6, 513
  attitudes toward, 339, 513–519
  Blacks, 512, 521, 533
  cross-cultural views of, 518–519
  as daughters, 530–531
  double standard of aging, 515–518

economic issues of, 520, 521–522
  ethnicity and, 512, 533–534
  exercises about, 514, 517, 526
  family relationships of, 529–532
  as grandmothers, 531–534
  love relationships of, 517–518
  media's portrayal of, 513–514
  menopause and, 522–528
  as mothers, 529–530
  osteoporosis and, 410, 424
  personal reflections by, 536–538
  relationships with younger men, 517–518
  retirement and, 513, 519–522
  and rewriting life stories, 536–538
  and satisfaction with life, 534–536
  sexuality of, 339–340
  social aspects of lives of, 529–538
  statistics on, 513
  widowhood, 532–533
  work and, 519–520
Olympic Games, 139
On Women Turning 50 (Rountree), 536
Operational definition, 16, 214
Orgasm, 326–327, 328, 329, 338, 342
Orgasmic phase, of sexual response cycle,
  326–327
Osteoporosis, 410, 424, 445
Ova, 126, 128, 363
Ovarian cancer, 410
Ovaries, 126, 127, 523
Overweight
  dieting and, 449, 450
  discrimination against overweight people,
    447, 449
  media portrayal of, 47, 449, 450
Ovulation, 128

Pain
  of childbirth, 370, 371, 372
  during intercourse, 342–343
  menstrual pain, 128–129
Painful intercourse, 342–343
Pakistan, 103, 483
Panic attacks, 442–443
Pap smear test, 409
Parents. *See also* Family; Fathers; Mothers
  adolescents' feelings about, 150–151
  and aggression of children, 106–107
  behavior toward infant boys and girls,
    89–90, 104
  child care responsibilities of, 268–269, 376
  decision not to be parents, 385–388
  and educational plans for daughters, 144
  gender typing and, 89–90, 104–108
  and independence in children, 107
  and mathematics abilities of children, 180
  moral reasoning by, 217

Parents *(Continued)*
   motivations for parenthood, 387–388
   of older women, 530–531
   sex education and, 330–331, 349, 350
   television and, 118–119
Part-time work, 271
Peer marriages, 296
Peers. *See also* Friendships
   during adolescence, 152–153
   during childhood, 108–111
   differential treatment and, 109–111
   gender prejudice and, 109, 110
   gender segregation and, 109, 153
   gender typing and, 108–111
   rejection of nontraditional behavior by, 108
Penis, 326, 329, 401
Penis envy, 94–95, 457
Penn State, 173
Pension plans, 521
Performance. *See also* Competence
   explaining successful performance, 188
   as leaders, 226–227
   and menstrual cycle, 133
Persistence of attachment, 299
Person-centered explanations, for scarcity of
   women in certain occupations, 261
Personal adjustment
   abortion and, 354–355
   androgyny and, 74, 140
   of children of lesbian mothers, 380–382
   of lesbians, 303–304
   after rape, 484–486
   to retirement, 520–521
   work and, 270–272
Personal ads, 281
Personal relationships. *See* Interpersonal
   relationships; Love relationships
Personal space, 201–202, 209
Personality
   birth control and, 349
   children's stereotypes about, 99–101
   gender stereotypes about, 36–37, 47,
      99–101
Persons with a disability. *See* Disabilities
Persuasion, 227–229
Peru, 103, 477
Phallic stage, 94
Philosophy, gender stereotypes in, 38–39
Phobias, 442–443
Physical abilities, and menstrual cycle, 133
Physical abuse. *See* Abuse of women
Physical attractiveness. *See* Attractiveness
Physical health. *See also* Childbirth;
   Pregnancy
   of abused women, 499
   AIDS, 347, 396, 402, 416–421, 428
   alcohol abuse, 303, 425–427

athletics and, 138–139
biases of medical profession against
   women, 396–400
breast cancer, 405–410
breastfeeding and, 384–835
cardiovascular disease, 400, 402, 404–405,
   423, 424, 449
in developing countries, 400–402
disabilities, 411–416
female genital mutilation, 401–402, 559
gender comparisons in health care and
   health status, 396–397, 403–404
health insurance and, 350, 399–400
hormone replacement therapy, 405, 410,
   524–525
hysterectomy, 409
life expectancy, 402–403
osteoporosis, 410, 424, 445
overweight and, 449
and physician-patient relationship, 400,
   402–403
after rape, 404
reproductive system cancer, 408–410
research biases on, 16
sexually transmitted diseases other than
   AIDS, 421–422
smoking, 366, 404, 423–425
substance abuse, 423–429
work and, 271
Physical violence. *See* Violence
Physicians. *See* Medical profession
Pituitary gland, 125–128
Placenta, 363
Plateau phase, of sexual response cycle, 326
Play. *See also* Toys
   and "gender-inappropriate" behavior in
      boys, 105–106
   gender segregation in, 109, 153
   gender typing and play with "gender-
      appropriate" toys, 104–105, 107
Playboy, 343
Pleasantness, 58–59, 61, 113
PMS. *See* Premenstrual syndrome (PMS)
Politicians, 226, 559
Pornography, 487–488
Portuguese Americans, 151. *See also*
   Latinas/os
"Post-abortion syndrome," 354
Postpartum blues, 382
Postpartum depression, 382–383
Postpartum period, 382
Posttraumatic stress disorder (PTSD),
   485–486
Posture, 202–203
Poverty. *See also* Developing countries
   abuse of women and, 499
   of Blacks, 297, 521, 533

depression and, 437
after divorce, 300
ethnicity and, 297, 455–456, 521, 533
health problems and, 404
of Native Americans, 455–456
of older women, 520, 521–522
of single mothers, 356
welfare and, 239, 240–241
of women with disabilities, 414
of women worldwide, 401
Power. *See also* Aggression; Violence against
women
assertiveness, 225–226
communication patterns and, 209
feminist therapy and, 460–462
influenceability, 229
leadership, 226–227
in love relationship, 286–287
in marriage, 295–296
persuasion, 227–229
sexual harassment and, 468, 471
and sexual relationships between therapists
and clients, 452–453
Practical significance, 18
Pregnancy. *See also* Abortion; Birth control;
Childbirth
abuse during, 498
attitudes toward pregnant women, 366–368
biology of, 363
emotional reactions to, 364–366
employment and, 368–369
exercises about, 367
and expectations about childbirth, 371
and fetal alcohol syndrome, 426
home pregnancy test, 363
length of, 363
and obstacles to birth control, 349–351
physical reactions to, 363–364
sexuality during, 364
statistics on, 369
teen pregnancies, 345–347, 346n, 355–356,
366
unintended pregnancies, 347, 355–356
Prejudice. *See also* Ableism; Ageism; Gender
stereotypes; Homophobia; Racism;
Sexism; Theme 2 (differential treatment)
definition of, 37
peers and gender prejudice, 109, 110
Premenstrual syndrome (PMS)
controversy on, 129–130
coping with, 132
definition of, 129
explanations of, 129–130, 131
menstrual joy, 131–32
mood swings, 130–131
prevalence of, 130
research bias on, 18, 130–131

Prenatal period
atypical prenatal development, 85–86
definition of, 82
development of genitals during, 84
normal prenatal development, 83–85
Prepared childbirth, 372–373
Prescription drugs
abuse of, 428
for psychological disorders, 458, 460
Profeminists, 551–552
Professions. *See* specific professions
Professors, 250, 258
Progesterone, 126, 128, 383
Promotions, 248–250
Prostaglandins, 129
Prozac, 132, 441
Psychoanalytic theory, 94–95, 311–312, 457
Psychodynamic therapy, 457
Psychological adjustment. *See* Personal
adjustment
Psychological disorders
agoraphobia, 442–443
antisocial personality disorder, 434, 501
anxiety disorders, 442–443
definition of, 434
depression, 435–441
drug therapies for, 451, 458, 460
eating disorders and related problems,
444–450
gender comparisons on, 434
phobias, 442–443
posttraumatic stress disorder (PTSD),
485–486
psychotherapy for, 451–462
social phobias, 442
specific phobias, 442
treatment of, 451–462
Psychology, feminization of, 11, 12, 256–257,
545–546
Psychology of women. *See also* headings
beginning with Themes
central concepts and definitions in, 5–9
critical thinking and, 21–22
current status of, 12–13
developing more inclusive psychology of
women, 546–547
early studies on gender comparisons,
10–11
emergence of, as discipline, 11–12
feminist approaches in, 6–7, 8
and feminization of psychology, 11, 12,
256–257, 545–546
future of discipline of, 545–548
history of, 10–13
interdisciplinary nature of, 12–13
research on, 14–22
sex and gender as concepts in, 5–6

Psychology of women *(Continued)*
  similarities versus differences perspectives
    on, 7–9, 216
  social biases as concepts in, 6
  themes of book, 27–29
  women of color and, 22–26
Psychology of Women Quarterly, 12
Psychotherapy. *See also* Drug therapies
  for abused women and abusers, 504
  cognitive-behavioral approach to, 344–345,
    458
  couples therapy for battered women and
    batterers, 504
  definition of, 451
  feminist therapy, 460–462
  gender-sensitive therapy, 460–462
  misdiagnosis in, 437, 451–452
  nonsexist therapy, 460
  preferences about therapists, 459
  psychodynamic therapy, 457
  sexism and, 437, 451–453
  sexual orientation issues in, 304
  for sexual problems, 344–345
  sexual relationships between therapists and
    clients, 452–453
  therapists' views on lesbian adjustment, 304
  traditional therapies, 456–460
  with women of color, 453–456
PTSD. *See* Posttraumatic stress disorder
  (PTSD)
Puberty. *See also* Adolescence
  definition of, 124
  physical changes during, 124–28
Publication of research findings, 19–21
Puerto Ricans, 54, 107–108. *See also*
  Latinas/os

Quid pro quo harassment, 470

Race. *See* Ethnicity; and specific ethnic and
  racial groups
Racism, 6, 22. *See also* Discrimination;
  Ethnicity; and specific ethnic and racial
  groups
Radical feminism, 7
Radio talk shows, 46
Raloxifene, 410
Rape
  acquaintance rape, 478–482, 493
  attitudes toward, 480, 481–482, 486
  and blaming the victim, 50, 468, 470, 487,
    491
  child sexual abuse, 312, 488–490
  compared with other forms of violence
    against women, 468, 470
  cross-cultural patterns, 477–478, 483, 487

definition of, 335, 477
depression following, 439
exercises about, 478, 480
fear of, 483
frequency of, 482–483
health problems following, 404
long-term adjustment after rape, 485–486
marital rape, 490–491
myths about, 486–488
pornography and, 487–488
prevention of, 491–494
reactions during rape, 484
reactions immediately after rape, 484–485
short-term adjustment to, 484–485
society's prevention of, 493–494
statistics on, 479, 482–483
by strangers, 487, 491–493
underreporting of, 487
Rape in Marriage (Russell), 491
Reading disability, 169–170
Recovered memory perspective, 489–490
Refugees, 454–455, 534. *See also* Immigrants
Relational model, 215–216
Relationships. *See* Friendships; Interpersonal
  relationships; Love relationships
Religion
  AIDS and, 419
  birth control and, 351
  discrimination against women in, 37
  gender stereotypes in, 39–40, 48
  homosexuality and, 552
  marriage and, 295, 296–297
  men's movement and, 552–553
  women clergy in, 39–40
Religious approach, to men's movement,
  552–553
Reproductive system cancer, 408–410
Research
  on achievement motivation, 180
  biased samples in, 163
  biases in, 14–22, 163, 182, 560
  bipolar scales on femininity and
    masculinity, 71–72
  box-score approach to summarizing
    multiple studies, 165
  communicating the findings, 15, 19–20
  comparison-groups approach to, 546–547
  confounding variable in, 16–17, 118
  critical thinking about, 21–22
  data interpretation, 15, 18–19
  designing the study, 15, 16–17
  experimenter choice in, 16
  experimenter expectancy in, 17–18, 163
  frequency distribution, 163–164
  on gender comparisons, 163–166
  gender of experimenter in, 16

hypothesis formulation in, 14–15
medical research, 398–400
meta-analysis technique, 165–166, 168–169, 189, 212, 294–295, 335
operational definition in, 16, 214
performing the study, 15, 17–18
practical significance in, 18
statistical significance in, 18
summarizing multiple studies, 165–166
validity of test, 173
Whites as traditional norm for, 16, 22, 546
Researcher expectancy, 17, 163
Resolution phase, of sexual response cycle, 327
Retirement, 513, 519–522
Rhythm method of birth control, 347
Roe v. Wade, 352
Rohypnol ("roofie"), 479
Role strain, 270–271
Romantic relationships. *See* Love relationships
RU 486, 352
Ruminative style, as response to depression, 440, 441
Russia, 559
Rutgers University, 173

Sadness. *See also* Depression
after abortion, 354
decoding from facial expressions, 207, 208
family discussions about, 105, 151
as normal, 436
Safer sex, 421
Salary
comparable worth and, 246
cross-cultural patterns in, 245–246
discrimination in, 236, 244–248
gender comparisons in salary requests, 247
of people with disabilities, 414
and power in marriage, 295
in sweatshops, 256
women's reactions to lower salaries, 246–248
San Diego State University, 557
Sandwich generation, 530–531
SAT, 169, 172–174, 180
Satisfaction. *See* Happiness
Saudi Arabia, 334
Scandinavia, 223
Schema, definition of, 95
Scholastic Aptitude Test (SAT), 169, 172–174, 180
Schools. *See* Education; Teachers
Science ability, 142–143
Scotland, 55
Scripts. *See* Sexual scripts

Secondary sex characteristics, 125
Secret Paths (Apter), 536
Sedatives, 458
Segregation by gender. *See* Gender segregation
Self-concept, 136–141
Self-confidence, 65–66, 185–188, 258, 270
Self-defense, 493
Self-disclosure, 219, 286
Self-efficacy, 349, 354
Self-esteem
in adolescence, 140
androgyny and, 74, 140
children's books and, 115–116
lesbian and gay identity and, 252, 303
Self-fulfilling prophecy
definition of, 69
gender stereotypes and, 68–69
menstrual pain and, 129
Self-in-relation theory, 215–216
Senegal, 255
Sensate focus, 344
Serbian forces, 477
Sesame Street, 117
Seventeen, 46–47, 134, 138
Sex. *See also* headings beginning with Gender
definition of, 5
distinction between gender and, 5–6
Sex chromosomes, 83
Sex differences. *See* Gender comparisons
Sex education, 330–332, 349, 351
Sex guilt, 349
Sex Roles, 12
Sex similarities. *See* Gender similarities; Theme 1 (gender similarities)
Sex-role stereotypes. *See* Gender stereotypes
Sex therapy, 344–345
Sexism. *See also* Discrimination; Gender stereotypes; Theme 2 (differential treatment)
ambivalent sexism, 60, 61
Ambivalent Sexism Inventory, 60, 61
attitudes toward women's competence, 57–58
benevolent sexism, 61
complexity of contemporary sexism, 55–61
cross-cultural sexism, 61
definition of, 6
in early studies of gender comparisons, 10–11
hostile sexism, 61
in interpersonal interactions, 55–57
in language, 40–45
"niceness"/pleasantness of women and girls, 58–59, 61, 113
psychotherapy and, 437, 451–453

Sexism *(Continued)*
  in research, 14–22
  in schools, 111–114, 142–144, 145
Sexual abuse. *See also* Rape; Sexual
    harassment
  of children, 312, 488–490
  by psychotherapists, 452–453
Sexual assault. *See also* Rape
  definition of, 477
Sexual Assertiveness Scale for Women, 337,
    338
Sexual coercion. *See* Rape
Sexual desire phase, 326
Sexual dysfunctions. *See* Sexual
    problems/dysfunctions
Sexual harassment
  actions to take against, 474–476
  attitudes toward, 473–474
  in blue-collar jobs, 260
  compared with other forms of violence
      against women, 468, 470
  cross-cultural patterns on, 473
  definition of, 250
  effects of, on victim, 468, 473, 474
  exercise about, 469
  frequency of, 472–473
  in higher education, 471, 472, 473–474
  hostile work environment, 470–471
  making judgments about, 469
  in medical profession, 236, 258–259
  men's helpful responses to, 475
  in the military, 252
  quid pro quo harassment, 470
  reasons for importance of, 471–472
  society's response to, 475–476
  at work, 470–476
Sexual orientation and preference. *See also*
    Bisexual women; Gay males; Lesbians
  theoretical explanations about, 310–313
Sexual problems/dysfunctions
  definition of, 341
  female orgasmic disorder, 342
  gender roles and, 343–344
  painful intercourse, 342–343
  sexual unresponsiveness, 341–342
  therapy for, 344–345
Sexual relationships between therapists and
    clients, 452–453
Sexual response cycle, 326–327
Sexual scripts, 335
Sexual unresponsiveness, 341–342
Sexuality
  abortion, 352–355
  adolescent sexual behavior, 332–333
  AIDS and, 418–421
  birth control and, 345–352

  characteristics important for sexual partner,
      280–281, 343–344
  communication about, 336–338, 479, 481
  cross-cultural patterns in, 308, 334
  disabilities and, 415
  double standard, 333–334, 343
  ethnicity and, 308, 332, 406
  exercises about, 328, 333, 337, 351
  female sexual anatomy, 324–26
  gender comparisons in sexual resins cycle,
      327, 329
  guilt about, 349
  of lesbians, 338
  and living together, 287
  in marriage, 294, 335
  masturbation, 336
  media portrayal of, 324, 332
  of older women, 339–340
  orgasm, 326–327
  during pregnancy, 364
  in romance novels, 332
  safer sex, 421
  sex education, 330–332
  sexual activities, 335–336
  sexual response cycle, 326–327
  sexual scripts and, 335
  sexually transmitted diseases other than
      AIDS, 421–422
Sexually transmitted diseases (STDs)
  acquired immunodeficiency syndrome
      (AIDS), 347, 396, 402, 416–421
  chlamydia, 421, 422
  genital herpes, 421, 422
  genital warts, 421, 422
  gonorrhea, 421, 422
  syphilis, 421, 422
Shelters for battered women, 505
Sierra Leone, 255, 401
Sikh women, 528
Similarities perspective, 8–9, 27–28, 216. *See
    also* Gender comparisons; Theme 1
    (gender similarities)
Singapore, 487
Single women
  abortions for, 353
  advantages and disadvantages of being
      single, 316–317
  attitudes toward, 315, 316
  Black single women, 317–318
  characteristics of, 314–315
  ethnicity and, 317–318
  as mothers, 269, 355–356
  never-married women, 314–315
  statistics on, 314, 317
Situation-centered explanations, for scarcity of
    women in certain occupations, 261–262

Slimness, emphasis on, 137, 365, 439, 445–448
Smiling, 87, 205–206, 210
Smoking, 366, 404, 423–425
SMPY. *See* Study of Mathematically Precocious Youth (SMPY)
Social behavior. *See also* Interpersonal relationships; Love relationships
    aggression, 221–225
    assertiveness, 225–226
    communication patterns, 198–211
    day care and, 269–270
    gender comparisons on, 87
    helping and caring, 212–220
    during infancy, 87
    influenceability, 229
    leadership, 226–227
    persuasion, 227–229
Social biases. *See* Biases
Social class. *See also* Ethnicity
    abortion and, 353
    abuse of women and, 499–500
    birth control and, 349
    body image and, 448
    breastfeeding and, 384
    and children's gender stereotypes, 102
    mortality and, 402
Social cognitive approach
    biased judgments about women and men, 66–67
    definition of, 64
    exaggerating contrast between women and men, 65
    gender polarization, 65
    to gender stereotypes, 64–68
    normative male, 28, 65–66
Social constructionism, 8–9, 93, 197–198, 221–222, 312–313
Social constructionist approach
    to aggression, 221–222
    definition of, 312
    to gender differences, 197–198
    to sexual orientation, 312–313
Social explanations, for gender differences in cognitive abilities, 179–181
Social learning theory
    of gender differences in communication patterns, 209–210
    of gender typing, 96–97
    of mate selection, 284
    of sexual orientation, 312
Social phobias, 442
Social Security benefits, 521
Social status, 209
Social work profession, 255
Sociocultural explanations, of sexual orientation, 311–312

South Korea, 498
Spain, 103
Spatial abilities
    definition of, 174
    gender comparisons, 166–167, 174–177
    genetic explanation for gender differences in, 178
    hormones and, 178
    mental rotation, 176–177
    spatial perception, 174–176
    spatial visualization, 174
    tests of, 175
Spatial perception, 174–176
Spatial visualization, 174
Specific phobias, 442
Speech. *See* Verbal communication
Sperm, 83, 363
Spermicidal foams and creams, 348
Sports. *See* Athletics
Spouse abuse. *See* Abuse of women
Stanford University Medical School, 258–259
Statistical significance, 18
STDs. *See* Sexually transmitted diseases (STDs)
Stereotypes. *See* Gender stereotypes; Gender typing
Sticky floor, 249
Stone Center, Wellesley College, 215
Stress
    of Black women, 454
    divorce and, 299
    of infertility, 389
    of refugees, 454–455
Study of Mathematically Precocious Youth (SMPY), 172–173
Substance abuse
    alcohol abuse, 303, 425–427
    illegal drugs, 428
    prescription drugs, 428
    smoking, 366, 404, 423–425
Success
    attributions for own success of failure, 188–190
    attributions of, and ethnicity, 67
    explaining successful performance, 188
    fear of success, 184–185
Suicide and suicide attempts, 402, 456, 499, 547
Sweatshops, 256
Sweden, 334
Switzerland, 245–246
Symptom Checklist-90-R, 303
Syphilis, 421, 422

Taiwan, 518
Talkativeness, 199

Tanzania, 518
TAT, 183
Teachers. *See also* Education; Professors
  gender bias of, 112–113, 142–144, 145, 180
  lesbians and gays as, 251
  salaries of, 244
  sex education and, 251, 331–332, 349
  sex of, 111–112, 144
  as traditional female occupation, 255
Teen, 138
Teenagers. *See* Adolescence
Television
  for children, 116–119
  exercise about, 48
  gender stereotypes on, 46–50, 116–119
  hours of viewing, 116
  menstruation on, 134
  nonverbal communication on, 201
  older women's portrayal on, 513–514
  parents and, 118–119
  rape on, 487
  women of color on, 48
Temperament during infancy, 86–87
Tests. *See* specific tests
Test-taking strategies, 180
Test validity, 173
Textbooks
  math textbooks, 180
  medical textbook, 398
Thailand, 103
Thematic Apperception Test (TAT), 183
Theme 1 (gender similarities), 27–28, 29,
    36–37, 163, 165, 167–168, 190, 202, 216,
    257–258, 284, 286, 288, 329, 396. *See also*
    Gender comparisons
Theme 2 (differential treatment), 28, 37, 57,
    62, 106, 109–111, 134, 202, 396, 397, 427.
    See also Ableism; Ageism; Discrimination;
    Gender stereotypes; Homophobia;
    Racism; Sexism
Theme 3 (invisibility), 28–29, 37, 38, 46, 134,
    182, 263, 307, 343, 362, 397, 412, 512
Theme 4 (variability), 29, 129, 130, 133, 153,
    163, 207–208, 290–291, 315, 364, 366,
    380, 408, 409, 411, 520, 522, 534, 547
Therapy. *See* Psychotherapy
Tonga, 223
Touch, 203–204
Toys. *See also* Play
  advertising of, 118
  and gender of infants, 91–92
  gender typing and play with "gender-
    appropriate" toys, 104–105, 107
Traditional marriage, 295
Traditional therapies, 456–460
Tranquilizers, 458
Treatment discrimination, 244–254

Trimester, 363
Tubal ligation, 348
Turkey, 559

UCLA, 554
Uganda, 477, 559
Undifferentiated people, 73
Union College, 174
Universities. *See* Higher education; and
    specific universities
University of California at Berkeley, 173
University of Colorado, 557
University of Hawaii, 288
University of Toronto, 285–286
Unmarried-couple household, 287–288
Uterine cancer, 409
Uterus, 126, 127

Vagina, 325–326
Vaginal orgasm, 327
Validity of test, 173
Vanatinai Island, 221–222
Vanity Fair, 514
Variability among women. *See* Theme 4
    (variability)
Variables
  confounding variable, 16–17, 118
  definition of, 16
  gender as a stimulus variable, 28
  gender as a subject variable, 27–28
Vasectomy, 348
Vasocongestion, 326
Venezuela, 55
Verbal ability
  brain lateralization and, 178
  gender comparisons, 168–170
  reading disability, 169–170
  research on, 168–169
  verbal fluency, 168
Verbal communication. *See also*
    Communication patterns; Language
  content of language, 199–201
  in friendships, 152–153
  language style, 199
  in love relationships, 294
  persuasion and, 228
  about sexuality, 336–338, 479, 481
  talkativeness, 199
Verbal fluency, 168
Veterinary medicine, 256–257
Video games, 225
Vietnamese Americans, 25
Vietnamese refugees, 534
Violence against women. *See also* Aggression
  abuse of women, 496–507
  and blaming the victim, 50, 468, 470, 487,
    491, 503

child sexual abuse, 312, 488–490
  depression and, 439
  impact of generally, 468, 470
  in media, 49–50, 494
  rape, 477–496
  sexual assault, 477
  sexual harassment, 468, 469, 470–477
Visibility. *See* Theme 3 (invisibility)
Vocational occupations, 148
Vogue, 514

Wage gap, 244–248
Wages. *See* Salary
Weddings. *See* Marriage
Welfare, 239, 240–241, 347, 379
Wellesley College, 151, 215, 248
Whites
  achievement motivation of, 183
  AIDS and, 416
  alcohol abuse by, 426
  androgyny of, 75
  attributions of success and, 67
  birth control and, 349
  body image and, 448
  breastfeeding and, 384
  career aspirations and romance during
    college, 148–149, 155
  children's gender stereotypes, 102–103
  depression and, 438–439
  disabilities and, 412–413
  divorce and, 298
  empty-nest syndrome and, 530
  feminism and, 548–549
  gender stereotypes about, 53
  gender typing and, 107, 108
  higher education and, 144, 145
  idealized white women in advertising,
    137–138
  illegal drugs and, 428
  as lesbians, 307
  mammograms and, 406
  marriage of, 292, 293
  menarche and, 125
  menopause and, 528
  as norm, 16, 22, 26, 139, 546
  pap smears and, 409
  poverty of, 533
  pregnancy and, 368
  privileged status of, 22–23, 139
  promotions for, 249
  retirement and, 520
  salary discrimination and, 244, 245
  sex education and, 331
  sexuality and, 332
  single women, 317
  smoking and, 424–425
  weight dissatisfaction and, 137

  welfare and, 240
  work outside of home, 237–238
Widowhood, 532–533
Withdrawal birth control method, 347
Wolffian ducts, 83
Women & Health, 397
Women for a Change (Zepatos & Kaufman),
    561
Women of color. *See* Ethnicity
Women's education. *See* Education
Women's employment. *See* Work
Women's Health, 397
Women's Health Issues, 397
Women's movement. *See also* Feminism
  in North America, 558
  worldwide women's movement, 558–560
Women's studies courses, 557–558
Work. *See also* specific occupations and
    professions
  background factors related to women's
    employment, 237–244
  blue-collar jobs, 259–260
  and career aspirations during adolescence,
    146–149, 155
  children and maternal employment, 269–270
  in children's books, 115–116
  children's gender stereotypes about, 101,
    102, 114
  chilly climate at, 258–259, 470–471
  communication about, 199, 200
  comparable worth and, 246
  denial of personal disadvantage and,
    247–248
  discrimination in hiring patterns, 241–243
  discrimination in promotions, 248–250
  discrimination in the workplace, 55–56, 58,
    244–254
  domestic work, 255
  dual-career marriages, 265–268
  employed women in the media, 46–47
  evaluation in the workplace, 250
  exercises about, 239, 247, 248, 262
  garment work, 255–256
  gender segregation among and within
    occupations, 246
  gender stereotypes about, in children, 101,
    102, 114
  and geographical constraints on dual-career
    marriages, 266
  glass ceiling in, 249
  glass escalator in, 249
  guidelines for correction of discrimination
    at, 252–253
  hiring patterns for, 241–243
  homemakers, 262–264
  lesbians' experiences in the workplace,
    251–252

Work *(Continued)*
   marriage and, 265–268
   media biases on employed mothers, 21
   mental health and, 271–272
   nontraditional employment, 143–144,
      147–148, 256–260
   older women and, 519–520
   part-time employment, 271
   personal adjustment and, 270–272
   personal characteristics related to women's
      employment, 237–240, 257–258
   personal life coordinated with, 264–272
   person-centered explanations for scarcity
      of women in certain occupations, 261
   physical health and, 271
   pregnant women and, 368–369
   research biases on employed mothers, 14
   role strain and, 270–271
   salary discrimination, 236, 244–248
   sexual harassment at, 468, 469, 470–477

   situation-centered explanations for scarcity
      of women in certain occupations,
      261–262
   statistics on, 236, 259, 519
   sticky floor metaphor, 249
   traditional employment, 246, 254–56
   vocational occupations, 254–262
   and women with disabilities, 412–414
Working women, definition of, 236
World Conference on Women (Beijing),
   559–560

X chromosome, 83, 402, 436

Y chromosome, 83
Yale University Medical School, 237
Yin and yang, 40
YM, 138
York University, 547

Photo Credits

Literary Credits

Demo 13.1. Making judgements about sexual harassment from Bursik, K., "Perception of sexual harassment in an academic context," *Sex Roles, 27,* 401–412.

Figure 14.2. Three bars from 18-bar graph, Figure 1, top of page 283, from Gannon, L. & Ekstrom, B. (1993). Attitudes toward menopause: The influence of sociocultural paradigms. *Psychology of Women Quarterly, 17,* 275–288.

Figure 14.3. Figure 1 on page 456 from Mitchell, V. & Helson, R. (1990). Women's prime of life: Is it the 50s? *Psychology of Women Quarterly, 14,* 451–470.